ART AND THE M

A CRITICAL READER

EDITED BY TANYA LEIGHTON

TATE PUBLISHING
IN ASSOCIATION WITH AFTERALL

First published 2008
by order of the Tate Trustees
by Tate Publishing, a division
of Tate Enterprises Ltd
Millbank, London SW1P 4RG
www.tate.org.uk/publishing

In association with:
Afterall
Central Saint Martins College of Art and Design
University of the Arts London
107–109 Charing Cross Road
London WC2H 0DU
www.afterall.org

A catalogue record for this book is available from the British Library.

ISBN 978-1-85437-625-1

Distributed in the United States and Canada
by Harry N. Abrams Inc., New York.

Library of Congress Control Number:
2007934791

Design by Kaisa Lassinaro
Printed by Graphicom SPA, Italy

Afterall is a research and publishing group based at Central Saint Martins College of Art and Design, University of the Arts London. This book has been produced by Afterall and published by Tate Publishing.

Afterall Readers Editor
Charles Esche

Afterall Series Editors
Charles Esche and Mark Lewis

Cover images

Front: Dan Graham, *Body Press*, 1970–72.
Courtesy Marian Goodman Gallery, New York & Paris

Back: Charles and Ray Eames, *Glimpses of the USA*,
Moscow World's Fair auditorium, 1959 © 2008 Eames Office LLC

Peter Kubelka, *The Invisible Cinema*, 1970. Courtesy Anthology
Film Archives. All rights reserved

Art and the Moving Image Editor
Tanya Leighton

Managing Editor
Caroline Woodley

Associate Editor
Lucy Steeds

Copy Editor
Deirdre O'Dwyer

Editorial Assistant and Picture Researcher
Gemma Sharpe

This publication was made possible through the support of the Arts and Humanities Research Council.

Contents

PREFACE
Charles Esche

Art and the Moving Image is the second critical reader to be produced by Afterall in collaboration with Tate Publishing. The reader evolved out of a series of seminars and lectures organised at Tate Modern in 2002 by Mark Lewis and Michael Newman in collaboration with Andrew Brighton. It follows *Art and Social Change* as part of a series documenting significant tendencies in contemporary art through historical texts and new commissions.

This reader considers the development of the moving image since the 1960s and tracks the changes that have occurred in the reception and understanding of the aesthetic, social and technical ideas that have informed the fields of moving-image art and cinema itself. The traditional distinction between art and cinema is one that is increasingly difficult to maintain, and it is the condition of increasing mutability that informs every aspect of this book. The texts contained herein discuss in depth the changing relationship between moving-image art and cinema; for instance, relating how experimental film work eventually gave way to video art in the 60s and 70s, once the introduction of video cameras in the US and Europe and the technology of moving-image reproduction became economically accessible to more than just a few artists and experimental film-makers. Since that time, it seems that the march of the video, and later digital, image in art contexts has been relentless. It must now be obvious to even an occasional gallery or museum visitor that the moving image has become a privileged form for artistic experimentation and communication. This book includes new translations of important commentaries by authors such as Sabeth Buchmann and Jean-Christophe Royoux. New texts have been commissioned from Elizabeth Bennett Hupp, Bill Horrigan, William Kaizen, John Kelsey and Federico Windhausen. These combined with previously unpublished texts by Alexander Alberro, John Rajchman, Gregor Stemmrich, Andrew V. Uroskie and Jonathan Walley make for a collection of discoveries for even the most informed reader.

We are very grateful to Tanya Leighton, who, as the editor of this book, has made intelligent and rigorous selections. This reader would not have been possible without her dedication to research over an extended period. Also instrumental have been the support of Central Saint Martins College of Art and Design (University of the Arts London) and the English Arts and Humanities Research Council, which provided the initial impetus for the project. I would additionally like to thank Caroline Woodley for her attentiveness to detail throughout the process and, finally, all the writers who kindly lent their work to the reader as well as those who contributed with comments and advice at various stages.

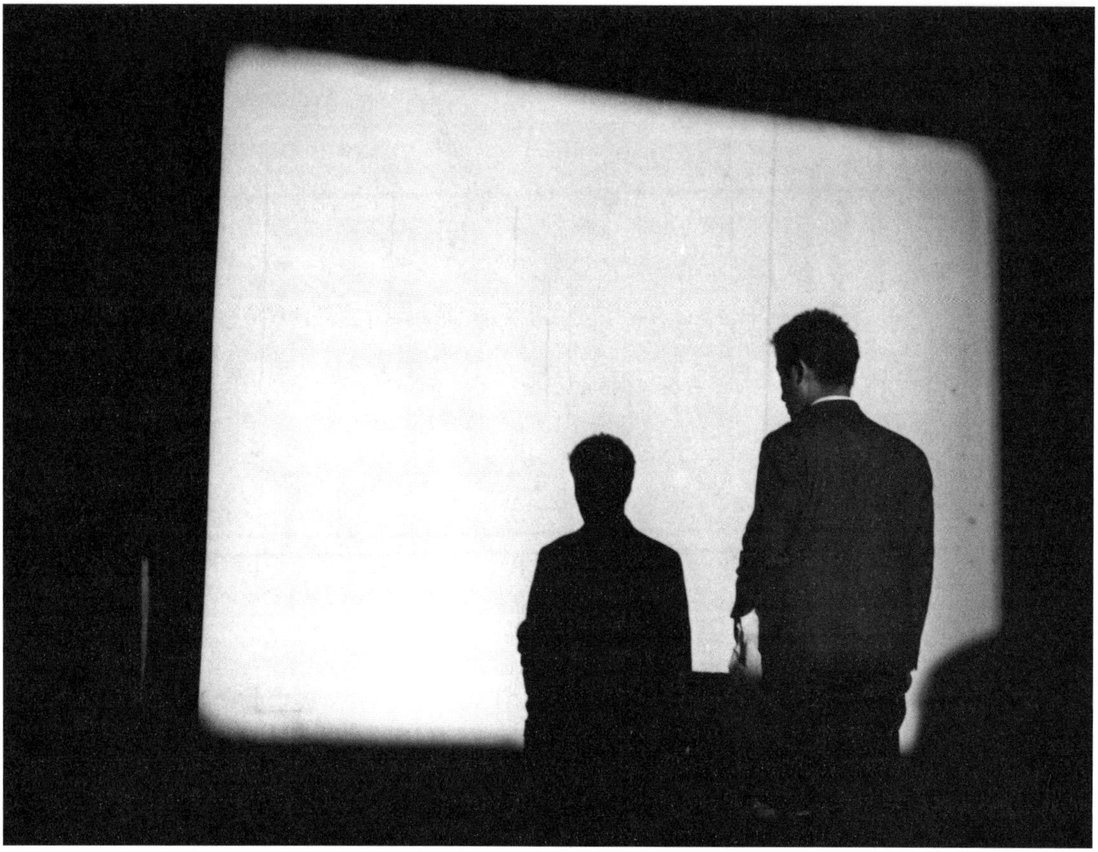

Nam June Paik, *Zen for Film*, 1964. 16mm film installation. Photo © 2008 Peter Moore estate & VAGA, New York

INTRODUCTION
Tanya Leighton

Since the beginning of the 1960s the international contemporary art scene has undergone a significant transformation. Artists have gravitated to a range of moving-image practices and technologies, exchanging the white cube of the exhibition space for the black box of image projection. Given the pervasive convergence of art and moving images, the claim that we are now witnessing the 'flowering' of cinematic and televisual forms in visual art, and that the practice or 'medium' of film and video installation is now the dominant form of contemporary art is hardly surprising.[1] In fact, in terms of visibility in large-scale exhibitions such as documenta or the Venice Biennale, one may go so far as to say that large-scale cinematic modes of projection have quantitatively surpassed traditional mediums such as painting and sculpture — a situation that would have been unimaginable forty years ago. This dominance of the projected image is reflected in an array of installations that run the gambit from projected celluloid film installations, to single- and multiple-projections of analogue and digital video, to multimedia environments, sculptural film objects, computer- and net-based installations and more. Significantly, it was only ten years ago that American critic and curator Bruce Jenkins could still claim that film, 'now in the company of video, holography, and new forms of computer-based imaging', continues to reside 'on a fault line discernible only well below the surface of the art world infrastructure'.[2]

Many artists and critics, including Korean Fluxus artist Nam June Paik (a catalytic figure for video art), predicted this altered status of the work of art in the age of information. Paik's pronouncement that 'As the collage technique replaced oil-paint, the cathode ray tube will replace the canvas' retains a certain validity, in the sense that moving images are now ubiquitous in contemporary art.[3] Yet, what exactly lies behind this conviction, beyond a technological determinism? Why has there been a turn to moving images in contemporary art? How did the projected image find its way into the museum and into the art historical discourse of modernity? How have moving images redefined what we think of as 'art'? How might they have affected our viewing experience? *Art and the Moving Image: A Critical Reader* attempts to confront these and other related questions as it charts and re-evaluates the terms

1 See George Baker, *Gerard Byrne: Books, Magazines, and Newspapers*, New York: Lukas & Sternberg, 2003.
2 Bruce Jenkins, 'The Machine in the Museum; or The Seventh Art in Search of Authorization', *Space, Site, Intervention: Situating Installation Art* (ed. Erika Suderberg), Minneapolis and London: University of Minnesota Press, 2000, p.263.
3 Hal Foster, Rosalind Krauss, Yve-Alain Bois and Benjamin Buchloh, *Art Since 1900: Modernism, Antimodernism, Postmodernism*, London and New York: Thames and Hudson, 2005, p.561.

of debate that have surrounded film and video's ruptured and irregular entry into the wider body of the visual arts. The book brings together seminal, rare and new analyses representative of the range of writing on this subject in order to help negotiate the difficult field of moving images, its historical models and the meaning of its transformations. It is both a collection of new essays and an anthology of republished ones, some in new and first translations and several revised for the occasion. It explores what happens to the moving image when it is transposed from the black box to the white cube, when cinema is 'exhibited' by being re-sited within a museum or gallery context. This debate develops in tandem with artistic practices, which stand at odds to more spectacular forms of image production and circulation. Thus, the subject of this book is lodged in the interstices between more established and seemingly coherent cultural domains: the visual arts, cinema (in its classical and avant-garde guises) and television (in its commercial and public variants). It is hoped that with access to the texts in *Art and the Moving Image* readers will begin to acquire a more complex understanding of the multiple issues surrounding this unbridled field. In the absence of a comprehensive body of critical thought and art historical analysis of the subject, this book is offered as a first attempt to bring the field into focus.

One of the key issues motivating this publication is to explore precisely the 'ambivalent' relation of video to the art world, before, in Martha Rosler's terms, it came to shed its 'utopian moment'.[4] Whereas art historical accounts of this field have tended to draw on the paradigm of Minimalism, discussing film and video installations in the gallery largely in terms of phenomenological space and perception, the aim here is to highlight the different historical moments of this transition whilst providing an adequate history of film and video installation. The ambition of many of the essays is to historicise the radical aesthetic of projected-image practices of the 60s and 70s, and not simply for the sake of revivalism. Rather, the strength of such reflections is that, from a distance, key works of the past can shed new light on contemporary moving-image installations. More explicitly, *Art and the Moving Image* concentrates on the site of the gallery and, indeed, in the case of 'intermedia' events (as coined by Fluxus artist Dick Higgins) or early video production, on moving images' deliberate exit from the constraints of this

4 In an essay titled 'Video: Shedding The Utopian Moment', Martha Rosler discusses the transformative impulses that drove the utopian hopes of early video art. Such a utopian moment, she claims, was 'encouraged by the events of the 1960s. Attention to the conduct of social life, including a questioning of its ultimate aims, had inevitable effects on intellectual and artists pursuits. Communications and systems theories of art making, based partly on the visionary theories of Marshall McLuhan and Buckminster Fuller, as well as on the Structuralism of Claude-Levi Strauss ... displaced the expressive models of art that had held sway in the West since the early post-War period. Artists looked to a new shaping and interventionist self-image (if not a shamanistic-magical one), seeking yet another route to power for art, in counterpoint — whether discordant or harmonious — to the shaping power of the mass media over Western Culture.' See Martha Rosler, 'Video: Shedding the Utopian Moment', in Doug Hall and Sally Jo Fifer (eds.), *Illuminating Video*, New York: Aperture/The Bay Area Video Coalition, 1991, p.31–50.

5 Michael Snow's *Two Sides to Every Story* (1974), for example, is exemplary of the spatial film-environments and Structural-Conceptual-Minimal cinema that emerged in the late 1960s and early 70s.

6 There is a general perception held by artists, critics and curators that a similar rift exists between hard-core 'new media artists' (Masaki Fujihata, Luc Courchesne) and art world 'media artists' (Eija-Liisa Ahtila, Isaac Julien, Gary Hill).

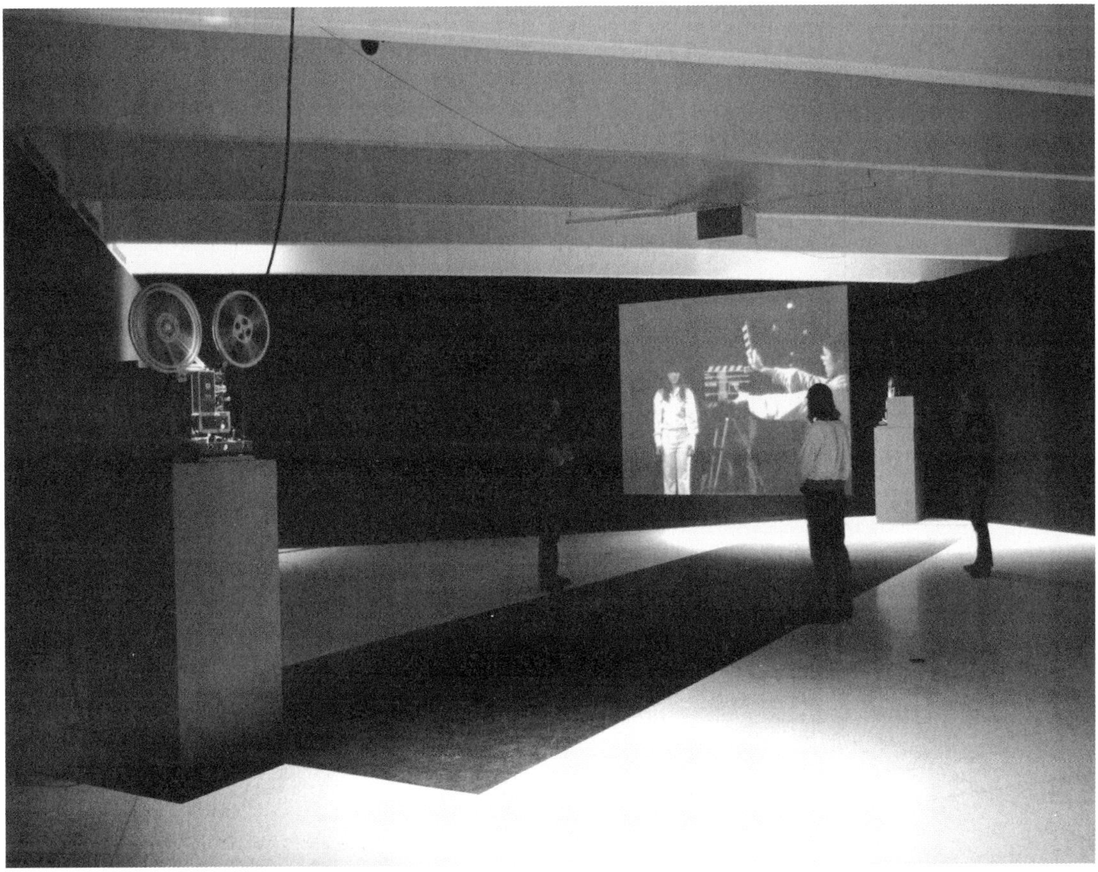

Michael Snow, *Two Sides to Every Story*, 1974. 16mm film installation. Courtesy Walker Art Center, Minneapolis

domain. It also focuses on the work of artists who innovatively employ multiple-screen, multimedia installation or forms of expanded cinemas in their work, artists who draw attention to the environment in which the work is projected and, in Frederic Jameson's terms, 'spatialise' media.[5]

Another key concern is to recognise the dangers of fragmentation in the field and the absence of a historical and formal account of the constituents of moving images. Therefore, many texts seek to link the art- and film-historical accounts of this period. Avant-garde or experimental film-makers on the one hand, and visual artists on the other, each have different modes of practice, histories, institutions, economic structures and critical languages, yet they very often share similar aesthetic concerns. To a great extent the problem of fragmentation has been caused by the formalist, high modernist allegiances of much of the experimental film world that sought to establish equal footing with the other 'high' arts. As Jonathan Walley's essay in this volume seeks to understand, the question remains whether this gap is indeed bridgeable.[6] It is in presenting a cross-section of filmic practices and juxtaposing studies of early works with contemporary ones that *Art and the Moving Image* seeks to provide new critical frameworks, to encourage a reconsideration of these histories and an understanding of how our perception of and relationship to the moving image in art has changed.

As French film critic Raymond Bellour has asked, somewhat disingenuously, 'what is a poor critic to do' now that cinema is 'redistributed, transformed, mimicked and reinstalled'? The transition between what is still called cinema and the one-thousand-and-one ways of presenting moving images within the site of the gallery, as Bellour writes elsewhere, begs further consideration of the kind of cinema that existed before, and this new, vague and ungraspable 'other'.[7] With projected images seemingly slipping out of control, how can we begin to understand the art of the moving image today? Such a question is difficult to answer without considering the typology of set-ups, modes and techniques, or without acknowledging the slippage between media and how they can metamorphose into multiple versions depending on their various viewing contexts. Thus, many of the essays collected here attempt to address this metamorphosis and the significant and diverse effects this potentially has on the viewer and on the work of art's meaning. Several of the authors insist on setting the record straight, on discriminating between film's and video's various modes, on revisiting their roots, arguing that to do so is critical to our understanding of the present. While some essays are theoretical, making brief reference to individual works in order to flesh out larger narratives, others involve intricate interpretations of individual moving-image installations. Case studies range from Andy Warhol's Exploding Plastic Inevitable (1966) to Bruce Nauman's corridor installations (1969–74), as well as to Marcel Broodthaers's *Section Cinéma* (1971–72) and Hélio Oiticica's 'quasi-cinemas' from the same period. Studies on recent artworks include Pierre Huyghe's *The Third Memory* (1999), Janet Cardiff and George Bures Miller's *The Paradise Institute* (2001), the cinematic projects of Eija-Liisa Ahtila (1993 – ongoing) and Bernadette Corporation's temporary underground film factory *Pedestrian Cinema* (2006–07).

In order to navigate the various discussions within this field, the book is divided into three different sections — 'Histories and Revisions', 'The Agonistic Relationship between Video and Television' and 'From Cinema to Post-Cinema' — while remaining sensitive to the temporal unfolding of the debates. 'Histories and Revisions' includes discussions of film's anomalous status and reception by the art world; the confusion of forms and media in early multiple-screen and multimedia installations; and the 'post-Minimal' turn and the temporalisation of space. 'The Agonistic Relationship between Video and Television' covers video's contradictory relationship to the field of art and the contested site of the exhibition space; the construction of alternative programmes for production, distribution and exhibition; video's different traditions and effects (for instance, how video art diverged from film while extending the medium of television within a real/present-time/space continuum); and how artists' video projects and televisual interventions effected transformations in the public sphere and cultural politics. 'From Cinema to Post-Cinema' includes the relationship of large-scale cinematic projections to classical cinema (their role and impact on the viewer), media archaeology, technical transformation, obsolescence and the future of film and video in the digital age.

The problem that *Art and the Moving Image* addresses in general is the association of art with technology, and in particular the relationship of visual art to projected images and the technologies of image reproduction. By 'projected images' I mean for the most part any gallery-based artwork that includes temporal images or time-based media (for example, film, slides, video, holographic and photographic or computer, digital, real-time projections). While some prefer the term 'moving image' — recalling expressions such as *moving pictures* and *motion pictures* (the word *image* embracing the abstract, non-figurative and non-objective) — for others, the term 'moving image' risks misleading the reader and needs some qualification. Invoking the notion of the 'image' is always a delicate matter; its methodological status within art historical discourse is a hotly debated topic, particularly since the arrival of visual studies. So, although it might seem transparent enough, it is questionable whether 'moving image' can provide sufficient clarity. The objections are three-fold. The concept of the 'moving image' is imprecise since it implies that movement is located at the level of the (filmic or televisual) image.[8] This is a reversal of the mechanism of film projection where actual movement is not, of course, 'in' the image itself but in the projector, though in video the scanning function is 'inside' of the image as it is constantly redrawn. The second point is that since so many of the essays here are concerned with a demystification (or 'stilling') of movement on an imaginary or ideological level, it is debatable whether 'moving image' is accurate enough. The third concern is that 'moving image' is an all-too generic term that might detract from a more specific, apparatical analysis of the relations — discursive, institutional, technical, etc. — between art and film.[9] Whereas the preceding objections are not insubstantial, in the end the term — which came to be through common usage — does portray the object of study sufficiently well. Bearing in mind that this book takes as its starting point the lecture series *Moving Images* at Tate Modern in spring 2002, organised by Mark Lewis and Andrew Brighton, I decided to retain the term 'moving image', although I use it interchangeably with the term 'projected image' here. It's obvious, but significant nevertheless, to emphasise that all categories — be they 'television', 'video art', 'the cinematic' or other — are artificial and similarly indeterminate; their presumed boundaries are in fact permeable. To assume the stability of any artistic (or non-artistic) media is to fail to appreciate that different image-making practices frequently cohabit the same technologies: video, for instance, encompasses home movies, digital film, commercial television, internet broadcasts and video art.[10] Every term presents different dilemmas, complexly intertwining with others. Avant-garde cinema, for example, has been variously described as 'personal', 'independent', 'amateur', 'artisanal', 'underground',

7 See Raymond Bellour, 'La querelle des dispositifs/Battle of the images', *Art Press*, no.262, November 2000, pp.48–52.

8 I am grateful to Eric de Bruyn for these observations. Email correspondence 24 January 2005.

9 Arguably, this being one of the shortcomings of, for instance, the 'Hall of Mirrors' exhibition (Museum of Contemporary Art, Los Angeles, 1996).

10 David Joselit, 'The Video Public Sphere', *Art Journal*, vol.59 no.2, Summer 2000, pp.46–53.

'experimental', 'concrete'. The 'cinematic' is problematic within this context because it indicates limits on video, Structural film, performance-based work and so on. In other words, the 'cinematic' proposes only one kind of relationship to the moving image in art while this book discusses many, of which some have little or nothing to do with the cinematic *per se*.[11]

With such an amplified discussion of the terms, it may be assumed that histories of artists' spatial experiments with film and video are available and well articulated. However, although significant critical attention has been paid to video and new media, and although 'film and video installation' is of great theoretical interest, there has been relatively little debate within Anglo-American criticism about the aesthetic, social and political significance of this field.[12] P. Adams Sitney's *Visionary Film*, the seminal high modernist book on moving images, for example, focuses on single-screen films but has little or nothing to say about expanded cinema, while most other theoretical and analytical contributions to the field of film and video installation have appeared in exhibition catalogues.[13] When comparing — if it's even feasible to do so — the scholarly output on this subject with that of video art and, to a lesser extent, experimental film, for example, the lack of attention to the art of the projected-image installation is evident. By comparison, however, due to economic incentives and the broader cultural context, new media is receiving a tremendous amount of coverage.

Whilst the popularity of film and video installation in contemporary art has been attributed to many factors — not least to the increasing availability and affordability of digital cameras, video projectors and editing programmes since the mid-90s — explicating reasons for their peripheral location and slight neglect within the established discipline of art history is not so straightforward. In search of provisional answers, the concerns and topics explored in the following pages allow the reader to become acquainted with the intersections between the world of art and that of film and television — an arena that has been called a 'videosphere', '*un autre cinéma*', a 'tertiary cinema' and a 'filmic topology', to name a few of the terms. In addition, the exact dynamics of moving-image artistic practices, their convergences, disparities and tensions are traced from the 60s onwards. If there is one area on which many of the writers in this book converge, it is the question of the projected image's interstitial status: the uneasy assimilation of these practices within an

11 Thanks to William Kaizen for pointing this out.

12 As Tamara Trodd, organiser of the conference 'Screen/Space: The Projected Image in Contemporary Art' at the University of Edinburgh in April 2007, writes: 'Astonishingly, it seems this may be the first major conference on the projected image in contemporary art to be organised by a UK university. This seems all the more surprising given the prominence and high profile internationally of British artists working with projected images'. Email correspondence with Trodd, 7 December 2006.

13 Exhibition catalogues on the subject of notable interest include: Kerry Brougher, *Art and Film Since 1945: Hall of Mirrors*, Los Angeles: The Museum of Contemporary Art, 1996; Chrissie Iles, *Into the Light: The Projected Image in American Art 1964–1977*, New York: Whitney Museum of American Art, 2001 (arguably a path-breaking exhibition for, in Tamara Trodd's words, 'putting the question of the projected image in the gallery space on the agenda for contemporary art, and in opening out theorisations of the projected image beyond the critical agendas of the 1960s and 70s'); Matthias Michalka, *X-Screen: Film Installations and Actions in the 1960s and 1970s*, Vienna: Museum Moderner Kunst Stiftung Ludwig, 2004; Stan Douglas, Christopher Eamon, Joachim Jaeger and Gabriele Knapstein, *Beyond Cinema: The Art of Projection*, Berlin: Hamburger Bahnhof, 2006; Harun Farocki and Antje Ehmann, *Cinema*

expanded field of scholarship, or within 'the physical, institutional or discursive space of either the art gallery or the cinematic theatre' (Andrew Uroskie; this volume, p.398).

One of the most compelling issues one faces in editing such a collection of texts is to order the scattered and radically heterogeneous works within this field, without imposing a false sense of homogeneity. In this sense the majority of contributions trace the movement of inconsistency and bias within the historical terrain of film and video installation art. They do not aim to represent a definitive survey of all moving-image practices or all new media. The focus is more selective, they represent — to cite art historian Eric de Bruyn — a constellation of ambivalent moments within the field, moments that are narrowly and ambitiously structured by contrastingly articulated positions. The texts aim to discover the critical reception of moving images in light of art historical perspectives, revealing the underlying paradoxes and anomalies within this history, while attempting to understand what kinds of moving images there are, and what their differences and limitations might be. There are two major omissions in the reader. The first is the presence of non-NATO/Western artists, and the second is the broad topic of New Media. The former was influenced by my focus on the extensive material available during research based in New York and Berlin. The second by the fact that New Media has been amply theorised in recent years. Such exclusions can only be acknowledged by the inescapable limitations of space that made difficult decisions necessary.

I The Projected Image in the 1960s and 70s

1. An Expanded Cinema

I am not a film-maker. For me, film is a prolongation of language. I started with poetry, then visual art and finally cinema, which combines several elements of the arts. By that I mean writing (poetry), the object (visual art) and the image (film). What is really difficult is of course the harmony between elements.

Marcel Broodthaers (discussing his film *Une discussion inaugurale* in 1968)

The decade of the 1960s is the apposite place to begin as this period marks the point when artists' film production emerged as a recognisable category

Like Never Before, Vienna: Generali Foundation, 2006. Significantly, Tate Modern's director, Vincent Todoli, claimed in the foreword to the 2004–05 catalogue to *Time Zones: Recent Film and Video* (curated by Jessica Morgan and Gregor Muir) that this exhibition 'constitutes Tate Modern's *first* to concentrate on [the] moving image' (my emphasis). Exceptions include Gene Youngblood's classic *Expanded Cinema*, New York: E.P. Dutton and Co., 1970 (which has been described as the manifestly psychedelic West Coast version of expanded cinema), and anthologies such as John G. Hanhardt's *Video Culture: A Critical Investigation*, New York: Visual Studies Workshop Press, 1986 (now more than twenty years old); D. Hall and S. Fifer's *Illuminating Video*, *op. cit.*; Ursula Frohne's *Video Cult/ures, Multimediale Installationen der 90er Jahre*, Karlsruhe and Cologne: ZKM Center for Art and Media, 1999; Edwin Carels, Mark Kremer and Dieter Roelstraete's *Projectie: Technologie als Metafoor*, Antwerp: Museum van Hedendaagse Kunst Antwerpen, 2006 (in Flemish only). To my knowledge few other comprehensive books devoted to this field have been published in recent years.

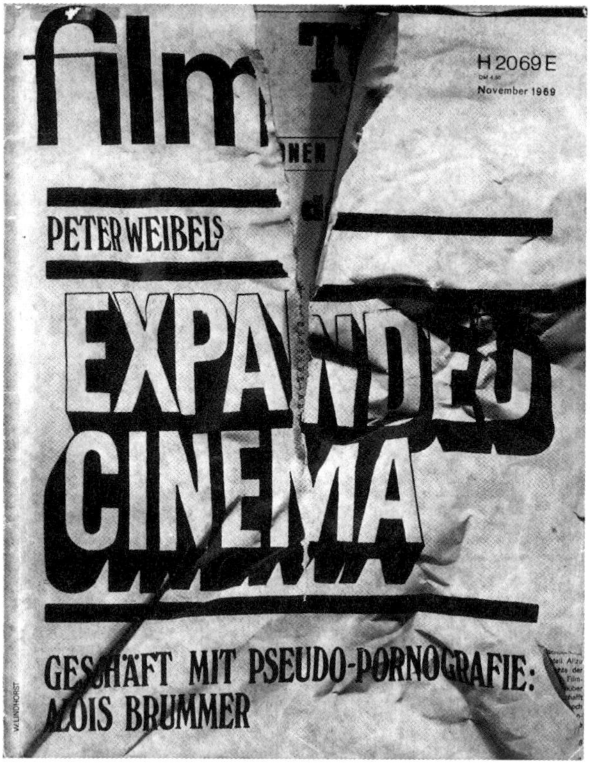

Cover of *film* designed by Peter Weibel, November 1969. Photo © 2008 Peter Weibel

of film art. It saw the contemporary exodus of film from the theatre towards the site of the gallery (and an emphasis on screening situations); the beginnings of an 'intermedia' condition; the permeation of boundaries between art and film; and the creation of hybrid filmic objects, installations, performances and events. As art historian Pamela M. Lee writes of VALIE EXPORT and Peter Weibel's shared conception of expanded cinema in the 60s, their practice focused in part on the 'scene of projection — the particularities attending the screening of the work itself'. Examinations of the relationships between reality and apparatus, and the reconceptualisation of film's inherent *illusionism* to the *material* of film, Lee and Weibel argued in 1967, paved the way for numerous new artistic possibilities, such as film installation and the film-environment. Artists, at this time, surpassed merely incorporating media imagery into painting, taking up moving-image technology itself—compelled as they were to do so under the influence of a newly mediated reality brought about by the ubiquitous televisual image. In fact, a general uptake of mass-mediation and mass-manufacturing technologies occurred in the art of the 60s, from Pop and Minimalism to post-Minimalism.

The focus on the 60s has to do not only with the greater hybridity between art forms that was established during the decade but also with access. The decades after World War II were a time when access to 16mm-film equipment (at least in the US and Britain) was reasonably affordable and uncomplicated, and video became available from the late 60s onwards, when Sony released the first domestic video equipment onto the market. The period also marked the beginning of widespread state support for the production of media workshops that encouraged different forms of experimentation. With the acceleration of new technologies, and as film gradually gave way to new forms of electronic information in the 70s, there was also an embrace of recovered or displaced media discarded by the industry. Against the totalising logic of mass communication, a number of artists took to film to explore the phenomenological and physiological conditions of perceptual experience for the viewer, and to exploit the realm between the autonomous space of the museum and the spectacular realm of the mass media.

While Nam June Paik made his notorious, imageless *Zen For Film* from 1962 to 1964 (in which clear leader was run through the projector), his famous exhibition 'Exposition of Music—Electronic Television', which opened on 11 March 1963 in Galerie Parnass, Wuppertal-Elberfeld, used television monitors to display modified broadcast images and abstract electronic patterns. During the same year, another Fluxus-affiliated artist, Wolf Vostell, showed altered television monitors ('dé-collage') and staged performances as conduits for newly distorted broadcast messages at the Smolin Gallery in New York. Throughout the decade, further exhibitions implicitly and explicitly problematised the conventional distinctions between 'art and technology' and involved other experimental art media and technological inventions. They included Maurice Tuchman's 'Art and Technology Program' at the Los Angeles Museum of Art in 1967; 'Cybernetic Serendipity' at the ICA in London in 1968, curated by Jasia Reichardt; 'The Machine: As Seen at the End of the Mechanical Age', curated by Pontus Hulten at the Museum of Modern Art in New York in 1968; 'Television as Creative Medium' at the Howard Wise Gallery in New York, organised by Wise in 1969 (the first gallery exhibition devoted exclusively to video as an art form); and art historian Jack Burnham's exhibition 'Software, Information Technology: Its New Meaning for Art' at the Jewish Museum in New York, 1970. One of the prevalent attitudes held by artists, engineers and curators (for example, John Cage, Robert Rauschenberg, Billy Klüver and Jack Burnham) was that art possessed special and redemptive powers that, when combined with technology, could counteract what was perceived as the latter's deleterious effects. This humanistic view was characterised by the utopian ideal of fusing art and technology, believing that it was unrealistic for art and technology to develop separately if some kind of revolution was to ensue.

A particularly famous series of 'intermedia' events that reveal the unquestionable impact

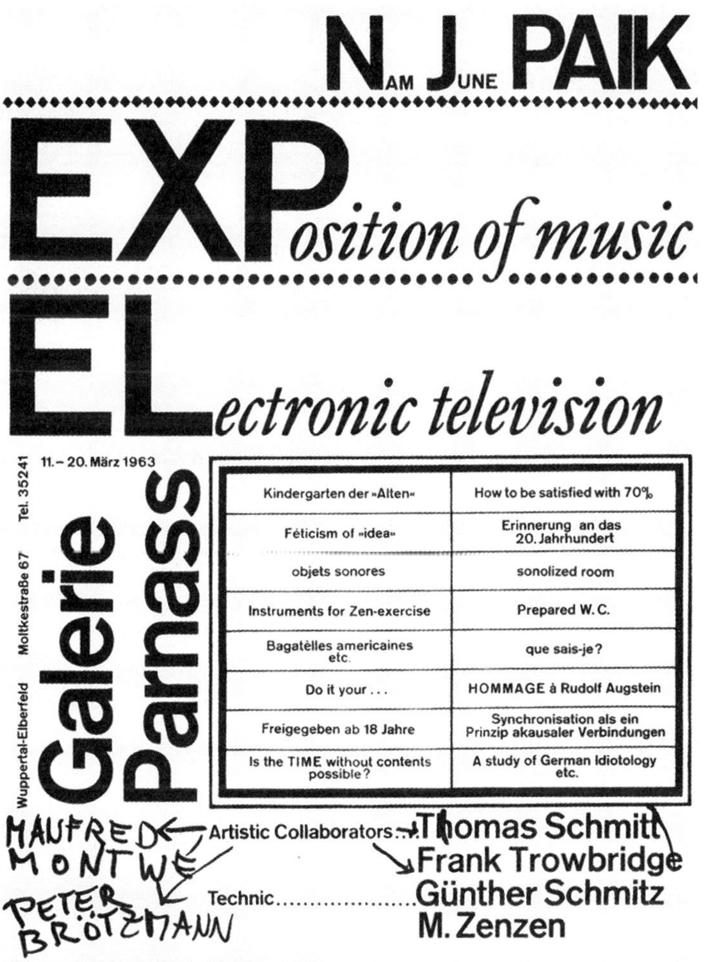

Nam June Paik, poster for *Exposition of Music – Electronic Television*, 57.5×42cm, March 1963. Photo © 2008 Günter Knop

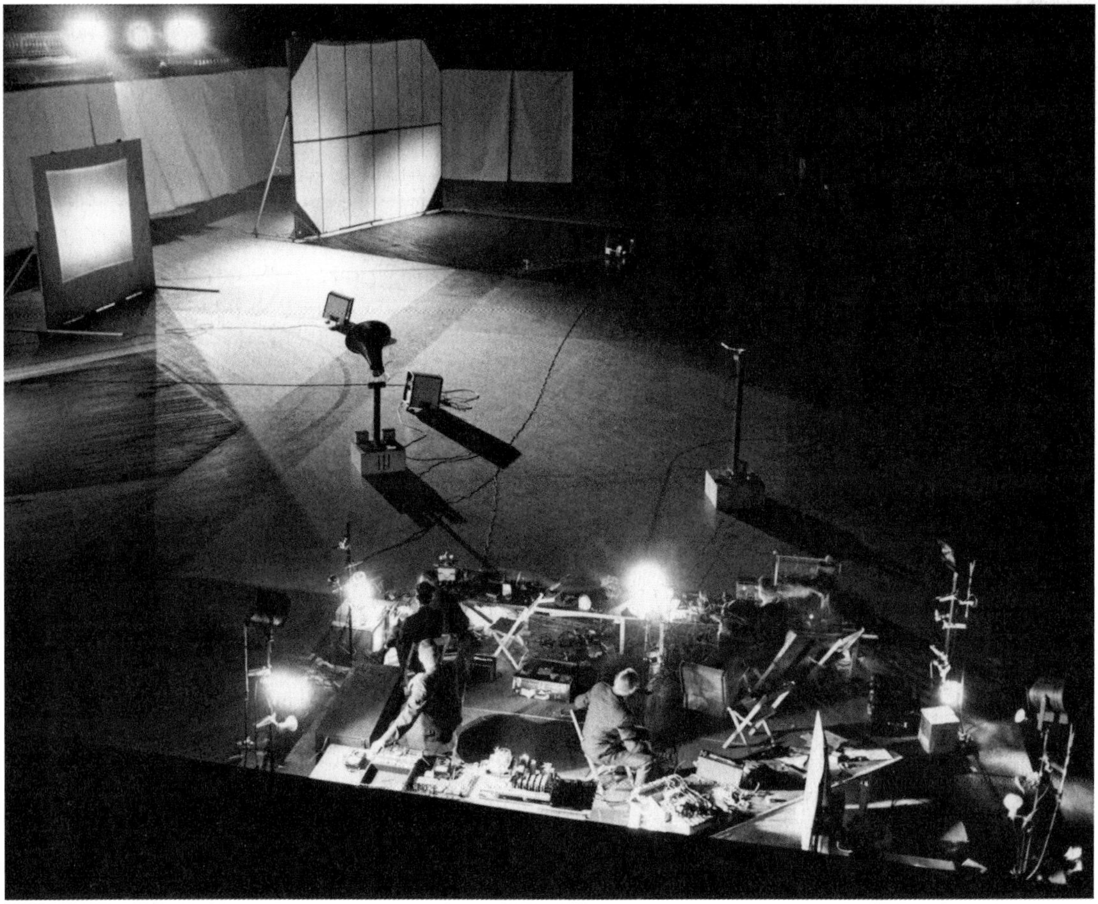

and centrality of science and technology on the art of the 60s was '9 Evenings: Theatre and Engineering', a series of performances hosted at the 69th Regimental Armory in New York in 1966. '9 Evenings' brought together forty engineers (including Klüver and Fred Waldhauer) and ten contemporary artists, musicians, dancers and performers associated with the Judson Memorial Church (Cage, Lucinda Child, Öyvind Fahlström, Alex Hay, Yvonne Rainer, Steve Paxton, Rauschenberg, David Tudor and Robert Whitman) to collaborate on performances incorporating new technology. From this series of performances developed the non-profit organisation E.A.T. (Experiments in Art and Technology). While '9 Evenings' was detested at the time by the local press, it did pose significant questions as to what constituted the relationship between art and technology, and it came to stand as an icon for subsequent collaborations — meetings between E.A.T. organisers and local artists are said to have initiated an unprecedented call for institutionally supported access to technology and the arts.[14] E.A.T. also initiated other interdisciplinary events and projects, for example, 'Some More Beginning' (1968), held at the Brooklyn Museum, New York, and arguably the first international exhibition of art and technology. These artist-engineer collaborations climaxed in the 70s with E.A.T.'s design conceived for the extravagant pavilion commissioned by

'9 Evenings: Theatre and Engineering', New York, 1966. Photo © 2008 Peter Moore estate & VAGA, New York

Facing page: Tony Conrad, frames from *The Flicker*, 1965–66. 16mm black-and-white film, sound, 30mins. Courtesy Anthology Film Archives. All rights reserved

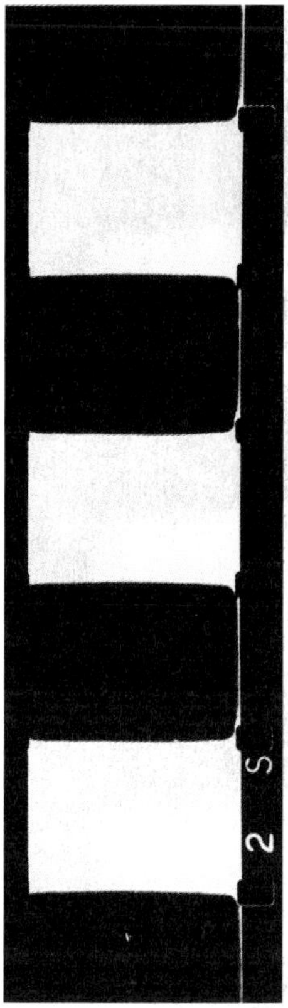

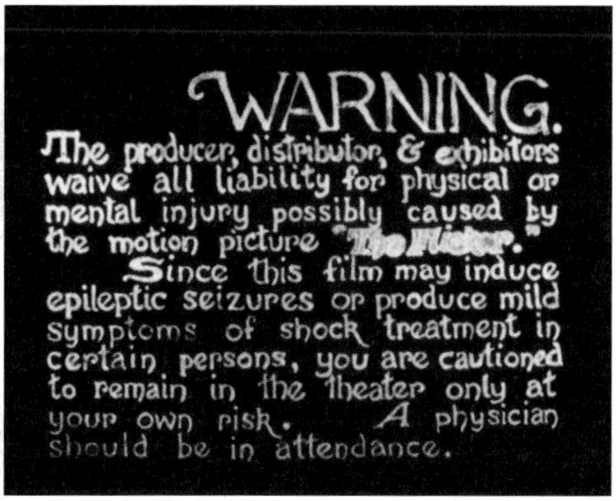

Pepsi-Cola for Expo '70 in Osaka, Japan.

Just prior to '9 Evenings', Robert Whitman debuted *Prune Flat* at the multiple-venue 'Expanded Cinema Festival' in New York in 1965. As art historian Branden W. Joseph has written, this series of occurrences that radically altered the relationships between film, performance and the audience, positioned the artist prominently within the newly emerging art form of 'expanded cinema' in the 60s.[15] Whitman's *Shower* (c.1964), a *trompe l'oeil* image of a woman showering in a functioning metal shower stall, was 'amazing', Jonas Mekas wrote in his movie journal, 'because it pushed cinema into another field of unexplored and new possibilities'.[16] Whitman's so-called 'cinema pieces' that combined live action, film and objects innovatively utilised the spatio-temporal possibilities of moving-image technologies to confound viewers' habitual ways of categorising experiences of illusion and reality. They took place in a new hybridised space at the limits of theatre — somewhere between the white cube and the black box.

The 'flicker films' pioneered by Peter Kubelka in Vienna, and developed by Tony Conrad, Paul Sharits and others, are also exemplary, if unusual, forms of 'expanded cinema' — unusual in that they are not typically considered in such terms. Gilles Deleuze noted in *Cinema 2* that Conrad's *The Flicker* (1965–66) helped to acknowledge the introduction of a 'third epoch' in film: a 'cinema of expansion without camera, and also without screen or film stock', a cinema in which 'anything can be used as a screen, the body of a protagonist or even the bodies of the spectators; anything can replace the film stock, in a virtual film which now only goes on in the head, behind the pupils'.[17] Other 'expanded cinema' events that prefigured the large-scale theatre works of the 70s and 80s and which serve as precedents for subsequent experiments with moving images in the gallery are best exemplified by 'intermedia' works such as Jordan Belson's legendary vortex concerts at Morrison Planetarium in San Francisco in the late 50s, or the pioneering light, film and performance pieces of the 60s multimedia collective USCO; Stan VanDerBeek's *Movie-Drome* (1963); Andy Warhol's Exploding Plastic Inevitable (1966); Mark Boyle and Joan Hill's

14 For a full introduction to E.A.T. and *9 Evenings*, see Pamela M. Lee, 'Introduction: Eros and Technics and Civilization', in Lee's *Chronophobia: On Time in the Art of the 1960s*, Cambridge, Mass. and London: The MIT Press, pp.5–34.

15 Branden W. Joseph, 'Plastic Empathy: The Ghost of Robert Whitman', *Grey Room* 25, Fall 2006, pp.64–91.

16 Jonas Mekas, 'Movie Journals', *Village Voice*, 3 June 1965.

17 Gilles Deleuze, *Cinema 2: The Time-Image* (trans. Hugh Tomlinson and Robert Galeta), Minneapolis: University of Minnesota Press, 1989, p.215 (translation modified), quoted in Branden W. Joseph, *Beyond the Dream Syndicate: Tony Conrad and the Arts after Cage*, New York: Zone Books, forthcoming in 2008.

Son et Lumiére for Earth, Air, Fire and Water (1966); John Cage and Ronald Nameth's *HPSCHD* (1969); Hélio Oiticica's *CC5 Hendrix-War* (1973); and Carolee Schneemann's *Snows* (1967).

For VanDerBeek the expansion beyond the medium's boundaries was an attempt to remedy the lack of cultural communication reflected in the global crisis of the period. Expanding art to encompass broader political systems of distribution, social regulation and mechanisms of information. Through his *Movie-Drome* he sought to create a worldwide satellite communication network intended to effect levels of the unconscious and act as an emotional denominator across all people and cultures.[18] If *Movie-Drome* aimed to unite all men in utopian cultural conditions, celebrating the capacity of electronics to effect a 'cultural intercom', Warhol's multiple-screen, expanded cinema production the EPI bombarded and disorientated viewers. Branden W. Joseph argues that the EPI's contradictory experimental environment, where different media clashed against each other with intensely distracting, shock-like effects, was completely at odds with other similarly enveloping electronic environments, such as the desire of Charles and Ray Eames for ideological naturalisation — in projects like *Think* (at the IBM Pavilion at the New York World's Fair in 1964) — that 'actually produced a more active form of suture, an identification with and subjection to the electronic image', or Marshall McLuhan's descriptions of a new 'auditory' electronic space that claimed to unify viewers in a twentieth-century global village, and saw the return of spectators to self-presence (Branden W. Joseph; this volume, p.105).

Artists such as Marcel Broodthaers, Dan Graham, David Lamelas, Bruce Nauman, Richard Serra and Robert Smithson, intersecting with the diverse practices of post-Minimalism in the late 60s and early 70s, engaged in critical investigations with film as a medium within the domain of visual arts to resist the technological and ideological forces of the globalised marketplace. Argentinian artist David Lamelas's *Time as Activity* (1969), conceived for Kunsthalle Düsseldorf, offers an opportunity to reflect on the *positive* potential of film. Based on a model of site-specificity and 'anti-narrative', his film presents three 4-minute-long, stationary views of the area immediately surrounding the Kunsthalle. In negating action and narrative, *Time as Activity* proposes a way of operating politically within spectacle, without allowing that which is shown to be hidden in the nothingness it shows and presented as an *image* itself. It refuses and frustrates the normative processes by which the mass media imposes subjective identification with its social apparatus. To invoke Walter Benjamin — and as paraphrased by the philosopher Giorgio Agamben in his essay 'Repetition and Stoppage: Guy Debord's Technique of Montage' — it 'exhibits the image as image and thus to allow the appearance of "imagelessness", which [...] is the refuge of all images'.[19] Agamben (extending also Deleuze's thoughts on cinema) suggests that film be understood not as representation — that is, as image and hence politics — but rather as gesture.

The late 60s also witnessed the regular appearance of film and later video criticism in art magazines — some of the most interesting of which included

Artforum, the cross-disciplinary magazine *Aspen* and the German magazine *Interfunktionen*. In particular, it was critics such as Annette Michelson and Rosalind Krauss who resisted the specialisation of disciplines and explored the nexus between the different avant-gardes in film and art.[20] As film historian David Bordwell has commented on Michelson's support of avant-garde film, her 'philosophically informed essays [have] helped make the study of avant-garde film part of modern art criticism and history'.[21] Michelson appealed to a new vocabulary of film, one based on art-critical training, rather than of the then-extant discourse of film criticism. She also called for a radicalised understanding of the viewer's perception from filmic action to the particular temporalities of the medium — a commitment that fostered a profound self-critique at the heart of modernist art criticism. Her appreciation and discussion of Canadian artist and film-maker Michael Snow's film *Wavelength* (1967) precisely underscores what Michelson saw as a unification of many kinds of critical opinion. She saw *Wavelength* as overcoming the split between 'narrative' and 'non-narrative', and transcending distinctions between 'linear' and 'vertical', 'prose' and 'poetic' forms, 'realistic' and 'mythopoeic', 'vertical' and 'horizontal' — styles of continuity and montage that had previously been key concerns for film theory.[22] Of course critics were not alone in analysing the connection between art and film, as artists and film-makers also made significant contributions — Malcolm Le Grice's 'The History We Need' or Peter Wollen's 'The Two Avant-Gardes' (the latter published in this volume), particularly so.[23]

Histories of the moving image are also controversially set against discourses in other fields, including those of independent film-making, classical cinema and the historical avant-garde of the 1920s, or linked art historically to modernist painting and sculpture and experimental forms such as process and body art, happenings, experimental theatre and performance. Although it is impossible here to cover these connections in full, it is important to highlight the so-called 'anti-production' or 'cine-sabotage' development of Situationist and Lettriste cinema, because their radicalism is too easily overlooked. Gil J. Wolman, one of the central figures in Isidore Isou's Lettrist movement, created *L'Anticoncept* (*The Anticoncept*) in 1951 — an imageless film projected on a large white weather balloon. Another film that dispensed with images and narrative altogether was Debord's *Hurlements en faveur de Sade* (*Howlings in favour of de Sade*) of 1952, which consisted of alternating

18 B.W. Joseph also discusses VanDerBeek in 'Plastic Empathy', *op. cit.*

19 Giorgio Agamben, 'Face au cinema et à l'Histoire, à propos de Jean-Luc Godard', *Le Monde des Livres*, 6 October 1995.

20 For a full account of film's appearance in art magazines, see Eric de Bruyn, *The Filmic Anomaly: Moments in Post-Minimalism (1966–1970)*, unpublished dissertation, New York: Graduate Faculty in Art History, The City University of New York, 2002, pp.2–5. Many of de Bruyn's essays on post-Minimalism and the 'filmic anomaly' have been particularly helpful in understanding the fragmented nature of this field, and it is from many of his insightful comments that these notes develop.

21 David Bordwell, *Making Meaning: Inference and Rhetoric in the Interpretation of Cinema*, Cambridge, Mass.: Harvard University Press, 1989, p.61.

22 See Malcolm Turvey's introduction to *Camera Obscura, Camera Lucida: Essays in Honor of Annette Michelson* (ed. Richard Allen and Malcolm Turvey), Amsterdam: Amsterdam University Press, 2002, p.27.

23 See Malcolm LeGrice, 'The History We Need', *Film as Film: Formal Experiment in Film 1910–1975* (3 May–17 June, 1979). 'Film as Film' was curated for the Hayward Gallery by David Curtis and Richard Francis. The exhibition was originally conceived by Brigit Hein and Wulf Herzogenrath at the Kölnisher Kunstverein in 1978.

Marcel Duchamp, still from *Anemic Cinema*, 1925–26. 16mm black-and-white film, silent, 7mins © 2008 Succession Marcel Duchamp/ADAGP, Paris & DACS, London

Facing page: Takahiko iimura, *A Loop Seen as a Line*, 1972.16mm film installation

black-and-white leader accompanied by voiceovers reading mainly found text fragments intercut with periods of silence of varying lengths. Such affronts to cinematic conventions have been described not so much as works of art or experiments that revolutionised the medium of film, but rather as tactical constructions that intended to provoke real social change — revolutionising and reinventing the structure of life itself. Situationist and Lettriste counter-cinema is pre-eminent in its encouragement of entirely new relationships between spectators and projected images.

2. The Problem of the Medium

> [A]ny technology gradually creates a totally new human environment. Environments are not passive wrappings but active processes [...]
> Marshall McLuhan

Two concepts frequently referred to in discussions about moving images and art are 'medium-specificity' and the 'post-medium condition'. The former notion refers to the traditional way in which mediums have been specified, for example, as painting, sculpture, photography and so on. The latter — a term identified by art historian Rosalind Krauss (drawing on analysis by Fredric Jameson) — endorses the rejection of traditional media in favour of hybrid artistic forms and technologies, displacing formalist definitions of the medium and the perpetuation of distinct artistic traditions.

Echoed in a quote by semiotician Roland Barthes, a persistent concern with the obliteration of medium-boundaries flourished in the 60s: 'Nothing separates the Eisensteinian frame from the Greuzean tableau ... nothing separates the epic-theatre scene from the Eisensteinian frame.'[24] Conceptual, Minimalist and Process art turned towards a 'dematerialisation' of art into idea. The object in the context of Minimalism acknowledged the ambient space and the viewing subject, elaborating its phenomenological concerns and giving way to 'process' and 'situation' — as famously described by the artist Robert Morris.[25] 'Even the most unalterable property, shape, does not remain constant', Morris claimed — extending Marcel Duchamp's notion that it is the viewer who completes the work — 'for with each shift in position the viewer also constantly changes the apparent shape of the work'.[26] As sculpture in the hands of Richard Serra gave way to temporality (*Splashing*, 1968) — so film became simultaneously temporal, spatial and 'physicalised' with the likes of Takahiko iimura (*A Loop Seen As A Line*, 1972), Anthony McCall (*Line Describing a Cone*, 1973), or Paul Sharits (*Sound Strip/Film Strip*, 1971), as the beam of the projector or other elements of the film system were exploited with a new 'sensitivity' towards the space of projection or exhibition.[27] For artists such as Joan Jonas,

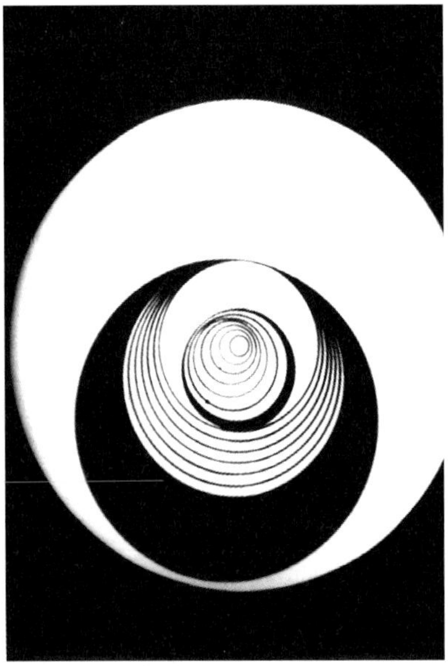

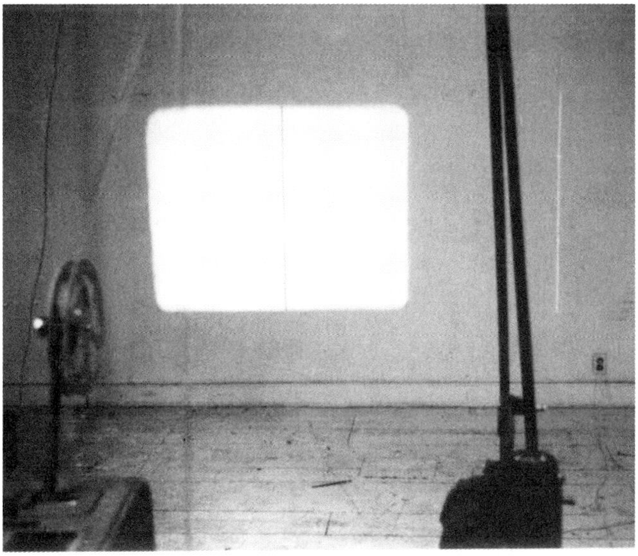

Lynda Benglis, Bruce Nauman and Vito Acconci, among others, specific media such as painting, sculpture, drawing and film were gradually abandoned in favour of what was deemed a higher integrity for art — a new hybridisation of forms and an expansion to immaterial 'supports', such as performance, video and installation art.

Other artists continued to act in response to the necessity for material specificity, wedded as they were to foregrounding the intrinsic properties of the medium as the very substance of their work. In Britain during the late 70s and early 80s, many avant-garde film-makers gathered around the London Film-Makers Co-op, such as Peter Gidal, Malcolm Le Grice, Nicky Hamlyn, Tony Hill, Annabel Nicolson, Jane Rigby and Tony Sinden, were engaged in exploring the materiality of film. Malcolm Le Grice's series of film performances — for example, *Horror Film* (1971), *Love Story 3* (1972) and *Preproduction* (1973) — drew attention to the physicality and spatiality of the film apparatus, while asserting the dominance of film's physical parameters in the viewing experience itself.

P. Adams Sitney's term 'Structural film' — first coined in the eponymous essay in *Film Culture* in 1969 — 'was initially defined *against* related modernist ideals. Sitney enumerated Structural film's four characteristics — fixed frame, loop printing, flicker and rephotography off the screen ... '[28] He saw its principle 'axiom', its potentiality, not as the dismissal or 'condensation' of film's temporality, but rather as the 'elongation' of the temporal.[29] As defined by film historian David James, 'Structural', or 'Conceptual', film, had an 'essential [...] concern with materials and language' which 'took the form of a general subordination of interest in representation, especially of narrative, and a corresponding emphasis on the materials and resources of the medium, on the conditions of production and display and on the specific kinds of signification of which film is capable'.[30] The inherently self-reflexive

24 Roland Barthes, 'Diderot, Brecht, Eisenstein', *The Responsibility of Forms* (trans. Richard Howard), Berkeley: University of California Press, 1991, pp.90–91. Quoted in G. Baker, *Gerard Byrne, op. cit.*, p.35.
25 Quoted by T.J. Demos, in 'The Art of Darkness: On Steve McQueen', *October*, no.114, Fall 2005, p.78.
26 See Robert Morris, 'Notes on Sculpture', *Continuous Project Altered Daily: The Writings of Robert Morris*, Cambridge, Mass.: The MIT Press, 2000. Duchamp's attack on the modernist myth of visual purity is best exemplified in his focus on the presentational rather than the representational in Anemic Cinema (1925–26), an abstract film intended for projection on to a two-way mirror.
27 T.J. Demos, 'The Art of Darkness: On Steve McQueen', *op. cit.*, p.78.
28 See B.W. Joseph, *Beyond the Dream Syndicate*, *op. cit.*
29 P. Adams Sitney, 'Structural Film' (1969), *Film Culture Reader* (ed. P. Adams Sitney), New York: Cooper Square Press, 2000, p.332.
30 David E. James, *Allegories of Cinema: American Film in the Sixties*, Princeton: Princeton University Press, 1989. Quoted in Genevieve Yue's 'The Last Picture Show: Film and Video Installation in the Late '60s and Early '70s', www.sensesofcinema.com/contents/03/28/last_picture_show_installation_60s_70s.html#3

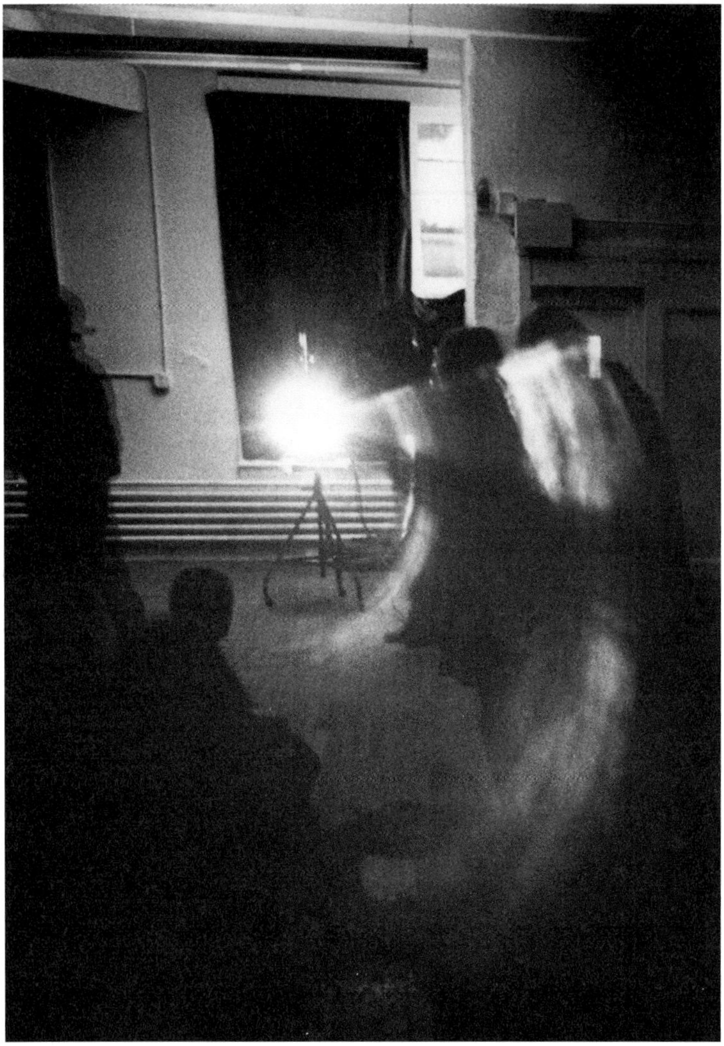

characteristic of the work of 'Structuralist' film-makers, according to Sitney, supposedly induced a more meditative, contemplative mode of viewing that marked a paradigmatic shift within modernist aesthetics. Sitney's 'Structural Film' article was the subject of a terse attack by George Maciunas and others who asserted that many of the characteristics Sitney enshrined already existed in works associated with Fluxus artists. Peter Gidal, the main theorist of the rather austere Marxist concept of 'Structural/Materialist film', was similarly intent on confronting the materiality of film and its representation. In 1976, the British Film Institute published his seminal article 'Theory and Definition of Structural/Materialist Film' in its *Structural Film Anthology*, which forged a new theoretical framework for the British avant-garde — a framework that was an important influence on a whole generation of younger artists and film-makers, most notably acclaimed film-maker John Smith. Gidal used the term 'Structural/Materialist' polemically in order to recognise the work that P. Adams Sitney had canonised, and to try to distance himself from what he saw as Sitney's idealism.

Unlike film, however, whose intrinsic properties could be easily foregrounded as the very substance of the work, the question of video's ontological 'specificity' was much more complex, its formal language more difficult to articulate. Some artists would agree with Bill Viola's remark, from the early days of video art, that, 'like Structural film', the medium of video is 'the content'. Other artists, such as Vito Acconci, Bruce Nauman and David Hall, while expressing discontent with medium-specific definitions in general, and critically engaged as they were with inventing new supports and spaces for art, did however see in video a specific characteristic — namely mediation — that was to become a central subject in their work. Andy Warhol's quadruple film-

Anthony McCall, *Line Describing a Cone*, 1973. 16mm film installation. Photo © 2008 Peter Moore estate & VAGA, New York

video portrait of Edie Sedgwick, *Outer and Inner Space* (1965), is considered one of the earliest works to reflect on mediation, on film's relationship to video and televisual liveness. It is precisely this aspect of mediation in video that Nauman took up in his various participatory 'corridor' pieces of the late 60s and early 70s (for example, *Live Taped Video Corridor* and *Going Around the Corner Piece*, both from 1970). These consisted of claustrophobic enclosures that introduced delay, liveness and 'performance' — in the sense of 'performing' as a spectator, rather than passively 'viewing' — into video. Spectator participation, art historian Janet Kraynak argues, is consistently figured in these environments as strangely alienating encounters where the viewer 'continually confronts a collapse of identification between her experience as a body/subject and her image or representation' (this volume, p.229).

Acconci and Hall also aggressively addressed spectator participation and the collapse of identification between the self and its image, the artist and the audience. Acconci's *Centers* (1971) points to video's immediacy and how the 'now-ness of communication' is both opened and foreclosed in television. Art historian William Kaizen writes of the 'phatic' communication at work in Acconci's *Centers*, that it elicits the palpable experience of televisions' lopsided immediacy (this volume p.270). By pointing at the viewer in a virtual present, Acconci urges viewers to consider their own reflections within the paradoxical contradiction of televisual 'now-ness'. His work, as Kaizen says, lays bare the fact that television and video always run up against their own reality, that they are never as transparent, immediate or as instantaneous as they might first appear.

If there is a difficulty in specifying and articulating the formal language of video, it may be attributed to its instantaneity — the quality of its being able to produce the image simultaneously as it transmits it — as well as its controversial 'lack of physicality'. Adapting the title of one of Gary Hill's video works, it has been said that video seems 'stuck, ontologically speaking "between cinema and a hard place" — the hard place of television'.[31] Another view of video considered its paradoxical containment within the sculptural box of the television set. Nam June Paik's early work explored this paradox in depth and almost always used monitors in his installations (*Participation TV*, 1963; *Magnet TV*, 1965; *TV Buddha*, 1974; *Candle TV*, 1975). Joan Jonas's *Vertical Roll* of 1972 references this quite explicitly. In a sense it was the boxy physicality of video that gave it an *entrée* into the gallery world.

Numerous articles — long before Krauss's influential essay 'Video and the Aesthetics of Narcissism' (1976, republished in this volume) and her pronouncement that narcissism was the medium of video — discussed the problem of the medium of video and television, including, most notably, the work of Marshall McLuhan.[32] McLuhan famously theorised televisual images

31 H. Foster, et. al., *Art Since 1900*, *op. cit.*, p.562.
32 See, for example, Marshall McLuhan, *Understanding Media: The Extensions of Man*, New York: McGraw-Hill, 1964.

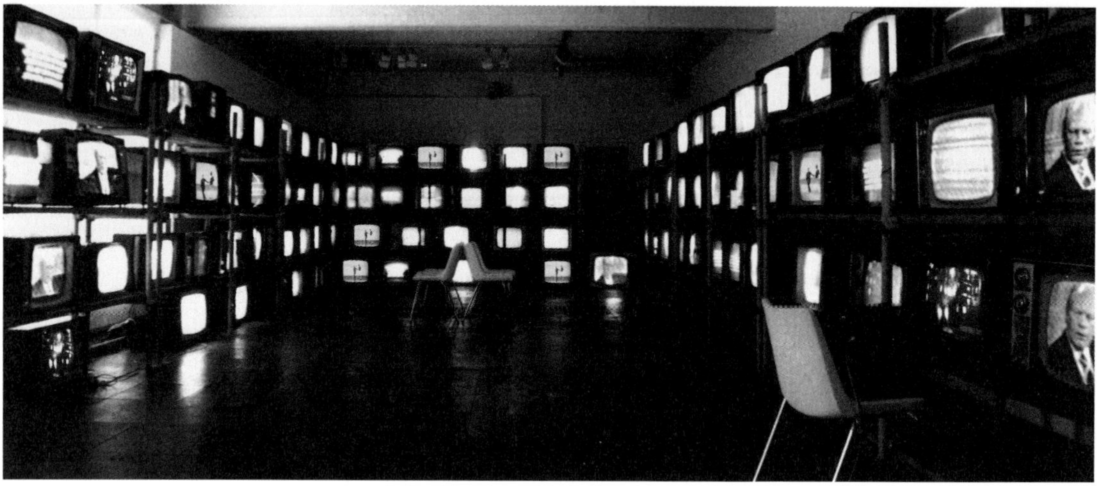

as projective 'tactile promptings', arguing that television and video are not primarily visual media but are an extension of touch rather than sight. He pronounced:

> The mode of the TV image has nothing in common with film or photo, except that it offers also a nonverbal gestalt or posture of forms. With TV, the viewer is the screen. He is bombarded with light impulses that James Joyce called 'the Charge of the Light Brigade' imbuing his 'soulskin with sobconscious inklings'. The TV image is visually low in data. The TV image is not a still shot. It is not photo in any sense, but a ceaselessly forming contour of things limned by the scanning-finger.[33]

Video was one place where problems related to the mass media as a medium were formulated and considered in detail, using the legacy of Modernism but moving in a 'postmodern' direction regarding the self and its constitution.[34]

Contrary to what Krauss wrote in the 70s, when she did consider video as a medium and did specify its 'formal language', she has recently appealed to an idea of 'differential specificity', a re-articulation of a medium as such. She has written of the strategies of post-Minimalist artists that they 'expanded' rather than negated previously conceived notions of artistic mediums, and created a new mode of specificity that could act upon the world in new ways. Krauss points to the practice of video as central to this condition, where ideas override the centrality of a particular medium. Belgian artist Marcel Broodthaers's use of primitive cinema is a significant example of the 'redemptive possibilities encoded at the birth of a given technical support'.[35] As film-maker Keith Sanborn has pointed out, even this essentially high-modernist formulation, however, can also be seen to function retroactively as incipiently postmodernist, much like the films and written work — not to mention the digital work — of film-makers such as Hollis Frampton.

As we have seen, encounters between art and moving images cannot be defined *exclusively* by their mere material specificity or ontological security (in terms of the film or video medium itself), and analysing media art in terms

David Hall, *101 TV Sets*, Serpentine Gallery, London, 1975

of the medium alone is not particularly helpful.[36] As art historian David Joselit asserted: 'If the art of the '60s and '70s had anything to teach us, it was that aesthetic problems no longer needed to be couched in one form or another but could migrate across different material substrates at will.'[37] Therefore, in attempting any legitimate genealogy of media art or any analysis of film and video works, their institutional, discursive and cultural contexts must also be taken into account.

3. The Institutional Context

Following film critic Annette Michelson's 'radical aspiration' of the avant-garde — a desire that sought to secure a recognition of film's specificity and a reconsideration of its aims in opposition to Hollywood cinema — film-makers and artists in the 60s and 70s ended in an ambiguous situation where they were both pushing film out of the black box and into the white cube of the gallery while still sometimes trying to keep it in the black box and rejecting visual art's own conventions. Jonas Mekas, who in the 60s had set out to chart the contours of American experimental cinema, noted: 'The medium of cinema is breaking out and taking over and is going blindly and by itself. Where to nobody knows ... '[38] At the same time that Mekas was questioning where film was heading, some artists and film-makers expressly avoided the white cube. Peter Wollen and Malcolm Le Grice, for example, were particularly suspicious of the space of the gallery, and Peter Kubelka designed *The Invisible Cinema* (Anthology Film Archives, New York, 1970–74) — a highly unusual cinema theatre where everything was painted black or covered in black velvet with blinkered seats — to eliminate any distraction or possibility of interaction from surrounding spectators, in complete contrast to viewing conditions in the space of the gallery. As film-maker Stan Brakhage commented of *The Invisible Cinema*, 'people really had a sense of drifting in a black space, a black box, and black ahead of you, nothing visible except the screen'.[39] Anthology Film Archives, founded by Mekas, Kubelka, Brakhage and P. Adams Sitney in 1970, was, and still is, a pantheon for experimental cinema dedicated to the black box and the self-awareness of film — a strongly modernist gesture — even while recognising the worth of work like Anthony McCall's sculptural films.

33 *Ibid.* (From the second edition, New York: Signet, 1966, p.273 (VIII).)

34 Thanks to William Kaizen for his observations on the question of the medium.

35 Rosalind Krauss argues – if rather idealistically – for using the term 'technical support' as a way of repelling the unwanted positivism of the term 'medium', a term she claims for the most part refers to the specific material support for a traditional aesthetic genre, whereas '"Technical support" has the virtue of both acknowledging the recent obsolescence of most traditional aesthetic mediums ... while it also welcomes the layered mechanisms of new technologies that make a simple, unitary identification of the work's physical support (is the "support" of film the celluloid strip, the screen, the splices of the edited footage, the projector's beam of light, the circular reels?)'; see Rosalind Krauss, 'Two Moments from the Post-Medium Condition', *October*, no.116, Spring 2006, p.56.

36 See Jonathan Crary, *Techniques of the Observer: On Vision and Modernity in the Nineteenth Century*, Cambridge, Mass.: The MIT Press, 1990, pp.30–31, and William Kaizen's summary of Crary's suggestion of the discursiveness of a given medium (this volume, note number 21, pp.260–61).

37 David Joselit, '"Into the Light: Image in American Art 1964–1977"; Whitney Museum of American Art, New York', *Artforum*, January 2002, pp.135–36

38 Jonas Mekas, 'Movie Journals', *Village Voice,* 11 November 1965.

39 Quoted in Sky Sitney, 'The Search for The Invisible Cinema', *Grey Room* 19, Spring 2005, p.108.

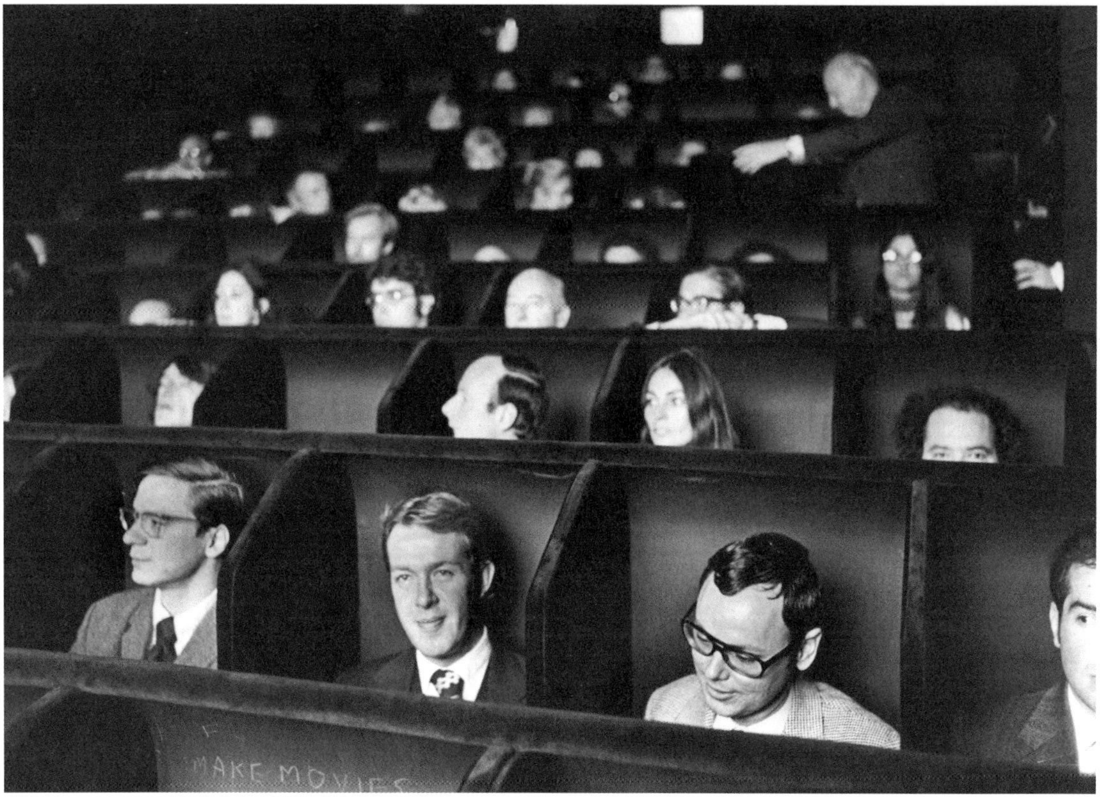

Peter Kubelka, *The Invisible Cinema*, 1970. Courtesy Anthology Film Archives.

Critical debates about new ideas of representation, fuelled by the collapse of disciplinary boundaries, created a new model of specificity—a concern not with medium-specificity so much as a medium's 'site-specificity'—one that created a new kind of consideration towards the space of projection or exhibition. Art historian Alexander Alberro reminds us that the meaning of film and video installations is not merely a question of material or materiality, nor of a work's thematic content; rather, they are 'intricately dependent on the way a particular work comes together in formal terms and dialogically negotiates the site of its display' (this volume, p.424).

However, as Eric de Bruyn states, this 'should not automatically lead to the conclusion that the frame determines the work. It is the frame as such that many of the works problematise', and it is rather the 'shifting network of various public spheres' that one needs to consider.[40] The term 'public spheres' here embodies the meaning of an oppositional dynamic—a dynamic, as the scholar Miriam Hansen originally intended in her definition of 'public', which denotes 'a discursive matrix or process through which social experience is articulated, interpreted, negotiated, and contested in an intersubjective, potentially collective, and oppositional form'.[41] Through analysis of 'performative' film works from the 60s and 70s that drew attention to their architectural surroundings and critiqued the manipulative powers of the media, de Bruyn proposes to consider post-Minimal film not just through the 'prism of its dialectical relation to modernism', but to 'dominant publicity' as well. Post-Minimalist experiments, such as Marcel Broodthaers's *Le Corbeau et le renard* (1967) and David Lamelas's *Film Script (Manipulation of Meaning)* (1972), for example, forged new and important relations between artistic practices and the public sphere. The intention of such works to engage viewers' 'social horizons of experience' points to a 'politics of counterpublicity' not equitable with a tactic of direct political engagement with the media, but rather a certain awareness that alternative models to the homogenised public sphere of mass culture were needed.[42] It is the 'emphatic shadow that inserts itself between the viewer and the image' that many artists and film-makers have thematised in their work.[43] It has been argued that the 'work' of Broodthaers's *Section Cinéma*, for instance, was not just in placing the cinematic apparatus and the interstices between the viewer and projector on display; rather, it was in exhibiting the intersection of relations between production and reception.

By the mid-60s film's anomalous status as art was gradually beginning to change as multimedia experiments proliferated. As Jonas Mekas reported, 'suddenly, the intermedia shows are all over the town ... now, with five, six, seven-year perspective, these far-far-out and anti-art works begin to fall into the same thousand-year-old treasury of all art'.[44] However, although film and video installation has now become a staple in contemporary art, Mekas's statement is not quite as correct as he may have anticipated in the late 60s. As we know, this period did not guarantee film's seamless assimilation into the wider body of the visual arts. And even today projected-image art, when considered alongside more traditional media or 'technical supports', still experiences intrinsic difficulties regarding its modes of display, marketability and collectable status.

André Bazin argued that cinema was tainted because it drew inspiration from all the other arts and offered nothing in exchange except reality. One of painting's most insistent proponents, Michael Fried, condemned the hybrid activity of (post-)Minimalism as 'theatre', the veritable enemy of modernist art, into which its forms could only degenerate: 'The success, even the survival, of the arts has come increasingly to depend on their ability to defeat theatre.'[45] One register of the difficulty of the institution of art in embracing the moving image has to do with the fact the medium itself is inherently vague and difficult to locate. Raising Bazin's famous vexed question on the ontology of cinema — 'Qu'est-ce que le cinéma?' — film historian Mary Anne Doane argues: 'The answer to the question "Where is the film?" is less assured than

40 Eric de Bruyn, 'The Expanded Field of Cinema, or Exercise on the Perimeter of a Square', *X-Screen: Film Installations and Actions in the 1960s and 1970s* (ed. Matthias Michalka), Vienna: Museum Moderner Kunst Stiftung Ludwig, 2004, pp.154–55.

41 Miriam Hansen, 'Early Cinema, Late Cinema: Transformations of the Public Sphere', *Viewing Positions: Ways of Seeing Film* (ed. Linda Williams), New Brunswick and New York: Rutgers University Press, 1995, p.140; quoted in Eric de Bruyn, 'Shadows of the Spectacle', *Argos Festival Brussels*, Brussels: Argos, 2003, p.46.

42 *Ibid.*, pp.48 and 56.

43 *Ibid.*, p.47.

44 Jonas Mekas, 'Movie Journals', *Village Voice*, 11 November 1965.

45 Michael Fried's *'Art and Objecthood'* appeared in *Artforum*, vol.5 no.10, June 1967, pp.12–23.

that concerning the physical location of a painting. Is it the celluloid strip, the projected image, the viewer's apprehension of the illusion of motion?'[46] For projection, Doane continues, 'complicates the question of the location of the image. The screen intercepts a beam of light but the perception of the moving image takes place somewhere in between projector and screen, and the temporary, ephemeral nature of that image is reaffirmed by its continual movement and change.' Part of the problem is also that film was the paradigm for Modernism in and of itself. There was no traditional lexicon of film which Modernism could reject or reinvent in formal terms; rather, film was formally modern at the moment of its invention.

No doubt the multiple temporalities of film and video have contributed to the success of moving-image installations in contemporary art, yet, paradoxically, they also account for a certain level of critical blindness and historical oversight. Temporality has traditionally been seen as a fundamental constraint on the reception and integration of moving images within the institutions of art and art history, with static objects being favoured more than 'dematerialised', time-based technologies. The unique qualities of film, video and digital media have often been considered their Achilles heel with regard to their status as art. In addition, the failure of art institutions in the past to recognise fully the necessity and relevance of artists working within the parameters of the field of the moving image could result from moving images' associations with commercialism, spectacularisation and triviality. Regarding film, Bruce Jenkins has argued that its 'undeniable complicity in the wholesale transmission of repressive ideologies dressed in the glamour of the silver screen' seemed to have presented a deficiency in the medium.[47] The acknowledgement of film's 'indexical illusionism' — its privileged relation to the Real and possession of a certain 'that has been quality' that semiotician Roland Barthes called its indexical nature in *Camera Lucida* — as well as its 'ephemerality and illusionary basis', even its 'collaborative origins', similarly might have traditionally accounted for its being less than readily accepted within the institutions of art.[48]

Some of the more productive artistic engagements with film, however, have used these very deficiencies to their own advantage, combining narrative or anti- or counter-narrative strategies borrowed from spectacle culture to challenge how the moving image is encountered in our media society. Perhaps the anxiety around the 'cinematisation' (or 'televisuality') of art has to do with its unrepresentability, with the 'denial of the accelerating abstraction linked to capitalism, with a clinging to the idea of the materiality of the image, its touchability, its concreteness'.[49] Art historian George Baker suggests that one way to measure critically the most important projects that utilise moving

46 Mary Anne Doane, 'The Location of the Image: Projection and Scale in the Cinema', paper presented at 'The Art of Projection: A Symposium on the Cinematographic and Art', Hamburger Bahnhof and Kino Arsenal, Berlin, 29 October 2006.

47 B. Jenkins, 'The Machine in the Museum; or The Seventh Art in Search of Authorization', *op. cit.*, p.266.

48 *Ibid.*

49 M. Doane, 'The Location of the Image: Projection and Scale in the Cinema', *op. cit.*

50 G. Baker, *Gerard Byrne*, *op. cit.*, p.42.

51 For an analysis of how art distracts and how it is received in distraction, see

images might be to follow those that attempt in some manner 'to give form to social forces that can no longer be represented, that are themselves in fact a form of the unrepresentable'.[50] In other words, since representational images in contemporary art and culture can be said to engage more broadly with the abstract or the unrepresentable, the question is how can images concretise or give form to and transform the power of abstraction?

II Contemporary Moving-Image Practice

1. The Viewer and Suture

Today, moving-image installations in galleries and museums, rather than always adopting the single vantage perspective of classical cinema, or causing the spectator to be within a closed diegetic illusionary universe, are often comprised of a multitude of competing images and presentations that mobilise the viewer through the exhibition space, undercutting the 'false absolutisation of time to which cinema is prone'.[51] One might say that this freeing of film from its flat, fixed-screen perspective, from its *disciplined* conditions of narrative and representational plenitude, is analogous to the notion of 'the death of the author' and the empowerment of the viewer (as analysed by Barthes in the 50s and 60s). The phenomenological presence of the viewer and the viewing space became crucial to understanding how a work of art communicates. As Peter Wollen writes in 'The Two Avant-Gardes': 'van Doesburg, in 1929, already anticipated many of the ideas of "expanded cinema", realised decades later: "The spectator space will become part of the film space. The separation of 'projection surface' is abolished. The spectator will no longer observe the film, like a theatrical presentation, but will participate in it optically and acoustically."' (This volume, p.174.)[52] All of this takes place at the risk of illegibility. To paraphrase Hal Foster, 'the death of the author' could mean not 'the birth of the reader', as Barthes speculated in his 1968 eponymous essay, so much as the bewilderment of the viewer.

The classic argument of 70s 'apparatus theory' in film theory, as developed by Jean-Louis Baudry, speaks to related questions of spectatorship, identification, subjectivity and ideology.[53] It forcefully contends that the power of illusion in cinema resides less in the content of films than in the instruments and institutions that make and exhibit them. The cinematic apparatus constructs its subject as a solitary voyeur, 'blanking out' all distractions, every sign of an exhibitionist gaze. The conditions of exhibition that, according to Baudry, immobilise spectators in the darkness force the spectator to give up returning the gaze of the spectacle, to abandon their

Peter Osborne, 'Distracted Reception: Time, Art and Technology', *Time Zones: Recent Film and Video*, London: Tate, 2004, p.72.

52 Quoted in Eric de Bruyn, 'The Expanded Field of Cinema, or Exercise on the Perimeter of a Square', *op. cit.*, p.155

53 See Jean-Louis Baudry's 'Ideological Effects of the Basic Cinematographic Apparatus' and 'The Apparatus: Metaphysical Approaches to the Impression of Reality in Cinema', in Philip Rosen (ed.), *Narrative, Apparatus, Ideology: A Film Theory Reader*, New York: Columbia University Press, 1986, pp.286–318.

critical faculties and surrender to the power of the illusion: 'Projection and reflection take place in a closed space, and those who remain there, whether they know it or not (but they do not), find themselves chained, captured, and captivated.'[54] Such captivation supposedly causes the spectator to regress to a state of primitive narcissism in which the distinction between oneself and one's environment, and between perception and representation, are lost.

'Suture theory', as it is known, became predominant in the field of film studies in the 70s and 80s and grew out of a burgeoning interest in linguistics, semiotics and psychoanalysis. Proponents of this theory, including Raymond Bellour, Christian Metz, Colin MacCabe and Stephen Heath, while diverging in specifics, all suggested ways in which cinematic discourse engaged the psychic processes of the spectator. Bellour and others were unified in an overarching interest in how the classical realist film effaced all marks of its cinematic construction and established a subject position that bound the spectator to the world of fiction. By masking the operation of cinematic narration, this 'suturing' was believed to produce a seamless and transparent work.[55] Narrative, editing, music and other devices have been said to foster the regression of the subject during the viewing experience and help to create what Baudry calls the 'subject effect' of cinema.[56] Through such devices the spectator's psychic experience is exploited to aid the suspension of disbelief, securing the spectator's identification of his or her own perceptions with that of the film.

This 'contemplative immersion' or 'absorption' by the artwork or film does not operate reflexively; it draws attention away from its existence as a construct. It avoids laying bare its own 'discursive conditions of enunciation'. Rather, it rests on cinema's 'reality effect' — 'the constitutive illusion of presenting the spectator with an unmediated view of the world and projecting him/her in a distracted state to another place and time'.[57] Characteristically, contemporary film and video installations with their articulations of spatiality are, on the contrary, contextual. They take place in the actual time and place of the viewer. They often exhibit the material conditions of the filmic or digital apparatus, or confront the viewer through a mode of direct address, rather than via a mode of contemplative attention familiar to classical cinema.[58] The spatio-temporal conditions of film and video in art spaces raise the problem of distraction, and pose a set of questions such as: how can moving-image installations distract from distraction without simply reproducing distraction, and how can they retain their criticality by provoking attention to distraction without falling prey to contemplative immersion?[59] Continuing a study of Siegfried Kracauer and Walter Benjamin's analysis of distraction, theorist Peter Osborne suggests that one of the conditions of reception

54 J. Baudry, 'Ideological Effects of the Basic Cinematographic Apparatus', *op. cit.*, p.309.

55 Jeff Smith, 'Unheard Melodies? A Critique of Psychoanalytic Theories of Film Music', *Post-Theory: Reconstructing Film Studies* (ed. David Bordwell and Noël Carroll), Wisconsin: The University of Wisconsin Press, 1996, pp.232–33.

56 See Jean-Louis Baudry, 'The Apparatus', *Camera Obscura*, no.1, December 1976, pp.104–26.

57 See E. de Bruyn's discussion of this theme in 'Shadows of the Spectacle', *op. cit.*, pp.44–45.

58 *Ibid.*

59 P. Osborne, 'Distracted Reception: Time, Art and Technology', *op. cit.*, pp.66–75.

60 See Siegfried Kracauer, 'Cult of Distraction: On Berlin's Picture Palaces'

of film and video installations points to a 'deepening of distracted perception'.[60] In questioning how time is socialised through the spatial articulations of temporal relations, how the 'character of collectivity' works in the reception of contemporary film and video art and the impact of the 'broader, historical time within which it is inscribed and upon which it draws', Osborne suggests that one measure of judgment for a moving-image installation — 'one new task of apperception' — could be the degree to which it exposes 'new reflective rhythms of absorption and distraction, new articulations of duration' within the complex 'network of its temporal connections (psychic, social, historical)'.[61]

2. Obsolescence

> [N]o activity can become an art until its proper epoch has ended and it has dwindled, as an aid to gut survival, into total obsolescence.
> Hollis Frampton

Hollis Frampton's now classic article 'For a Metahistory of Film: Commonplace Notes and Hypotheses', first published in Annette Michelson's guest-edited special film issue of *Artforum* in September 1971, offers an ontological account of the origins of experimental cinema and an analysis of the relationship between still photography and film.[62] 'For a Metahistory of Film' signalled an unprecedented rupture with previous cinematic avant-gardes, shifting the emphasis from the limit condition of film itself — the material of celluloid, *the frame* and photographic illusion — to a consideration of the projection apparatus, the 'total film machine', and the possibilities of what he termed the 'infinite cinema', '(or of all knowledge, which amounts to the same thing)'.[63] Frampton emphasised that film could no longer be considered independent of the 'event' of projection. He argued: 'If filmstrip and project are parts of the same machine, then "a film" may be defined operationally as "whatever will pass through a projector" [...] The least thing that will do that is nothing at all. Such a film has been made. It is the only *unique* film in existence.' No activity, including film, could become art until its 'proper epoch' had ended and diminished into total obsolescence. According to Frampton, it was only with the advent of video that the motion-picture camera became available as an art-making tool. Only as a model of useless artistic innovation could cinema survive — not in the service of some social, political or ideological function, as he claimed for all the various art cinemas of the previous years.

A significant body of contemporary work is based on artists' recovery of devices such as the slide projector, 16mm loopers, animation and on

(1926), *The Mass Ornament: Weimar Essays* (ed. and trans. Thomas Y. Levin), Cambridge, Mass.: Harvard University Press, 1995, pp.323–28, and Walter Benjamin, 'The Work of Art in the Age of Mechanical Reproduction', *Illuminations* (trans. Harry Zohn), New York: Schocken, 1968. *On modes of attention,* see also Jonathan Crary, *Suspensions of Perception: Attention, Spectacle and Modern Culture*, Cambridge, Mass. and London: The MIT Press, 1999.

61 P. Osborne, 'Distracted Reception: Time, Art and Technology', *op. cit.*, p.73.

62 Due to a forthcoming anthology of Frampton's writing, we were not able to reprint the article in this volume.

63 All Frampton quotes from 'For A Metahistory of Film: Commonplace Notes and Hypotheses', *Artforum*, September 1971, pp.32–35.

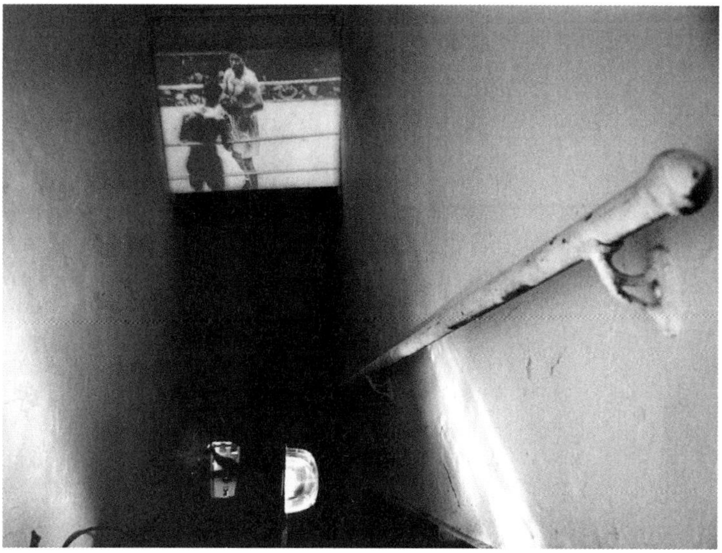

James Coleman, *Box (ahhareturnabout)*, performed by Olwen Fouere & Roger Doyle, Julian Pretto Gallery, New York, 1977. Courtesy Marian Goodman Gallery, New York & Paris

the production of new mediums from the remnants of old forms. Artists such as these strive to deflect the cinematic mechanism of suture, to rupture the traditional modes of viewing moving images through reconsideration of obsolete technologies and in rescuing earlier cinematic models. Rosalind Krauss describes this appreciation and appropriation for outmoded devices in terms of 'self-differing' mediums (the embrace of hybridity within self-reflexive projects). Irish artist James Coleman, for instance, utilises 16mm-film projectors (*Box (ahhareturnabout)*, 1977) and slide projectors for his 'heterogenous assemblages' of large-scale, multilayered dissolves of projected images and audio narrations (*Background*, 1991–94; *Lapsus Exposure*, 1992–94; and *INITIALS* 1993–94) to transform and mutate what has been called 'a radical sharing of forms'. The American artist Allan Sekula frequently employs single, projected, medium-format slides as 'technical support' in works such as *Prayer for the Americans* (1999–2003); while South African artist William Kentridge's 'drawings for projection' exploit the support of animation in such work as *Shadow Procession* (1999) and *7 Fragments for Georges Méliès* (2003). American film-maker Ken Jacobs's *Nervous System* has involved an extraordinary number of performances that mine existing films with specially-modified 16mm projectors, propellers and individual lenses for audience members to view the projected images; and British artist Tacita Dean regularly exploits the ambiguity of film, playing with obsolescence both symbolically and materially in works such as *Disappearance at Sea* (1996), *Fernsehturm* (*Television Tower*, 2001) and *Jukebox 2* (2001). It has been suggested that to find new expression in surpassed modes, to create what has been called a sort of 'archaeology of outmoded forms', might not only encouragingly complicate media history, it may also enable us to grasp the inner complexity of such mediums and bring about a radical reconsideration of the cinematisation of culture. The embrace of these outmoded forms of media might be a by-product of new media that can open up cultural history, standing as 'ciphers of surpassed aesthetic and social experiences that contemporary artists can recover critically'.[64]

64 H. Foster, et. al., 'The Predicament of Contemporary Art', *Art Since 1900*, *op. cit.*, p.767.
65 The majority of the following arguments on the immersive effects of the virtual image are Hal Foster's. See *Art Since 1900*, *op. cit.*, pp.655, 676, 677 and 767.
66 W. Benjamin, 'The Work of Art in the Age of Mechanical Reproduction', *op. cit.*, p.232.

3. Immersion

We are lost between the abyss within us and the boundless horizons outside of us.
Robert Smithson

Early video art and, to a degree, the practices of expanded cinema in the 60s and 70s can be understood as attempts to articulate the aesthetics of the moving image outside or against the specifically cinematic — in the former case through an association with the immediacy of performance as a branch of the visual arts, and in the latter through the idea of breaking down genre distinctions in a quest for a perceptual synthesis. Much recent work, however, is reclaiming the cinematic as a departure from such strategies towards more internal, psychological experiences. It has been argued that the shift from the sculptural priorities of the 'multi-screen clusters of monitors' of the 80s to those approaches that draw upon and highlight the language, qualities and values of the single, large-scale projected image in space, or from an emphasis on the three-dimensional object (the 'box') and an essentially theatrical use of the physical environment to the illusory dissolution of the boundary between the viewing subject and the projection screen, opens up a new psychological space for a more inclusive sensory involvement. Often the aesthetic mimicry of the cinematic by the electronic and the fusion of the 'tactile power' of the electronic media with the powers of the filmic attributes of the image transform the image into a site for a complete sensory immersion.

Contrary to the kind of rupturing devices employed in some of the above-mentioned installations and in contrast to Warhol's early monocular films like *Sleep* (1963) and *Empire* (1964) that introduced the unwavering gaze and extended duration into visual art, or the closed-circuit video installations of the late 60s and 70s — such as Ira Schneider and Frank Gillette's multiple-monitor installation *Wipe Cycle* (1969), Peter Campus's *Interface* (1972) or Dan Graham's 'Time Delay Rooms' — that assertively engaged other kinds of spectatorship and made explicit and disconcerting the cultural imperatives to identify with the televisual public sphere and the media culture at large, there is a treacherous tendency in contemporary immersive projection spaces. These environments, art historian Liz Kotz points out, align video more closely with the large-scale spectacularised photographic work of, for example, Jeff Wall and Andreas Gursky. For while some might consider highly mediated 'technophiliac extravaganzas' — for example Bill Viola's multiple-projection *Five Angels for the Millennium* (2001) with its diaphanous, larger-than-life-size images — that envelope and immerse the viewer to be exhilarating, even mesmerising, others contend that such installations that seduce and captivate the viewer are particularly disturbing because of their 'rush of special effects'[65] and their proximity to 'illusion-promoting spectacles and dubious speculations'.[66] In other words, they could be thought to be problematic because, rather than offering alternatives to spectacle, they simulate the slickness of television or film, aestheticising or 'artifying' already well-known experiences of the mind-blowing intensities produced by the media culture at large. Such anxiety is not new, however. Concern with expanded cinema's proximity to advanced forms of capital in the 60s and 70s was forcefully expressed by several of expanded cinema's critics, for example, Max Kozloff in his criticism of '9 Evenings' or of Robert Whitman's work more generally.

Such immersive installations, where the viewer appears to *merge* with the projected image, and which are described in terms of effecting a kind of sublime experience and 'technological mysticism' or 'spiritual immediacy', have been perceived as having an affirmative relation to dominant society because of the seemingly passive mode of perceptual and social experience they appear to support. Such highly mediated, 'derealised' installations that provoke visual splendour and foster passive perception are in danger of heightening artifice, of rendering the space of exhibition even more virtualised than cinema itself. The problem with projection spaces that overwhelm and engulf the viewer is no longer simply a concern with distraction. In contrast to the phenomenological acuity of Minimalist installations in the 60s and 70s or the institutional critique of the 80s and early 90s, for example, wall-sized or often room-sized projections and sculptures of epic scale are frequently disparaged for their lack of critical awareness and political relevance today. Installations that call for mesmerising sensorial and captivating immersive experiences are also problematic because of their desire for a kind of 'cultic reenchantment', in the words of Hal Foster, or for a reinvestment of 'technological representation with mythological representation, even religious experience', according to Benjamin Buchloh. Foster argues that installations such as Viola's seem keen to enact a kind of 'techno-sublime' or 'bewitching mysticism' through complete media immersion to effect what Walter Benjamin called, in relation to film, 'the blue flower in the land of technology'.[67]

Indeed, the historical emergence of fascism and the modern technological apparatus it required has been a position to argue for the ideological functions of electronic media and their use in art. Benjamin's writings on the fascist dimension of manipulated immediacy in 'The Work of Art in the Age of Mechanical Reproduction' might be argued to be still pertinent today. In a final note to his essay, Benjamin writes: 'In big parades and monster rallies, in sports events and in war, all of which nowadays are captured by camera and sound recording, the masses are brought face to face with themselves.'[68] What this suggests to Foster is that the fetishisation of mechanisms of control brought about through the increase in televisual technologies — TV, video, computers — has supported a 'fascistic subject'.[69] At least as often, however, it is argued that new media brings about increased democratic potential. In activist art circles, we could think, for instance,

67 H. Foster, et. al., *Art Since 1900*, *op. cit.*, p.676.

68 See Allen Meek, 'Benjamin, the televisual and the "fascistic subject"', www.latrobe.edu.au/screeningthepast/firstrelease/fir998/AMfr4e.htm; and W. Benjamin, *Illuminations*, *op. cit.*, p.251.

69 Hal Foster, 'Postmodernism in parallax', *October*, no.63, 1993, p.8, quoted in A. Meek, 'Benjamin, the televisual and the "fascistic subject"', *op. cit.*

70 Email correspondence with William Kaizen, 23 March 2007.

71 H. Foster, et. al., *Art Since 1900*, *op. cit.*, p.655.

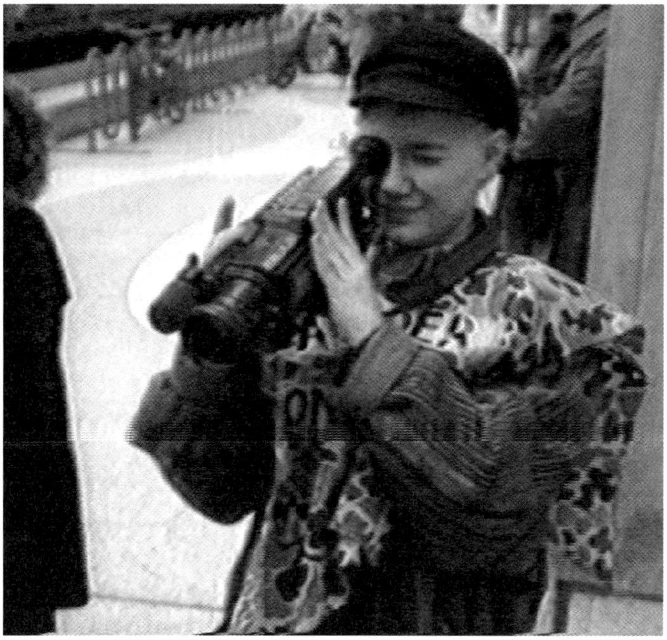

of public-access television and community-based cable initiatives such as Videofreex, People's Video Theatre, Global Village, Top Value Television, Raindance Corporation and Paper Tiger Television Collective. Technologies of control have been used here to justify greater citizen-based participation.[70] Yet the critique of media embedded in the intellectual culture of the 1930s may well still be accurate regarding the tendency, in much new media, to reinvest technological representation with mythological imagery and in the desire for an intensification of myth.

Such arguments would indicate that the new mobility and immersive effect of the virtual image in all-encompassing projective spaces might come at a significant cost since they not only entail the captivity of the viewer, but at the same time they require the emptying or abandoning of the physical space entirely.[71] It is thought that these immersive projected environments might confound bodily perception and technological mediation to the point where the viewer is neither discouraged from trying to extract himself from the matrix of the filmic event nor from aligning himself with the point of view of the camera. The viewer, therefore, is more likely to fall victim to the manipulations of the apparatus, such as Baudry defined it, and experience projective identification through 'suturing' devices that could become even more aggressive than those of classical cinema.

4. Replay/Remake

You don't have to search for new images, ones never seen before, but you do have to utilise the existing ones in such a way that they become new.
Harun Farocki

Poaching freely from the mass media and the entertainment industry, both in form and content, appropriating and reusing spectacular forms, is one of the hallmarks of contemporary projected images. While some large-scale projected installations today re-enlist techniques of visual excess without so much as a thought as to how such forms might need to be purged, deflected, denied or negated, others demonstrate at least a consciousness of the ambiguities of the mass media's seduction. The replay/remake is a technique that has been used effectively to achieve this, mimicking distraction without simply reproducing it. Artists and film-makers such as Eija-Liisa Ahtila, Hartmut Bitomsky, Janet

Paper Tiger Television, *Paper Tiger Production no.195: Operation Storm the Media*, 1991

Cardiff, Stan Douglas, Douglas Gordon, Steve McQueen, Pipilotti Rist, Marcel Odenbach, Tony Oursler, Keith Sanborn, Lorna Simpson, Rosemarie Trockel, Gillian Wearing and Jane and Louise Wilson intentionally strive in very different ways to break the type of experience common to classical cinema, for example, by refusing linear narrative in preference for devices grounded in a kind of polyphonic discourse (following Mikhail Bakhtin) that mirror, double, split, echo and multiply the projected image to produce image-spaces of a highly psychological nature (in what Hal Foster has called the 'traumatic' sublime). Ahtila's *The House* (2002) and Sanborn's video *Operation Double Trouble* (2003) are textbook examples. Sanborn shows us that the question of form is in a way the most political: What is it we see? What is the destiny of the image? Through a simple gesture of doubling the filmic image, he creates an effective reworking — a 'disturbing echo' — of a recent propaganda movie made by the United States Navy and Marine Corps.

Engagements with the quotation of cinematic and televisual modes have ranged from American artist Jack Goldstein's 70s films that transformed and restaged stock film footage — one, for instance where the MGM lion's roar, simply isolated on a red background, is looped over and over — to Chris Marker's 'Constructivist-evoking', five-stacked monitor installation *Silent Movie* (1995) and Morgan Fisher's *Standard Gauge* (1984). More recently one might consider French artist Pierre Huyghe's double- or multiple-screen projections, where films often become 'scores' for new films — new 'chains of representations', as he calls them. Huyghe's *Remake* (1995) is based on Hitchcock's *Rear Window*, and his *Les incivils* (*The Uncivils*, 1995) derives from Pier Paolo Pasolini's *Hawks and Sparrows*, wherein he enlisted the actual actors from Pasolini's film as a way of 'embodying' the original. Huyghe's *L'Ellipse* (*Ellipsis*, 1998) is also an anomalous kind of remake of Wim Wenders's *The American Friend* (1977). The understanding of representation in practices such as Huyghe's is that they are concerned with doubling events with new representations; submitting historical

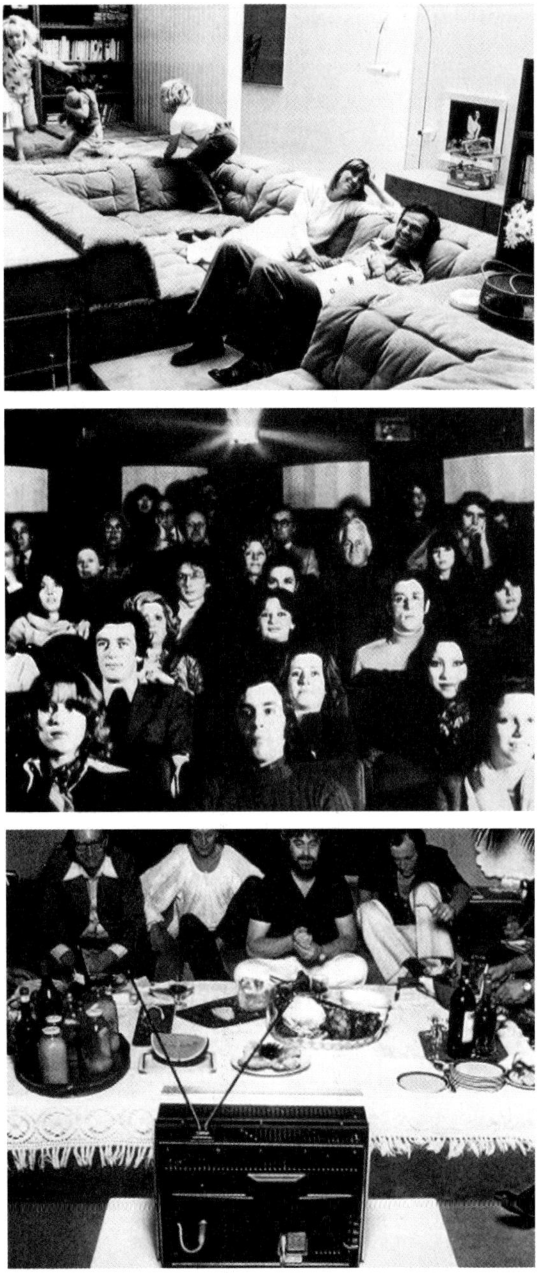

Guy Debord, stills from *In Girum Imus Nocte Et Consumimur Igni* (*We Go Round and Round in the Night and Are Consumed by Fire*), 1978. 35mm black-and-white film, sound, 100mins

representations to further repetitions; and disseminating events, representations and images in certain ways, and in disregard for spectacle's alienating spectacle. But Huyghe does not simply call our attention to figures of filmic vocabulary, as has been suggested; rather, he 'undoes' them in peculiar and significant ways. Contrary to earlier artists' commitment to counter-spectacle Huyghe's *Third Memory* (1999)— a remake of Sidney Lumet's 1975 film *Dog Day Afternoon*—and his DIA installation *Streamside Follies* (2003) are exemplary in their employment of projection techniques to paradoxically embrace spectularisation in order to launch a critique against it.

Equally notable in this regard is Colombian artist François Bucher's project *Television (an address)* (ongoing since 2002) and American artist Andrea Frasers's *Soldadera (Scenes from 'Un Banquete en Tetlapayac', a film by Olivier Debroise)* (1998/2002), which is focused on the dysfunctional ties between artists and benefactors. Bucher's *Television (an address)* presents two simultaneously projected live feeds that reflect on the image of television by retransmitting it inside of an altered playing field. Bucher signals the question 'what is live?'—opening up a reflection on the implications of a paradoxical *transmission of a transmission*, where the televisual image and its rhetoric of truthfulness is brought to task. Fraser's use of double-projection in *Soldadera* reinstates a visual component that her practice has typically resisted, but offers as an image on this ground a 'deflated, pseudoprojection that offers little of the technical wizardry, the elaborate art direction and soundtracks, or the narrative interest we have come to expect from projection's most accomplished practioners'.[72] The arrested, repeated shots in *Soldadera* imply a desire for incompleteness, for a perpetual deferment and frustration against the totalising impulse characteristic of spectacle.

This endless displacing of perception bears a certain resemblance to the theorisation of 'spectacle' suggested by Guy Debord in his films and writing. In *Society of the Spectacle* (1967), his 'manifesto' for modernity, capitalism and everyday life in the late-twentieth century, Debord writes: 'The spectacle proclaims the predominance of appearances and asserts that all human life, which is to say all social life, is mere appearance.'[73] Spectacle brings us an image of our era that has totalised itself, emptied itself of beliefs, traditions, contents, latency and sacredness, and replaced them with commodities. A pure form of separation now controls the perception and memory of the world, and reveals the alluring and alienating nothingness of all things. In different ways works such as those by Bucher, Fraser and Huyghe imagine new artistic strategies and tactics *within* the violence of spectacle, subversions that could be said to fracture what Debord called the 'empire of modern passivity' and awaken us from the 'permanent coma', in Robert Smithson's words, imposed by Hollywood and television.[74]

72 James Meyer, 'The Strong and the Weak: Andrea Fraser and the Conceptual Legacy', *Grey Room*, no.17, Fall 2004, p.103.

73 Guy Debord, *Society of the Spectacle*, New York: Zone Books, 1995, p.14.

74 See Robert Smithson, 'A Cinematic Atopia', *Artforum*, vol.10, September 1971, pp.53–55. Smithson conceived the ultimate film experience: an 'underground' cinema in a cave or abandoned mine, where the only film ever to be shown would be one of the cinema's construction.

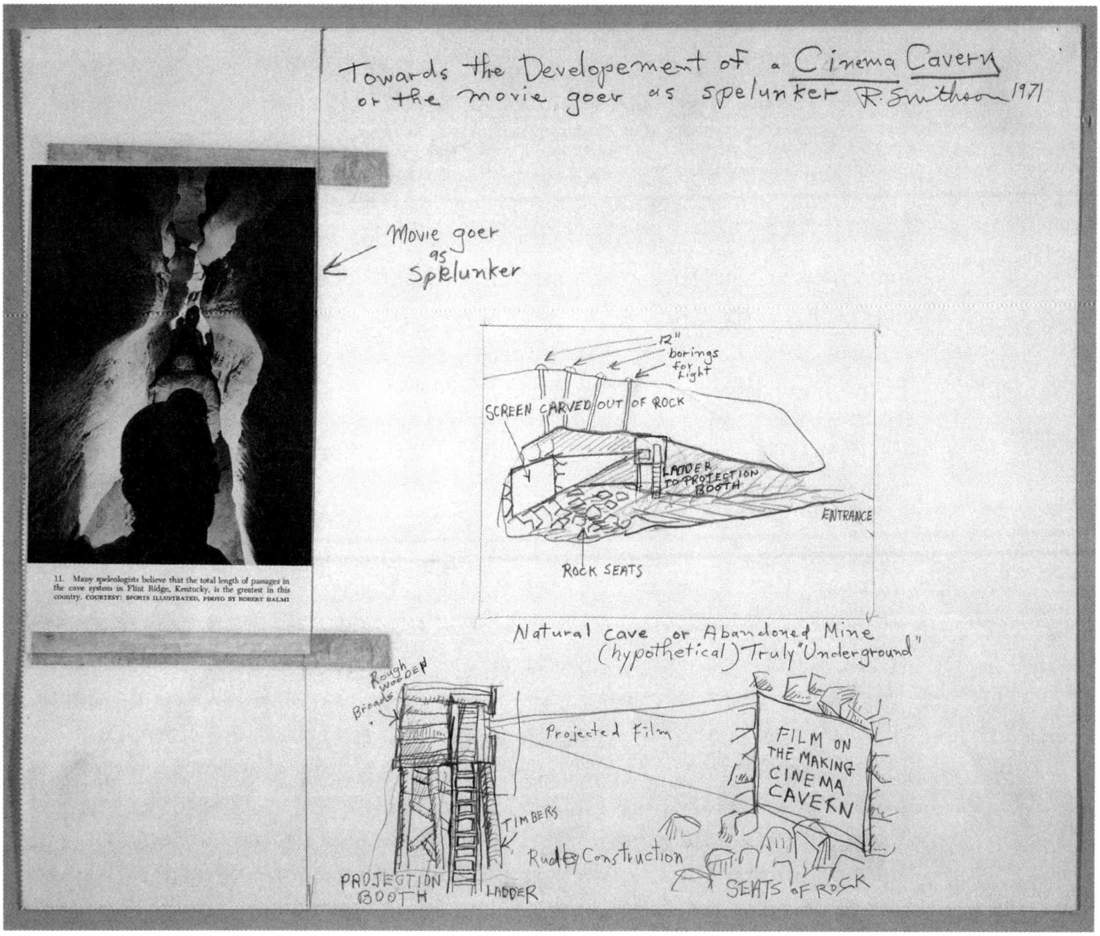

5. Slowness/The Still

A further opportunity for mobilising the image — another possible site of resistance in our era of fully realised nihilism (the spectacle) — could be found in 'stillness'. British film historian Laura Mulvey points out that there is a paradox in the ability of projection technologies to reveal in retrospect the material complexity, and thus to enhance the spectatorial experience, of the historic cinema through a 'displacement that breaks the bond of specificity'.[75] The still photographic image can be recovered under the new technological conditions as a site for a critical distance between the conflicting temporalities of the inscription of film's own history and the progression of the narrative. Douglas Gordon's *24-hour Psycho* (1993), in which he slowed the original Hitchcock film down to a thirteenth of its normal speed, is a classic example. Other contemporary moving-image works, such as those by Francis Alÿs,

75 See Laura Mulvey, 'Stillness In The Moving Image: Ways of Visualising Time and Its Passing', in Tanya Leighton and Pavel Büchler (eds.), *Saving The Image: Art After Film*, Manchester: Manchester Metropolitan University, 2003, p.81

76 Laura Mulvey, *Death 24× a Second: Stillness and the Moving Image*, London: Reaktion Books, 2006, p.102.

Angela Bulloch, David Claerbout, Mark Lewis, Jeroen de Rijke and Willem de Rooij, Wolfgang Staehle and Fiona Tan, are similarly pervaded by a striking absence of movement. They yield an ambiguous stillness, a 'dynamic stasis' (as media theorist Thomas Y. Levin characterises it), more commonly associated with photography than with film. Alÿs's *Zocalo May 20* (1999), for instance, only shows uninterrupted footage of Mexico City's central plaza, and Staehle's *Empire 24/7* presents a single webcam shot of New York's Empire State Building (recalling Warhol's 1964 film *Empire*). Technically, however, Staehle's *Empire 24/7* is not so much a continuous transmission as a periodically refreshed one, where every five seconds or so a new still replaces the last one. These works are static images, yet at the same time they are moving; they create a heightened awareness of time's passing. In slowing down, halting the image or simply showing it as it is, slowness perhaps becomes a new and vital artistic strategy, one that brings about renewed attention to an 'archaeology' of time. Works conducted through an electronic or digital medium open up cinema to an aesthetics of slow motion and to a materiality allied to the traditions of avant-garde film (though often with little acknowledgement of this earlier experimental film work). By subjecting moving pictures to playful manipulations, in effect what we see are not moving images at all but a succession of still frames, frames that heighten the fragility of the illusion of real time in cinema. It is in such playfulness, Mulvey concludes, that cinema can find a way back to its essential stillness, its double temporality. While the flow of the image at 24 frames per second tends to assert a 'now-ness', stillness, on the contrary, allows access to the film's registration, its 'then-ness'. It is at this point 'that cinema meets the still photograph, both registering a moment of time frozen and thus fossilized'.[76] Cinema undresses photography, so to speak, as the latter performs the same function reciprocally.

The compression of time (i.e. ellipsis) in many filmic works today has been discussed exactly in terms of a 'new kind of slowness'. Thomas Y. Levin has noted that one of the characteristics of surveillance and CCTV imaging in particular, one of the 'temporal signatures of surveillance', is a kind of 'recalibration of eventhood'. Given how little 'happens' in surveillance feed, he argues, we consequently revise our expectations as to what constitutes an 'event'. The proliferation of such imaging in contemporary cinema has produced new narrative forms, including what Levin

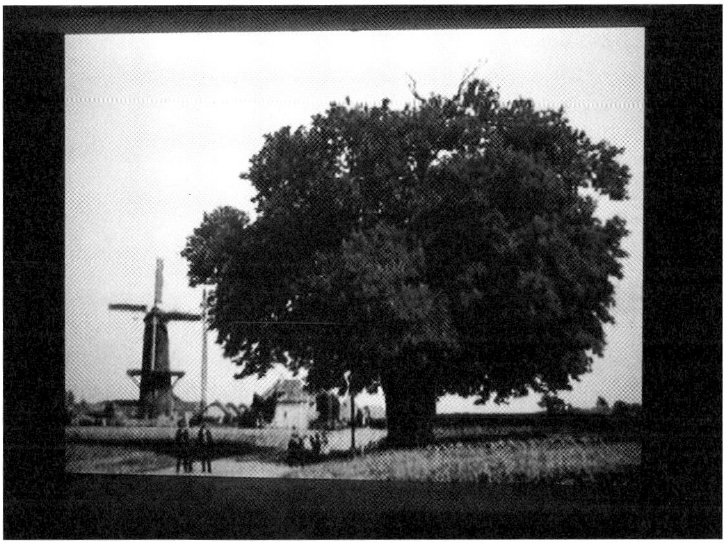

David Claerbout, *Ruurlo, Bocurlo-scheweg 1910*, 1998. Installation view. Collection MuHKA

Previous page: Robert Smithson, *Towards the Development of a Cinema Cavern*, photo collage, 33cm×40.6cm, 1971 © 2008 Robert Smithson estate/DACS, London & VAGA, New York. Courtesy James Cohan Gallery, New York

calls an 'expressive rhetorics of surveillance'. What is key in such narrative mobilisations of surveillance, Levin argues, is the question of 'the temporal signature of the surveillant time'. In reference to Michael Haneke's film *Caché*, he asks: 'Is what we see here indeed an observing time? Who's watching? Why are they watching? Is there actually a watching? Or is it instead a figure of memory, of anxiety ... ?' The rhetorical function of surveillance in these unanswered questions at the centre of *Caché* remains, Levin suggests, 'a central feature of our current media historical landscape'.[77]

Such examples of various returns in contemporary projected-image practice — obsolescence, immersion, replay/remake, slowness/the still — do not exist in a vacuum and they are not new to the realm of the projected image; we might recall their antecedents in earlier movements, in the Historical Avant-Garde, in post-Minimal Film and in Conceptual Film. Just as there are no aesthetic movements of any kind untouched by cross-fertilisation from previous practices — Surrealism emerged partly as an outgrowth of Dada, Neo-Conceptualism draws on Conceptualism and so on — the art of the contemporary projected image combines and restores, consciously and unconsciously, tactics and themes from the media archive of the past. A critical practice utilising projection technologies needs to be attentive to the character of returns such as those mentioned above, and to reflect upon the various genealogies that attend the moving image. The significance of comprehending and examining the legacies and paradoxes of these histories is that it establishes a productive distance from the subject under focus, which is essential for understanding the broader context in which the work arises and vital for the construction of new historicities.[78] This volume wants to breach small gaps and to consider the ruptures and discontinuities of histories of the projected image without invoking a misleading sense of uniformity. The goal is that *Art and the Moving Image* will encourage a discursive arena, one necessarily marked by conflict, but also one suggestive of new and richer horizons.

77 Levin's comments were presented in a public lecture at *The Art of Projection: A Symposium on The Cinematographic and Art*, Hamburger Bahnhof and Kino Arsenal, Berlin, 28 October 2006, and subsequently discussed in email correspondence with the author, 3 July 2007.

78 See J. Meyer's comments to this effect in 'The Strong and the Weak: Andrea Fraser and the Conceptual Legacy', *op. cit.*

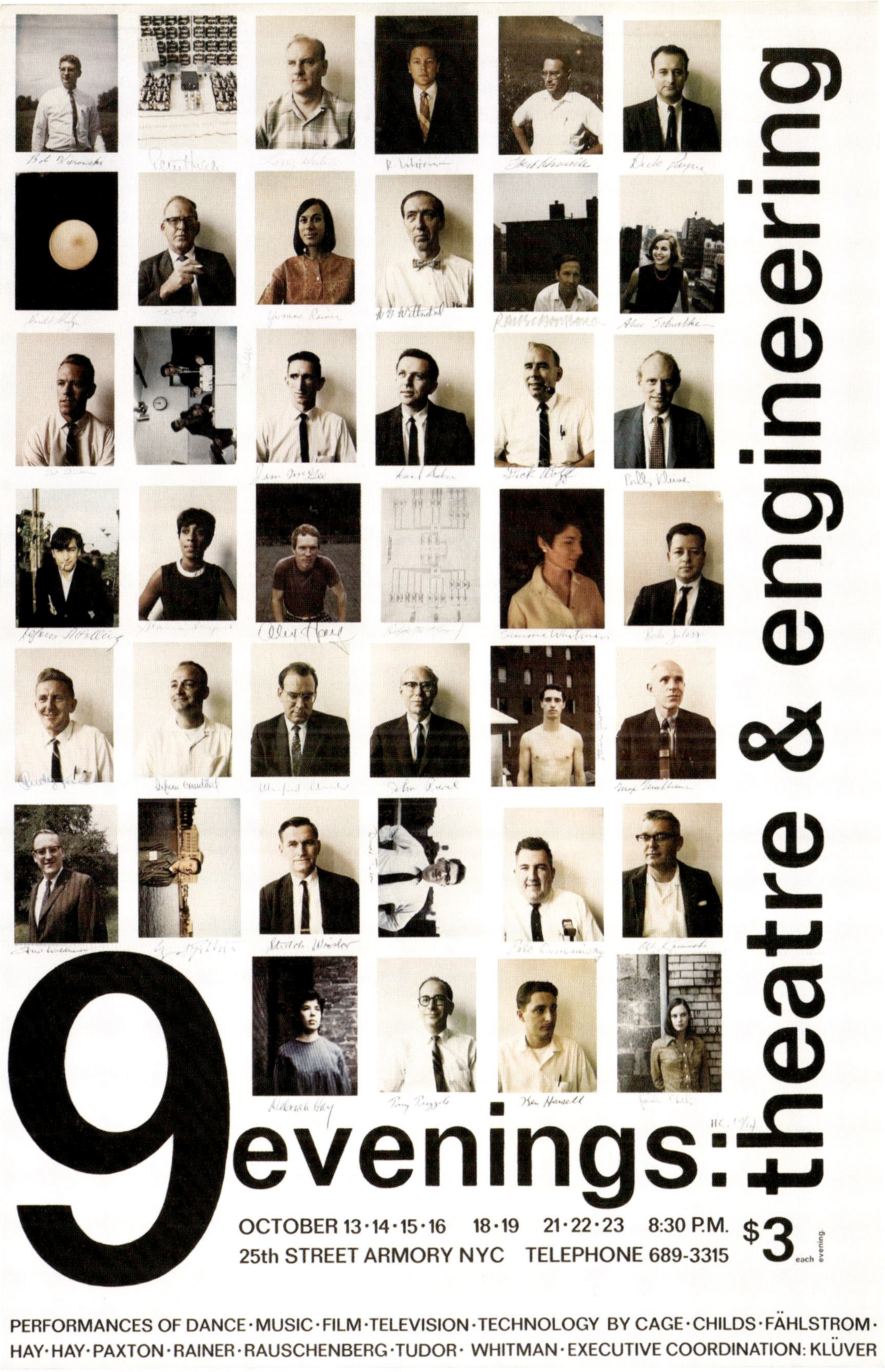
9 evenings: theatre & engineering
OCTOBER 13·14·15·16 18·19 21·22·23 8:30 P.M.
25th STREET ARMORY NYC TELEPHONE 689-3315
$3 each evening.
PERFORMANCES OF DANCE·MUSIC·FILM·TELEVISION·TECHNOLOGY BY CAGE·CHILDS·FÄHLSTROM·
HAY·HAY·PAXTON·RAINER·RAUSCHENBERG·TUDOR· WHITMAN·EXECUTIVE COORDINATION: KLÜVER

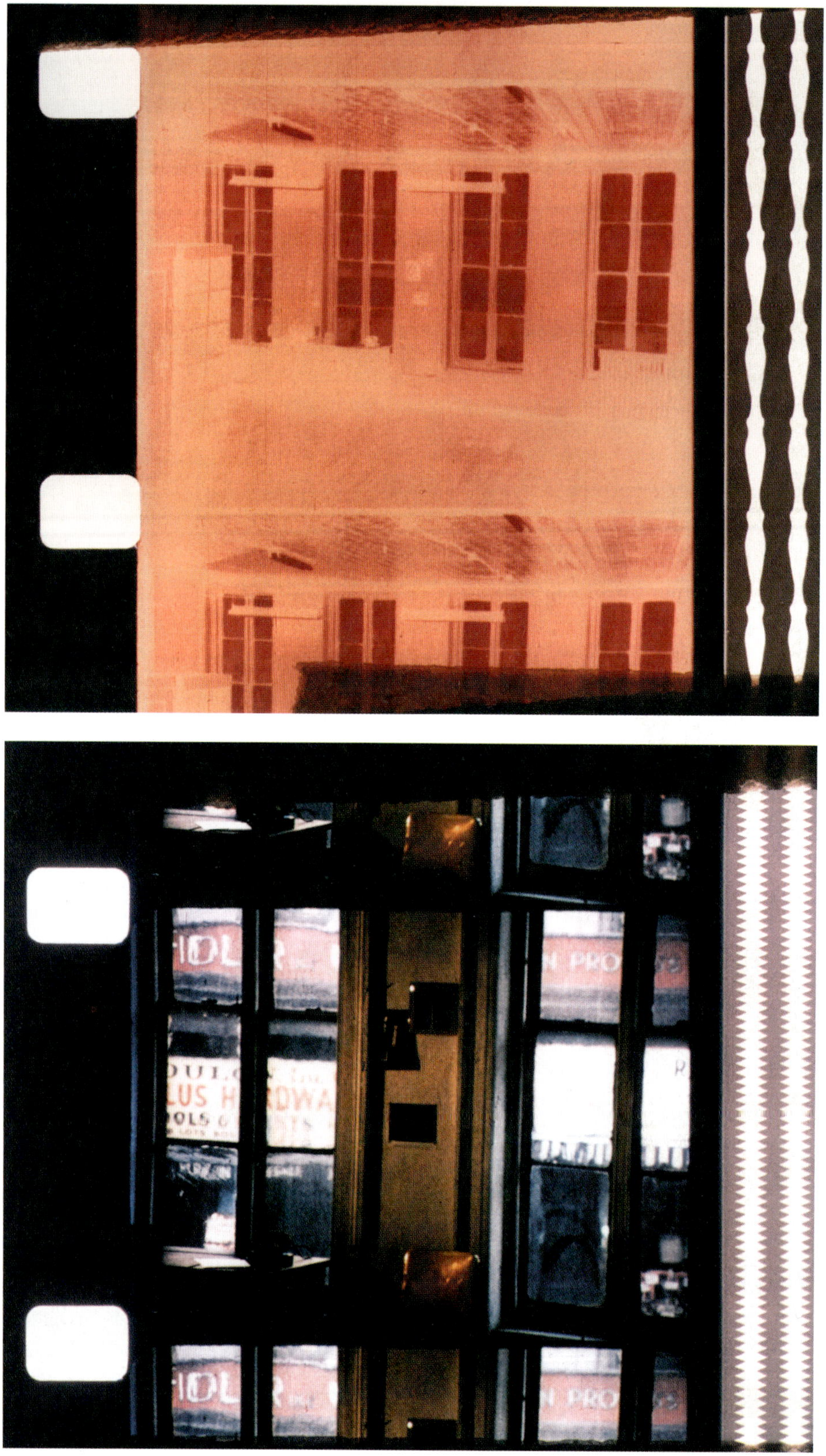

Previous page: '9 Evenings: Theatre and Engineering' poster designed by Robert Rauschenberg, 1966 © 2008 DACS, London & VAGA, New York. Courtesy EAT

Michael Snow, frames from *Wavelength*, 1967. 16mm colour film, sound, 45mins

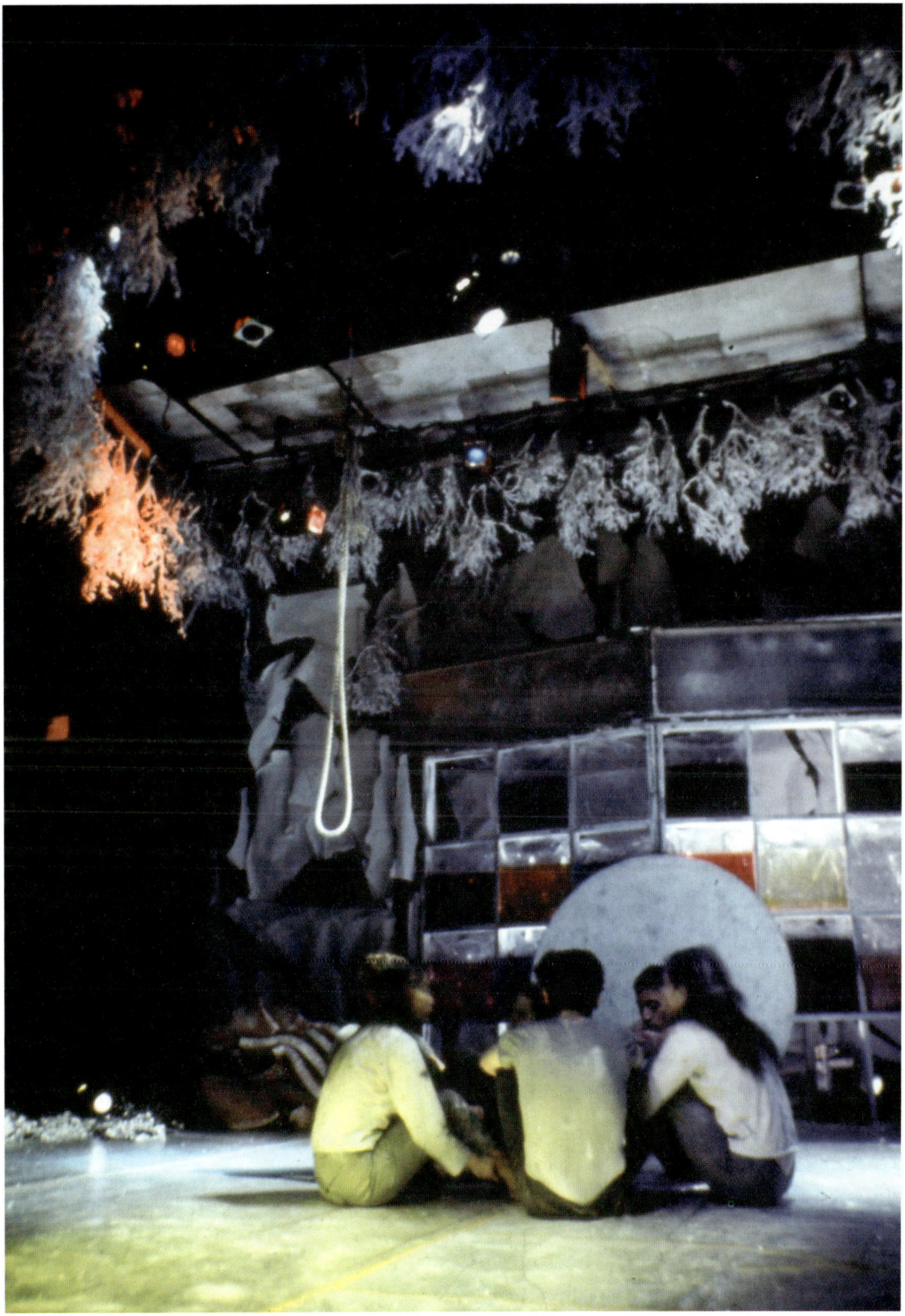

Carolee Schneemann, *Snows*, Kinetic Theater Performance, Martinique Theatre, New York, 1967. Photo © 2008 Herbert Migdol

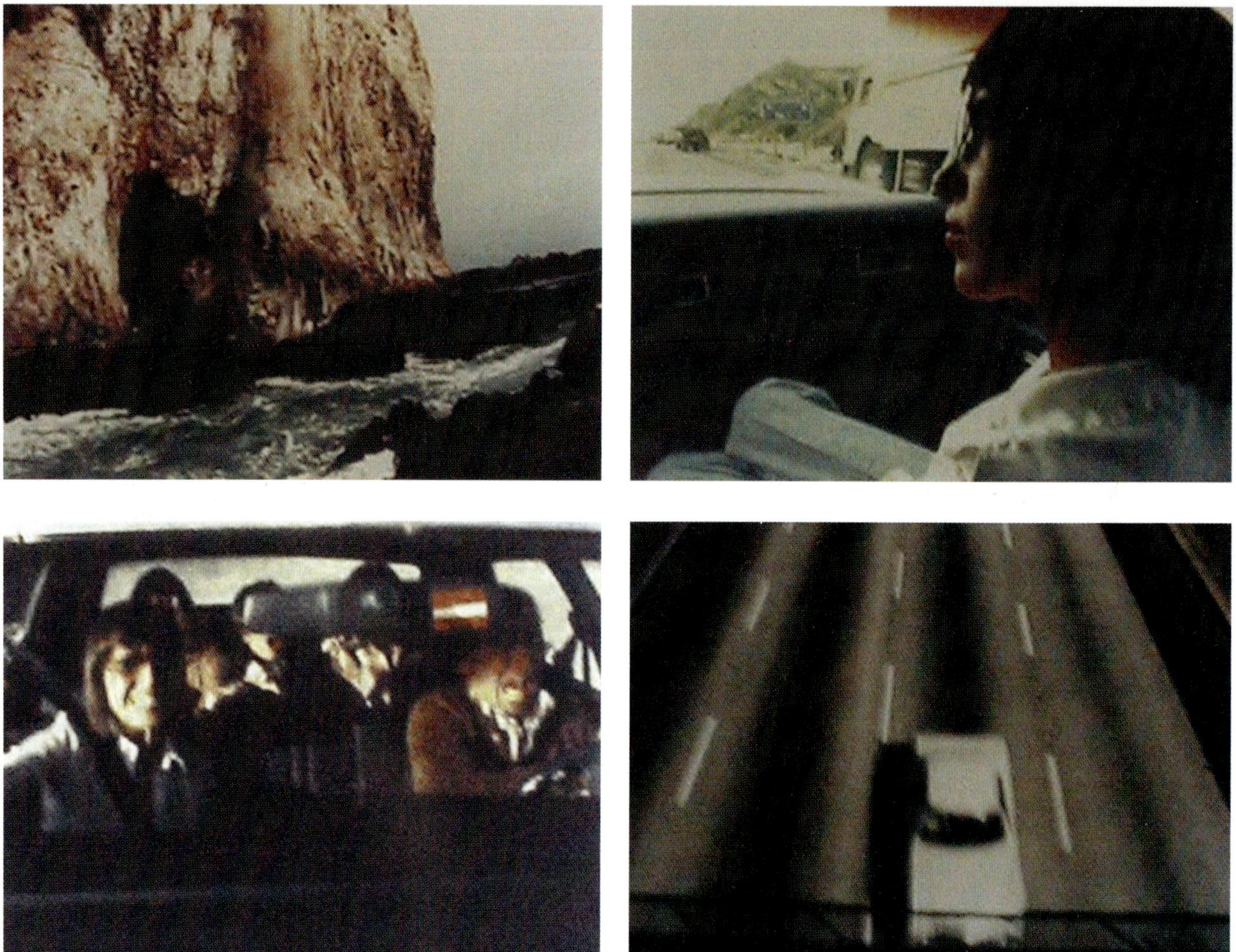

David Lamelas, *A Fiction,* 1975. 8 C-Prints from *The Desert People*, 1974.
Courtesy Monika Sprüth & Philomene Magers, Cologne, Munich & London

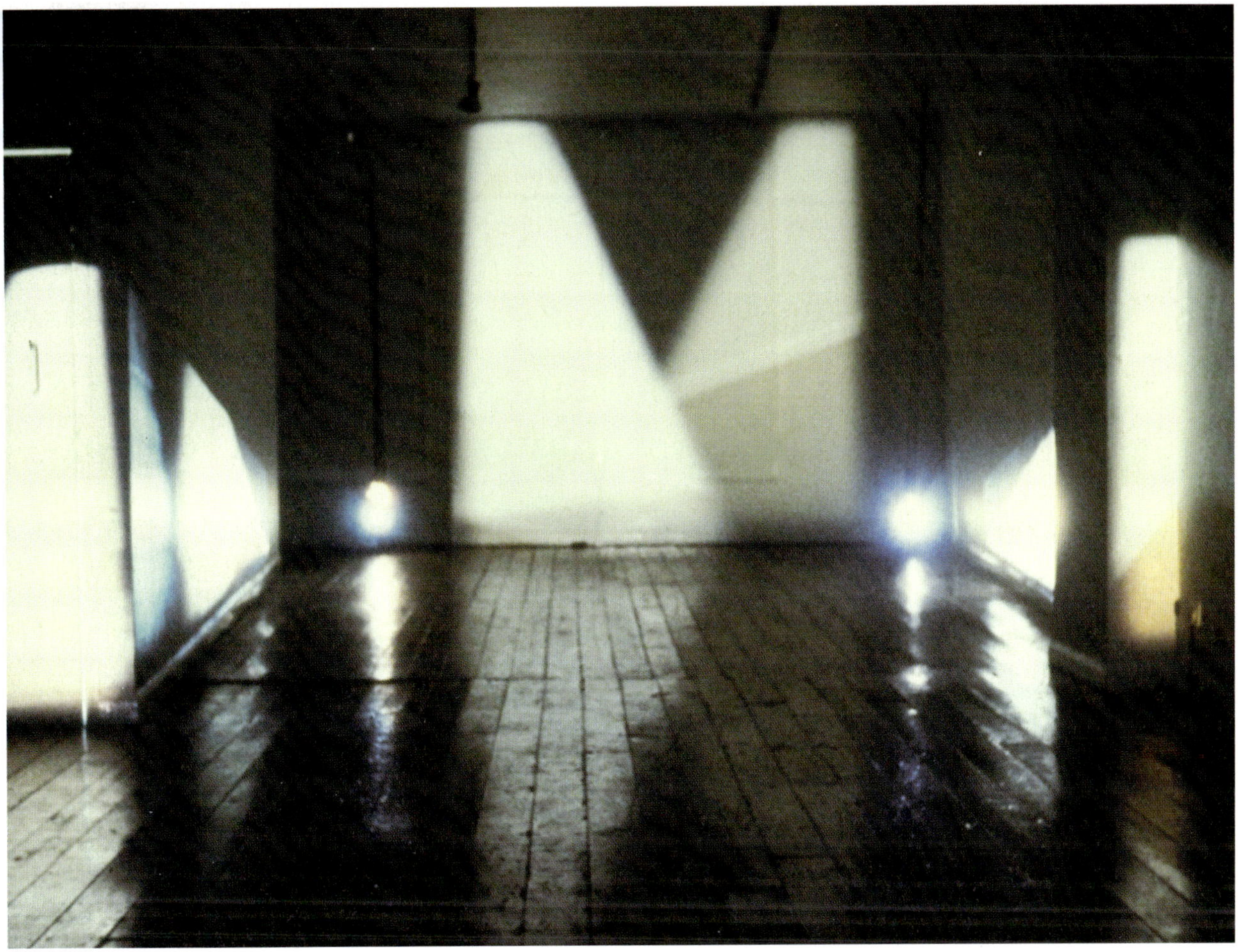

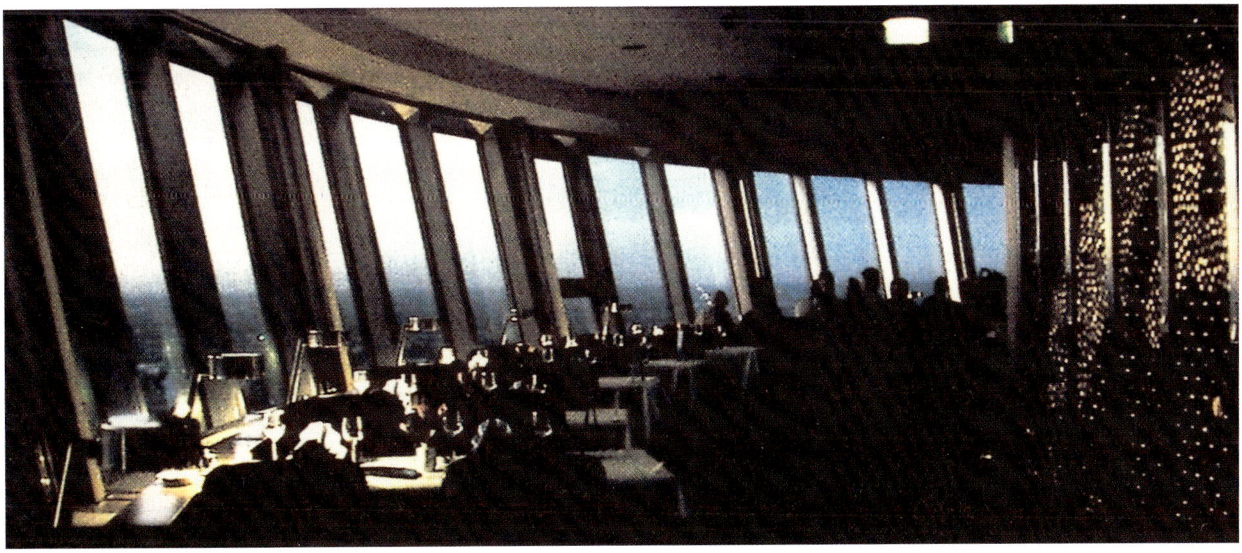

Jane Rigby, *Ambient Vision*, Acme Gallery, London, 1979. 16mm film installation. Courtesy British Artists Film & Video Study Collection, Central Saint Martins, London

Tacita Dean, still from *Fernsehturm* (*Television Tower*), 2001. 16mm colour anamorphic film, optical sound, 44mins. Courtesy the artist, Frith Street Gallery, London & Marian Goodman Gallery, New York & Paris

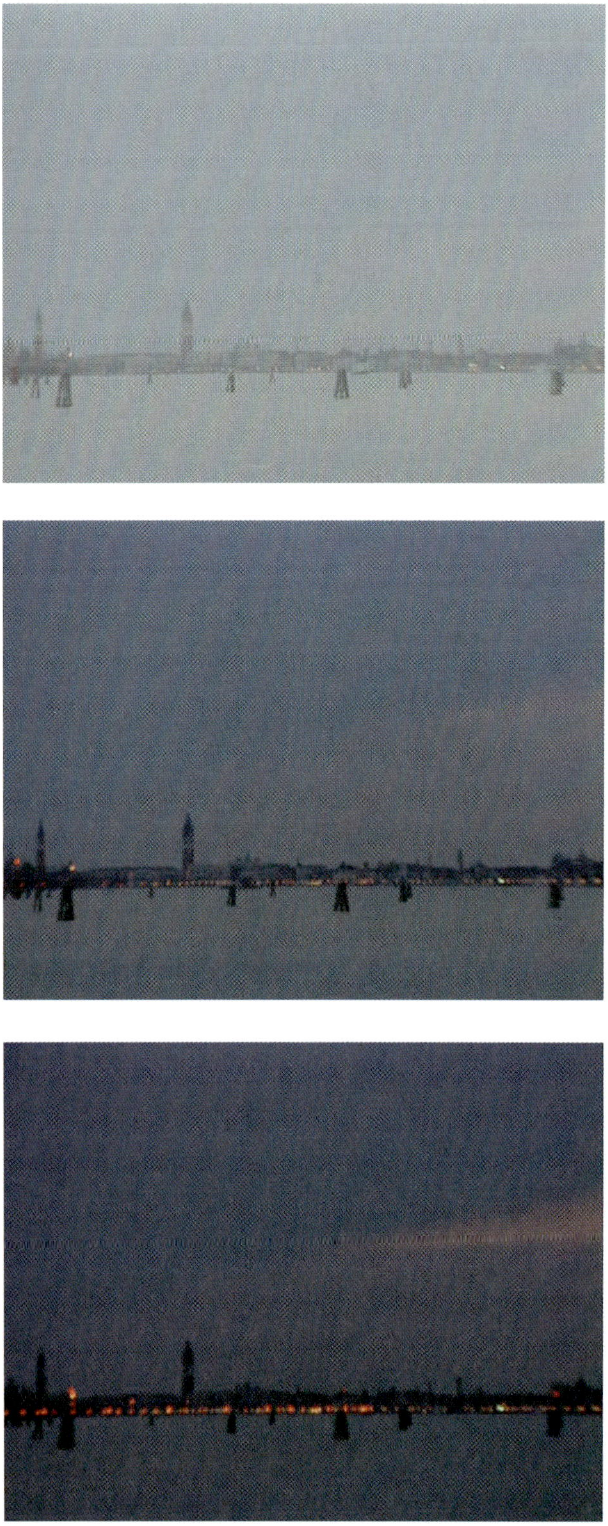

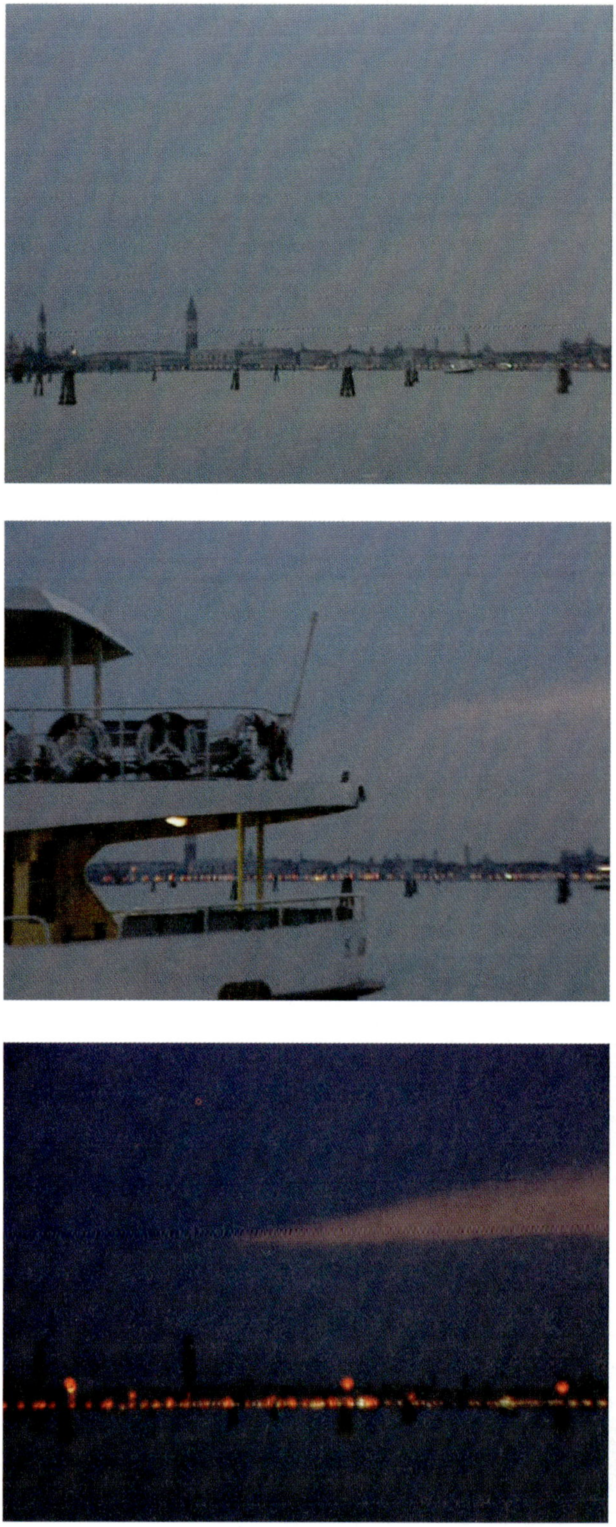

Thierry Kuntzel, stills from *Venises*, 1995. 8mm colour film, silent, 8mins. Courtesy Galerie Yvon Lambert, Paris

Facing page: Eija-Liisa Ahtila, still from *The House*, 2002. Photo © 2008 Crystal Eye Ltd, Helsinki. Courtesy Marian Goodman Gallery, New York & Paris

Allan Sekula, *Prayer for the Americans*, 1999–2004. Slide projection. Courtesy Christopher Grimes Gallery, Santa Monica

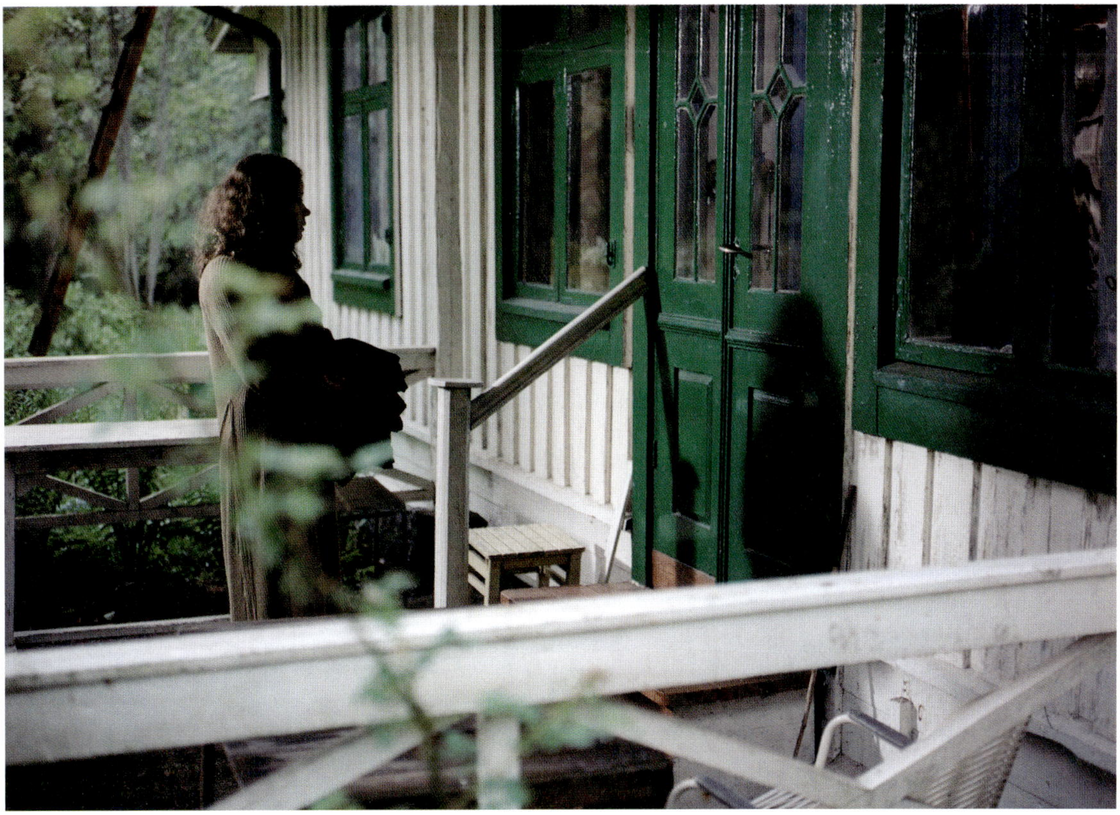

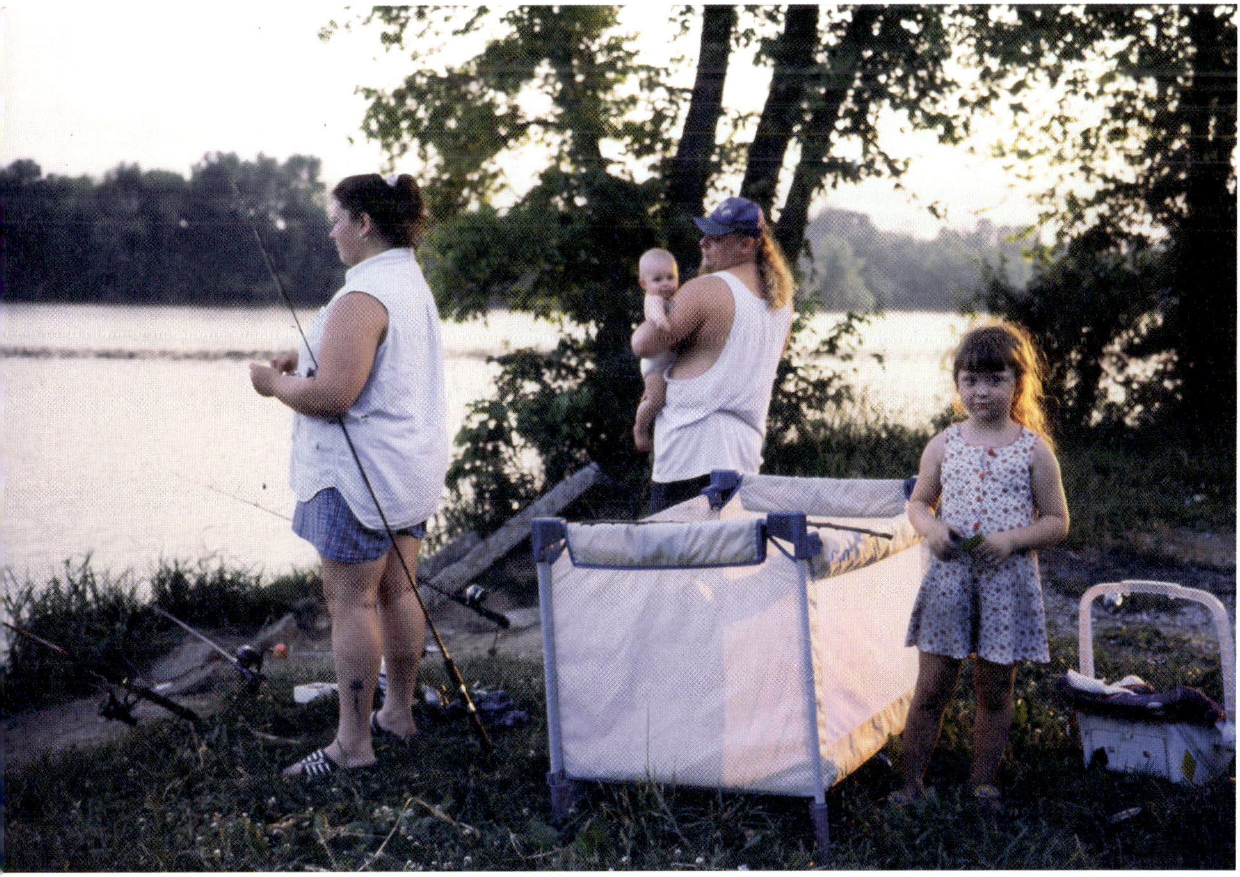

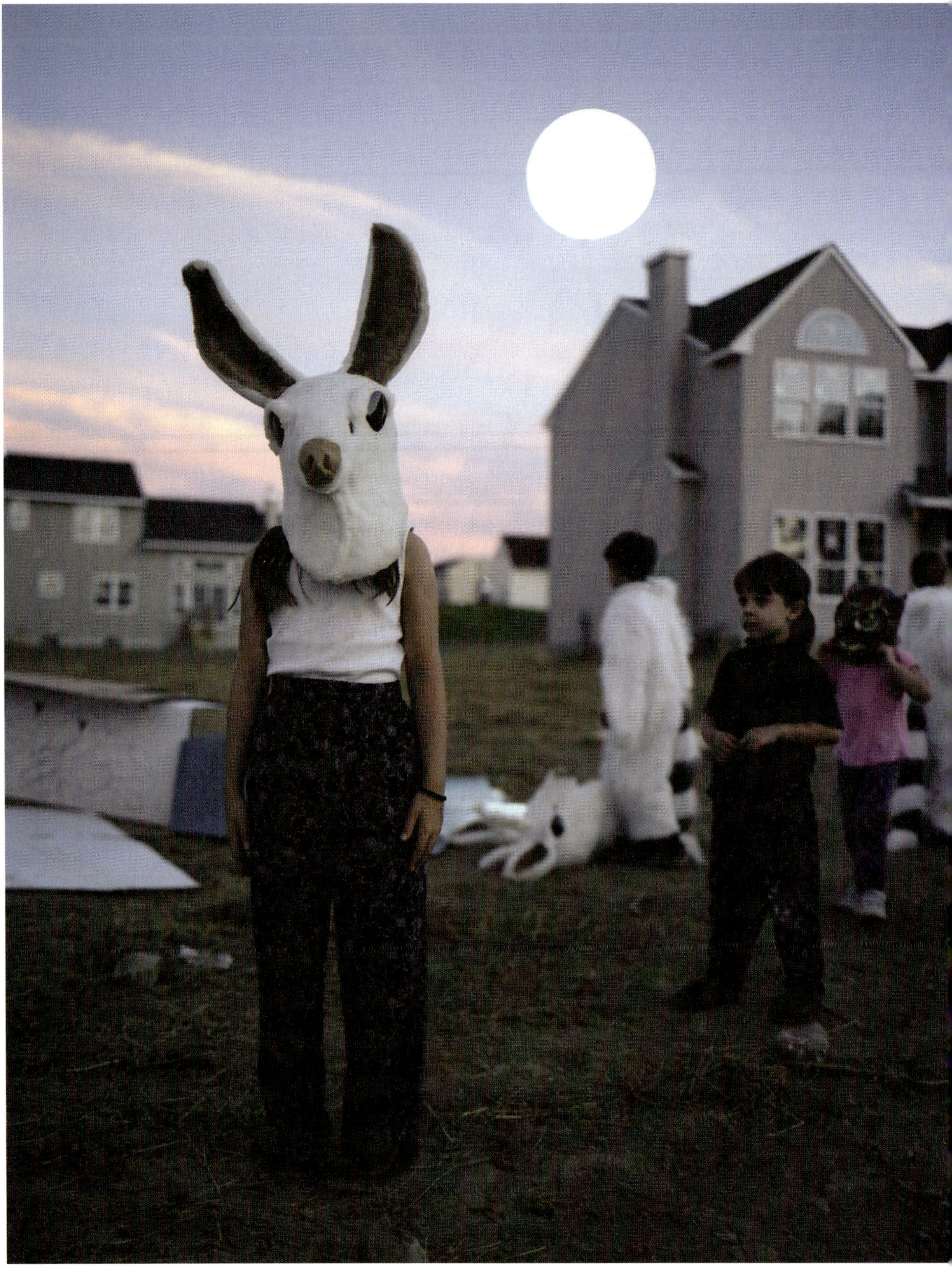

Pierre Huyghe, still from *Streamside Day* screened as part of *Streamside Day Follies*, 2003. Mixed media. Courtesy Marian Goodman Gallery, New York & Paris

–I– Histories and Revisions

The first part of this reader explores some of the major divisive topics reflected within the history of moving images and art, as it traces the historical and theoretical legacy of film's entry into the art world and the transformed status of the art object within the conflictual arena of artistic practice in the 1960s and 70s. This terrain includes the 'intermedia' movement of Fluxus; 'Structural cinema'; 'expanded cinema'; early multiple-screen installations and multimedia environments; and 'post-Minimal' and phenomenological filmic experiments.

The 60s witnessed the ambivalent moment of film's introduction to the art world. Film – presented as art – had limited access to art institutions, and the legacy of Fluxus films is arguably still one of the least assimilable of all. In 'Fluxfilms in Three False Starts', Bruce Jenkins writes that Fluxus films shift 'incongruously between a pared-down formalism and broad parody, alternately cerebral and sentient'. Unable to be categorised within any of the rubrics of alternative cinematic practice – 'direct', 'personal', 'poetic', 'expanded', 'underground' – critical recognition of Fluxus films was not forthcoming from either the leading protagonists of the cinematic avant-garde or mainstream reviewers. Comprising a set of forty-or-so experimental films produced by around two dozen artists associated with the movement (including George Maciunas, Jackson Mac Low, Yoko Ono, Nam June Paik and Paul Sharits), Fluxus cinema was openly critical towards abstract films and countered the 'painterly' or 'poetic' visionary experience of previous avant-garde films with references to the materiality (or dematerialisation) of the medium, as well as the institutional, functional, minimal and quotidian. While Fluxus films were produced as loops and single-screen pieces, George Maciunas had proposed a multiple-screen film installation, *Film Wallpaper*, in 1967, that would bring the film loops together for spatial contemplation within a gallery-based viewing area. Fluxus films that attempted to assault conventions, Jenkins argues, represent a paradigm shift in the parameters of film experience, the nature of the film object and in the position of the spectator.

Stan VanDerBeek's proposal and manifesto '"Culture: Intercom" and Expanded Cinema' calls artists to invent a new world language, a non-verbal one comprised primarily of moving pictures and new image-making devices – what he calls an 'experience machine', a 'culture de-compression chamber', a 'culture-intercom'– in an attempt to remedy the lack of cultural intercommunication reflected in the global crisis of the 60s. Between 1957 and 1965 VanDerBeek conceived and created *Movie-Drome* – a conceptual multiplex theatre, intended for the development of image-events and performances, and as a training ground for new 'image tools'.[1] Built in upstate New York, *Movie-Drome* was a 31-foot-high, aluminium, spherical dome, where thousands of images (moving and still) were projected onto the domed screen by a dozen 16mm film and slide projectors.[2] This prototype networked theatre is said to have functioned like an immersive three-dimensional image-library or life theatre. Its 'visual velocity' divided audiences' expectations while it opened up images to processes of continual reinterpretation and defamiliarisation. In its idealised form as a global satellite communications centre, these domes were intended to receive images via direct broadcast and in dialogue with other centres (in a process of 'intra-communitronics'), storing and remixing them in immediate feedback

1 *Move-Movies* was a similar multiple-screen projection/'movie-mural' created by VanDerBeek, and presented at the New Cinema Festival at the Film-Maker's Cinematheque in 1965. *Move-Movies* consisted of a two-screen projection as well as five portable projectors that were carried around the theatre and occasionally projected onto the audience.

2 These notes on VanDerBeek stem from Gloria Hwang Sutton's excellent examination of *Movie-Drome* and expanded cinema's influence on media art practices in general in 'Visual Velocity: *Movie-Drome* and the Anticipation of Immersive Subjectivity in Expanded Cinema Practices of the 1960s' (unpublished), and 'Movie-Drome: Networking the Subject', *Future Cinema*, (eds. Jeffrey Shaw and Peter Weibel), Cambridge, Mass. and Karlsruhe: The MIT Press and ZKM/Center for Art and Media, 2003, pp.136–38.

presentations. Set against a fear of a dystopian future, VanDerBeek's manifesto has been said to convey a sincere, if somewhat naive, reaction against technology's alienating tendency, and that *Movie-Drome* registered the inverted-utopian cultural conditions largely ignored by Marshall McLuhan and other media 'visionaries'.[3] As art historian Gloria Hwang Sutton writes: '[...] by generating an immersive subject that relied on more than just visual input, *Movie-Drome* makes evident expanded cinema was not exclusively invested in image refinement or depiction. Even in its half-realized state, the project confirms that expanded cinema attempted to address broader political systems of distribution, social regulation and the mechanization of information.'

Beatriz Colomina writes: 'We sit in front of our computers on our ergonomically perfected chairs, staring with a fixed gaze at many simultaneously "open" windows through which different kinds of information stream towards us. We hardly even notice it. It seems natural, as if we were simply breathing in the information.' In 'Enclosed by Images: The Eameses' Multimedia Architecture', Colomina examines the multiple, simultaneous images that surround and distract us, making clear that: 'Designers, architects and artists were involved from the beginning [in domains ranging from experimental cinema to the establishment of military war rooms], playing a crucial role in the evolution of the multi-screen and multimedia techniques for presentation of information.' Focusing on the film *Glimpses of the USA* by Charles and Ray Eames, produced for the 1959 'American National Exhibition in Moscow' (site of the famous 'Kitchen Debate' between Richard Nixon and Nikita Khrushchev on the virtues of the American way of life), Colomina explores the role the Eameses' enormous multiple-screen film projection played in Cold War operations.

Branden W. Joseph's essay '"My Mind Spilt Open": Andy Warhol's Exploding Plastic Inevitable' (the title is derived from a line in the Velvet Underground's song 'I Heard Her Call My Name') discusses the production of the EPI – Warhol's expanded multimedia event – along with many phases of Warhol's collaboration with the Velvet Underground and his lesser-known musical collaborations with composer La Monte Young, film-maker Barbara Rubin and the brief rock-group project with Claes and Patti Oldenburg. Unlike Warhol's canonical single- and double-screen cinematic works – such as *Sleep* (1963), *Empire* (1964) and *Chelsea Girls* (1966) – the EPI, Joseph suggests, has not been taken seriously as a work of art. In order to understand and theorise the EPI's place within the histories of avant-garde and media arts, Joseph draws upon extensive archival research into previously little-known Warhol collaborations and interventions into popular media (music and television among them) to argue that the EPI can be understood as a particular instance of the emerging dystopic 'media spaces' discussed by Marshall McLuhan and William S. Burroughs. Citing another of the Eameses' multimedia works, *Think* (1964) at the IBM Pavilion, New York World's Fair, Joseph agrees with Colomina that the Eameses' multiple-screen and multimedia exhibitions effected a new kind of attention in distraction. He argues that the EPI succeeded like the Eameses' project in 'channeling the newly emerging dislocating effects of electronic technology to the contemporary operations of commercial mass media', only he claims that the EPI did so far more intensely without cohering to the norms of popular spectacle. As opposed to the ideological naturalisations of the type put forward by the Eames and the 'orchestral, resonating unity' and 'subjective self-possession' that McLuhan advocated in his holistic image of the global village, Joseph links the EPI's 'contemporary, capital-driven, technological dislocations with more volatile forms of social and libidinal transformations'. Ultimately, he outlines the EPI's potential for evading the media's controlling effects within a more active, participatory form of 'suture' and the possibilities for liberation within a new mode of distraction.

'The Museum of Attractions: Marcel Broodthaers and the *Section Cinéma*' is one of a series of essays by Eric de Bruyn on Belgian artist Marcel Broodthaers that map different stages in the artist's involvement with the interrelations of artistic and filmic practices. The first text, 'Marcel Broodthaers: *Cinéma Modèle*', to paraphrase de Bruyn, focuses on the 'morality tale' of *Le Corbeau et le Renard* (1967), and is concerned with the (re)mediations of the different levels of writing and representation in the work – how boundaries between different media in

3 G.H. Sutton, 'Visual Velocity: *Movie-Drome* and the Anticipation of Immersive Subjectivity in Expanded Cinema Practices of the 1960s', *op. cit.*

Broodthaers's work are dislocated in an endless play of negation. The second stage of the project, 'The Museum of Attractions: Marcel Broodthaers and the *Section Cinéma*' (published in this volume), analyses the issues of presentation, exhibition and the media public sphere. The final stage, 'On the Museum as Film Décor: Marcel Broodthaers and *La Bataille de Waterloo*', considers the '*décor*', in which the presence of the artwork and gallery installation almost threatens to disappear into a fully mediated state. All three essays reveal Broodthaers's concern with the processes and uses of historical memory versus the progressive spatialisation of time within media society and his attempts to weaken or counter this historical force from within.

Particular emphasis has been placed upon the legacy of 'Structural film' (or 'Structural-Materialist film') in recent re-examinations of the relevance of moving-image installations and expanded cinema in cinema studies and art history, and Federico Windhausen's essay 'Paul Sharits and the Active Spectator' responds to this development with a close analysis of one so-called Structuralist film-maker's shift from single-screen films to film installations. Drawing upon rare archival materials as well as Sharits's own published texts and interviews, Windhausen's essay aims to rectify the general oversight of the artist's installation work by art and film historians. His essay contributes to a revived dialogue on Sharits by reintroducing the film-maker's multiple-screen works of the 1970s to readers today, situating the pieces he termed 'locational' within a larger project. As Windhausen notes, despite evidence of the film-maker's many divergent impulses and the occasionally confusing array of theoretical and artistic influences and models mentioned in Sharits's writings, a consistent set of interests and concerns can be found within his syncretic practice. Windhausen acknowledges the contradictions and paradoxes that emerge within Sharits's theoretical pluralism, yet he also identifies two goals that Sharits pursued throughout his career: the expansion of filmic composition and the expansion of the parameters of spectatorial experience. Focusing on the set-up of Sharits's installation works, Windhausen argues that foregrounding the apparatus is simply one strategy within a didactic project that develops new compositions for a new temporal cinema.

In 'Bare Lives', Pamela M. Lee discusses media works by Carole Schneeman, Joan Jonas and VALIE EXPORT from the 1960s and 70s. She does so in contrast to the ways in which these works have previously been considered in art history, and specifically how they have been analysed under the theoretical lens of 'body art'. Lee sees little correspondence with the essentialised body of a particular feminist aesthetic that 'body art' focused upon; rather, she argues that it may be more appropriate to understand the radical convergence of 'a violently screened body ... and the body's own proactive *screening*' in terms of Foucault's concept (and Agamben's elaboration) of the 'biopolitical' – the right of death and power over life. Such a right, Lee argues, has a medium-specific dimension, in that sexualised subjects were and continue to be reproduced 'in and *as* media'. Lee argues that works by Schneeman, Jonas and EXPORT are significant mediations on the emergent biopolitics in the 60s because they shifted between divergent and parasitic relations of sexuality, while acting out the workings of biopolitical production and fracturing the rules to which they are bound. It is precisely these forms of communications media, Lee argues, that give the body its contingent power.

Sabeth Buchmann's 'Leisure 73' discusses the filmic collaborations of artist Hélio Oiticica and film-maker Neville D'Almeida. Buchmann examines the 'quasi-cinemas' (multiple slide-projected installations) as a continuation of the participatory objects and interactive environments that Oiticica devised in the context of the *Tropicalismo* movement – a group founded in Brazil in the 60s, comprised of political activists, writers, film-makers, musicians and visual artists. Buchmann claims that it is within this context that Oiticica's appropriations of filmic media generally, and cinema in particular, should be understood. Citing *CC5 Hendrix-War* (1973) as exemplary of their highly heterogeneous references to Brazilian, European and US-American cultures and counter-cultures, Buchmann argues that it implies the possibility of overcoming a social morale based on capitalist systems of production and consumption. She concludes that Oiticica's 'collage-media' positioned itself somewhere 'between the critical negativity of the historic avant-garde and the aesthetic positivity of queer underground cinema', and that it would be impossible to imagine 'without the "queer Babylon" of Hollywood cinema'.

Peter Wollen's article 'The Two Avant-Gardes' is an important contribution to discussions that occurred in the 1970s around the different practices of visual artists and film-makers and the difficulty of differentiating between them. Partly based on Peter Gidal's assertions in the manifesto-like essay 'Theory and Definition of Structural Materialist Film',[4] Wollen's text is considered influential – especially within European assessments of avant-garde practice – because it is claimed that it helped to revive another model of the avant-garde.[5] As Eric de Bruyn has noted, Wollen confronted and juxtaposed (within a framework based on Julia Kristeva's notion of 'intertexuality') what he saw as two strong tendencies of filmic work in the 60s and 70s: formalist and political. Within the formalist camp he identified the origins in the Co-op Movement from North America and in the so-called 'Structural-Materialist cinema' of Peter Gidal, Malcolm Le Grice and so on; and within the political camp as those stemming from Soviet cinema in the 1920s (Sergei Eisenstein and Dziga Vertoz) to European film-makers in the 60s (Jean-Luc Godard and Straub-Huillet). The former applied Greenbergian criteria of modernist painting to an examination of film and its inherent specificities – the flatness of the filmic image, grain, light, movement – in order to create alternative worldviews; while the latter (the 'counter-cinema' of Wollen and Laura Mulvey, for example) were committed to political strategies of agitation that questioned the construction of ideologies and mediations of meaning within mass culture. De Bruyn has argued that while the two did have certain denominators in common (for example, a consideration of the process of signification), Wollen foresaw an unbridgeable gap between them. As such his text does not acknowledge the fact that a complex reception of Godardian and Brechtian aesthetics took place among American (post-)Minimalist artists, and that a convergence between the two avant-gardes occured within the space of the gallery as early as 1975. Wollen and other film-makers treated gallery spaces suspiciously at the time, thereby contributing to the fissure between the two practices.

Jonathan Walley's essay 'Modes of Film Practice in the Avant-Garde' considers the complicated relationship between two bodies of film art in the avant-garde: the 'avant-garde' or 'experimental' film and 'artists' film' or 'projected-image art'. Referencing the work of David Bordwell, Kristin Thompson and Janet Steiger, he employs the concept of a mode of film practice – comprised of the aims and methods of film production, channels of distribution, venues and conventions of exhibition and viewing strategies – to characterise the two groups of work and their distinct histories, institutions, economics and critical languages. Walley focuses on spatial works by both groups, such as gallery-based film installations, tracing the different ways that the two groups conceive of film's temporal and spatial dimensions and their effects on the activities of spectators. He addresses art historical discussions of Anthony McCall's work, and in particular *Line Describing a Cone* (1973), that have appeared in the wake of McCall's recent 're-emergence' as a film artist. He claims that these discussions overlook the historical existence of a distinct artistic tradition of avant-garde cinema understood as a mode of film practice different from the practices of the gallery art world. Walley cites the importance of the institutional context of avant-garde cinema in work such as McCall's from the 70s. He makes reference to the category of what he terms 'paracinema' – phenomena that are considered 'cinematic' but that are not embodied in the materials of film as traditionally defined – in order to make concrete the distinction between film and cinema, where the latter is understood to encompass more than the raw physical materials of the film medium. Making such a distinction enables us, Walley argues, to recognise how non-filmic 'paracinematic' work nonetheless engages aesthetic preoccupations specific to the tradition of avant-garde film. The 'paracinema' explorations of Tony Conrad, Malcolm Le Grice, Annabel Nicolson, Takahiko iimura, Lis Rhodes and Paul Sharits turned away from the medium-specific materialism attributed to so-called 'Structural film' in order to address cinematic conventions beyond the material register. Hence, while such spatial film works were often designed for the gallery, they should be differentiated from contemporaneous film work by gallery artists. The two respective bodies of film art, though related in some respects, ultimately represent different artistic traditions that have been developed, experienced and theorised under different historical circumstances. Walley concludes: 'While the two modes of film practice in the avant-garde may, like the double helix, "spiral around each other without ever quite meeting", the individuals who operate within these modes have more freedom of movement.'

4 Peter Gidal, 'Theory and Definition of Structural Materialist Film', *Structural Film Anthology*, London: British Film Institute, 1976.

5 The following summary develops from Eric de Bruyn's discussion of 'The Two Avant-Gardes' in *The Filmic Anomaly: Moments in Post-Minimalism (1966–1970)*, unpublished dissertation, New York: Graduate Faculty in Art History, The City University of New York, 2002. p.157.

FLUXFILMS IN THREE FALSE STARTS
Bruce Jenkins

1. Metro George Maciunas[1]

Let's have some new clichés.
Samuel Goldwyn

The realm of jokes knows no boundaries.
Sigmund Freud

There are at least two Fluxus cinemas: one consisting of forty-odd short films, most dating from the mid-1960s; the other, potentially open-ended, embracing virtually any motion picture seen in a Fluxus way. Jonas Mekas, the indefatigable chronicler of the history of American avant-garde film-making and a co-editor of *Film Culture*, the main journal for independent film-makers, described an instance of the latter in recollecting George Maciunas's response to Vittorio De Sica's *Miracle in Milan* and its Fluxus event — peasants watching a sunset.[2]

Maciunas seems to have divided his cinematic attentions between overseeing production on the various reels of Fluxfilms and monitoring the wider arena of Fluxus activity on-screen. Included in the extraordinary paper trail that constituted his real lifework are files on 'films liked and noted'; clippings of ads for 'Used 8mm Silent' films (including such standards as *The Birth of a Nation* and *Tarzan of the Apes*, starring Elmo Lincoln); listings for prints of a wide range of silent comedy (early Chaplins, later Keatons and even the less-heralded work of Chester Conklin, Snub Pollard and Mack Swain); and a pastiche of offerings for railroad movies, Pearl White serials, war documentaries and vintage sports films. Found in the same files are mail-order ads for the 8mm viewers, film splitters, reels and cans and other low-end devices and materials that were employed in the making, packaging and marketing of the Fluxfilms.

Maciunas's fascination with film and film history — the 'pre-history' of the Fluxfilms, as it were — was apparent in the aesthetic genealogies he often crafted for the movement at large. In these graphic timelines charting the cultural milieus and artistic practices he thought to have prefigured Fluxus,

1 The comparison to the Hollywood studio system implied by this section's title is suggested in part by the role Maciunas assumed in the production of the Fluxfilms — a role not unlike that of a producer. The comparison also has been invoked by Jonas Mekas, quoted in Tod Lippy, 'Disappearing Act: The Radical Reductivism of Fluxus Film', in Cornelia Lauf and Susan Hapgood (eds.), *FluxAttitudes* (exh. cat.), Ghent: Imschoot Uitgevers, 1991, p.35.

2 Conversation with Jonas Mekas at Anthology Film Archives, New York, June 1991.

GEORGE MACIUNAS (DEC.5,1969): SOME COMMENTS ON *STRUCTURAL FILM* BY P.ADAMS SITNEY *(FILM CULTURE NO.47,1969)*

We have heard of *3 EMPTIES* and *3 NOTHINGS* (response of Vietnamese villagers), *3 HOLIES, 3 TRUTHS,* etc. and now P.Adams Sitney has contributed *3 ERRORS:* (wrong terminology, wrong examples-chronology and wrong sources for origins).

category	error	cause of error	proposed correction of error
terminology	Term of *Structural Film* is semantically incorrect, since structure does not mean or imply simple. Structure is an arrangement of parts according either to complex or simple design, pattern or organization. Complex structures: fugue, sonata, serial form, indeterminate statics of concrete frame, desoxyribose nucleic acid molecule. Simple structures: continuous crescendo, pivot support beam, helium molecule, *So Sho* painting, *Haiku*, held tone, etc.	Misplaced dictionary and ignorance of recent *art-philosophy* such as definitions of *Concept-art* and *Structure-art* by Henry Flynt in his *General Aesthetics*, or *Concept Art* essay in *An Anthology, 1963*	(As proposed in *Expanded Arts Diagram*, by G.Maciunas, *Film Culture No.43, 1966)* Monomorphic structure *(having a single, simple form; exhibiting essentially one structural pattern)* Neo-Haiku. This monomorphism tends to border on *Concept-art*, since it emphasizes an image or idea of generalization from particulars rather than particularization (arrangement into particular design or pattern) of generalities. In *Concept-art* realization of form is therefore irrelevant, since it is an art of which the material is *concepts* (closely bound with language), rather than particular form of film, sound, etc.
chronology of each category  single staccato	no examples given	Cliquishness and ignorance of film-makers outside the *Coop.* or *Cinematheque* circle.	George Brecht: *Two Durations, 3 lamp events, 1961* Dick Higgins: *Constellation no.4, 1960; Plunk, 1964* Eric Andersen: *Opus 74, 1965* Anonymous: *Eye Blink, 1966*
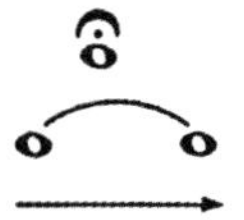 linear progress, held image, tone, straight development.	Andy Warhol: *Sleep, 1963-4; Eat, 1964.* John Cavanaugh: *The Dragon's Claw, 1965* Paul Sharits: *Ray Gun Virus, Piece Mandala, N:O:T:H:I:N:G.* Joyce Wieland: *Sailboat, etc. 1967*	same as above	La Monte Young: *Composition 1960 No.9*, realized in 1965 Jackson Mac Low: *Tree Movie, 1961.* Nam June Paik: *Zen for Film, 1962-4.* Dick Higgins: *Invocation of Canyons & Boulders for Stan Brakhage, 1963* (endless eating motion of mouth) Brion Gysin: *Flicker machine, 1963-4.* George Brecht: *Black Movie, 1965* Paul Sharits: *Sears, 1965* (single frame exposure of Sears catalogue pages), *Wrist trick, Word Movie, etc.* John Cavanaugh: *The Dragon's Claw, 1965* (flicker) Milan Knizak: *Pause, 1966* James Riddle: *9 Minutes, 1966* George Maciunas: *10 feet, 1000 frames, Artype (lines) 1966*
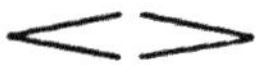 arithmetic or algebraic progression. transition, zoom f stop or focus change; crescendo or decrescendo	Tony Conrad: *The Flicker, 1966* Michael Snow: *Wavelength, 1967* Ernie Gehr: *Wait, Moments, etc. 1968* George Landow: *Bardo Follies*	same as above	Nam June Paik: *Empire State Building, 1964* (f stop change) George Brecht: *Entry–Exit, 1962* realized in 1965 (black to white transition, either by f stop change or devel.) Takehisa Kosugi: *Film & Film for Mekas, 1965* Chieko Shiomi: *Disappearing Music for Face, 1965-6* Tony Conrad: *The Flicker, 1966* George Maciunas: *Artype (dots), 1966* Michael Snow: *Wavelength, 1967,* Ernie Gehr films, 1968, George Landow: *Bardo Follies,* Ayo: *Rainbow, 1968-9.* (color wheel: yellow to green)
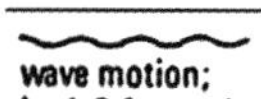 wave motion; back & forward	no examples given		Paul Sharits: *Dots, 1965* Yoko Ono: *Number 4, 1965* (buttock movement of walker) Michael Snow: *◄—►, 1968*
readymades & found film	George Landow: *Fleming Faloon, 1965*		Nam June Paik: *Zen for Film, 1962-4* (film with dust) George Landow: *Fleming Faloon, 1965* Albert M. Fine: *Readymade, 1966* (color test strip)
origins and precursors	Peter Kubelka: *Arnulf Rainer, 1958,* which is not monomorphic but polymorphic (complex) in structure. Andy Warhol: *Sleep, 1963-4,* which to begin with is a plagiarized version of Jackson Mac Low's *Tree Movie, 1961* just as his *Eat, 1964* is a plagiarized version of Dick Higgins' *Invocation...* or his *Empire, 1964* a plagiarized version of Nam June Paik's *Empire State Building.*	Ignorance of precursory monomorphic examples in other art forms, such as music, events and even film.	Zen chant, Haiku poem, So Sho painting, Eric Satie: *Vexations* John Cage: *4'3", 1952* (silence) Yves Klein: *Monotone Symphony, Blue Movie etc. 1958* La Monte Young: *Composition 1960 No.7 & 9, etc.* (drawn continuous line, held tone, etc.) George Brecht: *Drip Music, 1959; Direction (—► ◄—), 3 Yellow events* (for slide projector), *Word Event (Exit), 2 Vehicle events (start, stop)* & many other 1961 pieces. Ben Vautier: *Intermission,* & many other 1961 pieces. Nam June Paik: most of his 1960-61 compositions. Robert Morris: *Print* (till ink runs out) Walter De Maria: *Beach Crawl, 1960.* Etc. etc. etc.

George Maciunas, *Some Comments on Structural Film*, 1969. Courtesy Anthology Film Archives.

Maciunas typically invoked a wide range of film forms — from mainstream 'Walt Disney Spectacles' and the comedies of Charlie Chaplin and Buster Keaton to the latest avant-garde works of Ed Emshwiller, Takahiko iimura, Ken Jacobs and Stan VanDerBeek.[3] Like *Film Culture*, with which Maciunas maintained a long association as a graphic designer, his passion for film was strong enough to embrace both the classic and the contemporary, the studio feature and the experimental short.

Cinema frequently served for Maciunas as an antecedent art form and at times as a productive metaphor for articulating Fluxus strategies and principles. Films could be invoked to clarify key aspects of Fluxus practice. In an analysis of monomorphic structure — the 'single, simple form' that underlay many of the early Fluxus scores and performances — for example, Maciunas cited comic strategies in the film work of Keaton and countered with the Marx Brothers:

> Watch Buster Keaton. He'll never have two gags at the same time. They follow one another very quickly, but they will not be simultaneous. And if they're simultaneous, usually they're bad gags. That's one reason I think Marx Brothers are not that good on gags because they just overcrowd them.[4]

But what finally may have linked the cinephilia of Maciunas to the cultural intervention of Fluxus were the populist roots of film and the central role of humour in both enterprises. The appeal of humour for Maciunas ('I was mostly concerned with humour, I mean like that's my main interest, is humour')[5] seems to have been grounded, at least partially, in early cinematic models. Like other anti-art movements in the last century, the burgeoning Fluxus enterprise recognised in these popular entertainments not only the aggression endemic to every comedic form but also a distinctly antisocial, anti-bourgeois sensibility at play in the physical humour, sight gags, caricatures and parody of classic silent comedy.

As Maciunas seemed well aware, film comedy illuminated an inverted world in which the weak triumphed, hypocrisy was unmasked and the maintenance of law and order fell onto the sloping shoulders of the blundering cops at Keystone. Comedy's corrosive external gaze was matched in the work of artists such as Chaplin and Keaton by reflexive strategies that bared formal aspects of the medium. Sight gags revolved around the limited palette of black-and-white filming, spatial distortions intrinsic to the medium's two-dimensionality or reversals of motion and direction that derived from shifts in the movement of the filmstrip. These were privileged moments in which

3 See 'Expanded Arts Diagram', *Film Culture*, no.43, Winter 1966, p.7; 'Fluxus (Its Historical Development and Relationship to Avant-Garde Movements)' (c.1966), reproduced in Jon Hendricks (ed.), *Fluxus Codex*, Detroit and New York: The Gilbert and Lila Silverman Fluxus Collection, in association with Harry N. Abrams, 1988, p.350; and 'Diagram of Historical Development of Fluxus and Other 4 Dimensional, Aural, Optic, Olfactory, Epithelial and Tactile Art Forms', reproduced in *ibid.*, p.329–32.

4 'Transcript of the Videotaped Interview with George Maciunas by Larry Miller, March 24, 1978', in Jon Hendricks (ed.), *Fluxus etc./Addenda I: The Gilbert and Lila Silverman Collection* (exh. cat.), New York: Ink &, 1983, p.27.

5 *Ibid.*, p.22.

the sight gag made visible the mechanics of film and, for a moment, granted us participatory entry into the making of the work.

Of the new movies (mostly silent and black-and-white) that Maciunas commissioned, collected and often completed under the Fluxfilm imprimatur, many can be described as comedies, and they share with their more mainstream predecessors both an outward parodic focus and an inward reflexive gaze. In Maciunas's hands, however, the reflexive aspect of silent comedy assumed a concrete and often punningly literal form in works in which parody is enacted on the material level rather than within a fiction. His brief *10 Feet* (Fluxfilm no.7, 1966), for example, transforms the filmstrip into a ruler calibrated to the titled 10 feet. Similarly, James Riddle's lengthier study *9 Minutes* (Fluxfilm no.6, 1966) shifts the screen into a flashing digital clock that progresses second-by-second for its titled duration. In *End after 9* (Fluxfilm no.3, 1966), an unattributed short made by Maciunas, the title not only predicts the content but, in a comic reversal of the relationship between text and title, also makes up the main portion of the film, which ends after a split-second montage of the numbers one through nine. Even Yoko Ono's politically engaged *No.4* (Fluxfilm no.16, 1964/65) maintains a punning relationship with the medium. While its title is suggestive of Maciunas's purely functional numbering system, the '4' proves a remarkably perspicuous figure in describing the content of the film — a series of buttocks in motion shot in close-up to create mobile compositions of quartered biomorphic masses.[6]

A fuller figure of the performer emerged in a subgenre of 'comedies' that embraced the more performative aspects of Fluxus. In the silent film *Shout* (Fluxfilm no.22, 1966), attributed to Jeff Perkins and photographed by Yoko Ono, the film-maker squares off with fellow artist Anthony Cox in a shouting match that — given the limitations of the silent cinema — is comically incomplete. The relationship of performance to the visual boundaries of the medium is wryly explored in the untitled Fluxfilm no.36 (1970), made by the Australian artists Peter Kennedy and Mike Paar. Here a performer is visible only below the ankles against a backdrop of bare floor seen from directly overheard. As the feet slowly begin to edge clockwise around the frame of the film, we hear the coaching directions ('Lovely, keep going') of an offscreen partner, who assists in the completion of this circuit. Not unlike Marcel Duchamp's critique of the medium in his film *Anemic Cinema* (1926) (consisting of rotoscopes embossed with nonsense texts that alternate with depth-producing spiral forms), the film creates a ludicrous spectacle of the conflation of the space of performance with the material limits of the film frame.

6 For a sense of the political underpinnings of the piece, see Ono's notes on her expanded remake of *No.4* in 'Yoko Ono on Yoko Ono', *Film Culture*, no.48–49, Winter–Spring 1970, p.32: 'This film, in fact, is like an aimless petition signed by people with their anuses.'

7 The definitive account of this tradition of experimental film-making is P. Adams Sitney's appropriately titled *Visionary Film: The American Avant-Garde*, New York: Oxford University Press, 1974.

8 For an account of Brakhage's life and work in Boulder, see his interview in the Maciunas-designed special issue of *Film Culture*, no.30, Fall 1963. For a brief account of Baillie's early activities in Canyon, see 'A Brief History of Canyon Cinema', in *Canyon Cinema Catalog 6*, 1988, p.v.

9 *Film-Makers' Cooperative Catalogue*, no.5, New York: New American Cinema Group, 1971, p.153.

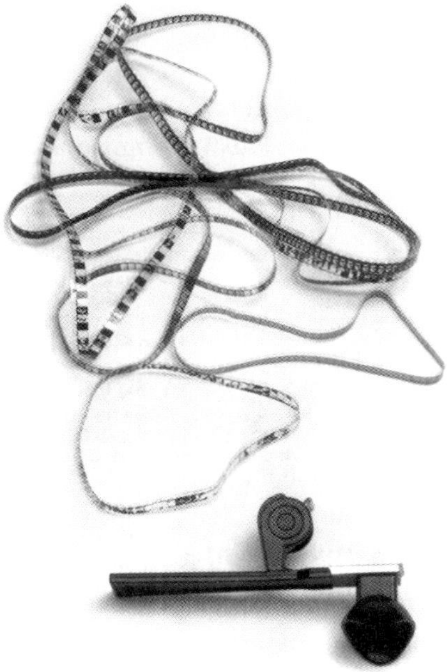

George Maciunas, 8mm Fluxfilm loops and 8mm hand-held viewer. Courtesy Robert Watts Studio Archive, New York

The target of Fluxfilm humour, however, was often directed less at the medium in general or the social order *per se* and more at the hierarchies internal to the contemporary art world — especially the deadly earnest, serious film culture represented by the leading form of avant-garde film-making of the day, the personal and poetic (or, more properly, 'mythopoeic') cinemas of artists such as Kenneth Anger, Bruce Baillie and Stan Brakhage.[7] These anti-art-film strategies employed by the Fluxfilms were multiple; they ranged from jettisoning the personal or visionary content of the poetic films to dispensing with significant aspects of their formal innovations, particularly the complex editing schemes and expressive cinematography that marked the intervention of the personal into this most impersonal of media. In place of personal content, the Fluxfilms countered with the institutional, the functional and/or the minimal. Some of the films, such as Nam June Paik's *Zen for Film* (Fluxfilm no.1, 1962/64), made of a roll of clear leader, or John Cavanaugh's flickering Fluxfilm no.5 (1965), eliminated the image completely; others, the 'readymades' such as Robert Watts's moving X-ray study *Trace No.22* (Fluxfilm no.11, c.1965) or Albert Fine's loop of a colour test strip in Fluxfilm no.24 (1966), consisted solely of found footage. Maciunas himself developed one of the more effective means to make 'cameraless' movies by applying art type directly onto the filmstrip, as in his *Artype* (Fluxfilm no.20, 1966). Still others — Joe Jones, Yoko Ono and Mieko (Chieko) Shiomi — subverted the motion of motion pictures by producing unedited, fixed-frame, slow-motion portraits of mundane activities.

Less formal but more parodic in its humorous assault on the poetic impulse was Dick Higgins's sole film for Fluxus, *Invocation of Canyons and Boulders for Stan Brakhage* (Fluxfilm no.2, 1963). The title punningly invokes two avant-garde film-making icons: Brakhage, through the double designation of his name and adopted hometown, Boulder, Colorado; and Baillie, by reference to his hometown, Canyon, California, and his independent film-distribution service, Canyon Cinema.[8] In a perverse variation of both Brakhage's and Baillie's strikingly visual, highly personal autobiographical mode — a neo-romantic exploration of the inner psyche that venerates the external gaze of the camera (and sets in motion the 'I/eye' paradigm of visionary film-making) — Higgins films himself simply in facial close-up in the act of chewing. While only a few seconds long, and consisting of a series of extreme close-ups of his masticating mouth in motion, the film was made to be shown in endless looped versions. According to one account: 'Higgins's movie ... started at 8 p.m. and at 1 a.m., when I left, it was still running.'[9]

Jackson Mac Low's 1961 score for the unrealised Fluxfilm *Tree* Movie* similarly parodied the romantic imagery of the poetic film while challenging the claims of personal authorship and the visionary experience. His film score (not unlike other early Fluxus event scores) involved a simple three-step production:

> Select a tree.* Set up and focus a movie camera so that the tree* fills most of the picture. Turn on the camera and leave it on without moving it for any number of hours. If the camera is about to run out of film, substitute a camera with fresh film. The two cameras may be alternated in this way any number of times. Sound recording equipment may be turned on simultaneously with the movie cameras. Beginning at any point in the film, any length of it may be projected at a showing.
> * For the word 'tree' one may substitute 'mountain', 'sea', 'flower', 'lake', etc.[10]

Maciunas embraced this impersonal encounter between the camera and the natural world and included the idea for the Mac Low feature among his earliest proposed festivals of Fluxfilms, advising presenters to 'just film from tripod a tree for an hour or so'.[11] Mac Low's work, along with the Higgins film, later served Maciunas in a critique of another major avant-garde film practitioner of the period, Andy Warhol. As Maciunas complained: '[Warhol's] *Sleep*, 1963 ... to begin with is a plagiarised version of Jackson Mac Low's *Tree* Movie*, 1961 just as his *Eat*, 1964 is a plagiarised version of Dick Higgins's *Invocation.*'[12] Whether or not he was inspired by Mac Low's concept, Warhol's underground movies of the mid-1960s and the experimental films of Fluxus existed in mutually exclusive arenas. Despite formal similarities and a shared contempt for the poetic cinema, Warhol's work, produced in the context of Pop Art, was predicated on voyeurism and the fetishistic power of the moving image, while a film like *Tree* Movie* was rooted in a desire to dematerialise the medium in order to bridge the gap between art and life. And, of course, most notably, Warhol's work actually was realised; Mac Low's did not even need to be.[13]

The decentralisation and democratisation of the production process implied by Maciunas's approach to presenting (and creating) *Tree* Movie* represented a transgression of the highly individualistic, personal and handcrafted 'style' of the then current avant-garde practice. For Maciunas, film was — much as the critic Walter Benjamin had described it nearly three decades earlier — the archetypal mechanically reproducible medium and,

10 J. Hendricks (ed.), *Fluxus Codex*, *op. cit.* (note 3), p.399.

11 Letter from Maciunas to George Brecht, 21 July 1964, quoted in *ibid.*

12 Maciunas was not only challenging the originality of Warhol's underground-film aesthetic but also calling into question the claims of P. Adams Sitney's then-influential essay 'Structural Film'. At the end of a revised version of that essay, published in P. Adams Sitney (ed.), *Film Culture Reader*, New York: Praeger, 1970, pp.326–48, Sitney included Maciunas's 'Some Comments on *Structural Film* by P. Adams Sitney (*Film Culture*, no.47, 1969)', a chart-like rebuttal of his own critical models (p.349).

13 Mac Low eventually did produce three versions of *Tree* Movie*, but not until 1971 and 1972, and on video, not film. The videotaped realisations (consisting of a mimosa tree on the rooftop garden of film-maker Shirley Clarke's Chelsea Hotel suite, a sugar maple on a Pennsylvania farm and a tree in Central Park) were shown in two four-hour programmes at the Anthology Film Archives in New York City on 25 and 26 January 1975. See Jackson Mac Low, 'Wie George Maciunas die New Yorker Avantgarde kennenlernte', in René Block (ed.), *1962 Wiesbaden Fluxus 1982: Eine kleine Geschichte von Fluxus in drei Teilen* (exh. cat.), Wiesbaden and Berlin: Harlekin Art and Berliner Künstlerprogramm des DAAD, 1983, pp.123–25.

14 As Benjamin notes: 'In the case of films, mechanical reproduction is not,

as such, an ideal medium for the multiple.[14] Like the array of plastic boxes that served as supports for the Fluxus editions of games and scores, paperworks and appropriated readymades, the celluloid-based medium embodied in its own material origins the industrial, impersonal facticity of the age of reproduction. Or to put it in more practical terms, with film, Fluxus art could be produced literally by the yard.

Tied to these unorthodox productions were equally unconventional distribution plans and modes of exhibition. Maciunas intended many of the Fluxfilms to be cut into small-format (8mm) loops for inclusion in Fluxyearboxes or inexpensively sold along with handheld viewers. Others were produced in various static forms. These were printed as serial stills, as with Higgins's *Invocation*, or proto-flip-book imagery (dubbed 'poor man's movies'), as with Shiomi's *Disappearing Music for Face* (Fluxfilm no.4, 1966), and marketed along with the boxes and scores.[15] Still others were designed to be 'expanded' into multimedia environments replete with design plans and suggested sound components, all under the rubric of Film Wallpaper. While plans for such room-sized projections appeared frequently in Fluxus publications and newsletters, the only documented presentations of such pieces were a two-screen projection by Paul Sharits (1966) and a smaller, 'capsule' version in a 3-foot cube created for the Fluxfest presentation of John Lennon and Yoko Ono in 1970.[16]

The role of the individual Fluxus artist was diminished by these production and presentation methods, but Maciunas's involvement remained very much hands-on. He rented the camera equipment, purchased the film stock, shot the title sequences, placed the lab orders for prints and paid the bills, spliced together the programmes and personally prepared and mailed prints to film festivals in the United States and Europe. It was his numbering system that identified the films and his imprimatur that could either embrace or exclude work from Fluxus. He ordered and reordered the versions, creating a packaged short programme and a companion selection that extended it to feature length.

Despite his efforts, the films received only scant critical attention and limited public screenings. The 1965 Ann Arbor Film Festival, the venue Maciunas had selected for the first public screening of a short programme of Fluxfilms, accorded the artists and their work recognition

as with literature and painting, an external condition for mass distribution. Mechanical reproduction is inherent in the very technique of film production. This technique not only permits in the most direct way but virtually causes mass distribution.' See 'The Work of Art in the Age of Mechanical Reproduction', *Illuminations*, New York: Schocken Books, 1973, p.244.

15 See a 1962 Fluxus newsletter on the plans for 'Fluxus Yearbook-Box', in J. Hendricks (ed.), *Fluxus etc./Addenda I: The Gilbert and Lila Silverman Collection*, *op. cit.* (note 4), p.140.

16 Maciunas wrote to Ken Friedman in the summer of 1967 that twenty of the films would be available in loop form for Film Wallpaper. Information about creating such wall environments was published in the Fluxus newsletter of December 1968 and in an announcement for Fluxfest Kits of December 1969. See J. Hendricks (ed.), *Fluxus Codex*, *op. cit.* (note 3), pp.64–65.

in the form of the Moss Tent Award, a lightweight, high-count poplin mountain tent.[17] Other minor awards followed, including the Tracy Atkinson Award of fifty dollars from the Milwaukee Art Center and modest fees for screenings at a few university and film-society venues.[18] Maciunas loaned a print to the Fluxus artist Ken Friedman for West Coast screenings, shipped another to Milan Knízák in Prague, and eventually deposited a long and a short programme with the Film-Makers' Cooperative in New York.

Critical recognition for the Fluxfilms was forthcoming neither from the champions of the cinematic avant-garde nor from mainstream reviewers: the former regarded the work as 'subversive', and the latter regarded it not at all.[19] The only significant acknowledgment of the work and of Maciunas's central role as the producer of Fluxfilms during this period came in the autumn of 1968 from the Friends of New Cinema, an organisation that provided experimental film-makers with small but strategic funding.[20] As the award letter stated:

> The Friends of New Cinema has undertaken to award a grant for your support and encouragement in your work in experimental films. The Friends expect to be able to send you the sum of $40.00 per month for the period of twelve months. [...] Best wishes for your continued good work.[21]

Enclosed was a cheque for forty dollars made out to George Maciunas.

2. The Fluxfilms: (no) Lights, (no) Camera, (no) Action

> All of the beautiful and poetic young film-makers of the new American cinema have been making dirty, nude movies lately because we are told not to — naughty aren't we?
> Jack Smith

> The movies are a Revolution.
> Taylor Mead

In the 1960s the arena of alternative film-making was alive with possibilties — new forms, new subjects, new techniques. The critic Annette Michelson, in a landmark lecture given at the 1965 New York Film Festival, distinguished within the new cinemas two aspects of the 'radical aspiration': the political and the formal.[22] In his influential midstream survey of the new forms of American cinema, the critic Sheldon Renan pared the movement into several contrasting forms beginning with 'sexy films and sexless films'.[23] Jonas Mekas, then a film critic for the *Village Voice*, suggested in a 1964 review a simpler polar division between 'two extremes: the slow and the quick', as exemplified on the one hand by the long-take features of Andy Warhol and on the other by the kinetic, highly edited work of Stan Brakhage.[24]

Within this formally and ideologically bifurcated arena of 'other' cinemas, enter the Fluxfilms, forty or so short experimental films produced by two dozen or so artists associated with Fluxus. While few of these artists were film-makers — several were composers and musicians, a few writers and poets and the rest a mixture of lapsed scientists, graphic designers and painters — their work, although indelibly 'Fluxus', flowed in several of the critical crosscurrents charted by Mekas, Michelson and Renan. A sizable portion of the films seemed to fit the Mekas model, while the paradigm advanced by Michelson could be seen in certain ideological thrusts (leftist, anti-establishment, anti-bourgeois) whose radicalism, however, was signaled more by bared bottoms and the accompanying formal baring of the device than by clenched fists. As Renan noted, the *derrière* was often at the forefront of the new cinema.[25]

Formally, the Fluxfilms tended to cluster around the polar extremes of the Mekas model. The 'slow' included several Minimalist works, such as Nam June Paik's *Zen for Film* or George Brecht's *Entrance — Exit* (Fluxfilm no.10, 1962/65) that relied on unvaried (or very gradually developing) presentations of basic film materials — clear leader, black leader, sound, silence.[26] Another significant group of 'slow' films, made by the participants in a remarkable single production session that took place in 1966 at the apartment of the Fluxus artist and photographer Peter Moore, made use of a high-speed, slow-motion camera to produce works that, when projected at normal speed, resulted in highly distended portraits, performances and motion studies.

The first of these, *Disappearing Music for Face*, was based on a performance score by the Japanese artist Mieko (Chieko) Shiomi that read simply: 'Performers begin the piece with a smile and during the duration of the piece, change the smile very gradually to no-smile.'[27] The film version, shot by Moore, featured one performer, Yoko Ono. In an image oddly reminiscent

17 This initial programme may have contained as few as eight of the Fluxfilms, the number listed for screening a few months later, in early February, at the programme's New York City debut at the Film-Makers' Cinematheque (from a photocopy in Barbara Moore's files). The Ann Arbor award was duly noted in Maciunas's file on the Fluxfilms (now in the Gilbert and Lila Silverman Fluxus Collection, Detroit) and used in the *Film-Makers' Cooperative Catalogue* to promote the rental of the short (approximately 40-minute) version. In these first catalogue listings, Maciunas (under F for Fluxus) is given the designation d/b/a ('doing business as') to indicate his unique role as entrepreneur in the Fluxfilms venture.

18 In the *Fluxnewletter* of 8 March 1967, Maciunas reported that the programme 'was already exhibited in several cities in USA (New York, Los Angeles, San Francisco, Boulder, Ann Arbor, etc.) France and Czechoslovakia'. Cited in J. Hendricks (ed.), *Fluxus etc./ Addenda I: The Gilbert and Lila Silverman Collection*, *op. cit.* (note 4), p.172.

19 In discussing the subversive nature of the Fluxus films (as compared to the Structural film), P. Adams Sitney, in a postscript to his revised 'Structural Film', *op. cit.* (note 12), p.346, suggests that the Fluxus works are mere 'tautologies'.

20 In Sheldon Renan's classic book, *An Introduction to the American Underground Film*, New York: E.P. Dutton, 1967, p.220, the Friends of the New Cinema is briefly acknowledged in a section on 'financing', midway between a listing of major foundation support (e.g. Ford, Rockefeller, Guggenheim) and novel individual contributions ('Robert Nelson received a cheque for $2,500 in a box of jelly beans, sent by a woman in Pennsylvania who admired his films').

21 This letter is in Maciunas's alphabetical files (from his estate, part of which is now on deposit at Anthology Film Archives, New York) inside the first folder marked 'misc.'

22 See Annette Michelson, 'Film and the Radical Aspiration', *Film Culture*, no.42, Fall 1966, pp.34–42 and 136.

23 S. Renan, *An Introduction to the American Underground Film*, *op. cit.* (note 20), p.17.

24 See Jonas Mekas, *Movie Journal: The Rise of a New American Cinema, 1959–1971*, New York: Collier, 1972, p.158.

25 'Much of the popularity of underground films is based on the expectation that they will include large dollops of sex' (S. Renan, *An Introduction to the American Underground Film*, *op. cit.* (note 20), p. 31).

26 George Brecht incorporated a simple electronic score for the audio portion of *Entrance–Exit* that shifted in tone from a sine wave to white noise (as the film image shifts from white to black). For a fuller treatment of the Brecht audio score, see Douglas Kahn's 'The Latest: Fluxus and Music', in *In the Spirit of Fluxus* (exh. cat.), Minneapolis: Walker Art Center, 1993, p.110.

27 See 'Fluxorchestra Circular Letter No.2', reproduced in J. Hendricks (ed.), *Fluxus etc./Addenda I: The Gilbert and Lila Silverman Collection*, *op. cit.* (note 4), p.160.

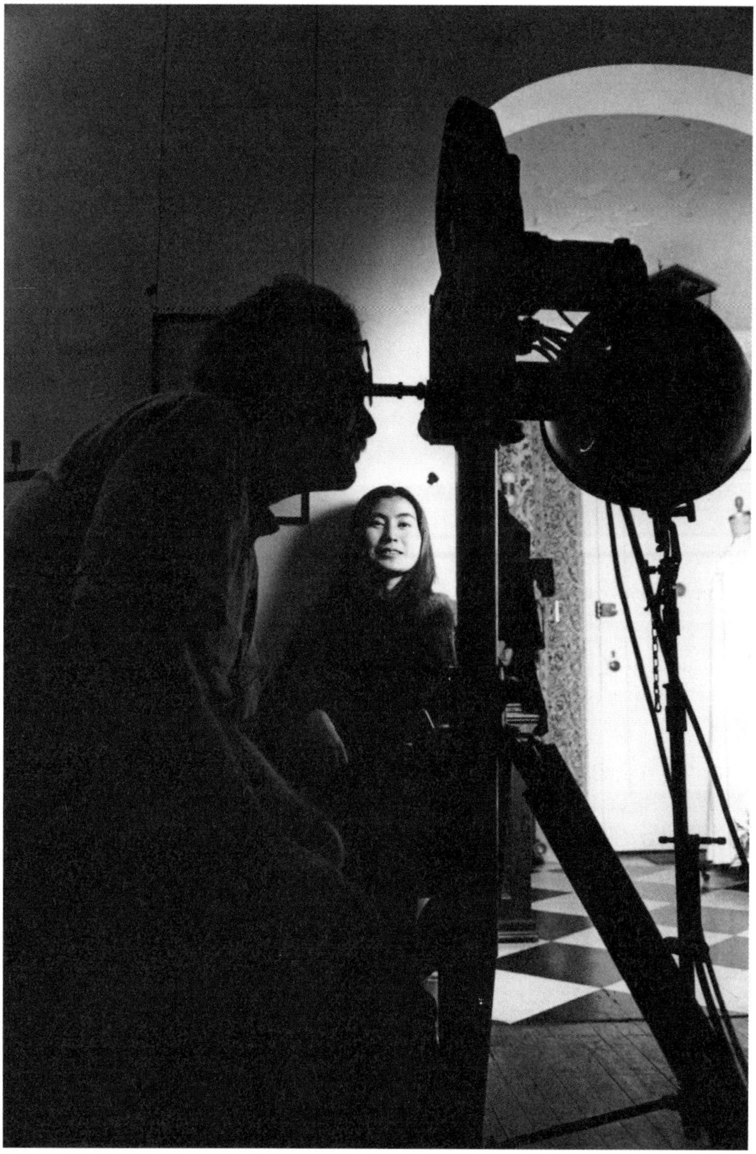

of Fernand Léger's fragmented film portrait of the French model Kiki in his *Ballet mécanique* (1924), Ono's face is segmented and seen only in an extreme close-up of its lower portion (mouth, chin and cheeks). The Shiomi score's gradual shift from smile to 'no-smile' — filmed by Moore in 8 seconds of real time — is distended into just over 11 minutes of screen time. The slightly off-centre framing captures the infinitesimal movements of lips and teeth, chin and cheeks, that coalesce in the return to an expressionless lower face.[28]

As if the camera merely tilted up, *Eyeblink* (Fluxfilm no.9, unattributed) takes as its subject the upper-right portion of Ono's face. As in *Disappearing Music for Face*, the action consists in a single facial activity — here the blinking of an eye, perhaps the ultimate monomorphic act; and again, this action is distended. Despite the slow motion, the blink is relatively brief, and the film ends as it began with a long stare into the camera, an act that transgresses a long-standing cinematic taboo and, in so doing, bares the contradictory positions of viewer and viewed (spatially adjacent but temporally disjunct) while miming the monocular lens and eyepiece of the film camera.[29]

Ono's final contribution to these productions, her own film *No.1* (Fluxfilm no.14, 1966), presents a lyrical, slow-motion study of a burning match that vividly references both the classic motion-study experiments of still photographers such as Harold Edgerton and the nature studies of film-makers such as Jean Painlevé, whose work was done in the service of both science and the spectacle. More in the mode of the pseudo-scientific is Pieter Vanderbeek's

Peter Moore filming Yoko Ono for Fluxfilms, 1966. Photo by Christopher Moore © 2008 Peter Moore estate & VAGA, New York

5 O'Clock in the Morning (Fluxfilm no.17, 1966), a slow-motion, balletic display of a quartet of potato-shaped rocks and a foursome of chestnuts falling onto a flat white surface. Over the course of 5 minutes, the bounces and rotations of these forms gradually dissipate, and the film concludes only after all movement has lapsed into a fixity of chance composition. And finally, the scientific merges with the personal in Joe Jones's *Smoking* (Fluxfilm no.18, 1966), a monomorphic self-portrait of the artist exhaling.

In contrast to the distended actions of these 'slow' films, several artists, including Fluxus impresario George Maciunas, the German visual and performance artist Wolf Vostell, the Danish composer Eric Andersen and most especially the young American film-maker Paul Sharits, experimented with single-frame film-making to produce an array of 'quick' works. Their films — which make use of animation, pixilation, collage, décollage — exhibited brevity in both their rapid-fire montage and brief running times. Based on single, one-twenty-fourth of a second exposures that pressed against the boundaries of the visible, these films both parodied and exceeded the visual velocity of even the 'quickest' of the personal and poetic films of the time. Yet, like the static films of Jones, Ono and Shiomi, the transgression was not limited to the formal but readily extended to the subjects and narratives advanced in the work. The ecstatic pace of the imagery opened onto neither autobiography nor revelation nor an approximation of the visionary experience. In their stead the quick films proffered pages from the Sears catalogue, pixilated portrayals of proper toilet use, the interior decor of a cramped 1960s apartment and fragments from a day of German television.

Among the earliest completed pieces in this group was Wolf Vostell's pioneering *Sun in Your Head* (Fluxfilm no.23, 1963). Working with broadcast material shot by a film camera directly off the television screen, Vostell's work subverts the givens of then-current personal film practice by eschewing the personal and the cinematic and embracing instead the impersonal and videographic. At the same time, he subverts the intention of the original material by transforming it into a cinematic object. Consisting of 'TV screen distortions and interferences',[30] the film includes not only examples of the material support — the thick dark raster bar and electronic screen — but also a sampling of the genres that dominated television programming of the period. Included are pixilated news footage of a space capsule splashdown, fragments from a programme called *Magazin der Woche* and further news segments that mix reportage of a massive street demonstration with a gathering of business and/or government leaders. The film concludes with an extended,

28 For a description and analysis of this work, see D. Kahn in *In the Spirit of Fluxus*, *op. cit.* (note 26), p.107.

29 In the version of this film deposited at Anthology Film Archives, New York, there are several significant differences from the print in the Gilbert and Lila Silverman Fluxus Collection described here. First, the image is flipped left to right. More serious is missing footage at the head and tail of the film that produces an opening image of Ono with eye closed and an ending image abruptly cut to black, plunging the screen into a darkness recalling the closed-eye performer at the beginning.

30 This is part of the standard description of the work written by Maciunas (c.1966) for a distribution circular offering the Fluxfilms for rental (photocopy in the Gilbert and Lila Silverman Fluxus Collection, Detroit).

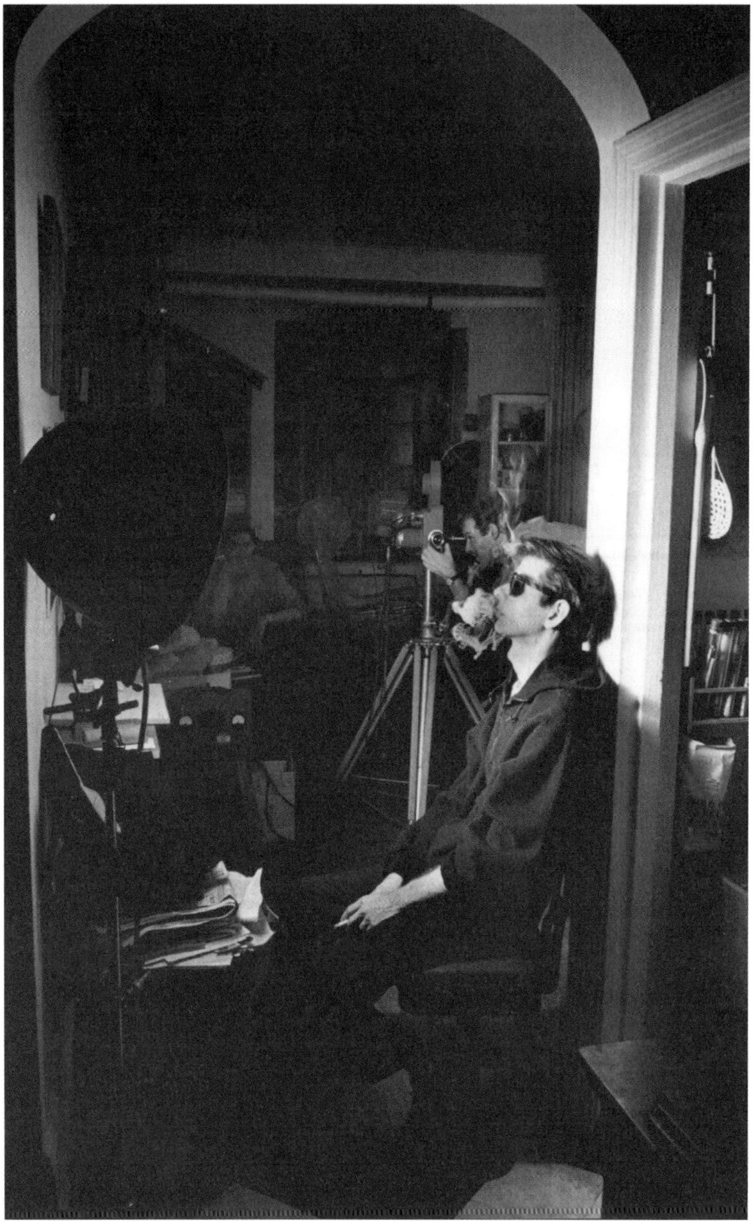

though highly edited, montage of scenes from a standard World War II documentary on the US Air Force — replete with close-ups of pilots, gauges and propellers — inflected with Vostell's videographic interventions.

A companion piece of sorts to Vostell's inventory of the typical contents of television is Eric Andersen's *Opus 74 version 2* (Fluxfilm no.19, 1965). This very brief film presents a rapid-eye tour in single-frame exposures of the view, so to speak, from the other side of the television screen — the reverse field of the room that is adjacent to the on-screen world of the TV set. In 4-second cycles, Andersen inventories the rectilinear environs of an apartment from kitchen to living room, dining table to bookshelves, hi-fi and records, paintings on the wall, jeans hanging in the closet and many other quotidian details. The effect of this rush of imagery — barely comprehensible even after several repetitions in the course of the film — is to mark out an ironic space between the exhilaration of the technique and the deadpan nature of the imagery. Andersen challenges the expressivity of this form of filmic self-portrait and counters the attendant visionary experience with a cascade of the commonplace.

Though only peripherally involved with Fluxus, the artist Paul Sharits emerged in the late 1960s as the most ambitious of the Fluxus film-makers. In his single-frame works, Sharits attempted to fashion a new poetics for experimental cinema that would be concrete rather than abstract, employing a monomorphic structure in place of the heteroclitic forms of then-current

Peter Moore filming Joe Jones for Fluxfilms, 1966. Photo by Christopher Moore © 2008 Peter Moore estate & VAGA, New York practice, grounded in and referring to the materiality of the medium rather than miming the 'painterly' or the 'poetic'. His Fluxfilms represented the most systematic attempt to found an entire experimental film form upon a limited set of formal directives that might be called Fluxus.[31] As he boldly claimed in introducing his work at an international experimental film festival in 1967: 'At the risk of sounding immodest, by re-examining the basic mechanisms of motion pictures and by making these fundamentals explicitly concrete, I feel as though I am working toward a completely new conception of cinema.'[32] Although his manifesto eventually veered off into a discussion of 'meditational-visionary experience', Sharits's critique of 'abstract films' and his desire to 'abandon imitation and illusion' set out the terms for a new, distinctly Fluxist cinema, one that would prove influential to emerging independent film and video practices.[33]

Sharits's contributions to the Fluxfilms were a number of modest, single-frame films. The simplest, *Dots 1 & 2* (Fluxfilm no.27, 1965), resembled Maciunas's *Artype* and involved simple variations of art-type dots animated by single-frame exposures. The result is expansive fields of white and black dots that undergo shifts and reversals in pattern, scale and direction of movement. By comparison, his *Sears Catalogue 1–3* (Fluxfilm no.26, 1965) is a complex work with strong formal and thematic links to Vostell. Like *Sun in Your Head*, *Sears Catalogue* takes its imagery from the mass media, here converting the pages of a mid-1960s edition of the mail-order catalogue into a pixilated portrait of commerce and desire that comically reinforces Vostell's tacit critique of the mass media and its links to business and state control.[34] And, like Andersen's kinetic home movie, the film bombards us with images of extraordinary banality.

Structured after its source, *Sears Catalogue* is organised according to a plan that refers to the gender divisions of an idealised, 'modern', white, middle-class American family and its attendant material trappings, with a decidedly ironic reading of family-style consumption. This minute-long movie begins with a burst of catalogue imagery of products for the physically infirm: a female model sits in a Sears wheelchair, and men model various styles of Sears trusses and back braces. Sharits then shifts into the male world of tyres, tools and auto accessories. The women's section, an amalgam of lingerie imagery and bathroom accessories, is disrupted by flash frames of such 'male' items as auto parts and a heavy-duty hose with a phallic nozzle. The film ends with a more traditional coupling, as Sears-attired models (a man and a woman in drawn illustration) seem simultaneously to celebrate their

31 While never elaborated as a priori for Fluxfilm production, these principles were invoked by Maciunas in 'Some Comments on *Structural Film*', in P. Adams Sitney (ed.), *Film Culture Reader*, *op. cit.* (note 12).

32 From his address to the Fourth International Experimental Film Competition in 1967 at Knokke-Le-Zoute, Belgium, as cited in Paul Sharits, 'Notes on Films: 1966–1968', *Film Culture*, no.47, Summer 1969, p.13.

33 In his essay 'Disappearing Act' (C. Lauf and S. Hapgood (eds.), *FluxAttitudes*, *op. cit.* (note 1)), Tod Lippy discusses the impact of Fluxfilms on the development of the various forms of 'Structural' and 'Structural-Materialist' film-making during the late 1960s and early 70s in the United States and Western Europe.

34 This aspect of Vostell's work, particularly in relation to his use of video, is examined in John G. Hanhardt, 'Video in Fluxus', *Art & Text*, no.37, September 1990, pp.86–91.

marriage (images of hands exchanging wedding bands) and their liaison with Sears (as they happily hold up the company's credit card).

Sharits's major work for Fluxus, however, was the sound-and-colour *Word Movie* (Fluxfilm no.30, 1966). Consisting of nothing but the titled items of language, *Word Movie* mixes the verbal (in the form of pseudo-instructional voice-over commentaries by a male and a female narrator, broken into alternating single-world units) with the visual, as a series of fifty or so words are repeatedly flashed, one at a time, onto the screen. As in *Sears Catalogue*, Sharits converts a normative text — the woman intones directions for cutting a paper pattern for an art project; the man lectures on the relationship between neural impulses and muscle movement — into a visceral experience. The effect of this assaultive blend of verbal and visual language, of informational and nonsensical sequences, is to exceed comprehension and reduce the elements to their media instantiations as sound and image, or, as Sharits suggested, to create the sense of 'one 3 ¾ minute long word'.[35]

The radical aspiration Renan cited — the uninhibited representation of human sexuality — found its proponents within Fluxus as well. Robert Watts's *Trace No.22*, for example, features a detailed view of the human anatomy — so detailed that we are privy (via its use of X-ray footage) to the intimate workings of the mouth and tongue, jawbone and oesophagus, in vivid portrayals of sipping, chewing, panting and speaking. More graphic, though less penetrating, are the fleshy portraits presented in Watts's *Trace No.24* (Fluxfilm no.13, circa 1965) and *Trace No.23* (Fluxfilm no.12, circa 1965) that are reminiscent of the appropriated soft-core pornographic imagery that recurs in his collages, objects and installations. The first of these begins, like Vostell's film, with material filmed directly off the television screen — here, two static images of Marilyn Monroe in Billy Wilder's *The Seven Year Itch*. Monroe's public display of sexuality is given a more graphic, private articulation in the succeeding imagery shot by Watts: the shadowy interior of a loft space strewn with sheets of plastic and inhabited by a naked woman writhing half-hidden in the translucent debris.

In *Trace No.23*, Watts's most ambitious Fluxfilm, sexual imagery is embedded within a formal examination of the relation of the rectangular film frame to the space defined by the circular movements of the camera. The film opens with a series of pans that follow a painted white line (perhaps the service line of an outdoor tennis court) first past a white cut-out of the numeral 4 and then, in succession, past a hand pointing to the line, a hand and a foot pointing and an outstretched arm, now situated in a meadow, that seems to be directing the camera's movement toward a scenic view. In the main body of the film, the camera moves past a woman reclining nude on the grass, a chair,

35 *Canyon Cinema Catalog 5*, 1982, p.239.
36 'Movie Journals by Jonas Mekas', *Village Voice*, 11 November 1965; reproduced in *Film Culture*, no.43, *op. cit.* (note 3), p.11.

a hot dog-like object and more cut-out numbers. Shifting from the formal to the venal, the woman begins a series of suggestive actions, sliding the hot dog-like object between her legs and, in a reversal of that movement, pulling up a polka-dotted wiener and pulling a series of wieners from under one armpit. The film concludes with a perverse sexual pun as an egg-like object (the apparent product of the actions in the previous scene) is shown floating down a leaf-strewn stream.

Multiple nudity in the service of the political is the subject of Fluxus's magnum opus of up-frontness, Yoko Ono's *No. 4*. Bringing together a number of artists both from within Fluxus (Geoffrey and Bici Hendricks, Benjamin Patterson and Ono herself) and from without (Carolee Schneemann, James Tenney, Pieter Vanderbeek and Anthony Cox), the film focuses on the bared bottoms of these performers walking in place. As Ono's actors go through their paces, the work begins to open onto subtle questions of sexual identity, the physiology of gender cues and the shifting codes of sexual difference. In the end, this fusion of gender opposition bespeaks a more global desire for cultural rapprochement. *No. 4* seems to locate in the body stripped bare a common ground upon which the various forms of cinematic radicalism can come together—the formal in league with the political, the static melding with the kinetic, the sensual embracing the ideational.

3. Somewhere Over the Rainbow Movie

Even the shock of discovering that the Wizard was a humbug was a shock I felt as a child, a shock to a child's faith in adults.
Salman Rushdie

My TV is not always interesting,
but not always uninteresting.
As nature,
who is beautiful,
not because it changes beautifully,
but because it
simply changes.
Nam June Paik

One of the least assimilable legacies of Fluxus activity is a set of forty-odd experimental films produced in the 1960s. Viewed as a group a quarter-century after they were made, these films contest easy description, shifting incongruously between a pared-down formalism and broad parody, alternately cerebral and sentient. Yet despite the extremes of their surface variation, they reveal fundamental affinities. As Jonas Mekas, then himself an aspiring experimental film-maker, noted in one of the earliest reviews of this new expanded media scene: 'Light is there; motion is there; the screen is there; and the filmed image, very often, is there; but it cannot be described or experienced in terms you describe or experience the Griffith cinema, the Godard cinema, or even Brakhage cinema.'[36]

Mekas's characterisation proved in many ways to be prophetic, for Fluxfilms represented nothing less than a paradigm shift in what the Soviet film-maker and theorist Sergei Eisenstein had called 'the film sense'. As such, the films were misdescribed, improperly experienced, generally maligned by critics and virtually ignored by every segment — straight or hip, mainstream or avant-garde — of the film-going public.[37] Their degree of 'otherness' was all the more striking given the enormous changes wrought in the early part of the decade through the work of Jean-Luc Godard, who had opened up the narrative feature film to varied new content (political analyses, cinephilic homages, reflexive exercises of and on the medium) and Brakhage, who had redirected the medium inward toward the personal, private realms of intimate experience (birth, sex, death) and the visions of the camera I/eye. Godard and Brakhage spearheaded new cinemas — the *nouvelle vague* in France and the New American Cinema in the United States, respectively — that embraced surprisingly heteroclitic practices and yet could be accounted for by the form and extent of their rejection of classic narrative cinema.

So in the beginning there were 'the movies', and they were good (according to Godard) and bad (according to Brakhage). Then, unburdened by either the seriousness of the Godardian intervention or the shame of the Brakhagean attitude toward mainstream media, came the Fluxfilms, which maintained an immaculate conception of the cinema that was at once childlike and cunning. Listen again to Jonas Mekas: 'Nam Paik, Peter Kubelka, George Maciunas have made movies where they did away with the image itself, where the light becomes the image.'[38] Of this group, it was Paik who made the first Fluxfilm and who attempted to make of his *Zen for Film* an archetypal first film through a gesture that seems both infantile and recherché: he took a roll of 16mm clear leader and projected it as a film.

In much of the same way that *The Jazz Singer* (1927) has been mythologised as the first sound motion picture, the Fluxfilm was born on the evening of 8 May 1964, at the Fluxhall on Canal Street with the first public screening of Paik's *Zen for Film*. Conceived sometime in 1962, the film gestated until that day in 1964, when, at Maciunas's invitation, Paik showed it as part of the six-week Fluxus Concerts series of performances and events. The new work emerged on-screen slightly undersized, barely filling out half of a home movie-sized screen that was positioned at the front of the loft space adjacent to an upright piano and a double bass. Visible already were the scratches and dust particles that would continue to accumulate on the print, injecting new content into and onto subsequent screenings.

37 In one of the few critical appraisals of the Fluxfilms, P. Adams Sitney inaccurately described one of the three films he invokes ('*End after 9* ... is simply academy leader from 1 to 9') and concludes by dismissively labelling the Fluxfilms 'subversive'. See Sitney's postcript to his 'Structural Film', *op. cit.* (note 12), p. 345–46.

38 Review, *Village Voice*, 25 June 1964; reproduced in *Film Culture*, no.43, *op. cit.* (note 3), p.11.

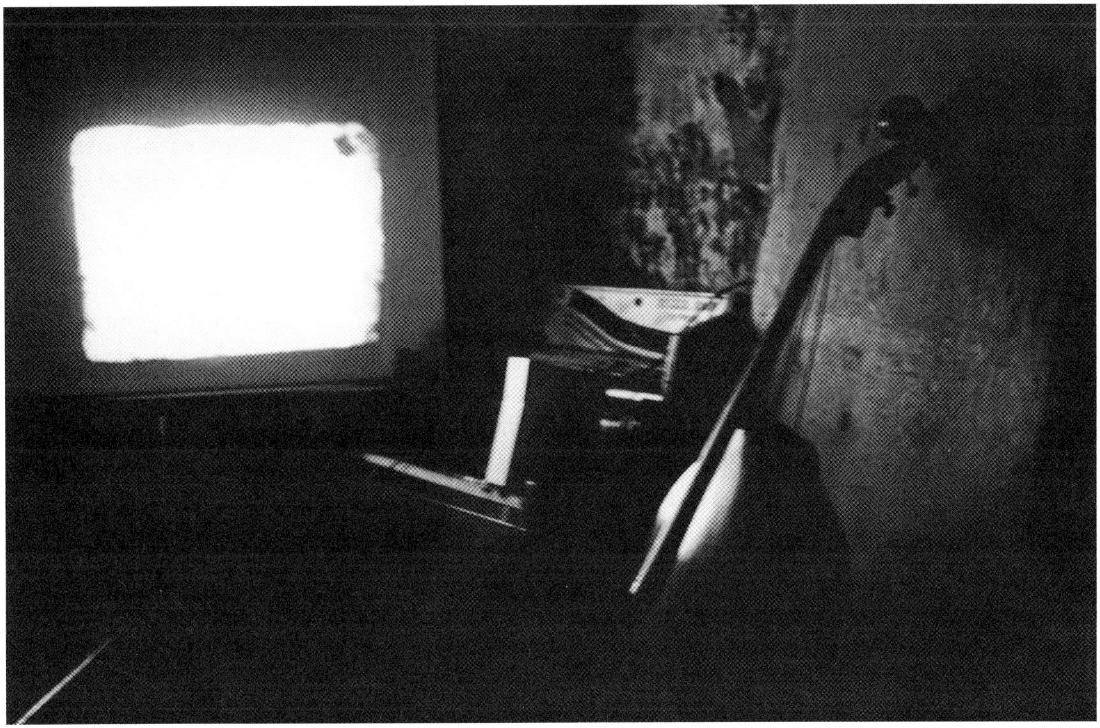

The product of both Duchampian appropriation and a childlike desire for immediate gratification, *Zen for Film* was a model Fluxus work that effectively fixed the material and aesthetic terms for the production of the subsequent Fluxfilms. Quickly and inexpensively produced by circumventing the standard technologies of production (camera, lights, sets) and post-production (editing, opticals, sound mixing), the film consisted of about a thousand feet of 16mm clear leader with a running time of nearly 30 minutes. With one simple gesture, Paik had opted out of the duplicity of the representational by making an aggressively presentational, imageless and anti-illusionist work. While his film foregrounded the materials of the medium by presenting on-screen the generally unseen — that is, repressed — physical support of cinema (i.e. blank celluloid), *Zen for Film* marked a more radical intervention into the nature of a medium that seemed no longer stable, fixed, 'finished'.

Zen for Film subtly shifted the intrinsic temporality of the film medium, instilled a performative aspect into the screening context, and, in the process, liberated the viewer from the manipulations of both the commercial *and* the alternative cinema. In contrast to the 'pastness' of filmic representation, with its indexical claims to capturing actual, pre-existing phenomena, Paik posited a concrete 'present' in his moving-image tale of the celluloid's journey through the transport mechanism of the projector. And in contrast to the frozen discourse of more traditional forms of cinema, this tale would be unique in each telling. Like some Heisenbergian allegory, *Zen for Film* was visibly changed by each viewing and maintained on its celluloid surface a record

World premiere of Nam June Paik's *Zen for Film*, Luxhall, 1964. Photo © 2008 Peter Moore estate & VAGA, New York

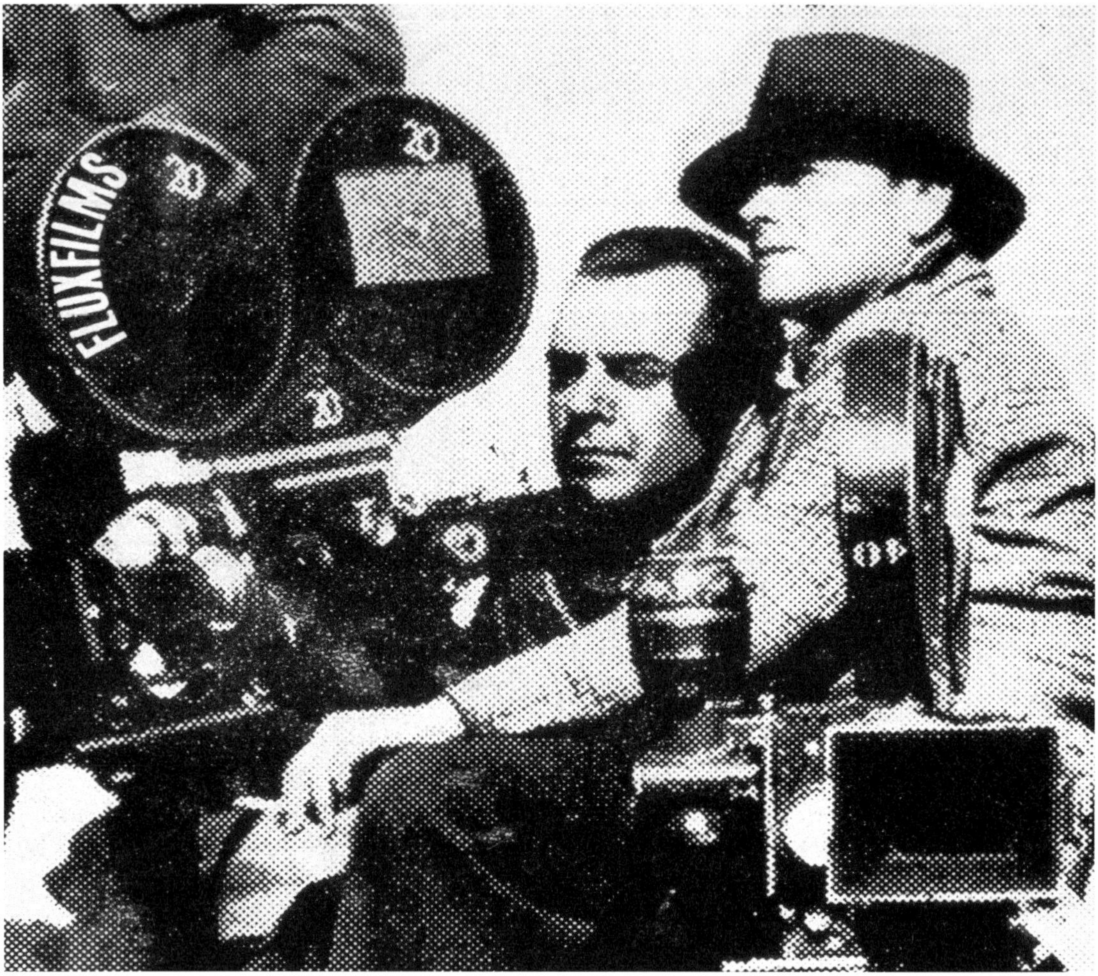

Fluxfilms label designed by George Maciunas, offset lithograph on paper, 8.3×8.3cm. Collection Walker Art Center, Minneapolis

of those observations and screenings in the form of accumulated scratches, dust, dirt, rips and splices.

With this shift came a correspondingly fundamental change in the position of the spectator. Redirecting attention toward what had previously seemed distinctly background features of the medium — the arena of visual noise — *Zen for Film* indulges and exposes our primal, moth-like fascination with this luminous medium and playfully modulates the range of attraction from the micro level of constant frame-by-frame change to the macro level of a seemingly static blank screen. Paik seems to have isolated this distinctive feature of the medium and displayed it with such brute facticity that the film could, at once, both invite intensive scrutiny and elicit absolute boredom. In this way, *Zen for Film* sacrificed the spectacle in the name of the spectator and empowered the viewer by exposing the emptiness of cinema's sound-image wizardry.

39 Brecht's statement appeared originally in 'Something About Fluxus', *FLuxus cc fiVe ThReE* (Fluxus newspaper no.4, June 1964).

Like much Fluxus work, Paik's film challenged conventional notions about the standard practice and appropriate content of the cinema. In the process, *Zen for Film* domesticated the power of this powerful medium, reducing the silver screen to the proportions of the home movie and offering the viewer control over the parameters of the film experience. George Brecht advised practicing this mastery over the moving image, suggesting that one go to see Paik's movie and 'then go to your neighbourhood theater and see it again'.[39] Maciunas expanded such options by offering a boxed version of *Zen for Film* that ensured both mastery and (partial) ownership of the medium. With its oppositional stance toward mainstream and avant-garde cinemas alike, *Zen for Film* prefigured much of Fluxus film-making and posited a 'Fluxus cinema' that exists whenever artistic control—whether by force of laughter or logic—shifts back to the viewer.

'CULTURE: INTERCOM' AND EXPANDED CINEMA: A PROPOSAL AND MANIFESTO

Stan VanDerBeek

primetime

for the moment this world
and the idea of this world
curve together in the mind
resembling each other ...
this cockfleshhouse ... starkplane and running man
sunsight handdance life, looking at life
comes, coming to be part of itself

to this vast analogy of space and time
that curve off and together in the mind
movement ... light ... it is clear we do not have
a fixed point of view
our mouth is not our hand, timebent, manspan
our eyes are not our ears, virtuallook, age leg
image move, motion itself is moving
if I think it's different it's an illusion
the world is an idea, man is an idea
in the revolving door of the universe ...

if I can, I will
take it from there ...

It is imperative that we quickly find some way for the level of world understanding to rise to a new human scale. This scale is the world. The risks are the life or death of this world. Man is running the machines of his own invention, while the machine that is man runs the risk of running wild.

Technological research, development and involvement have almost completely outdistanced our emotional and socio-'logical' comprehension. It is imperative that every member of the world community join the twentieth century as quickly as possible. Technical power and cultural 'over-reach' are placing the fulcrum of man's intelligence so far outside himself, so quickly, that he cannot judge the results of his acts before he commits them. The process of life as an experiment on earth has never been made clearer. Man does not have time to talk to himself, man does not have means to talk to other men — the world hangs by a thread of verbs and nouns. It is imperative that the world's artists invent a non-verbal international language.

I propose the following:

That immediate research begin on the possibility of a picture-language based on motion pictures.

That we combine audio-visual devices into an educational tool: an experience machine or 'culture-intercom'.

That audio-visual research centres be established on an international scale to explore the existing audio-visual devices and procedures, develop new image-making devices and store and transfer image materials, motion pictures, television, computers, video-tape, etc.

That artists be trained on an international basis in the use of these image tools.

That prototype theatres, called 'Movie-Dromes', be developed immediately, incorporating the use of such projection hardware.

I shall call these prototype presentations: 'Movie-Murals', 'Ethos-Cinema', 'Newsreel of Dreams', 'Feedback', 'Image Libraries'.

The 'Movie-Drome' would operate as follows: in a spherical dome, simultaneous images of all sorts would be projected on the entire dome-screen. The audience lies down at the outer edge of the dome, feet towards the centre; thus almost the complete field of view is taken up by the dome-screen. Thousands of images would be projected on to this screen.

This image-flow could be compared to the 'collage' form of the newspaper, or the three-ring circus (both of which suffuse the audience with an abundance of facts and data). The audience takes what it can or wants from the presentation and makes its own conclusions. Each member of the audience will build his own references and realisations from the image-flow.

A particular example: an hour-long presentation using all sorts of multiplex images, depicting Western civilization since the time of the Egyptians to the present through a rapid panoply of graphics and light calling upon thousands of images, both still and in motion, with appropriate 'sound-images'. The last three-thousand years of Western life would be compressed into such an aspect ratio that the audience could grasp the flow of man, time and forms of life that has led us up to this very moment, using the past and immediate present to help realise the likely future.

Endless filmic and imagistic variations of this idea are possible in science, maths, geography, art, poetry, dance, biology, etc. This idea could be endlessly varied by each culture group and nationality that took it on as a project, and presented in turn to other groups.

The purpose and effect of such image flow and image density (also to be called 'visual velocity') is both to deal with logical understanding and to penetrate to unconscious levels, to reach for the emotional denominator of all men, the non-verbal basis of human life, thought and understanding, and to inspire all men to goodwill and 'inter- and intro-realisation'. When I talk of the Movie-Dromes as image libraries, it is understood that techniques such as videotape and computer inter-play would be used and thus they would be real communication and storage centres. Each dome could receive its images by satellite from a worldwide library source, store them and programme a feedback presentation to the local community. 'Intra-communitronics', or dialogues with other centres, would be likely, and instant reference material via transmission television and telephone could be called for and received at 186,000 mps from anywhere in the world. Thus I call this presentation a 'newsreel of ideas, of dreams, a movie-mural, a kinetic-library, a culture de-compression chamber, a culture-intercom'. My concept is in effect the maximum use of the information devices that we now have at our disposal.

If an individual is exposed to an overwhelming information experience, it might be possible to re-order the structure of motion pictures as we know them. Cinema would become a 'performing' art and image library. Such centres would have artists in residence who will orchestrate the image material at their disposal, integrating it with live actors and performers, leading to a totally new international art cinema form. In probing for the 'emotional denominator', it would be possible by the visual 'power' of such a presentation to 'reach' any age or culture group regardless of background. There are an estimated 700 million people who are unlettered in the world: we have no time to lose or miscalculate.

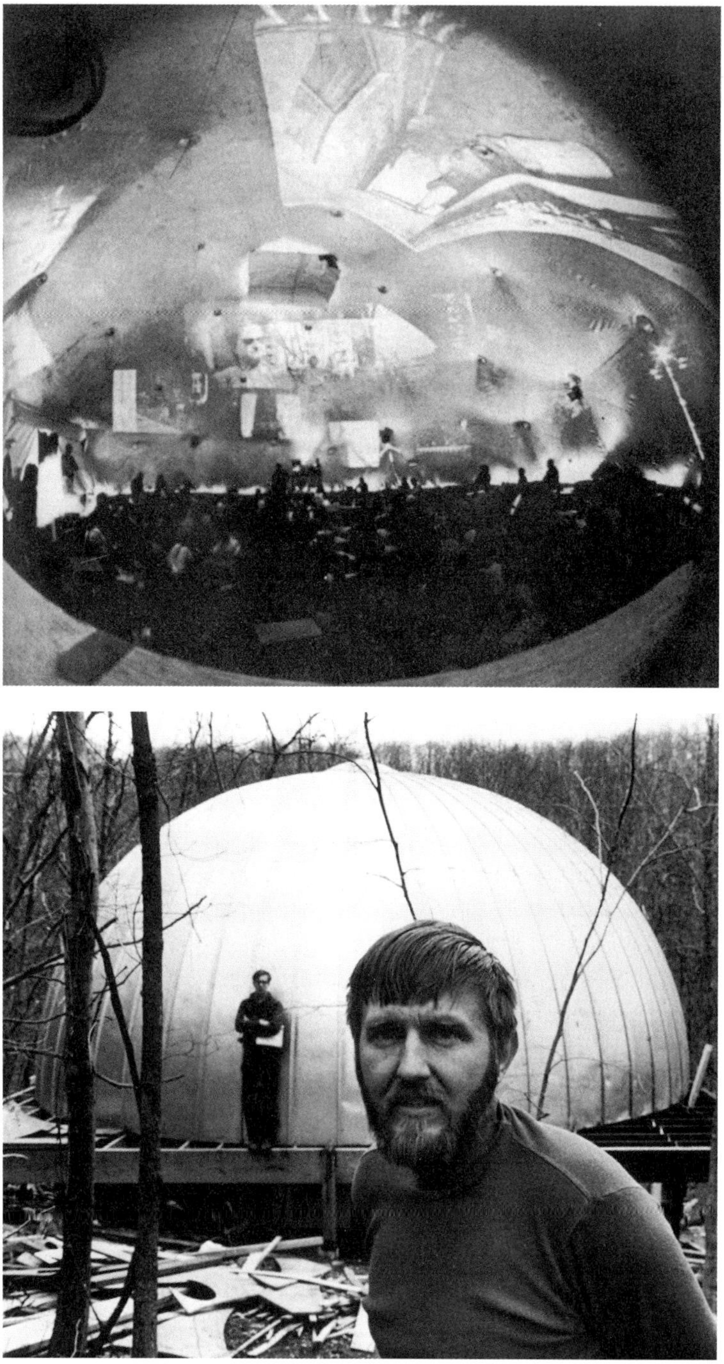

Stan VanDerBeek's *Movie-Drome* (interior), Stony Point, New York, 1963, and VanDerBeek in front of his *Movie-Drome*, 1966. Photo © 2008 Lenny Lipton. Courtesy Anthology Film Archives. All rights reserved

ENCLOSED BY IMAGES: THE EAMESES' MULTIMEDIA ARCHITECTURE

Beatriz Colomina

– I –

We are surrounded today, everywhere, all the time, by arrays of multiple, simultaneous images. In the streets, airports, shopping centres and gyms but also on our computers and television sets. The idea of a single image commanding our attention has faded away. It seems as if we need to be distracted in order to concentrate. As if we — all of us living in this new kind of space, the space of information — could be diagnosed *en masse* with attention deficit disorder. The state of distraction in the metropolis, described so eloquently by Walter Benjamin early in the twentieth century, seems to have been replaced by a new form of distraction, which is to say a new form of attention. Rather than wander cinematically through the city, we now look in one direction and see many juxtaposed moving images, more than we can possibly synthesise or reduce to a single impression. We sit in front of our computers on our ergonomically perfected chairs, staring with a fixed gaze at many simultaneously 'open' windows through which different kinds of information stream toward us. We hardly even notice it. It seems natural, as if we were simply breathing in the information.

How would one go about writing a history of this form of perception? Should one go back to the organisation of television studios, with their walls of monitors from which the director chooses the camera angle that will be presented to the viewer; or should one go to Cape Canaveral and look at its Mission Control Centre; or should one even go back to World War II, when so-called 'situation rooms' were envisioned with multiple projections bringing information from all over the world and presenting it side-by-side for instant analysis by leaders and military commanders?

But it is not simply the military, or war technology, that has defined this new form of perception. Designers, architects and artists were involved from the beginning, playing a crucial role in the evolution of multi-screen and multimedia techniques for presentation of information. While artists' use of these techniques tends to be associated with the 'happenings' and 'expanded cinema' of the 1960s, architects were involved much earlier and in very different contexts, not only military operations but also governmental propaganda campaigns.

Take the 1959 American National Exhibition in Moscow, where the US government enlisted some of the country's most sophisticated designers. Site of the famous Kitchen Debate between Richard Nixon and Nikita Khrushchev, the exhibition was a Cold War operation in which Charles and Ray Eameses' multi-screen technique turned out to be a powerful weapon.

To reconstruct a little bit of the atmosphere: the USA and USSR had agreed in 1958 to exchange national exhibits on 'science, technology and culture'. The Soviet exhibition opened in the New York Coliseum at Columbus Circle in New York City in June of 1959 and the American exhibition opened in Sokolniki Park in Moscow in July of the same year. Vice-President Nixon, in Moscow to open the exhibition, engaged in a heated debate with Khrushchev over the virtues of the American way of life. The exchange became known as the Kitchen Debate because it took place — in an event that appeared impromptu but was actually staged by the Americans — in the kitchen of a suburban house split in half to allow easy viewing. The Russians called the house the 'Splitnik', a pun on Sputnik, the satellite the Soviets had put into orbit two years before.

What is remarkable about this debate is the focus. As historian Elaine Tyler May has noted, instead of discussing 'missiles, bombs, or even modes of government ... [the two leaders] argued over the relative merits of American and Soviet washing machines, televisions and electric ranges'.[1] For Nixon, American superiority rested on the ideal of the suburban home, complete with modern appliances and distinct gender roles. He proclaimed that this 'model' suburban home represented nothing less than American freedom:

> To us, diversity, the right to choose, is the most important thing. [...] We don't have one decision made at the top by one government official. [...] We have many different manufacturers and many different kinds of washing machines so that the housewife has a choice.[2]

The American exhibition in Moscow captivated both the national and international media. Newspapers, illustrated magazines and television networks reported on the event. Symptomatically, *Life* magazine put the wives instead of the politicians on its cover. Pat Nixon appears as the prototype of the American woman depicted in advertisements of the 1950s: slim, well groomed, fashionable, happy. In contrast, the Soviet ladies appear stocky and dowdy, and while two of them, Mrs Khrushchev and Mrs Mikoyan, look proudly toward the camera, the third one, Mrs Kozlov, in what Roland Barthes may have seen as the *punctum* of this photograph, can't keep her eyes off Pat Nixon's dress.[3]

Envy — that is what the American exhibition seems to have been designed to produce (despite vigorous denials by Nixon in his debate with Khrushchev: 'We do not claim to astonish the Soviet people.')[4] But not envy of

1 Elaine Tyler May, *Homeward Bound: American Families in the Cold War Era*, New York: Basic Books, 1988, p.16. See also Karal Ann Marling, *As Seen on TV: The Visual Culture of Everyday Life in the 1950s*, Cambridge, Mass.: Harvard University Press, 1994.

2 Quoted in E.T. May, *Homeward Bound, op. cit.*, p.17. For transcripts of the debate, see 'The Two Worlds: A Day-Long Debate', *The New York Times*, 25 July 1959, pp.1–3; 'When Nixon Took on Khrushchev', a report of the meeting and the text of Nixon's address at the opening of the American National Exhibition in Moscow on 24 July 1959, printed in 'Setting Russia Straight On Facts about U.S.', *U.S. News and World Report*, 3 August 1959, pp.36–39 and 70–72; 'Encounter', *Newsweek*, 3 August 1959, pp.15–19; and 'Better to See Once', *Time*, 3 August 1959, pp.12–14.

3 *Life*, 10 August 1959.

4 Khrushchev: 'You Americans expect that the Soviet people will be amazed. It is not so. We have all these things in our new apartments.' Nixon:

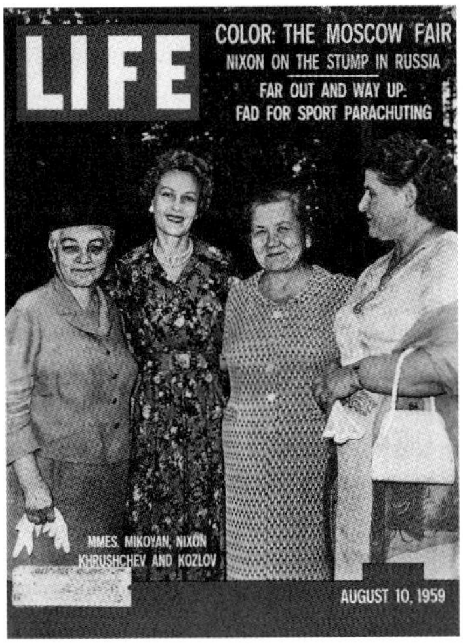

Cover of *Life*, August 1959

scientific, military or industrial achievements. Envy of washing machines, dishwashers, colour televisions, suburban houses, lawnmowers, supermarkets stocked full of groceries, Cadillac convertibles, make-up colours, lipstick, spike-heeled shoes, hi-fi sets, cake mixes, TV dinners, Pepsi-Cola and so on. 'What is this,' the newspaper *Izvestia* asked itself in its news report, 'a national exhibit of a great country or a branch department store? Where is American science, American industry and particularly their factory techniques?'[5] And a Russian teacher is quoted by the *Wall Street Journal*: 'You have lots of dolls, furniture, dishes, but where are your technical exhibits?'[6] Even American newspapers described the main pavilion of the exhibition as a 'lush bargain basement', but one that, due to the dust of a crumbling concrete floor, 48 hours after the opening, already looked as if it 'had barely survived a fire sale'.[7]

It was for this context that the Eameses produced their film, *Glimpses of the USA*, projecting it onto seven 20-by-30-foot screens suspended within a vast (250 feet in diameter) golden geodesic dome designed by Buckminster Fuller. More than 2,200 still and moving images (some from Billy Wilder's *Some Like It Hot*, 1959) presented 'a typical work day' in the life of the United States in 9 minutes and 'a typical weekend day' in 3 minutes.[8] Thousands and thousands of images were pulled from many different sources, including photo archives (such as Magnum Photos; Photo Researchers; and the magazines *Fortune*, *Holiday*, *Life*, *Look*, the *Saturday Evening Post*, *Sports Illustrated*, *Sunset* and *Time*), individual photographers (such as Ferenc Berko, Julius Shulman, Ezra Stoller, Ernst Braun, George Zimbel and Charles Eames) and friends and associates of the Eameses (including Eliot Noyes, George Nelson, Alexander Girard, Eero Saarinen, Billy Wilder, Don Albinson and Robert Staples).[9] The images were combined into seven separate film reels and projected simultaneously through seven interlocked projectors. Fuller later said that nobody had done anything like this before and that advertisers and film-makers would soon follow the Eameses.[10]

The Eameses did not simply install their film in Fuller's space. They were involved in the organisation of the whole exhibition from the beginning. George Nelson, who had been commissioned by the United States Information Agency (USIA) to design the exhibition, and Jack Masey from the USIA brought them into the team. According to Nelson, it was in an evening meeting in the Eames House in Los Angeles, culminating three days of discussions, where

'We do not claim to astonish the Soviet people.' *U.S. News & World Report*, 3 August 1959, pp.36–37.

5 Quoted in Alan L. Otten, 'Russians Eagerly Tour U.S. Exhibit Despite Cool Official Attitude', *The Wall Street Journal*, 28 July 1959, p.16, col.4.

6 *Ibid.*

7 Max Frankel, 'Dust From Floor Plagues U.S. Fair', *The New York Times*, 28 July 1959, p.12, col.3.

8 John Neuhart, Marilyn Neuhart and Ray Eames, *Eames Design: The Work of the Office of Charles and Ray Eames*, New York: Harry N. Abrams, 1989, pp.238–41. See also Hélène Lipstadt, 'Natural Overlap: Charles and Ray Eames and the Federal Government', *The Work of Charles and Ray Eames: A Legacy of Invention* (ed. Donald Albrecht), New York: Abrams, 1997, pp.160–66.

9 Eames Archives, Library of Congress, Washington DC, box 202.

10 Letter from Buckminster Fuller to Ms Camp, 7 November 1973, Eames Archives, Library of Congress, Washington DC, box 30.

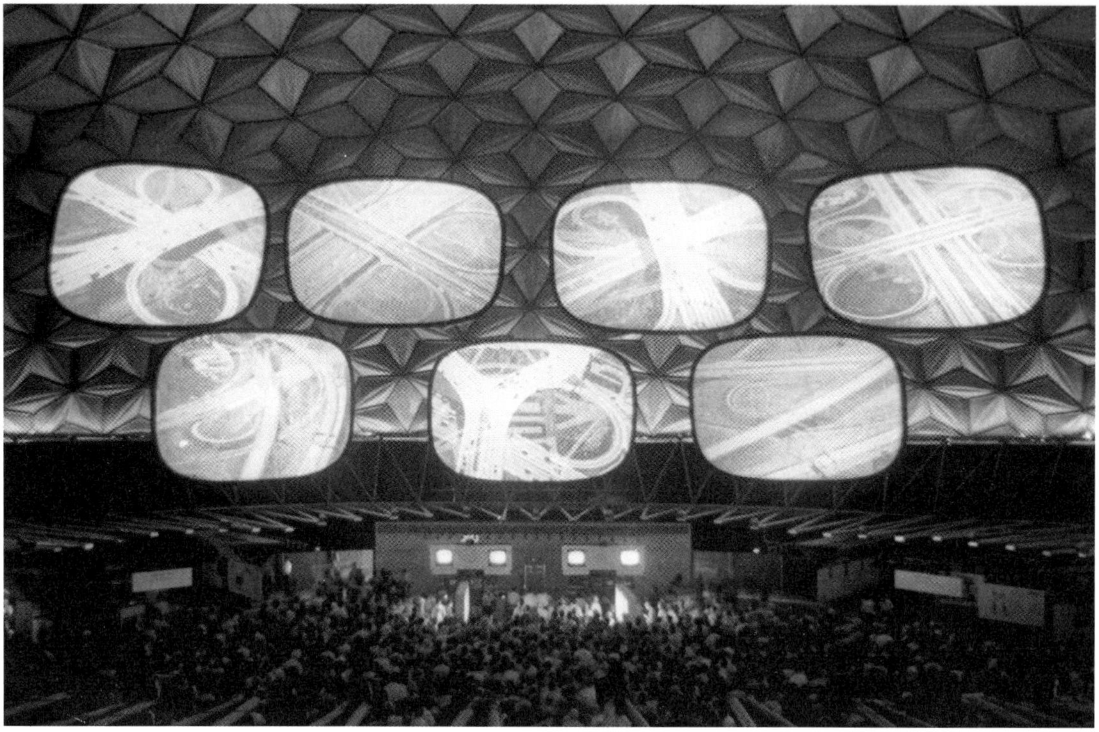

'all the basic decisions for the fair were made. Present were Nelson, Ray and Charles (the latter occasionally swooping past on a swing hung from the ceiling), the movie director Billy Wilder and Masey.'[11] According to Nelson, by the end of the evening a basic scheme had emerged:

> [1] A dome (by Bucky Fuller).
> [2] A glass pavilion (by Welton Beckett) 'as a kind of bazaar stuffed full of things, [the] idea being that consumer products represented one of the areas in which we were most effective, as well as one in which the Russians ... were more interested'.
> [3] An introductory film by the Eameses, since the team felt that the '80,000 square feet of exhibition space was not enough to communicate more than a small fraction of what we wanted to say'.[12]

In addition, the USIA had already contracted for the inclusion of Disney's Circarama, a 360-degree motion picture which offered a 20-minute tour of American cities and tourist attractions and which played to about a thousand Russians an hour;[13] an architecture exhibit curated by Peter Blake; a fashion show curated by Eleanor Lambert; a packaging exhibition by the New York Museum of Modern Art's Associate Curator of Design, Mildred Constantine; and Edward Steichen's famous photographic exhibit 'The Family of Man'.[14] The exhibition also included a full-scale, ranch-style suburban house, put up by a Long Island builder and furnished by Macy's. It was in the kitchen of this fourteen-thousand-dollar, six-room house filled with appliances that the Kitchen Debate began, with an argument over automatic washers.

Charles and Ray Eames, *Glimpses of the USA*, Moscow World's Fair auditorium, 1959 © 2008 Eames Office LLC

The multi-screen performance turned out to be one of the most popular exhibits at the fair (second only to the cars and colour televisions).[15] *Time* magazine called it the 'smash hit of the fair',[16] *The Wall Street Journal* described it as the 'real bomb shell', and US officials believed this was 'the real pile-driver of the fair'.[17] Groups of five-thousand people were brought into the dome every 45 minutes, sixteen times a day, for the duration of the fair.[18] Close to three-million people saw the show, and the floor had to be resurfaced three or four times during the six-week exhibition.[19]

The Eameses were not just popular entertainers in an official exhibition. *Glimpses of the USA* was not just a series of images inside a dome. The huge array of suspended screens defined a space, a space within a space. The Eameses were self-consciously architects of a new kind of space. The film breaks with the fixed perspectival view of the world. In fact, we find ourselves in a space that can be apprehended only with the high technology of telescopes, zoom lenses, aeroplanes, night-vision cameras and so on, and where there is no privileged point of view. It is not simply that many of the individual images that make up *Glimpses* have been taken with these instruments. More importantly, the relationship between the images re-enacts the operation of the technologies.

The film starts with images from outer space on all the screens: stars across the sky, seven constellations, seven star clusters, nebulae, etc., then moves through aerial views of the city at night, from higher up to closer in, until city lights from the air fill the screens. The early morning comes with aerial views of landscapes from different parts of the country: deserts, mountains, hills, seas, farms, suburban developments, urban neighborhoods. When the camera eyes finally descend to the ground, we see close-ups of newspapers and milk bottles at doors. But still no people, only traces of their existence on earth.

Not by chance, the first signs of human life are centred upon the house and domestic space. From the stars at night and the aerial views, the cameras zoom to the most intimate scenes: 'people having breakfast at home, men leaving for work, kissing their wives, kissing the baby, being given lunchboxes, getting into cars, waving good-bye, children leaving for school, being given

11 Stanley Abercrombie, *George Nelson: The Design of Modern Design*, Cambridge, Mass.: The MIT Press, 1995, p.163.

12 *Ibid.*, p.164.

13 Max Frankel, 'Image of America at Issue in Soviet', *The New York Times*, 23 August 1959. 'Circarama' had already been shown in the 1958 World's Fair in Brussels.

14 S. Abercrombie, *George Nelson*, *op. cit.*, p.167.

15 'The seven-screen quickie is intended as a general introduction to the fair. According to the votes of Russians, however, it is the most popular exhibit after the automobiles and the color television.' M. Frankel, 'Image of America at Issue in Soviet', *op. cit.*

16 'Watching the thousands of colorful glimpses of the U.S. and its people, the Russians were entranced, and the slides are the smash hit of the fair.' 'The U.S. in Moscow: Russia Comes to the Fair', *Time*, 3 August 1959, p.14.

17 'And Mr. Khrushchev watched unsmilingly as the real bombshell exploded — a huge exhibit of typical American scenes flashed on seven huge ceiling screens. Each screen shows a different scene but all seven at each moment are on the same general subject — housing, transportation, jazz and so forth. US officials believe this is the real pile-driver of the fair, and the premier's phlegmatic attitude — not even smiling when seven huge Marilyn Monroes dashed on the screen or when Mr. Nixon pointed out golfing scenes — showed his unhappiness with the display.' A.L. Otten, 'Russians Eagerly Tour U.S. Exhibit Despite Cool Official Attitude', *op. cit.*

18 M. Frankel, 'Dust From Floor Plagues U.S. Fair', *op. cit.*, p.12, col.3.

19 From interview with Billy Wilder by Pat Kirkham in 1993. Pat Kirkham, *Charles and Ray Eames: Designers of the Twentieth Century*, Cambridge, Mass.: The MIT Press, 1995, p.324.

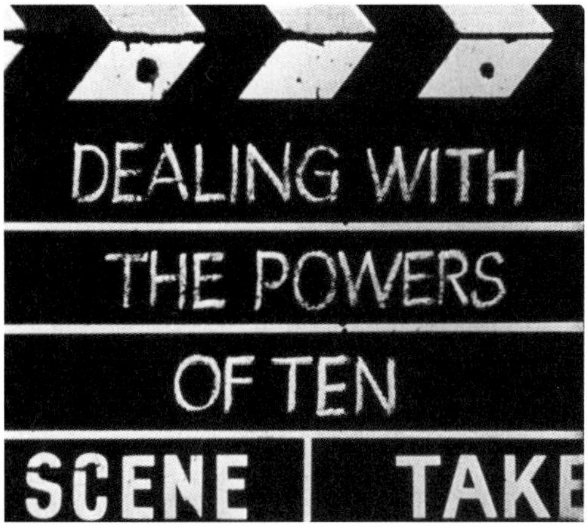

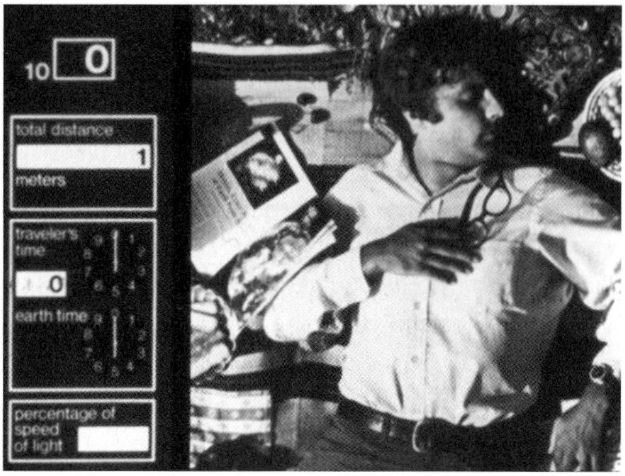

lunchboxes, saying good-bye to dog, piling into station wagons and cars, getting into school buses, baby crying'.[20]

As with the Eameses' later and much better-known film *Powers of Ten* (1968),[21] which, incidentally, reused images of the night sky from *Glimpses of the USA*,[22] the film moves from outer space to the close-up details of everyday life. As the working script of the film indicates, the close-ups are: 'last sips of coffee' of men before leaving for work, 'children washing hands before dinner', 'housewives on the phone with clerks (supermarket food shelves in b.g.)' and so on.[23] In *Powers of Ten*, the movement will be set in reverse, from the domestic setting of a picnic spread with a man sleeping beside a woman in a park in Chicago, out into the atmosphere, and then back down inside the body through the skin of the man's wrist to microscopic cells and to the atomic level. Even if *Powers of Ten*, initially produced for the Commission on College Physics, was a scientific, more advanced film, in which space is measured in seconds, the logic of both films (*Glimpses* and *Powers of Ten*) is the same. Intimate domesticity is suspended within an entirely new spatial system — a system that was the product of esoteric scientific-military research but that had entered the everyday public imagination with the launching of Sputnik in 1957. Fantasies that had long circulated in science fiction had become reality. This shift from research and fantasy to tangible fact made new forms of communicating to a mass audience possible.[24] The Eameses' innovative technique did not simply present the audience with a new way of seeing things. Rather, it gave form to a new mode of perception that was already in everybody's mind.

Glimpses breaks with the linear narrative of film to bring snippets of information, an ever-changing mosaic image of American life. And yet the message of the film is linear and eerily consistent with the official message represented by the Kitchen Debate. From the stars in the sky at the beginning of the film — which the narrative insists are the same in the Soviet Union as they are in the USA — to the people kissing their goodnights and the forget-me-not flowers in the last image, the film emphasised universal emotions, while at the same time it unambiguously reinforced the material abundance of one country.[25] From the parking lots of factories, which the narrative describes

Charles and Ray Eames, stills from *Powers of Ten*, 1968. 16mm colour film, sound, 9mins © 2008 Eames Office LLC

as filled with the cars of workers, to the aerial views of suburban houses with a blue swimming pool in each yard, to the close-ups of shopping carts and shelves full of goodies in supermarkets and housewives cooking dinner in kitchens equipped with every imaginable appliance, the message of the film was clear: we are the same, but, on the material level, we have more.

Glimpses, like the 'Splitnik' house where the Kitchen Debate took place, displaced the USA-USSR debate from the arms and space race to the battle of the appliances. And yet the overall effect of the film is that of an extraordinarily powerful viewing technology, a hyper-viewing mechanism, which is hard to imagine outside the very space programme the exhibition was trying to downplay. In fact, this extreme mode of viewing goes beyond the old fantasy of the eye in the sky. If *Glimpses* simulates the operation of satellite surveillance, it exposes more than the details of life in the streets. It penetrates the most intimate spaces and reveals every secret. Domestic life itself becomes the target, the source of pride or insecurity. The Americans, made insecure by the thought of a Russian eye looking down on them, countered by exposing more than that eye could ever see (or at least pretending to, since 'a day in the life of the USA' became an image of the 'Good Life' without ghettos, poverty, domestic violence or depression).

Glimpses simply intensified an existing mode of perception. In fact, it synthesised several already existing modes that were manifest in television, space programmes and military operations. As is typical of all the Eameses' work, it was the simplicity and clarity of this synthesis that made it immediately accessible to all.[26]

– II –

What kind of genealogy can one make of the Eameses' development of this astonishingly successful technique?

It was not the first time they had deployed multiple screens. In fact, the Eameses were involved in one of the first multimedia presentations on record, if not the first. Again, it was George Nelson who set up the commission.

20 Taken from the working script of *Glimpses*, Eames Archives, Library of Congress, Washington DC, box 202.

21 *Powers of Ten* was based on the 1957 book by Kees Boeke, *Cosmic View: The Universe in Forty Jumps*. The film was produced for the Commission on College Physics. An updated and more developed version was produced in 1977. In the second version the starting point is still a picnic scene, but it takes place in a park bordering Lake Michigan in Chicago. See J. Neuhart, M. Neuhart and R. Eames, *Eames Design*, *op. cit.*, pp.336–37 and 440–41.

22 See handwritten notes on the manuscript of the first version of *Powers of Ten*, Eames Archives, Library of Congress, Washington DC, box 207. The film is still referred to as *Cosmic View*.

23 Working script of *Glimpses*, Eames Archives, Library of Congress, Washington DC, box 202.

24 In 1970, in the context of Charles Eames's third Charles Eliot Norton Lecture at Harvard University, where he once again insisted on the need to incorporate media into the classroom, he still spoke of changing forms of communications with reference to Sputnik: 'In post-Sputnik panic, a great demand for taping science lectures; when they were shown on television, distribution cost ended up as 100:1 of production cost; no way to run a railroad.' Eames Archives, Library of Congress, Washington DC, box 217, folder 10.

25 Apparently even the forget-me-not flowers were understood in precisely the intended way, as symbols of friendship and loyalty. According to the Eameses, the audience could be heard saying '*nezabutki*', 'forget-me-not', as the flowers appeared on the screen as the last image of the film. J. Neuhart, M. Neuhart and R. Eames, *Eames Design*, *op. cit.*, p.241.

26 For example, *Powers of Ten* was a 'sketch film' to be presented at an 'assembly of one thousand of America's top physicists', but the Eameses decided that it should 'appeal to a ten year-old as well as a physicist'. Paul Schrader, 'Poetry of Ideas: The Films of Charles Eames', *Film Quarterly* 23, no.3, Spring 1970, p.10.

In 1952 he had been asked to make a study for the Department of Fine Arts at the University of Georgia in Athens, and he brought along Ray and Charles Eames and Alexander Girard. Instead of writing a report, they decided to collaborate on a 'show for a typical class' of 55 minutes. Nelson referred to it as *Art X*, while the Eames called it *A Rough Sketch for a Sample Lesson for a Hypothetical Course*. The subject of the lesson was 'Communications',[27] and the stated goals included 'the breaking down of barriers between fields of learning ... making people a little more intuitive ... [and] increasing communication between people and things'.[28] The performance included a live narrator, multiple images (still and moving pictures) and even smells and sounds (music and narration). Charles Eames later said: 'We used a lot of sound, sometimes carried to a very high volume so you would actually feel the vibrations.'[29] The idea was to produce an intense sensory environment so as to 'heighten awareness'. The effect was so convincing that apparently some people even smelled things when no smells were introduced, only a suggestion in an image or a sound (for example, the smell of oil in the machinery).[30]

It was a major production. Nelson described the team arriving in Athens 'burdened with only slightly less equipment than Ringling Brothers. This included a movie projector, three slide projectors, three screens, three or four tape recorders, cans of films, boxes of slides and reels of magnetic tape. Girard brought a collection of bottled synthetic odours that were to be fed into the auditorium during the show through air-conditioning ducts.'[31] The reference to the circus was not accidental. Talking to a reporter for *Vogue* magazine, Charles later argued: '*Sample Lesson* was a blast on all senses, a super-saturated three-ring circus. Simultaneously the students were assaulted by three sets of slides, two tape recorders, a motion picture with sound and peripheral panels for further distraction.'[32]

The circus was one of the Eameses' lifetime fascinations — so much so that in the 1940s, when they were out of work and money, they were about to audition for parts at the circus.[33] They would have been clowns, but ultimately a contract to make plywood furniture allowed them to continue as designers. And from the mid 1940s on they took hundreds and hundreds of photographs of the circus, which they used in many contexts, including *Circus* (a 180-slide, three-screen slide show accompanied by a soundtrack featuring circus music and other sounds recorded at the circus), presented as part of the Charles Eliot Norton Lectures at Harvard University that Charles delivered in 1970, and the film *Clown Face* (1971), a training film about 'the precise and classical art of applying makeup' made for Bill Ballentine, director of the Clown College of Ringling Brothers Barnum & Bailey Circus. The Eameses had been friends with

27 'Grist for Atlanta paper version', manuscript in the Eames Archives, Library of Congress, Washington DC, box 217, folder 15.
28 J. Neuhart, M. Neuhart and R. Eames, *Eames Design*, *op. cit.*, p.177.
29 Owen Gingerich, 'A Conversation with Charles Eames', *The American Scholar* 46, no.3, Summer 1977, p.331.
30 *Ibid.*
31 S. Abercrombie, *George Nelson*, *op. cit.*, p.145, quoting George Nelson's manuscript 'The Georgia Experiment: An Industrial Approach to Problems of Education' from October 1954.
32 Allene Talmey, 'Eames', *Vogue*, 15 August 1959, p.144.
33 Beatriz Colomina, 'Reflections on the Eames House', *The Work of Charles and Ray Eames: A Legacy of Invention* (ed. Donald Albrecht),

the Ballentines since the late 1940s when the Eameses had photographed the circus's behind-the-scenes activities during an engagement in Los Angeles.[34] Charles was on the board of the Ringling Brothers College and often referred to the circus as an example of what design and art should be — not self-expression but precise discipline:

> Everything in the circus is pushing the possible beyond the limit — bears do not really ride on bicycles, people do not really execute three and a half turn somersaults in the air from a board to a ball, and until recently no one dressed the way fliers do. [...] Yet within this apparent freewheeling license, we find a discipline which is almost unbelievable. [...] The circus may look like the epitome of pleasure, but the person flying on a high wire, or executing a balancing act, or being shot from a cannon must take his pleasure very, very seriously. In the same vein, the scientist, in his laboratory, is pushing the possible beyond the limit and he too must take his pleasure very seriously.[35]

The circus, as an event that offered a multiplicity of simultaneous experiences that cannot be taken in entirely by the viewer, was the Eameses' model for their design of multimedia exhibitions and the fast-cutting technique of their films and slide shows, where the objective was always to communicate the maximum amount of information in a way that was both pleasurable and effective.[36]

But the technological model for multi-screen, multimedia presentations may have been provided by the White House Situation Room, which was designed in those same years to bring information in simultaneously from numerous sources around the world so that the president and military commanders could make decisions. It is not without irony, in that sense, that the Eameses read the organisation of the circus as a form of crisis control. In a circus, Charles said, 'there is a strict hierarchy of events, and an elimination of choice under stress, so that one event can automatically follow another. [...] There is a recognized mission for everyone involved. In a crisis there can be no question as to what needs to be done.'[37] A number of the Eameses' friends were involved in the secret military project of the War Rooms, including Buckminster Fuller, Eero Saarinen and Henry Dreyfuss, whose unrealised design involved a wall of parallel projected images of different kinds of information.[38] It is not clear that the Eameses knew anything about the project during the War years, but it is very likely, given their friendship with Fuller, Saarinen and Dreyfuss, that they would have found out after the War. In 1970, in the context of his second Norton Lecture at Harvard University, Charles referred to the War Rooms as a model for city management:

New York: Abrams, 1997, p.128.

34 J. Neuhart, M. Neuhart and R. Eames, *Eames Design*, *op. cit.*, p.373; Bill Ballentine, *Clown Alley*, Boston: Little, Brown and Company, 1982.

35 Charles Eames, 'Language of Vision: The Nuts and Bolts', *Bulletin of the American Academy of Arts and Sciences* 28, no.1, October 1974, pp.17–18.

36 J. Neuhart, M. Neuhart and R. Eames, *Eames Design*, *op. cit.*, p.91.

37 Charles Eames, 'Language of Vision: The Nuts and Bolts', *op. cit.* See also typescript of the actual lecture in Eames Archives, Library of Congress, Washington DC, box 217, folder 12.

38 Barry Katz, 'The Arts of War: "Visual Presentation" and National Intelligence', *Design Issues* 12, no.2, Summer 1996, pp.3–21. I am grateful to Dennis Doordan for pointing out this article to me.

In the management of a city, linear discourse certainly can't cope. We imagine a City Room or a World Health Room (rather like a War Room) where all the information from satellite monitors and other sources could be monitored; [Fuller's World Game is an example.] ... The city problem involves conflicting interest and points of view. So the place where information is correlated also has to be a place where each group can try out plans for its own changing needs.[39]

The overall theme of the Norton Lectures was announced as 'Problems Relating to Visual Communication and the Visual Environment', and a consistent theme was the 'necessity to devise visual models for matters of practical concern where linear description isn't enough'. György Kepes's *Language of Vision* (1944) was a constant reference point for the Eameses.[40] The 'language of vision' was seen as a 'real threat to the discontinuity' (between the arts, between university departments, between art and everyday life, etc.) that the Eameses were always fighting.[41] Architecture ('a most non-discontinuous art') was seen as both the ultimate model for discontinuity and where the new technologies should be implemented.

A number of wartime research projects, including work on communications, ballistics and experimental computers, had quickly developed after the War into a full-fledged theory of information flow, most famously with the publication of Claude Shannon's *Mathematical Theory of Communication* in 1949, which formalised the idea of an information channel from sender to recipient whose efficiency could be measured in terms of speed and noise.

This sense of information flow organised the *Sample Lesson* performance. The Eameses said 'we were trying to cram into a short time, a class hour, the most background material possible'.[42] As part of the project, the Eameses produced *A Communication Primer*, a film that presents the theory of information, explaining Shannon's famous diagram of the passage of information. The film was subsequently developed in an effort to present current ideas in communication theory to architects and planners and to encourage them to use these ideas in their work. The basic idea was to integrate architecture and information flow.

If the great heroes of the Renaissance were, for the Eameses, 'people concerned with ways of modeling/imaging ... not with self-expression or bravura. ... Brunelleschi, but not Michelangelo',[43] the great architects of our time would be the ones concerned with the new forms of communication, particularly computers:

39 Partial transcript of Norton Lectures, Eames Archives, Library of Congress, Washington DC, box 217, folder 10. Square brackets appear in original.

40 See György Kepes, *Language of Vision*. Chicago: Paul Theobald, 1944.

41 See, for example, Charles Eames's manuscript 'On Reducing Discontinuity', for a talk to the American Academy of Arts and Sciences in 1976: 'My wife and I had made a commitment to disregard the sacred enclosure around a special set of phenomena called art; in our view preoccupation with respecting that boundary leads to an unfortunate and unwarranted limitation on the aesthetic experience.' Eames Archives, Library of Congress, Washington DC, box 217, folder 17.

42 O. Gingerich, 'A Conversation with Charles Eames', *op. cit.*, p.332.

43 Charles Eames is referring here to 'Professor Lawrence Hill's Renaissance'. Notes for second Norton Lecture, Eames Archives, Library of Congress, Washington DC, box 217, folder 10.

> It appeared to us that the real current problems for architects now — the problems that a Brunelleschi, say, would gravitate to — are problems of organization of information. For city planning, for regional planning, the first need is clear, accessible models of current states-of-affairs, drawn from a data base that only a computer can handle for you.[44]

The logic of information flow was further developed in the Eameses' 1955 film *House: After Five Years of Living*. The film was made entirely from thousands of colour slides the Eameses had been taking of their home over the first five years of its life.[45] The images are shown in quick succession (a technique called 'fast cutting', for which the Eameses won an Emmy Award in 1960) and accompanied by music by Elmer Bernstein.[46] As Michael Braune wrote in 1966:

> The interesting point about this method of film making is not only that it is relatively simple to produce and that rather more information can be conveyed than when there is movement on the screen, but that it corresponds surprisingly closely with the way in which the brain normally records the images it receives. I would assume that it also corresponds rather closely with the way Eames's own thought processes tend to work. I think it symptomatic, for instance, that he is extremely interested in computers ... and that one of the essential characteristics of computers is their need to separate information into components before being able to assemble them into a large number of different wholes.[47]

This technique was developed even further in *Glimpses*, which is organised around a strict logic of information transmission. The role of the designer is to orchestrate a particular flow of information. The central principle is one of compression. At the end of the design meeting in the Eames House, in preparation for the American exhibition in Moscow, the idea of the film emerged precisely 'as a way of compressing into a small volume the tremendous quantity of information' they wanted to present, which would have been impossible to do in the eighty-thousand square feet of the exhibition.[48] The space of the multi-screen film, like the space of the computer, compresses physical space. Each screen shows a different scene, but all seven at each moment are on the same general subject — housing, transportation, jazz and so forth. As *The New York Times* described it: 'Perhaps fifty clover-leaf highway intersections are shown in just a few seconds. So are dozens of housing projects, bridges, skyscrapers scenes, supermarkets, universities, museums, theatres, churches, farms, laboratories and much more.'[49]

44 '"Communications Primer" was a recommendation to architects to recognize the need for more complex information ... for new kinds of *models* of information.' Charles Eames, 'Grist for Atlanta paper version' (manuscript), Eames Archives, Library of Congress, Washington DC, box 217, folder 15.

45 B. Colomina, 'Reflections on the Eames House', *op. cit.*, p. 126–49.

46 Charles and Ray Eames won an Emmy Award for Graphics for their rapid cutting experiments in *The Fabulous Fifties*, a television programme broadcast on the CBS network on 22 January 1960. It included six film segments made by the Eames Office. P. Schrader, 'Poetry of Ideas: The Films of Charles Eames', *op. cit.*, p.3.

47 Michael Braune, 'The Wit of Technology', *Architectural Design* 36, September 1966, p.452.

48 See S. Abercrombie, *George Nelson*, *op. cit.*, pp.163–64.

49 M. Frankel, 'Image of America at Issue in Soviet', *op. cit.*

According to the Eameses, repetition was done for credibility. They said: 'If, for example, we were to show a freeway interchange, somebody would look at it and say, "We have one at Smolensk and one at Minsk; we have two, they have one" — that kind of thing. So we conceived the idea of having the imagery come on in multiple forms, as in the *Rough Sketch for a Sample Lesson*.'[50] But the issue was much more than one of efficiency of communication or the polemical need to have multiple examples. The idea was, as with the *Sample Lesson*, to produce sensory overload. As the Eameses had suggested to *Vogue*, *Sample Lesson* tried to provide many forms of 'distraction' instead of asking students to concentrate on a singular message.[51] The audience drifts through a multimedia space that exceeds their capacity to absorb it. The Eames-Nelson team thought that the most important thing to communicate to undergraduates was a sense of the relationships between things, what the Eameses would later call 'connections' among seemingly unrelated phenomena. Nelson and the Eameses argued that this awareness of relationships between seemingly unrelated phenomena is achieved by 'high-speed techniques'. They produced an excessive input from different directions that has to be synthesised by the audience. Likewise, Charles said of *Glimpses*:

> We wanted to have a credible number of images, but not so many that they couldn't be scanned in the time allotted. At the same time, the number of images had to be large enough so that people wouldn't be exactly sure how many they have seen. We arrived at the number seven. With four images, you always knew there were four, but by the time you got up to eight images you weren't quite sure. They were very big images — the width across four of them was half the length of a football field.[52]

One journalist described it as 'information overload — an avalanche of related data that comes at a viewer too fast for him to cull and reject it ... a 12-minute blitz'. The viewer is overwhelmed. More than anything, the Eameses wanted an emotional response, produced as much by the excess of images as by their content. They said:

> At the Moscow World's Fair in 1959 — when we used seven screens over an area that was over half the length of a football field — that was just a desperate attempt to make a credible statement to a group of people in Moscow when words had almost ceased to have meaning. We were telling

50 O. Gingerich, 'A Conversation with Charles Eames', *op. cit.*, pp.332–33.
51 Allene Talmey, 'Eames', *Vogue*, 15 August 1959, p.144.
52 O. Gingerich, 'A Conversation with Charles Eames', *op. cit.*, p.333.
53 Digby Diehl, 'West Q&A: Charles Eames', manuscript in the Eames Archives, Library of Congress, Washington DC, box 24, folders 4–5. Published as 'Charles Eames: Q&A', *Los Angeles Times West Magazine*, 8 October 1972. Reprinted in Digby Diehl, *Supertalk*, New York: Doubleday, 1974.
54 Mina Hamilton, 'Films at the Fair II', *Industrial Design*, May 1964, pp.37–41.
55 Arthur A. Cohen, *Herbert Bayer: The Complete Work*, Cambridge, Mass.: The MIT Press, 1994, p.292. Mary Anne Staniszewski, *The Power of Display: A History of Exhibition Installations at the Museum of Modern Art*, Cambridge, Mass.: The MIT Press, 1998, pp.25–28.
56 Script of the IBM film *View from the People Wall* for the Ovoid Theater at the New York World's Fair in 1964, Eames Archives, Library of Congress, Washington DC.

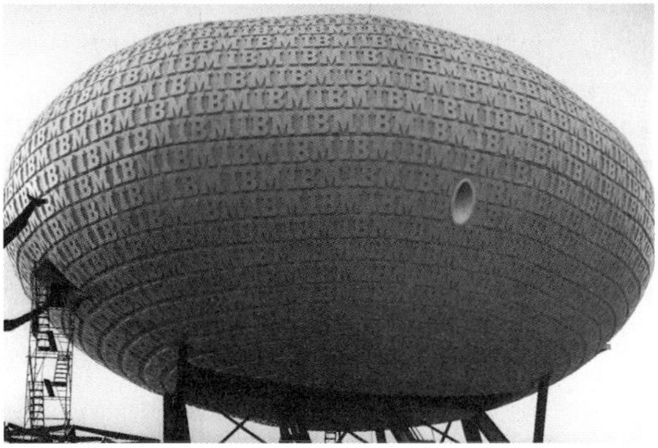

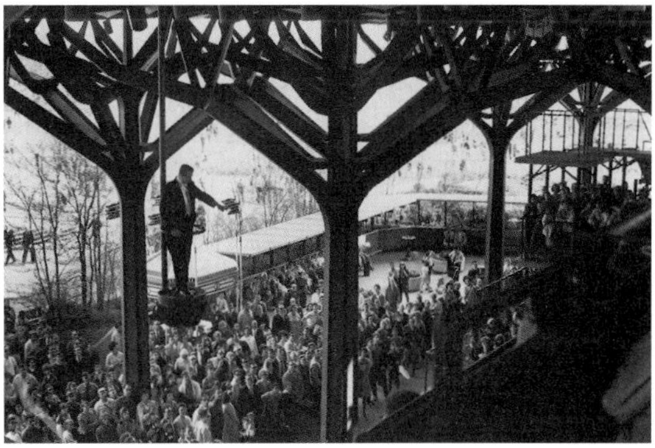

the story straight, and we wanted to do it in 12 minutes, with images; but we found that we couldn't really give credibility to it in a linear way. However when we could put 50 images on the screen for a certain subject in a matter of 10 seconds, we got a kind of breadth which we felt we couldn't get any other way.[53]

The multi-screen technique went through one more significant development at the 1964 World's Fair in New York. In the IBM Ovoid Theater designed by the Saarinen office, visitors could board the 'people wall' to be greeted by a 'host' dressed in coat-tails, who slowly dropped down from the IBM ovoid; the seated, five-hundred-person audience was then lifted up hydraulically from the ground level into the dark interior of the egg where they were surrounded by fourteen screens on which the Eameses projected the film *Think*.[54] To enter the theatre is no longer to cross the threshold, to pass through the ceremonial space of the entrance, as in a traditional public building. To *enter* here is to be lifted in front of a multiplicity of screens. The screens wrap the audience in a way that is reminiscent of Herbert Bayer's 1930 'diagram of the field of vision', produced as a sketch for the installation of an architecture and furniture exhibition.[55] The eye cannot escape the screens and each screen is bordered by other screens. Unlike the screens in Moscow, those in the IBM building are of different sizes and shapes. But once again the eye has to jump around from image to image and can never fully catch up with all of them and their diverse contents. Fragments are presented to be momentarily linked together. The film is organised by the same logic of compression. Each momentary connection is replaced with another. The speed of the film is meant to be the speed of the mind. The 'host' welcomes the audience to 'the IBM Information Machine':

> ... a machine designed to help me give you a lot of information in a very short time. [...] The machine brings you information in much the same way as your mind gets it — in fragments and glimpses — sometimes relating to the same idea or incident. Like making toast in the morning.[56]

Eero Saarinen & Associates, IBM Pavilion for the New York World's Fair, 1964–65

Already in 1959, the design team (Nelson, the Eameses, etc.) had used exactly the same term — 'information machine' — to describe the role of Fuller's dome in Moscow, taking it from the title of a 1957 film the Eameses had prepared for the 1958 Brussels World's Fair. In addition to the multi-screens, the dome housed a huge RAMAC 305 computer, an 'electronic brain' which offered written replies to 3,500 questions about life in the United States.[57] The architecture was conceived from the very start as a combination of structure, multi-screen film and computer. Each technology creates an architecture in which inside and outside, entering and leaving, meant entirely different things, and yet they coexisted. All were housed by the same physical structure — Fuller's dome — but each defined a different kind of space to be explored in different ways. From the *Sample Lesson* in 1953 to IBM in 1964, the Eameses treated architecture as a multichannel information machine. And, equally, multimedia installations as a kind of architecture.

– III –

All of the Eameses' designs can be understood as multi-screen performances: they provide a framework in which objects can be placed and replaced. Even the parts of their furniture can be rearranged. Spaces are defined as arrays of information collected and constantly changed by the users.

This is the space of the media. The space of a newspaper or an illustrated magazine is a grid in which information is arranged and rearranged as it comes in: a space the reader navigates in his or her own way, at a glance, or by fully entering a particular story. The reader, viewer, consumer, constructs the space, participating actively in the design. It is a space where continuities are made through 'cutting'. The same is true of the space of newsreels and television. The logic of the Eameses' multi-screens is simply the logic of the mass media.

It is not by chance that Charles Eames was always nostalgic for the time of his set-design job for MGM in the early 1940s, continuously arranging and rearranging existing props at short notice.[58] All Eames architecture can be understood as set design. The Eameses even present themselves like Hollywood figures, as if in a movie or an advertisement, always so happy, with the ever-changing array of objects as their backdrop.

This logic of architecture as a set for staging the good life was central to the design of the Moscow exhibition. Even the famous kitchen, for example, was cut in half not only to allow viewing by visitors but, most importantly, to turn it into a photo op for the Kitchen Debate. Photographers and journalists knew already the night before that they had to be there, choosing their angle. Architecture was reorganised to produce a certain image. Charles had already spoken, in 1950, of our time as the era of communication. He was acutely aware that the new media were displacing the old role of architecture. And

57 'U.S. Gives Soviet Glittering Show', *The New York Times*, 25 July 1959.
58 B. Colomina, 'Reflections on the Eames House', *op. cit.*, p.129.
59 O. Gingerich, 'A Conversation with Charles Eames', *op. cit.*, p.327.
60 '*Powers of Ten* — Gregotti' (handwritten notes), Eames Archives, Library of Congress, Washington DC, box 217, folder 11.
61 Charles Eames, speaking in a film about a storage system the Eameses had designed. Quoted in Ralph Caplan, 'Making Connections: The Work of Charles and Ray Eames', *Connections: The Work of Charles and Ray Eames* (exh. cat.), Los Angeles: Frederick S. Wight Art Gallery, University of California, 1976, p.15.
62 *Ibid.*, p.43.
63 *Ibid.*, p.45.

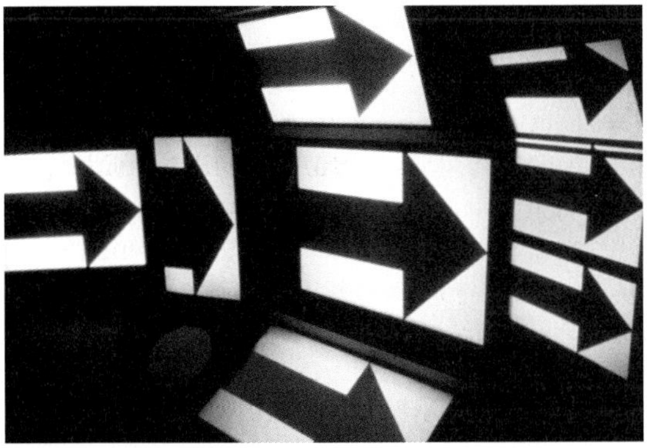

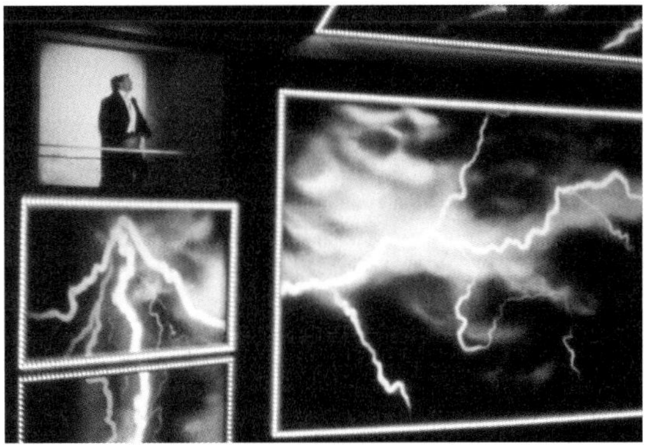

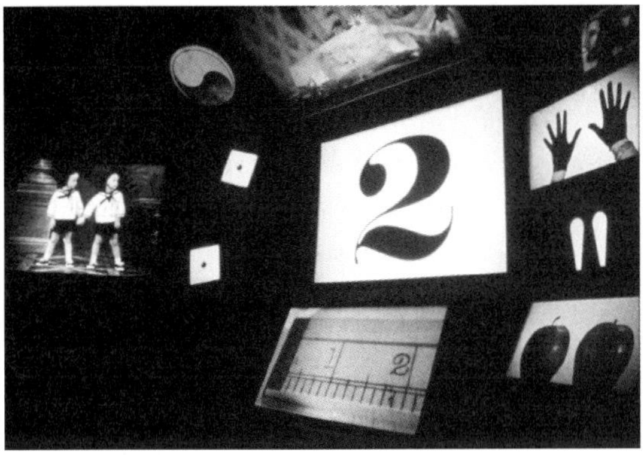

Charles and Ray Eames, *Think*, a 22-screen presentation projected in the IBM Pavilion New York World's Fair 1964–65 © 2008 Eames Office LLC

yet everything for the Eameses, in this world of communication that they were embracing so happily, was architecture: 'The chairs are architecture, the films — they have a structure, just as the front page of a newspaper has a structure. The chairs are literally like architecture in miniature ... architecture you can get your hands on.'[59] In the notes for a letter to Italian architect Vittorio Gregotti accompanying a copy of *Powers of Ten*, they write: 'In the past fifty years the world has gradually been finding out something that architects have always known, that is, that *everything* is architecture. The problems of environment have become more and more interrelated. This is a sketch for a film that shows something of how large — and small — our environment is.'[60]

In every sense, Eames architecture is all about the space of information. Perhaps we can talk no longer about 'space' but rather about 'structure' or, more precisely, about time. Structure, for the Eameses, is organisation in time. The details that are central to Mies van der Rohe's architecture are replaced by what the Eameses call the 'connections'. As Charles said in a film about a storage system they had designed: 'The details are not details. They make the product. The connections, the connections, the connections.'[61] But, as Ralph Caplan pointed out, the connections in their work are not only between such 'disparate materials as wood and steel' or between 'seemingly alien disciplines' like physics and the circus, but also between ideas. Their technique of 'information overload', used in films and multimedia presentations, as well as in their trademark 'information wall' in exhibitions, was not used to 'overtax the viewer's brain' but precisely to offer a 'broad menu of options' and to create an 'impulse to make connections'.[62]

For the Eameses, structure was not linear. They often reflected on the impossibility of linear discourse. The structure of their exhibitions has been compared to that of a scholarly paper, loaded with footnotes, where 'the highest level of participation consists in getting fascinated by the pieces and connecting them for oneself'.[63] Seemingly static structures, like the frames of their buildings or of their plywood cabinets, are but frameworks for positioning ever-changing objects. And the frame itself is, anyway, meant to be changed all the time. These changes, this ever-fluctuating movement, can never be pinned down.

Mies van der Rohe's exhibition of his work at the Museum of Modern Art in New York in 1947 was significant, according to the Eameses, not because of the individual exhibits, but because of the way the architect had organised them.[64] The organisational system of the exhibition communicated, in their view, the idea of Mies's architecture better than any single object (model, drawing, photograph) on display. When Charles published his photographs of the Mies exhibition in *Arts & Architecture*, he wrote: 'The significant thing seems to be the way in which he [Mies] has taken documents of his architecture and furniture and used them as elements in creating a space that says, "this is what its all about".'[65]

The Eameses' multi-screen presentations, exhibition technique and films are likewise significant not because of the individual factoids they offer, or even the story they tell, but because of the way the factoids are used as elements in creating a space that says 'this is what [the space of information is] all about'.

Like all architects, the Eameses controlled the space they produced. The most important factor was to regulate the flow of information. They prepared extremely detailed technical instructions for the running of even their simplest three-screen slide show.[66] Performances were carefully planned to appear as effortless as a circus act. Timing and the elimination of 'noise' were the major considerations. Their office produced masses of documents, even drawings showing the rise and fall of intensity through the course of a film, literally defining the space they wanted to produce, or, more precisely, the existing space of the media that they wanted to intensify.

With *Glimpses*, the Eameses retained complete control over their work by turning up in Moscow only 48 hours before the opening, as Peter Blake recalls it, 'dressed like a boy scout and a girl scout', clutching the reels of the film.[67] A photograph shows the smiling couple descending from the plane, reels in Charles's hands, posing for the camera. As he later put it:

> Theoretically, it was a statement made by our State Department, and yet we did it entirely here and it was never seen by anyone from our government until they saw it in Moscow. [...] If you ask for criticism, you get it. If you don't, there is a chance everyone will be too busy to worry about it.[68]

64 B. Colomina, 'Reflections on the Eames House', *op. cit.*, p.146.

65 Charles Eames, 'Mies van der Rohe', *Arts & Architecture* 64, no.12, December 1947, p.27.

66 'To show a 3-Screen slide show', 14-page manuscript in Eames Archives detailing the necessary preparations for an 'Eames 3 screen 6 projectors slide show' with 'sound' and 'picture operation procedure', illustrated with multiple drawings, Eames Archives, Library of Congress, Washington DC, box 211, folder 10.

67 Peter Blake, in 'An Eames Celebration: The Several Worlds of Charles and Ray Eames', WNET Television, New York, 3 February 1975. Quoted in P. Kirkham, *Charles and Ray Eames*, *op. cit.*, p.320.

68 O. Gingerich, 'A Conversation with Charles Eames', *op. cit.*, p.333.

The experience for the audience in Moscow was almost overwhelming. Journalists speak of too many images, too much information, too fast. For the MTV and the Internet generation watching the film today, it would not be fast enough, and yet we do not seem to have come that much further, either. The logic of the Internet was already spelled out in the Eameses' multi-screen projects.

Coming out of the War mentality, the Eameses' innovations in the world of communication, their exhibitions, films and multi-screen performances transformed the status of architecture. Their highly controlled flows of simultaneous images provided a space, an enclosure — the kind of space we now occupy continuously without thinking.

'MY MIND SPLIT OPEN': ANDY WARHOL'S EXPLODING PLASTIC INEVITABLE

Branden W. Joseph

> At no point in time, no matter how utopian, will anyone win the masses over to a higher art; they can be won over only to one nearer to them.
> Walter Benjamin

In 1968 a fledgling critic by the name of Wayne McGuire sent an unsolicited article to *Crawdaddy!* magazine proclaiming the Velvet Underground to be 'prophets of a new age, of breakthrough on an electronic: intermedia: total scale'.[1] Describing them as 'the only true intermedia group in the country', McGuire situated them within the context of Andy Warhol's Exploding Plastic Inevitable, or EPI, an overwhelming expanded cinema production collaboratively orchestrated from 1966 to 1967.[2] At the height of its development, the Exploding Plastic Inevitable included three to five film projectors, often showing different reels of the same film simultaneously; a similar number of slide projectors, movable by hand so that their images swept the auditorium; four variable-speed strobe lights; three moving spots with an assortment of coloured gels; several pistol lights; a mirror ball hung from the ceiling and another on the floor; as many as three loudspeakers blaring different pop records at once; one to two sets by the Velvet Underground and Nico; and the dancing of Gerard Malanga and Mary Woronov or Ingrid Superstar, complete with props and lights that projected their shadows high onto the wall. Advertisements for the EPI emphasised the variety of included effects, touting in addition to Warhol and the music:

> Superstars Gerard Malanga And Mary Woronov On Film On Stage On Vinyl: Live music, dancing, ultra sounds, visions, lightworks by Daniel

1 Wayne McGuire, 'The Boston Sound', *Crawdaddy!*, August 1968; reproduced in Albin Zak III (ed.), *The Velvet Underground Companion: Four Decades of Commentary*, New York: Schirmer Books, 1997, p.18.

2 W. McGuire, 'The Boston Sound', *op. cit.*, p.25. The last Velvet Underground concert to be associated with the Exploding Plastic Inevitable seems to have occurred in May of 1967 at Steve Paul's Scene in New York City. The final performances with Nico occurred at the Boston Tea Party in Boston on 26–27 May 1967. Concert posters show that the group continued to be billed as 'Andy Warhol's Velvet Underground', however, until at least July 1967. The *San Francisco Oracle* apparently ran a small advertisement announcing 'The [*sic*] Andy Warhol's "EPI" with The Velvet Underground' for a 20 December 1967 performance at The Cinematheque Coffeehouse Palace of Pleasure, but there seems to be no mention of the Exploding Plastic Inevitable in 1968. For dates and a history of the Velvet Underground and the EPI, see Victor Bockris and Gerard Malanga, *Up-Tight: The Velvet Underground Story*, London: Omnibus Books, 1983. See also the concert and poster listing on The Velvet Underground Web Page, available at http://members.aol.com/olandem/vu.html

3 Advertisement for 'Andy Warhol's Velvet Underground and Nico' at 23 St Mark's Place (The Dom), *East Village Other*, 15 April 1966, p.5. For some of the most informative (although not always positive) descriptions of the EPI, see, among others, V. Bockris and G. Malanga, *Up-Tight*, *op. cit.*; John Wilcock, 'A "High" School of Music and Art', *East Village Other*, 15 April 1966, p.5; Paul Jay Robbins, 'Andy Warhol and the Night on Fire', *Los Angeles Free Press*, 13 May 1966, p.12; Michaela Williams, 'Warhol's Brutal Assemblage: Non-Stop Horror Show', *Chicago Daily News*, 22 June 1966, p.34; and Barry Lord, 'Velvet Underground in Hamilton', *Arts Canada* 105, February 1967, pp.15–17.

4 See Timothy Jacobs, 'The Velvet Underground', *Vibrations* 2, July 1967,

> Williams; color slides by Jackie Cassen, discotheque, refreshments, Ingrid Superstar, food, celebrities, and movies, including: *Vinyl, Sleep, Eat, Kiss, Empire, Whips, Faces, Harlot, Hedy, Couch, Banana, Blow Job*, etc., etc., etc. all in the same place at the same time.[3]

The cumulative effect was one of disruptive multiplicity and layering, as the Velvet Underground, Nico and other of Warhol's superstars appeared amidst the barrage of sounds, lights, images and performance. Critics who saw the shows consistently labelled the effect 'decadence' or 'perversion'.[4] While noting the showing of such anodyne films as *Eat* (1964), they more consistently pointed to such scenes as Malanga's sadomasochistic reprogramming in *Vinyl* (1965); Mario Montez's drag in films like *Harlot* (1964), *Mario Banana* (1964) and *More Milk, Yvette* (1965); the slyly allusive activity of *Blow Job* (1964); or the explicitly pornographic engagements in *Couch* (1964)—all accompanied by the Velvet Underground's lengthy, atonal improvisations and dark, provocative songs like 'Heroin', 'Venus in Furs' and 'Sister Ray'.[5] 'It is no accident,' noted McGuire:

> that the Velvet Underground was an organic element in Andy Warhol's Exploding Plastic Inevitable. The now defunct Inevitable remains as the strongest and most developed example of intermedia art. Although productions ... have since achieved greater technical dexterity on a visual plane, no one has yet managed to communicate a guiding spirit through the complex form as well as Warhol and the Underground.[6]

Elaborating on this guiding spirit, McGuire related Warhol to William S. Burroughs—as the 'two oracles' of the time—and proceeded to explain that:

> Put in a nutshell, the real question is: how can we control and humanize an increasingly uncontrollable and proliferating technology, an overpoweringly dehumanizing technology, when the value foundation for that attempted humanization is rapidly disintegrating and when the attempt by humans to control such power (who would be the master programmer?) would most certainly be corrupting in the extreme?[7]

n.p.; Kevin Kelly, 'O, Andy, How Sad', unattributed clipping (review of EPI performance at the ICA, Boston, 29 October 1966) in scrapbook vol.2 small, p.1, Archives Study Center, The Andy Warhol Museum, Pittsburgh (hereafter cited as Warhol Archive); Richard Mortifoglio, 'The Velvet Underground and Nico', in A. Zak III (ed.), *The Velvet Underground Companion*, *op. cit.*, pp.57–62; PJ Robbins, 'Andy Warhol and the Night on Fire', *op. cit.*, p.12; and M. Williams, 'Warhol's Brutal Assemblage', *op. cit.*

5 It is important to note that in performance with the Exploding Plastic Inevitable, much of the Velvet Underground's set consisted of long, dissonant improvisations (often erroneously described in reviews as tuning up) much different from the songs heard on the released albums. Known by such titles as 'Melody Laughter' or 'The Nothing Song', these improvisations often took up more than half of an evening's performance. See, for instance, the recording of the full EPI performance at the Valleydale Ballroom in Columbus, Ohio on 4 November 1966, released on CD as *If It's Too Loud for You Move Back!* An excerpt of the Valleydale Ballroom performance of 'Melody Laughter' was included on disk two of the five CD set, *Peel Slowly and See* (Polygram 31452 7077-2). This cut, unfortunately, falsifies the effect by editing the over 28-minute improvisation into a 10-minute-and-43-second format more closely resembling a conventional song structure. Such experimental improvisations by the Velvet Underground are similar to John Cale's former associate, Cornelius Cardew's contemporary work in London with the free-noise improvisational group AMM. Compare, for example, the improvisations at the Valleydale Ballroom with those on *AMMMusic 1966* (Machless Recordings).

6 W. McGuire, 'The Boston Sound', *op. cit.*, p.24.

7 *Ibid.*, p.21.

McGuire was not alone in setting the EPI at the forefront of the develepment of intermedia artforms. In 1966 Jonas Mekas credited 'The Plastic Inevitables' with being 'the loudest and most dynamic exploration platform' for the new 'intermedia shows and groups'.[8] Nor was McGuire the only writer to relate the Exploding Plastic Inevitable to such social and technological developments. A few months later, Bob Stark of the Detroit underground paper *The Fifth Estate* published a more concise, but no less intriguing, review of *The Velvet Underground and Nico* album. Neglecting the conventional format of the record review or any attempt at qualitative evaluation, Stark was prompted instead to ask: 'Have you ... ever considered what your role in society will be after the impending Cybernetic revolution?' Like McGuire, he then proceeded to relate Warhol and the Velvet Underground to Burroughs's 'Nova Police', to the displacement of a traditional humanist subjectivity and to the then unimaginable possibility of a future in which 'everybody can have one computer or machine which he or she can sit and watch all day'. He asked:

> What will you (yes, YOU) do, when machines do all the manual labour and computers run all the machines?
>
> On a much larger scale, how will you as a part of society be able to maintain your ego role as The Superior Being on Earth when machines have replaced you and all your work functions and can do a better job? And who will program the computers? You, maybe? Or maybe your elected representatives? Or maybe the computers themselves? Then what will you do?
>
> ... I can only suggest places to look which brings us to the subject of the article ... The one group working in the context of Rock that presents a system which represents anything more than their own personal temporary answers to any of these questions is the Velvet Underground.[9]

8 Jonas Mekas, 'On the Plastic Inevitables and the Strobe Light' (26 May 1966), in *Movie Journal: The Rise of a New American Cinema, 1959–1971*, New York: Macmillan, 1972, p.242. This article is also cited by McGuire.

9 Bob Stark, 'The Velvet Underground', *The Fifth Estate*, 14 November 1968, p.11. Stark almost certainly also had the context of the Exploding Plastic Inevitable in mind. The EPI had been well-received in the Detroit-Ann Arbor area where it played some four times in 1966–67. *The Fifth Estate* had previously reported on Warhol and the Velvets' appearance at the Michigan 'Mod Wedding' ('Warhol Here for Mod Wedding', *The Fifth Estate*, 15 November 1966, p.2).

10 In the face of their own observations both Stark and McGuire end up advocating variants of direct action liberationism that their meditations on technology would seem to preclude. For his part, Stark concedes that: 'I know a lot of questions but only a few answers.' In McGuire's case, his provocative characterisation of the EPI is somewhat undermined by a typical 1960s mysticism and an affirmation of the possibility of experiencing, in music, 'pure essence and perpetual presence' (W. McGuire, 'The Boston Sound', *op. cit.*, p.23), tellingly connected with an interest in the writing of Mel Lyman, later an 'acid fascist' commune leader, but who worked for a time with Jonas Mekas. In the 1966 'Expanded Arts' issue of *Film Culture*, Lyman is listed as available for 'A full evening show alone or together with Eben Siven, Ronna Page, Jonas Mekas, light, images, voice, human presence' (*Film Culture* 43, 1966, n.p.).

11 Robert Mazzocco, 'aaaaaa ... ', *New York Review of Books* 12, no.8, 24 April 1969, p.36.

12 W. McGuire, 'The Boston Sound', *op. cit.*, p.22.

13 On the rock band project, see Glenn O'Brien, 'Andy Warhol: Interview', *High Times*, August 1977, p.34 (partially reproduced in V. Bockris and G. Malanga, *Up-Tight*, *op. cit.*, p.25); Patti Oldenburg, quoted in Victor Bockris, *Warhol*, New York: Da Capo, 1997, p.147; and La Monte Young, 'Question à La Monte Young', in Bernard Blistène, et. al. (eds.), *Andy Warhol: Cinéma*, Paris: Centre Georges Pompidou, 1990, p.55. Additional information, including the project's date and its connection to the context of happenings, derives from the unpublished transcript of an interview with La Monte Young and Marian Zazeela by Legs McNeil and Gillian McCain, New York City, 1995. I am thankful to Legs McNeil for providing me with a copy of this interview.

14 Young's departure after a couple of rehearsals is noted in L. Young, 'Question à La Monte Young', *op. cit.*, p.55, as well as L. McNeil and G. McCain, unpublished transcript, *op. cit.* Although he does not give a specific reason for the group's breakup, Warhol recalled that: 'We met

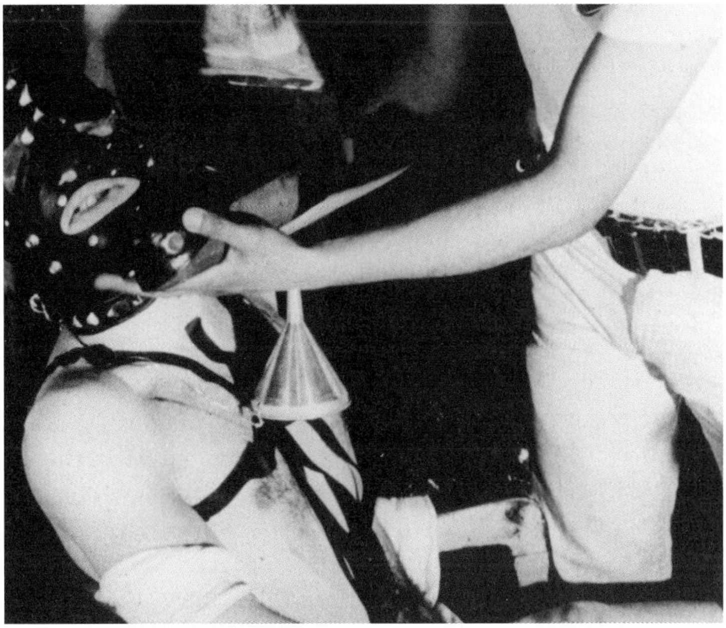

If I am drawn to the testimony of Stark and McGuire to begin an analysis of the Exploding Plastic Inevitable, it is not on account of their conclusions; far from it. For neither one does, ultimately, arrive at satisfactory answers to the provocative questions that they pose.[10] Rather, it is for the manner in which their invocations of cybernetics, automation, the dissolution of humanist subjectivity and Burroughsian visions of social control foreground, with particular concision, a constellation of ideas that hovered insistently about Warhol's late-60s production — his relationship to what a reviewer of *a*, Warhol's tape-recorded novel from the same period, called 'a bizarre new class, *untermenschen* prefigurations of the technological millennium'.[11] But I am also drawn to the fact that certain individuals, like Stark and McGuire, saw in the apparent darkness and chaos of the EPI a possibility of transformation, if not liberation, a possibility that was both within and somehow at odds with the general ethos of the 60s, one that was, in McGuire's words, 'bathed in a strange light, a demon light electric'.[12]

—

Far from Warhol's first foray into popular music, the Exploding Plastic Inevitable actually resulted from a longer line of related investigations. These began as far back as early 1963, when Warhol collaborated with Claes and Patti Oldenburg on an ill-fated attempt to form a rock band. This somewhat unlikely project included Patti Oldenburg as lead singer, Warhol and the artist Lucas Samaras as her backups (Warhol, by his own admission, 'singing badly'), the artists Larry Poons and Walter De Maria on guitar and drums, Minimalist composer La Monte Young on saxophone, and Jasper Johns, who was apparently enlisted to contribute the lyrics.[13] Although Warhol could not remember the specific role played by Claes Oldenburg, the project appears to have been conceived along the lines of other of Oldenburg's performances such as *Sports* (1962) and *Store Days* (1961–62), earlier happening-type events that appropriated similar sites of popular spectacle and consumption. After only a few rehearsals, however, the project folded when Young, who unlike Warhol did not share the Oldenburgs' interest in commercial culture, abandoned the group.[14] Despite the theatricality and Zen-like humour of Young's earlier, proto-Fluxus pieces like *Piano Piece for David Tudor #1*

Andy Warhol, still from *Vinyl*, 1965. 16mm black-and-white film, sound, 67mins © 2008 The Andy Warhol Museum, Pittsburgh, PA, a museum of Carnegie Institute. All rights reserved. Courtesy The Andy Warhol Museum

(1960) — in which a piano was fed a bale of hay — the Minimalist aesthetic he was developing at the time staunchly opposed popular forms of amusement. As Young announced at the important series of concerts he organised at Yoko Ono's loft in 1960 and 1961, the purpose of his work was 'not entertainment'.[15]

Despite this apparently fundamental divide, Warhol and Young would enter into another collaboration in the fall of 1964. As a last-minute addition to the Second Annual New York Film Festival, Warhol had been invited to project a collection of his films, not in the theatre, but in the mezzanine lobby of Lincoln Center's Philharmonic Hall.[16] In response, Warhol produced an installation that featured excerpts from his films *Eat* (1963), *Sleep* (1963), *Kiss* (1963–64) and *Haircut* (1963), each of which was shown individually on a separate Fairchild 400 projector, a machine recently developed to enable easy home viewing by back-projecting 8mm film cartridges onto small, television-sized screens.[17]

Warhol's film production had already been associated with commercial culture, either through his explicit adoption of television as a model in, for instance, the unfinished film project *Soap Opera* (1964) or by using pop radio as a soundtrack to the premiere of *Sleep*. In the context of Lincoln Center, therefore, his choice of the small, back-lit Fairchild projectors initially appears as a characteristically Pop conflation of cinema and TV.[18] The promotional literature surrounding the event seems to reflect just such a position. Whereas the Festival promoted itself as the celebration of 'a new cultural reality in New York: the belated and triumphant acceptance of film as high art', Warhol's participation was officially described as a 'festival side show' and 'extra-added-attraction'.[19] Warhol, however, clearly regarded the marginalised and subordinate position accorded his films as a slight, one that he still resented bitterly over a decade-and-a-half later.[20]

Warhol responded by adopting Young's Minimalist strategy of reductive negation. By transferring a single, 3-minute segment from each of his films onto the repeating loop cartridges, Warhol further reduced their already minimal variation and eliminated any appreciable development while extending their duration indefinitely by means of continuous repetition.

ten times, and there were fights between Lucas and Patti over the music or something.' See G. O'Brien, 'Andy Warhol: Interview', *op. cit.*, p.34; reproduced in V. Bockris and G. Malanga, *Up-Tight*, *op. cit.*, p.25.

15 Cited in K. Robert Schwarz, *Minimalists*, London: Phaidon, 1996, p.32. Young's statement referred to all of the series' performances.

16 For accounts of this installation, see David Bourdon, *Warhol*, New York: Harry N. Abrams, 1989, p.190; L. Young, 'Question à La Monte Young', *op. cit.*, p.55: Eugene Archer, 'Festival Bringing Pop Artist's Films to Lincoln Center', *The New York Times*, 12 September 1964, p.15; and Joseph Gelmis, 'Russian "Hamlet" Shown as Film Festival Opens', *New York Newsday*, 15 September 1964.

17 Warhol's copies of the advertisement for the Cine Magnetics, Inc., Fairchild 400 projector and instructions for its use are preserved in Time Capsule 65, Warhol Archives. Callie Angell, head of The Warhol Film Project, has determined that the excerpt from *Haircut* was from what is now designated *Haircut (No.2)*, and not *Haircut (No.1)*, which has been preserved and is currently in circulation.

18 On the relation of Warhol's films to television, see Callie Angell, 'Andy Warhol, Filmmaker', in *The Andy Warhol Museum*, Pittsburgh: The Andy Warhol Museum, 1994, pp.139–40. On the inclusion of a radio at the premiere of *Sleep*, see Angell, *The Films of Andy Warhol: Part II*, New York: Whitney Museum of American Art, 1994, p.11. The Fairchild 400's resemblance to television is noted both in the advertisement found in Time Capsule 65, and in 'Festival Side Show', one-page typed press release, in Time Capsule 37, Warhol Archives. This last document describes Warhol's film excerpts as lasting 20 minutes. Given the unanimity of the other descriptions of the installation, however, this 20-minute loop — which was the capacity of a full film cassette — likely consisted of the shorter, repeated film segments.

19 'Festival Side Show', *op. cit.*;

As reported in a press release: 'The quartet of Warhol films, according to the artist's definition, are "endless."'[21] The soundtrack provided by Young complemented the installation's visuals perfectly. Realising a version of his *Composition 1960 #9* — the score for which consists of a horizontal line — Young and Marian Zazeela performed a single sustained tone on a bowed brass mortar. Then, dubbing a separate but identical recording to accompany each of Warhol's films, Young had all four tapes broadcast simultaneously and at an ear-splitting volume. In a manner similar to the 'continuous frequency environments', or Dream Houses, that Young would conceive at around the same time, the amplification of his soundtracks would not only have filled the lobby, but would have melded the four tones into an acoustical structure that interacted both with their surroundings and each other.[22]

The result was of a complex sonic environment of slowly shifting sound waves that replaced traditional compositional variation with the phenomenological interaction of listener and sound. Ambulant spectators, enveloped within the sound and passing through different complexes of standing waves, would become sensitised to the subtle acoustical differences audible at different points in space and thereby become cognizant of the role played by their own movements and perceptions in the production of the musical experience.[23] In this way the installation formed a semi-autonomous zone that acted to negate, rather than embrace, the realm of commercial culture, allowing for a consciousness of individual perception and an experience of bodily depth against the expropriating alienation of spectacle. Exemplifying a Minimalist strategy of 'reducing the stimulus to next to nothing', as Young's close associate, Robert Morris, summarised it, the installation 'turn[ed] the focus on the individual, as if to say, "whatever you got in the past you brought along anyway, so now really work at it."'[24]

Warhol's film loops operated in a similar manner. Their visual reduction and temporally extended repetition so minimised the aesthetic experience as to throw the viewer back onto an attentiveness to his or her own perceptual engagement with the work, thereby exemplifying Warhol's comment that

and Amos Vogel, 'Film at Lincoln Center', 3-page typed press release, copy located in the Billy Rose Theater Collection, Performing Arts Library, New York Public Library, file 'Festivals-Cinema-US-NY-1964'.

20 See Warhol's comments in Andy Warhol and Pat Hackett, *Popism: The Warhol Sixties*, New York: Harcourt Brace Jovanovich, 1980, p.211. It wouldn't have helped matters that Jean-Luc Godard, with whom Warhol seems to have felt some rivalry, had not one but two films, *A Woman Is a Woman* and *Band à Part*, screened as part of the festival.

21 'Festival Side Show', *op. cit.*

22 La Monte Young references Dream Houses in 'from concert program notes, 1964', in La Monte Young and Marian Zazeela, *Selected Writings*, Munich: Heiner Friedrich, 1969, n.p. In another text dating from 1969, Young and Zazeela date the concept to 1962 (L. Young and M. Zazeela, *Selected Writings*, *op. cit.*, n.p.).

23 As Young and Zazeela explained of the analogous situation in their Dream Houses: 'When a continuous frequency is sounded in an enclosed space such as a room, the air in the room is arranged into high and low pressure areas. In the high pressure areas the sound is louder, and in the low pressure areas the sound is softer. Since a sine wave has only one frequency component, the pattern of high and low pressure areas is easy to locate in space. Further, concurrently sounding sine waves of different frequencies will provide an environment in which the loudness of each frequency will vary audibly at different points in the room, given sufficient amplification. This phenomenon can rarely be appreciated in most musical situations and makes the listener's position and movement in the space an integral part of the sound composition.' See *ibid.*, n.p.

24 Robert Morris, 'Letters to John Cage', *October* 81, Summer 1997, p.73.

his 'first films using the stationary objects were ... made to help the audience get more acquainted with themselves'.[25] As with Young's music, this afforded a certain critical distance from the temporal and perceptual organisation of spectacle, an organisation Warhol once described in terms of 'the same plots and the same shots and the same cuts over and over again' of 'all the most popular action shows on TV'. As he went on to explain: 'Apparently most people love watching the same basic thing, as long as the details are different. But I'm just the opposite: if I'm going to sit and watch the same thing I saw the night before, I don't want it to be essentially the same — I want it to be *exactly* the same.'[26]

Despite his temporary artistic alliance with Young, Warhol would almost certainly have recognised in the strategies of Minimalism a mimetic relation to the same logic of seriality that it denied.[27] Indeed, while each of Warhol's individual film loops displayed a stark, minimal repetition, the collection of the four projectors together amounted to differences in details, instantiating much the same logic of pseudo-differentiation that Warhol disparaged in commercial TV. Situated at what Hal Foster has termed 'the crux of Minimalism', Warhol's Lincoln Center installation occupied a pivotal, but ultimately provisional and perhaps fragile, moment of dialectical tension between a resistant, modernist autonomy and a postmodern aesthetic collapse into the expanded field being colonised by capital at that time.[28]

Like the Oldenburgs' rock group project, Warhol's Lincoln Center installation would be short lived. For in addition to producing an environment of subtle acoustical interactions that could only be achieved though amplification, the volume of the installation's soundtracks staged an evident and aggressive intervention into the space of the Lincoln Center Festival. In an act that recalled the censorship of Warhol's *Thirteen Most Wanted Men* at the 1964 New York World's Fair (which was painted over in silver at the instigation of the exhibition's organisers), officials at Lincoln Center almost immediately directed Young to reduce the volume. Realising that its critical edge would be blunted and its integral Minimalist aesthetic destroyed, Young

25 Gretchen Berg, 'Nothing to Lose: An Interview with Andy Warhol' (1967), *Andy Warhol: Film Factory* (ed. Michael O'Pray), London: British Film Institute, 1989, p.58.

26 A. Warhol and P. Hackett, *Popism*, *op. cit.*, p.50 (emphasis in original). Here and throughout, my discussion of 'spectacle' is, of course, made in reference to Guy Debord, *The Society of the Spectacle* (trans. Donald Nicholson-Smith), New York: Zone Books, 1995.

27 This would have been clear, for example, in the relationship between Warhol's installation of *Brillo* and other box sculptures at the Stable Gallery in 1964 and the serial objects developed by Minimalist sculptors.

28 Hal Foster, 'The Crux of Minimalism', *The Return of the Real*, Cambridge, Mass.: The MIT Press, 1996, pp.35–69.

29 John Cale worked with La Monte Young, Marian Zazeela and Tony Conrad as part of the Theatre of Eternal Music from 1963 through the end of 1965. Judging from 'Loop', the first recording issued by the Velvet Underground, it was at least in part Cale's relationship to the Minimalist aesthetic that interested Warhol in the group. 'Loop', released on side two of the flexi-disk included in the 'Fab' issue of *Aspen Magazine* co-edited by Warhol, was composed and probably realised almost exclusively by Cale *(Aspen Magazine* 1, no.3, December 1966, n.p.). To a degree far beyond even the most experimental of the group's other releases, 'Loop' exemplifies the minimalist aesthetic with which Young and Cale were involved. 7½ minutes of continuously undulating feedback, 'Loop' ends with a locked groove which — like the film loops in Warhol's Lincoln Center installation — extends the duration of the piece indefinitely by means of repetition. (Cale's 'Loop' is the prototype for Lou Reed's later two-album *Metal Machine Music* of 1975, which also ended with a repeating locked groove.) A slightly earlier instrumental improvisation by the Velvet Underground titled 'Noise' was included as part of a sound collage in the 'Electric Newspaper' issue of the *East Village Other* recorded on 6 August 1966 and released as ESP-Disk 1034. The Velvets' contribution is well-hidden within the audio collage.

reacted by withdrawing his soundtracks completely, leaving Warhol's loops running harmlessly on the Grand Promenade for the remainder of the festival.

—

In the first phase of his collaboration with the Velvet Underground (one of whose members, John Cale, had worked extensively with Young),[29] Warhol would exacerbate the dialectic put into play within his Lincoln Center installation, increasing the aggressive negation of popular spectacle even as his promotion of a rock group tied him to it all the more completely. Initially entitled *Andy Warhol's Up-Tight*, the performance made its now infamous debut at a dinner for the New York Society for Clinical Psychiatry held at Delmonico's Hotel on 13 January 1966. In that incarnation, in which Warhol screened several of his films before appearing on stage with the Velvet Underground, Nico, Edie Sedgwick and Malanga, the incessant, multimedia barrage of the Exploding Plastic Inevitable had not yet been fully implemented. Instead, once the concert began the audience found themselves subjected to the guerrilla-type assaults of film-maker Barbara Rubin, who, with the help of Jonas Mekas, thrust floodlights and running movie cameras into their faces. Careening from table to table, Rubin and Mekas filmed the hapless psychiatrists' responses to blunt and embarrassing sexual questions such as 'Does he eat you out?' or 'Is his penis big enough?' and aggressively stated interjections like 'You're making too much noise'.[30]

These and other similarly filmed interventions by Rubin played an integral role in all of the *Up-Tight* performances. The shock they effected was intended not only to destroy the audience's traditionally contemplative attitude toward the spectacle taking place on stage but also to make them — as exemplars of bourgeois culture, norms and comportment — reveal themselves and the society of which they were a part as 'up-tight'.[31] As John Wilcock noted of the group's appearance at Rutgers University on 9 March 1966:

> There's something about authoritarian creeps which is triggered instantly by the tiniest glimmering of anarchistic freedom and Barbara

30 On the performance at Delmonico's, see A. Warhol and P. Hackett, *Popism*, *op. cit.*, p.147; Grace Glueck, 'Syndromes Pop at Delmonico's', *The New York Times*, 14 January 1966; and Seymour Krim, 'Andy Warhol's "Velvet Underground": Shock Treatment for Psychiatrists', *New York Herald Tribune*, 14 January 1966. See also accounts of the performance of *Andy Warhol's Up-Tight* at the Film-makers' Cinematheque in New York, which took place from 8–13 February 1966, in Archer Winston, 'Reviewing Stand: Andy Warhol at Cinematheque', *New York Post*, 9 February 1966; Bosley Crowther, 'The Screen: Andy Warhol's "More Milk, Yvette" Bows', *The New York Times*, 9 February 1966, p.32; and 'Reprinted from the Fire Island News', in Andy Warhol et. al., *Andy Warhol's Index (Book)*, New York: Random House, 1967, n.p. The Film-makers' Cinematheque press release for this event describes a screening of Warhol's film *More Milk, Yvette* to be accompanied by an appearance of the Velvet Underground and Nico, Edie Sedgwick, Gerard Malanga and Barbara Rubin. (This listing is, no doubt, the source of the widespread but erroneous idea that the Velvet Underground provided the soundtrack to *More Milk, Yvette*.) Crowther's review indicates that *More Milk, Yvette* was shown in double-screen projection with Warhol's film, *The Velvet Underground*, followed by a double-screen showing of *Lupe*. The event is described in the press release as 'the second in the projected UP-TIGHT series, the first of which was held at the psychiatrists' convention at the Delmonico Hotel in January' ('Special Press Screening of a Film by Andy Warhol', one-page press release, late January or early February, 1966, Anthology Film Archives, New York, file 'Warhol, Andy. Prog Notes, Pres rel, ... ').

31 I am using the term 'bourgeois' with regard to Rubin's activities advisedly, in reference to what seems the specifically historical avant-garde underpinnings of her interventions.

> [Rubin] exploits it ruthlessly. Her continuing cycle of day-by-day documentaries — she was busy filming now — is aptly entitled, the Uptight Series. It invariably depicts the helplessness of people who are blowing their cool, losing control.[32]

Already at Delmonico's the effect of such explicitly avant-garde interventions was to instantly and powerfully divide the representatives of the new culture from those of the old.[33] 'You want to do something for mental health?' asked one of the enraged psychiatrists of a reporter for *The New York Times*. 'Kill the story.'[34]

Another, lesser-known, activity within the *Up-Tight* series reveals the group's interest in intervening in the mass media as one of the exemplary sites of bourgeois ideology. Instead of a concert this involved a disruptive and chaotic appearance by Warhol, Rubin and members of the Velvet Underground and the East Village band the Fugs on David Susskind's television programme. During the course of the show, Rubin and Danny Williams's filming, Ed Saunders's political advocacy of oral-genital relations and Cale's languid caressing of Malanga with a cattle whip caused the TV host to angrily lose his cool. Halfway through the taping, as Wilcock reported: 'Susskind is getting rattled. The roving cameramen, the disorderly group, the smell of pot, the occasional clicks, shrieks and catcalls from Barbara are apparently so much more than he expected.'[35] Halfway through the taping Susskind and his staff abruptly decided to cancel the second hour of the programme.

In the later, more fully developed version of the Exploding Plastic Inevitable, this aspect of direct, personal confrontation between performer and audience was replaced by the more encompassing, multimedia experience familiar to Stark and McGuire.[36] By the end of March 1966, with the waning of Rubin's participation and the full development of the projections and light show, the term 'up-tight' had come to take on a different meaning. As noted at the time by Ingrid Superstar: 'Up-tight means to have so many different

32 John Wilcock, 'On the Road with the Exploding Plastic Inevitable', in *The Autobiography and Sex Life of Andy Warhol*, New York: Other Scenes, 1971, n.p.

33 See Van M. Cagle's discussion of the Delmonico's event in *Reconstructing Pop/Subculture: Art, Rock, and Andy Warhol*, Thousand Oaks, California: Sage, 1995, pp.4–8.

34 Cited in G. Glueck, 'Syndromes Pop at Delmonico's', *op. cit.*

35 John Wilcock, 'Other Scenes', *East Village Other*, 15 February 1966, p.4. Wilcock's article reports this event in detail. At the bottom of the accompanying photograph, in which Cale and Malanga are clearly visible, the caption identifies the event as 'Barbara Rubin, The Uptight Series'.

36 One notable relapse into a directly confrontational style occurred in Ann Arbor, where 'someone yelled "Andy Warhol's queer" and got hit ten times with the blinding [spot] light. Warhol never smiled once' (David Freedman, 'Andy Warhol and the Plastic Quadrangle', unattributed clipping, scrapbook vol.10 large, p.72, Warhol Archives).

37 Ingrid Superstar, 'Movie Party at the Factory: A Trip and a Half', one page typed manuscript, dated 26 March 1966, Time Capsule -7, Warhol Archives (punctuation slightly altered). The first phase of the EPI, which I have been referencing under the title *Up-Tight* seems to have come to an end in March 1966, concurrently with the adoption of a more intense use of strobe lights. Warhol reports that strobes were initially used at the group's first appearance in Ann Arbor (V. Bockris and G. Malanga, *Up-Tight*, *op. cit.*, p.29). This occurred as part of the Fourth Ann Arbor Film Festival at the University of Michigan on 12 March 1966. In posters for this performance, however, it was still billed as *Up-Tight with Andy Warhol*. See Ingrid Superstar's description in V. Bockris and G. Malanga, *Up-Tight*, *op. cit.*, p.29. The title Exploding Plastic Inevitable seems to have debuted during the April 1966 performances at the Dom on St. Mark's Place in New York.

38 Marshall McLuhan and Quentin Fiore, *The Medium Is the Massage: An Inventory of Effects*, New York: Bantam Books, 1967, n.p. (emphasis in original).

39 Marshall McLuhan, 'The Agenbite of Outwit' (1963), *Media Research: Technology, Art, Communication* (ed. Michel A. Moos), Amsterdam: G+B Arts International, 1997, pp.123–24.

40 Marshall McLuhan, *Understanding Media: The Extensions of Man*, New York: McGraw-Hill, 1964, p.327.

41 *Ibid.*, p.314.

42 M. McLuhan, 'The Agenbite of Outwit', *op. cit.*, p.124.

confusing things going on at one time, to attract or detract the audience's attention in order to confuse them and make them nervous. Sometimes it even makes us nervous.'[37]

—

To a certain extent, considerations such as those by Stark and McGuire had been prompted by Marshall McLuhan, who included the Exploding Plastic Inevitable in his popular pictographic handbook *The Medium Is the Massage* of 1967. As indicated on the subsequent two-page spread (illustrated with a Roy Lichtenstein-like, comic-book 'BANG'), the EPI represented the 'auditory space' of electric media, which, as McLuhan explained, was multidirectional, synaesthetic and interactive. 'The ear favours no particular "point of view",' McLuhan observed. 'We are *enveloped* by sound. It forms a seamless web around us.'[38] As he explained more precisely in an earlier article, 'The Agenbite of Outwit', such an auditory space designated:

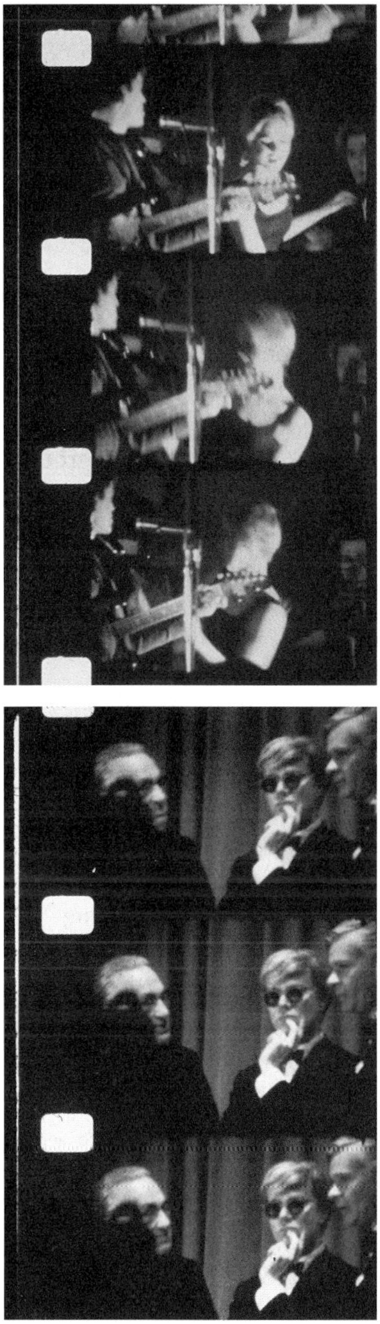

Andy Warhol's *Up-Tight*, New York Society for Clinical Psychiatry dinner, Delmonico's Hotel, New York, 13 January 1966. Film by Jonas Mekas

> any pattern in which the components co-exist without direct lineal hook-up or connection, creating a field of simultaneous relations [which] is auditory, even though some of its aspects can be seen ... They form a mosaic or corporate image whose parts are interpenetrating. Such is also the kind of order that tends to exist in a city or a culture. It is a kind of orchestral, resonating unity.[39]

Prior to implicating the EPI, the privileged site of McLuhan's electronic space was television. Although the TV image was flat, the children of the electronic age, who sit, in McLuhan's descriptions, with a characteristic closeness to the screen, were enveloped by the scanning electrons beamed forth from the cathode-ray tube, 'bombarded', as McLuhan put it, 'by atoms that reveal the outside as inside in an endless adventure amidst blurred images and mysterious contours'.[40] Within this all-encompassing, audio-visual environment, the flickering half-presence of television's (then) low level of resolution was seen to create a 'mosaic' that called forth the spectators' 'participatory' in-filling and a synaesthetic, multisensory response. 'The TV image,' McLuhan explained in *Understanding Media,* 'requires each instant that we "close" the spaces in the mesh by a convulsive sensuous participation that is profoundly kinetic and tactile.'[41] For McLuhan, the ultimate result of such electronic media was to be both the return to an organically 'retribalised' global village — 'where everything happens to everyone at the same time: [and] everyone knows about, and therefore participates in, everything that is happening the moment it happens'[42] — and an equally holistic transformation

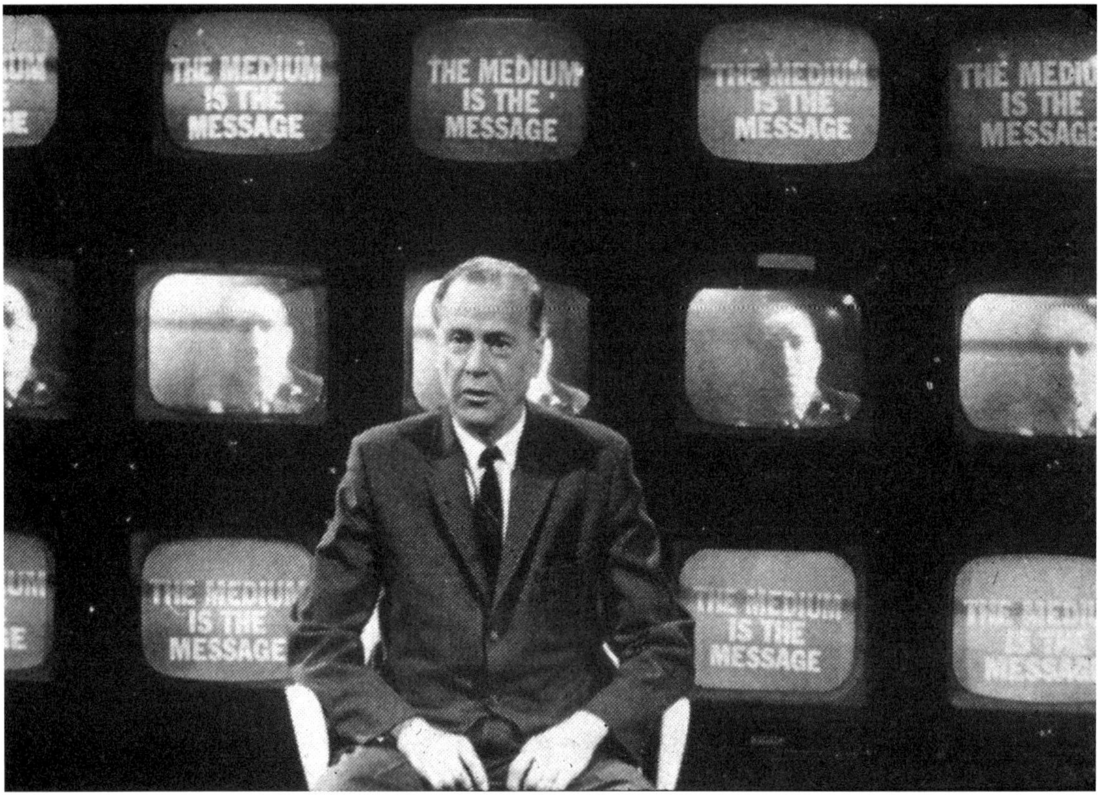

Marshall McLuhan

of the individual into 'a complex and depth-structured person emotionally aware of his total interdependence with the rest of human society'.[43] In an inverse, but no less ideological, appeal to the great 'Family of Man', McLuhan's 'tribal' imagery sought to naturalise the decade's thoroughly technological transformations (to such a point, in fact, that *The Medium Is the Massage* illustrated this idea with Nat Farbman's photograph of Beschuana villagers from the famous exhibition by Edward Steichen).[44]

To date, the reception of the Exploding Plastic Inevitable remains unproblematically tied to McLuhan's apologetics. In the book *Up-Tight,* Victor Bockris and Gerard Malanga declare that a 'formal definition ... of the aims of the E.P.I.' could be found in McLuhan's statement that: 'Our new [electronic] environment compels commitment and participation. We have become irrevocably involved with, and responsible for, each other.'[45] More generally, Gene Youngblood claimed expanded cinema as 'a paradigm for an entirely different kind of audiovisual experience, a tribal language that expresses not ideas but collective group consciousness'.[46] Following McLuhan's claim of an impending return to self-presence, Youngblood further explained that: 'We are tragically in need of new vision: expanded cinema is the beginning of that vision. We shall be released. We will bring down the wall. We'll be reunited with our reflection.'[47]

By all accounts, however, viewers of the Exploding Plastic Inevitable did not feel returned to tribal unity or subjective self-possession so much as uprooted and disoriented by the incessant bombardment of audio-visual shocks. Art Seidenbaum of the *Los Angeles Times* described it as 'like ducking in the midst of shrapnel, not knowing what's hitting next from where'.[48] Another reporter noted more precisely and dispassionately that: 'It's a dislocation of the senses — a breaking down of ordinary responses.'[49] 'At a slight distance,' wrote reviewer Michaela Williams, 'the Exploding Plastic Inevitable seems like a Fun Machine. People move into it and become nothing more than parts of it, receptors essential to its functioning but subordinate to it and manipulated by it.'[50] She later declared of Warhol:

> He has indeed put together a total environment, but it is an assemblage that actually vibrates with menace, cynicism and perversion. To experience it is to be brutalized, helpless.
>
> ... The strobe lights blaze, spots dart, flickering pistol lights start in on [the audience] and their humanness is destroyed; they are fragments, cutouts waving Reynolds Wrap reflectors to ward off their total disintegration.

'Eventually,' she concluded, in lines that the group would quote gleefully in subsequent advertisements, 'the reverberations in your ears stop. But what do you do with what you still hear in your brain? The Flowers of Evil are in full bloom with the Exploding Plastic Inevitable; let's hope it's killed before it spreads.'[51]

—

Without mentioning McLuhan, George Maciunas's 1966 *Expanded Arts Diagram* traced the genealogy of the Exploding Plastic Inevitable from international expositions and world fairs, to Disney-esque spectacles, to the multiple-screen projections of expanded cinema, a category headed by the name of Charles Eames.[52] Indeed, in 1964 — the year before

43 M. McLuhan, *Understanding Media*, *op. cit.*, pp.50–51.

44 The Farbman image reproduced in *The Medium is the Massage* to illustrate the phrase 'The new electronic interdependence recreates the world in the image of a global village' is taken from Edward Steichen, *The Family of Man*, New York: The Museum of Modern Art, 1955, p.120.

45 V. Bockris and G. Malanga, *Up-Tight*, *op. cit.*, p.36; see also p.26 and 42.

46 Gene Youngblood, *Expanded Cinema*, New York: Dutton, 1970, p.387.

47 *Ibid.*, p.49. Tellingly, Youngblood avoids a direct discussion of the EPI in favour of Ronald Nameth's film of the performance, which effectively tames the overall effect. See *ibid.*, pp.102–05. Nameth's film is perceptively characterised by Richard Whitehall: 'From Warhol's intermedia, the sharp cry of pain and desperation which seems to be the heart of all his work, Nameth has employed a pulsation of light and sound to modulate an event into an abstraction' ('Nameth/Warhol Replace Arc with Strobe', *Los Angeles Free Press*, 5 January 1968, p.16).

48 Art Seidenbaum, 'Andy Peace-pimple Puts a New Complexion on Night Life', *Los Angeles Times Calendar*, 15 May 1966, p.3.

49 Susy Dooley, 'An "Experience"— Warhol Version', unattributed clipping (review of first Chicago show at Poor Richard's, 1966), scrapbook vol.10 large, p.70, Warhol Archives. See also Jonas Mekas's comments on the fragmentation of the ego, in 'On the Plastic Inevitables and the Strobe Light', *op. cit.*, p.242; and Stephen Koch's description of the EPI, in *Stargazer: The Life, World and Films of Andy Warhol* (2nd edition), New York: Marion Boyars, 1991, pp.70–72.

50 Michaela Williams, 'Andy Warhol and His Marvelous Fun Machine', unattributed clipping (preview of first Chicago show at Poor Richard's, 1966), scrapbook vol.10 large, p.62, Warhol Archives.

51 M. Williams, 'Warhol's Brutal Assemblage', *op. cit.*, p.34. Compare with the advertisement 'Andy Warhol's Exploding Plastic Inevitable Returns', *Village Voice*, 29 September 1966, p.22 (the final seven words of the Williams quotation are omitted).

52 *Film Culture* no.47, special issue on 'Expanded Arts', 1959 (reproduced on p.54 in this volume). As we shall see, Maciunas's perceptive notation of Warhol's relationship to 'exhibitionism, sadism, perversion, sex, etc.' is not unimportant.

the Cinematheque's first 'Expanded Cinema Festival'—the publication of McLuhan's *Understanding Media* would likely have been overshadowed by Charles and Ray Eames's *Think* presentation in the IBM Pavilion at the New York World's Fair. The Eameses's audience—lifted hydraulically before a vast hemispherical wall of movie and slide projections—was bombarded by information at a pace too rapid to be fully absorbed. More so than television, the *Think* installation—with its literal mosaic of screens, its fragments of information and its synaesthetic, or at least multisensory, engagement exemplified McLuhan's descriptions of an 'auditory', electronic space.

Although lacking the full visceral impact of the EPI, visitors nonetheless found the IBM Pavilion 'occasionally confusing', 'frustrating' and 'too fragmented to be entirely successful'.[53] In his 'Movie Journal', Jonas Mekas described the experience as 'A very busy performance[,] confused, overcrowded, perfectly unfunctional, and, I would dare say, silly.'[54] In part, such disorientation attests to the displacement of earlier forms of more focused spectacular attentiveness established with the sound film.[55] Like the Eameses's 1959 installation, *Glimpses of the USA* (reproduced in the same issue of *Film Culture* as Maciunas's *Expanded Arts Diagram*), the IBM Pavilion was a privileged site of the type of perceptual retraining that Jonathan Crary has revealed as integral to capitalism's dynamic of de- and re-territorialisation. The 'IBM information machine', as the installation was called, sought to naturalise the newly developing, technologically mediated modes of absorbing the augmented speeds and diversity of stimuli within an emerging information economy. These modes of subjective assimilation were now to be claimed as actually truer to human perception. Although 'the pace of the show', as one observer recalled, 'is so fast that a person does not have enough time to weed out what he wants to see or not see', the tuxedoed IBM 'host' explained that the installation actually 'brings you information in much the same way as your mind gets it—in fragments and glimpses—sometimes relating to the same idea or incident. Like making toast in the morning'.[56]

Think derived from years of the Eameses's research into the most effective means of communicating multiple stimuli.[57] According to Beatriz Colomina, they had found that the 'awareness of relationships between seemingly unrelated phenomena [was] achieved by "high speed techniques"' that 'produce an excessive input from different directions that has to be synthesized by the audience'. The IBM Pavilion, channelling the newly

53 Mina Hamilton, 'Films at the Fair 2', *Industrial Design*, May 1964, pp.36–38; quoted in Pat Kirkham, *Charles and Ray Eames: Designers of the Twentieth Century*, Cambridge, Mass.: The MIT Press, 1995, p.325 and 328.

54 Jonas Mekas, 'Movies at the World's Fair', 9 July 1964; reproduced in *Film Culture* 43, 1966, p.11.

55 On the relation of spectacle to the conjunction of sound and vision in the sound film and early television, see Jonathan Crary, 'Spectacle, Attention, Counter-Memory', *October* 50, Fall 1989, pp.97–107. It is part of the argument of this paper that the transformations that Crary sees in television in the 1970s begin to be visible within the culture at this moment in the mid-1960s. On the transformation in television, see Jonathan Crary, 'Eclipse of the Spectacle', *Art after Modernism: Rethinking Representation* (ed. Brian Wallis), Boston: David R. Godine, 1984, pp.283–94.

56 M. Hamilton, 'Films at the Fair 2', *op. cit.*, pp.36–38; quoted in P. Kirkham, *Charles and Ray Eames*, *op. cit.*, p.325, and IBM 'host', quoted in Beatriz Colomina, 'Enclosed by Images: The Eameses' Multimedia Architecture',

emerging dislocating effects of electronic technology to the contemporary operations of commercial mass media, rendered the audience's 'impulse to make connections', as Colomina observes, into a form of 'participation', the desired result of which was to surpass intellectual engagement in favour of an 'emotional response, produced as much by the excess of images as [by] their content'.[58]

While McLuhan generally presented such an interactive participation as leading to the holism of the global village, the controlling effect of this new mode of distraction was not entirely absent from his discussions either. Although apparently unable to elucidate its significance fully, he nonetheless broached it toward the end of *Understanding Media*. 'In the course of many studies of audience reactions to TV teaching,' McLuhan observed,

> there recurs this puzzling fact. The viewers feel that the teacher has a dimension almost of sacredness. This feeling does not have its basis in concepts or ideas, but seems to creep in uninvited and unexplained. It baffles both the students and the analysts of their reactions. Surely, there could be no more telling touch to tip us off to the character of TV. This is not so much a visual as a tactual-auditory medium that involves all of our senses in depth interplay. For people long accustomed to the merely visual experience of the typographic and photographic varieties, it would seem to be the *synesthesia*, or tactual depth of TV experience, that dislocates them from their usual attitudes of passivity and detachment.[59]

As in the IBM Pavilion, then, the 'participatory' closing of an auditory, mosaic space — the individual's connection of diverse, fragmentary bits of information — actually produces a more active form of suture, an identification with and subjection to the electronic image. 'Potentially,' remarked McLuhan, television 'can transform the Presidency into a monarchic dynasty. A merely elective Presidency scarcely affords the depth of dedication and commitment demanded by the TV form.'[60]

For both McLuhan and the Eameses the forms of perceptual training and interpellation produced by electronic media were understood to bypass conscious assimilation in order to impact sub-individual or automatic processes. Seen from this perspective, the mutual, participatory involvement and proximity within the global village — the contact over distance allowed by electronic communication — reveals itself as a subjective permeability to external forces of signification. In a 1964 review of the conflictual, electronic

Grey Room 02, Winter 2001, p.20. Please note that the latter text is reproduced in the current volume.

57 See Colomina, *ibid.*, *passim*; and Sheldon Renan, *An Introduction to the American Underground Film*, New York: E.P. Dutton and Co., 1967, pp.229–33.

58 B. Colomina, 'Enclosed by Images', *op. cit.*, p.19 and 23. Colomina relates the Eameses' installations to the media on p.20.

59 M. McLuhan, *Understanding Media*, *op. cit.*, p.336 (emphasis in original).

60 *Ibid.*, p.336. Reviewer Art Seidenbaum sensed a similar dimension in the multisensory impact of the EPI. 'Andy [Warhol] is providing the stimulus for us,' he wrote, 'our rock, our master. All we have to be is passive, the empty vacuum bags which he will fill with his genius' ('Andy Peacepimple Puts a New Complexion on Night Life', *op. cit.*, p.3). The student reviewers from Columbia University, however, saw more clearly the distinction between the EPI and the strategies of identification at work in multimedia events more directly aligned with capital. As they wrote laconically in contrasting the EPI with Murray the K's World: 'Inside, the screens carry photos

battlegrounds of *Naked Lunch* (1959) and *Nova Express* (1964), McLuhan's habitual discourse underwent a highly symptomatic rupture, temporarily drawing back the ideological veil of tribalisation to reveal the more nefarious dimensions of this electronic space. Burroughs, he noted, presents:

> a paradigm of a future in which there can be no spectators but only participants. All men are totally involved in the insides of all men. There is no privacy and no private parts. In a world in which we are all ingesting and digesting one another there can be no obscenity or pornography or decency. Such is the law of electric media which stretch the nerves to form a global membrane of enclosure.[61]

It is certainly a coincidence that Warhol characterised Pop art — in terms that recall McLuhan's descriptions of television and electronic space — as 'taking the outside and putting it on the inside or taking the inside and putting it on the outside'.[62] Yet it is, I would suggest, this dimension of the global village — its spatial and subjective interpenetration — that was modelled by the Exploding Plastic Inevitable. Within it spectators became keenly aware of the sub-individual transformations effected by media technologies.[63] Surpassing then current perceptual norms more intensely than had the IBM Pavilion, the EPI formed a similarly enveloping 'membrane of enclosure', a vast electronic environment, the space of which Warhol momentarily even contemplated furnishing with individual television sets on every table.[64]

—

In his 1967 *Introduction to the American Underground Film*, Sheldon Renan explicitly defined 'expanded cinema' in terms of the dissolution of the medium: it was, in his words, 'cinema expanded to the point at which the effect of film may be produced without the use of film at all'.[65] More recently, Rosalind Krauss has described the related historical development of television and the advent of such intermedia arts. The artistic adoption

and movies of Murray, Murray with a motorcycle, and the Playboy Bunny softball team. Soon there is a shot of the team with Murray.' Calling Murray the K's World a 'veneer, a thin covering over Murray's real talent: making money', they concluded that 'Warhol still has the best entertainment in New York' (Mitch Susskind and Leslie Gottesman, 'Keep Your Cool: An Exploding World', *Columbia Daily Spectator*, 27 April 1966). It is worth noting that Murray the K's World (which cynically announced that 'the individual [presumably other than Murray] *is* the focal point') was explicitly based on McLuhan's ideas about electronic media (Jane Tamerin, 'Sights and Sounds of the New Night Life', *New York Herald Tribune*, 17 April 1966, p.14).

61 Marshall McLuhan, 'Notes on Burroughs' (1964), in *Media Research*, *op. cit.*, p.89.

62 Warhol, quoted in G. Berg, 'Nothing to Lose', *op. cit.*, p.57. Hal Foster has also noted this quotation, making an argument about Warhol's place within a 'pathological public sphere' that is relevant to the arguments about the space of electronic media developed below ('Death in America', *October* 75, Winter 1996, pp.37–59).

63 Reporter David Freedman, for instance, described spending days following a performance 'trying to recover his sensibilities from the onslaught' ('Andy Warhol and the Plastic Quadrangle', *op. cit.*, n.p.).

64 During the first EPI performance at the Dom, Wilcock reported: 'Somebody was watching the late news on a tiny, portable television set. "Wow!" said Andy. "Wouldn't it be great if we could have one of those on every table?"' ('A "High" School of Music and Art', *op. cit.*, p.5).

65 S. Renan, *An Introduction to the American Underground Film*, *op. cit.*, p.227.

66 Rosalind Krauss, *'A Voyage on the North Sea': Art in the Age of the Post-Medium Condition*, New York: Thames and Hudson, 1999, p.24.

67 *Ibid.*, p.53.

68 *Ibid.*, p.44.

69 See, most notably, Jonas Mekas, 'Notes after Reseeing the Movies of Andy Warhol', in M. O'Pray (ed.), *Andy Warhol: Film Factory*, *op. cit.*, pp.37–39; and P. Adams Sitney, *Visionary Film: The American Avant-Garde* (3rd edition), New York: Oxford University Press, 2002, pp.348–52.

70 J. Mekas, 'On the Plastic Inevitables and the Strobe Light', *op. cit.*, p.243.

71 R. Krauss, *'A Voyage on the North Sea'*, *op. cit.*, p.31. Film-maker Hollis Frampton similarly speaks of the 'metaphoric simultaneity' of video

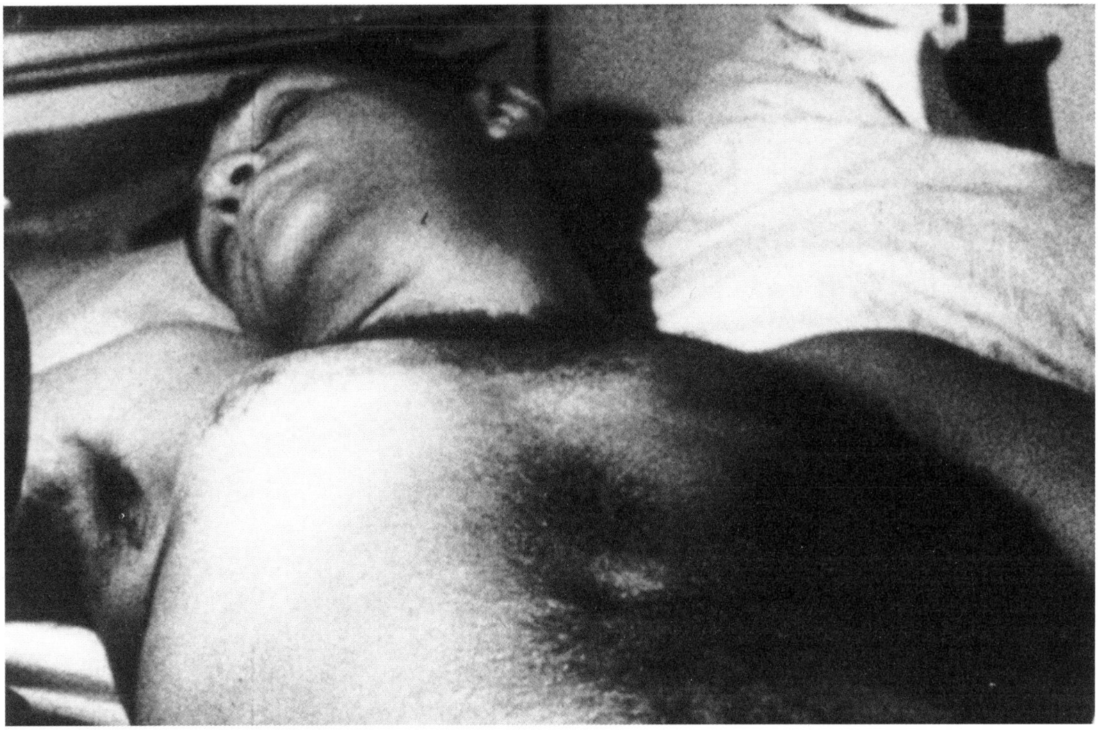

Andy Warhol, still from *Sleep*, 1963. 16mm black-and-white film, silent, 5hrs 21mins at 16fps © 2008 The Andy Warhol Museum, Pittsburgh, PA, a museum of Carnegie Institute. All rights reserved. Courtesy The Andy Warhol Museum

of the Portapak video recorder, she explains in '*A Voyage on the North Sea*', effectively extinguished the modernist practice of Structural film and 'shatter[ed] the notion of medium-specificity', opening onto a 'post-medium' condition where aesthetics and capital could permeate all aspects of culture.[66] Far from a postmodern concession of oppositional art, however, Krauss appealed to Walter Benjamin's idea of allegorical appropriation to argue that 'it is precisely the onset of higher orders of technology … which allows us, by rendering older techniques outmoded, to grasp the inner complexity of the mediums those techniques support'.[67] For an artist like Marcel Broodthaers, she explains, the late-60s advent of television, electronics and intermedia prompted a Benjaminian recovery of early, artisanal film as 'a medium whose specificity is to be found in its condition as self-differing.'[68]

Warhol's earliest films, like *Sleep*, *Kiss* or *Empire*, which Broodthaers might have seen in Belgium at the Experimental Film Festival in Knokke-le-Zoute, have long been related to both the recuperation of early cinema and the development of Structural film.[69] Neither interest, however, characterises the EPI. For far from redeeming earlier cinematic models, the Exploding Plastic Inevitable, which Mekas described as 'all Here and Now and the Future',[70] employed Warhol's films as components of an intermedia space with all the impure promiscuity that Krauss ascribes to television: 'a discursive chaos, a heterogeneity of activities that could not be theorized as coherent or conceived of as having something like an essence or unifying core'.[71]

Yet the appropriation of an outmoded medium was only one of the oppositional strategies theorised by Benjamin, who similarly regarded the moment of a technology's emergence as dialectical. In the famous 'Work of Art' essay and the *Passagenwerk*, Benjamin described technologies — *'at historical turning points'*[72] — as developing within social and subjective complexes of perceptual modalities and habitual actions. The largely unconsciously developed habits that emerged with the advent of new technologies and that came to the fore in artistic modes of distraction, he argued, could be channelled in either progressive or reactionary directions, mobilised through identification with either proletarian workers or with Hollywood stars and *Führer* cults. While aware of the latter, regressive outcomes, Benjamin nonetheless defended the possibility of anticipatory, artistic operations to reveal (as in a dream) the repressed potentials of these unconscious aspects of subject formation.[73] At the moment of its emergence, early film, he maintained, performed two oppositional functions: expressing the institutional sedimentations of habitual actions and revealing within them repressed or hidden potentials.[74] Bursting asunder the offices, factories and other 'prison-worlds' of institutional power, cinematic disjunctions (as anticipated by Dadaist montage) revealed 'entirely new structural formations' of the depicted subject and opened onto new possibilities and articulations.[75] 'On the one hand,' he explained of this optical unconscious,

> film *furthers insight into the necessities governing our lives* by its use of close-ups, by its accentuation of hidden details in familiar objects, and by its exploration of commonplace milieux through the ingenious guidance of the camera; on the other hand, *it manages to assure us of a vast and unsuspected field of action* [*Spielraum*].[76]

In 1935 Theodor Adorno would find Benjamin's theory of distraction unconvincing.[77] Yet Benjamin's argument was largely confined to the cinema of the 20s; and while he would concede that the advent of sound film had delivered the political promise of early cinema to the forces of fascism and

as realised in the 'dissolve', in *Circles of Confusion*, Rochester, New York: Visual Studies Workshop Press, 1983, p.167. As he comments further on p.163: 'Photons impress upon the random delirium of silver halide crystals in the film emulsion an illusion of order, electrons warp the ordered video raster, determinate as a crystal lattice, into an illusion of delirium.'

72 Walter Benjamin, 'The Work of Art in the Age of Its Technological Reproducibility: Third Version' (1939), in *Selected Writings*, vol.4 (ed. Howard Eiland and Michael W. Jennings), Cambridge, Mass.: Harvard University Press, 2003, p.268 (emphasis in original).

73 It is in this way, as Benjamin explained in the *Passagenwerk*, that the superstructure 'expresses' the lived conditions of the masses. See Walter Benjamin, *The Arcades Project* (trans. Howard Eiland and Kevin McLaughlin), Cambridge, Mass.: Harvard University Press, 1999, p.392. Such 'dream images', as he called them — the arcades were one; film, in a different way, another — were ambiguously intertwined sites that manifest at the same time the immanent forces of utopian longing and those of ideological repression (pp.4–5 and 388–404 [convolute K]).

74 See Benjamin's comments on the film's revelation of habitual actions in 'The Work of Art in the Age of Its Technological Reproducibility: Third Version', *op. cit.*, p.266.

75 'Our bars and city streets, our offices and furnished rooms, our railroad stations and our factories seemed to close relentlessly around us. Then came film and exploded this prison-world with the dynamite of the split second, so that now we can set off calmly on journeys of adventure among its far-flung debris' (W. Benjamin, 'The Work of Art in the Age of Its Technological Reproducibility: Third Version', *op. cit.*, p.265). The earlier translation famously rendered the last part of the citation as 'in the midst of its far-flung ruins and debris, we calmly and adventurously go traveling' (W. Benjamin, 'The Work of Art in the Age of Mechanical Reproduction', *Illuminations* (trans. Harry Zohn), New York: Schocken Books, 1969, p.236). 'Entirely new structural formations' is taken from the *Illuminations* translation; the revised translation renders the phrase as 'entirely new structures of matter'.

76 W. Benjamin, 'The Work of Art in the Age of Its Technological Reproducibility: Third Version', *op. cit.*, p.265 (emphasis added). This dynamic formed the contemporary dialectical counterpart to the outmoded dream images of

capital, he firmly defended the 'revolutionary primacy of the silent film'. At its emergence, he maintained, a new technology incites a mixture of 'reactions that [are] hard to control and hence politically dangerous' to instituted powers.[78] While such reactions only become progressive or reactionary in the artistic and sociological assemblages that they form, it is their initial, ambiguous duality that the anticipatory artist must be given to understand.[79] 'The artist,' as Gilles Deleuze summarised, glossing Benjamin by means of Hans-Jürgen Syberberg, 'is always in the situation of saying simultaneously: I claim new methods, and I am afraid that the new methods may invalidate all will to art, or make it into a business, a pornography, a Hitlerism ... '[80]

Responding to contemporary economic and sociological developments, the mid-60s saw the earlier, spectacular regime of perception that had emerged with the sound film giving way to new forms of electronic information. It was at this historical turning point that Warhol's Exploding Plastic Inevitable emerged to contest ideological naturalisations of the type posed by McLuhan and the Eameses.[81] Forming a contradictory, experimental space, the EPI trafficked in emergent technological forces still lingering on the threshold before their complete subsumption within the market.[82] As opposed to naturalisation, the EPI produced a dislocating, environmental montage where different media interfered and competed with one another, accelerating their distracting, shock-like effects to produce the three-dimensional, multimedia equivalent of a *moiré*. Such was described by reviewer Larry McCombs, who noted the manner in which: 'The lights have become a dim blue flicker, but a flicker that goes faster and slower and pauses now and then, just as your eyes get used to each kind of flicker.' 'Too much happening', he continued:

> it doesn't go together. But sometimes it does — suddenly the beat of the music, the movements of the various films, the pose of the dancers, blend into something meaningful, but before your mind can grab it, it's become

the nineteenth-century arcades, which, in the midst of a commercial space, reveal (as their unconscious) the immense field of constructive possibilities of iron and steel building technologies.

77 In Ronald Taylor (ed.), *Aesthetics and Politics*, London: Verso, 1980, p.123. See Giorgio Agamben's discussion of parts of this correspondence, in 'The Prince and the Frog', *Infancy and History: Essays on the Destruction of Experience* (trans. Liz Heron), London: Verso, 1993, pp.107–24.

78 R. Taylor (ed.), *Aesthetics and Politics*, *op. cit.*, p.140.

79 I am thinking here of Benjamin's famous idea of ambiguity as 'the manifest imaging of dialectic, the law of dialectics at a standstill' (*The Arcades Project*, *op. cit.*, p.10). In early film this law was to be found in the coexistence of a certain level of critique or negation, brought on by the shock effect produced by cinematic technology, and a consumability — as 'something stirring, useful, ultimately heartening' by which this effect was 'brought closer' to the masses who did not thereby reject it as they would more distant forms of high art. See *The Arcades Project*, *op. cit.*, p.395; and 'The Work of Art in the Age of Its Technological Reproducibility: Third Version', *op. cit.*, p.264. It was the very volatility of this moment of combined reception that Benjamin saw as a necessary, although not sufficient, condition for the audiences' awakening to their lived situation and that called for a political channelling in one direction or another.

80 Gilles Deleuze, *Cinema 2: The Time-Image* (trans. Hugh Tomlinson and Robert Galeta), Minneapolis: University of Minnesota Press, 1989, p.266 (ellipses in original). The context of Deleuze's remark is both a commentary on Benjamin and a meditation on the possibilities of a resistant art in the age of television.

81 And others, such as spiritualism or an idea of the EPI's merely illustrating an LSD trip. For their part, the members of the EPI consistently rejected both interpretations. See comments in Barrie Hale, 'The Warhol Happening', *The Telegram* (Toronto), 14 November 1966, p.44; and Judy Altman, 'Warhol "Happening": It's Like a Noisy Bomb', *Philadelphia Daily News*, 12 December 1966, p.4.

82 Benjamin comments on this 'threshold' in *The Arcades Project*, *op. cit.*, p.898.

random and confusing again. Your head tries to sort something out, make sense of something. The noise is getting to you. You want to scream, or throw yourself about with the dancers, something, anything![83]

The EPI, as Wayne McGuire noted, rejected the many 'false resolutions' of the time, refusing both McLuhan's rhetoric of retribalisation and the Eameses' attempted naturalisation onto images of nuclear families and morning toast. Instead, Warhol's multimedia presentation linked contemporary, capital-driven, technological dislocations with more volatile forms of social and libidinal transformations, signalled in part by the 'decadent' contents of both his films and the lyrics of the Velvet Underground.[84] This was indeed 'a demon light electric', an ambiguous and threatening form of deterritorialisation, played out to the volume, feedback, length and shifting tempos of a music that failed (in extended bouts of dissonant improvisation) to cohere comfortably within the norms of popular spectacle. Within this environment, however, identifications were not disarticulated entirely into some kind of postmodern flux; the EPI was not simply a bricolage of existing signifiers, practices and codes.[85] Rather, it formed a multiplicitous situation or 'image' in which the possibilities of subjective transformation were opened to forms of political appropriation. Not primarily by the proletarian mass or the official, and often essentialist, counterculture, but by delinquents, drag queens, addicts and hustlers: a 'group', as Kathy Acker observed about the Factory, 'who at that time no decent person, not even a hippy, would recognise as being human'. It was a group, however, that would later emerge within punk and a politicised gay subculture.[86]

In 1967, therefore, as artists such as Robert Smithson, Dan Graham and Mel Bochner were exploring post-industrial suburban landscapes and

83 Larry McCombs, 'Chicago Happenings', *Boston Broadside*, July 1966, in scrapbook vol.2 small, p.7, Warhol Archives.

84 On the relationship of capitalist dislocations to the emergence of liberationist struggles, see Ernesto Laclau and Chantal Mouffe, *Hegemony and Socialist Strategy: Towards a Radical Democratic Politics*, London: Verso, 1985, especially pp.160–61; and Ernesto Laclau, 'New Reflections on the Revolution of Our Time', *New Reflections on the Revolution of Our Time*, London: Verso, 1990, pp.3–85.

85 Thus, although it intersects with it, the EPI is not fully assimilable to the critique of late capitalist culture developed by Fredric Jameson. Nor is it adequately characterised from a cultural studies approach like that of Dick Hebdige, which seeks a subversiveness within the displacement of existing codes via certain rituals of consumption. See Dick Hebdige, *Subculture: The Meaning of Style*, London: Routledge, 1979, especially p.102ff. Warhol's work with the EPI is ultimately more productive (not least through its augmentation of technological dislocations) than either of these models would seem to allow. On issues of subcultural resistance in relation to modern art, see Thomas Crow's indispensable 'Modernism and Mass Culture in the Visual Arts', in *Modern Art in the Common Culture*, New Haven: Yale University Press, 1996, pp.3–37. Crow's article — which is more Adornan in nature, and thus distinct from the argument about subcultural resistance developed here — references at the beginning the 'Happenings' of Warhol, among others.

86 Kathy Acker's quote is found in 'Blue Valentine', in M. O'Pray (ed.), *Andy Warhol: Film Factory*, *op. cit.*, p.65. See also Peter Wollen's comments at the end of 'Raiding the Icebox', in *ibid.*, pp.25–26. Jon Savage has also noted the role played by the image of the Velvet Underground and Warhol's Factory for the development of British punk in 'The New Hippies', in Ian Burch (ed.), *The Book with No Name*, London: Omnibus, 1981, p.40, cited in Simon Frith and Stuart Home, *Art into Pop*, London: Methuen, 1987, p.131.

87 Jonathan Crary points to the relation of the suburban 'non-sites' investigated by Smithson and 'what might be called the "tele-visual" city' of the new electronic media in 'J.G. Ballard and the Promiscuity of Forms', *Zone* 1/2, 1986: pp.159–65. Works such as Mel Bochner's *Alfaville, Godard's Apocalypse* (1968; which critiques Godard's humanism on the basis of Warhol, Burroughs and Roger Corman) and, later, Dan Graham's *Rock My Religion* (1982–84; which allegorises this moment of passage from art to popular music) take up issues raised by the EPI and, I would contend, form part of its extended artistic reception.

88 'And all this time you probably thought the Velvet Underground was talking about drugs, homosexuality and sadomasochism. Look a bit closer' (W. McGuire, 'The Boston Sound', *op. cit.*, p.45).

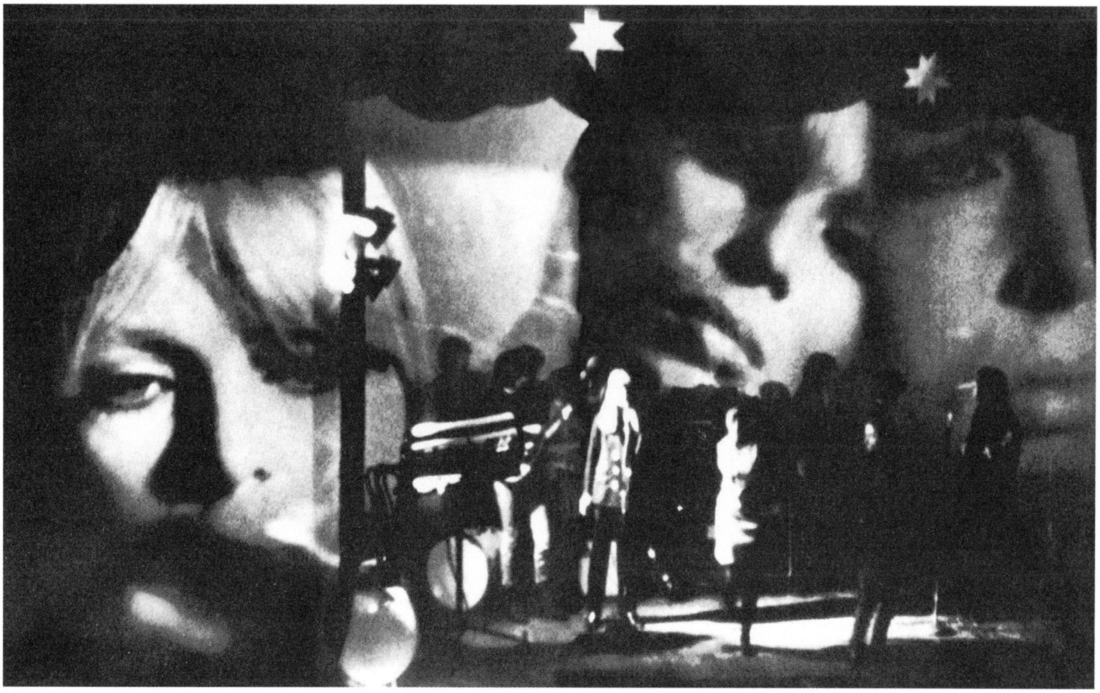

The Exploding Plastic Inevitable, c.1966. Photo © 2008 Steve Schapiro

the serialised pages of magazines, Warhol was not simply touring the country with a rock band but was occupying the newly emerging spaces of information.[87] Rather than merely capitalising on them, however, the Exploding Plastic Inevitable acted to articulate these zones within the taut ambiguities of a contemporary dream image, one that would be seized upon by emergent forces of subcultural resistance. Today, at the outset of the twenty-first century, Warhol's formerly futuristic 'brutal assemblage' has no doubt itself become outmoded. Yet in its time the EPI mobilised the conflictual, deterritorialised forces of electronic media toward the explosion of a newly developing, post-institutional prison-world ... amongst the far-flung debris of which some, at least, would find it possible — less calmly, perhaps, but no less adventurously — to go travelling.[88]

THE MUSEUM OF ATTRACTIONS: MARCEL BROODTHAERS AND THE *SECTION CINÉMA*

Eric de Bruyn

The thought is almost as old as the medium itself: cinema resembles a kind of writing. With sardonic relish, Marcel Broodthaers would often visit this analogy during his short-lived career. In a manuscript called *Projet pour un texte*, for instance, we find the following comment: 'And here I am cruelly torn between something immobile that has already been written and the comic movement that animates 24 images per second.'[1] The tragicomic effect of such an idea is registered in an eponymous film of 1969. Broodthaers is filmed in his garden while absorbed in the process of writing a text. However, the text is never completed because the rain that constantly pours down on him washes the ink off the page.

For Broodthaers, cinema functioned as a curious device of simultaneous inscription and erasure — an invention of a technological age that was both stillborn and still remained to be born. He asks us to consider cinema as a project, therefore, and not as a projection. 'At the origin of my intentions there was this idea of cinema that dispenses with the notion of movement', the artist wrote in 1967.[2] This resistance to the directional force of film was geared to his refusal of a cinema of narrative absorption. The diegetic universe of classical cinema, with its projective unity of word and image, offers the spectator a vision of spatial totality. Broodthaers always eyed such a perceptual 'conquest of space' with great suspicion. The spatialised logic of classical cinema, after all, mimics the universal structure of the commodity — a structure that Broodthaers advises underpins the cultural field as a whole: 'If we are concerned with reification, then Art is a particular representation of the phenomenon — a form of tautology.'[3]

Broodthaers frequently observed how a process of instrumentalisation has come to pervade the cultural sphere. In 1967 he could still propose,

1 As cited in Jean-Christophe Royoux, 'The Cinematographic Model in the Work of Marcel Broodthaers', in *Marcel Broodthaers: Cinéma*, Barcelona: Fundació Antoni Tàpies, 1997, p.305. 'Projet pour un texte' dates from 1969 or 1970. A facsimile of the text is printed in the Barcelona catalogue on pp.184–85. Royoux's essay provides an extensive, if poetic, reading of Broodthaers's text.

2 Marcel Broodthaers, 'Le D est plus grand que le T', in *Marcel Broodthaers: Cinéma*, *op. cit.*, p.319.

3 Without doubt Benjamin Buchloh has done most to develop this basic theme in Marcel Broodthaers's work. See, for instance, his 'Marcel Broodthaers: Allegories of the Avant-Garde', *Artforum*, vol.18 no.9, May 1980, pp.52–59; 'Open Letter, Industrial Poems', *October*, no.42, Fall 1987, pp.67–100; and 'Contemplating Publicity: Marcel Broodthaers' Section Publicité', in *Musée d'Art Moderne, Département des Aigles, Section Publicité*, New York: Marian Goodman Gallery, 1995, pp.87–99.

4 M. Broodthaers, 'Le D est plus grand que le T', *op. cit.*, p.319.

5 M. Broodthaers, 'Projet pour un texte', in *Marcel Broodthaers: Cinéma*, *op. cit.*, pp.184–85.

6 The text becomes rather ambivalent at this point: 'Aussi dans certains aspects du conceptual Art, souvent le film est un intermédiare banal où l'idée joue le rôle principal du sujet. Mais le sujet

partially in jest, that we consider 'film stock as a place for storing ideas — a rather special kind of can'.[4] But by 1969 he was to lament the progressive reduction of film to the transmission of an idea: 'Thus in certain kinds of conceptual art, the film is often a banal intermediary in which the idea plays the main role of subject.'[5] Art thus assumes the status of publicity. Unless, that is, the acknowledgement of art's current status as a documentary of received ideas might form a method to regain critical ground.[6]

Hence Broodthaers's cinema was not simply one of arrested motion; it remained wrapped in the contradiction between a static image and a moving image. His cinema presents a text that is in the process of being written and has already been written — a text that in animating the present is immediately inscribed as past. The velocity of such a cinematic writing, it appears, can never escape the gravitational force of historicity. However, in order to appreciate the curious temporality of this cinematographic method, we will need to draw the contours of its space of public performance.

I propose to address this task in relation to a specific theatre of film exhibition that was designed by Broodthaers. I am referring to the *Section Cinéma* that forms the seventh installment of his well-known museum fiction called the *Musée d'art Moderne, Département des Aigles* — a project, which ran for four years, from 1968 to 1972, and saw twelve different editions before being dissolved at 'documenta 5'. The *Section Cinéma* was located in a cellar at Burgplatz 12 in Düsseldorf, from January 1971 to October 1972.[7] In a figurative sense, this subterranean space functioned as both a foundational and archaeological site, which continuously wavered between a state of construction and dismantlement. In a more literal sense, the *Section Cinéma* fulfilled the combined function of storage facility, meeting place, production studio, film theatre and museum space.

Allow me to enter the first piece of evidence. Here is the masked artist enveloped in a swirl of smoke while he holds up a copy of a book for all to see. The tome is titled *L'Invention du cinéma (1832–1897)*, and it forms the first volume of George Sadoul's classic *Histoire générale du cinema*, published in 1948. This book finds its place as 'fig.1' in the cinema section of the museum. It is important to note the connection that this masked self-portrait makes between cinema, or rather early cinema, and an enunciative mode of direct address.[8] In this fashion, the silent gesture of the artist introduces a model of performativity that shall recur throughout the following discussion.

n'est-il pas réduit par cette platitude du style de transmission, sinon absorbé et rejeté dans un documentaire des idées reçues, parfois original?'

7 The *Section Cinéma* was preceded by the *Cinéma Modèle*, which opened on 15 November 1970, at the same location. For further details of this history, see *Marcel Broodthaers: Cinéma*, *op. cit.*

8 The museum series was succeeded by a series of *décors*, which superimposed the models of the retrospective exhibition and the installation. While the critical projects of the museum and the décors should not be confused with each other, the *Section Cinéma* does prefigure the later *Décor: A Conquest by Marcel Broodthaers* of 1975, which treated the gallery as a stage set replete with klieg lights and film props. For more on this subject see my 'On the Museum as Film Décor: Marcel Broodthaers and *La Bataille de Waterloo*', *Trans*, no.8, 2000, pp.76–91.

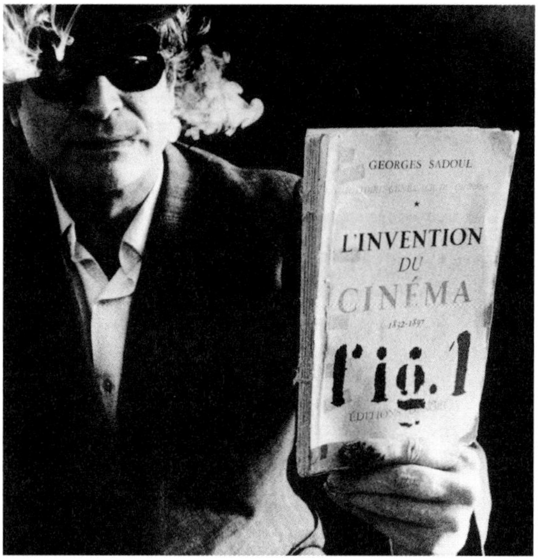

At this point, I can imagine two possible objections to my angle of approach. The first is of a factual nature. Sadoul's narrative in *L'Invention du cinéma* ends in 1897 with the birth of cinema proper, and the book is therefore not concerned with the history of early or primitive cinema. However, I will maintain that the true topic of Broodthaers's cinema is formed by the non-synchronous relation between the two founding moments of cinema's technical invention and its industrial-commercial (re-)invention. I shall demonstrate how the historical figure of early cinema functioned for the artist as a form of counter-memory to the progressive homogenisation of the public sphere under the 'vigilant eyes of the industrial mamas and papas'.[9]

The second objection might well concern my use of the term performativity. This linguistic category has gained widespread currency in recent discussions of contemporary art and, in particular, in the field of performance studies. For our purpose, however, we need not engage the full historical and theoretical range of this complex debate. It shall suffice at present to define the performative as a statement that carries no significance beyond its actual time and place of utterance. The performative, in other words, designates a mode of direct address that highlights its own conditions of enunciation. A performative utterance exhibits its own act of speech, as it were, and is therefore opposed to the usual suppression of the author's voice in historical narration. On the other hand, by exposing the contingency of its position of speech, the performative statement is denied any transcendent authority. This fact was once celebrated during the 1960s as the death of the Author, but it remains to be seen whether Broodthaers paid more than lip service to such a revolutionary liberation of language.

To return to the film, the hand of the masked artist thrusts the book forward into our view. Broodthaers, we might say, is made present through this gesture, but he does not assume an affirmative presence in the process. Nothing is declared except the act itself, or, at the very least, the exact content of this act remains undetermined. The book-object appears to be offered as evidence in the court of history, yet no final judgment is passed. What this proposition ultimately 'figures' is a pure gesture of citation. The speech act is exhibited as 'fig.1': one figure selected from a possible range of ready-made statements. However, 'fig.1' does not provide the key to break the code. Broodthaers does not invite us to engage in a hermeneutic activity of source interpretation. 'Fig.1' offers no stable referent — e.g. the historical thesis or signified of Sadoul — but becomes mobilised by Broodthaers's gesture as an empty sign within a discursive network of exchange. In sum, the gesture might

Marcel Broodthaers holding Georges Sadoul's *L'Invention du Cinema*, 1971. Photo © 2008 Joaquim Romero Frias

be called strategic, although we have not established the exact operative terrain of this tactic.

The writer has only the power 'to mix writings, to counter the ones with the others, in such a way as never to rest on any one of them'.[10] As Roland Barthes insisted, the performative act is fundamentally a writerly act. The writer's hand performs a pure gesture of inscription that is divorced of any voice. Indeed, on closer inspection, we see that Broodthaers's index finger is blackened as if stained by the ink of a pen. *As if*, but not in truth, because Broodthaers has clearly altered the image after the fact. Once more we are reminded of the performative nature of writing that 'can only imitate a gesture that is always anterior, never original', and a gesture, moreover, that we experience as being simultaneously comic and tragic in kind.[11]

Broodthaers's cinema certainly resembles the intertextual nature of an *écriture* as theorised by Barthes. His films range across the genres of narrative, documentary and experimental film without, finally, fitting into any single category, and individual films are often submitted to a process of recombination and recycling. Yet, Barthes's model of performativity can be taken only so far in the artist's case. As we shall see, the artist does not embrace the more utopian aspect of an *écriture* that knows no other time than that of enunciation, where every text is eternally written here and now. The theatrical gesture of Broodthaers is, on the contrary, not cut off from the past, but feigns a return to what might be called the primal scene of cinema. This historical dimension of Broodthaers's cinema should never be lost from sight.

If we now widen our frame of vision, we can see arranged against a white-washed wall a set of twelve objects, among which are a pipe, a smoke bomb, a clock, a calendar, a mirror, a winder and a mask such as the one worn by Broodthaers in the photograph. An inscription, such as 'fig.1', 'fig.2', 'fig.12', etc., accompanies each of these objects. A chest contains a second set of twelve objects, including Sadoul's book. And, finally, against an adjacent wall stands a mock piano beneath a framed sign that carries the bilingual title of this artifice — namely 'Musée-Museum'.

The majority of these objects starred as props in Broodthaers's previous films, such as the series of short silent movies based upon René Magritte's painting *Ceci n'est pas une pipe*. The first in the series was *La Pipe (Magritte)* of 1969. The film was shot with a stationary camera that registered all the possible combinations of an empty white wall, a pipe, a clock and billowing smoke. To this original footage, Broodthaers later added the engraved captions 'Figure I', 'Figure II' or 'Figures', according to a now familiar system.

9 Programme note by Marcel Broodthaers for a screening of *Un film de Charles Baudelaire* in 1974 at the Studio Arenberg, Brussels; see *Marcel Broodthaers: Cinéma*, *op. cit.*, p.121. I have discussed the Baudelaire film in 'Marcel Broodthaers: *Cinéma Modèle*', *Texte zur Kunst*, vol.8 no.29, March 1998, pp.33–49.

10 Roland Barthes, 'The Death of the Author', (trans. Stephen Heath), *Image-Music-Text*, New York: Hill and Wang, 1977, p.146.

11 Barthes's example is that of Flaubert's Bouvard and Pécuchet, whom he describes as 'those eternal copyists, at once sublime and comic and whose profound ridiculousness indicates precisely the truth of writing'. See R. Barthes, 'The Death of the Author', *op. cit.*, p.145.

Facing page:
Marcel Broodthaers, frames from *Ceci ne serait pas une pipe (Un Film de Musée d'Art Moderne)*, 1969–71

On the level of the individual film, i.e. *La Pipe*, Broodthaers obsessively, if not perversely, mimics a capitalist logic of serial reproduction — similar images are repeated over and over again until all difference blurs into the identical. The only indication of a possible alternation in meaning from one sequence to the next is given by the captions that are appended to the image of the recurrent objects. The captions substitute for the lived experience of the object, operating in a similar way to the fashion slogans of publicity, but without offering the same comforting illusion of content. The instrumental language of advertising that once was cited by Magritte at one remove has now swallowed his painting whole, or so it seems. 'Matter has gone up in smoke,' Broodthaers declared in 1971, and 'the object is spoken, written or filmed language'.[12] Sometimes the pipe is, in fact, obscured by the rising smoke, but in less literal terms the material object can be said to recede behind the captioned image of a phantom pipe. The pipe, as Broodthaers says, is represented as filmed language. However, things do not end here.

One might conjecture that the materiality of the static pipe is still registered by the spectator, albeit indirectly in the discontinuous stammer of the filmstrip with its many abrupt cuts. Furthermore, we might ask, what *is* the intrinsic role of this pipe? In watching the film, we appear to attend the rushes of an improbable film — a film without intrinsic organisation or direction. In addition to this internal dispersion of figures, Broodthaers set an external process of multiplication in motion. The footage of *La Pipe* was itself submitted to an incessant operation of recombination that produced numerous variants, such as *Ceci ne serait pas une pipe* or *La Pipe (Gestalt, Abbildung, Figur, Bild)*. This method of serialisation was pushed to the point that it becomes impossible to always determine what constitutes a unique or finished work.

The frontality of the image in *La Pipe*, which is intermittently underscored by the engraved captions, is typical of Broodthaers's early films. But despite this inscription of a silent voice, the speaker himself remains absent. Indeed, whose speech is figured here? What mode of communication is being performed? In the catalogue to the 1972 *Section des Figures* of Broodthaers's museum, we encounter the following instruction: 'Read the text of Michel Foucault's *This is not a pipe*.' Let us, for the moment, take this advice of Broodthaers to heart. Following the artist's lead, we must come to the conclusion that Broodthaers's strange method of filming by numbers strives to linger on the threshold of symbolic speech. The object is given a figurative assignment within a language system, which, however, remains without a definite, spatial organisation. Objects show up, as it were, without any subject being there to claim them, to delegate them to their proper place.

12 Marcel Broodthaers, 'La Figure O', *Kurt Schwitters*, Düsseldorf: Städtische Kunsthalle, 1971, p.25.
13 Michel Foucault, *This Is Not a Pipe* (trans. James Harkness), Berkeley: University of California Press, 1983, p.37.
14 Marcel Broodthaers, 'Gare au defi! Pop art, Jim Dine, and the Influence of René Magritte' (1963, trans. Paul Schmidt), *October*, no.42, Fall 1987, p.34.
15 *Ibid.*
16 M. Foucault, *This Is Not a Pipe*, *op. cit.*, p.30.

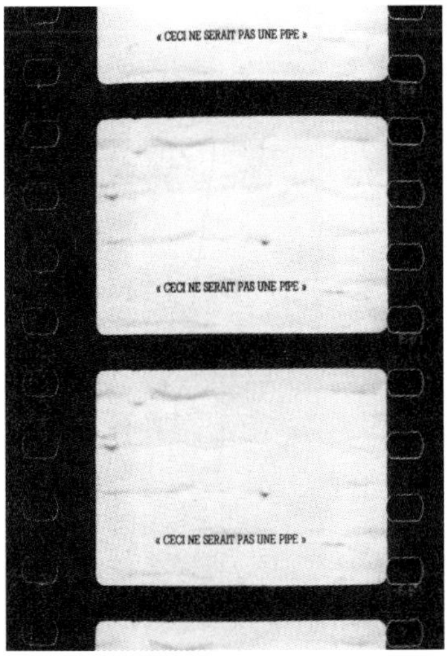

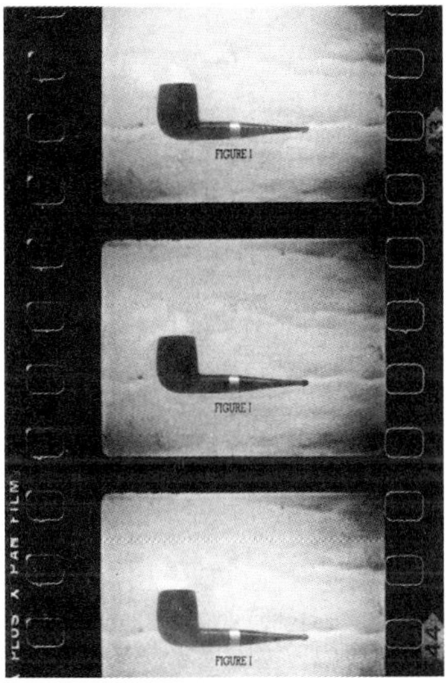

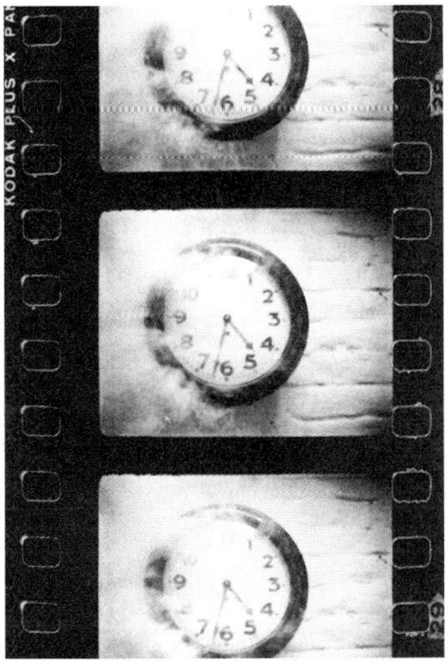

Broodthaers's figures are thus activated as 'burrowing words', which, as Foucault claims, dig their treacherous tunnels beneath the seemingly smooth surface of Magritte's pictures. As the former argued, the Belgian painter 'secretly mines a space he seems to maintain in the old arrangement'.[13] And his choice of words is remarkably close to that of Broodthaers, who once remarked that 'Magritte aimed at the development of a poetic language to undermine that upon which we depend'.[14] Yet the affirmative realm of language that was targeted by Broodthaers was not that of everyday speech, as it was for Magritte. Broodthaers was more concerned with the pervasive babble of publicity that had come to saturate all spheres of life in late capitalism. 'Is there any other explanation,' he asks, 'than the context of a world devoted to advertisements, overproduction and horoscopes?'[15] Magritte, he confesses, was to disagree with him, and considered the younger artist too much of a sociologist.

Where Broodthaers and Magritte do agree, however, is in showing up the false authority of a mode of affirmative speech that was personified in Foucault's text by the figure of the teacher. To paraphrase the latter, the teacher sets out to show how everything is solidly anchored within a pedagogic space. Hence a film 'shows' an image that 'shows' the form of a pipe; a caption inscribed by the zealous instructor 'shows' that the pipe is really what is meant. Yet scarcely has he stated, 'This is a pipe', before he must correct himself and stutter, 'This is not a pipe, but an image of a pipe', 'This is not a pipe but a figure saying this is not a pipe', etc., etc.[16] The baffled master must then lower his extended pointer and turn towards the class in order to face the uproarious students.

The story now takes a quite familiar turn. The figure of the simulacrum was the counter-measure that Post-Structuralism adopted to destroy the false hegemony of the pedagogical or masterful discourse of Foucault's instructor. Not the figure of resemblance, that is, which only serves the needs of representation, but similitude as structured by a logic of pure repetition. The similar provides an opening onto a series of differences, of contiguities and displacements; that is, a series without closure. In short, the utopian imagination is refigured as an endless play of signs, a text that is eternally written here and now. But, as always, the utopian imagination remains nourished by its own historical context. Famously, Foucault's essay ended on the wistful note: 'A day will come when, by means of similitude relayed indefinitely along the length of a series, the image itself, along with the name it bears, will lose its identity. Campbell, Campbell, Campbell, Campbell.'[17]

Can this simulacral series provide an alternative to the dissemblance of modern art? Can the simulacrum form an antidote to that phantasm, which, as Broodthaers has observed, 'flickers along the peripheries of our history like a shadow play'?[18] Is the fiction of art's autonomy simply to be dissolved in the here and now of similitude? Surely such a conclusion does not rhyme with the enunciative condition of Broodthaers's cinema, which, as I have stated before, is doubly inscribed within both the present and the past.

At first sight, the *Section Cinéma* appears to support exactly such a reading. It appears to insist on the simulacral character of the displayed objects. As the artist stated in an interview, the submission of these objects to an identical numbering system undoes their proper identity. They become, that is, 'interchangeable elements on the stage of a theatre'; and, as a result, 'their destiny is ruined'.[19] However, the ensemble of objects bears a double assignment. First of all, there exist two sets of objects. One is scattered across the architectural space, including a chair and a ceiling lamp. The other is contained within a coffer, like the assortment of toys in a child's play chest. Furthermore, the numerical series has received a double articulation. Broodthaers offers not only the alternative of 'fig.1' versus 'fig.2', but also the possibility of their symbolical combination, as in the 'fig.1 & 2' of the film winder or the 'fig.12' of the clock. In other words, the purely equivalent status of these numbered ready-mades does not rule out their assimilation within a specific ideological or narrative order of language. According to the artist the objects are susceptible to assuming a 'moral' role within the spatial continuum of any diegetic universe whether projected by the social apparatus of the museum or the cinema. 'If we are to believe what the inscription says,' Broodthaers considers, 'then the object takes on an illustrative character referring to a kind of novel about society.'[20]

However, this moral figure does not spell the end of our series. Despite the vacillation of these objects between the space of similitude and that of representation, between a differential and a moral value, Broodthaers claims that a further value remains in evidence. The objects retain an obstinate presence that resists their complete sublation within either the spatialised domain of affirmative speech or the dematerialised realm of the simulacral. Progress, movement, all this comic animation, momentarily falters when confronted with the materiality of an 'already written' trace; with, that is, a 'readable texture' of wood, glass, metal and fabric. This texture,

17 *Ibid.*, p.54.
18 Marcel Broodthaers, 'To be *bien pensant* ... or not to be. To be blind' (1975, trans. Paul Schmidt), *October*, no.42, Fall 1987, p.35.
19 Marcel Broodthaers, after an interview with Irmeline Lebeer, 'Ten Thousand Francs Reward' (1974, trans. Paul Schmidt), *October*, no.42, Fall 1987, p.43.
20 *Ibid.*
21 *Ibid.*
22 M. Foucault, *This Is Not a Pipe*, *op. cit.*, p.34.
23 M. Broodthaers, 'To be *bien pensant* ... or not to be. To be blind', *op. cit.*

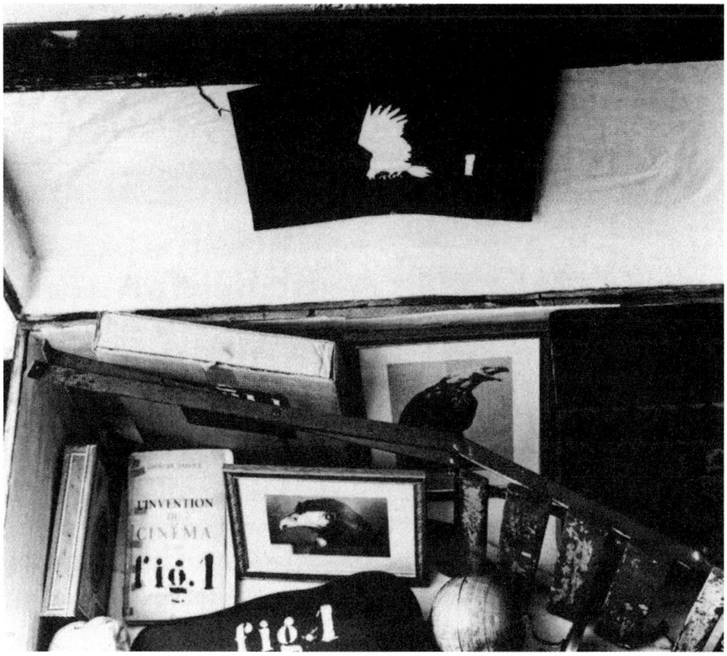

Marcel Broodthaers, detail from *Section Cinéma*, 1971. Photo © 2008 Maria Gilissen

Broodthaers maintains, avoids the levelling process of technological reproduction. 'I would never have obtained this kind of complexity,' he concludes, 'with technological objects, whose singleness condemns the mind to monomania: minimal art, robot, computer.'[21] But, even now, the series is not complete.

At the opening of the *Section Cinéma*, Broodthaers announced that he would withdraw the displayed objects and place them on sale. The ensemble of objects, he contended, could not achieve a permanent place in a museum that leads, after all, to a fictional existence. After being sold to the Mönchengladbach Museum, the only clues referring to the once present objects were the painted abbreviations 'fig.' on the wall, to which a further word was added: 'silence'. In the absence of any enunciative markers the expressive function of this noun seems to oscillate between the imperative — 'Be silent!' — and the descriptive — 'Here reigns silence.' Stencilled onto the wall, the word 'silence' wavers between a performative and an affirmative mode of speech.

Let me suggest how we might locate the historical significance of this simple, yet enigmatic noun 'silence' by starting one last time with Foucault. 'All that is needed,' he writes, is that 'a figure resemble an object ... and that alone is enough for there to slip into the pure play of the painting a statement — obvious, banal, repeated a thousand times yet almost silent. (It is like an infinite murmur — haunting, enclosing the silence of the figures, investing it, mastering it, extricating the silence from itself and finally reversing it within the domain of things that can be named.)'[22] Modernism, liked the hushed space of the museum itself, was a silent art, but could nonetheless not stop the reifying process of naming to which Foucault alludes. Contemporary art, as Broodthaers would counter, has reversed the tactic of modernism. It is no longer silent but is overrun by a rhetoric that transforms it into a mere advertisement for a fashionable theory. All that commentaries on art will reflect, therefore, are the results of a shift in economy. Which leads the artist to the sombre conclusion that it is doubtful whether such commentaries can be considered political.[23]

Yet, we might also take the stencilled word 'silence' in its most obvious sense — namely, as a reference to the sound stage of cinema, and, by extension, to the technological history of cinema itself. That is, not only as a reference to the off-screen silence that reigns in narrative cinema, but also to the very absence of sound in silent movies. Indeed, language was only to slowly penetrate the distinctly non-narrative realm of silent movies, and with this permeation of early film by narration came a homogenisation of its space concurrent with the rise of the major commercial studios.

This diversity at the beginning of cinema did not just concern a differential specificity of the medium, as Rosalind Krauss has recently suggested. She has noted the correspondence between the look of early film and that of Broodthaers's films with their 'uneven exposures spliced together and their flickering gait'.[24] However, this comparison can be taken a step further. The heterogeneity of early cinema on the formal level was mirrored in the composite character of its public sphere — a claim that, I suggest, holds for Broodthaers's cinema as well. The performative gesture of Broodthaers, therefore, extends across the spectacular backdrop of a mediatised society and it is *there*, against the homogenised background of publicity, that we can begin to read its most critical significance.

This thesis will have to await future development, but not without a brief indication of how one might proceed. To this purpose, Tom Gunning's celebrated notion of a 'cinema of attractions' will prove helpful.[25] The cinema of attractions refers to a pre-classical period of film that lasted until circa 1907. Gunning opposes this phrase to the more common one of primitive film since he argues that early film established a specific mode of spectatorship that is repressed, and not simply superseded, by the narrative film genre of Hollywood. He contrasts, for instance, the frequent use of a mode of direct address in early cinema to the absorptive structure of classical cinema. 'Theatrical display,' in Gunning's summary of early film experience, 'dominates over narrative absorption, emphasising the direct stimulation of shock or surprise at the expense of unfolding a story or creating a diegetic universe.'[26] Thus early cinema offered a popular attraction in the tradition of vaudeville or burlesque — a filmic event that was orchestrated by the live presence of a cinema showman.

It has often been stated that Broodthaers assumed the outmoded roles of the collector and amateur. To these types we might add the historical figure of the cinema showman. The function of this performer was to adapt the film programme to the changing circumstances of architectural setting and social events and to elicit the active engagement of the audience. Just as the exhibition practice of Broodthaers was characterised by its endless reshuffling of content, its shifting relation to the institutional context and its theatrical

24 Rosalind Krauss, *'A Voyage on the North Sea': Art in the Age of the Post-Medium Condition*, London: Thames & Hudson, 1999, p.43.

25 Tom Gunning, 'The Cinema of Attractions: Early Film, Its Spectator and the Avant-Garde', *Early Cinema: Space Frame Narrative* (ed. Thomas Elsaesser), London: British Film Institute, 1990, pp.58–59. The following discussion also draws on Miriam Hansen, 'Early Cinema, Late Cinema: Transformations of the Public Sphere', *Viewing Positions: Ways of Seeing Film* (ed. Linda Williams), New Brunswick: Rutgers University Press, 1994, pp.134–52.

26 T. Gunning, 'The Cinema of Attractions: Early Film, Its Spectator and the Avant-Garde', *op. cit.*, p.59.

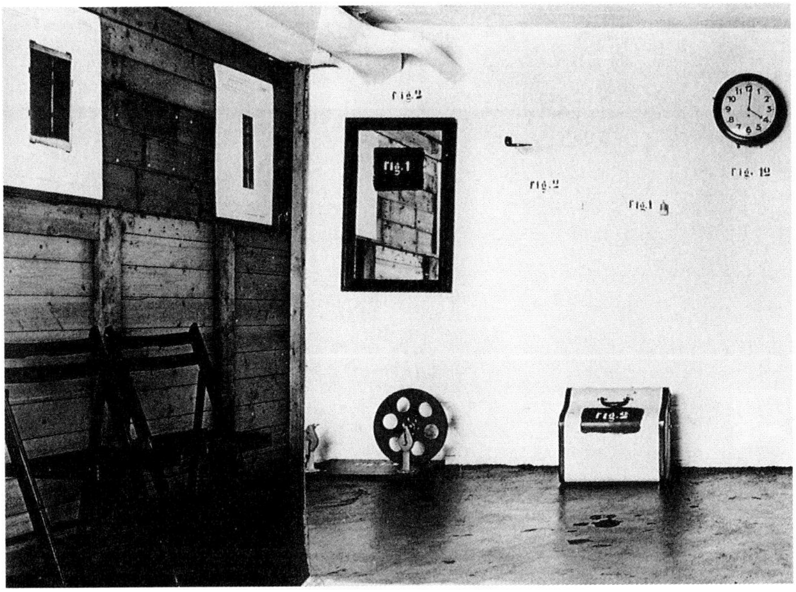

mode of presentation, the *Section Cinéma* can be described as a *mise-en-scène* of the composite public sphere of early cinema. It re-enacted the primal conflict between a performative and reproductive mode of cinema that pre-dated the final rise of the studio system and its industrial organisation of the public sphere. This *mise-en-scène*, however, functioned only as a theatre of memory, for it could not reverse the erosion of social experience already underway.

To back up my claim, I might end by referring to the film programme that Broodthaers screened in the *Section Cinéma*. This programme achieved a deliberate alternation and confusion between different cinematic genres. It begins with a quasi-documentary about the founding of the Musée d'Art Moderne called *Une discussion inaugurale* (1968) that follows a meandering trajectory with no conclusion. Secondly, a combined travelogue and historical fiction called *Un Voyage à Waterloo (Napoléon 1769–1969)*, starring Broodthaers sporting a false nose. Thirdly, a group of found films consisting of a heterogeneous set of newsreel and commercial fragments that were edited together by Broodthaers, and a compilation of film excerpts called 'Charlie als Filmstar' that was put together by the German film rental company Globus. The films were projected by the artist onto a white screen on which the abbreviations 'fig.12', 'fig.2', 'fig.1', 'fig.A' had been stencilled.

What Broodthaers's cinematic project demonstrates, in sum, is a process of continuous disorganisation. Yet, by these very means, *Section Cinéma* provides a faint glimmer of an alternative public sphere. It indicates a social horizon of experience that can only enter representation in a fragmented form. *Section Cinéma* thus commemorates the unrealised, utopian potential of modern technology. A potential, furthermore, that is seized only in the fleeting moment of an arrested image. I have attempted to show where this interpretation of Broodthaers's project overlaps with arguments that have been advanced elsewhere. However, in the face of current events I am led to conceive of Broodthaers's project in the following, more particular fashion. If the gesture enacted by *Section Cinéma* can be thought to have a redemptive potential then this can be found in the countering of a museum of attractions by the imminent reality of the museum as spectacle.

Marcel Broodthaers, *Section Cinéma*, 1971. Interior view of the inner room. Photo © 2008 Joaquim Romero Frías

PAUL SHARITS AND THE ACTIVE SPECTATOR

Federico Windhausen

In 1976, during the most productive decade of Paul Sharits's career, film critic Fred Camper reviewed a pair of his single-screen films for *Soho Weekly News*. Inserted between Camper's formal analysis of the first film, *Word Movie* (Fluxfilm no.29, 1966), and the second, *Color Sound Frames* (1974), is a provocative (and admirably straightforward) paragraph that articulates the response of a critic challenged by new work in film:

> Sharits's films do offer much to the eye; watching them requires a very active viewer; their rapidity energises one's perception. But finally, for me, they do not have the internal mysteries of structure, the strange disparities of rhythms, the surprising and unexplainable imagery of the film-makers I think of as more traditional 'artists'. I find it much more interesting to think about them in relation to the projector and the filmstrip behind me. It may be that Sharits wants this, that he is trying to create a cinema in which films do not achieve their meaning only via their optical effect on the viewer, but rather to create films that demand that the relationship between screen, image, projector, film and viewer be considered. The schematic ways in which his films are structured and the ways they refer to filmstrip and projection should encourage the viewer to consider these things rather than looking passively at the screen.[1]

Presumably comparing Sharits to film-makers such as Stan Brakhage (about whom he had written extensively), Camper juxtaposes two modes of spectatorial experience here. In the mode he prefers, the viewer's attention is held by an unpredictable or surprising array of stylistic features ('imagery', 'rhythms' and 'structure'); this viewing experience can be characterised in terms of the emotional or affective responses experienced in the moment of spectatorship. The opposed mode includes visual engagement as well, but it also seems designed to compel intellectual contemplation. Through the form of the film, the critic intuits that a different set of expectations have been placed upon him as a viewer, and he realises that the more familiar joining of visual apprehension to states of transfixed absorption might have been replaced in the newer scenario by shifts of attention, even by physical activities of alternation. For instance, it seems likely that, on occasion, when Camper thinks about the materials and processes of the cinema during a Sharits screening, he will look away from the screen in order to observe the machine in motion behind him. Sharits facilitates this kind of activity through the layouts of his film installations, which aim to make explicit the 'relationship' to which Camper refers.

Camper's review neglects to mention the film-maker's non-theatrical work, which first appeared in gallery and museum spaces five years earlier, but those installations (termed 'locational') seem to have informed his comments nevertheless. One critic's reasons for not mentioning them (likely related to the space limitations of short film reviews) are less interesting in this context than the symptomatic nature of the omission. Few critics and scholars of contemporary art and experimental film have written about Sharits in the past two decades, and even fewer have looked beyond the canonical single-screen films in order to consider his installations. The neglect of Sharits's locational pieces has been motivated, in part, by aesthetic judgments (such as the cinephile critic's preference for more 'traditional', single-screen experimental films and the politically-inclined academic's commitment to more explicitly topical work in film and video) and facilitated by institutional obstacles (such as the archival and curatorial inattention that prevented further display of the film installations until around 2000).[2] More recently, however, a re-examination of the relevance of moving-image installations and 'expanded cinema' has been undertaken in cinema studies and art history, with particular emphasis being placed upon the legacy of Structural film.

Assuming a readership that is, in all likelihood, best acquainted with films such as *N:O:T:H:I:N:G* (1968), *T,O,U,C,H,I,N,G* (1968) and *S:TREAM:S:S:ECTION:S:ECTION:S:S:ECTIONED* (1968–70), this study seeks to contribute to a revived dialogue by placing Sharits's films of the 1960s and his multiple-screen film installations from the first half of the 70s in the context of a set of ideas that he develops throughout his career. In the selective chronicle that follows, the filmic work is connected, sometimes conceptually and sometimes historically, to various aspects of spectatorial experience as they are articulated in texts written by Sharits, both published and unpublished, and by his contemporaneous critics in art and film. The literature requires careful navigation. At different points in his career — and even within a single essay — Sharits asserts that his work displays or embodies detachment and immersion, the abstract and the concrete, illusionism and anti-illusionism, literalism and symbolism, playfulness and didacticism, expressive creation and procedural anti-composition. He has a pronounced capacity for theoretical overreach, which tends to complicate efforts at identifying the concepts most relevant to the film-maker in his practice. Critics and scholars writing after the early 1980s generally avoid this issue, usually by ignoring his writings altogether.

1 Fred Camper, 'Paul Sharits', *Soho Weekly News*, 22 April 1976, p.32.

2 In 2000, the Burchfield-Penney Art Center in Buffalo, New York mounted a retrospective exhibition titled 'The Filmic Art of Paul Sharits', which included a reconstruction of Sharits's film installation *Third Degree* (1982). Unfortunately, as a result of technical difficulties, the work was projected vertically, not horizontally as in the original version. One year later, the Whitney Museum of American Art in New York displayed a version of *Shutter Interface* (1975) as part of the retrospective group exhibition 'Into the Light: The Projected Image in American Art 1964–1977'. Since lost negatives prevented the full reconstruction of the work, which Sharits had displayed as a four-screen installation in the 1970s, the Whitney's version had only two screens. Nonetheless, both exhibitions made important contributions to a modest resurgence of interest in his installations.

The conceptually oriented periodisation offered here addresses some of the problems generated by Sharits's overly inclusive statements, in large part by concentrating on viewer response and aesthetic experience, topics that appear consistently in his writings and in the critical literature.[3] Since this study pays particular attention to the fact that he modifies his views regarding these matters over time, it shows, in subsequent sections, how the formal transformation of Sharits's work after 1970 is accompanied by changes in his treatment of the topics of affect and intellectual reflection in aesthetic experience. The following section argues that from the mid-60s to the end of the decade, as he explores a set of aesthetic issues articulated within Soviet modernism, Sharits conceives of the viewer's experience in terms of feeling and physiological response. He expects that the combination of non-narrative content and novel physiological effects encountered in his films will generate intense feelings, and that somehow the viewer will be prompted to think about the cinema and human perception analytically. Sharits repeatedly explains that the optimal viewing experience for his films should include a developing awareness of the materials and processes of the cinema (based in the particular features foregrounded by the film being viewed), along with more self-directed considerations of one's own ability to perceive and apprehend a variety of visual and aural phenomena. The subsequent section argues that Sharits's work shifts emphasis during the first half of the 70s, when he ceases to refer to affect and emotion. He produces articles and lectures dealing with more academic subjects, such as the significance of his work for research projects and educational programmes, and this coincides with his deployment of new formal structures for directing the viewer's attention.

Taken as a whole, this study comprises a scholarly reply to Camper, whose review covers one film from each of the two aforementioned phases of the film-maker's career. It responds, in other words, to a speculative approach ('it may be that Sharits wants this') with a research-based, historical account of the film-maker's objectives and assumptions.

—

In Sharits's brief autobiographical statements about his early work, he recalls utilising strategies of inversion and reversal to question conventional beliefs and expectations regarding the temporality of specific art forms and media. Thus portrayed, he sounds like a typical artist of his era. Sharits claims, for example, that in the period between 1958 and 1965 he was working mostly in photography, sculpture and abstract painting:

> These so-called 'all-at-once' modes were, for me, also temporal objects ... the complexity of the photograph and painting unfold in perceptual time and sculpture temporally unfolds in the observers' movement around/through it.[4]

At the same moment, he produces a counterpoint to these works in his 'quasi-narrative films', in which he seeks to contain the 'temporal film object' within 'a single, instantaneous image-compound'. Described in terms of a 'haiku immediacy', the films were 'plotted out in my mind's eye as all-at-once structural fabrics'. No film produced by Sharits after 1964 conforms to this early ideal of atemporal presence; for much of the remainder of the decade, he explores effects of immediacy in a sort of subgenre within experimental cinema called the flicker film, which is depicted by Sharits as a form of 'neural transmission' in which 'the retina screen is a target'.[5]

These films belong to the second phase of his work, which lasts from 1965 until around 1970. They are conceived, in part, through forms of pre-design that are 'in a way similar to musical scores and modular drawings', and therefore quite unlike the more concentrated filmic structures of the earlier phase.[6] The first work from this period, *Ray Gun Virus* (1965), is a colour flicker film comprised of rhythmic, shifting patterns generated by the alternation of darker and lighter monochromatic frames; subsequent colour flicker films from the second half of the 1960s include violent, sexual and comic imagery.[7] At the core of Sharits's earliest formulations of his reflexive cinema lie physiological response and experiential intensity, both of which he had been considering in the years leading up to *Ray Gun Virus*. His earliest published text on spectatorial response is a collection of notes from 1966 titled 'Movie Cookbook', where he refers to the notion of pure feeling that appears in Kasimir Malevich's 1927 publication *The Non-Objective World*, the subject of Sharits's Master of Fine Arts thesis (also dated 1966), and to the supposedly Eisensteinian notion that a montage sequence can produce 'emergent images' in the viewer's mind.[8] This stage of Sharits's development, in which modernist theories inform the production of his flicker films of the 1960s, merits deeper analysis but, since my overall goal is to provide an overview of his ideas about the spectator's experience, a few points will have to suffice.

When Sharits writes of his desire to generate a type of spectatorial response to *Ray Gun Virus* that consists of 'direct, empty, intense, non-humourous, non-serious *feeling* (what concerned Malevich ... his "desert")',[9] he is citing a trope in Malevich's text. Malevich advocates a Suprematist art that 'reaches a "desert" in which nothing can be perceived but feeling',

3 Limitations of space prevent me from delineating the points of convergence and divergence between my treatment of these issues and William Wees's fine study of 'ecstasy and analysis', or the address of 'eye and mind', in three films by Michael Snow. See William C. Wees, *Light Moving in Time: Studies in the Visual Aesthetics of Avant-Garde Film*, Berkeley: University of California Press, 1992, pp.153–71.

4 Paul Sharits, 'Statement Regarding Multiple Screen/Sound "Locational" Film Environments-Installations (1976)', *Film Culture*, no.65–66, 1978, p.79.

5 All quotations from this paragraph can be found in Paul Sharits, 'Notes on Films/1966–1968', *Film Culture*, no.47, Summer 1969, pp.13–14.

6 P. Sharits, 'Exhibition/Frozen Frames', 1974, *Film Culture*, no.65–66, 1978, p.81.

7 Sharits's films of the 1960s have been analysed extensively (excepting the seminal *Razor Blades*, the neglect of which is perhaps related to the minor practical obstacle of its two-projector requirement). See Regina Cornwell, 'Paul Sharits: Illusion and Object', *Artforum*, vol.10 no.1, September 1971, pp.56–62; Rosalind Krauss, 'Paul Sharits' (1976), *Film Culture*, no.65–66, 1978; P. Adams Sitney, *Visionary Film: The American Avant-Garde 1943–1978*, New York: Oxford University Press, 1979, pp.385–89; W.C. Wees, *Light Moving in Time*, *op. cit.*, pp.146–52. Sharits's films are compared to other flicker films from the period in the following texts: Regina Cornwell, 'Some Formalist Tendencies in the Current American Avant-garde Film', *Kansas Quarterly*, vol.4 no.2, 1972, pp. 65–66; Malcolm Le Grice, *Abstract Film and Beyond*, London: Studio Vista, 1977, pp.105–07; Maureen Cheryn Turim, *Abstraction in Avant-Garde Films*, Ann Arbor: University of Michigan Research Press, 1985, pp.93–105; Nicky Hamlyn, *Film Art Phenomena*, London: British Film Institute, 2003, pp.57–71.

8 Paul Sharits, 'Movie Cookbook', *Film Culture*, no.65–66, 1978, p.109. This text was published more than ten years after it was written. The artist's reading of Eisenstein is dated 1963.

9 *Ibid.*

a desert 'filled with the spirit of non-objective sensation'.[10] In unpublished notes for *Ray Gun Virus*, another reference to the desert trope is preceded by terms such as 'meaningless', 'non-discursive', 'immediate' and 'experiential but deeply sensed'.[11] Since Sharits ties the 'non-narrative' cinema to what he calls the 'non-referential', he might appear to be sympathetic to the work of abstract animators, but he views their films as overly concerned with painting's 'aesthetics and pictorial principles' and with 'demonstrations of optics'.[12] No single practitioner assumes the place of a 'model' in Sharits's syncretic practice, since the film-maker allows himself the freedom to borrow, revise or discard any number of elements from the theories and conceptual frameworks that engage his interest. Accordingly, he attempts to revise Eisenstein as he combines the film-maker's ideas with those of Malevich.

Sharits does not explain his understanding of the concept of the emergent in his 1966 text, but he does endorse, a decade later, Eisenstein's essay 'The Filmic Fourth Dimension', stating that he is 'in general agreement' with the film-maker's 'visual ("montage") model of the aural overtone'.[13] As far as I can tell, the emergent and the overtone are similar terms for Sharits, perhaps even identical. Eisenstein's discussion of overtonal montage touches on the juxtaposition of shots to create visual resonances which, like the musical overtone, 'cannot be traced in the static frame ... Overtonal conflicts, foreseen but unwritten in the score, cannot emerge without the dialectical process of the passage of the film through the projection apparatus, or that of the performance by a symphony orchestra.'[14] In other words, the emergent to which Sharits refers is generated when the viewer sees images that cannot be located in any single frame. Sharits's own films, for example, include fast-moving flicker effects that stimulate the retina at a faster rate than the brain can process, causing the images that were perceived in the just-past to be seen in conjunction with the images being perceived in the present (as if superimposed). In 1966, Sharits takes Eisenstein to be prescribing that 'emergent images arising from juxtaposition must relate directly back to the films' literal, narrative content'.[15] Objecting to this perceived mandate, Sharits maintains that he 'would have liked to have had the "emergents" as the whole of the film'.[16] In addition, since he rejects not only non-filmic representational imagery but also Eisenstein's explicitly political aims, Sharits replaces the Soviet film-maker's ideologically enlightened spectator with his interpretation of Malevich on the topic of affect. The Suprematist artist's depiction of painting as a physical manifestation of the painter's expressive feelings is elided, however, in favour of his promotion of an abstract art that generates a 'non-objective sensation' in the viewer.

10 Kasimir Malevich, *The Non-Objective World* (trans. Howard Dearstyne), Chicago: Paul Theobald and Company, 1959, pp.67–68.

11 Letter from the artist to Rosalind Krauss (undated), *Ray Gun Virus* folder, files of Burchfield-Penney Art Center, Buffalo, New York, n.p.

12 P. Sharits, 'Notes on Films/1966–1968', *op. cit.*, p.13.

13 Paul Sharits, 'Hearing: Seeing', 1976, *Film Culture*, no.65–66, 1978, p.75.

14 Sergei Eisenstein, 'The Filmic Fourth Dimension', *Film Form: Essays in Film Theory* (trans. Jay Leyda), New York: Harcourt Brace & Company, 1949, p.69.

15 *Ibid.*

16 P. Sharits, 'Movie Cookbook', *op. cit.*, p.109.

17 P. Sharits, 'Notes on Films/1966–1968', *op. cit.*, p.13.

18 *Ibid.*, p.15. In an interview from 1980, Sharits claimed that since various details of the imagery in *N:O:T:H:I:N:G* are initially difficult to decipher, or seem to be 'illogical', the film 'seems to be something but it is not. Everything is

The flicker is a particularly valuable format in the context of these goals, since it uses light and montage to 'generate visual forms ("open-eye phosphemes")' and impact the 'individual psycho-physical subjectivities of consciousness'.[17] Even when discussing flicker films that include recognisable images of people and objects — such as *N:O:T:H:I:N:G* and *T,O,U,C,H,I,N,G* — Sharits claims to be working on the 'subtraction of potentially discursive-symbolic-dramatic-narrative meaning' and the 'creation of new, filmic levels of meaning', which, although they 'may be partially associative ... are intended to be primarily plastic, even physiological'.[18] The first (subtractive) goal would appear to be neo-Suprematist; the second (generative) goal extracts from Eisenstein the idea that there are levels of meaning and types of response to which the cinema has privileged access. Both objectives are served by another feature of the flicker films: their status as 'two vector, symmetric works in which the first part's forward structure is countered by the second part's retrograde direction'.[19] The intended effect of the films' montage-based mandalas is 'the suspension of linear time and spatial direction'. Faced with the absence of 'non-filmic images and [cinematic] stories', the viewer's 'consciousness is freed to turn inward upon itself' and discover 'the immediate reality of experiencing the film'.[20]

Another version of the emergent is first mentioned in relation to *S:TREAM:S:S:ECTION:S:ECTION:S:S:ECTIONED*. A six-screen version of the film would have been the first of Sharits's locational installations, had insufficient funding not forced him to scale the work down, first to four screens and finally to the single-screen, theatrical film that exists now. The completed work, which has been analysed elsewhere by Stuart Liebman, covers both fresh and familiar territory, occupying a singularly transitional place in Sharits's career.[21] The film's imagery is carefully balanced between illusionistic and anti-illusionistic elements, and the continual interplay of both links it back, in a general sense, to his previous films, which tend to alternate between flicker effects of flatness and depth. Heretofore unseen in his work, however, is the film's 'scratch aesthetic', which displays dense layerings of markings and images. White, vertical, emulsion scratches accumulate over continually changing footage of a volatile water current, seen through different superimposed images; six looped, spoken words, each beginning with the prefix 'exo-', are slowly made to coalesce aurally on the soundtrack; and at seemingly-random moments, a beeping sound coincides with the visual jump caused by a conspicuous, horizontal filmstrip splice. When Sharits discusses *S:TREAM:S:S:ECTION:S:ECTION:S:S:ECTIONED* in a 1971 letter to his gallerist Klaus Kertess, he calls

using contradictions. Things are happening in the wrong order and stuff, and everything is going backwards, getting mixed-up in time.' He also recalls 'thinking about' Malevich's idea of nothingness and emptiness when working on *N:O:T:H:I:N:G*. See Yann Beauvais, 'Interview with Paul Sharits', *Scratch Book, 1983/1998* (ed. Yann Beauvais and Jean-Damien Collins), Paris: Light Cone, 1999, p.362.

19 Paul Sharits, 'Postscript as Preface' (1973), *Film Culture*, no.65–66, 1978, p.5.

20 P. Sharits, 'Notes on Films/1966–1968', *op. cit.*, p.14.

21 Stuart Liebman, 'Paul Sharits's *S:TREAM:S:S:ECTION:S:ECTION:S:S:ECTIONED*: Paradigm Lost, or Adventures of the Dialectic', *Millennium Film Journal*, no.16/17/18, Fall/Winter 1986–87, pp.190–94.

it his 'water-to-film-current work', since the scratches slowly displace the film's initial images of the stream.[22]

It is in the same letter that the film-maker broaches the concept of the emergent again, tacitly maintaining a line of continuity with his earlier work. He writes that the film's images and sounds 'interweave' into 'a new-emergent, percept-mixed "whole"' when they are experienced simultaneously.[23] Instead of citing Eisenstein on this occasion, he compares the experience he is trying to generate to 'the sort of thing which happens in La Monte Youngs' use of two slightly out of phase "continuous" sine tones where you hear "pulses" which "aren't there"'. Sharits's mention of Young's sine-tone installations suggests that he has begun to think in terms of audio-visual environments that will contain longer, more open-ended perceptual experiences. This area of Sharits's work seems to have been productively informed by a number of issues raised by artists interested in twentieth-century experimental music and sound art (including the question of how machine-facilitated techniques and processes — such as modulation, oscillation and phasing — can be applied to non-musical practices). He even goes so far as to state: 'In making films, I have always been more interested in speech patterns, music and temporal pulses in nature than in the visual arts for exemplary models of composition.'[24] The issue of his 'interest' is far more complicated than his claim indicates, but it is evident that Sharits's appreciation for and research into the work of composers such as Young and Steve Reich informs his use of looped and spatialised sounds within film environments. This is a rich topic, but one that falls beyond the scope of this essay.

Sharits actually comes much closer to realising the intended effect of 'a new-emergent, percept-mixed "whole"' in *Shutter Interface* (1975), a later locational piece that combines four overlapping screens of flickering colours with a variety of beep tones (set to coincide with each flicker filmstrip's black frames). Liebman's description captures the effect:

> As the sound's dynamic level rises and moves back and forth underneath the images, the colors seem to become more vibrant. As one watches, the quadraphonic whine fuses inextricably with the optical flux, reinforcing the glowing spatial environment which the piece creates.

Notably, Liebman asserts that the 'ancient dream' realised by the installation — 'of removing the barriers between sight and sound to create compound synesthetic sensations' — is one that 'we know Eisenstein shared'.[25] Sharits, writing to Kertess, terms this 'a "heterodyne effect" between vision and hearing', but since his statements regarding *Shutter Interface* belong

22 Letter from the artist to Klaus Kertess, 26 August 1971, *S:TREAM:S:S:ECTION:S:ECTION:S:S:ECTIONED* folder, files of Burchfield-Penney Art Center, Buffalo, New York, n.p.

23 *Ibid.*

24 P. Sharits, 'Hearing: Seeing', *op. cit.*, p.70.

25 Stuart Liebman, 'Apparent Motion and Film Structure: Paul Sharits's *Shutter Interface*', *Millennium Film Journal*, no.2, Spring/Summer 1978, p.107. Liebman's article is an exceptionally insightful analysis of the physiological phenomena that Sharits explores throughout his career.

26 Sharits also mentions 'an emergent psychophysiological heterodyne effect' in an essay from the same period as his letter to Kertess. There he suggests that

to his more predominantly analytic phase, he does not explicitly connect the installation's effects to his earlier ideas.[26]

At least two versions of the emergent appear in Sharits's writings, with the early one being primarily visual and the later one bridging image and sound, sight and hearing. The first focuses on a range of phenomena that can be generated by tapping into the unique attributes of eye-brain relations; in the flicker films, these phenomena include optical after-images (retinal traces) and vivid closed-eye illusions (which draw upon the memory traces of visual stimuli).[27] The second has its place in the concerns Sharits articulates in 'Hearing: Seeing' (1976/78), an essay in which he explains that he is interested in 'how operational analogues can be constructed between ways of seeing and ways of hearing' and that sound film 'appeared to be the most natural medium for testing what thresholds of relatedness might exist between [both]'. (It should be noted that he denies being 'captivated' by synaesthesia as a concept, however, because he is exploring not only sensorial merging but also the analytic uncovering of 'levels of ultimate difference between the two systems'.)[28] His pursuit of synaesthetic experiences is distinguished by a precise understanding of the perceptual psychology of moving-image illusions (the phi phenomenon in particular and apparent motion in general) and by his knowledge of modern music (which is somewhat more patchwork).

In one statement about *Ray Gun Virus*, Sharits writes:

> Given the fact of retinal inertia and the flickering shutter mechanism of film projection, one may generate virtual forms, create actual motion (rather than illustrate it), build actual color-space (rather than picture it), and be involved in actual time (immediate presence).[29]

Exploiting the capacities and limitations of both the film projector and the human perceptual system, Sharits seeks to engage spectators who, by allowing themselves to become *immersed* in a multifaceted perceptual experience, can become newly conscious of and connected to the 'actual', thereby gaining a degree of aesthetic *distance*. The viewer must apprehend each Sharits film in 'its own reality' — as a projected moving image and a filmstrip moving through a machine in the viewing room — if he or she is to arrive at the goal of 'totally new levels of awareness'.[30]

Sharits often suggests that his films can achieve, at this intersection of cognition and technical processes, a high degree of transmissive purity; but neither of the features he mentions most often — the flicker film's lack of conventional content and its activation of neural response — can *necessarily* produce the 'turn[ing] inward upon itself' of the spectator's consciousness.

'a controlled continuous collision of sound and image' based on Eisenstein's idea of vertical montage may be used to generate such an effect. See Paul Sharits, 'Words Per Page' (1970/72), *Film Culture*, no.65–66, 1978, p.41.

27 Since Sharits believes that the effect of being immersed in colours and images both seen and imagined produces a uniquely aesthetic experience, he asserts that *Ray Gun Virus*, for example, is not 'a psychological testing device', in Paul Sharits, *Sound Recording*, no.69.20, Museum of Modern Art Archives, New York, 1 April 1969.

28 P. Sharits, 'Hearing: Seeing', *op. cit.*, p.70.

29 P. Sharits, 'Notes on Films/ 1966–1968', *op. cit.*, p.13.

30 *Ibid.*, p.15.

As one film scholar has noted, films such as *Ray Gun Virus* can be easily interpreted as playful, offering 'the perversity of a pleasure derived from an appreciation of a skillful offense', since 'one is seduced even as one is threatened by the fleeting color glimpses, fades and flashes, the mystery of effects one has not known before'.[31] On occasion, Sharits does acknowledge the possibility of a playful response to his films,[32] but during the early years of his bid for artistic legitimacy, he promotes the notion that his films function as initially aggressive 'tools for turning perception inward'.[33]

During the second half of the 1960s, the joining of intense feeling, physiological response and non-narrative content is said to yield not only a demystified understanding of phenomenal reality but also an existential experience of some sort. Describing his work as 'occasions for meditational-visionary experience', Sharits suggests that 'the viewer [of *Ray Gun Virus*] is left to his own reconstruction of self, left with a screen upon which his retina may project its own patterns'.[34] Ideally, the aesthetic experience sought by the film-maker should strengthen the viewer's ties to the phenomenal world through a renewed awareness of the cinematic setup, while also facilitating an exploration of internal states. By the end of the 1960s, Sharits begins to reconsider his goals, and in the following decade they will no longer be restricted to the attainment of an expanded consciousness of external and interior conditions.

Discussions of affect, feeling and spectatorial experience in general disappear from Sharits's writings during the third phase of his career. The direct causes of this development are considerably more difficult to identify than possible catalysts. In a note written in 1969, Sharits discusses the work of artists Robert Morris and Carl Andre, before speculating 'it seems that to project an image onto a wall one must also project a parody of the assumption that it is viable to do so'.[35] Both the statement and its placement following references to Morris and Andre suggest that the recent North American critique of particular sculptural conventions — related to the object's position in space, for example — had influenced his thinking about art forms and media by the end of his second phase. Since the large majority of contemporary artists and critics admired and read by Sharits shared a reluctance to discuss aesthetic experience in terms of emotion, feeling or affect, it is possible that their silence had an influence on the film-maker's thinking.[36]

In contrast, numerous statements offer clear indicators of his thinking about the future direction of his work. In a 1969 'Cineprobe' screening-discussion held at the Museum of Modern Art in New York, Sharits explains that the flicker is not 'the thing I'm trying to do, exactly', adding that he

31 M.C. Turim, *Abstraction in Avant-Garde Films*, *op. cit.*, p.101.

32 For one explicit discussion of the topic of play, see the first and second pages of Paul Sharits and Gary Garrels, 'Interview', *Mediums of Language*, Cambridge, Mass.: Hayden Gallery and The MIT Press, 1982, n.p. Note that this comment on playful responses to his work is offered long after the close of his third phase. During the early 1970s, Sharits is more likely to discuss play in relation to theory, as in Sharits, 'A Cinematics Model for Film Studies in Higher Education' (1974), *Film Culture*, no.65–66, 1978, p.64.

33 P. Sharits, 'Notes on Films/1966–1968', *op. cit.*, p.14.

34 *Ibid.*, p.14.

35 P. Sharits, 'Postscript as Preface', *op. cit.*, p.11.

had viewed Peter Kubelka's *Arnulf Rainer* (1958/60) only as recently as the previous year, and that he has yet to see Tony Conrad's *The Flicker* (1965–66).[37] He criticises the 'pretension' of fixed, directed attention in conventional movie theatres, but he also tells his audience that he is not interested in 'psychedelic environments' as an alternative, presumably because they are associated with a condition of self-absorbed, narcoticised spectatorship that seems far removed from the effects of engagement and distantiation he values (and finds in the work of colleagues such as Hollis Frampton). More than once during his talk, he describes his films as maps, explaining that in the future he will seek to provide for the viewer a 'map of the projection process, without the esoteric qualities, very straightforward', while also 'making films that could be thought of more as locations'. Various notes and remarks from this period show that he has reconsidered the relevance of the standard theatrical viewing situation (now subject to 'parody'), along with the importance of the mobility of the spectator, an issue first addressed much earlier in his career, when he was producing 'sculpture [that] temporally unfolds in the observers' movement around/through it'.[38]

The move away from a reliance on the most conventional cinematic viewing conditions is accompanied by a changed view of the iconography of his films. Despite Sharits's initial rejection of the notion that his cinematic imagery of the 1960s could be possessed of referential or symbolic significance, he revises his views in the following decade, claiming that he had been attempting a marriage of formalist reflexivity and psychological meaning. In the mid-1970s, he retrospectively periodises his renunciation of the 'emotional-dramatic-psychological structures' and 'formalist tactics' of the second phase, situating the change in his thinking within the two or three years following the completion of *T,O,U,C,H,I,N,G* in the fall of 1968.[39] Looking back on the final section of *T,O,U,C,H,I,N,G*, he writes:

> I wanted to visualise 'inverse pain' as a kind of imploding reverberation of the picture edge — the screen appears to collapse, in rhythmic pulses, into itself. This latter mode — of introducing shapes into the frame, which were reflective of the film frame's perimeter-shape, and which acted as a commentary on the state of consciousness of the film's protagonist at that point in the (backwards) 'narrative' — struck me later as being somewhat too related to strategies of painting, as did other aspects of my films of that early period.

Resolving after 1968 to 'remove from my work all influences of painting' along with any formal features referring or corresponding to emotional states,

36 In 1976, affect returns as a topic when Sharits explains that he values 'more sophisticated levels of "feeling", derived from intense contemplation of filmic realities', over the representation of 'emotionality' of his earlier work. He does not elaborate upon this changed notion of feeling, however. See P. Sharits, 'Hearing: Seeing', *op. cit.*, p.72.

37 P. Sharits, *Sound Recording*, *op. cit.*

38 P. Sharits, 'Statement Regarding Multiple Screen/Sound "Locational" Film Environments-Installations (1976)', *Film Culture*, no.65–66, 1978, p.79.

39 P. Sharits, 'Cinema as Cognition: Introductory Remarks' (1975), *Film Culture*, no.65–66, 1978, p.77.

Facing page: Paul Sharits, drawing and notes for *Soundstrip/ Filmstrip*, graphite on paper, 21.6×28cm, 1971–72 © 2008 Paul Sharits estate. Courtesy the Burchfield-Penney Art Center Archives

he renews his commitment to 'filmic realities'.[40] As he pursues this objective in the five years comprising his third phase, Sharits restricts himself to the production of only two kinds of images: abstract colour flickers (as in *Shutter Interface*) and shots of rephotographed filmic phenomena (such as coloured frames, frame lines, film grain, sprocket holes and the optical soundtrack code).[41]

'Specimen' is the term he employs for the latter image type, and the immediate connotation it carries is scientific. When depicting his work as a research-oriented endeavour, as he does on occasion in the 1970s, Sharits seems to be looking for points of resonance between the ideas and methods of the sciences, on the one hand, and those of a new approach to cinema, on the other.[42] Yet he appears to be primarily invested in a rhetorical appeal to scientific legitimacy, not a sustained investigation of possible connections.[43] A more productive way of looking at the film-maker's use of 'specimen' is historical: the term calls attention to an analytic aspiration that is particularly pronounced between 1970 and 1975. This third stage of his work is the period of Sharits's deepest commitment to a reflexive aesthetic, to the realisation of a modernist ideal concentrated on the 'intense contemplation of filmic realities'.[44] Since he remains concerned to demonstrate or prove the legitimacy of his project, however, he is at pains to display the broadening of his intellectual interests in the writings of his third phase. Most notably, he argues for a research-oriented approach that would set his filmic output within the context of a larger, more academic project.[45]

As Sharits embarks upon the construction of his locational film installations, his earlier ideas about abstract feeling are supplanted by reflections on an abstraction of another sort, namely time — a topic that has the beneficial effect of unifying some of his interests after 1969. One major mode of inquiry prevalent during this period is diagnostic, pertaining to the identification of the cinema's fundamental elements.[46] In a typical example excerpted from the working notes for his first completed locational piece, the four-screen *Sound Strip/Film Strip* (1971), he writes:

> [E]ssential to the concept of the movie (or any expressive use of time) is the sectioning of the continuous time reality (beats, words, frames) ... What we want to do is, not negate the sectioning of time, but reveal the nature of the illusionary continuity of film time.[47]

40 P. Sharits, 'Hearing: Seeing', *op. cit.*, p.72.

41 Other single-screen works, such as the *Analytical Studies* series (1971–76), also belong to this phase, and they represent a different manifestation of the analytic aspiration addressed by this study.

42 See, for example, the course description in P. Sharits, 'A Cinematics Model for Film Studies in Higher Education', *op. cit.*, p.57.

43 Sharits does resist the conversion of art into a form of pseudo-scientific inquiry, however, since he is far more concerned with philosophical import, preferring to portray his work as 'prototheoretical'. See P. Sharits, 'Cinema as Cognition: Introductory Remarks', *op. cit.*, p.77.

44 P. Sharits, 'Hearing: Seeing', *op. cit.*, p.72.

45 See P. Sharits, 'A Cinematics Model for Film Studies in Higher Education', *op. cit.*, pp.43–68.

46 'Ontological' is a word used frequently by Sharits to describe this mode, but since he never clearly resolves the contradictions raised by his alternation between essentialist and historicist claims, I avoid employing the term. ('Diagnostic' appears in P. Sharits, 'Statement Regarding Multiple Screen/ Sound "Locational" Film Environments-Installations (1976)', *op. cit.*, p.80). Similar contradictions were pointed

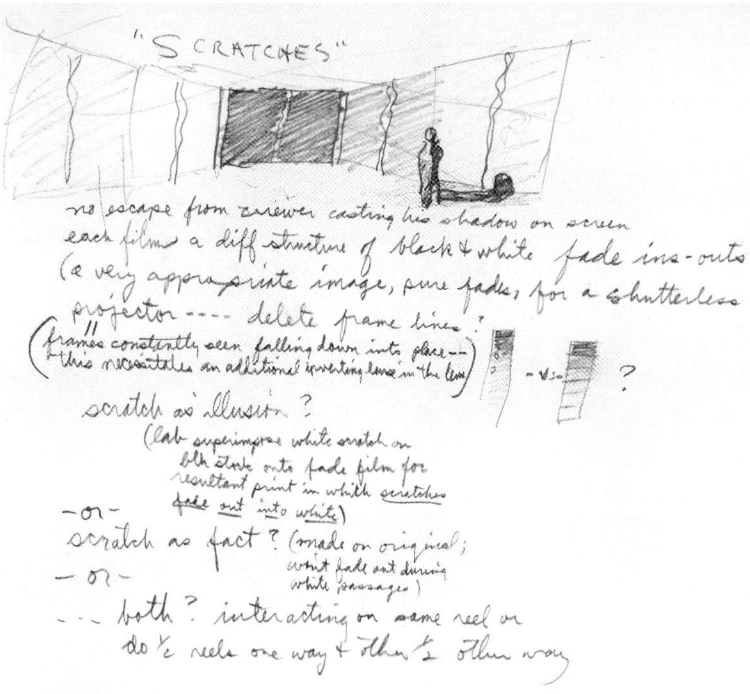

The other major mode of investigation deals with the spectator's subjective experience, and it is labelled 'phenomenological' by Sharits.[48] His readings in this area, which are not restricted to texts written by proponents of phenomenology, can be exceptionally instructive. An essay by Vilém Flusser, archived with his notes for *Shutter Interface*, lists 'the various levels of time' pertaining to the cinema, including 'the linear time in which the pictures of scenes follow each other', 'the time in which each picture itself moves' and 'the time in which it takes for us to read each picture'—all of which Sharits expects his viewer to consider in a number of works.[49] Abraham Moles's book *Information Theory and Esthetic Perception*, a text Sharits studied and taught, distinguishes between two dominant types of 'physical time' experienced in perception: 'one rather well defined; the other more fluid, more variable, the extension of the immediately perceptible duration; the latter is the temporal field of consciousness'.[50] The experience of time unmoored from fixed markers

out by Regina Cornwell, who noted that Sharits's essay 'Words Per Page' is divided between two models of artistic practice, art-as-research and essentialist. See her article 'Structural Film: Ten Years Later', *TDR (The Drama Review)*, vol.3 no.23, September 1979, pp.87–88. For an interpretation of Sharits as a Greenbergian essentialist (later revised, somewhat, in his *S:TREAM:S:S:ECTION:S:ECTION:S:S:ECTIONED* article), see Stuart Liebman, *Paul Sharits*, Minneapolis: Film in the Cities and Walker Art Center, 1981. For a historicist reading (which mistakenly claims that Sharits produced video installations), see Jonathan Walley, 'The Material of Film and the Idea of Cinema: Contrasting Practices in Sixties and Seventies Avant-Garde Film', *October*, no.103, Winter 2003, pp.15–30.

47 Paul Sharits, untitled notes, *Sound Strip/Film Strip* folder, Files of Burchfield-Penney Art Center, Buffalo, New York, n.p.

48 A sketch of Sharits's readings in phenomenology is provided in the collection of his notes titled '-UR(i)N(ul)LS:STREAM:S:S:ECTION:s:s:ECTIONED:(A)(lysis)JO: "1968-70"', *Film Culture*, no.65-66, 1978, pp.8–10; see also P. Sharits, 'A Cinematics Model for Film Studies in Higher Education', *op. cit.*, pp.62–63.

49 Vilém Flusser, 'Line and Surface', *Main Currents in Modern Thought*, vol.3 no.29, January–February 1973, pp.101–02; a copy of this article is included in Paul Sharits, *Shutter Interface* folder, files of Burchfield-Penney Art Center, Buffalo, New York.

50 Abraham Moles, *Information Theory and Esthetic Perception* (trans. Joel E. Cohen), Urbana and London: University of Illinois Press, 1966, p.198.

can be heightened in the environment created by a flicker film, as affirmed by neurophysiologist W. Grey Walter's study of flicker effects. In a book that Sharits describes as 'nearly poetic',[51] Walter notes that 'Sometimes the sense of time is lost or disturbed' in his test subjects, and that one of them felt as if 'he had been "pushed sideways in time"'.[52] During the half-decade in which images of monochromatic frames and filmic material dominate Sharits's practice, each installation solicits a variety of temporal experiences made possible because the viewing space is less constricting than a movie theatre, while also presenting a prominent display of the materials and processes used to construct the 'time reality' of Sharits's cinema.

A few critics from the era single out time as important. Annette Michelson observes in 1974 that the move into the gallery is 'a first step ... toward the clarification and redefinition of a filmic temporality',[53] a claim further developed two years later by her colleague Rosalind Krauss, in a catalogue essay on *Sound Strip/Film Strip*. In *Sound Strip/Film Strip*, scratches are overlaid upon and represented within rephotographed filmstrips, confounding the viewer's sense of the visible differences between documents of past scratch marks and 'actual' damage (on the strips being projected). Writing of the film's image of a scratched filmstrip, Krauss observes: 'As document, seen through projection, it holds past and present in a strange synthetic relation to one another. We realise that the material support of Film is being shown to us from within the context of Time.'[54]

The scratches and strips in the installation's four screens move horizontally, appearing to traverse past adjacent screen borders. This illusion of extension is created by Sharits's innovative removal of projector mechanisms — specifically the gripper arm and shutter — designed to keep the filmstrip moving in place at a standardised speed and to prevent the eye from seeing frame borders as they pass through the light gate.[55] Taking the projector out of phase, Krauss notes that Sharits's modification 'provides us with the image of the static, material object of the strip, coupled with its continuous glide into the condition of time'.[56] In other words, the installation directs the viewer's attention to the cinema's dual status 'as an *object*, before or after projection ... and as a temporal *process*, while it is being "projected"', in Sharits's words.[57]

51 P. Sharits, 'Locational Film Pieces', *Film Culture*, no.65–66, 1978, p.124.
52 W. Grey Walter, *The Living Brain*, New York: W.W. Norton and Company, 1953, p.107.
53 Annette Michelson, 'Paul Sharits and the Critique of Illusionism: An Introduction', 1974, *Film Culture*, no.65–66, 1978, p.87.
54 R. Krauss, 'Paul Sharits', *op. cit.*, p.92.
55 P. Sharits, 'Words Per Page', *op. cit.*, pp.40–41. Surprisingly, the literature includes no mention of Sharits's technical modifications (discussing only their visual effects) until 2003; see J. Walley, 'The Material of Film and the Idea of Cinema', *op. cit.*, pp.18–19, and N. Hamlyn, *Film Art Phenomena*, *op. cit.*, pp.60–61.
56 R. Krauss, 'Paul Sharits', *op. cit.*, p.93.
57 P. Sharits, 'Words Per Page', *op. cit.*, p.35.
58 R. Krauss, 'Paul Sharits', *op. cit.*, p.93.
59 In doing so, the article also shows how the techniques utilised for the installations differ markedly from those used in the single-screen flicker films of the 60s.
60 Letter from the artist to 'Lefty', 22 November 1971, *Sound Strip/Film Strip* folder, files of Burchfield-Penney Art Center, Buffalo, New York, p.1.
61 A. Michelson, 'Paul Sharits and the Critique of Illusionism', *op. cit.*, p.88.

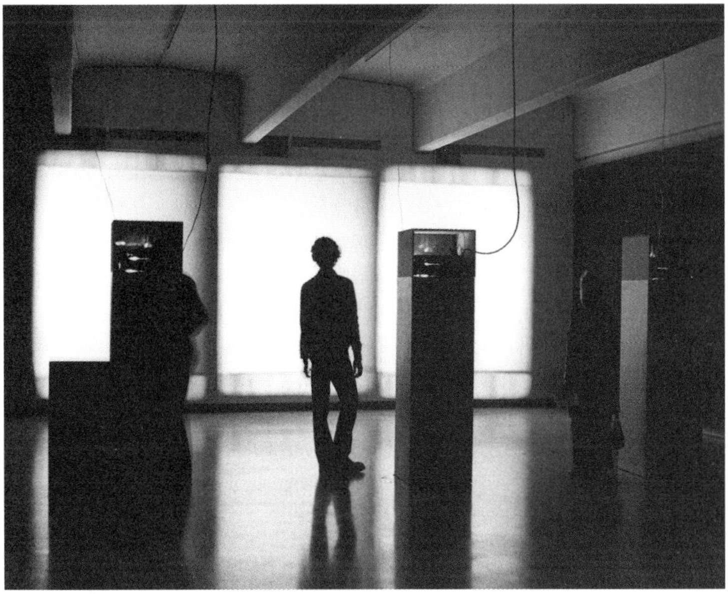

Paul Sharits, *SYN-CHRONOUSOUND-TRACKS*, Walker Art Center, Minneapolis, 1973–74. Super 8 film installation

Perhaps most significantly, Krauss constructs an analogy between the formal strategies employed by the film-maker and the cognitive processes and perceptual experiences of the spectator. Asserting that the subject of *Sound Strip/Film Strip* is 'time, in relation to what might be called the analytic mode of consciousness', she divides up two cognitive states — absorptive viewing and detached analysis — schematically, in order to link each to a different aspect of the installation — acceleration and deceleration.[58] For Krauss, the normative experience of watching a narrative film is 'about being caught up in the flow of time', and Sharits's laterally moving filmstrip-images correspond to this present-tense feeling of continuous progression. In contrast, the reflective, analytic act — 'the standing back from experience in order to ask what it is and how it is made' — finds its formal complement in the visible retardation of movement and reversal of direction afforded by Sharits's mechanical alterations during rephotography. Throughout the first half of the 1970s, critics and academics often emphasised the analytic dimension of experimental film at the expense of spectatorial experiences related to 'flow', but Krauss's text is distinguished within this literature because it argues that Sharits's formal innovations can generate a sense of present-tense immediacy while simultaneously directing viewers toward an analytic posture.[59] In writings and interviews from the period, however, Sharits clearly demonstrated a preference for discussions focused on the analytic dimension.

For the film-maker, 'the essential (sculptural) idea of activating a space with sound and image' is joined, in his installations, with 'the equally essential idea that the piece be ongoing (no beginning or end)'.[60] As Michelson explains in her essay on the three-screen, variable-movement installation *SYNCHRONOUSOUNDTRACKS* (1973–74), 'systematic permutation' is viewed 'as analytic of the temporal and spatial aspects of the filmic material'; thus, all of the locational installations utilise continuous film loops.[61] Sharits first writes about the loop in a statement about his dual-screen film *Razor Blades* (1965–68), which he describes as follows:

> Since *Razor Blades* ends as it began, an infinite loop is suggested — metric time is destroyed. Apart from the beginning and ending footage, which

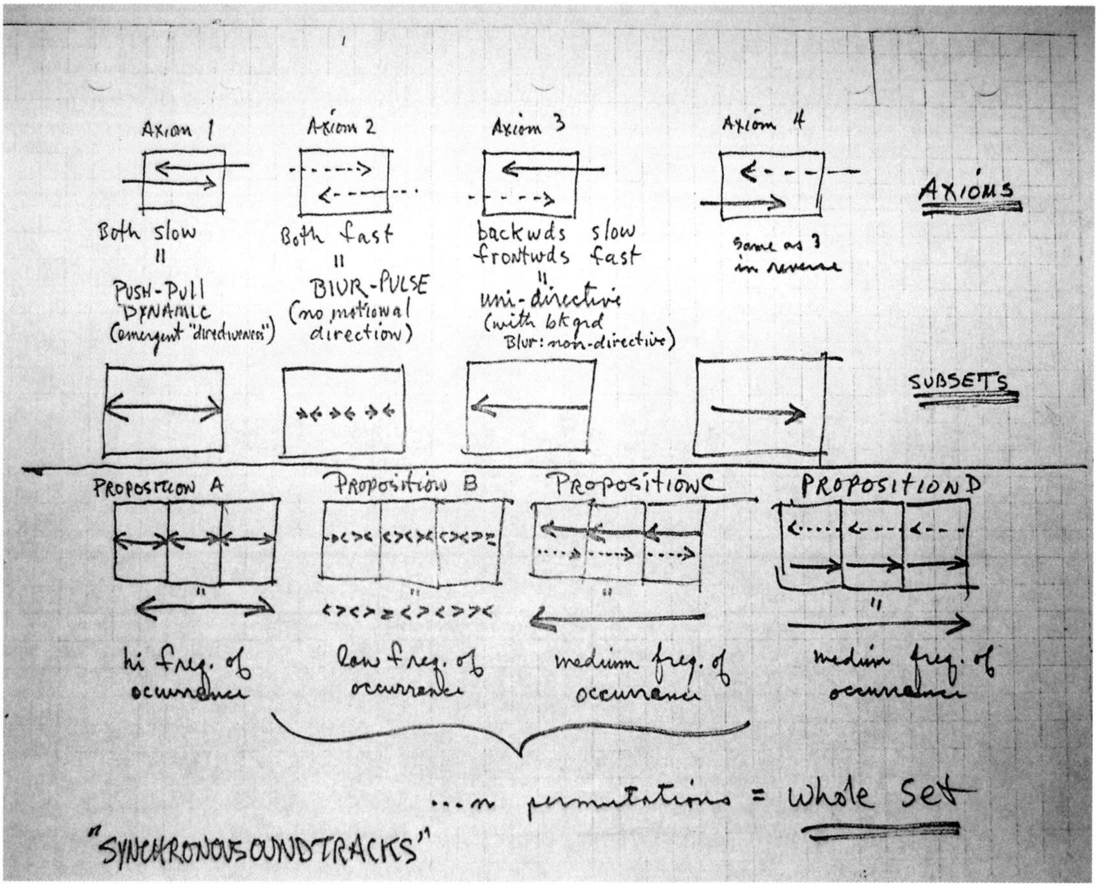

Paul Sharits, *S/ynchronou/s/ oundtrack/s/*, study for *SYNCHRONOUSOUNDTRACKS*, 28×21.6cm, 1972 © 2008 Paul Sharits estate. Courtesy the Burchfield-Penney Art Center Archives

> is linear, the film is made up of 14 loops which, staggered, play against ('slice' back and forth, interpenetrate) each-other [*sic*]. Each loop, in itself, is made so that one can chart variations in one's own consciousness of speed, rhythm and image recognition; when these loops are projected side by side, so that both images are seen as one large image, because of their differences in cycle length, this variability of consciousness is geometrically increased; since there are constantly different pairs of images on the screen, the repetitive characteristic of loops is transcended.[62]

Sharits is much more precise in this passage than in other writings from the 1960s. Note that he does not merely suggest that the loop allows the spectator to 'chart' changes in the work itself—he claims that 'the variability of consciousness', the perceiving agent's own changing recognition of 'speed, rhythm and image', should be a primary object of reflection. Years later, in an interview about the installations, he reiterates this goal when he asserts that 'there's a lot of internal variation which is testing one's ability to realise that there is variation', since the installations are composed along a 'polytemporal scale so the time measure is always shifting slightly'.[63] Even the relations between initially synchronised elements of the work are subjected to change, as various mechanical contingencies are allowed to impact upon projection and display. In the case of *SYNCHRONOUSOUNDTRACKS*, which utilises Super 8-film cartridges modified for loop projection, the issue of variations is important enough to be flagged twice for gallery visitors: in an explanatory statement that includes an approximation of the total duration of original variations (roughly one month) and in a 'paradigmatic diagram' that maps out 'the most primary types of possible variations'.[64]

Following the locational installation's placement in 'an open, free, public location', there are three crucial, interconnected features to the loop in Sharits's practice: a lack of fixed duration for film spectatorship; a 'non-developmental ... dynamic of oscillations and cycles'; and a 'diagnostic analysis of the qualities and functions of film as a physical-perceptual fact', according to the only text he devotes exclusively to the installations.[65] Writing roughly one year later, in 1975, he mentions an additional feature not included in his short piece on the locational works, a sort of 'infrastructural "blow up"' that encompasses film scores, 'diagrams, films-as-objects, written language and whatever else is necessary to form the conjugations and punctuations between the projected works, which will enable them to be properly read by others'.[66] In a sense, this added element is not novel, considering that Sharits planned to display filmstrips encased in Plexiglass outside screenings of his flicker films, as part of an ongoing exhibition called 'Frozen Film Frames'. Sharits's 'blow up' is intended to directly affect the viewer's experience of the 'rapidity' (to use Camper's word) of the shorter, non-looped, theatrical films, a quality signaled by one critic's assertion that *Ray Gun Virus* 'reads like a projected diagram which slips by too fast to comprehend fully'.[67] But in the case of the installations, it is apparent that the gallery-based mode of display expands the objects of attention beyond the screen; the loop structure encourages repeated viewings; and the variable-movement technique allows for closer inspection at slower rates of movement (in the non-flicker works). If one accepts that the rapidity of images is less of an obstacle to comprehension in the installations, this raises the question of why Sharits explicitly affirms the importance of this added feature as late as the mid-1970s, years after the single-screen film began to assume a considerably less central role in his practice.

A possible answer lies in Sharits's ongoing concerns over whether his work will be 'properly read' by spectators. On the one hand, he certainly values the pleasures that can accompany the discernment of a film's formal properties unfolding in time; on the other hand, as we have seen, the exploration and expansion of visual and aural experience cannot be

62 P. Sharits, 'Notes on Films/1966–1968', *op. cit.*, p.5.

63 Linda Cathcart, 'An Interview with Paul Sharits' (1976), *Film Culture*, no.65–66, 1978, p.107.

64 Paul Sharits, undated text, *SYNCHRONOUSOUNDTRACKS* folder, files of Burchfield-Penney Art Center, Buffalo, New York, n.p. *SYNCHRONOUSOUNDTRACKS* was first exhibited at the Bykert Gallery in New York City in the spring of 1974.

65 P. Sharits, 'Statement Regarding Multiple Screen/Sound "Locational" Film Environments-Installations (1976)', *op. cit.*, pp.79–80. For a brief analysis of this article, see John G. Hanhardt, 'Interrogating the Cinematic Apparatus: Notes on "3rd Degree" by Paul Sharits', in *The Filmic Art of Paul Sharits* (exh. cat.), Buffalo, New York: Burchfield-Penney Art Center and Buffalo State College, 2000, pp.7–8.

66 P. Sharits, 'Cinema as Cognition', *op. cit.*, p.78.

67 Douglas Crimp, 'New York Letter', *Art International*, vol.3 no.17, March 1973, p.42.

Facing page:
Paul Sharits, study for *Episodic Generation*, 1975
© 2008 Paul Sharits estate. Courtesy the Burchfield-Penney Art Center Archives

properly described as his sole objective.[68] It would seem that, for Sharits, the presence of the analytic spectator is never guaranteed or taken as a given, even after half a decade of installations designed to facilitate abstract reflection. Some time later, during the production of *Episodic Generation* (1978), a scratched-strip and variable-movement installation, which would have fitted easily into Sharits's third phase, he mentions in an unpublished note that he is trying to prevent his serial imagery from becoming 'wallpaper decoration'.[69] Presumably, he is aware that the problem might be exacerbated by the same looped structure he uses to allow the viewer to 'chart variations'. For it is from within structures of *fixed* duration — utilised most famously in Michael Snow's *Wavelength* (1967) — that a number of other North American and British film-makers explore, in the late 1960s and early 70s, their own strategies for producing attentive spectators. In this context, Sharits's denotation of the conceptual dimension of each piece takes on not only a didactic but also a countervailing function, as diagrammatic and discursive texts are used to guide film viewers who are now possessed of the novel option of merely casting a glance.

By the time *Episodic Generation* is completed, however, the configuration of aesthetic issues has changed yet again, with the onset of the fourth phase of Sharits's career, which approximately lasts from 1976 until 1982. During these years, the analytic aspiration loses quite a bit of the urgency it had exhibited earlier, and, consequently, Sharits publishes far fewer texts, incorporates psychologically resonant imagery of human bodies into his films again and even likens *Declarative Mode* (1976–77), a dual flicker installation, to a Romantic 'tone poem', calling it 'my break from "Structural film"'.[70] The reasons for these changes are numerous, but it is enough to say, for now, that Sharits is affected by and participates in a larger shift of values within artistic and filmic practices of the period. Rather than renounce the earlier manifestations of his aesthetic, he simply opts for inclusiveness and diversity.

—

In 1969, a film-goer at the Museum of Modern Art in New York asks Sharits: 'Are you concerned with the audience?' He replies that his concerns are 'just problems that are necessary for me to work out'.[71] This study has sought to demonstrate otherwise, by dating his concern for spectatorial response at least as far back as the early 1960s, and by showing that he seeks to emphasise different aspects of aesthetic experience at different stages of his career.

The answer he provides, disingenuous though it may seem in retrospect, stands as further evidence of the film-maker's many divergent impulses. These include the desire to ascribe convoluted philosophical meanings to his work (a tendency admittedly downplayed here) and the need to make 'straightforward', even 'obvious' installations (for the MoMA audience he cites Wittgenstein on the value of such qualities). Not only conceptual contradictions of various kinds but also significant gaps between intention and execution abound in Sharits's work. There are still many other lines of development to explore.

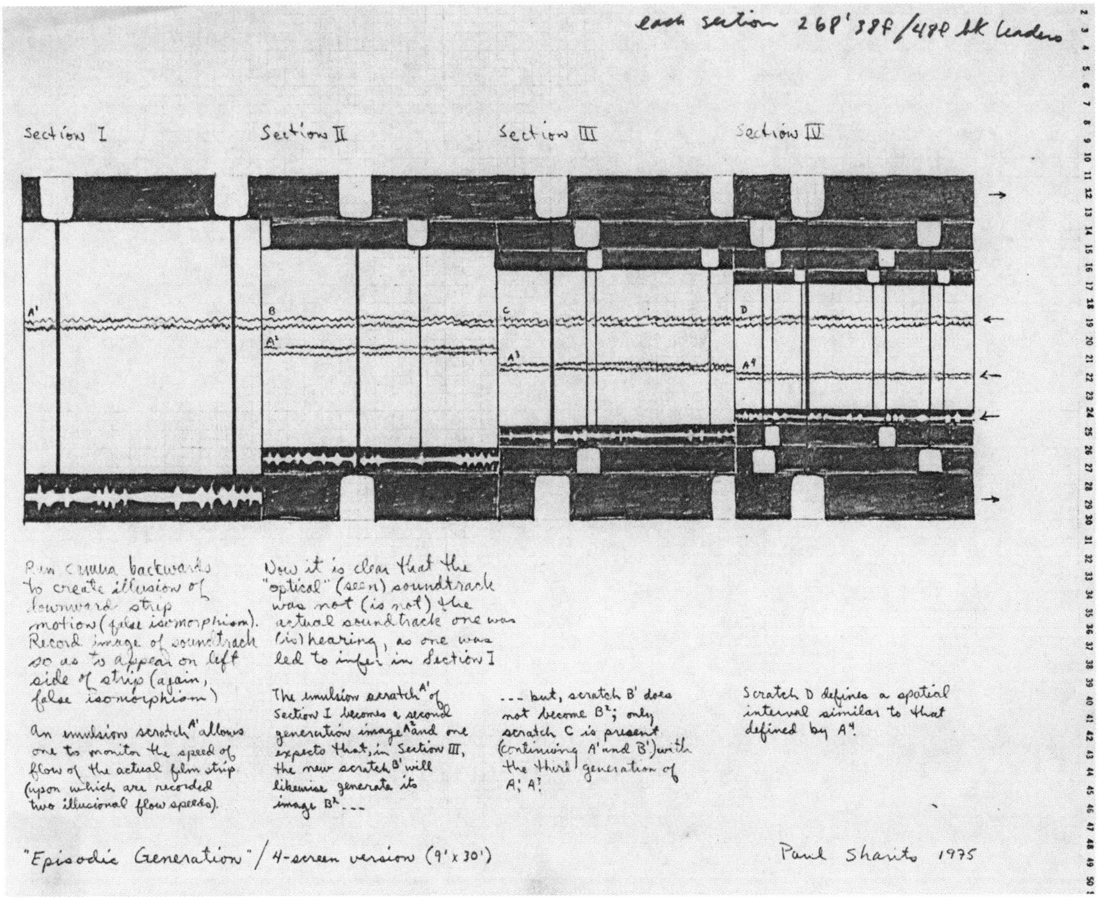

It remains to be seen, however, whether the resurgence of interest in Structural film will generate discussion and debate about the installations and writings of this particular film-maker. At any rate, it seems unlikely that the primary impetus behind a major reconsideration of Sharits's corpus will originate with contemporary scholars of film and art, most of whom have seen very few of his films or installations. Such a development will probably depend upon future institutional commitments to restoration and display. In the meantime, the existing prints and negatives continue to languish.

68 One can easily imagine an aesthete's purely sensual response to Sharits's work. Even as obstinate a critic of 'preplanned' films as Stan Brakhage offered appreciative comments (Sharits's files include letters expressing Brakhage's praise for *Analytical Studies III: Color Frame Passages*, from 1973 to 1974, and the single-screen version of *Declarative Mode*). For Brakhage's criticism of Sharits's contemporaries, see Stan Brakhage, 'Stan Brakhage at Millennium: November 4, 1977', *Millennium Film Journal*, vol.16/17/18, Fall/Winter 1986–87, pp.297–307. He does add: 'But I know that there are limits.'

69 Paul Sharits, '"The 8-Datum Level Blow Out" or Why *Episodic Generation* is just "4" (physical) generations' (undated), *Episodic Generation* folder, files of Burchfield-Penney Art Center, Buffalo, New York, n.p.

70 Paul Sharits, untitled text (undated), *Declarative Mode* folder, files of Burchfield-Penney Art Center, Buffalo, New York, n.p.

71 P. Sharits, *Sound Recording*, *op. cit.*

This essay could not have been written without the research assistance of Nancy Weekly at the Burchfield-Penney Art Center in Buffalo and Robert Haller at Anthology Film Archives in New York City. I also thank Malcolm Turvey for comments on an earlier manuscript.

BARE LIVES
Pamela M. Lee

In the 1960s and 70s, the image of the body crossed by violence was a brute fact of everyday life, and was the visual and phenomenal horizon of the world. A survey of the visual record of that moment — a moment that saw state authority clash aggressively with public interest — bears witness to the struggle between violence and enlightenment. The many forms of this damaged body — the lifeless shell of a fallen protestor, a man taking a bullet in the temple, a monk being consumed by fire — were endlessly pictured in magazines and newspapers, flashed night after night on television screens, and presented as real-time spectacle through video transmission. This was, in short, a mediated body: abstracted, parsed, regulated and controlled, submitted to the logic of a new multimedia technocracy. It was under the post-War reign of this logic that the corpus of political democracy would then give way to the corpse of degraded life, for the ubiquity of this body was coextensive with the violence of the world, be it in Birmingham, Chicago, My Lai, Kent State or Hanoi.

At the same time as this proliferation of mediated bodies, many women artists — Carolee Schneemann, VALIE EXPORT, Joan Jonas and many others — began making work in which bodies themselves took on the status of media. Male artists would make such work, too, but women had an especially important role to play in this scenario. By performing task-oriented movements, grand gestures or intimate actions, they treated their bodies as agents, or 'extensions', to follow the McLuhanesque rhetoric of the day. Art historians and critics have used the term 'body art' to describe this work, which typically placed the body under conditions of great physical duress or vulnerability in both public and private performances. More often than not, these bodies were also stripped bare, naked rather than nude. Critical here was that these 'bare lives' found their material fallout in what was then considered the most experimental forms of new media. Jonas, for instance, found her naked alter ego in spirals of feedback loops and the techniques of de-synchronisation[1]; EXPORT would deploy her own as both projection and screen; Schneemann's screened and screening presence incarnated the radical extremes of both life and death. Vibrant with the stirrings of sexual revolution, the appearance of this body likewise signalled the limit condition of a desperate and mediated life.

1 On Jonas and 'de-synchronization', see Douglas Crimp, 'De-synchronization in Joan Jonas's Performances', *Joan Jonas: Scripts and Descriptions 1968–1982*, Berkeley: University of California, Berkeley, 1983, pp.8–10.

Although this body was placed in an intensely precarious position, for many it came to stand as an article of faith. Indeed, the conventional wisdom about this work argues that the body presented here was a unified and essential whole: the expression of a feminised core historically oppressed by the prejudices of culture. That Schneemann, EXPORT and Jonas used advanced time-based media in these works — projections, feedback systems, video monitors, other such technologies — seemed to confirm the will to self-representation that is commonly understood as a benchmark of feminist art.[2]

But what are we to make of the radical convergence of a violently screened body, on the one hand, and the body's own proactive *screening*, on the other? How can we square the opposition between state-sponsored death and willful life, the emergencies in South East Asia (and elsewhere) and the mandates of feminist autonomy? Although we can hardly dismiss the notion of 'body art' as a descriptive category, this category may prove a red herring for examining the practice of Schneemann, EXPORT and Jonas as *media* artists: artists whose films, videos and projections are inseparable from their performances. The cruelty of women's historical oppression brooks no contradiction; the ways in which the body has been considered in the art historical record demand revisiting. For the body organised by media — and in turn the body wrested from technology — is far from the flesh and blood, 'organic' thing. While this body might well indeed be recalcitrant and material, these works of these artists, decidedly feminist in disposition, share little with the essentialised corpus of a particular feminist aesthetic.

The relationship between the body screened and the screening body instead revolves around a third term: the *biopolitical*. This concept, famously theorised by Michel Foucault, allows us to understand the radical premise posed by the work of Schneemann, EXPORT and Jonas. In his 1978 work *The History of Sexuality*, Foucault gave this concept its first meaning, using it to indicate the ways in which the sphere of life (and implicitly sex) had become integrated into the mechanisms, and thus politics, of sovereign authority: 'the right of death and power over life'. His formulation stemmed from his rejection of what he called the 'repressive hypothesis', the belief that modernity's attitudes towards sex, as crystallised in the drawing room mores of Victorian culture, was organised around the virtual and literal censorship of sex. For Foucault the situation was precisely the opposite: the generalised deployment of sex was in fact an essential aspect of modernity:

> What occurred in the eighteenth century in some Western countries was an event bound up with the development of capitalism, was a different phenomenon having perhaps a wider impact than the new morality; this was nothing less than the entry of life into history, that is, the entry of

2 This is to leave aside the question as to whether or not there is a 'feminine aesthetic'. The topic is too long to consider in this essay, but suffice it to say that among the most sophisticated accounts of the problematic derive from feminist film theory. Among many other texts, see Theresa de Lauretis, 'Rethinking Women's Cinema: Aesthetics and Feminist Theory', *Technologies of Gender*, Indianapolis and Bloomington: Indiana University Press, 1987, pp.127–48.

phenomena peculiar to the life of the human species into the order of knowledge and power, into the sphere of political techniques [...] In the space for movement thus conquered, and broadening and organizing that space, methods of power and knowledge assumed responsibility for the life processes and undertook to control and modify them.[3]

In the wake of Foucault's profoundly influential interpretation, philosophers and critics have further embroidered upon this notion of the biopolitical, applying it to realms beyond the history of sexuality.[4] Giorgio Agamben, for example, explores the biopolitical as the threshold of 'bare life' in the long history of political theory from Aristotle to Carl Schmitt to Hannah Arendt. 'The entry of *zoe* into the sphere of the polis,' he writes, 'the politicization of bare life as such — constitutes the decisive event of modernity and signals a radical transformation of the political-philosophical categories of classical thought.'[5] For Agamben, the fate of biopolitics in the twentieth century has catastrophic consequences, finding its most corrupt paradigm in the concentration camp. 'Only because politics in our age had been entirely transformed into biopolitics,' he argues, 'was it possible for politics to be constituted as totalitarian politics to a degree hitherto unknown.'[6] 'The state of exception' that constitutes the field of sovereign power finds its modern incarnation in the realm of biopolitics.

Both Foucault and Agamben describe how an array of social institutions — juridical, medical and incarceral — have internalised biopolitical production. These authors analyse the technologies of biopolitical production: Foucault treats the technologies of modern sexuality, Agamben the technologies of domination. This discussion, however, localises biopolitical production to the media culture of the 1960s and early 70s, a moment variously described as the era of 'Television's War',[7] and a time when the question of reproducibility for women's bodies represented a historically acute facet of the right of death and power over life.[8] That right, we shall see, had a medium-specific dimension: the reproduction of sexualised subjects was (and doubtlessly continues to be) coextensive with its reproducibility both *in* and *as* media.

The oeuvres of Schneemann, EXPORT and Jonas are each distinct meditations on the emergent biopolitics attending 1960s media culture and the claims to transparency — the politics of illusionism — that culture would make. Their practices demonstrate the conflicted and parasitic relation between what Foucault calls the 'deployment of alliance' and the 'deployment of sexuality' constitutive of modern conceptions of sexuality. A 'deployment of alliance' is 'built around a system of rules defining the permitted and the forbidden, the licit and illicit', whereas 'the deployment of sexuality operates

3 Michel Foucault, *The History of Sexuality: An Introduction, Vol.1*, New York: Vintage, 1990, p.142.
4 In addition to Agamben's reading, discussed below, the notion of the biopolitical is explicit to recent accounts of globalisation, most notably Michael Hardt and Antonio Negri, *Empire*, Cambridge, Mass.: Harvard University Press, 2000.
5 Giorgio Agamben, *Homo Sacer: Sovereign Power and Bare Life*, Stanford: Stanford University Press, 1995, p.4.
6 *Ibid.*, p.120.
7 Michael J. Arlan, *Living Room War*, New York: Syracuse University Press, 1997.

according to mobile, polymorphous and contingent techniques of power'.[9] For all three artists, the movement of the body between these systems — as something conscripted by a system of rules as well as that which interrupts its mechanisms — accords the body its contingent power.

Carolee Schneemann: Life Against Death in the Multimedia Age

'For the TV Generation, Multimedia Techniques Bombard and Overload the Senses for Fun and Profit.'[10] On 16 September 1967, *The New York Times* waxed hyperbolic about the latest, most fantastical forms of new visual media, all deployed, so the text argued, in the service of entertainment and capital. 'A new method of communication is developing in our society,' Grace Glueck wrote, 'the technique of multimedia.'

> Its jarring combinations of stimuli — sounds, light, colors, smells and moving images — aim at reaching audiences by a supersaturated attack on all the senses, not just eye or ear.[11]

Glueck threw the most diverse elements into this rather heady mix: presentations by the Scott Paper Company, which increased its profits by eleven percent due to its use of strobe lights, slide projections and rock music in their sales pitch meetings, 'total environment' discotheques, such as the Cheetah and the Electric Circus, and innovative treatments in endocrinology. Of course she also made mention of art, referring to various sculptural, cinematic and musical practices, including the work of Otto Piene, Len Lye, USCO and the twitchy, computer-generated compositions of Morton Subotnick. Carolee Schneemann is the only woman artist mentioned in the article; Glueck describes Schneemann's kinetic theatre piece *Snows* (1967), which featured a complex relay system and the projection of media images, as an unbridled affirmation of multimedia's new experiential possibilities.

Nothing could be more misleading than this account. If Schneemann believed that film, video, television and the range of new media 'bombarded' and 'overloaded' its imagined audience, she used such media for something quite other than these journalistic imperatives of 'fun and profit'. If *Snows*, as we shall see, in fact provided unflinching political commentary, a later work, which ostensibly bore no relationship to media at all, delivered one of the most incisive verdicts on media's effects on the body. In her performance *Interior Scroll* (1975), where the artist's naked body takes centre stage, Schneemann reads the following text:

8 Indeed, this is the historical moment of the birth-control pill and its sweeping implications for the regulation of female sexuality and its liberation. On the wide-ranging debates on this topic, see Lara V. Marks, *Sexual Chemistry*, New Haven: Yale University Press, 2001.

9 M. Foucault, *The History of Sexuality*, *op. cit.*, p.106.

10 Grace Glueck, 'For the TV Generation, Multimedia Techniques Bombard and Overload the Senses for Fun and Profit', *The New York Times*, 16 September 1967, pp.35 and 37.

11 *Ibid.*, p.35.

I met a happy man
a Structuralist film-maker
— but don't call me that
it's something else I do —
he said we are fond of you
you are charming
but don't ask us
to look at your films
we cannot look at the personal clutter
the persistence of feelings
the hand-touch sensibility
the diaristic indulgence
the painterly mess
the dense gestalt
the primitive techniques [...][12]

While reading, Schneemann pulls a strip of paper out of her vagina. Slowly unfurling the coiled text inch by inch, she reads part of a monologue from her film *Kitch's Last Meal* (1973–78). The documentary images of the performance are indelible, picturing the artist standing on a table, knees bent and naked but for some smears of paint shadowing her breasts, lining her arms, circling her face. Little wonder, then, that the performance has accrued canonic status in the annals of body art. As a performative meditation on what Schneemann calls 'vulvic space' — the architectural, sexual and symbolic space of the vagina — a sense of creative embodiment finds its material expression in a metaphorical birthing of language.

But the interior scroll that ushers forth from her body is not just any scroll, not just any text. Instead, this scroll serves as a metonym for the *vertical* scroll that is film. Schneemann collapses the temporal structure of film, in which the flickering image rolls out frame after frame to produce an illusion of visual coherence, with the body, a body that has seemingly *internalised and then projected* that medium. *Interior Scroll*, after all, was inspired in part by two experimental films by women: Sharon Hennesey's *What I Want* and Anne Severson's *Near the Big Chakra*. In addition, the text archly refers to the largely exclusive boys club of 1960s avant-garde cinema, the Structuralist film-makers who could little bear Schneemann's filmic 'indulgences'.[13] 'Structural film', as defined by P. Adam Sitney in 1969, 'insists on its shape and what content it has is minimal and subsidiary to the outline'.[14] Whatever the usefulness of this definition today, *Interior Scroll* indicts this kind of filmic vocabulary through implicating the position of the body relative to it. On the occasion of its second performance in 1977, Schneemann penned the following stream-of-conscious reflections on the medium's relation to the body:

12 Carolee Schneemann, 'Interior Scroll', *More Than Meat Joy*, New York: Documentext, 1997, p.238.
13 Schneemann recalls that her monologue was as much directed to the critics of her films as it was the artists themselves, and it was by no means limited to men.
14 P. Adam Sitney, 'Structural Film', *Experimental Cinema: The Film Reader* (ed. Wheeler Winston Dixon and Gwendolyn Audrey Foster), London and New York: Routledge, 2002, p.226.
15 C. Schneemann, *More Than Meat Joy*, *op. cit.*, p.236.
16 The term 'expanded cinema' needs to be defined relative to its North American and European contexts.

Live body action steps into area of discrepancy between film which even in most intensive physical conviction remains in the mind-eye permits the passive viewing separation projection an illusion step into the fissure between live action and filmic images the tension is there between the distancing of audience perception and fixity of projection an actual reality triggering filmic reality as coherent present.[15]

To 'step into the fissure between live action and filmic images' was Schneemann's strategy for interrupting 'passive viewing', for more often than not the 'passive viewing' situation bound up with the communications media stemmed from the biopolitical imaging of the body, the power to command its representation as either violence or *Eros*.

Schneemann, as it turned out, had been preoccupied with this issue for well over a decade. She began her first sustained investigations into film with the works *Fuses* (1964–67) and *Viet Flakes* (1965); the subsequent performance *Snows* would make use of the later film in a mixed-media performance. The radical contrast between the two films plots out two biopolitical trajectories: one presents an image of life through its graphic representation of loving sexuality; the other shores up the image of death in the atrocity images streaming endlessly out of South East Asia. These intersect at the point where *Eros* and *Thanatos* are subjected to the technocratic implications of new media in the 1960s, dramatising the degree to which the body screened and abstracted in contemporary culture later would run up against its material double in everyday life.

A 16mm film in both colour and black-and-white, *Fuses* is a notorious critical contribution to the 1960s movement known as 'expanded cinema', sometimes known more generically as 'abstract film'.[16] This 18-minute film, the first of what Schneemann called her 'autobiographical trilogy', is a benchmark of proto-feminist cinema, anticipating both the will to self-representation emblematic of Second Wave Feminism and the imperatives of the sexual revolution more generally.[17] *Fuses* witnesses Schneemann and the composer James Tenney engaged in a protracted session of intense lovemaking, a montage of flesh in which the layering and manipulation of multiple images conspire to produce a work of great visual density. Schneemann made the film in an implicit dialogue with Stan Brakhage, a good friend of the artist since the late 1950s. (Schneemann and Tenney feature prominently in Brakhage's *Cat's Cradle* of 1959.) Yet if Brakhage's aesthetic would prove formative to artists experimenting with film and projection in the 1960s, his film *Window Water Baby Moving* (1959) gave Schneemann pause. In it, Brakhage records his first wife Jane giving birth to their son. For Schneemann, the recording of the birth scene by Brakhage's

As Malcolm Le Grice writes, Peter Weibel used it as early as 1967 to describe specifically formal developments within cinema, particularly those concerning 'the reality of the projection situation itself'. As formulated by Gene Youngblood (whose book of the same title was published in 1970), expanded cinema refers more broadly to the cinematic exploration of 'expanding consciousness' in a peculiar marriage of the psychedelic and technological (Malcolm Le Grice, *Abstract Film and Beyond*, Cambridge, Mass.: The MIT Press, 1977, p.121.)

17 Schneemann's autobiographical trilogy includes *Fuses*, *Plumb Line* (1971) and *Kitch's Last Meal* (1973–78).

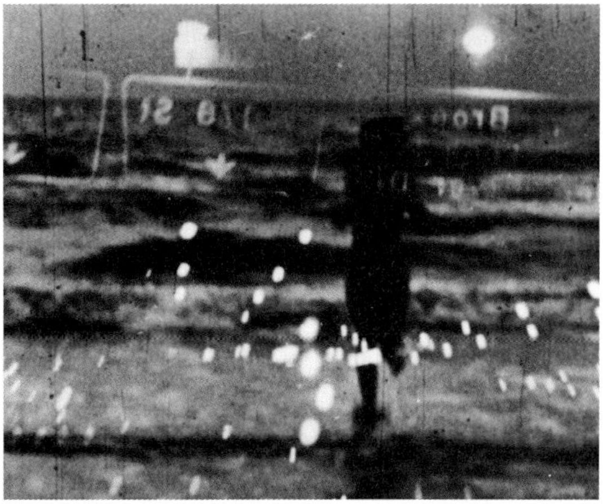

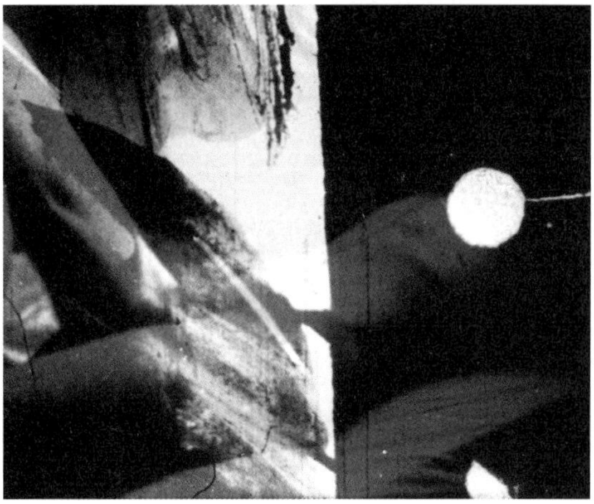

Carolee Schneemann, stills from *Fuses*, 1964–67. 16mm colour film, silent, 22mins

camera eye verged dangerously towards a gesture of masculine appropriation.

Fuses came as a kind of ambivalent response to that appropriation, but, in Schneemann's film, visual access to the body is granted equally to both partners. (Even Schneeman's cat, Kitch, who surveys the goings-on with supreme feline indifference, stands in as a surrogate viewer for the audience.) In *Fuses*, everything is laid open to vision, everything is laid bare. Everything intimate is rendered explicit, laying waste to the border war between the private and spectacular: it is a filmic demonstration of what Lauren Berlant calls the 'intimate public sphere'.[18] 'The fuck', as Schneemann referred to the action, as if it were an actor in the third person, is presented without apology, spurning any kind of veiling soft-focus. Genital sexuality is granted total visibility: cunt, cock and balls move in and out of the frame as relentless formal devices. If conventional pornography treats the female body as a passive object of visual consumption — an inert heap of flesh submitted to phallocratic violence — in *Fuses*, the sexual intertwining of two intimates is a promise of parity. The ever-shifting terrain of those bodies and the multiple perspectives the film affords of them offers a non-monolithic vision of the sexual act. In *Fuses*, *Eros* takes on a phenomenological aspect.

At once celebrated and reviled for its unblinking sexuality, *Fuses* was also regarded as a demonstration piece of the new cinema, stressing 'the material tendency of recent formal work'.[19] Gene Youngblood was among the first critics to review *Fuses*,[20] describing its aesthetic of 'fragmentation' that 'not only prevents narrative continuity, therefore focusing on individual image-events, but also closely approximates the actual experience of sex in which the body of one's partner becomes fragmented into tactile zones and exaggerated mental images'.[21]

We might also turn the generalised notion of 'abstract film' on its head to stress the abstracting tendencies of media in general: their capacity to rationalise and thus manage the body as a function of biopolitical technocracy. As a work veering between the poles of experimental cinema and pornography, *Fuses* plays with that notion in revealing a body teetering between abstraction and figuration, at once shifting out of its recognisable materiality as a visual image and insisting upon the unabashed physicality of its performers.

At numerous points in *Fuses*, the spectator struggles to identify the body. Then, just as quickly, the genital imagery becomes unavoidable — as Schneemann laughingly paraphrased Youngblood, the film brazenly featured 'a 90-foot penis in cinemascope'[22] — only to shift just as dramatically to its more explicitly formal aesthetic. 'There were whole sections,' she recalled, 'where the film is chopped up and laid out onto either black or transparent leader and taped down [...] I soaked it in all sorts of acids and dyes to see what would happen. I cut out details of imagery and repeated them.'[23] These gestures were matched in degree and kind by the movement of the film itself, which sees the coupling of the male and female body as a set of fluid, kinetic relations, variously spliced with scenes that are anything but erotically charged. Kitch takes in the scene by the window; curtains blow; a view of crashing surf suggests an oceanic force. In keeping with that marine metaphor — or rather Freudian trope — the rhythm of the film has itself been described as 'oceanic', an almost tidal ambience in which distinctions between self and other, subject and object, abstraction and figuration are overcome.

At one point the film washes into an open blank expanse, a device not unfamiliar in the new cinema. It is, as Schneemann puts it, an 'indecipherable whiteness' suggesting 'that orgasmic space where you are out beyond wherever you are'.[24] That white field, in other words, stood for pleasure beyond the sensate. Pleasure in excess of the limits of rational being. That the actual footage was 'a snowstorm with cows in it', does little to diminish Schneemann's formal sensibility. This is a body unmoored from the traditional spatio-temporal coordinates of both narrative and pornographic film.

It is thus telling that the next 'abstract' film Schneemann made took on scenes of whiteness — a blanket of media — as a metaphorical snow. Here, though, the body was no longer a screen for orgiastic bliss, porous and open to the desire of another, but a body submitted to the flipside of the biopolitical coin: the right of death and power over life as witnessed in the accelerating violence of the late 1960s. In *Viet Flakes*, Schneemann confronted the media images coming daily out of Vietnam. The proliferation of these images as mass media produced for Schneemann their own form of 'collective insanity', sprawled as they were across newspapers, televisions, magazines and both public and domestic space. As I have written elsewhere, that film would serve as the backdrop for *Snows*, which was performed for eight nights at New York's Martinique Theatre.[25] Insofar as *Snows* was a performance about the 'image' of Vietnam in the mass media, it also provided commentary on the *technology* of the media that produced that image. The living room war brought those images into constant circulation, and for Schneemann, as for so many others,

18 See Lauren Berlant, 'Introduction: The Intimate Public Sphere', *The Queen of America Goes to Washington City*, Durham: Duke University Press, 1997.
19 M. Le Grice, *Abstract Film and Beyond*, *op. cit.*, p.121.
20 Gene Youngblood, *Expanded Cinema*, New York: Dutton, 1970, p.41.
21 *Ibid.*, p.119.
22 Kate Haug, 'An Interview with Carolee Schneemann', *Experimental Cinema*, *op. cit.*, p.176.
23 Carolee Schneemann quoted in G. Youngblood, *Expanded Cinema*, *op. cit.*, p.119.
24 K. Haug, 'An Interview with Carolee Schneemann', *op. cit.*, p.181.
25 For an expanded discussion of *Snows*, see my 'Bridget Riley's Eye/Body Problem', in *Chronophobia: On Time in the Art of the 1960s*, Cambridge, Mass.: The MIT Press, 2004.

they called up the dilemmas of the *reality* of the mass media, understood not just as mere representation — a passive mirroring of events and things outside it — but as a spatio-temporal projection of material consequence in its own right.[26]

In keeping with the complexities of the situation, enormous technical input was demanded of *Snows*.[27] Participants of the group Experiments in Art and Technology facilitated the construction of an interactive relay system between performers and audience. It was important for Schneemann that the images, however horrific, did not immediately register as pictures from the war; she was bent on keeping the roles of the performers flexible, open to cues established by the audience.

> The imagery of *Snows* is ambiguous, shifting metaphors in which the performers are merely themselves, as well as victim, torturer and tortured, aggressor, love and beloved. A dozen audience seats were wired with contact microphones; when people in these seats shifted about, the contact microphones amplified the sound which in turn was channeled into a scr converter and changed the moving light machines.[28]

Schneemann further justified the use of a complex relay system through the following terms:

> I wanted to have these systems of interference, so that even after I could make the most complex, determined sequences of projections [...] there could be some system to interrupt them so that the performers or participants would also be constantly off-guard [...] we were always sort of lost in the process of the piece and on edge because we were being retriggered. What we were responding to was complex.[29]

Schneemann's work provided a means to interfere in the system of images but that interference itself underscored the body's mediation through the visual environment. The notion that one was 'retriggered' or 'reconditioned' by visual cues produced, for Schneemann, something of the phenomenal confusion one confronted in the barrage of images streaming rapid fire out of Vietnam. How to respond? How to locate oneself in relation to a conflict deeply mystified by both distance and the media? *Snows*, Schneemann recalls, 'had to do with the toughening of the materiality of the media [...] they're here now, they're entering [...] and they're *changing* my body'.[30]

26 I borrow the expression 'the reality of the mass media' from a book of the same name by Niklas Luhmann, whose systems-based accounts of social organisation find their counterpart in the logic of mass media. Niklas Luhmann, *The Reality of Mass Media*, Stanford: Stanford University Press, 2000.

27 From a statement (typed) on technical aspects of *Snows* and E.A.T. (in E.A.T. journal), see Carolee Schneemann papers, The Getty Research Institute, Los Angeles, Accession no.940003. As Schneeman observed: 'My problems with technology are concrete, personal; my difficulties with using technicians are mechanical. I want to work with the gestures of machines: to expose their mechanical action as part of the total environment to which it contributes its particular effect. I would like technicians to be interchangeable with performers whenever possible.'

28 Carolee Schneemann papers, The Getty Research Institute, Los Angeles, Accession no.95001, fldr 2.1 b. box 2/1967–71.

29 Interview with the artist, New York, 12 October 2000.

30 *Ibid.*

31 VALIE EXPORT, 'The Real and Its Double: The Body', *Discourse* 11, Fall–Winter 1988–89, pp.5 and 7.

32 Peter Weibel, 'Avant-Garde Film in Austria: Current Activities', *Studio International*, vol.190 no.978, November/December 1975, p.214.

VALIE EXPORT: Within, Without and Throughout the Apparatus

Technology as the sum of all tools serves thus not only the cultural transformation of nature, but also the tendency to transform and dissolve the body itself precisely inasmuch as technology is cultural activity [...] Technologies of reproduction pose the question about the body, and above all, the female body, most radically.[31]
VALIE EXPORT

Schneemann's work plays at the extremes of the biopolitics within the technoculture of the 1960s, the point at which *Eros* and death are submitted to media representation but inverted by the artist through tactics of bodily interference. In Vienna at roughly the same moment, VALIE EXPORT was embarking on her own investigation of the intersection between the body and media, in which the technologies of reproducing subjects were especially critical to female subjectivity. Vienna's experimental cinema and art scene was legendary by 1968, ranging from the avant-garde film of Peter Kubelka and Kurt Kren (an older generation of film-makers than that which concerns me here) to the dramaturgical excesses of Vienna Actionists Günther Brus, Hermann Nitsch and Otto Mühl.[32] Where a woman artist could position herself in relation to this milieu — one with an aggressively masculinist reputation — proved a foundational question to EXPORT's practice. In 1967, for instance, EXPORT was one of the founding members of the Austrian Film-Makers Cooperative; and more often than not, she would locate that question at the point where body and the media converged to produce its own set of psychosexual, cultural and political identifications. That body would take on the character of a sign, becoming a kind of code. EXPORT's very persona as an artist participates in this thinking: in 1966, she famously adopted the name VALIE EXPORT as her pseudonym, borrowing from the realm of commodity culture and the circulation of its advertising imago ('Smart Export' was one of the most popular brands of cigarettes in Austria at the time). EXPORT's presentation as an artist self-consciously appropriated both the verbal and visual rhetoric of that culture to comment upon the reproduction of women's bare lives.

EXPORT's work of the late 1960s and early 70s examines the reproduction of sexual difference in the projection of sexual behaviours in the media.[33] She does so by stressing the *publicness* of representations of sexual difference: how the formation of feminine sexuality, in particular, is always subjected to the mechanisms of representational power, forces coextensive with what is assumed to be private and internalised. Foucault is at pains to point out in *The History of Sexuality* that the alleged repression of sexuality within modernity was, in actuality, that which generated sexuality as 'a discursive fact'; institutional apparatuses produced a public language —

33 Chrissie Iles, 'VALIE EXPORT: Body/Space/Splitting/Projection', *Ob/De+Con(Struction)* (exh. cat.), Philadelphia: Moore College of Art and Design, 2001, p.35. As Iles puts it, EXPORT's was a 'determination to challenge the mediation of the female body by technology'.

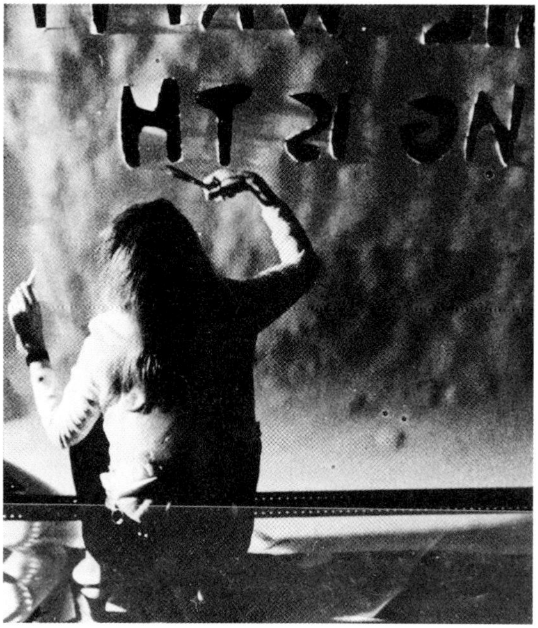

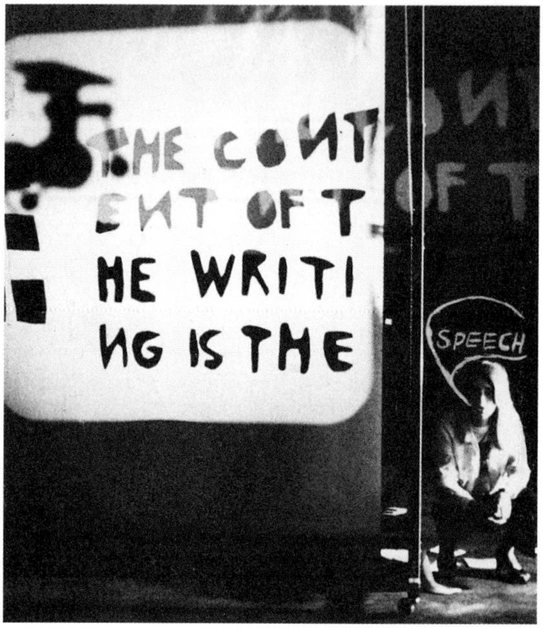

a public representation — around sex, with its own rules and distinct genealogy.[34] EXPORT's practice converges with this sensibility by treating the body as part and parcel to the technological apparatus of media.

EXPORT's collaborations with Peter Weibel subscribed broadly to a shared conception of expanded movies or cinema. In contrast to the distinctly psychedelic, even 'West Coast' iteration of expanded cinema advocated by Gene Youngblood, Weibel and EXPORT's reading of the term in part focused on the scene of projection — the particularities attending the screening of the work itself. As EXPORT herself put it:

> In 1967, Peter Weibel and I developed our 'expanded cinema' in Vienna. We examined the relationship between reality and the apparatus that registered it. [...] The expansion of our film work proceeded initially from the material concept; thus the 'illusion' film was transformed into the material film, and in this way the foundations of the film medium were reflected. [...] The formal arrangement of the elements of film, whereby elements are exchanged or replaced by others ... had an effect which was artistically liberating and yielded a wealth of new possibilities, such as film installations and the film-environment.[35]

According to this definition, expanded cinema is a serious engagement with the 'formal arrangement of film', of which projection represents the ultimate part. The projection itself, as so many of EXPORT's and Weibel's works imply, is a kind of phantasm: a cone of hot air, a beam of light, clouds of dust. The projection is thus both the literal and metaphorical analogue for the illusions of film. Yet, however transient and ephemeral, however bound to the province of shadows, projection's effects are no less material or concrete, no less part of 'reality'. It is in this sense that the projection is the cinematic scene of ideology;

VALIE EXPORT, *Cutting*, 1967/68. Photos © 2008 Peter Hassmann. Courtesy Charim Galerie, Vienna and it is in exploring the apparatus that EXPORT will come to locate the biopolitics of sexual difference.

It hardly needs saying that questions of the apparatus, the ensemble of discrete technical and psychic operations that combine to produce cinematic meaning and its 'reality', is a central category of film theory, evoking a range of debates in the work of Jean-Louis Baudry, Christian Metz, Jean-Louis Comolli and Jacqueline Rose.[36] EXPORT herself has made clear reference to these accounts, which provide a theoretical armature for her conviction that expanded cinema challenged 'the structures and conditions of visual and emotional communication, so as to render our amputated sense of perception capable of perception again'.[37] In 'Ideological Effects of the Basic Cinematographic Apparatus', his canonical discussion of the cinematic apparatus of 1970, Baudry draws upon the language of Louis Althusser (who in turn was drawing in part on Jacques Lacan) to argue that 'the meaning effect produced does not depend only on the content of the images but also on the material procedures by which an image of continuity, dependent on the persistence of vision, is restored from discontinuous elements'.[38] 'The cinematographic apparatus' and the 'hallucinatory reality it creates' demanded a particular kind of critical parsing generally understood as a function of ideology. As apparatus theory was subsequently elaborated by Baudry and Metz, the production of ideology was increasingly located in the specific relation between camera and viewing subject. As if anticipating the mandates of apparatus theory (which would subsequently find among its most cogent articulations in feminist film theory),[39] EXPORT (sometimes with Weibel) would engage the structural terms of multimedia by embedding her own material presence within it.[40] Like so many artists of the 1960s and early 70s — Peter Campus, Anthony McCall, Mary Lucier or Malcolm Le Grice, for example — these investigations took form at the site of the work's projection.[41]

In *Address Redress* of 1968, EXPORT and Weibel engaged projection more literally to demonstrate the way media reproduces its audience through an attendant set of regulations and socialised behaviors — a virtual

34 M. Foucault, *The History of Sexuality*, *op. cit.*, p.11.

35 VALIE EXPORT, 'Expanded Cinema as Expanded Reality' (an edited version of a lecture delivered by EXPORT at 'The Essential Frame — Austrian Independent Film 1995–2003', a two-day programme of screenings and talks on Austrian independent film-making, curated by Mark Webber and held in London, 31 May–1 June 2003). Posted online at www.sensesofcinema.com/contents/03/28/expanded_cinema.html

36 In addition to Baudry, the canonical essays include: Christian Metz, 'The Imaginary Signifier', *Screen*, vol.16 no.2, Summer 1975, pp.14–16; Jean-Louis Comoli, 'Techniques and Ideology: Camera, Perspective, Depth of Field', *Movies and Methods Vol II* (ed. Bill Nichols), Berkeley: University of California Press, Berkeley, 1985, pp.40–57; and the feminist critique of apparatus theory in Jacqueline Rose, 'The Cinematic Apparatus — Problems in Current Theory', *Sexuality in the Field of Vision*, London: Verso, 1986, pp.199–215. Also see Stephen Heath and Teresa de Lauretis (eds.), *The Cinematic Apparatus*, London: Macmillan, 1980.

37 V. EXPORT, 'Expanded Cinema as Expanded Reality', *op. cit.*

38 Jean-Louis Baudry, 'Ideological Effects of the Basic Cinematographic Apparatus', reprinted in *Narrative, Apparatus, Ideology: A Film Theory Reader* (ed. Phillip Rosen), New York: Columbia University Press, 1986, pp.306–07.

39 See, for example, J. Rose, 'The Cinematic Apparatus — Problems in Current Theory', *op. cit.*

40 Silvia Eiblmayr, for instance, notes that EXPORT turns her body into a 'movie screen' or takes on the 'status of a picture'. See Silvia Eiblmayr, '"Split Reality": The Structure of Representation in VALIE EXPORT's Work', *VALIE EXPORT* (exhibition catatalogue), Linz: Oberösterreichisches Landesmuseum, 1992, p.117.

41 On the American history of this phenomena, see Chrissie Iles, *Into the Light: The Projected Image in American Art* (exh. cat.), New York: Whitney Museum of American Art, 2002.

deployment of alliance, to borrow Foucault's terms. Although superficially about the autonomy of the live performer engaged in its projection, *Address Redress* (1968) takes on the thematics of mass psychology through an image recalling the visual archive of fascism. The projection features the scene of a crowd: hundreds of spectators are pressed up against a protective railing, creating a visual field unerring in its regularity and completeness. A performer (EXPORT or Weibel or any actor) was invited to stand before the film and make declarations, tell a joke, air complaints or discourse on whatever topic she chose. Periodically (and regularly) the crowd erupts into rounds of applause, as if to affirm the statements just made by the performer. Here EXPORT and Weibel enact a curious inversion. As audience members, we are expected to voice approval or dissent through the ritualised displays of opinion — cheering or booing. In *Address Redress*, however, the tables are turned, bringing out a paradoxical effect: the projected image seems to answer whatever we may be saying, but its response is already determined in advance, a function of the looping and repetition of the projection mechanism. *Address Redress*, in other words, does not so much *react* to the subject's behavior; instead, it reproduces that behaviour through the appearance of affirmation.

These issues found an acutely feminist reading in works in which EXPORT's body is conflated with the projection event to become the locus of expanded cinema. They include EXPORT's two most notorious performances: *Tap and Touch Cinema,* (1968) and *Genital Panic* (1969). Read together, they articulate the metaphorical penetration of the body by media and explore how the female body, in turn, confronts its own visual representation as the phenomenal horizon of its world, its physical environment. In *Tap and Touch Cinema*, for instance, EXPORT stood on a busy street in Vienna with a box strapped to her chest. The box, made to resemble a stage, was open on both ends; passersby, solicited by Weibel, were entreated to feel EXPORT's bare breasts hidden behind the box's makeshift curtains. *Genital Panic* saw EXPORT enter into the space of a darkened theatre known for screening erotic films.[42] With her hair wildly teased and the crotch cut out of her pants, EXPORT roamed up and down the aisles of the theatre inveighing against the cinematic reproduction of women's bodies as sexualised objects of visual consumption.

Both *Tap and Touch Cinema* and *Genital Panic* speak to the filmic mediation of the female body relative to its spatial — specifically architectural — dimensions. Both blur the line between what is typically regarded as private or internal to female sexuality and what is deemed exposed and public in its pornographic representation: in the realm of biopolitics, where the licit and illicit is legislated by very public forms of discourse, such distinctions are themselves illusory. *Tap and Touch Cinema,* on the one hand,

42 There is some controversy as to what kind of theatre this actually was, although it is now widely accepted that this was not a pornographic movie theatre as it has been suggested in some accounts. Nor was EXPORT holding a gun during her performance, as it has also been claimed. On this history, see Kristin Stiles, 'Corpora Vilia', in *Ob/De+Con(Struction), op. cit.*, note 7, p.32.

43 Quoted in Andrea Jahn, 'The Encounter with the Gaze behind the Mask', in *Joan Jonas: Performance, Video, Installation 1968–2000* (exh. cat.), Ostfildern-Ruit: Hatje Cantz Verlag, note 14, p.57.

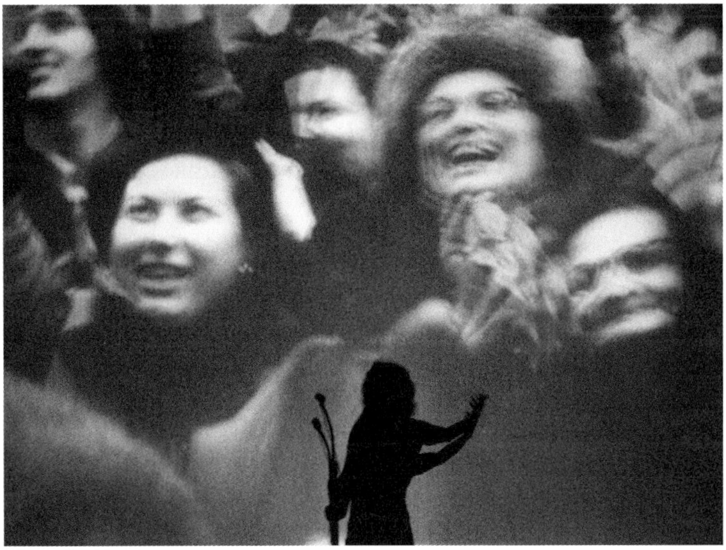

VALIE EXPORT, *Address Redress*, 1968. Courtesy Charim Galerie, Vienna

enlists the artist's body as the architectural locus for the theatrical projection of female sexuality. The 'theatre', the domain of phantasms, of images, is a cavity coextensive with the artist's material body, here made open and available. Calling the work *Tap and Touch Cinema*, EXPORT stresses the haptic implications or physical consequences of the filmic medium, however much pornography is claimed as the realm of fantasy. She does so by situating that body in the harsh light of the public sphere, as if the clandestine world of pornographic cinema and its accoutrements — the upturned collar, the trench coats that disguise, the gestures that take place in theatres of darkness — was itself exposed in its nakedly public aspect. In contrast, *Genital Panic* takes the figure of the naked woman *off* the screen and into the aisles of the theatre itself, thereby confusing the terms of the visual object with the subject of spectatorship.

No work addresses this conceit more completely than EXPORT's *Adjoined Dislocations* (1973 and 1975) in which the artist strapped two 8mm cameras to her front and back, at once filming the body's relationship to its surroundings and becoming the implied object of the two recordings. Her body is quite literally armoured by — if not sutured into — the technologies of the apparatus. The films represent an experience of the body divided between recto and verso, but the panoramic sweep provided by the imagery of both does less to consolidate an image of bodily coherence than to produce a sense of dislocation, registering the temporal split between the movements of a simultaneous coming and going. The gesture is crucial to the reproduction of bare lives — the reproduction of the female body through its virtual dissection in media.

Joan Jonas: Bare Lives as Interrupted Signals

I like to reveal the mechanics of illusion.[43]
Joan Jonas

Jonas, a New York-based artist, began working a short time after Schneemann and EXPORT. While she also made films, many of her performances were primarily organised around the medium of video. Influenced by the radical dance innovations of the Judson Memorial Church — she participated in workshops led by Yvonne Rainer, Deborah Hay and Trisha Brown —

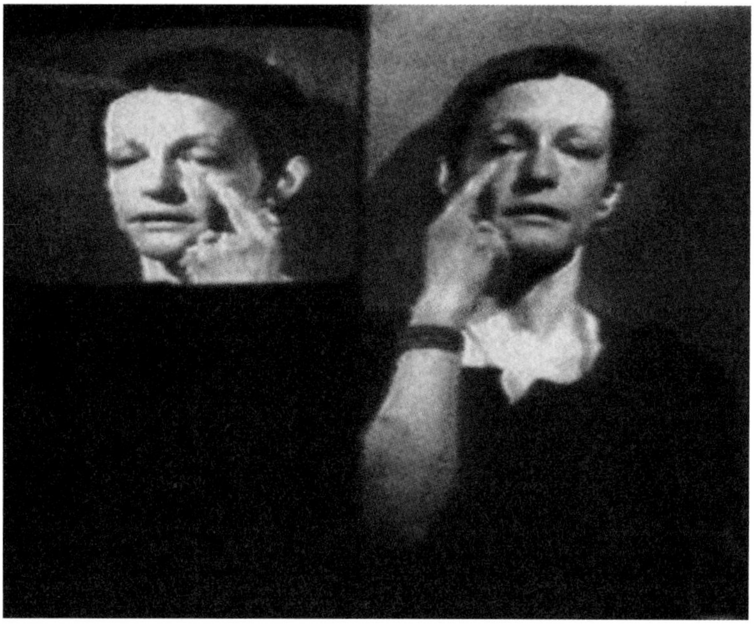

Joan Jonas, still from *Left Side Right Side*, 1972. Black-and-white video, sound, 9mins. Courtesy Electronic Arts Intermix

Jonas's understanding of task-oriented and Minimalist dance was critical to the spare, repetitious work she would later produce. Just as EXPORT considered the dimensionality of the female body as it was coordinated in expanded cinema, Jonas treated the body's spatial abstraction in video. This thinking, however, ran contrary to the conventional artistic politics of video in the late 1960s and early 70s, which centred on both the rhetoric of its immediacy and the conviction that video, as opposed to television, was a democratising medium. Video, in other words, was championed largely for its real-time properties: it was seen as a mode of representation that shored up the transparency of communication and those it represented.

But Jonas would invert the use of video and its associated technologies in the service of *disarticulating* the body: both the body's imagined integrity and its seeming capacity to communicate in an unmediated fashion. While this was a moment in which the stakes of art and politics were especially high, Jonas's implicit approach to video's representational imperatives was not in keeping with traditional activist aesthetics. For Jonas, the devices of the mirror, first, and the feedback signal, second, act as metonyms for video's presentation of the body imagined as coherent, spatially and temporally immanent. Far from subscribing to the visual recuperation of the body, a gesture advanced in certain feminist artistic circles, Jonas's work challenged the irreducibility of that body in terms of the mediated space it would occupy.[44] As Douglas Crimp has argued, the sense of dislocation so critical to her practice often took the form of *de-synchronization*: the disjunctive temporality between the body's action and its subsequent representation, a kind of endless (and fruitless) attempt to mesh the lived presence of the body with its mediated double in its surroundings.[45] Crucially, this kind of doubling within her art, whether produced through mirrors or feedback loops, thematises the technological reproduction of the female body *not* in terms of maternal plenitiude — not in terms of psychic identification — but as a type of loss.[46]

Consider Jonas's use of mirrors in her performances, which then pointedly undermine the expectations of bodily identification experienced on approaching those reflective surfaces.[47] *Left Side Right Side* (1972) for instance, plays with the distortions produced by and within the culture of media as allegorised by the mirror. As Jonas writes:

> What interested me in the piece was the construction of a self-reflective loop through which I regarded myself simultaneously in a mirror and a video monitor, both of which faced me while a video camera recorded the paired images through which I watched my two selves, the one in the mirror, which was reversed left and right, and the one in the monitor, which was a displacement of my own subjective orientation out into the space in front of me.[48]

In short, Jonas would use both mirrors and video monitors to expose the delay between movement and representation; they served in her hands as devices of fragmentation or even dis-identification. Rather than consolidating the image of the body as reproduced in video transmission, Jonas's performance was a critical parsing of that body, dividing it into left and right, corresponding to the breakdown of binocular vision. The resulting video documents the confusion generated in her attempt to distinguish left from right during her performance. 'The formal tensions,' she observed, 'remained tied to the kind of psychic tension that was behind the work as a whole.'[49]

The temporal delay between self and its mirror image found a more technologically mediated analogue in works that followed, particularly the performance *Funnel* (1974), which implicated the audience in its complex representation of space. Performed in both New York and Rome, *Funnel* involved a spatially ambiguous stage set that changed continuously throughout the work's duration: it was comprised of live performance, video images and sound. Two cloth curtain walls were hung from the ceiling perpendicular to the stage, breaking up the area into three sections. They appeared to recede dramatically into the background — like the funnel that is a visual cone — producing an illusion of radical depth for the audience facing them. As the performance wore on, the curtains were progressively stripped back so that the space was flattened over the course of Jonas's action. Other props were revealed in the process: cones and horizontal bars and a large hoop, but also video monitors and cameras. As Jonas explains the action:

> A monitor placed in the left foreground reflected what was beside it, before it, and behind it, depending on the camera angle. One stationary camera was placed in front of the audience about twenty feet from

44 Joan Jonas (with Rosalind Krauss), 'Seven Years', *Drama Review*, vol.19 no.1, March 1975, p.13.

45 See D. Crimp, 'De-synchronization in Joan Jonas's Performances', *op. cit.*, pp.8–10.

46 Or, as Rosalind Krauss would argue, it is a kind of narcissism. Rosalind Krauss, 'Video: The Aesthetics of Narcissism', *Video Culture: A Critical Investigation* (ed. John Hanhardt), Rochester, New York: Video Studies Workshop Press, 1986, pp.179-91. Please note that this essay is reproduced in the current volume.

47 This is why, one imagines, references to Lacan's canonical account of the mirror stage are so prevalent in the literature on Jonas. See e.g. A. Jahn, 'The Encounter with the Gaze Behind the Mask', *op. cit.*, p.64.

48 J. Jonas, 'Seven Years', *op. cit.*, p.14.

49 *Ibid.*, p.15.

the set, transferring an image to the monitor, a detail of the performance seen simultaneously with my activity [...] A second portable camera was used for alternate angles of vision.[50]

Jonas's description attests to the complexity of the space — the disjunction between the illusionistic depth of the stage and the elusive realms of the video monitor. Her activities within both registers of space, at once altering the physical coordinates of the stage and captured by the television screen, would set into motion a virtual hall of mirrors. 'The intent,' she suggested, 'was to play with the illusion of the flat video image and to relate the space of the monitor and its image to that of the real space. The actual space is sometimes as ambiguous as that of the TV.'[51]

Like many of her works from the period, *Funnel* takes place at the ambiguous nexus between 'real' space and media space. As Crimp has suggested: 'Presenting real space as an impenetrable illusion, Jonas has made the experience of performance equivalent ... to film and videotape.'[52] When Jonas alters the image on the television through feedback, she reveals how the representational integrity of the female body in media is, in fact, the product of a set of interrupted signals. The body itself takes on the status of information. Like information, not only does it become something to regulate and manage, but something to be analysed and dispersed.

Vertical Roll (1972), Jonas's best-known video, demonstrates how bare lives function like interrupted signals, feedback loops endlessly filtered through the temporality of the video monitor. In *Vertical Roll*, there are no props, no costumes, just the stripped down mechanisms of video camera, monitor and the body staged before it. The video is organised around an encounter of sorts: a performance of the body and 'the vertical roll that results from two out-of-sync frequencies, the frequency signal sent to the monitor and the frequency by which it is interrupted'.[53] Jonas instrumentalises the temporal delay between signals for both representational and structural effect; she does so to the point where the video's 'narrative' founders on the non-contemporaneity of its technology. As the video stutters along, its image broken at regular intervals, body parts appear in frame: an arm, a hand, a leg, a midriff. No image remains still, however, and no image is stable enough to produce anything close to a coherent body. Jonas uses sound as well to emphasise the non-synchronous quality of the image: a spoon striking a mirror, for example, or two blocks of wood struck together function as a primitive soundtrack that underscores the halting movement of the medium.

Yet the body dispersed and parsed by the signal is at the same time that which both interrupts and constructs its illusion. In several frames, Jonas places her hand face down parallel to the ground, while the movement

50 *Ibid.*, p.17.
51 *Ibid.*, p.18.
52 Douglas Crimp, 'Joan Jonas's Performance Works', *Studio International*, vol.192 no.982, July/August 1976, p.10.
53 Joan Jonas, *Scripts and Descriptions 1968–1983* (ed. Douglas Crimp), Berkeley and Eindhoven: University Art Museum and Stedelijk Van Abbesmuseum, 1983, p.130.
54 M. Foucault, *The History of Sexuality*, *op. cit.*, p.73.

of the roll produces the appearance of the artist clapping. It is by virtue of such forced illusions that *Vertical Roll* exposes the seams behind the flow of visual information that would otherwise appear seamless. When Jonas directly faces the camera at the end of the video, breaking out of the circuit between video and monitor, we sense the self-conscious movement of her body as a form of information in its own right, as its own signal, with all its implications for the mobilisation of other 'signals' contiguous with that body's representation.

It is this sense that Jonas, EXPORT and Schneemann understand bare lives not only in terms of their limit conditions — of the sovereign power of life and death wielded over them — but in the possibilities of *performing* the mechanics of biopolitical production. Each sees those mechanisms as technocratic in kind; each treats sexuality as a discursive fact in its mediation. Confronting those mechanisms in their work, implicating their bodies as communications media, they evoke Foucault's mandate for a biopolitics of pleasure — and power along with it:

> We need to take these mechanisms seriously, therefore, and reverse the direction of our analysis; rather than assuming a generally acknowledged repression, and an ignorance measured against what we are supposed to know, we must begin with these positive mechanisms, insofar as they produce knowledge, multiply discourse, induce pleasure and generate power ... In short, we must define the strategies of power that are immanent in this will to knowledge.[54]

LEISURE 73
Sabeth Buchmann

–I–

At a time when the combination of youth and pop culture, protest and social movements, avant-garde film and electronic mass media promised far-reaching cultural upheavals, the artist Hélio Oiticica (1937–80) — mostly in collaboration with the film-maker Neville D'Almeida — was developing his 'quasi-cinemas'. These consisted of installation-like combinations of slide projections and audio tracks that were a continuation of the participatory objects and interactive environments Oiticica had made in Brazil in the 1960s within the context of *Tropicalismo* — a broad movement of political activists, writers, film-makers, musicians and artists. Oiticica became well-known, in particular, for his *Parangolés*, samba costumes which, in his words 'still retained features of a universal tendency to go back to myths, to incorporate sense-impressions'; they 'represented the beginning, the origin of my concept of a "New Objectivity" and of *Tropicália*.'[1] Oiticica's installation called *Tropicália* referred to the 'organic architecture of the *favelas* in Rio de Janeiro (and later to other types of *favelas*, like the *palafitas* with their pole dwellings by the Amazon), and especially to the discovery of the anonymous, *ad hoc* constructions in large urban areas — the art of the street, of the unfinished, of empty space etc.'[2]

The name Oiticica gave to his environment had a programmatic element to it inasmuch as *Tropicalismo* was the name of a politically left, pop-cultural group that was formed in 1967 to oppose the military regime that had come to power in Brazil in 1964, as well as to protest against the economic and cultural hegemony of the US and Western Europe. Nevertheless, Oiticica felt closely connected to New York's subculture as well as its popular culture, having come into close contact with them at the beginning of the 1970s, after having received a grant from the Guggenheim Foundation and moved to the city as a result. There are, for example, references in the 'quasi-cinemas' to the glamour culture surrounding Andy Warhol and to the slide shows of underground film-maker Jack Smith, which appealed to Oiticica's taste

1 See Hélio Oiticica, 'Tropicália', in Sabine Breitwieser (ed.), *Vivências/Lebenserfahrung/Life Experience* (exh. cat.), Vienna: Generali Foundation, 2000, p.262.

2 *Ibid.*

3 See Carlos Basualdo, 'Waiting for the Internal Sun: Notes on Hélio Oiticica's Quasi-Cinemas', in Carlos Basualdo (ed.), *Hélio Oiticica's: Quasi-Cinemas* (exh. cat.), Cologne, Columbus and New York: Kölnischer Kunstverein, Wexner Center for the Arts, and New Museum of Contemporary Art, in association with Hatje Cantz, 2001, p.41.

4 Oswald de Andrade, 'Manifesto Antropófago/Anthropophagisches Manifest/Anthropophagite Manifesto' (trans. Thomas Sandführ and Jeffrey Hoff), reprinted in Elke aus dem Moore and Giorgio Ronna (eds.), *Entre Pindorama*, Nuremberg: Verlag für Moderne Kunst, 2005, pp.26–31. It is a coincidence that Joaquim Pedro, Mário and Oswald shared the surname de Andrade — the three individuals were not related. With thanks to

for so-called 'hybrid' kinds of art, of which there are a string of examples in the Brazilian *Cinema Novo* movement of the 1960s. Indeed, Oiticica appeared in the 1968 film 'Câncer' by Glauber Rocha, who called it 'an underground film shot in 16mm'.[3] Within this trajectory one could also mention the legendary film *Macunaima* (1969), directed by Joaquim Pedro de Andrade and based on a short story published in 1928 by Mário de Andrade. That same year the poet Oswald de Andrade produced his 'Manifesto Antropófago'.[4] The very title of de Andrade's manifesto was programmatic insofar as anthropophagy means cannibalism. The poet was referring to the ritual of the Tupi Indians who, quite literally, incorporated those enemies they felt to be more powerful than themselves, in order to obtain their strength and be able to face them on a superior level. Hence de Andrade formulated his most famous motto: 'Tupi or not Tupi is the question.' (Thomas Sandführ has called this de Andrade's 'version of Hamlet's dilemma'.)[5] Just as European modernism had appropriated 'foreign' — that is, pre-modern and 'exotic' — forms of representation from Africa and Asia, so Brazilian artists and intellectuals should show scant respect in appropriating European culture, which they had up until then only ever tried to emulate and combine with local traditions. In the process of working through external influences, de Andrade recognised the historical trauma of relinquishing to the colonial powers of Portugal and Europe, against which he proposed an artistic eclecticism that would not only 'eclipse the existing asymmetries' but also 'emphasise the reciprocity of influences'.[6]

As Ruda de Andrade, grandson of the poet, writes, de Andrade was demanding nothing less than 'the Caribbean Revolution':

> Greater than the French Revolution. A revolution of the tropics, the end result of an historical process, that he had dreamt up in the manifesto: A revolution, whose final consequence would be the abolition of the patriarchal, capitalist system and the ringing in of a new era of sacred idleness [courtesy of technological progress] — the idleness of the indigenous population which the Europeans had destroyed through the introduction of slavery and the production system.[7]

Key ideas of the senior de Andrade's appear in a text that Oiticica wrote to accompany his *Tropicália* environment — for example, when he advocates the reciprocal absorption and penetration of diverse cultural practices and types of experience, especially those that, from the perspective of 'progressive' industrial societies, are perceived as regressive and primitive.[8] At the beginning

Paula Braga for this information.

5 Thomas Sandführ, 'Só a Antropofagia nos une — Assimilation und Differenz in der Figur des Anthropophagen', in E. aus dem Moore and G. Ronna (eds.), *Entre Pindorama*, *op. cit.*, p.47.

6 *Ibid.*

7 Ruda de Andrade, 'História Devorada/Verschlungene Geschichte', in E. aus dem Moore and G. Ronna (eds.), *Entre Pindorama*, *op. cit.*, p.54.

8 See H. Oiticica, 'Tropicália', *op. cit.*, p.262.

of his artistic career, Oiticica had adhered to the programme of Concretism, which was popular in Brazil in the 1950s; later, in his Conceptual phase, he was to take up de Andrade's ideas again and integrate them into his version of *Tropicalismo*.

> *Tropicália* is the very first conscious attempt to put a wholly 'Brazilian' stamp on the contemporary context of the avant-garde and on the various forms of national art in general.[9]

Yet, as artist and author Ricardo Basbaum writes:

> the politics of *Tropicalismo* were completely different from the *Antropofagia* of the 1920s. It was no longer a question of redefining the country and its traditions as a new nation, but of liberating people's desires, needs and senses through new forms of behaviour and action and, more to the point, in the context of McLuhan's global village with all its far-reaching possibilities for communication.[10]

Oiticica's involvement in Brazilian *Modernismo* had given him a special affinity for combining the avant-garde with folk and popular culture in the way he portrayed others and expressed himself. This also proved to be effective in his early experiments with film and cinema. Thus, his 'quasi-cinemas' contain highly heterogeneous and inter-connected references to Brazilian, European and US-American cultures and counter-cultures. They allow one to glimpse the eventual possibility of overcoming a social and moral code based on capitalist production and consumerism. I intend to demonstrate this using Oiticica's work *CC5 Hendrix-War* (1973)—recently recreated in the exhibition 'X-Screen' at the Museum Moderner Kunst Stiftung Ludwig in Vienna—as an example.[11] The reference to Jimi Hendrix can be understood as an allusion to those mythical, black heroes in Brazilian and Cuban literature who reject demeaning and badly-paid forms of physical labour and factory work because they are deeply rooted in the institution of slavery.[12]

This is the context in which one should understand Oiticica's invention of the term 'creleisure'—a neologism based on a punning amalgamation of 'creativity' and 'leisure'. Its implicit reference to the leisure culture of the proletariat was meant to counter both the elitist views of art by the bourgeoisie and the production ethos of the proletariat as expressed in Concrete art. The artist wrote:

> Not to occupy a specific place, in space and time, as well as to live pleasure or not to know the time of laziness, is and can be the activity to which

9 *Ibid.*

10 Richardo Basbaum, 'Antropofagia and the Strategies of Permanent Hybridization/Antropofagia und Strategien permanenter Hybridisierung', in E. aus dem Moore and G. Ronna (eds.), *Entre Pindorama*, *op. cit.*, p.64.

11 See Matthias Michalka (ed.), *X-Screen: Film Installations and Actions in the 1960s and 1970s* (exh. cat.), Vienna: MUMOK, Museum Moderner Kunst Stiftung Ludwig, 2004.

12 See Stephanie Dennison and Lisa Shaw, *Popular Cinema in Brazil: 1930–2001*, Manchester: Manchester University Press, 2004, p.21.

13 Hélio Oiticica, 'Creleisure', in *Hélio Oiticica* (exh. cat.), Barcelona, Paris, Rio de Janeiro and Rotterdam: Fundació Antoni Tàpies, Galerie nationale du Jeu de Paume, Projeto Hélio Oiticica and Witte de With Center for Contemporary Art, 1992, p.135.

the 'creator' may dedicate himself. [...] Is *Creleisure* creation of leisure or belief in leisure? [crer = to believe, tn.] — I don't know, maybe both, maybe neither. The dimwits can quit at this point, because they will never understand: it is stupidity which predominates in art criticism — luckily they were punished by their own indifference to pleasure, to leisure, or to cannibalistic supra-states, though this identification does not interest me here.[13]

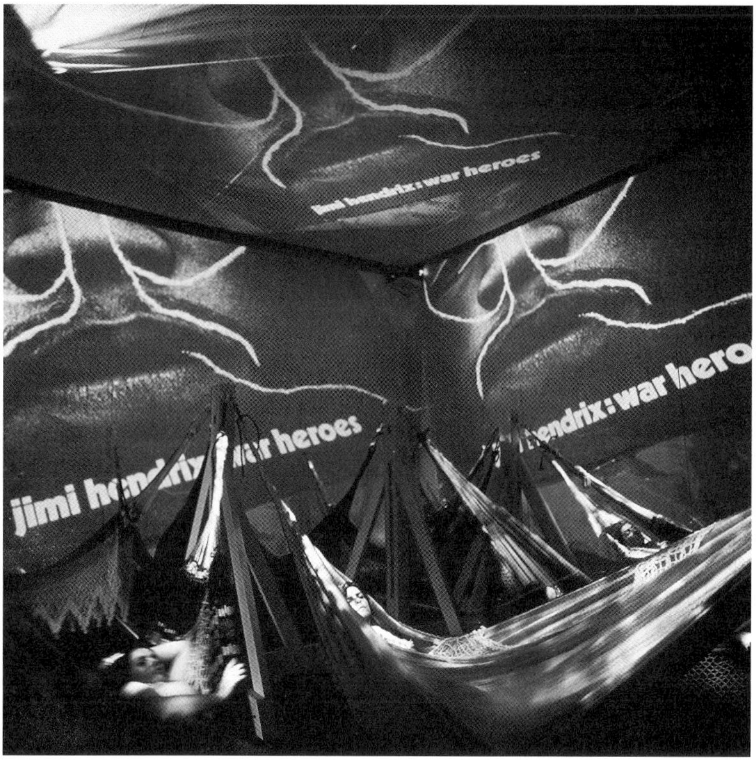

Hélio Oiticica and Neville D'Almeida, *01-CC5 (Trash-iscapes/Cosmo-coca Programa in Progress)*, 1973/2003. Courtesy Cesar Oiticica Filho and MUMOK

Oiticica openly employed his belief as a 'living' way of experiencing the world polemically against those whom he saw as agents of a value system geared towards the prevailing dictates of labour and production. Using the example *CC5 Hendrix-War*, I intend to argue that the 'quasi-cinemas' reveal tensions between the critical negativity of the (neo-)avant-garde (in Oiticica's case this means the production-orientated tradition of constructivist languages of images and objects) and the positivity of a (post-)avant-garde aesthetic (characterised by a fetishised, sexualised appropriation of mass-media images). Unlike the environments that Oiticica made at the end of the 1960s, in this case it isn't the gallery, the museum or urban spaces that are transformed into places of 'creative leisure'. Here, the *topos* of creativity is in no way linked to romantic, possibly escapist ideas of pre-industrial craftsmanship, but rather to an aspect of the culture industry that, like no other, embodies Walter Benjamin's conditions for the work of art in the age of its technical reproducibility. This interpretation finds support in Carlos Basualdo's essay 'Waiting for the Internal Sun: Notes on Hélio Oiticica's Quasi-Cinemas'. Basualdo suggests that one should read Oiticica's 'quasi-cinemas' as an attempt to create models of subjectivity (as the result of value-added labour) to which no opposition could be expected either from the then avant-garde or from the left:

> What emerges from the texts [i.e. the texts of Oiticica] is no longer the concrete artist who forces art to fulfil its modern promise, extending it to the world through the viewer's active participation, but rather the inventor of ways of life, reconfiguring his work on the basis of a systematic consideration of the relations between the different regimes of labour and

> the subjective formations to which they give rise. At the centre of this effort of intellectual reordering in Oiticica's late production one finds his relation to cinema, and the series of works in which the artist addressed the cinematographic image, works that were given the collective name of quasi-cinemas.[14]

Thus, the association of cinema with 'creleisure' that was central to the 'quasi-cinemas' was aimed only partly at the class struggle of a proletariat bound to the prevailing ethos of production; in addition, Oiticica's artistic model envisaged an experience of time and space that ran counter to the prevailing order. According to Basualdo, the concept of 'invention' is therefore not predicated on the connection between artist and work but on the 'life form' as such — a claim that can be related to Michel Foucault's and Giorgio Agamben's theories on modern biopower. Artist and critic Ricardo Basbaum applies these theories to works by Lygia Clark, an artist who was close to Oiticica. For example, he shows that the way in which *Tropicalismo* redirected cannibalistic strategies to the area of media culture signifies a biopolitical turning-point.[15] The question remains whether this assertion addresses the full implications of what Foucault calls the appropriation of life by modern regimes of power and what Agamben describes as the totalitarian means of control.[16] Alternatively, one could argue against Peter Bürger's assertion that the social dreams of the (post-)avant-garde had failed because they had been institutionalised or made part of the culture industry (or both), and advance the thesis that these dreams had been realised at least as far as the social acceptance of a modern way of life was concerned.

– II –

CC5 Hendrix-War belongs to the so-called 'block-experiments in cosmococa' that occupy a special place within the 'quasi-cinemas'. Conceived as a 'program in progress',[17] seven of the eight *Cosmococas* were made in collaboration with others, and the first five with D'Almeida. These five consist of room-sized installations with slide projections, cassette recordings, various materials and things to sit and lie on. Oiticica's role was to arrange the installation, including choosing the soundtrack and photographic images, while D'Almeida took charge of 'painting' everything with cocaine powder, applying it as if it were make-up. The use of cocaine represents only one of the many double and multiple meanings contained within Oiticica's (and D'Almeida's) idea of 'creleisure'. The use of make-up can also be read as a form of exaggerated and trashy appropriation of the portraits and names of celebrities — taken from books, record covers and magazines — which served as images for the slides shown in the *Cosmococas*. Included alongside Jimi Hendrix were Luis Buñuel, Yoko Ono, Martin Heidegger, Marilyn Monroe, John Cage and the Rolling Stones, among others. It seems reasonable to assume that Oiticica's selection should be understood as a homage to those figures in literature, film, philosophy and art who constituted, at that time, his artistic and intellectual pantheon. He intended to change their significance not only in accordance with the principles of *Antropofagia*, but also in relation to his critique of modernism and universalism. He wrote:

> In a long article which I am preparing, 'In search of the Supra-sensorial', all these problems are posed and proposed: the old problem to the 'return to myth', the problem of the national culture, of the definitive suppression of the 'work of art' (transformed into consumption in the capitalist structure), of creativity on the collective level, in opposition to the reigning of conformity, of the use of hallucinogenic drugs on the collective plane (also showing a considerable difference between the proposition here and Timothy Leary and his followers in the U.S.), of the expansion of individual consciousness onto the creative plane, of the incomparable difference in the expressiveness, intellectually, of Blacks in relation to Whites and of the creation of Brazilian myth of 'miscegenation'.[18]

It is Oiticica's vision of a socially transgressive consumption of drugs that gives its name to his *Cosmococas*; he refers unequivocally to the coca plant and, therefore, to the ultimate source of cocaine and of its medicinal, spiritual and economic importance for the Incas, whose empire disappeared with the colonisation of Latin America. For Oiticica this is also one of the historic starting points for the question of how to undermine the ruling capitalist system of production and consumption, together with its complicit colonial exploitation and patriarchal way of thinking. According to Basualdo, this complicity also manifested itself in the Kennedy administration's attempts to establish local markets in South American countries in the name of democratisation and 'developmentalism', which were meant to act, among other things, as a bulwark against local left-wing forces.[19] In a letter to Lygia Clark dated 11 July 1974, Oiticica places in a historical perspective the use of cocaine (referred to as PRIMA in his writings) as a highly specific form of oppositional subjectivity:

> Because marijuana tribalizes and PRIMA isolates, the Incas were powerful in their individuality and succumbed to the Spanish because they were SPARTAN (united in masculine Fraternity to make War); for me the PRIMA-INCA thing is the future; the SPARTAN thing is the past.[20]

In this way Oiticica's model of 'creleisure' combines a forgotten culture with subcultural practices. In reference to the poet Haroldo de Campos, Basualdo writes that the *Cosmococas* represented a systematic attempt at 'organised delirium' — something that was not at all that unusual in the context

14 C. Basualdo, 'Waiting for the Internal Sun: Notes on Hélio Oiticica's Quasi-Cinemas', *op. cit.*, p.40.

15 R. Basbaum, 'Antropofagia and the Strategies of Permanent Hybridization/ Antropofagia und Strategien permanenter Hybridisierung', *op. cit.*, p.64.

16 See Michel Foucault, *The History of Sexuality: An Introduction* (trans. Robert Hurley), New York: Pantheon, 1978; and Giorgio Agamben, *Homo Sacer: Sovereign Power and Bare Life* (trans. Daniel Heller-Roazen), Stanford University Press, 1998.

17 See Palo Alto: 'Block-Experiments in Cosmococa-Program in Progress', in *Hélio Oiticicia: Quasi-Cinemas*, *op. cit.*, p.97.

18 See H. Oiticica, 'Tropicália', *op. cit.*, p.264.

19 See C. Basualdo, 'Waiting for the Internal Sun: Notes on Hélio Oiticica's Quasi-Cinemas', *op. cit.*, p.42.

20 *Ibid.*

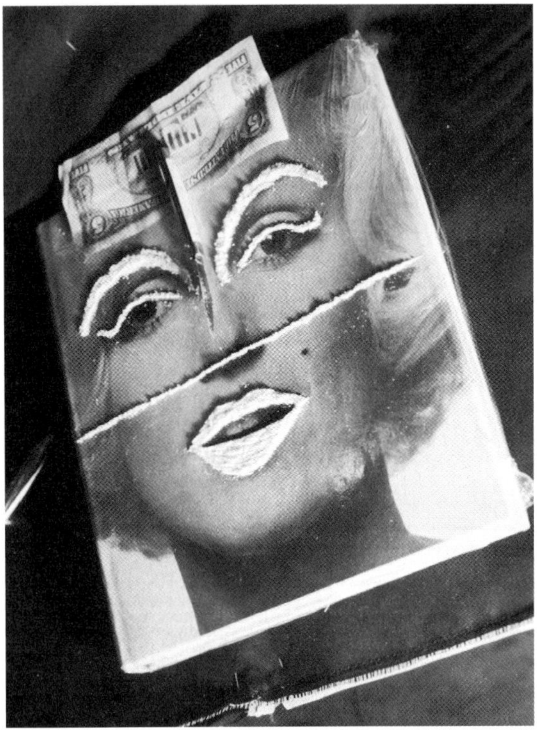

Hélio Oiticica and Neville D'Almeida, *23-CC3 (Maileryn/ Cosmococa Programa in Progress)*, 1973/2003. Courtesy Galerie Lelong, New York

of revolutionary calls to change society through the expansion of perception and consciousness, as the exhibition 'X-Screen' clearly demonstrated with its documents on so-called LSD-art.[21] Thus, in a text written on the occasion of his 1969 exhibition 'Eden' at London's Whitechapel Art Gallery, Oiticica speaks of 'supra-sensory' fields of perception, distinguishable from the deterministic Op art model of stimulus and response, and from all purely mechanical forms of interactivity.[22] However, that does not mean that Oiticica's perceptual model was sited outside the parameters of (the culture) industry. Rather, based on the analogy between pigment and cocaine, a possible collusion between art and cinema, on the one hand, and the underground and illegality, on the other, is revealed. After all, his (idealistic) view of taking cocaine contains the promise not only of seeing, hearing and feeling more, but also the hope of removing the legitimacy of those bourgeois, capitalist values of which high culture and the culture industry in general were agents, according to Oiticica. This is why Basualdo believes that the stimulating effect of cocaine represented for Oiticica an antidote to the power he thought was inherent in the dialectic between alienated labour and de-sublimated consumption.[23] If one accepts Basualdo's idea, it would mean that Oiticica saw the use of cocaine as a possible means of opposing the way that the subject was reified by the producer-and-consumer model practised by the stimulation industry, and of replacing it with a form of boundless enjoyment that was as much individualised as it was collectivised. According to this model, the use of cocaine could be understood as a deviant attempt to re-sublimate a leisure culture (making it consequently an aesthetic experience), which — unlike the avant-gardes of modernism — was no longer (whether unconsciously or with the aim of being critically compensated) in thrall to the worker-and-producer morality of patriarchal, bourgeois capitalism.[24]

Seen from this angle, the 'illegal' consumption of the incunables of intellectual history, of the avant-garde and of Hollywood seems in no way arbitrary. Titles such as *CC2-Onooject*, which is attached to slides of Yoko Ono's book *Grapefruit* and *What is a thing?* by Martin Heidegger, or *CC3 Maileryn* — which refers to a portrait of Marilyn Monroe from a Norman Mailer novel — are reminiscent of Oswald de Andrade's strategy of incorporating aspects of European and non-European art, literature and cultural history into a work — a strategy that reutilised popular and folkloric forms of representation in multiple ways. Oiticica shares with the poet and thinker of Brazilian

Modernismo a predilection for transforming found footage along onomatopoeic lines to give an acoustic quality to material. Related to this is an emphasis on the haptic-tactile as well as on the imaginative-intellectual perception of things. For example, objects such as matchboxes, Coca-Cola signs, knives and pencils that were used in the pictorial montages can be read not only as multi-layered signs but also as tools. Thus, a penknife is both a substitute for a palette knife and a metaphor for editing films — an instance that brings out the imaginative-conceptual as well as the material-artisanal dimensions of Oiticica's cinematic model. Since the portrait of Buñuel appears in Oiticica's cosmos, it is possible that the knife here refers to his famous Surrealist film *Un chien andalou* (1929).

An important characteristic of the *Cosmococas* is the script-like instructions that form the basis of each installation.[25] This is reminiscent of the performance directions developed in the Fluxus movement at the beginning of the 1960s and radicalised by Conceptual art to distinguish between the actual process of making a work and its linguistic definition. Oiticica's reference to Yoko Ono can be read in this way, for example. His instructions are divided into 'public' and 'private performances'; that is, they could be staged either in a specific, public place and at a fixed time, or at an unspecified time in private — an idea that makes it clear that Oiticica's participatory, Conceptual art owes much to the avant-garde vision of making art part of life itself.

I will begin with the instructions for the 'public performance' of *CC5 Hendrix-War*. Oiticica designated his loft as the site for the action:

> At babylonests, lower-middle NEST:
> 81 2nd Ave: #4,
> NYC

Details of the time follow:

> August 26th 1973
> from 2 am to 3:30 am[26]

It seems likely that Oiticica's decision to call his loft 'Babylonests' is a direct nod to Kenneth Anger's book *Hollywood Babylon* (1959); in other words, Oiticica was concerned to relate the locations of his 'quasi-cinemas' unmistakably to queer underground films, which in turn had parallels with Brazilian cinema of the 1940s and 50s and its popular drag performances.[27]

On this point Basualdo quotes a letter by Oiticica to the poet Wally Salomâo, his friend. In the letter the artist expresses his enthusiasm for Jack Smith, who performed his famous slide shows in his East Village loft, beginning in the morning and sometimes spending as long as half-an-hour

21 *Ibid.*
22 See H. Oiticica, 'Eden', in S. Breitwieser (ed.), *Vivências*, *op. cit.*, p.12.
23 *Ibid.*
24 *Ibid.*
25 '(t)he instructions for *CC1–CC6* are reproduced here from English typescripts provided by Projeto Hélio Oiticica', see C. Basualdo (ed.), *Hélio Oiticica's Quasi-Cinemas*, *op. cit.*, p.109.
26 See C. Basualdo (ed.), *Hélio Oiticica's: Quasi-Cinemas*, *op. cit.*, p.115.
27 See S. Dennison and L. Shaw, *Popular Cinema in Brazil*, *op. cit.*, p.20.

to show three slides. According to Oiticica's report, the film-maker would move through the space, interrupting the projection in various places, continually changing the projector in order to cut up the slides. What remained was projected onto the surrounding environment:

> [I]t was a kind of quasi-cinema, for me just as much cinema as you can imagine: the same complex simplicity that you feel in Godard: more than that, in my view: the images, the duration of each slide on the screen etc. was brilliant and extremely important: sound-track of AM radio music ... Latin malagüeña music, incredible things, telephone cars in traffic etc; it ended at one in the morning: I went away transformed![28]

Under the influence of a 'quasi-cinematographic experience', Oiticica developed his early attempts at non-narrative montage into an expanded form of what he called 'collage-media'. This work contained images in which he sought to incorporate a sense of time and space — something already evident in his Conceptual works. In the context of Oiticica's ideas about 'super-sensory fields of perception', Smith's performances corresponded closely to this vision of being able to experience time and space both physically and mentally — an experience Oiticica hoped would take one beyond a purely illusionistic, representational reading of images. He therefore suggested to those who carried out his instructions that they take charge of their own performances in giving actual form to the principle of 'collage-media', and varying it accordingly. Everything should be in flux and nothing should stay in the same place.' For example, just as visitors to *CC5 Hendrix-War* can exchange their traditionally vertical position for a horizontal one, so they have the opportunity of including their own body in the quasi-cinematic space that they see around them. Luis Camnitzer writes about Oiticica's perceptual model: 'Whatever happens there only takes place *with* the viewer, not *for* the viewer.'[29]

Thus, it is not so much the collage of images, objects and sounds in *CC5 Hendrix-War* that appear to give one an audio-visual experience comparable with the classic visit to the cinema as a physical way in which one perceives time and space. Bearing in mind that film is light in motion, in this particular case it is the movement of one's own body that constitutes the cinematographic principle.

While the so-called 'public performance' of *CC5 Hendrix-War* is a unique event specific to a particular time and place, the second variation, as described in directions for the 'private performance', can be repeated without any restriction on location or time. Intended for four or more private

28 Letter from the artist to Wally Salomâo, 25 March 1971, in the archives of Projeto Hélio Oiticica; quoted in the exhibition brochure *Hélio Oiticica e a cena Americano* (*Hélio Oiticica and the American Scene*), held from 11 December 1998 to 28 March 1999 at the Centro de Arte Hélio Oiticica in Rio de Janeiro; see C. Basualdo, 'Waiting for the Internal Sun: Notes on Hélio Oiticica's Quasi-Cinemas', *op. cit.*, p.40.

29 Quoted from an unpublished original manuscript: Luis Camnitzer, *Contextualization and Resistance: Conceptualism in Latin American Art*, 4 September 2002.

30 H. Oiticica, *CC5 Hendrix-War*, in C. Basualdo (ed.), *Hélio Oiticica. Quasi-Cinemas*, *op. cit.*, p.116.

31 See Maurizio Lazzarato, *Videophilosophie. Zeitwahrnehmung im Postfordismus*, Berlin: b_books, 2002, p.8.

32 Henri Bergson quoted in *ibid.* Although Bergson correctly described the conditions governing the development of mechanical and thermodynamic machines, he did not foresee that what

rooms, for interior as well as exterior walls, Oiticica gave instructions that the four sets of slides should be shown in multiple variations. According to his instructions, the event should begin immediately after waking up; all those living in the flat or house should make sure that the slides are shown continuously; and Hendrix's record should be played.

> Projection-interludes at operator's will: not as: WASTE TIME rather as INVENTED TIME: as the day lengthens and the soundsandslides repeat-repeat-repeat themselves so should the operators direct everything towards DANCE to the extent of inviting OTHERS from ELSEWHERE.[30]

For this reason Oiticica suggests that his instructions be followed as if they were for a non-stop cinema performance open to all, and that its duration, development and internal dynamics should be decided by those taking part. Here the principle of simultaneous and diachronic repetition is concerned not only with the way that the individual viewing subject creates a phenomenological image of a spatial here and a temporal now, but also with the way that this subject experiences a variety of physical interactions with others. In the combination of all these factors one can see an attempt to bring together the temporal qualities of contemplation, doing nothing, dance, delirium, etc., with those of creative productivity.

Pointers to Oiticica's concept of time can be found in his numerous texts, wherein he refers to the phenomenological speculations of Maurice Merleau-Ponty and Henri Bergson. In order to gain a better understanding of his concept of 'creleisure', it seems to me that Bergson's philosophical creed, which states that there is more 'reality and creativity' in the act of 'perception' than there is 'in understanding and reasoning', is of relevance.[31] Bergson formulated his theories under the impact of the first Industrial Revolution and of the scientific approach to production and labour that accompanied it. Bergson said that this had helped to produce an 'artificial body' which demanded a 'different mind'.[32] If the mind wished to resist the accumulation of capital and therefore the growth of material reality, it had to be seen in relation to the passing of time. Not, however, in the sense of a rationalistically conceived, forward-moving chronology or linear progression, but in terms of the intuitive and synthetic aspects of memory; and by that Bergson meant the physical movements of contraction and expansion.[33] Due to its non-chronological nature, the past was being continually annulled by the present. Time, or rather our perception of time, thus appeared to be split or internally differentiated.

he considered to be the necessary inclusion of the psyche would also assume a machine-like form. According to him, the development of the artificial body has reached a level where 'material resistance has almost disappeared'. In view of their tendency towards 'mystical mechanics' and spiritualism, one does not have to share the conclusions that Bergson draws from his extremely original reflections about the artificial body of the Industrial Revolution, in order to hold fast to his ideas and use them freely.

33 Henri Bergson, *Matter and Memory* (trans. N.M. Paul and W.S. Palmer), London: Allen and Unwin, 1911.

In this sense Oiticica's instructions represent manoeuvres in the field of perceptual aesthetics, which, rather like the written plans for US-American Minimal and Conceptual art, attempt to define possible forms of resistance to the industrial and social fragmentation and serialisation of time and space by creating a new physical relationship between the individual and the work of art. If, therefore, Oiticica's working model excludes being reduced to the laws governing the genres and mediums of painting, photography, objects, sound, language, etc., then it does so to annul the naturalistic and rationalistic categories of time and space inherent within them, by combining all the mentioned elements together in an irreversible process. In contrast with work-specific, passive forms of participatory, multimedia installations, however, Oiticica had in mind a meta-media, active form of virtual-cinema, using popular images, rock and avant-garde music, queer performance and drug use — both depicted and real. The reference to Bergson's theory of perception makes clear beyond doubt that it was by no means an idealistic, naive belief in authenticating perception that underlay Oiticica's animation of aesthetic experience.

In this regard, it seems to me revealing that Hendrix's *War Heroes* (1972), along with *Cry of Love* (1971), *Rainbow Bridge* (1971) and *Crash Landing* (1975), was one of the original LPs put together posthumously from material made in the recording studio. After their release, these records were spurned by Hendrix-afficionados because they were much more song-orientated — presumably for commercial reasons — than the freer, more instrumental style which characterised Hendrix's musical phase leading up to his death in 1970, in which he painted pictures with sounds. For example, in 'Machine Gun', the second track on the live album *Band of Gypsys* (1970), he imitated the sounds of a machine gun.[34] A possible connection can be made here with Oiticica's and D'Almeida's first collaborative film project, *Mangue Bangue*. As Basualdo explains, *Mangue* is the name of a red-light district in Rio, where Oiticica often hung out with friends and acquaintances who earned their money there, and *bangue* (pronounced bang) is the onomatopoeic form of the sound of a gun.[35] It is clear that Oiticica's *CC5 Hendrix-War* was a development of *Mangue Bangue*, and that it came out of the queer subculture of New York in the early 1970s. It's equally plain to see that Oiticica's choice to reference *War Heroes* can be traced back to Hendrix's solidarity with his 'black brothers fighting in Vietnam'.[36] Oiticica's title can be read as a reference to the Black Panthers Party and their self-conscious concept of blackness as a basis for radical politics. After initial links with white hippie culture, Hendrix became more and more attracted, under the influence of

34 I wish to thank Christoph Dreher and Diedrich Diederichsen for these references.

35 C. Basualdo, 'Waiting for the Internal Sun: Notes on Hélio Oiticica's Quasi-Cinemas', *op. cit.*, p.44. Since Oiticica went to New York straight after his exhibition at the Whitechapel Art Gallery in London in 1969, D'Almeida was meant to finish the film on his own.

36 http://panafricannews.blogspot.com/2006/06/stokely-carmichael-speaks-on-black.html

37 H. Oiticica, 'Tropicália', *op. cit.*, p.264.

38 See Oiticica's homage to Cara de Cavalo, who lived in the *favelas* and who was wanted by the police for several offences and was eventually shot dead by them. Hélio Oiticica, 'Cara de Cavalo', *Hélio Oiticica* (exh. cat.), *op. cit.*, p.25.

39 C. Bausaldo, 'Waiting for the

Miles Davis, to the political notion of blackness. Hand-in-hand with this was his interest in futuristic Afro-myths, such as the one according to which black slaves' ancestors had been born on another planet. There are similarities here with Oiticica's views about history and the social reality of Brazil. In one of his texts, written at the same time as his *Tropicália* installation was on view in Rio de Janeiro in 1967, he said: 'We are Blacks, Indios and Whites, all at the same time — our culture has nothing to do with European culture, even though it has, until now, been heavily suppressed by it.'[37] Oiticica's reference to Hendrix represents a 'self-reference' to *Tropicália* in an additional respect, since the environment included a sign saying 'Be an outlaw, be an hero'. This proved to be an ambiguous statement insofar as it referred, on the one hand, to the above-mentioned popular figures in Brazilian and Cuban literature, and, on the other, to the petty criminals in the poor areas of Rio de Janeiro.[38]

– III –

Oiticica's concept of 'creleisure' was to be given a new meaning during his time in New York. After his initial euphoria about the city, he commented in one of his letters about the demeaning slave labour to which the city owed its wealth. The artist experienced this first hand, for after his scholarship ran out, he had to accept every badly paid job going. Basualdo reports that Oiticica had been happy at first to be able to escape the repressions and censorship of the military dictatorship in Brazil, but then he had to endure the typical forms of exploitation that exist within an industrial society that thinks of itself as progressive.[39] Oiticica voiced his criticism at a time when wage levels and workers' rights were being undermined by the transfer of manufacturing facilities to so-called Tricont states, a phenomenon caused by the internationalisation of production processes and markets and made possible by the introduction of high technology.[40] Thus, artists who were in favour of social revolution saw a link between the establishment of dictatorial regimes and the expansion of low-wage industries in the so-called peripheries. Unlike those artists who were in thrall to the rationalistic logic of progress and to the New Man as outlined in the historic project of the avant-garde, artists such as Oiticica, Clark, Almir Mavignier and Ivan Serpa (Oiticica's teacher) placed their hopes in the still unexplored potential of a deviant subjectivity. As Paulo Herkenhoff states, '[i]n Brazil, under the 1964 dictatorship, madness represented fragility and a possibility of creative resistance by society towards the irrationality and will of the State and political repression'.[41]

Internal Sun: Notes on Hélio Oiticica's Quasi-Cinemas', *op. cit.*, p.47.

40 Alain Lipietz, 'Die Beziehungen zwischen Kapital und Arbeit am Vorabend des 21. Jahrhunderts', in *Leviathan, Berliner Zeitschrift für Sozialwissenschaft*, Berlin: Freie Universität Berlin, Humboldt-Universität zu Berlin und des Wissenschaftszentrum Berlin für Sozialforschung, 1991, p.78.

41 Paulo Herkenhoff, 'Lygia Clark', in *Lygia Clark* (exh. cat.), Barcelona: Fundació Antoni Tapiès, 1998, p.48.

Seen against this background, one can understand the affinity that Oiticica felt for Jack Smith's *magic believe systems*,[42] which were such a provocative contrast to the critical negativity of the avant-gardes. Just as Smith made Maria Montez — a successful Mexican actress in Hollywood in the 1940s who later disappeared from sight as a B-movie player[43] — into an adored queer icon, so Oiticica celebrated charismatic figures and phenomena from the underground, avant-garde and media cultures. Katja Diefenbach writes of Smith that 'as opposed to the anti-fetishistic, enlightenment thrust of 70s' Structuralist, feminist and Marxist film', he opened up 'the fetishistic surface of "exotic beauty" and "splendid narcissism" that Maria Montez brought to the screen, and made it available to "low camp" drag performances'.[44] The same thing can be said about Oiticica's attempt to break through the prevailing sexual order by fetishising male beauty and female glamour. As the illustrations from his 'quasi-cinemas' show, his appropriated images display not only a queer-coded predilection for aesthetic excess, but also a positive identification with physical pleasure, erotic wishes and sexual desire. Oiticica's process of 'collage-media' comes very close to the flashiest forms of affirmation found in a second-order star system, which would have been unthinkable without the 'queer Babylon' of Hollywood cinema — as his references to Anger, Smith and Warhol demonstrate. The conceptual world of the 'quasi-cinemas' is situated between the critical negativity of the historic avant-garde and the aesthetic positivity of queer underground cinema, and thus cannot really be measured against either of the categories of affirmation or critique suggested by Peter Bürger.[45]

In an essay on methods of sampling, Diedrich Diederichsen writes:

> [T]he strategies of pop music [...] were concerned, from the start, with using montage so as to be part of the world. It was characteristic of pop music from the beginning — and in this respect, interestingly enough, it represents a radicalisation of avant-garde ideas as well as of strategies developed by the culture industry — that the work of art, the performance, the song, the votive image of the star should be taken out into the world and should leave behind the protective space of art. This particular quality of the popular arts has, perhaps, always been present in rudimentary form, but in the post-war period it was industrialised and professionalised, with the result that it made possible the triumph of a cultural industry second only to the film industry; at the same time it created the conditions for pop music to gather about it the hopes of various counter cultures.[46]

42 See Jack Smith, 'The Perfect Filmic Appositeness of Maria Montez', in J. Hoberman and E. Leffingwell (eds.), *Wait For Me at the Bottom of the Pool. The Writings of Jack Smith*, New York and London: High Risk Books, 1997, pp.25–35.

43 Maria Montez experienced a queer reincarnation in the form of Mario Montez, a drag queen who appeared first in Smith's films and later in Warhol's films and *Screen Tests* (1963–66).

44 Katja Diefenbach, 'Sehr rasch und nicht zu innig. Diesseits der Überschreitung', Sabeth Buchmann, Alexander Mayer, Carolin Meunier, et. al. (eds.), *Wenn sonst nichts klappt: Wiederholung wiederholen in Kunst, Popkultur, Film, Musik, Alltag, Theorie und Praxis*, Hamburg and Berlin: Material Verlag und b_books, 2005, p.28.

45 See Peter Bürger, *Theorie der Avantgarde*, Frankfurt am Main: Suhrkamp, 1974.

46 Diedrich Diederichsen, 'Von der Makromontage zum Mikrosampling', in Sabeth Buchmann, Alexander Mayer, Carolin Meunier, et. al. (eds.), *Wenn sonst nichts klappt*, *op. cit.*, p.143.

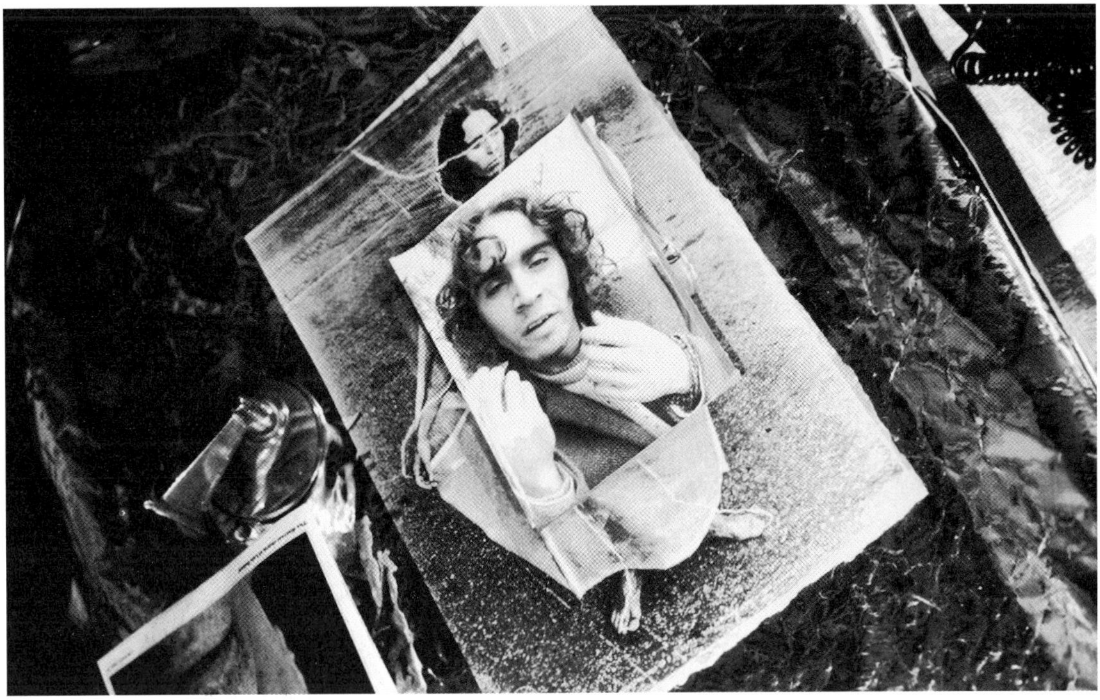

Hélio Oiticica and Neville D'Almeida, *01-CC1 (Trashiscapes/Cosmococa Programa in Progress)*, 1973/2003. Courtesy Galerie Lelong, New York

It seems to me that this throws light on all aspects of the ambivalent and diffuse position of Oiticia's 'quasi-cinemas', lying as they do between the avant-garde and the anti-avant-garde, between cinema and politics. Looked at in this way, the concept of the 'quasi-cinema' can be seen, at the very least, as a quasi-metaphor for the way life has been transformed by the media in the subcultural domain. The shattered hopes seemingly to be found there are made up of highly contradictory and unresolved ideas of deviant subjectivity, which are, nevertheless, aesthetically and politically more fruitful than those to be found in the relevant instructions for cultural activism or in the tales of the heroic (neo-)avant-gardes. The fact that Oiticica was less concerned with the movement of pictures than with the movement of bodies, emotions and desires serves to remind us of the biopolitical dimension discussed earlier in connection with Ricardo Basbaum's ideas on the contemporary reception of Brazilian *Modernismo* — for even Hollywood has long gone beyond the screen and permeated the bodies and souls of its consumers. It is against this background that the question arises as to whether we should look upon the 'quasi-cinemas' as a temporal phenomenon, specific to a past subculture, or whether we should see in them pictures and ideas of a deviant subjectivity with potential but also with ambivalent aspects, which can only be read in the context of an overarching analysis of the power of modern life.

Translated by Keith Hartley.

THE TWO AVANT-GARDES
Peter Wollen

Film history has developed unevenly, so that in Europe today there are two distinct avant-gardes. The first can be identified loosely with the Co-op movement. The second would include film-makers such as Godard, Straub and Huillet, Hanoun, Jancso. Naturally there are points of contact between these two groups and common characteristics, but they also differ quite sharply in many respects: aesthetic assumptions, institutional framework, type of financial support, type of critical backing, historical and cultural origin. There are other film-makers too who do not fit neatly into either camp, and films which fall somewhere in between or simply somewhere else — Jackie Raynal's *Deux Fois*, for instance — but in general the distinction holds good.

At the extreme, each would tend to deny the others the status of avant-garde at all. Books like Stephen Dwoskin's *Film Is* or David Curtis's *Experimental Film* do not discuss the crucial post-1968 work of Godard and Gorin, for example.[1] And supporters of Godard — and Godard himself — have often denounced the 'Co-op avant-garde' as hopelessly involved with the established bourgeois art world and its values. The reasons for dismissal are often quite beside the point and misplaced. By no means all the directors (to use a word taboo in the other camp) in one group work with narrative in 35mm, as you might sometimes imagine — Godard has worked in 16mm for years and recently with video (to open up another hornet's nest). Conversely, many Co-op film-makers are well aware of political issues and see themselves in some sense as militant. (Not that political militancy in itself is any guarantee of being avant-garde.)

The position is complicated too by the fact that in North America there is only one avant-garde, centred on the various Co-ops. There are no obvious equivalents of Godard or Straub-Huillet, although their influence can occasionally be seen — in Jon Jost's *Speaking Directly*, for example. Moreover, American critics and theorists of the avant-garde have long tended to overlook their European counterparts or see them as derivative. The Europeans — and perhaps particularly the English — then tend to react by stressing their own credentials, making claims to have occupied the same ground as the Americans earlier or independently. From outside, the quarrel often looks of secondary importance. After all, noone denies that the capital of narrative

1 Stephen Dwoskin, *Film Is...*, London: Peter Owen, 1975. David Curtis, *Experimental Cinema*, London: Studio Vista, 1971.

2 Standish Lawder, *The Cubist Cinema*, New York: New York University Press, 1975.

3 See Sophie Lissitzky-Kuppers, *El Lissitzky*, London: Thames and Hudson, 1968.

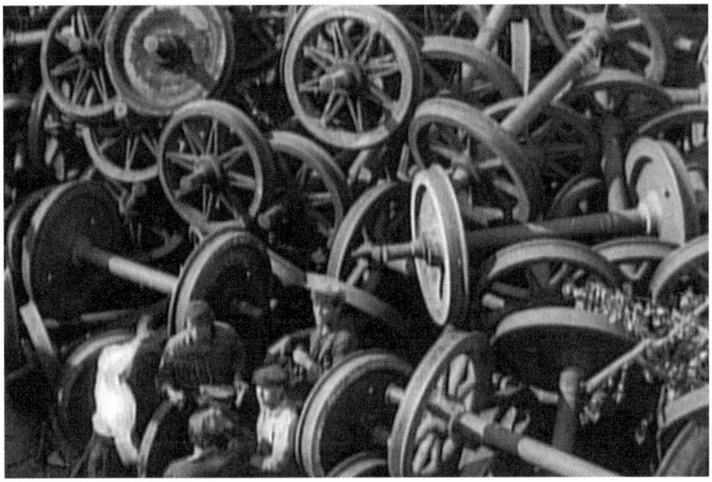

fiction 35mm film-making is Hollywood, however innovative European directors, such as Antonioni or Fellini or Truffaut may be. In the same way, New York is clearly the capital of the Co-op movement. Consequently, from New York, Godard looks much more distinctively European than Kren or Le Grice, a fact which simply reflects the realities of power in the art world, to which the Co-op movement is closely tied. Indeed, there is a sense in which avant-garde Co-op film-making in Europe is closer to New York than Californian film-making is, and the leading New York critics and tastemakers — Sitney, Michelson, etc. — are not appreciated in San Francisco any more than they are in London.

It seems to me much more important to try and understand what unites and separates Godard and Straub-Huillet on the one hand, and, say, Gidal and Wyborny on the other hand, than what unites and separates Europe and North America within the Co-op ambit. Moreover, I think the absence of any avant-garde of the Godard type in North America could ultimately prove a severe limitation on the development of the New American Cinema itself, narrowing its horizons and tying it unnecessarily closely to the future of the other visual arts, condemning it to a secondary status within the art world. Close relationship with 'art' — painting, post-painting, etc. — is both a strength and a weakness.

To understand further the split which has developed within the avant-garde it is necessary to go back into history. A similar split can be seen in the 1920s. On the one hand films were being made by Léger-Murphy, Picabia-Clair, Eggeling, Richter, Man Ray, Moholy-Nagy and others — many of them discussed in Standish Lawder's recent book on *The Cubist Cinema* — that were attempts to extend the scope of painting, to move outside the confines of the canvas, to introduce the dimension of time, to use light directly as well as colour and so on.[2] On the other hand, there were the Russian directors, whose films were clearly avant-garde but in a different sense: Eisenstein's *Strike*, Dovzhenko's *Zvenigora*, Vertov's *Man with the Movie Camera*. It was only at the very end of the decade that there was any real contact between the two groups — when Lissitizky (whose ideas about the electro-mechanical spectacle and admiration for Eggeling put him clearly in the 'painters' group) first met Vertov to discuss the Stuttgart *Film und Foto* exhibition,[3] and when Eisenstein met Richter on his first trip out of the Soviet Union and went with him to the conference at Le Sarraz, which turned out to mark the end rather than the beginning of an epoch.

Sergei Eisenstein, still from *Stachka* (*Strike*), 1924. 35mm black-and-white film, silent, 82mins

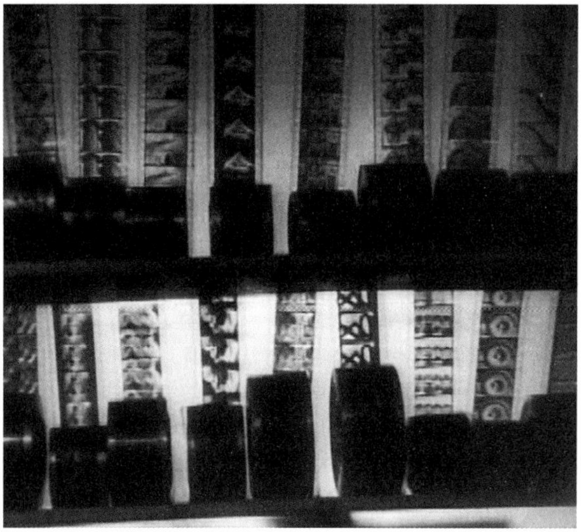

As today, part of the difference lies in the backgrounds of the people involved. One group came from painting. The other from theatre (Eisenstein) and futurist sound-poetry (Vertov) — Dovzhenko, in fact, had trained as a painter but deliberately gave it up, leaving all his painting materials behind him in Kharkov when he set off for Odessa and the film studios, seeking a complete break with his past. And, of course, there are premonitory links between these different currents of the 1920s and those of recent years — Godard and Gorin carried out their collaboration under the name of the Dziga Vertov group; van Doesburg, in 1929, already anticipated many of the ideas of 'expanded cinema', realised decades later: 'The spectator space will become part of the film space. The separation of "projection surface" is abolished. The spectator will no longer observe the film, like a theatrical presentation, but will participate in it optically and acoustically.'[4]

Painting, I think it can be argued, played the leading role in the development of modernism in the other arts. The break, the *coupure* — to use the Althusserian terminology — the shift of terrain that marked the substitution of one paradigm or problematic for another, the beginning of modernism, the work of the historic avant-garde, was a break that took place in painting pre-eminently, with the discoveries of Cubism. It is not hard to show how painting affected the other arts, how early Cubism had a decisive impact on Gertrude Stein and Ezra Pound, for example, in literature, and later on William Carlos Williams, Apollinaire, Marinetti, Mayakovsky, Khlebnikov — all were influenced at a crucial point by their encounter with Cubism. The innovations of Picasso, and Braque, were seen as having an implication beyond the history of painting itself. They were intuitively felt, I think, very early on, to represent a critical semiotic shift, a changed concept and practice of sign and signification, which we can now see to have been the opening-up of a space, a disjunction between signifier and signified and a change of emphasis from the problem of signified and reference, the classic problem of realism, to that of signifier and signified within the sign itself.[5]

When we look at the development of painting after the Cubist breakthrough, however, we see a constant trend towards an apparently even more radical development: the suppression of the signified altogether, an art of pure signifiers detached from meaning as much as from reference, from *Sinn* as much as from *Bedeutung*. This tendency towards abstraction could be justified in various ways — a transcendental signified could be postulated, in symbolist or spiritualist terms, a meaning located in the *Uberwelt* of pure ideas; a theory of formalism, of art as pure design, could be proposed;

Dziga Vertov, still from *Chelovek's kino-apparatom* (*Man with a Movie Camera*), 1929. 35mm black-and-white film, silent, 80mins

the work of art could be defended in terms of object-hood, pure presence; it could be explained as a solution to a problem, often set by the relationship between a signifier — a form of expression, in Hjelmslev's phrase — and its physical, material support (the matter or substance of expression).[6]

Literature, on the other hand, tended to fall back into forms of writing in which the signified clearly remained dominant. Modernism could be interpreted in terms of the expansion of subject-matter, new narrative techniques (stream of consciousness) or play on the paradoxes of meaning and reference (Pirandellism). It is significant, for instance, that so many of the most radical experiments, such as attempts at sound poetry, were the work of artists or writers working closely with painters: Arp, Schwitters, van Doesburg among them. In theatre the most radical developments were invariably associated with changes in set design and costume, including the use of masks: Meyerhold's Constructivist theatre in the Soviet Union, Schlemmer's Bauhaus theatre, Artaud. In this context, it should be added, Brecht appears as little more than a moderate.

Cinema is, of course, a form of art employing more than one channel, more than one sensory medium, and uses a multiplicity of different types of code. It has affinities with almost all the other arts. Music and verbal language, as well as natural or artificial noise, can form elements of the soundtrack. Theatre and dance can be elements of the pro-filmic event, placed in front of the camera to be photographed. Editing can be used to develop narrative or to produce a 'visual rhythm' by analogy with music. Film itself can be painted or paintings can be animated. Light can be used as a medium, and through projection a third dimension can be introduced, to produce a kind of mobile light sculpture. Cinema too has its own 'specifically cinematic' codes and materials, associated with the various phases of film production.[7]

As a result of this variety and multiplicity, ideas have fed into film-making from a variety of sources in the other arts. One powerful influence has come from painting, bringing with it a tendency to abstraction — pure light or colour; and non-figurative design — or deformation of conventional photographic imagery, involving prismatic fragmentation and splintering, the use of filters or stippled glass, mirror-shots, extreme and microscopic close-ups, bizarre angles, negative images, all of which are to be found in 1920s films. Editing tended to follow principles of association (related to poetry or dream) or analogies with music — shots of fixed length, repetition and variation, attempts at synesthetic effects, theories of counterpoint.

But this influence, and the films associated with it, are marked as much by what they excluded as what they included. Primarily of course verbal language was missing and also narrative. During the silent period, the absence of language was not foregrounded; it seemed a natural quality of film, but

4 Theo van Doesburg, 'Film as Pure Form' (trans. Standish Lawder), *Form*, Summer 1966; originally published in *Die Form*, 15 May 1929.

5 See Victor Burgin, 'Photographic Practice and Art Theory', *Studio International*, July/August 1975.

6 See Roland Barthes, *Elements of Semiology*, London: Hill and Wang, 1967.

7 See Christian Metz, *Language and Cinema*, The Hague: Mouton, 1974.

in retrospect its significance can be seen. Language is still excluded from an enormous number of avant-garde films, which are shown either silent or with electronic or other musical tracks. Again, there are real technical and financial reasons for this, but these practical disincentives coincide with an aesthetic itself founded on concepts of visual form and visual problems that exclude verbal language from their field, and may be actively hostile to it. This is part of the legacy of the Renaissance that has survived the modernist break almost unchallenged, except in isolated instances — Lissitzky, Duchamp, Picabia and, extremely important, recent Conceptualist work.

There is one further important point that must be made about the development of film in relation to art history. Film-makers at a certain point became dissatisfied with the search simply for 'kinetic solutions to pictorial problems',as in the films of Man Ray and Moholy-Nagy, and began to concentrate on what they saw as specifically cinematic problems.[8] Structural film-making over the last decade has thus represented a displacement of concerns from the art world to the film world rather than an extension. This way of thinking about art has remained one that film-makers have in common with painters and other visual artists, but an effort has been made to insist on the ontological autonomy of film. Thus, for instance, Gidal's work has foregrounded and been in a sense 'about' focus; Le Grice's work has foregrounded and been in a sense 'about' printing or projection. The tendency of painting to concentrate on its own sphere of materials and signification, to be self-reflexive, has been translated into specifically cinematic terms and concerns, though here again 'specifically cinematic' is taken to mean primarily the picture-track.

Thus the impact of avant-garde ideas from the world of visual arts has ended up pushing film-makers into a position of extreme 'purism' or 'essentialism'. Ironically, anti-illusionist, anti-realist film has ended up sharing many preoccupations in common with its worst enemies. A theorist like André Bazin, for instance, committed to realism and representationalism, based his commitment on an argument about cinematic ontology and essence that he saw in the photographic reproduction of the natural world. We now have, so to speak, both an extroverted and an introverted ontology of film, one seeking the soul of cinema in the nature of the pro-filmic event, the other in the nature of the cinematic process, the cone of light or the grain of silver. The frontier reached by this avant-garde has been an ever-narrowing preoccupation with pure film, with film 'about' film, a dissolution of signification into objecthood or tautology.[9] I should add, perhaps, that this tendency is even more marked in the United States than in Europe.

8 See Barbara Rose, 'The Films of Man Ray and Moholy-Nagy', *Artforum*, September 1971.

9 See Peter Wollen, 'Ontology and Materialism in Film', *Screen*, vol.17 no.1, 1976.

10 See Sergei Eisenstein, 'The Cinematographic Principle and the Ideogram', *Film Form*, New York: Harcourt, Brace and World, 1949.

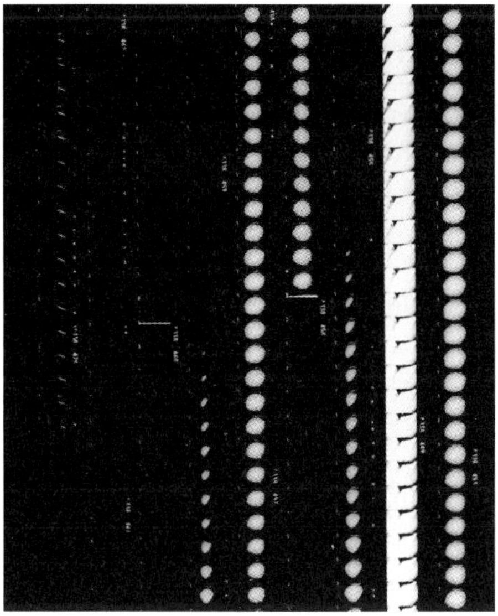

Where does the other avant-garde stand? Here, as one would expect, the tendency goes in the opposite direction. The Soviet directors of the 1920s, though they saw themselves in some sense as avant-garde, were also preoccupied with the problem of realism. For the most part they remained within the bounds of narrative cinema. The most clearly avant-garde passages and episodes in Eisenstein's films (experiments in intellectual montage) remain passages and episodes, which appear as interpolations within an otherwise homogeneous and classical narrative. There is no doubt that the dramaturgy is modernist rather than traditional — the crowd as hero, typage, *guignol* — but these are not features that can be attributed to a break with rather than a renovation of classical theatre. They are modes of achieving a heightened emotional effect or presenting an idea with unexpected vividness or force.

In Eisenstein's work the signified — content in the conventional sense — is always dominant and, of course, he went so far as to dismiss Vertov's *Man with the Movie Camera* as 'formalist jack-straws and unmotivated camera mischief',[10] contrasting its use of slow motion with Epstein's *La Chute de la Maison Usher*, in which, according to Eisenstein, it is used to heighten emotional pressure, to achieve an effect in terms of a desired content or goal. Vertov's film was, of course, a milestone for the avant-garde and it is a sign of its richness that it can be seen as a precursor both of *cinema-verité* and of Structural film, though also, evidently, a sign of its ambiguity, of its uncertainty caught between an ideology of photographic realism and one of formal innovation and experiment.

In broad terms, what we find with the Soviet film-makers is a recognition that a new type of content, a new realm of signifieds, demands formal innovation, on the level of the signifier, for its expression. Thus Eisenstein wanted to translate the dialectical materialism of his world-view from an approach to subject matter to an approach to form, through a theory of montage that was itself dialectical. The aesthetic was still content-based, it saw signifiers primarily as means of expression, but at the same time it demanded a radical transformation of those means. It was an aesthetic that had much in common with the avant-garde positions of, say, Léger or Man Ray, but which also kept a distance, a distance of which the fear of formalism is symptomatic. It is as if they felt that once the signifier was freed from bondage to the signified, it was certain to celebrate by doing away with its old master altogether in a fit of irresponsible ultra-leftism and utopianism. As we have seen, this was not so far wrong.

Peter Gidal, still from *Room Film 1973*, 1973. 16mm colour film, silent, 55mins

The case of Godard, working forty years or so later, is slightly different. In Godard's post-1968 films we glimpse something of an alternative route between contentism and formalism, a recognition that it is possible to work within the space opened up by the disjunction and dislocation of signifier and signified. Clearly Godard was influenced by Eisenstein's theory of dialectical montage, but he develops it in a much more radical way. In the last resort, for Eisenstein, conflict occurred primarily between the successive signifieds of images. Although he recognises a form of dialectical montage in the Suprematist paintings of Malevich, he himself remains within the confines of 'naturalism'. (Interestingly enough, he identifies a middle road between naturalism and abstraction, which he relates, somewhat surprisingly, to Balla and 'primitive Italian futurism'.)[11] Godard takes the idea of formal conflict and struggle and translates it into a concept of conflict, not between the content of images, but between different codes and between signifier and signified.

Thus, in *Le Gai Savoir*, which he began shooting before the events of May 1968, but completed after, Godard tries programatically to 'return to zero', to de-compose and then re-compose sounds and images. For Godard, conflict becomes not simply collision through juxtaposition, as in Eisenstein's model, but an act of negativity, a splitting apart of an apparently natural unity, a disjunction. Godard's view of bourgeois communication is one of a discourse gaining its power from its apparent naturalness, the impression of necessity that seems to bind a signifier to a signified, a sound to an image, in order to provide a convincing representation of the world. He wants not simply to represent an alternative 'world' or alternative 'world view', but to investigate the whole process of signification out of which a world-view or an ideology is constructed. *Le Gai Savoir* ends with the following words on the soundtrack: 'This film has not wished to, could not wish to explain the cinema or even constitute its object, but more modestly, to offer a few effective means for arriving there. This is not the film that must be made, but it shows how, if one is to make a film, one must necessarily follow some of the paths travelled here.'[12] In other words, the film deliberately suspends 'meaning', avoids any teleology or finality, in the interests of a destruction and re-assembly, a re-combination of the order of the sign as an experiment in the dissolution of old meanings and the generation of new ones from the semiotic process itself.

Put another way, *Le Gai Savoir* is not a film with a meaning, something to say about the world, nor is it a film 'about' film (which, after all, is simply a limited part of the world of interest in itself to film-makers and film students) but a film about the possibility of meaning itself, of generating new types of meaning. The array of sign-systems at work in the cinema are thus brought into a new kind of relationship with each other and with the world. Nor, of course, is Godard indifferent to what types of new meaning are produced. Although his work is open-ended, it does not offer itself simply for a delirium of interpretation, as though meaning could be read in at will by the spectator. Signifieds are neither fixed, or fixed as far as possible, as they are in

11 S. Eisenstein, 'A Dialectic Approach to Film Form', *Film Form*, *op. cit.*

12 Jean-Luc Godard, *Le Gai Savoir*, Paris, 1969. The script, 'mot-à-mot d'un film encore trop réviso', was published by the Union des Ecrivains formed during May 1968 in Paris. (My translation.)

conventional cinema, nor are they freed from any constraint, as though the end of a content-dominated art meant the end of any control over content.

In a sense, Godard's work goes back to the original breaking-point at which the modern avant-garde began — neither realist or expressionist, on the one hand, nor abstractionist, on the other. In the same way, Picasso's the *Demoiselles d'Avignon* (1907) is neither realist, expressionist or abstractionist. It dislocates signifier from signified, asserting — as such a dislocation must — the primacy of the first, without in any way dissolving the second. It is not a portrait group or a study of nudes in the representational tradition, but on the other hand, to see it simply as an investigation of painterly or formal problems or possibilities is to forget its original title, *Le Bordel Philosophique*. The same could be said, of course, about Duchamp's *The Large Glass* (1915–23). The battle between realism/illusion/'literature' in art, and abstraction/reflexiveness/Greenberg-modernism, is not so simple or all-encompassing as it may sometimes seem.

There are two other topics that should be mentioned here. The first is politics. As I suggested above, it is often too easily asserted that one avant-garde is 'political' and the other is not. Peter Gidal, for example, defends his films on grounds that clearly imply a political position. And the supporters of Godard and Straub-Huillet, by distinguishing their films from those of Karmitz or Pontecorvo, are constantly forced to assert that being 'political' is not in itself enough, that there must be a break with bourgeois norms of diegesis, subversion and deconstruction of codes — a line of argument which, unless it is thought through carefully or stopped arbitrarily at some safe point, leads inevitably straight into the positions of the other avant-garde. Nonetheless, in discussing Godard, the fact that his films deal explicitly with political issues and ideas is obviously important. He does not wish to cut himself off from the political Marxist culture in which he has steeped himself from before 1968 and increasingly since. This culture, moreover, is one of books and verbal language. The important point, though, is that a film like *Le Gai Savoir* — unlike some later work of Godard, as he fell under Brecht's influence — is not simply didactic or expository, but presents the language of Marxism itself, a deliberately chosen language, as itself problematic.

Politics — the influence and presence of Marxist writing — has been an obvious force of impetus and strength for Godard, but it also relates to another question — that of audience. On the whole, the Co-op avant-garde, happy though it would no doubt be to find a mass audience, is reconciled to its minority status. The consciously political film-maker, on the other hand, is often uneasy about this. The representatives of Marxist culture are on the whole aesthetically conservative and avant-gardism is damned as elitism. Godard, as is well-known, defended himself against this charge by citing Mao's dictum about the three types of struggle and placing his own work in film under the banner of scientific experiment, rather than class struggle, an instance in which theoretical work could be justified and take precedence over political work, in the short term at least. Yet it is also clear that it was pressure to rediscover a mass, popular audience which led to the artistic regroupment of *Tout Va Bien,* which abandons avant-gardism for a stylised didacticism, set within a classical realist frame, though with some Eisensteinian interpolations.

The second topic is that of 'intertextuality', to use Julia Kristeva's terminology.[13] One of the main characteristics of modernism, once the priority of immediate reference to the real world had been disputed, was the play of allusion within and between texts. Quotation, for instance, plays a crucial role in the *Demoiselles d'Avignon* and, indeed, in *The Large Glass.* In avant-garde writing it is only necessary to think of Pound and Joyce. Again, the effect is to break up the homogeneity of the work, to open up spaces between different texts and types of discourses. Godard has used the same strategy, not only on the soundtrack where whole passages from books are recited, but also on the picture-track, as in the quotations from Hollywood westerns and the *cinema novo* in *Vent d'Est.* Similarly, the films of Straub-Huillet are almost all 'layered' like a palimpsest — in this case, the space between texts is not only semantic but historical too, the different textual strata being the residues of different epochs and cultures.

It is significant perhaps that the latest films of Malcolm Le Grice have a similar quality of intertextuality in their quotation of Lumière and *Le Déjeuner sur l'Herbe* (1863). The Lumière film is especially interesting — in comparison with, for example, Bill Brand's re-make of Lumière's destruction-of-a-wall film.[14] It is not simply a series of optical re-combinations, like cinematic anagrams, but an investigation into narration itself, which by counterposing different narrative tones, so to speak, neither dissolves nor repeats Lumière's simple story, *L'Arroseur Arroseé* (1895), but foregrounds the process of narration itself. And this, as we have seen, is semiotically very different from foregrounding the process of projection. The way into narrative cinema is surely not forbidden to the avant-garde film-maker, any more than the way into verbal language.[15]

Cinema, I have stressed earlier, is a multiple system — the search for the specifically cinematic can be deceptively purist and reductive. For most people, after all, cinema is unthinkable without words and stories. To recognise this fact is by no means to accept a conventional Hollywood-oriented (or Bergman/Antonioni/Bunuel-oriented) attitude to the cinema and the place of stories and words within it. It is perhaps the idea, so strongly rooted by now, that film is a visual art that has brought about a blockage. Yet this idea is obviously a half-truth at best. The danger that threatens is that the introduction of words and stories — of signifieds — will simply bring back illusionism or representationalism in full flood. Clearly this fear is the converse of Eisenstein's anxiety about 'unmotivated camera mischief'. There are good reasons for these fears, but surely can they be overcome.

13 See Julia Kristeva, *Semeiotike*, Paris: Edition du Seuil, 1969.

14 See Ian Christie, 'Time and Motion Studies: Structural Cinema and the Work of Bill Brand', *Studio International*, June 1974.

15 The British landscape film-makers often use a new type of narrativity, in which both film-maker and 'nature' as causal agent play the role of protagonist. A pro-filmic event, which is a conventional signified ('landscape'), intervenes actively in the process of filming, determining operations on the 'specifically cinematic' codes.

I have tried to show how the two avant-gardes we find in Europe originated and what it is that holds them apart. To go further, I would have to discuss as well the institutional and economic framework in which film-makers find themselves. The basis of the Co-op movement, as has often been pointed out, lies in artisanal production, with film-makers who do as much as possible themselves at every stage of the film-making process. If there are performers involved they are usually few, generally friends of the film-maker, often other film-makers. The other avant-garde has its roots much more in the commercial system, and even when filming in 16mm Godard would use stars known in the commercial cinema. The difference is not simply one of budgets — Dwoskin or Wyborny have made films for TV as well as Godard, and Dwoskin's are clearly much more conventional, yet they are almost automatically assigned different cultural places. It is much more one of the film-makers' frame of reference, the places from which they come and the culture to which they relate.

The facts of uneven development mean too that it would be utopian to hope for a simple convergence of the two avant-gardes. The most revolutionary work, both of Godard and of Straub-Huillet, was done in 1968 — *Le Gai Savoir* and *The Bridegroom, the Comedienne and the Pimp*. In comparison, *Tout Va Bien* and *Moses and Aaron* are a step backwards. Godard works increasingly in isolation, cut off from any real collective work or movement. In *Le Gai Savoir*, Juliet Berto says towards the end that half the shots are missing from the film, and Jean-Pierre Léaud replies that they will be shot by other film-makers: Bertolucci, Straub, Glauber Rocha. We can see now how wrong Godard was in some of his judgements — the shots missing from his film could be supplied by the other avant-garde — and it is not clear that he has ever realised this.

Nonetheless, though a simple convergence is very unlikely, it is crucial that the two avant-gardes should be confronted and juxtaposed. History in the arts goes on, as Viktor Shklovsky long ago pointed out, by knight's moves. During the first decade of the twentieth century, when the historic avant-garde embarked on its path, the years of the *coupure*, the cinema was still in its infancy, scarcely out of the fairground and the nickelodeon, certainly not yet the Seventh Art. For this reason — and for others, including economic reasons — the avant-garde made itself felt late in the cinema and it is still very marginal, in comparison with painting or music or even writing. Yet in a way, the cinema offers more opportunities than any other art — the cross-fertilisation, so striking a feature of those early decades, the reciprocal interlocking and input between painting, writing, music, theatre, could take place within the field of cinema itself. This is not a plea for a great harmony, a synesthetic *Gesamtkunstwerk* in the Wagnerian sense. But cinema, because it is a multiple system, could develop and elaborate the semiotic shifts that marked the origins of the avant-garde in a uniquely complex way, a dialectical montage within and between a complex of codes. At least, writing now as a film-maker, that is the fantasy I like to entertain.

MODES OF FILM PRACTICE IN THE AVANT-GARDE

Jonathan Walley

Introduction: 'Artists and Film-makers'

> The dichotomy between avant-garde film (and video) makers, and artists 'working in film/video', still seems to be with us. Despite the important role being played by museums like the Whitney in bridging this divide, the two worlds sometimes seem like Crick and Watson's double helix, spiraling closely around one another without ever quite meeting.[1]
> Anthony McCall

> I think the relationship between film and art is a one-way love affair. Artists love film, but the film world is largely indifferent to the fact. In fact, it often irritates them — they deride it — because filmmaking is still essentially a craft.[2]
> Chrissie Iles

These statements exemplify the perception of a split between two bodies of filmic art. The first is typically called 'avant-garde' or 'experimental' film, while the second, comprised of works made in film or video but designed primarily for gallery exhibition, is called 'artists' film/video', 'projected-image art' or 'film/video installation'. While this distinction has been acknowledged by artists, scholars, curators, etc., it has been addressed only generally — often in colloquial terms — and its precise nature remains unclear.[3] There is not even agreement among the interested parties about whether or not a divide between 'artists and film-makers', as it is often put, exists in the first place. Moreover, the consequences of the split, if there is one, have yet to be thoroughly considered.

The Whitney Museum's 2001 exhibition 'Into the Light: The Projected Image in American Art 1964–1977' threw this vexing issue into bold relief. Organised by Whitney curator Chrissie Iles, 'Into the Light' featured nineteen installations involving film, video or other projected media (e.g. slides, holography). In her catalogue essay, Iles incorporated these installations into a history of contemporary projected-image art, a form that now dominates the art world.

1 Anthony McCall, '*Line Describing a Cone* and Related Films', *October*, no.103, Winter 2003, p.48.

2 George Baker, Matthew Buckingham, Hal Foster, Chrissie Iles, Anthony McCall and Malcolm Turvey, 'Round Table: The Projected Image in Contemporary Art', *October*, no.104, Spring 2003, p.74.

3 See also Brett Kashmere, 'Underground Film, Into the Light: Two Sides of the Projected Image in American Art, 1945–1975', *Synoptique*, no.8, March 2005, www.synoptique.ca/core/en/articles/kashmere_underground

4 Chrissie Iles, 'Re: Into the Light', email post in Frameworks archive, 29 October 2001, www.hi-beam.net/fw/index.html; Frameworks is an online experimental film discussion list with thousands of members internationally, including major figures in avant-garde film theory and practice.

5 G. Baker, et. al., 'Round Table: The Projected Image in Contemporary Art', *op. cit.*, p.72.

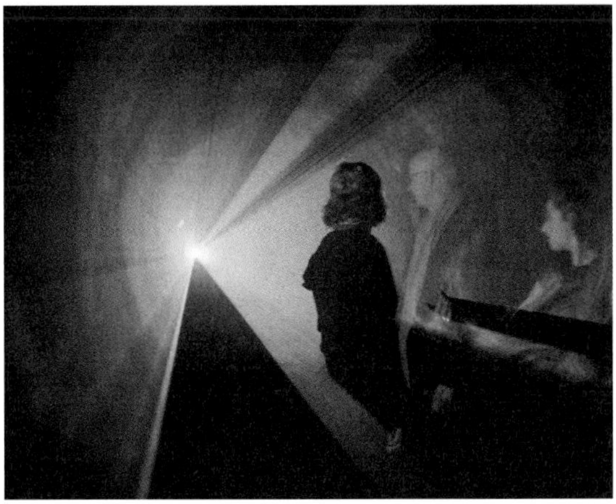

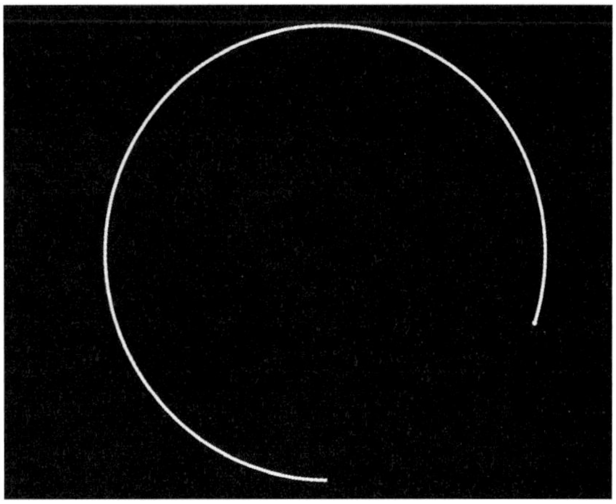

Iles's historiography was unusual because it included several pieces by artists whose film work had not previously been associated with the gallery art world, but with that thing called 'avant-garde cinema'. Iles herself noted the difference in acknowledging 'the film-makers in the show', who included Michael Snow, Paul Sharits and Anthony McCall.[4] Placing these film-makers within her lineage of projected-image art, Iles argued that their films were related to sculptural and process-based work of the 1970s. Film-makers like Sharits, McCall and Hollis Frampton, according to Iles, were 'exploring many of the same concerns' as artists in other media, which warranted her inclusion of their work.[5] The decision indeed brought important but rarely seen works to light, and Iles's art-historical contextualisation was compelling; at the same time, however, it raised the spectre of a split, even an unbridgeable gulf, between two camps of film art.

The situation of McCall's *Line Describing a Cone* (1973) was especially telling. The work is a three-dimensional film in which spectators, rather than watching an image on a screen, engage with the projector beam as it transforms, over 30 minutes, from a thin line to a hollow cone. The film was reconfigured for 'Into the Light' as a looped installation, and experienced as an ongoing, cyclical gallery work rather than being shown in the format typical of film exhibition venues — single screenings with distinct beginnings and endings. This raised questions about the relationship between the 'new' *Line Describing a Cone* and the 'old' version: was it best understood as a film or an art object, and what was the difference? Was the film better illuminated by the context of canonical avant-garde cinema — Maya Deren, Stan Brakhage, Ken Jacobs, et. al. — or that of film and video art — from Bill Viola, Bruce Nauman and Dan Graham to Matthew Barney, Pierre Huyghe and Shirin Neshat? Was the change that McCall's film had undergone for the Whitney's exhibition a distortion, or did it shed new light on a classic work? Such questions extend to the relationship between avant-garde film and the avant-garde in general, especially as museums are increasingly saturated with film and video art. McCall addressed this in a talk at the Whitney during the exhibition, making the 'double helix' analogy cited above.

Anthony McCall, *Line Describing a Cone*, Whitney Museum, 2002. 16mm film installation. Photo © 2008 Henry Graber

Right: Anthony McCall, frame from *Line Describing a Cone*, 1973

What does it mean to say that there are 'two worlds' of film art, or to distinguish between 'artists and film-makers'? Given the history of cross-fertilisation among all media in the avant-garde, can we make a distinction between so-called 'avant-garde film-makers' and 'artists working in film/video'? Is such a distinction even feasible? I believe that the answer to the latter questions is yes, and will offer here a model for thinking about the distinction between 'avant-garde cinema' proper, so to speak, and what I will refer to as 'artists' film' (including film and video, and especially the use of these media in installation formats).

Modes of Film Practice

The two bodies of work tentatively identified thus far as 'avant-garde cinema' and 'artists' film' constitute two different modes of film practice in the avant-garde. The term 'mode of film practice' refers to the cluster of historically bound institutions, practices and concepts that form a context within which cinematic media are used. In their groundbreaking book *The Classical Hollywood Cinema: Film Style and Mode of Production to 1960*, David Bordwell, Janet Staiger and Kristin Thompson explain the term this way:

> The concept of a mode of film practice situates textual processes in their most pertinent and proximate collective context. This context includes both a historically defined group of films and the material practices that create and sustain that group ... A mode of film practice, then, consists of a set of widely held stylistic norms sustained by and sustaining an integral mode of film production ... These formal and stylistic norms will be created, shaped, and supported within a mode of film production — a characteristic ensemble of economic aims, a specific division of labor, and particular ways of conceiving and executing the work of filmmaking.[6]

The authors note that a mode of film practice is not limited to the aims and methods of production, but extends to the channels of distribution, venues and conventions of exhibition and to the viewing strategies that characterise each mode and distinguish one from one another. For instance, Bordwell identifies art cinema (e.g. Godard, Fellini, Bergman) as a mode of film practice 'possessing a definite historical existence, a set of formal conventions, and implicit viewing procedures' distinct from classical Hollywood cinema.[7] Film historian Murray Smith has applied this term to avant-garde cinema, identifying it as a mode distinguishable from both Hollywood and art cinema: 'Such a practice is defined by an integrated set of economic, institutional, and aesthetic norms.'[8] Smith elaborates on some of these norms, tracing out

6 David Bordwell, Janet Staiger and Kristin Thompson, *The Classical Hollywood Cinema: Film Style and Mode of Production to 1960*, New York: Columbia University Press, 1985, p.XIV.

7 David Bordwell, 'Art Cinema as a Mode of Film Practice', *Film Criticism*, vol.1 no.4, Fall 1979, p.56.

8 Murray Smith, 'Modernism and the Avant-Gardes', *The Oxford Guide to Film Studies* (ed. John Hill and Pamela Church Gibson), Oxford: Oxford University Press, 1998, p.395.

9 D. Bordwell, J. Staiger and K. Thompson, *The Classical Hollywood Cinema*, *op. cit.*, p.xiv.

the shape, so to speak, of avant-garde film via a consideration of its history, major figures, animating theoretical concepts and perceived relationship to Hollywood and art cinema.

A mode of film practice, then, is a simultaneously historical, institutional and discursive context constituted by the norms of production, distribution, exhibition and reception of film art. These four categories overlap and shape one another over time. For instance, the production aims of artists inform critical reception, which in turn feeds back into the pool of aesthetic ideas upon which artists draw. Assumptions about the exhibition contexts in which works will be seen affect both artistic production and critical reception, as do changes in media technology. We shall see specific examples of how this works, but for now suffice it to say that the concept of modes of film practice provides a general model for characterising and differentiating between broad contexts in which cinematic media have been used, made into new forms, circulated, experienced and interpreted.

The benefit of this concept for the problem at hand — the 'artists and film-makers' split — is that it provides the widest array of differentiating factors. It enables us to see beyond aesthetics, subsuming aesthetics under its broader heading; the contexts of production, distribution, exhibition and reception are the material conditions under which aesthetic goals are formed by artists and recognised by spectators. As Bordwell and his co-authors explain, a mode of film practice is not limited to a genre, an oeuvre, aesthetic tendencies, etc., but cuts across these, placing them in the context of 'the historical conditions that have controlled and shaped textual processes'.[9] This is especially important here. The two modes of film practice in the avant-garde share aesthetic preoccupations and personnel (i.e. artists who have moved between both modes), which is often asserted as a reason *not* to distinguish between the two groups of film artists. When we expand our consideration of film in the avant-garde from these local factors to the more global perspective of modes of film practice, however, significant differences stand out. These differences, in turn, shed new light on apparent aesthetic affinities between the two bodies of work; the contrast between the two modes extends to the aims behind these aesthetic qualities and the circumstances under which they can be seen and understood.

Production and Distribution

In this section I consider some of the major points of distinction between the production and distribution of avant-garde cinema and artists' film. This section is not meant to be exhaustive, but to set out what I take to be the most important and widely applicable differences. Setting forth the major characteristics of the different 'infrastructures' of production and distribution will allow me to explain how these aspects of each mode of film practice bear on the aesthetics of avant-garde cinema and artists' film.

Avant-garde cinema's mode of production has been described in many ways: 'personal', 'independent', 'amateur', 'artisanal'. These labels all speak to the fact that avant-garde cinema breaks with other film-making traditions in which production is organised according to a hierarchical division of labour. Film historian Ed Small has called experimental film-making 'radically acollaborative', as typically the film-maker — not 'director', 'writer', or 'cinematographer' — controls every aspect of production from the initial conception of the film's idea, through writing and shooting, to post-production (editing and striking prints).[10] In many cases, as in films by Maya Deren, Kenneth Anger and George Kuchar, the film-maker also performs in the film. While there have been famous instances of collaboration among avant-garde film-makers (e.g. Ken Jacobs and Jack Smith, Maya Deren and Alexander Hammid), these are infrequent and do not represent a division of labour like that of other modes of production, as the collaborators still tend to share responsibility for the entire production. Acollaborative production is a core feature of avant-garde film's historical identity, one that has distinguished it from mainstream studio film-making and the capitalist aims its division of labour is often taken to represent.

Artists' film production, however, has become increasingly collaborative since it emerged as a recognisable category of film art in the 1960s. Some work even approaches the scale of mainstream film-making, such as Matthew Barney's *Cremaster* series and recent pieces by Bill Viola, but even smaller scale artists' film production often involves cinematographers, film editors, sound recordists and editors, composers, costume and set designers and performers. Sometimes this division of labour is acknowledged, as in Shirin Neshat's *Passage* (2001), which has a musical score by Philip Glass, or in the *Cremaster* films, which roll end credits in the manner of more conventional films; but more often no reference to the collaborative nature of artists' film appears in the works themselves or in accompanying texts (e.g. exhibition catalogues, critical writings, etc.) Thus, a more proximate reference point for artists' film might be independent art cinema, as it is there that the division of labour in production is subsumed under the rubric of the *auteur*, or film author — the person recognised as the creative conscience to whom the film's form and meaning is ultimately attributed. There are aesthetic reasons to draw an analogy between artists' film and art cinema, but it is also pertinent in terms of the way the labour of film production is represented in publicity and critical discourse around artists' film.

The distinction between artisanal and collaborative production extends to financing and the relationship of each to distribution and exhibition practices. Here we find some of the most pronounced differences between the two modes. McCall has said that 'the avant-garde film tradition is economically unsustainable and probably always has been, and yet somehow it goes on existing'.[11] While avant-garde cinema has rejected much else from mainstream film, it has adopted — albeit on a much smaller scale — commercial film distribution and exhibition, wherein set prices for film rentals and a share of ticket sales constitute the sole revenue film-makers see from their work. This, along with personal funds and occasional grants from arts foundations, is what sustains avant-garde film production. Given the size of the avant-garde film audience and relative rarity of screenings in all but the largest cities, avant-garde film production is generally not financially profitable. Mainstream feature film-making is done on a scale that makes it economically feasible, generating revenue via mass theatrical screenings substantial enough to sustain further production, but this economic model is problematic for film-makers who cannot release multiple prints of their films and whose work, after all, is not fashioned for mainstream tastes.

With rare exceptions, avant-garde film-makers do not sell prints of their films, and the occasional release of experimental films on video is aimed at the video sales and rental market and priced accordingly. Film-makers who do offer prints for sale simultaneously keep one or two circulating in the rental market; the ownership of a print by a private collector has no bearing on the rental price or circulation of other prints.

Artists' film has adopted an entirely different economic model, one that solves many of the financial problems lamented by avant-garde film-makers. The key difference is in how avant-garde film and artists' film regard the tangible, material object that film-making produces: the print.[12] Whereas the limited number of prints avant-garde film-makers strike is a function of their extraordinarily low budgets, in artists' film prints are purposefully scarce, as scarcity is what makes them valuable in the art market. We might characterise this difference as one of unintentional or unavoidable scarcity (as avant-garde film-makers cannot afford to strike multiple prints) versus intentional scarcity (as artists' films, like works of art in other media, are editioned). In McCall's words, the process of editioning films is a matter of 'finding a simple logic to justify the work's selling price that can fund the next project', which involves setting a price for each edition of the film that is a multiple of the cost of production, based in part on the number of editions made.[13] Of course, the notoriety of the artist plays a significant role in establishing the price of editions, a phenomenon not paralleled in the setting of rental prices by avant-garde film distributors.

Simply put, artists' film regards the film print as an art object in a way that avant-garde cinema does not. The same medium used in two different modes of film practice is subject to strikingly different processes based on distinct conceptions of its materials. As many film scholars have pointed out, the potentially limitless reproducibility of film prints was one factor that

10 Ed Small, *Direct Theory: Experimental Film/Video as Major Genre*, Carbondale: Southern Illinois University Press, 1994, pp.17–18.

11 Jonathan Walley, 'An Interview with Anthony McCall', *The Velvet Light Trap*, no.54, Fall 2004, p.70.

12 As opposed to the less tangible experience of viewing the film in projection.

13 G. Baker, et. al., 'Round Table: The Projected Image in Contemporary Art', *op. cit.*, pp.94–95.

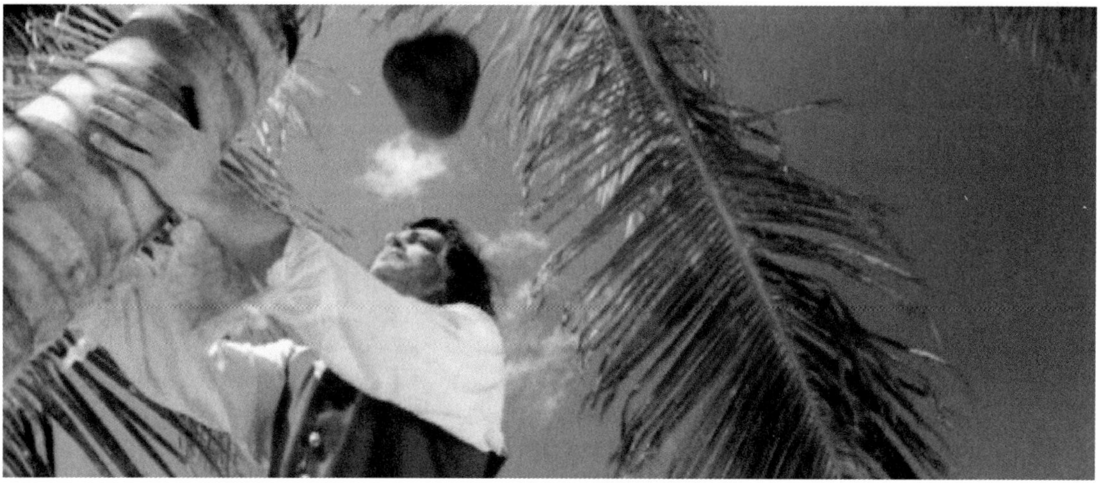

Rodney Graham, *Vexation Island*, 1997. Courtesy the artist and Lisson Gallery, London

prevented film's entry into the art world during the 1960s and 70s.[14] The art world has solved this problem by recourse to the same phenomenon that is regarded as a drawback in avant-garde cinema — scarcity of prints. The aura, supposedly a thing of the past in the age of mechanical reproduction, is maintained via control of just how much reproduction of artists' films takes place. In sum, it is not solely the inherent reproducibility of the film medium but the economic structures in which that medium is used that must be considered in an examination of the relationship between avant-garde cinema and artists' film.

The practice of editioning is aimed at selling the work rather than renting it, and because of this artists' film-making is potentially much more lucrative. This is one factor that enables the degree of collaboration in artists' film I have described; collaboration on this scale is expensive, as cinematographers, editors and actors have to be paid. In general, production budgets are higher in artists' film than in avant-garde cinema, and in many cases artists' films are at least partially financed by galleries, who also play a role in editioning. Higher budgets are also connected to the tendency toward higher production values, especially in more recent artists' film. 'Production values' is a somewhat vague term, subject to individual taste to some extent, and related to aesthetics as much as economics; I raise it here briefly to note a general sense that artists' film aims for a different kind of image quality than avant-garde cinema. Hal Foster has referred to this quality of contemporary artists' film as 'rampant pictorialism, which is also a rampant virtualism'; these terms connote both narrative and illusionism in contrast to abstraction and an emphasis on literal space that had been, by many accounts, the dominant concerns of earlier artists' film *and* avant-garde cinema.[15] Rosalind Krauss has been critical of attempts by certain artists to incorporate traditional painterly values in contemporary work with the photographic image.[16] Certainly, work produced for thousands or even millions of dollars — such as the *Cremaster* films and recent works by Neshat (*Pulse*, *Possessed* and *Passage*, all 2001) and Rodney Graham (*Vexation Island*, 1997; *City Self/Country Self*,

2000; and *A Reverie Interrupted by the Police*, 2003), all made collaboratively in 35mm colour film — possess a higher degree of visual polish than any avant-garde film could achieve. My point is not to criticise such works, but to suggest that different structures of production and distribution enable artists' films access to more material resources and thus different aesthetic possibilities. Once more, the mode of production and the preoccupation in artists' film with ambiguous narratives and a 'painterly' sensibility suggest it has more in common with art cinema than avant-garde film.

In contrasting the production and distribution structures of avant-garde cinema and artists' film, there is one key point I have not mentioned, as it is as much aesthetic as material. In avant-garde cinema, film is the artist's primary, often sole medium (sometimes excepting video). In artists' film, however, film is one medium among many, and artists' films are often part of a body of related works in a variety of media. Barney's *Cremaster* sculptural objects; Neshat's photographs (especially her *Women of Allah* series of the mid-90s, also collaboratively produced); Tacita Dean's drawings; Rosemarie Trockel's sculptures, drawings, books and woven pieces; and Graham's photographs and musical recordings are just a few of many examples of the nexus of works that creates a pool of themes and associations for the explication of films. In addition to providing points of reference for critics who seek the individual artist's sensibility in collaboratively produced films, these other art objects often subsidise work in projected images.

Among avant-garde film-makers, however, film is the centre of artistic practice. This is not to say that these film-makers adhere to medium-specificity theory, reducing the art of film to the brute materials and processes of the medium. But the medium and the aesthetic qualities it makes possible remain central preoccupations. Much attention has already been paid to the ways avant-garde film-makers and critics have investigated the 'essential' nature and purposes of the medium and its materials, processes and signifying practices. And as the medium has moved closer toward its long-predicted, long-delayed obsolescence, these preoccupations have become more pronounced. Film-makers and critics alike regularly bemoan the discontinuation of 16mm stock and equipment, and there is a long tradition in avant-garde film of celebrating outdated cinematic technologies and rediscovering possibilities in obsolete or aborted forms. This may have something to do with the total commitment to the film medium that avant-garde cinema's acollaborative mode of production entails — a defenciveness about the materials and processes of the craft of film-making, every aspect of which the artisanal film-maker knows intimately. The ongoing fascination with film is a crucial feature of avant-garde film

14 See David James, *Allegories of Cinema: American Film in the Sixties*, Princeton: Princeton University Press, 1989, pp.272–73; and Bruce Jenkins, 'The Machine in the Museum; or, The Seventh Art in Search of Authorization', *Space, Site, Intervention: Situating Installation Art* (ed. Erika Suderberg), Minneapolis: University of Minnesota Press, 2000, p.270.

15 G. Baker, et. al., 'Round Table: The Projected Image in Contemporary Art', *op. cit.*, p.75.

16 See Rosalind Krauss, '"... And Then Turn Away?" An Essay on James Coleman', *October*, no.81, Summer 1997, p.28. In this essay, it is Jeff Wall, *not* Coleman, who Krauss criticises.

culture's historical identity; its assertion of autonomy from the art world; and its systematic, obsessive investigation of all things filmic, which is not a feature of artists' film.

One dimension of this has been the exploration of film's spatial qualities — not screen space, but that of cinematic exhibition itself. I consider this phenomenon next, as it plays a central — though often misunderstood — role in perceptions about the two modes of film practice in the avant-garde.

Exhibition and Aesthetics: Cinematic Space

The difference between artists and film-makers is often expressed in terms of the 'white cube of the gallery' and the 'black box of the theatre', respectively. The white cube-black box dyad organises a number of oppositions between the art and film worlds: the sculptural space of artists' film opposes the theatrical film's two-dimensionality; the gallery's mobile viewer is distinguished from the seated cinema spectator; the gallery space enables freedom of choice and movement among viewers who come and go on their own time, while the theatrical space of film screenings putatively constricts the viewer's temporal and spatial experience. This last quality of film is often described as a barrier to film's entry into the art world, as it demands a temporal commitment quite different from that of looking at painting or sculpture. The installation format common among artists' films solves this problem, as film looping de-emphasises the beginning-middle-end structure of theatrical screening, freeing the spectator in time and space. Many artists' films designed for looping engage it in self-aware or playful ways. Rodney Graham's recent films, including *Vexation Island* and *City Self/Country Self*, possess simple narratives whose cyclical structures mirror (and mask) the looping. In Tacita Dean's pieces about lighthouses, *Disappearance at Sea (Cinemascope)* (1996) and *Disappearance at Sea II (Voyage de Guérison)* (1997), the circular scan of the lights on-screen parallels the motion of the loopers in the exhibition space, while repetitive imagery and lack of narrative development obscure the moment each loop begins again.

The ideas about film installation and spectatorship expressed in the white cube–black box distinction emerged out of the expanded, participatory art scene of the 1960s. Minimalism's conception of the relationship between artwork and viewer and the theorisation of this in terms of phenomenology emphasised the apperception of the literal space and time that the viewer and work co-occupied. Thus, the use of film in the gallery has been theorised under the rubric of the sculptural, in the expanded sense of that term in the art world. That is, the white cube–black box distinction implies that any filmic work embracing the space and forms of the gallery departs so dramatically from cinematic convention that such work is best explained in the language of another form. For instance, Iles describes *Line Describing a Cone* as combining 'the phenomenological reductivism of Minimalism with the participatory inclusiveness of Happenings to create an ephemeral projection event'.[17] Additionally, the film's three-dimensionality and open viewing space represent 'a complete reversal of conventional cinematic viewing'.[18]

McCall offered an alternative take on whether his film ultimately belongs in the white cube or the black box; after all, *Line Describing a Cone* had initially been made for theatrical screenings rather than a looped installation. He notes that while his 'solid light' films of the 1970s relate to sculpture,

> their meaning does depend ultimately on their being looked at as film. During the period these works were made they were first shown in avant-garde film showplaces, where they were looked at and thought about in relation to other films — such as work by Tony Conrad, Michael Snow, Malcolm Le Grice and Paul Sharits, for instance.[19]

McCall's claim about the relationship between the meaning of his work and its historical context is suggestive. A three-dimensional film can retain its identity as film rather than taking on the new identity of sculpture. In support of this idea, McCall names factors that shaped his films' aesthetics, including specific exhibition sites and a perceived relationship to a specific institutional and conceptual framework within which the spatiality of his films was legible as cinematic rather than sculptural. Considering avant-garde film-makers' notions of cinematic space reveals their distinctness from the aesthetics of space in artists' film.

Writing in 1960, film-maker Stan Brakhage acknowledged film's spatiality:

> Believe in [the illusion of film] blindly, and it will fool you ... Believe in it eye-wise, and the very comet of its overhead throw from projector to screen will intrigue you so deeply that its fingering play will move integrally with what's reflected, a comet-tail integrity which would lead back finally to the film's creator. I am meaning, simply, that the rhythms of change in the beam of illumination which now goes entirely over the heads of the audience would, in the work of art, contain in itself some quality of a spiritual experience.[20]

Here, the pursuit of heightened perception characteristic of avant-garde cinema from its beginnings includes making the spectator aware of the projector beam (predicting McCall's films); the space of the theatre between projector and screen; and the total system of screen, projector, beam, filmstrip, theatre and audience. Brakhage's comments demonstrate how avant-garde film-makers could conceive of their art as three-dimensional even in its conventional screening format, an idea echoed by Michael Snow in his notes

17 Chrissie Iles, 'Between the Still and Moving Image', *Into the Light: The Projected Image in American Art, 1964–1977* (exh. cat.), New York: Whitney Museum of American Art, 2001, p.45.

18 *Ibid.*

19 Quoted in Lisa Le Feuvre, 'Anthony McCall', *Tema Celeste*, no.94, December 2002, pp.57–58.

20 Stan Brakhage, 'Excerpt from *Metaphors on Vision*', *The Avant-Garde Film: A Reader of Theory and Criticism* (ed. P. Adams Sitney), New York: Anthology Film Archives, 1987, pp.125–26.

on his landmark experimental film *Wavelength* (1967): 'a definitive statement of pure film space and time, a balancing of "illusion" and "fact," all about seeing. *The space starts at the camera's (spectator's) eye, is in the air, then is on the screen, then is within the screen (the mind).*'[21]

The exploration of film space among experimental film-makers began in earnest in the late 1960s. Tentatively, we can identify three aspects of cinematic space in the discourses of avant-garde film. First is the space of the theatre and the activity of viewers within that space. Second is the space of what has been called the 'apparatus' or 'film machine', which extends beyond the screen to the projector and film reel normally behind the audience. Third, and somewhat more abstractly, are the institutional spaces that define avant-garde film and their ramifications for spectatorship. These are not necessarily distinct categories, but different points of emphasis among film-makers exploring film's spatiality.

The work of the London Film-Makers' Co-op encompasses all three conceptions of cinematic space in avant-garde film during the 1960s and 70s. The LFMC provides a rich case study of the relationship between the two worlds of art and film, as many Co-op film-makers were art-school trained and worked in other media. Nevertheless, the Co-op distinguished itself from the art world even as it took up the aesthetics of space that were simultaneously a preoccupation of artists, as A.L. Rees has demonstrated:

> From LFMC experimentation sprang a kind of filmmaking which was related to but finally distinct from the contemporary films of Gilbert and George, Gordon Matta-Clark and Marcel Broodthaers, to take a random sample of artists. In their cases, film extended or documented their practice in other media, as it still does for artists from Bruce Nauman to Tacita Dean. The LFMC — in the spirit of Deren and Brakhage as it happens — was committed to film as an independent art form. The conditions of making and projecting film were taken to be internal aspects of the art form, to be investigated as its major content ... New roles were explored for maker, for viewer, and for the space — the viewing space, be it cinema or installation, live performance or film projection — which stands between them.[22]

Many Co-op film-makers produced spatial film works; while some were designed for installation, many were intended to be shown in the conventional theatre space and screening format wherein the work was experienced all the way through from beginning to end. These spatial pieces grew out of the focus amongst Co-op film-makers on the relationship between film and spectatorial activity. The most prominent example of this emphasis was Structural/ Materialist film, which aimed to heighten viewers' awareness of the literal

21 Reprinted in Annette Michelson, 'Toward Snow', in P.A. Sitney (ed.), *The Avant-Garde Film*, *op. cit.*, p.173.

22 A.L. Rees, 'Locating the LFMC: The First Decade in Context', *Shoot Shoot Shoot: The First Decade of the London Film-makers' Cooperative and British Avant-Garde Film, 1966–76* (ed. Mark Webber), London: Lux, 2002, p.8.

23 Annabel Nicolson, untitled statement, *English Art Today: 1960–1976 (Part II)* (ed. Richard Cork), New York: Rizzoli, 1976, pp.458–59.

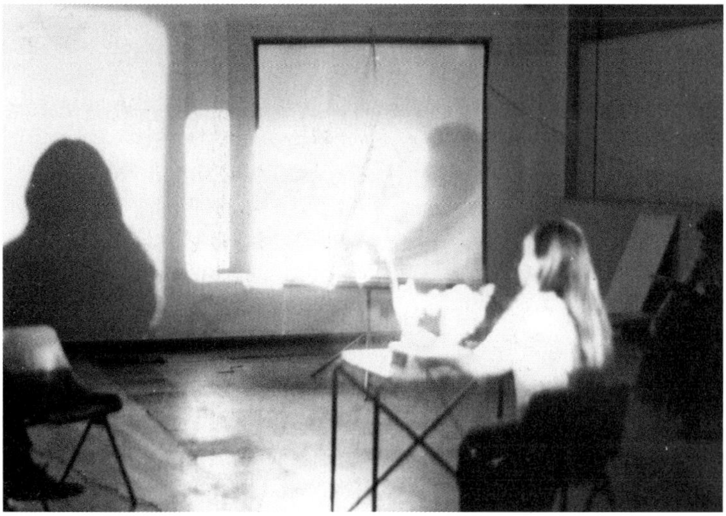

duration of a projection (as opposed to the illusionistic time of a narrative) and create an apperceptive experience in which viewers became aware of their own cognitive processes in response to the unfolding of the film over this duration. So 'activitated', the spectator putatively apprehended the formal and production processes of the film. While Structural/ Materialist film emphasised mental activity in time, some Co-op film-makers translated this into spatial terms, calling for physical self-awareness and bodily participation from the viewer. These works paralleled in space what Structural/Materialist films achieved in time; in each case, the works drew attention to the ways that film might activate and organise the viewing space beyond the screen.

The emphasis, in either case, was on the moment of projection, and this led many film-makers to envision time and space as inseparable elements of cinematic experience. In William Raban's *Take Measure* (1973), the filmstrip, once fed into the projector, is wound outward toward the screen and cut at that point. When the projector starts, the on-screen image of a footage counter measures the space between screen and projector, which in turn determines the duration of the film. In Annabel Nicolson's *Reel Time* (1973), the film ran in a wide loop from the projector, around the performance space, through a sewing machine at which Nicolson sat and back to the projector. As the film made its way repeatedly through the loop, it accumulated perforations made by the sewing machine; these appeared on the screen, simulatenously weakening the film. Nicolson noted that the film ended when the strip broke, making the duration of the piece a function of the object properties of filmstrip, projector and viewing space: 'Working with spatial projections inevitably called into play the whole of the performance/projection space, inseparable from its temporal qualities. The movement in and around the space determines how it is what it is.'[23]

In other spatial works, the projector beam was a concrete formal component. Malcolm Le Grice created a series of film performances in which he moved in the space between projector and screen, modulating the light beam. In *Horror Film 1* (1971), Le Grice performed movements in the path of multiple projectors, casting overlapping shadows onto the screen. Le Grice's actions vividly dramatised the shadow nature of all film projection, calling attention to the physicality — and spatiality — of the film system and asserting the primacy of these physical parameters in the film-viewing experience.

Annabel Nicolson, *Reel Time*, 1973. Courtesy Lux, London

In Lis Rhodes's *Light Music* (1975), the audience occupies the space between two facing screens. Under each screen is a projector aimed at the opposite screen. The two projector beams, made visible by smoke, articulate the space the audience occupies. The film's imagery — patterns of black-and-white bars of varying thickness — extends into the portion of the filmstrip that usually contains the optical soundtrack. Thus, the shifting images, visible both on-screen and in the air, are echoed by distinctive sonic patterns produced by these very images. Viewers must constantly choose where to stand and what to look at, turning their backs on one screen to look at another, or placing themselves between the screens to interact with the projector beams. The apprehension of temporal patterns on the screens is thus inextricably related to the viewers' position and movement in the three-dimensional space of the film. Indeed, the film's organisation of the viewing space is striking to watch, as some spectators line up along the edges of the space while others enter it to interact with the crossing beams. As one critic described it, 'the film becomes a collective event where the audience are invited to make interventions into the work itself'.[24]

The collectivity of these works is indeed important to consider. While many Co-op film-makers did make film installations, their investigations of film's spatiality began in the conventional film theatre and the familiar beginning-middle-end screening structure of commercial cinema. The format's clear spatial and temporal boundaries made film's organisation of time, space and spectatorial activity more palpable than in the installation format, in which time is undefined and spectators come and go at will. McCall makes precisely this argument — that the discrete screening and unified audience of cinema was a powerful form for his own testing of ideas about time, space and cinematic experience. To paraphrase McCall, the collective audience and bounded exhibition time of the cinema dissolved in the gallery into individual spectators making their own choices about the length of time they invested in the work.[25]

Hence, the reconfiguration of *Line Describing a Cone* for installation during 'Into the Light' potentially obscured the film's temporal structure — its slow development from line to cone — as well as the corresponding changes in the way the evolving shape of the projector beam organised audience position, movement and interaction. In this light, we can perceive *Line Describing a Cone* not as 'a complete reversal of conventional cinematic viewing', nor as a 'sculptural' work, but as a particularly vivid embodiment of ideas about film's essences, including its spatiality, as articulated by avant-garde film-makers in the early 1970s. We can also view its installation at the Whitney as an attempt to shift the film from one mode of film practice to another — from the aesthetics and exhibition conventions

24 Lisa le Feuvre, 'Lis Rhodes: Profile', on the LUX website: www.luxonline.org.uk/artists/lis_rhodes/essay(1).html

25 McCall's comments on these issues can be found in Scott MacDonald, 'Anthony McCall', in *A Critical Cinema 2*, Berkeley: University of California Press, 1992, pp.157–74; A. McCall, '*Line Describing a Cone* and Related Films', *it.*, pp.42–62; G. Baker, et. al., 'Round Table: The Projected Image in Contemporary Art', *op. cit.*; and Lisa Le Feuvre,

of avant-garde cinema to those of the art world, from the essentially cinematic to the essentially sculptural.

The exploration of cinema's spatial possibilities in the theatrical context eventually extended into the gallery. Nevertheless, the film-makers who took their work into this space continued to conceive of it cinematically. Their shifting of film from black box to white cube was not an attempt to attain 'art object' status for their work, as some critics have claimed, nor was it a turning away from film-ontological concerns.[26] Instead, these film-makers used the installation format to further enact ideas about cinematic space. In such work, questions about the relationship between the forms and institutions of avant-garde cinema and the art world come to the fore.

The film installations of Takahiko iimura revealed what he called 'the film system', the totality of machines, materials and space of film (what was being theorised as 'the apparatus' in cinema studies, and what Hollis Frampton named 'the film machine'). The gallery space enabled iimura to bring to light, all at once, the interconnected elements of the film system of which the on-screen image was only part. In *Projection Piece* (1968–72), two projectors, mounted side-by-side on stands, faced a third in the middle of the gallery. They were positioned so that one of the projectors stood in the path of the other's beam, casting a shadow in the lit frame on the wall behind. Two strips of film passed though enormous loops, through the two side-by-side projectors to the ceiling above them, across the ceiling to a spot on the wall several feet away, and then down through the exhibition space and back into the projectors once more. On each pass, the two filmstrips picked up dirt and scratches that appeared in the frame on the wall facing the projectors, creating an index of each strip's multiple passes through loop and projector. The contrast between the static projector shadow and the animated scratches on the opposite wall revealed two dimensions of cinematic time according to iimura: 'permanent and temporary'.[27] iimura's installations illuminated other cinematic dualities as well: they contrasted film as temporal experience with film as object (filmstrip, projector, screen and space); and the two-dimensional film image with the three-dimensional space of the 'film system'. iimura was careful *not* to equate the spatial qualities of his work with the sculptural: they were not to 'be seen as movie-sculpture consisting of the machines. The film-installations are a dialectic, positive and negative, which makes apparent what the film system is.'[28]

iimura's rethinking of cinema as dialectic — simultaneously temporal and spatial — was paralleled by Paul Sharits at roughly the same time. Sharits's film installations, multi-format gallery exhibitions and theoretical writings comprise an exhaustive project of researching the ontology of film and imagining new forms, materials and spaces for the medium. Designed

'Anthony McCall', *op. cit.*
26 See D. James, *Allegories of Cinema*, *op. cit.*, pp.272–73.
27 Takahiko iimura, 'On Film-Installation', *Millennium Film Journal*, no.2, Spring/Summer 1978, p.75.
28 *Ibid.*

for display in a gallery, Sharits's 'locational film environments'—including *Sound Strip/Film Strip* (1971), *Synchronousoundtracks* (1973–74) and *Shutter Interface* (1975)—aimed to 'allow [the] public to share with me a respect and enthusiasm for the primary structures of cinema'.[29] His investigation of these structures had led him, around 1970, to the same dualistic quality of iimura's installations. Film was simultaneously a tangible physical material occupying space and an ephemeral experience unfolding in time. Hence, film possessed a spatial dimension ultimately distinct from sculpture's. Moreover, the two poles of film's ontology were not separable:

> 'Film,' can occupy spaces other than that of the theatre; it can become 'Locational' (rather than suggesting-representing other locations) by existing in spaces whose shapes and scales of possible sound and image 'sizes' are part of the wholistic piece. I have found this form of filmmaking and display, using 'more than one projector', more and more meaningful (and imperative if I wish to truly actualize my intent of developing a clear ontological analysis of film's many mechanisms and dualisms).[30]

Sharits's presentation of film in the gallery naturally raised the question of his work's categorisation. Addressing this, Sharits made an early reference to the 'artists and film-makers' gap. Though his film installations had 'been generally better received in the museum-gallery context than in the theatrical art ("film-making") context', Sharits claimed:

> I do not regard myself as either a 'film-maker' or an 'artist who makes films'; rather, I view my activity as prototheoretical and I view myself as an artisan of infrastructural cinema.[31]

Though unwilling to commit to either side of the artists and film-makers split, it is significant that Sharits identified his work as cinematic rather than sculptural, invoked the artisanal mode of production of avant-garde film and cast his work as film ontological research, an aim that places him within the tradition of avant-garde film-making, with which he did indeed self-identify in other contexts. Indeed, it informed a multi-disciplinary pedagogy of film Sharits named 'cinematics', an approach to film instruction that reached beyond film-making craft and aesthetics and into avant-garde film's history, institutions and discourses.[32] That is, 'cinema' stands in Sharits's work for the totality of film-related phenomena subsumed under the heading 'mode of film practice'.

29 Paul Sharits, 'Statement Regarding Multiple Screen/Sound "Locational" Film Environments – Installations', *Film Culture*, no.65–66, 1978, p.79.
30 *Ibid.*
31 Paul Sharits, 'Cinema as Cognition: Introductory Remarks', *Film Culture*, no.65–66, Summer 1978, p.77.
32 Paul Sharits, 'A Cinematics Model for Film Studies in Higher Education', *Film Culture*, no.65–66, pp.43–68.
33 Jonathan Walley, 'The Material of Film and the Idea of Cinema: Contrasting Practices in Sixties and Seventies Avant-Garde Film', *October*, no.103, Winter 2003, pp.15–30; and Jonathan Walley, 'The Paracinema of Anthony McCall and Tony Conrad', *Avant-Garde Film* (ed. Dietrich Scheunemann), Amsterdam and New York: Rodopi, 2007, pp.355–82.

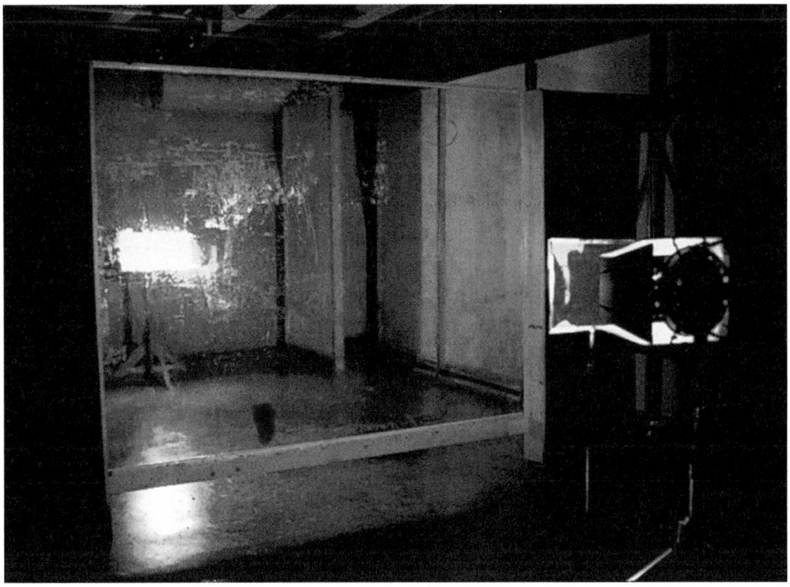

Tony Conrad, *Shadow File,* Wright State University Art Gallery Dayton, Ohio, 1975

A final and most unusual example of film installation is Tony Conrad's *Shadow File* (1975), a work employing no film, camera or projector. Though designed for a gallery, *Shadow File* is different from the works previously mentioned in that it had a projected running time rather than an indeterminant duration of looping. Because this running time was in the realm of months rather than hours and minutes, the installation format was more accommodating.

Shadow File consisted of an acetate diffusion screen suspended in a darkened gallery so that viewers could stand on either side of it. The screen was coated with photochromic paint, which changed colour when exposed to different types of light. One side of the photochromic screen was illuminated by visible light, which caused it to grow lighter, and the other by ultraviolet light, which made it darken. Thus, the screen was held in a state of equilibrium by the two contrasting light sources, unless a viewer blocked one of them. If said viewer stood still for several seconds, the space of their shadow on the screen would become lighter or darker depending on which light source they blocked. After several minutes, the shadow image 'stored' on the screen would revert to the equilibrium colour. Over a period of months, the screen would lose its sensitivity to light, at which point *Shadow File* was considered over.

Shadow File was part of a group of works Conrad made beginning in 1972 that he identified as films but that dispensed with one or all the materials of the medium. I have discussed these 'paracinematic' works elsewhere, along with similarly dematerialised film works by McCall and others.[33] Conrad's paracinema included the series *Yellow Movies* (1972–74), rectangular sheets of paper coated with house paint and allowed to yellow over long periods of time, and a group of unprojectable films subjected to frying, roasting, hammering or pickling. The genesis and aims of Conrad's paracinematic works are complex, as detailed in my other essays. For my purposes here, paracinema is important because it represents the dispersal of film across a variety of forms other than the medium as we know it, just as film installation extends film practice to non-theatrical spaces. But the wide array of materials, forms and spaces of paracinema and film installation have been, and remain, legible as film and, more specifically, as manifestations of the avant-garde film tradition.

Conrad, attracted to the 'hopelessly shabby integrity' of experimental film and its apparent incompatibility with the art market, made *Shadow File* in response to critical misunderstandings of *Yellow Movies* based on their apparent similarities to painting.[34] Like *Yellow Movies*, *Shadow File* amplified the investigation of duration in avant-garde film to a degree that the normal materials of film could not accommodate. In this respect, it extended two central trends in avant-garde film history: the radical re-thinking of the implications of film time and space for spectatorial activity and the search for alternative forms of film production and exhibition.

Conclusion

The assertion that works like *Shadow File*, *Yellow Movies* and *Horror Film I* are films is only possible in the context of a mode of film practice — a set of institutions and discourses that can alternatively be applied to other materials, making these recognisable as cinema. The reverse occurs in artists' film; that mode of film practice involves taking up the medium in a sculptural or performative context within which it is used, experienced and theorised differently. Film allowed artists like Robert Morris, Richard Serra, Dan Graham and Bruce Nauman — contemporaries of the film-makers surveyed here — to engage more directly with the temporal dimension of sculptural work theorised in the language of phenomenology and 'art process'. Hence, even certain artists' films that did not take the form of installation have been called 'sculptural'.[35] The ability of film to destabilise the space of the gallery via its illusory images also seems to have been appealing to artists; the prevalance of mirrors and other reflecting surfaces in artists' films or of disorienting camera (or even projector) movements suggests a desire to disrupt the viewer's comprehension of space.[36]

And while some critics have found 'pictorialism' and 'virtualism' in more recent artists' film, the associations with sculpture and the assumptions about viewer activity implied by the white cube-black box distinction are still prominent. Recent work by Neshat, Trockel, Douglas Gordon, Stan Douglas and Liisa Roberts, among many others, has been described in precisely these terms.[37]

34 Tony Conrad, 'Is This Penny Ante or a High Stakes Game? An Interventionist Approach to Experimental Filmmaking', *Millennium Film Journal*, no.43/44, Summer/Fall 2005, p.102; see also the programme notes for *Shadow File*, in William H. Spurlock (ed.), *Luminous Realities* (exh. cat.), Dayton: Wright State University Gallery, 1976.

35 These include *Railroad Turnbridge* (1967) and *Hand Catching Lead* (1968) by Serra, and *Thighing* (1967) and *Walking in an Exaggerated Manner Around the Perimeter of a Square* (1967–68) by Nauman.

36 I have in mind works like Morris's *Finch College Project* and *Mirror* (both 1969); Nauman's *Rotating Glass Walls* and *Spinning Spheres* (both 1970); Graham's *Body Press* (1970–72) and *Helix/Spiral* (1973); Dennis Oppenheim's *Echo* (1973) and *Gunfire* (1974); and many others.

37 In *Shirin Neshat: The Woman Moves* (Jörg and Ralf Raimo Jung, 2006), a documentary about her work, Neshat invokes the passive cinema viewer and argues that the three-dimensional space created by facing monitors in her installations encourages spectatorial activity. See also Chrissie Iles, 'The Mutability of Vision' *Scream and Scream Again: Film in Art* (exh. cat.), Oxford: Museum of Modern Art, 1996, n.p.; and, on Trockel's work, Joan Simon, 'Sculpture as Theater', *Art in America*, vol.91 no.6, June 2003, pp.90–97.

In emphasising the differences between avant-garde cinema and artists' film, I do not mean to suggest that there are no similarities or that certain works 'belong' to the discipline of film studies and others to art history. Nor are the institutions and histories of the two modes entirely separate. In examining the points of difference, however, we can get a clearer picture of the very phenomenon usually raised as a counter-argument to the 'artists and film-makers' split: the sharing of aesthetic interests, personnel, institutional support and critical languages that does indeed take place. The ways such areas of overlap have been conceived are themselves part of the two modes, as I hope the foregoing has suggested. The concept of modes of film practice is not meant, then, to impose boundaries on artists and art activity, but to illuminate distinctions that already exist and that are often acknowledged (at least tacitly) by artists and critics, who test, challenge and complicate them all the time. While the two modes of film practice in the avant-garde may, like the double helix, 'spiral around each other without ever quite meeting', the individuals who operate within these modes have more freedom of movement.

–II– The Agonistic Relationship Between Video and Television

The second part of this book examines the contradictory and vexed relationships amongst art, video, television and the contested site of the exhibition space. The essays were selected or commissioned in order to consider the changing modes of attention, address and reception in video and televisual works from the 1960s and 70s, and to evaluate the factors contributing to the proliferation of projected video in contemporary art.

Central issues are framed around a set of related questions: How does the new dominance of video projection provide a challenge to film or install a resistance to what Fredric Jameson has called video's 'total flow'? What differentiates video, film and television from one another? What are the key differences between video, film, and television? How do multiple-channel and closed-circuit video installations operate on the viewer's body, senses, mind? How do they envision, or work to decentre a different type of subject from the modernist contemplative one? How do they stage subjectivity, change psychological aspects of perception, manipulate time or challenge the audience's passive immersion into new forms of technology? What motivated the shift from 'viewing' an object to 'performing' in an interactive installation?

This section also examines how moving images have sought to act as counter publicity, dispel the illusion of Hollywood cinema or dis-identify with commercial television. Does television render cinema obsolete? What are the legacies of video art that oppose mass-cultural constructs? It aims to understand how these concerns might correspond with or differ from artists' use of the cinematic medium within our postmodern society of mass communication. It looks at what the digital holds in store and how it is transforming art and its observers.

The section begins with Gene Youngblood's text 'Hardware', an excerpt from 'The Videosphere', published in July 1970 in *Show* magazine, just prior to the release of Youngblood's *Expanded Cinema*. *Expanded Cinema* was the first book about video as an art medium, and was particularly influential in establishing the field of media arts. Taking his cue from Canadian cultural critic Marshall McLuhan, Youngblood examines what he calls 'the Paleocybernetic Age', 'the Videosphere' and 'the new nostalgia' within the context of 'the global intermedia network'. Youngblood traces a provocative evolution of cinematic language to speculate upon the vast emergent possibilities in cinema, video and video art. He concentrates on new technological 'extensions' of the medium – 'instruments of creative living', as he describes them, which include the advanced image-making technologies of computer films, television experiments and multiple-projection environments – that reshape physical, psychic and social aspects of human communication. Youngblood writes:

> *Television is not primarily an aesthetic medium ... It is neither an object nor a 'content'. Television is the art of communication itself, irrespective of message ... A number of contemporary artists* [he discusses Les Levine, Frank Gillotto, Ira Schneider, Allan Kaprow and others] *have realised that television, for the first time in history, provides the means by which one can control the movement of information throughout the environment ... The artist is concerned not so much with what is being communicated as with how it's communicated and the awareness of this process. Thus television becomes the world's first inherently objective art form.*[1]

1 Gene Youngblood, *Expanded Cinema*, New York: E.P. Dutton and Co., 1970, pp.337–38.

2 David Joselit, *American Art Since 1945*, London and New York: Thames and Hudson, 2003, p.156.

3 Hal Foster, Rosalind Krauss, Yve-Alain Bois and Benjamin Buchloh, *Art Since 1900: Modernism, Antimodernism,*

Youngblood argues that television makes us aware of our existence on a global scale by repeatedly showing us ourselves in a self-reflexive loop. Just as painting and sculpture turned inward with the advent of photography and its ability to show external truth, so cinema, Youngblood continues, is experiencing a parallel movement as television becomes evermore omnipresent. Branden W. Joseph notes that 'Gene Youngblood claimed expanded cinema as "a paradigm for an entirely different kind of audiovisual experience, a tribal language that expresses not ideas but collective group consciousness"'. Arguably, while *Expanded Cinema* has aged with its technocratic utopianism, it nevertheless remains a significant account of how technology enhances cinema or television beyond pure entertainment value, with a promise of liberation through new media; it also anticipates some of the key factors of digital aesthetics today, for example its embrace of interactivity.

Rosalind Krauss was not so optimistic about the liberating effects of video. In 'The Aesthetics of Narcissism', her classic essay from 1976, she discusses the formal procedures of video art as a conduit for exploring the self of the artist, relating this strategy to the Process art of the early 1970s. The work of Vito Acconci, Lynda Benglis, Peter Campus, Joan Jonas, Bruce Nauman, Richard Serrra and Nancy Holt employed real-time video as the means of acknowledging both the presence of the viewer and the production and transmission capabilities of video. Because these artists seemed more interested in images of the self than in objects in the world, Krauss had identified the psychological dimensions of narcissistic mirroring in these artist's works as the foundation of video art. Video, she argued, is conjoined with self-absorption. In other words, video, for Krauss at the time of writing, was not a physical medium but a psychological one: 'video's real medium is a psychological situation, the very terms of which are to withdraw attention from an external object – an Other – and invest it in the Self'. As David Joselit observes, while Krauss was largely critical of video's narcissistic impulse, she did note certain strategies of auto-reflection that possessed critical force – such as Jonas's *Vertical Roll*, which 'placed a body out-of-sync through mechanical reproduction'.[2] Furthermore, as other critics have noted, 'this narcissistic situation was never a perfect mirroring. In a sense it was closer to narcissism as understood by the French psychoanalyst Jacques Lacan in his celebrated "Mirror Stage" essay – a kind of mirroring that is always disturbed by a slight mediation, an identification with the image of the self that is always undercut by an alienation from this same image as a little alien.'[3]

In 'Tale of the Tape: *Radical Software*', Joselit argues that artists and theorists associated with *Radical Software* – the publication produced in the early 1970s by the video collective Raindance Corporation – emphasised an understanding of video diametrically opposed to Krauss's (on subjectivity and 'narcissism'), focusing instead on the social and interpellative characteristics of video, relating spectator, object and an other. In Acconci's video *Centers* (1971), for instance, rather than the work's collapsing 'into an undifferentiated ooze of subjectivity', '[w]hat is striking' about Krauss's reading, Joselit argues, is 'its occlusion of the obvious fact that in pointing at his reflected image on the playback monitor, Acconci simultaneously points out at the viewer of the tape. His "narcissism" – if that is what it is – is a thoroughly social act that interpellates the spectator as an object and an other.'

Krauss also saw in certain forms of video art – beyond those that she claimed simply embodied a display of narcissism – that the paradox of 'looking in by looking out' could be connected more explicitly with psychic energies. Citing Bruce Nauman's *Live Taped Video Corridor* (1970) as one such work that might suggest the 'forward trajectory of vision' through spatial decentring, she writes: 'It is an image of photography capturing and exploring a circuit of space from which we as subjects are naturally excluded.'[4] Janet Kraynak's essay 'Dependent Participation: Bruce Nauman's Environments' further considers this question of the participatory artwork within the art-historical framework of the late 60s and its specific expression in Nauman's early sculptural installations. Spectatorial participation, Kraynak argues, is a historical concept, not a static one, that resonates with and negotiates the emerging and unsettling technocratic space of the late 60s. What emerges in Kraynak's essay is the notion that participatory artworks at this time were part of larger social tensions in society, and that such confrontational or assaultive environments stand in contrast

Postmodernism, London and New York: Thames and Hudson, 2005.

4 Krauss's 'Impressionism: The Narcissism of Light', a precursor to the narcissism essay, was published in *Partisan Review*, vol.43 no.1, 1976, pp.102–12.

to today's 'benignly *inclusive*' installations. Rather than suggesting that such destabilising artworks operated outside the dominant system, Kraynak argues they are structurally inherent to it; that they embody tacit forms of control that mirror one of the central principles of technocratic society, that of 'dependent participation'. Art historically, Kraynak's approach presents an alternative model of explanation, one that weakens 'the oppositional logic of contemplative versus participatory artwork and their relative roles within the history of modernism'. Through the theoretical approach of the model of dependent participation, she concludes that multimedia installations 'can be seen to question one of the stakes upon which much progressive sculptural work of the 60s turned: namely the possibility (and benefits) of direct experience'. She identifies a cautionary tale in Nauman's oppressive yet seductive installations, one that questions 'participation as a panacea', a warning that, Kraynak reminds us, rings especially true today when dependent participation is 'increasingly the reality – and even the operative principle – of a global information society'.

Another group of artists – Lea Lublin, Marta Minujin and David Lamelas – working with (and counter to) the new technocratic media sphere of the late 1960s are discussed by Elizabeth Bennett. In 'After the Cull', a new commission for this volume, Bennett discusses media practice and discourse in Argentina while specifically evoking a discussion between 'culling for efficiency' and 'culling for latency'. Bennett uses the term 'culling' to describe the deliberate process of selectively removing individuals from a group based on predetermined criteria or standards, a process inherent to the production of mass media as 'real' events become information for passive consumption. 'Culling for efficiency', she explains, selects information that conforms to the commercial and practical restrictions of time and space as well as viewer expectation. 'Culling for latency', on the contrary, selects inactive information that necessitates the viewer's interactive, ontological presence. The latter assumes a way of revealing the processes and precepts of the culling. Bennett clarifies how the mass media in the late 60s and 70s selected standards by which to cull information differently from those collectively employed by Lublin, Minujin and Lamelas. She examines how media installations – specifically Lublin's *Fluvio Subtunal* (loosely translated as *Subterranean Current*, 1969), Minujin's *Simultaneidad en Simultaneidad* (*Simultaneity in Simultaneity*, 1966) and Lamelas's *Situación de tiempo* (*Situation of Time*, 1967) – reveal and question these processes in the mass media.

In another new commission for this book, William Kaizen deals with the problem of how to define video as an artistic medium. 'Live on Tape: Video, Liveness and the Immediate' situates a number of examples in the historical context of the emergence of video art and the debates over how video, as an extension of live television, differed from film. His essay explores the paradoxical claim made repeatedly in the reception of early video that it was 'immediate', in spite of the fact that it was a system designed for recording. Relating video to live television, he proposes that even when on tape, video's rhetorical immediacy came from a residual live presence that clung to it despite the spatial and temporal distance it imposed on what it presented. What is at stake in Kaizen's account is how communication takes place through this immediacy. He explores two works in detail, Andy Warhol's *Outer and Inner Space* (1965) and Acconci's *Centers*, as key episodes in the emergence of video as a means of reflecting on the larger regime of teletechnologies and the kinds of selfhood they proscribe.

Television, Kaizen suggests, is still very much with us, and Harun Farocki's cinematic work reminds us of exactly that – that we still belong to a system that permits the instant recording and retrieval of sounds and images, and where the digital retains certain aspects of video's immediacy. In 'The Art of the Possible: Notes About Some Installations by Harun Farocki', Christa Blümlinger continues to define the limit conditions of video, considering technological and aesthetical differences between the analogue and the digital, and between instrumental visual culture (such as electronic surveillance) versus the film image. She argues that video recycling comes out of a critical and historical impulse, capable of producing an archeology of different techniques and settings. Focusing on Farocki's double-screen installations, such as *I Thought I was Seeing Convicts* (2000) and *Auge/Maschine* (*Eye Machine*, 2001), she questions how the change from an essayistic cinematic presentation towards a double-screen video environment implies a change of device and form that radicalises the artist's enquiry into the possibilities of transcendent linear montage. Viewing the image as symbolic form in Farocki's work, Blümlinger argues, is just one difference. The real distinction, she writes, is with montage, with an essential operation between image and image, word and image, sound and image, a process that leads gradually towards thought, where the possible is part of the form. Extending Godard's analysis of video in *Numéro Deux* (*Number Two*, 1975) – where two monitors repeatedly appear as intersecting images – Farocki's installations, Blümlinger writes, spatialise the coexistence of images and force the viewer into a theatrical situation. Endowing projected images with a spatial character, she argues, creates a mental in-between space analogous to the invisible interval between two film frames. Blümlinger concludes that *I Thought I was Seeing Convicts* and *Eye Machine*, in confronting the relationship between automatically- and manually-produced images, or automatic versus cinematic vision, the relationship between industry and war and the closed-circuit effect of televisual imagery, present a highly symptomatic circulation of images in different media as objects for reflection.

Maurizio Lazzarato's essay 'Video, Flows and Real Time' responds to the work of Angela Melitopoulos, Nam June Paik and Bill Viola in order to elaborate the ontology of video. Drawing on the writing of these artists and on that of Gilles Deleuze and Henri Bergson, the video image and technology is discussed in terms of the deterritorialisation and synthesis of flows. He writes:

> *If cinema has already revealed that the world is a flow of images and this world of images is in a state of constant transformation, then video technology causes a further deterritorialisation of these flows. Video technology not only shows us the movement, the never-ending variation of images, but also the 'time-matter' from which the images are made (the electromagnetic waves). Video technology is a mechanical arrangement that establishes a relationship between a-significant flows (waves) and significant flows (the images). It is the first technical means of producing images that reflects the 'general decoding of the flows'.*

Another new commission, Bill Horrigan's essay titled 'Five Years Later', derives from a paper initially conceived and presented at the conference 'Moving Image as Art: Time-Based Media in the Art Gallery', at Tate Modern in 2001. Horrigan examines the transmigration of what was 'video art' into 'moving images in the gallery'. 'Five Years Later' is a narrative based on Horrigan's curatorial work at the Wexner Center for the Arts in Columbus, Ohio, since it opened in 1989 and inaugurated its first video installation, Julia Scher's *Occupational Placement*. From Scher's building-wide, multiple-monitor-surveillance installation piece, Horrigan traces a trajectory of projects and succession of 'trends', from the activist work of Paper Tiger Television to the video installations of Todd Haynes, Christine Vachon and Chris Marker, as well as the projections of Shirin Neshat, Phil Collins and William Kentridge.

HARDWARE: THE VIDEOSPHERE

Gene Youngblood

In 1948 approximately 200,000 American homes had television sets; fifteen television stations were broadcasting regularly. By 1958 some 520 stations were broadcasting to receivers in 42 million homes. Today there are tens of thousands of broadcasters and approximately 100 million homes have television sets. More than 95 per cent of American homes have TV sets today, approximately fourteen million of which are colour. In fact there are more TVs in US homes than telephones, bathtubs or refrigerators. TV antennas bristle from the rooftops of ghetto shacks that don't even have plumbing. An estimated quarter-billion television receivers are in use around the world.

Television is the software of the earth.

The videosphere is the *noosphere*—global organised intelligence—transformed into a perceivable state.

This implosive, self-revealing, consciousness-expanding process is irreversible. Global information is the natural enemy of local government, for it reveals the true context in which that government is operating. Global television is directly responsible for the political turmoil that is increasing around the world today. The political establishments sense this and are beginning to react. But it's too late. Television makes it impossible for governments to maintain the illusion of sovereignty and separatism which are essential for their existence. Television is one of the most evolutionary tools in the entire spectrum of technoanarchy.

Television, like the computer, is a sleeping giant. But those who are beginning to use it in revolutionary new ways are very much awake. The first generation of television babies has reached maturity having watched 15,000 hours of television while completing only 10,000 hours of formal education through high school. Yet television itself still has not left the breast of commercial sponsorship. Just as cinema had imitated theatre for seventy years, television has imitated cinema imitating theatre for twenty years. But the new generation with its transnational interplanetary video consciousness will not tolerate the miniaturised vaudeville that is television as presently employed. We will liberate the media.

Cheap, mass-produced, personalised radar sets and house to house closed-circuit television broadcasting soon will be available ...

Approximately 75 per cent of all TV homes in America are now 'all channel', that is, receiving UHF as well as VHF programming. It is estimated that 97 per cent will be all channel by 1974. Meanwhile there are fewer than

100 communities of more than 2500 population that do not have CATV systems now operating or with applications under consideration.

... The FCC recently granted permission for Microwave Communications, Inc. to compete with AT&T by offering CATV systems for rent at parts of a circuit for part of a day. AT&T charges for a whole circuit 24 hours a day. The first lines were to be available between Chicago and St Louis by July 1970.

... a new way to transmit CATV programs without laying down miles of cable has been developed ... a 'quasi-laser' broadcasting system with power requirements in the range of a flashlight battery. ... the system transmits up to fifteen miles and is 'virtually impervious' to atmospheric conditions.

... the New York County Lawyers Association currently is studying the question of whether the public, as owners of the airwaves, have a right to compel TV stations to provide free CATV service since it is the clearest reception.

... a two-way television system that can measure audience reactions instantly via cable and computer interface.

By autumn of this year, Bell Telephone's first commercial Picturephone service will be available to the public. ... AT&T will begin testing a variety of equipment that can read your gas and electric meters via the same lines.

... A laser videophone is now in operation at the headquarters of Nippon Electric Company in Japan, between buildings 300 yards apart.

... (Nippon Electric Company) has used lasers to transmit black-and-white television over a distance of three miles.

A laser-line telephone system that also carries black-and-white TV is now in operation in a high-rise office building in Moscow.

... 'demand TV' or 'telecommand' systems are expected by about 1978. This system will allow an individual to telephone regional video library/switchboards, ordering programmes from among thousands listed in catalogues. The programmes will be transmitted immediately by cable ...

Two networks in Japan are now so automated that two computers in headquarters connect 26 TV stations, schedule production work on 600 to 700 shows at a time, operate master switching controls, warm up equipment, select films and tapes and put them on the air. They do much the same for 33 radio stations.

... 'videofax' or 'homefax' process of facsimile replication and distribution by which one will receive newspapers, magazines and educational documents over home facsimile receivers. Although demonstrated as early as the 1930s homefax systems are only coming into commercial use. ... the facsimile revolution challenges current FCC regulations of content of CATV programmes. Since the 'content' of the facsimile system is a newspaper, present government rulings amount to an impairment of freedom of the press.

The three major satellite networks — the Comstat/Intelsat series, the US Defense Department series and the Soviet Molniyas series — ...

By 1972 no geographical area of the world will be without access to communications satellites.

Direct satellite-to-home TV is planned for NASA's Applications Technology Satellite-C scheduled for launch in 1974. According to a study made for NASA by Sylvania, home TV sets could be modified to pick up the signal for $100 to $150. Spokesmen for General Electric, however, maintain that the average American TV set could be converted to direct-from-satellite reception for about $50 and (in black-and-white at least) deliver a better picture than most sets get now. Comsat claims its 'local' satellite system would require no modifications of the home receiver.

Comsat officials say they can put a domestic satellite system into orbit within 24 months after receiving federal approval.

In September of 1969 the US and India signed a pact which will bring direct satellite-to-village television for 5000 villages in India. Manually-operated generators in each village will provide electricity to operate one community TV set and a ten-foot dish antenna that will reach out 22,300 miles over the Indian Ocean to receive programmes from two satellites. Next India hopes to have a TV satellite system that will reach directly into 560,000 villages by 1975, and for less than $200 million. Thus India has entered the television phase of the industrial equation considerably in advance of previous nations, having completely bypassed the ground relay stage and beginning with satellite television.

Within five years constant analysis of this planet via TV satellites will be a $2 billion industry .... Remote multispectral sensing capabilities of the satellites can distinguish between various types of crops such as wheat, oats and corn, and can also provide an early-warning system for the spread of insect infestation or crop disease, lack of adequate water, livestock movements, changes in grazing patterns, in forest and water tables and even wild animal and bird migrations may be continuously surveyed. By measuring light and heat emanations, the flows of traffic in and out of cities can be computed; patterns of human occupancy of buildings can be deduced from temperature changes — all from satellites thousands of miles above Earth.

Equipped with special high-resolution 5000-scanline cameras in a low 500-mile orbit, satellites have yielded picture resolution equivalent to 100-feet above ground. Higher resolution is possible, officials announced, but some countries would complain of 'invasion of privacy'.

The Nippon Electric Company of Tokyo has announced that its solid state flat TV set composed of light-emitting diodes will be released on the commercial market next year.

... it appears that flat wall TV sets will be on the commercial market by 1978 at the latest.

It is estimated that in 1975 your average colour TV set will cost less than $50.

... a TV receiver only 5-½-inches thick with a 13-inch screen.

... a TV tube with a screen 4×6 feet but only one-foot thick.

... a compact tubeless TV camera less than two-cubic-inches square (smaller than a man's hand) which utilises solid-state light sensors instead of the conventional photo-cathode screen.

... a high-resolution TV camera less than one pound and small enough to carry in a pocket ...

... a half-dollar-size TV screen

... a two-dimensional laser colour TV with a screen 10×6 ½ feet, composed of thousands of glass bars only two-millimeters thick ...

... transistorised TV sets with rechargeable 500-hour batteries.

... a 200-scanline system with picture definition so sharp that it may be transferred to 35 to 70mm film via laser for common movie theatre use.

... 'video Braille' ... a TV camera scans an area and the picture code is transmitted to 400 solenoid stimulators on the blind person's back, where the picture is translated onto the skin through plastic-tipped vibrators.

... most observers estimate that TV cameras small enough to fit in a human eye socket will be developed within the next ten years.

... television sets that translate foreign-language programs into the language of the receiver's local area ...

By 1972 more than 200,000 low cost videotape recorders will be in use in the United States, and the video cassette image-publishing industry will be well on its way to blanketing the Earth with audio-visual information. The videosphere will alter the minds of men and the architecture of our dwellings. 'There's a whole new story to be told,' says video artist Scott Bartlett, 'thanks to the new techniques. We must find out what we have to say because of our new technologies.'

VIDEO: THE AESTHETICS OF NARCISSISM
Rosalind Krauss

It was a commonplace of criticism in the 1960s that a strict application of symmetry *allowed* a painter 'to point to the centre of the canvas' and, in so doing, to invoke the internal structure of the picture object. Thus 'pointing to the centre' was made to serve as one of the many blocks in that intricately constructed arch by which the criticism of the last decade sought to connect art to ethics through the 'aesthetics of acknowledgement'. But what does it mean to point to the centre of a TV screen?

In a way that is surely conditioned by the attitudes of Pop art, artists' video is largely involved in parodying the critical terms of abstraction. Thus when Vito Acconci makes a videotape called *Centers* (1971), what he does is literalise the critical notion of 'pointing' by filming himself pointing to the centre of a television monitor, a gesture he sustains for the 23-minute running time of the work. The parodistic quality of Acconci's gesture, with its obvious debt to Duchampian irony, is clearly intended to disrupt and dispense with an entire critical tradition. It is meant to render nonsensical a critical engagement with the formal properties of a work or, indeed, a genre of works — such as 'video'. The kind of criticism *Centers* attacks is obviously one that takes seriously the formal qualities of a work or tries to assay the particular logic of a given medium. And yet, by its very *mise-en-scène*, *Centers* typifies the structural characteristics of the video medium. For *Centers* was made by Acconci's using the video monitor as a mirror. As we *look* at the artist sighting along his outstretched arm and forefinger toward the centre of the screen we are watching, what we see is a sustained tautology: a line of sight that begins at Acconci's plane of vision and ends at the eyes of his projected double. In that image of self-regard is configured a narcissism so endemic to works of video that I find myself wanting to generalise it as *the* condition of the entire genre. Yet, what would it mean to say: 'The medium of video is narcissism?'

For one thing, that remark tends to open up a rift between the nature of video and that of the other visual arts. Because that statement describes a psychological rather than a physical condition, and while we are accustomed to thinking of psychological states as the possible subject of works of art, we do not think of psychology as constituting their medium. Rather, the medium of painting, sculpture or film has much more to do with the objective, material factors specific to a particular form: pigment-bearing surfaces, matter extended through space, light projected through a moving strip of celluloid. That is, the notion of a medium contains the concept of an object-state, separate from the artist's own being, through which his intentions must pass.

Video depends — in order for anything to be experienced at all — on a set of physical mechanisms. So perhaps it would be easiest to say that this apparatus — both at its present and at its future levels of technology — comprises the television medium, and leave it at that. Yet with the subject of video, the ease of defining it in terms of its machinery does not seem to coincide with accuracy; and my own experience of video keeps urging me toward the psychological model.

Everyday speech contains an example of the word *medium* used in a psychological sense; the uncommon terrain for that common-enough usage is the world of parapsychology: telepathy, extrasensory perception and communication with an afterlife, for which people with certain kinds of psychic powers are understood to be mediums. Whether or not we give credence to the fact of mediumistic experience, we understand the referents for the language that describes it. We know, for instance, that configured within the parapsychological sense of the word *medium* is the image of a human receiver (and sender) of communications arising from an invisible source. Further, this term contains the notion that the human conduit exists in a particular relation to the message, which is one of temporal concurrence. Thus, when Freud lectures on the phenomenon of telepathic dreams, he tells his audience that the fact insisted upon by reports of such matters is that the dreams occur at the *same time* as the actual (but invariably distant) event.

Now, these are the two features of the everyday use of *medium* that are suggestive for a discussion of video: the simultaneous reception and projection of an image; and the human psyche used as a conduit, because most of the work produced over the very short span of video art's existence has used the human body as its central instrument. In the case of work on tape this has most often been the body of the artist-practitioner. In the case of video installations it has usually been the body of the responding viewer. And no matter whose body has been selected for the occasion, there is a further condition that is always present. Unlike the other visual arts, video is capable of recording and transmitting at the same time — producing instant feedback. The body is therefore as it were centred between two machines that are the opening and closing of a parenthesis. The first of these is the camera; the second is the monitor, which reprojects the performer's image with the immediacy of a mirror.

The effects of this centring are multiple. And nowhere are they more clearly named than in a tape made by Richard Serra, with the help of Nancy Holt, who made herself its willing and eloquent subject. The tape is called *Boomerang* (1974), and its situation is a recording studio in which Holt sits in a tightly framed close-up wearing a technician's headset. As Holt begins to talk, her words are fed back to her through the earphones she wears. Because the apparatus is attached to a recording instrument, there is a slight delay (of less than a second) between her actual locution and the audio feedback to which she is forced to listen. For the ten minutes of the tape, Holt describes her situation. She speaks of the way the feedback interferes with her normal

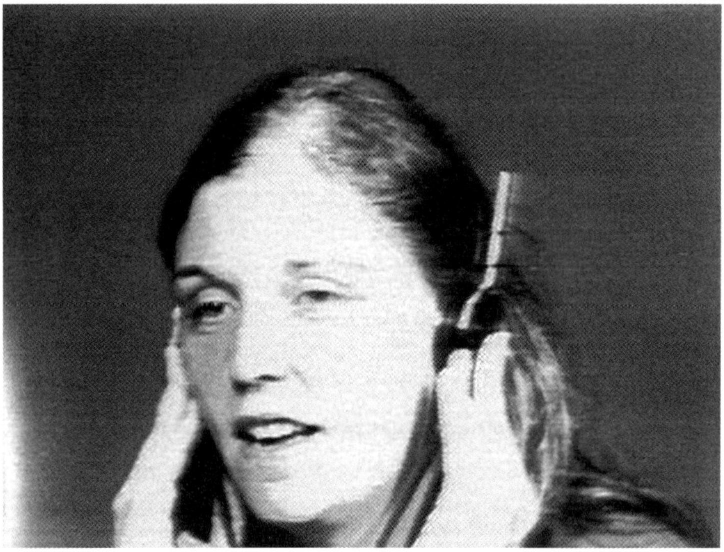

thought process and of the confusion caused by the lack of synchronism between her speech and what she hears of it. 'Sometimes,' she says, 'I find I can't quite say a word because I hear a first part come back and I forget the second part, or my head is stimulated in a new direction by the first half of the word.'

As we hear Holt speak and listen to that delayed voice echoing in her ears, we are witness to an extraordinary image of distraction. Because the audio delay keeps hypostatizing her words, she has great difficulty coinciding with herself as a subject. It is a situation, she says, that 'puts a distance between the words and their apprehension — their comprehension', a situation that is 'like a mirror reflection ... so that I am surrounded by me and my mind surrounds me ... there is no escape'.

The prison Holt both describes and enacts, from which there is no escape, could be called the prison of a collapsed present, that is, a present time that is completely severed from a sense of its own past. We get some feeling for what it is like to be stuck in that present when Holt at one point says: 'I'm throwing things out in the world and they are boomeranging back ... boomeranging ... eranginging ... anginging.' Through that distracted reverberation of a single word — and even word fragment — there forms an image of what it is like to be totally cut off from history, even, in this case, the immediate history of the sentence one has just spoken. Another word for that history from which Holt feels herself to be disconnected is *text*.

Most conventional performers are of course enacting or interpreting a text, whether that is a fixed choreography, a written script, a musical score or a sketchy set of notes around which to improvise. By the very fact of that relationship, the performance ties itself to the fact of something that existed before the given moment. Most immediately, this sense of something having come before refers to the specific text for the performance at hand. But in a larger way it evokes the more general historical relationship between a specific text and the history constructed by all the texts of a given genre. Independent of the gesture made within the present, this larger history is the source of meaning for that gesture. What Holt is describing in *Boomerang* is a situation in which the action of the mirror reflection (which is auditory in this case) severs her from a sense of text; from the prior words she has spoken, from the way language connects her both to her own past and to a world of objects. What she comes to is a space where, as she says: 'I am surrounded by me.'

Richard Serra, still from *Boomerang*, 1974. Colour video, sound, 11mins. Courtesy Video Data Bank

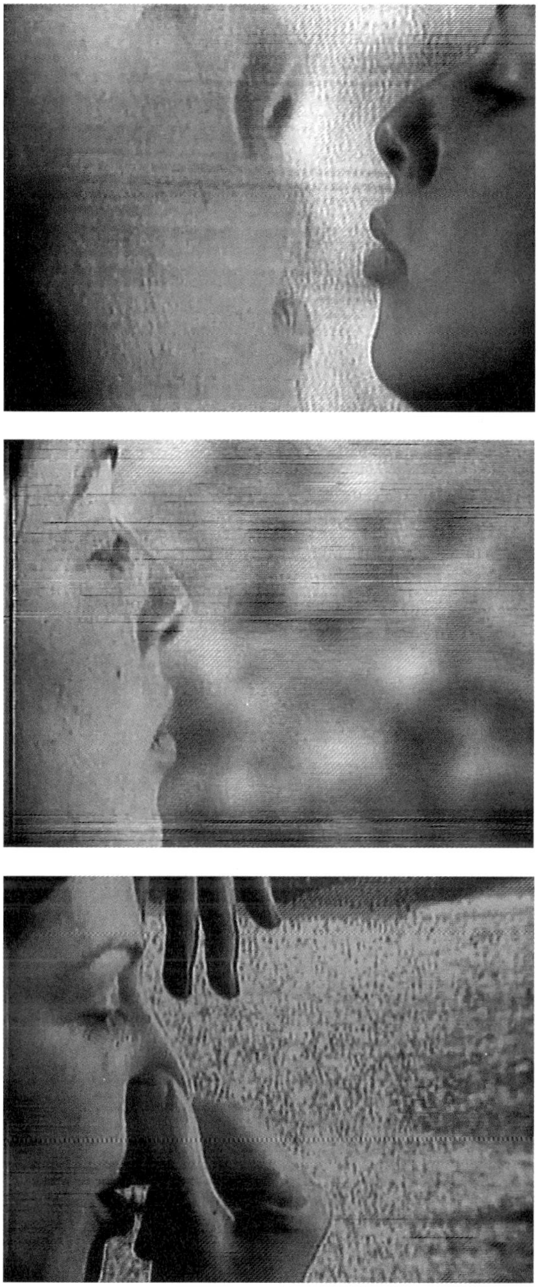

Lynda Benglis, stills from *Now*, 1973. Colour video, sound, 12mins. Courtesy Video Data Bank

Self-encapsulation — the body or psyche as its own surround — is everywhere to be found in the corpus of video art. Acconci's *Centers* is one instance, another is his *Air Time* (1973). In *Air Time* Acconci sits between the video camera and a large mirror, which he faces. For 35 minutes he addresses his own reflection with a monologue in which the terms *I* and *you* — although they are presumed to be referring to himself and an absent lover — are markers of the autonomous intercourse between Acconci and his own image. Both *Centers* and *Air Time* construct a situation of spatial closure, promoting a condition of self-reflection. The response of the performer is to a continually renewed image of himself. This image, supplanting the consciousness of anything prior to it, becomes the unchanging text of the performer. Skewered on his own reflection, he is committed to the text of perpetuating that image. So the temporal concomitant of this situation is, like the echo effect of *Boomerang*, the sense of a collapsed present.

Bruce Nauman's tapes are another example of the double effect of the performance for the monitor. In *Revolving Upside Down* (1968), Nauman films himself through a camera that has been rotated so that the floor on which he stands is at the top of the screen. For 60 very long minutes, Nauman slowly moves, turning on one foot, from the depths of his studio forward toward the monitor and then back again, repeating this activity until the tape runs out.

In Lynda Benglis's *Now* (1973), there is a similar levelling out of the effects of temporality. The tape is of Benglis's head in profile, performing against the backdrop of a large monitor on which an earlier tape of herself doing the same actions, but reversed left and right, is being replayed. The two profiles, one 'live', the other taped, move in mirrored synchrony with one another. As they do, Benglis's two profiles perform an autoerotic coupling, which, because it is being recorded, becomes the background for another generation of the same activity. Through this spiral of infinite regress, as the face merges with the double and triple reprojections of itself merging with itself, Benglis's voice is heard either issuing the command 'Now!' or asking: 'Is it now?' Clearly, Benglis is using the word *now* to underline the ambiguity of temporal reference: We realise that we do not know whether the sound of the voice is coming from the live or the taped source and, if from the latter, which level of taping. Just as we also realise that because of the activity of replaying the past generations, all layers of the 'now' are equally present.

But what is far more arresting in *Now* than the technological banality of the question 'Which "now" is intended?' is the way the tape enacts a collapsed present time. In that insistence it connects itself to the tapes by Nauman and Acconci already described, and ultimately to *Boomerang*. In all these examples the nature of video performance is specified as an activity of bracketing out the text and substituting for it the mirror reflection. The result of this substitution is the presentation of a self understood to have no past and, as well, no connection with any objects that are external to it. For the double that appears on the monitor cannot be called a true external object. Rather it is a displacement of the self that has the effect — as Holt's voice has in *Boomerang* — of transforming the performer's subjectivity into another, mirror object.

It is at this point that one might want to go back to the proposition with which this argument began and raise a particular objection. Even if it is agreed, one might ask, that the medium of video art is the psychological condition of the self split and doubled by the mirror reflection of synchronous feedback, how does that entail a 'rift' between video and the other arts? Isn't it rather a case of video's using a new technique to achieve continuity with the modernist intentions of the rest of the visual media? Specifically, isn't the mirror reflection a variation on the reflexive mode in which contemporary painting, sculpture and film have successfully entrenched themselves? Implicit in this question is the idea that autoreflection and reflexiveness refer to the same thing — that both are cases of consciousness doubling back upon itself in order to perform and portray a separation between forms of art and their contents, between the procedures of thought and their objects.[1] In its simplest form this question would be the following: Aside from their divergent technologies, what is the difference, *really*, between Vito Acconci's *Centers* and Jasper Johns's *American Flag*?

Answer: The difference is total. Reflection, when it is a case of mirroring, is a move toward an external symmetry; whereas reflexiveness is a strategy to achieve a radical asymmetry, from within. In his *American Flag*, Johns uses the synonomy between an image (the flag) and its ground (the limits of the picture surface) to unbalance the relationship between the terms *picture* and *painting*. By forcing us to see the actual wall on which the canvas hangs as the background for the pictorial object-as-a-whole, Johns drives a wedge between two types of figure/ground relationships: the one that is internal to the image

1 For example, this completely erroneous equation allows Max Kozloff to write that narcissism is 'the emotional correlate of the intellectual basis behind self-reflexive modern art'. See 'Pygmalion Reversed', *Artforum* 14, November 1975, p.37.

and the one that works from without to define this object as Painting. The figure/ground of a flat, bounded surface hung against a wall is isolated as a primary, categorical condition, within which the terms of the process of painting are given. The category Painting is established as an object (or a text) whose subject becomes this particular painting—*American Flag*. The flag is thus both the object of the picture *and* the subject of a more general object (Painting) to which *American Flag* can reflexively point. Reflexiveness is precisely this fracture into two categorically different entities that can elucidate one another insofar as their separateness is maintained.

Mirror reflection, on the other hand, implies the vanquishing of separateness. Its inherent movement is toward fusion. The self and its reflected image are of course literally separate. But the agency of reflection is a mode of appropriation, of illusionistically erasing the difference between subject and object. Facing mirrors on opposite walls squeeze out the real space between them. When we look at *Centers*, we see Acconci sighting along his arm to the centre of the screen we are watching. But latent in this setup is the monitor that he is, himself, looking at. There is no way for us to see *Centers* without reading that sustained connection between the artist and his double. So for us as for Acconci, video is a process that allows these two terms to fuse.

One could say that if the reflexiveness of modernist art is a *dédoublement,* or doubling back, in order to locate the object (and thus the objective conditions of one's experience), the mirror reflection of absolute feedback is a process of bracketing out the object. This is why it seems inappropriate to speak of a physical medium in relation to video. For the object (the electronic equipment and its capabilities) has become merely an appurtenance. And instead, video's real medium is a psychological situation, the very terms of which are to withdraw attention from an external object—an Other—and invest it in the Self. Therefore, it is not just any psychological condition one is speaking of. Rather, it is the condition of someone who has, in Freud's words, 'abandoned the investment of objects with libido and transformed object-libido into ego-libido'. And that is the specific condition of narcissism.

By making this connection, then, one can recast the opposition between the reflective and reflexive into the terms of the psychoanalytic project. Because it is there, too, in the drama of the couched subject, that the narcissistic reprojection of a frozen self is pitted against the analytic (or reflexive) mode.[2] One finds a particularly useful description of that struggle in the writing of Jacques Lacan.

2 Freud's pessimism about the prospects of treating the narcissistic character is based on his experience of the narcissist's inherent inability to enter into the analytic situation: 'Experience shows that persons suffering from the narcissistic neuroses have no capacity for transference, or only insufficient remnants of it. They turn from the physician, not in hostility, but in indifference. Therefore they are not to be influenced by him; what he says leaves them cold, makes no impression on them, and therefore the process of cure which can be carried through with others, the revivification of the pathogenic conflict and the overcoming of the resistance due to the repressions, cannot be effected with them. They remain as they are.' Sigmund Freud, *A General Introduction to Psychoanalysis* (trans. Joan Rivere), New York: Permabooks, 1953, p.455.

In *The Language of the Self*, Lacan begins by characterising the space of the therapeutic transaction as an extraordinary void created by the silence of the analyst. Into this void the patient projects the monologue of his own recitation, which Lacan calls 'the monumental construct of his narcissism'. Using this monologue to explain himself and his situation to his silent listener, the patient begins to experience a very deep frustration. And this frustration, Lacan charges, although it is initially thought to be provoked by the maddening silence of the analyst, is eventually discovered to have another source:

> Is it not rather a matter of frustration inherent in the very discourse of the subject? Does the subject not become engaged in an ever-growing dispossession of that being of his, concerning which — by dint of sincere portraits which leave its idea no less incoherent, of rectifications which do not succeed in freeing its essence, of stays and defences which do not prevent his statue from tottering, of narcissistic embraces which become like a puff of air in animating it — he ends up by recognizing that this being has never been anything more than his construct in the Imaginary and that this construct disappoints all his certitudes? For in this labour which he undertakes to reconstruct this construct *for another,* he finds again the fundamental alienation which made him construct it *like another one,* and which has always destined it to be stripped from him *by another.*[3]

What the patient comes to see is that this 'self' of his is a projected object and that his frustration is due to his own capture by this object with which he can never really coincide. Further, this 'state' that he has made and in which he believes is the basis for his 'static state', for the constantly 'renewed status of his alienation'. Narcissism is characterised, then, as the unchanging condition of a perpetual frustration.[4]

The process of analysis is one of breaking the hold of this fascination with the mirror; and in order to do so, the patient comes to see the distinction between his lived subjectivity and the fantasy projections of himself as object. 'In order for us to come back to a more dialectical view of the analytic experience,' Lacan writes, 'I would say that the analysis consists precisely in distinguishing the person lying on the analyst's couch from the person who is speaking. With the person listening [the analyst], that makes three persons present in the analytical situation, among whom it is the rule that the question ... be put: Where is the *moi* of the subject?'[5] The analytic project is then one in which the patient disengages from the 'statue' of his reflected self and, through a method of reflexiveness, rediscovers the real time of his own history. He exchanges the atemporality of repetition for the temporality of change.

3 Jacques Lacan, *The Language of the Self* (trans. Anthony Wilden), New York: Delta, 1968, p.11.

4 Explaining this frustration, Lacan points to the fact that even when 'the subject makes himself an object by striking a pose before the mirror, he could not possibly be satisfied with it, since even if he achieved his most perfect likeness in that image, it would still be the pleasure of the other that he would cause to be recognised in it'. *Ibid.*, p.12.

5 *Ibid.*, p.100. Although *moi* translates as 'ego', Wilden has presumably retained the French here in order to suggest the relationship between the different orders of the self by the implicit contrast between *moi* and *je*.

If psychoanalysis understands that the patient is engaged in a recovery of his being in terms of its real history, modernism has understood that the artist locates his own expressiveness through a discovery of the objective conditions of his medium and their history. That is, the very possibilities of finding his subjectivity necessitate that the artist recognise the material and historical independence of an external object (or medium).

In contradistinction to this, the feedback coil of video seems to be the instrument of a double repression: for through it consciousness of temporality and of separation between subject and object are simultaneously submerged. The result of this submergence is, for the maker and the viewer of most video art, a kind of weightless fall through the suspended space of narcissism.

There are, of course, a complex set of answers to the question of why video has attracted a growing set of practitioners and collectors. These answers would involve an analysis of everything from the problem of narcissism within the wider context of our culture to the specific inner workings of the present art market. Although I should like to postpone that analysis for a future essay, I do wish to make one connection here. And that is between the institution of a self formed by video feedback and the real situation that exists in the art world from which the makers of video come. In the last fifteen years that world has been deeply and disastrously affected by its relation to mass media. That an artist's work be published, reproduced and disseminated through the media has become, for the generation that has matured in the course of the last decade, virtually the *only* means of verifying its existence as art. The demand for instant replay in the media — in fact the creation of work that literally does not exist outside of that replay, as is true of Conceptual art and its nether side, body art — finds its obvious correlative in an aesthetic mode by which the self is created through the electronic device of feedback.

There exist, however, three phenomena within the corpus of video art that run counter to what I have been saying so far, or at least are somewhat tangential to it. They are: (1) tapes that exploit the medium in order to criticise it from within; (2) tapes that represent a physical assault on the video mechanism in order to break out of its psychological hold; and (3) installation forms of video, which use the medium as a subspecies of painting or sculpture. The first is represented by Serra's *Boomerang*. The second can be exemplified by Joan Jonas's *Vertical Roll* (1972). And the third is limited to certain of the installation works of Bruce Nauman and Peter Campus, particularly Campus's two companion pieces *mem* (1974) and *dor* (1975).

I have already described how narcissism is enacted in *Boomerang*. But what separates it from, say, Benglis's *Now*, is the critical distance it maintains on its own subject. This is primarily due to the fact that Serra employs audio rather than visual feedback. Because of this, the angle of vision we take on the subject does not coincide with the closed circuit of Holt's situation, but looks onto it from outside. Further, the narcissistic condition is given through the cerebrated form of language, which opens simultaneously onto the plane of expression and the plane of critical reflexiveness.

Joan Jonas, stills from *Vertical Roll*, 1972. Black-and-white video, sound, 20mins. Courtesy Video Data Bank

Significantly, Serra's separation from the subject of *Boomerang*, his position outside it, promotes an attitude toward time that is different from many other works of video. The tape's brevity—it is ten minutes long—is itself related to discourse: to how long it takes to shape and develop an argument and how long it takes for its receiver to get the 'point'. Latent within the opening situation of *Boomerang* is its own conclusion; when that is reached, it stops.

Vertical Roll is another case where time has been forced to enter the video situation, and where that time is understood as a propulsion toward an end. In this work access to a sense of time has come from fouling the stability of the projected image by desynchronising the frequencies of the signals on camera and monitor. The rhythmic roll of the image, as the bottom of its frame scans upward to hit the top of the screen, causes a sense of decomposition that seems to work against the grain of those 525 lines of which the video picture is made. Because one recognises it as intended, the vertical roll appears as the agency of a will that runs counter to an electronically stabilised condition. Through the effect of its constant wiping away of the image, one has a sense of a reflexive relation to the video grid and the ground or support for what happens to the image.

Out of this is born the subject of *Vertical Roll*, which visualises time as the course of a continuous dissolve through space. In it a sequence of images

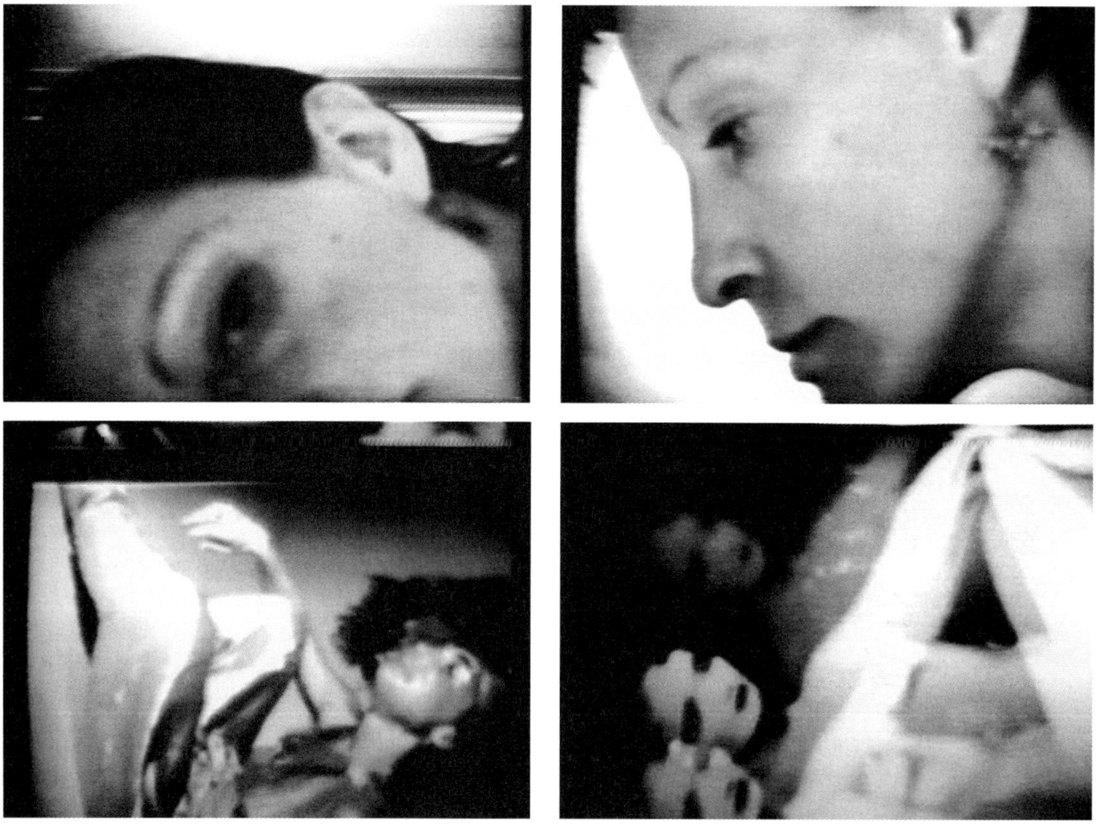

and actions are seen from different positions—both in terms of the camera's distance and its orientation to a horizontal ground. With the ordinary grammar of both film and video these shifts would have to be registered either by camera movement (in which the zoom is included as one possibility) or by cutting. And while it is true that Jonas has had to use these techniques in making *Vertical Roll,* the constant sweep of the image renders these movements invisible. That is, the grammar of the camera is eroded by the dislocating grip of the roll. As I have said, the illusion this creates is one of a continuous dissolve through time and space. The monitor, as an instrument, seems to be winding into itself a ribbon of experience, like a fishing line being taken up upon a reel, or like magnetic tape being wound upon a spool. The motion of continuous dissolve becomes, then, a metaphor for the physical reality not only of the scan lines of the video raster, but of the physical reality of the tape deck, whose reels objectify a finite amount of time.

Earlier, I described the paradigm situation of video as a body centred between the parenthesis of camera and monitor. Due to *Vertical Roll*'s visual reference through the monitor's action to the physical reality of the tape, one side of this parenthesis is made more active than the other. The monitor side of the double bracket becomes a reel through which one feels prefigured the imminence of a goal or terminus for the motion. That end is reached when Jonas, who has been performing the actions recorded on the tape, from within the coils of the camera/monitor circuit, breaks through the parenthetical closure of the feedback situation to face the camera directly—without the agency of the monitor's rolling image.

If it is the paired movement of the video scan and the tape reel that is isolated as a physical object in *Vertical Roll*, it is the stasis of the wall plane that is objectified in Campus's *mem* and *dor*. In both of the Campus works there is a triangular relationship created between: (1) a video camera; (2) an instrument that will project the live camera image onto the surface of a wall (at life- and over-life-size); and (3) the wall itself. The viewer's experience of the works is the sum of the cumulative positions his body assumes within the vectors formed by these three elements. When he stands outside the triangular field of the works, the viewer sees nothing but the large, luminous plane of one of the walls in a darkened room. Only when he moves into the range of the camera is he able to realise an image (his own) projected onto the wall's pictorial field. However, the conditions of seeing that image are rather special in both *mem* and *dor.*

In the latter the camera is placed in the hallway, leading to the room that contains the projector. Inside the room, the viewer is out of the range of the camera and therefore nothing appears on the wall surface. It is only as he leaves the room, or rather is poised at the threshold of the doorway that he is both illumined enough and far enough into the focal range of the camera to register as an image. Since that image projects onto the very wall through which the doorway leads, the viewer's relation to his own image must be totally peripheral; he is himself in a plane that is not only parallel to the plane of the illusion but continuous with it. His body is therefore both the substance of the image and, as well, the slightly displaced substance of the plane onto which the image is projected.

In *mem* both camera and projector are to one side of the wall plane, stationed in such a way that the range of the camera encompasses a very thin corridor-like slice of space that is parallel to, and almost fused with, the illumined wall. Due to this, the viewer must be practically up against the wall in order to register. As he moves far enough away from the wall in order to be able to see himself, the image blurs and distorts, but if he moves near enough to place himself in focus, he has formed such closure with the support for the image that he cannot really see it. Therefore in *mem*, as in *dor*, the body of the viewer becomes physically identified with the wall plane as the 'place' of the image.

There is a sense in which we could say that these two works by Campus simply take the live feedback of camera and monitor, which existed for the video artist while taping in his studio, and re-create it for the ordinary visitor to a gallery. However, *mem* and *dor* are not that simple, because built into their situation are two kinds of invisibility: the viewer's presence to the wall in which he is himself an absence and his relative absence from a view of the wall that becomes the condition for his projected presence upon its surface.

Campus's pieces acknowledge the very powerful narcissism that propels the viewer of these works forward and backward in front of the muralised field. And through the movement of his own body, his neck craning and head turning, the viewer is forced to recognise this motive as well. But the condition of these works is to acknowledge as separate the two surfaces on which the image is held — the one the viewer's body, the other the wall — and to make them register as absolutely distinct. It is in this distinction that the wall surface — the pictorial surface — is understood as an absolute Other, as part of the world of objects external to the self. Further, it is to specify that the mode of projecting oneself onto that surface entails recognising all the ways that one does not coincide with it.

There is, of course, a history of the art of the last fifteen years into which works like *mem* and *dor* insert themselves, although it is one about which little has been written. That history involves the activities of certain artists who have made work that conflates psychologistic and formal means to achieve very particular ends. The art of Robert Rauschenberg is a case in point. His work, in bringing together groupings of real objects and found images and suspending them within the static matrix of a pictorial field, attempts to convert that field into something we could call the plane of memory. In so doing, the static pictorial field is both psychologised and temporally distended. I have argued elsewhere that the impulse behind this move arose from questions that have to do with commodity fetishism.[6] Rauschenberg, among many other artists,

6 Rosalind Krauss 'Rauschenberg and the Materialized Image', *Artforum* 13, December 1974.

has been working against a situation in which painting and sculpture have been absorbed within a luxury market—absorbed so totally that their content has been deeply conditioned by their status as fetish prizes to be collected, and thereby consumed. In response, Rauschenberg's art asserts another, alternative relationship between the work of art and its viewer. And to do this, Rauschenberg has had recourse to the value of time: to the time it takes to read a text or a painting, to rehearse the activity of cognitive differentiation that that entails, to get its point. That is, he wishes to pit the temporal values of consciousness against the stasis of the commodity fetish.

Although responsive to the same considerations, the temporal values that were built into the Minimalist sculpture of the 1960s were primarily engaged with questions of perception. The viewer was therefore involved in a temporal decoding of issues of scale, placement or shape—issues that are inherently more abstract than, say, the contents of memory. Pure, as opposed to applied psychology, we might say. But in the work of certain younger sculptors, Joel Shapiro for example, the issues of Minimalism are being inserted into a space that, like Rauschenberg's pictorial field, defines itself as mnemonic. So that physical distance from a sculptural object is understood as being indistinguishable from temporal remove.

It is to this body of work that I would want to add Campus's art. The narcissistic enclosure inherent in the video medium becomes for him part of a psychologistic strategy by which he is able to examine the general conditions of pictorialism in relation to its viewers. It can, that is, critically account for narcissism as a form of bracketing out the world and its conditions at the same time as it can reassert the facticity of the object against the grain of the narcissistic drive toward projection.

TALE OF THE TAPE: *RADICAL SOFTWARE*

David Joselit

Over thirty years ago Ralph Lee Smith published an influential appeal concerning the future of cable access television (CATV) in the pages of *The Nation*. 'The Wired Nation' heralded nothing short of a revolution:

> As cable systems are installed in major U.S. cities and metropolitan areas, the stage is being set for a communications revolution — a revolution that some experts call 'The Wired Nation.' In addition to the telephone and to the radio and television programs now available, there can come into homes and into business places audio, video and facsimile transmissions that will provide newspapers, mail service, banking and shipping facilities, data from libraries and other storage centers, school curricula and other forms of information too numerous to specify. In short, every home and office will contain a communications center of a breadth and flexibility to influence every aspect of private and community life.[1]

Sound familiar? Substitute the word *Internet* for 'cable', and this passage could pass for a blurb from *Wired* magazine circa 1993 (though the difference between the simple adjective 'wired', which may modify any place — or no place — and Smith's phrase 'wired nation' indicates a growing consciousness and celebration of globalisation in the intervening years). It is well known that new media are habitually modelled on obsolescent networks of the recent past, but the amnesia surrounding the once great hopes for cable TV as a democratic force at the dawn of the 1970s is breathtaking. In books like Lev Manovich's influential *The Language of New Media*,[2] for instance, the rhetoric of the Internet is analysed through an extended comparison with cinema, while cable television, a far more pertinent and historically correct precursor, is all but ignored. There are good reasons for this: despite its status as big business, cinema retains vestiges of revolutionary heroism, whereas what counts for revolution in cable TV is the introduction of the History Channel into the menu. What's more, the thoroughgoing commercialisation of cable — its rapid devolution from an open form of communication to a highly standardised array of entertainment products — is perhaps too painful a reminder for Internet boosters that commerce and radical democracy are rarely if ever compatible.

1 Ralph Lee Smith, 'The Wired Nation', *The Nation*, 18 May 1970.

2 Lev Manovich, *The Language of New Media*, Cambridge, Mass.: The MIT Press, 2001.

3 See www.radicalsoftware.org

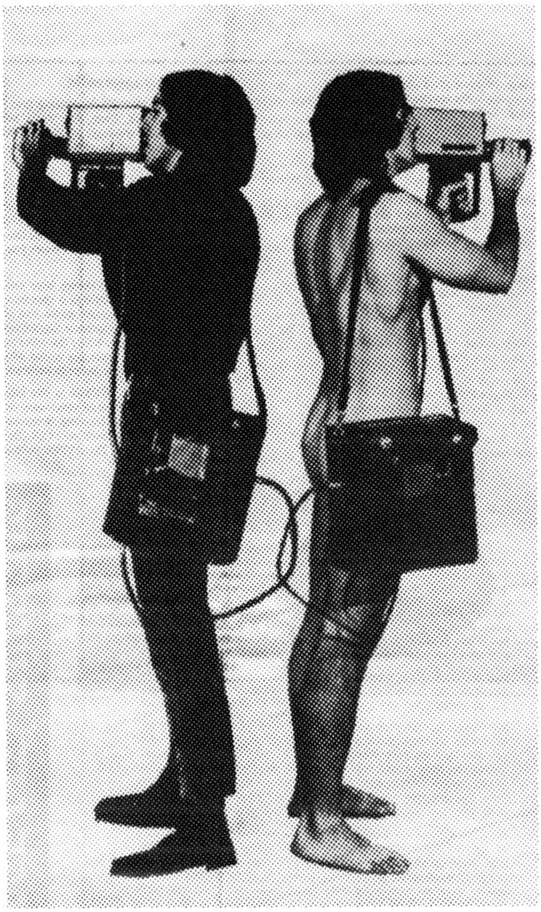

Three decades ago things were different. In order to garner the support of the Federal Communications Commission in the face of network opposition, cable operators professed a commitment to community programming in the years between 1966 and 1972 (the FCC had frozen cable expansion during this period in the one-hundred largest television markets). Community access channels seemed an effective means of legitimising cable and probably helped persuade the FCC to lift its ban. This openness to unconventional television was seized upon by a raucous community of video artists and activists equipped with a new technology — the Portapak — and underwritten by funding from the New York State Council on the Arts as well as private foundations. *Radical Software*,[3] a publication launched in 1970, served as a forum for this emerging movement. Its great virtue — and charm — was its wildly eclectic mix of discourses, including practical production advice, New Age prognostication and applied cybernetics. *Radical Software* was published from 1970 to 1974 by the Raindance Corporation, a video collective conceived by the artist Frank Gillette as a countercultural response to the RAND Corporation, which was conducting studies of the emerging cable industry in the early 1970s. Raindance's activities proceeded on two tracks — video-making and publishing — but all of its work came out of a fascination with media ecology. Influenced by the thought of Marshall McLuhan, Buckminster Fuller and anthropologist Gregory Bateson, the group asserted that social and psychic life are deeply intertwined with information technologies. Consequently, the artificial and oppressive structure of network TV, in which the capacity to produce programming is centralised like a massive accumulation of capital, constituted a major ecological disaster for the United States. Raindance believed that television could be democratised through the deployment of video — on the street, on cable television and in exhibition venues — and that this informational liberation could lead to political democratisation. To this purpose, its affiliates executed a number of informal videotapes allowing ordinary people on the street to address the camera. The group proposed and almost succeeded in funding a Center of Decentralized Television that would have been housed at the Jewish Museum, where the exhibition 'Software', a survey of artists engaged with information technologies, took place in 1970. But the lasting legacy of Raindance was *Radical Software*.

Detail of a spread from *Radical Software*, no.3, 1971 © 2008 Radical Software

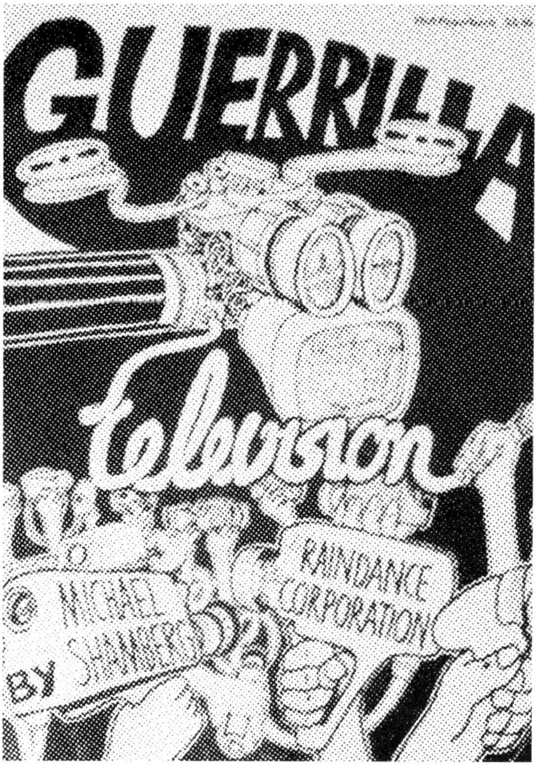

Radical Software was founded, edited and in its early issues primarily shaped by Beryl Korot and Phyllis Gershuny (now Phyllis Segura) with the assistance of several others, including Ira Schneider and Michael Shamberg, author of the important Raindance publication *Guerrilla Television* (1971).[4] In the first volume, printed as a large-format tabloid, funky illustrations recalling underground comics rub shoulders with technical charts, and dynamic compositions of text boxes are linked by vectors, transforming pages into flow charts recalling early computer code. The journal's freewheeling editorial policy is epitomised by the section titled 'Feedback' at the end of each issue of the first volume, where blurbs from various video groups or individuals are crudely pasted together on a skewed grid. Equally unconventional were the juxtapositions of feature articles. In the first number, for instance, texts ranged from Thea Sklover's highly technical account of a cable operators' conference in Chicago to Marco Vassi's 'Zen Tubes', which opens with the declaration:

> To write about ... to write ... about ...
> Tape is explaining a trip to someone who's never dropped acid.
> You have to say, it's like this.[5]

This wild veering from the intricacies of CATV to Acid Video captures the flavour of *Radical Software*. But underwriting such exuberant heterogeneity is a consistent and reasoned advocacy of feedback as a means of redressing media inequities. As a model of activism, feedback is a particularly nuanced approach, connoting both meaningful communication and the wilful jamming of communication through feedback noise. On the most basic level, video feedback is established in closed-circuit installations where viewers are recorded live and their images played back in real time on matrices of monitors. Gillette and Schneider explored this form in *Wipe Cycle* (1969), a work included in the pioneering video exhibition 'TV as a Creative Medium' at the Howard Wise Gallery in New York in 1969. *Wipe Cycle* consisted of a bank of nine monitors and a closed-circuit video camera that recorded live images of viewers as they approached. These fragments of footage were played on 8- and 16-second delays, jumping from monitor to monitor and interspersed with periods of live-broadcast TV and pre-recorded segments. Periodically the screens would be wiped clean. Gillette's description of the work in the exhibition brochure explicitly links it to an ethics of televisual

Cover of *Guerrilla Television*, 1971

Facing page: Ira Schneider and Frank Gillette, *Wipe Cycle*, 1969

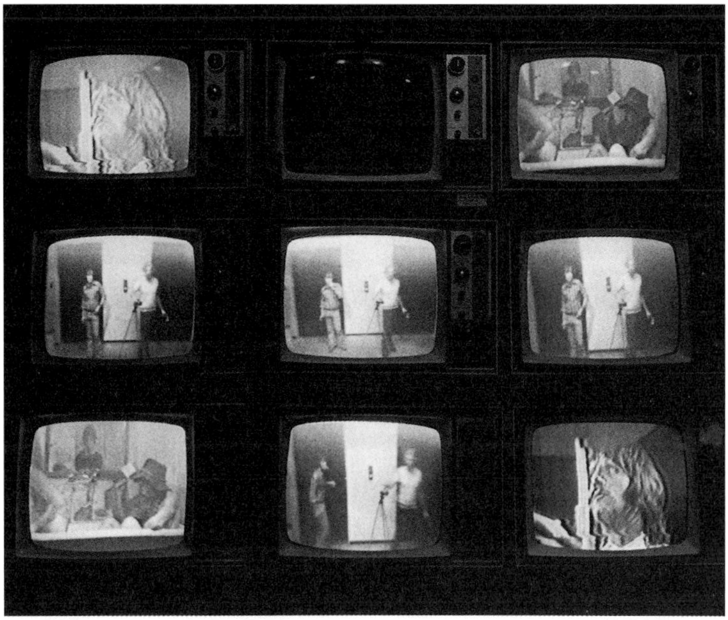

communication: 'The intent of this [image] overloading ... is to escape the automatic "information" experience of commercial television without totally divesting it of the usual content.'[6] In other words, *Wipe Cycle* was meant to break apart commercial television's accumulation of 'information' by giving the spectator a role in generating content. If the networks established a catastrophic centralisation of video production, closed-circuit video installation compensated for this disparity symbolically by introducing the viewer into the image.

What distinguished the editorial policy of *Radical Software* from other accounts of video in the 1970s—whose positions have been progressively balkanised by art and media historians alike—was its demonstration that works of video art like *Wipe Cycle* are structurally identical to video activism as practiced by Raindance and other community video collectives like Videofreex or Global Village. In *Radical Software* art and activism were shown to be formally equivalent on account of their shared practice of feedback. The symmetrical relationship between closed-circuit installations and cable TV that underlies this homology was addressed in a 1969 interview with Gillette and Schneider reprinted in the first issue of the magazine:

> FRANK: ... Now, television is usually understood in terms of a receiver. Our idea is to render that void. Television is something you feedback with as much as you receive with — which is a symbiosis — which works both ways. That's the vast potential of cable TV hooking up with portable equipment. ...
> IRA: Perhaps we should quickly run through these different television notions: CATV, CCTV (Closed Circuit TV), and UHF. The notion is that closed-circuit TV is akin to cable TV in that closed circuit, if we're talking about videotape or storage of information and playback, plays back from the recorder into a wire that runs into the monitor. CATV is an extension of this in that the wire-cable between the playback and the monitor is much longer.[7]

4 Michael Shamberg and Raindance Corporation, *Guerrilla Television*, New York: Holt, Rienhard and Winston, 1971.
5 Marco Vassi, 'Zen Tubes', *Radical Software*, vol.1 no.1, p.18.
6 Exhibition brochure for *TV as a Creative Medium*, Howard Wise Gallery, New York, 1969.
7 Jud Jalkut, 'Frank Gillette and Ira Schneider: Parts I and II of an interview', *Radical Software*, vol.1 no.1, Spring 1970, p.9.

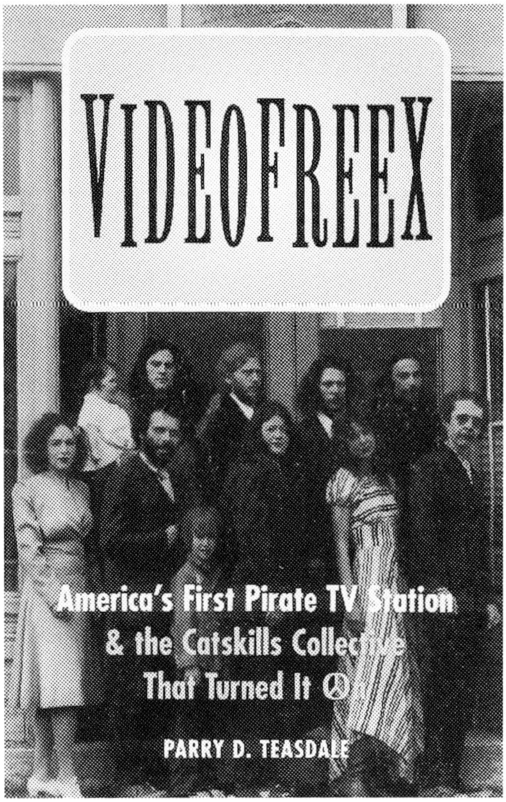

Parry D. Teasdale, *Videofreex: America's First Pirate TV Station & the Catskills Collective That Turned It On*, 1999

Two points deserve emphasis in this interchange. First, on a technological level cable television and closed-circuit TV are identical — as Schneider puts it, the only difference between them is the length of the cable required. But second, the 'software' recommended for CCTV and CATV is as closely related as the hardware. If *Wipe Cycle* was intended to introduce circuits of video feedback within the controlled environment of the gallery, it also served as a blueprint for guerrilla television — those efforts among video activists to respond to the centralisation of commercial television with feedback in the form of politically engaged documentaries to be broadcast on cable. It is consistent with the editorial programme of *Radical Software*, then, that Nam June Paik, who is sometimes criticised for his assiduous efforts to establish video as a purely aesthetic medium, contributed a text to the journal's first issue that proposed an expansive pedagogical role for video well beyond the art world. In 'Expanded Education for the Paperless Society', Paik recommends a thoroughgoing rethinking of higher education, including a systematic effort to record great thinkers on tape before they die. As he charmingly proposes with regard to the virtues of interviewing great philosophers: 'The interviewer should be a qualified philosopher himself ... so that Jaspers or Heidegger can talk as naturally as "Chelsea Girls".'[8]

It's hard to imagine Heidegger behaving as 'naturally' as one of Warhol's speed-driven trauma queens, but it's worth trying because such outlandish juxtapositions — which characterised early video art and activism — have largely been written out of history. Video of the 1970s is now primarily discussed as an art genre rooted in individual subjectivity or, in Rosalind Krauss's famous formulation, as a pure form of narcissism. In 'Video: The Aesthetics of Narcissism', a watershed 1976 essay first published in *October* (and reproduced in the current volume), Krauss suggested that Vito Acconci's *Centers* (1971), in which the artist videotapes himself pointing to the centre of the screen by tracking himself in the 'mirror' of the playback monitor, manifests 'a narcissism so endemic to works of video that I find myself wanting to generalize it as the condition of the entire genre'.[9] Krauss contends that the artist's reflection of him or herself in the video 'mirror' — a common

8 Nam June Paik, 'Expanded Education for the Paperless Society', *Radical Software*, vol.1 no.1, Spring 1970, p.7.
9 Rosalind Krauss, 'Video: The Aesthetics of Narcissism', as reprinted in the current volume, p.208.
10 R. Krauss, *ibid.*, p.213.
11 M. Shamberg and Raindance Corporation, *Guerrilla Television*, *op. cit.*, p.12.
12 Paul Ryan, 'Cable Television: The Raw and the Overcooked', *Radical Software*, vol.1 no.1, Spring 1970, p.12.

trope in the early 1970s — is the antithesis of modernist reflexivity, in which the conventions of an art medium are identified and represented as that medium's content. If reflexivity allows for a critical analysis of the aesthetic and historical relation between an author and his or her medium, mere reflection, according to Krauss, 'is a mode of appropriation, of illusionistically erasing the difference between subject and object'.[10] In other words, works like Acconci's *Centers* collapse into an undifferentiated ooze of subjectivity. What is striking about this reading — which has conditioned an entire generation's understanding of video — is its occlusion of the obvious fact that in pointing at his reflected image on the playback monitor, Acconci simultaneously points out at the viewer of the tape. His 'narcissism' — if that is what it is — is a thoroughly social act that interpellates the spectator as an object and an other. The artists and theorists associated with *Radical Software* emphasised this other dimension of the video mirror. The reading of 'narcissism' they produced is diametrically opposed to Krauss's.

Members of the Raindance Corporation dwelled on the therapeutic potential of video rather than its pathological dimension. As they saw it, one aspect of the ecological crisis occasioned by the centralisation of network television was a psychic blockage — a kind of media tumour — in which information flowed in one direction only, from TV to viewer, leaving the spectator little if any means of responding in kind. In Shamberg's *Guerrilla Television*, the situation was assessed in the following terms:

> In Media-America, our information structures are so designed as to minimize feedback. ... This makes for incredible cultural tension because on the one hand people cannot ignore media evolution, while on the other they require feedback for psychological balance. The result was the 1960s. Every conceivable special interest group, which was informationally disenfranchised, indulged in a sort of 'mass media therapy' where they created events to get coverage, and then rushed home to see the verification of their experience on TV.[11]

Here, Shamberg identifies the psyche of the viewer as a site for media activism. The 'mass media therapy' he recommends was enthusiastically embraced by several figures associated with *Radical Software*. Paul Ryan, for instance, advocated a process of 'infolding' by which one could see and incorporate one's behaviour objectively by watching it on videotape. In 'Cable Television: The Raw and the Overcooked', an essay published in the first issue of *Radical Software*, Ryan explained his technique:

> Working with encounter group leader Dennis Walsh, I videotaped while a girl stood in the middle of the group with her eyes closed and described how she thought people were reacting to her then and there. The contrast between her negative description and the positive responses to her that the playback revealed were both illuminating and encouraging for her. This was information infold. What she and the group put out was taken by the tape and given back to them.[12]

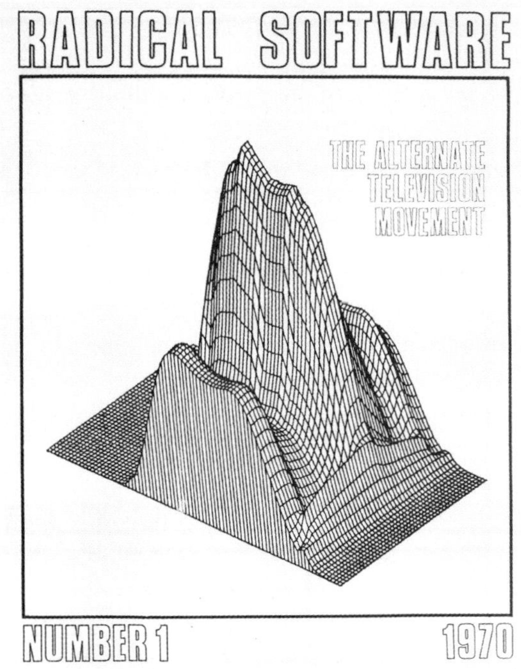

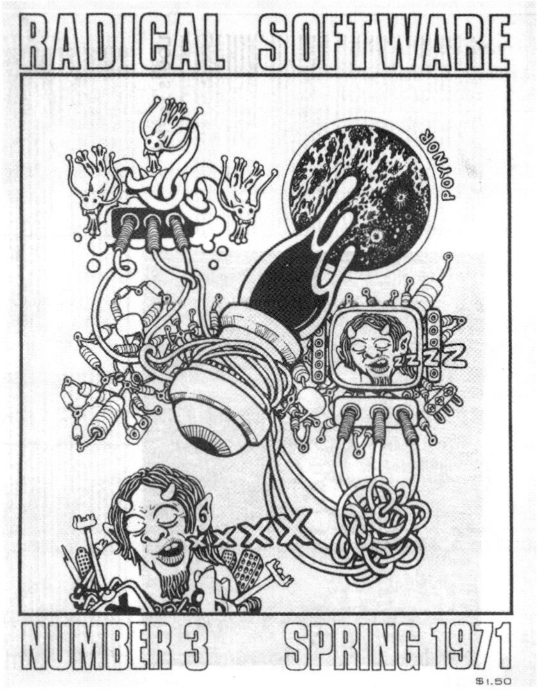

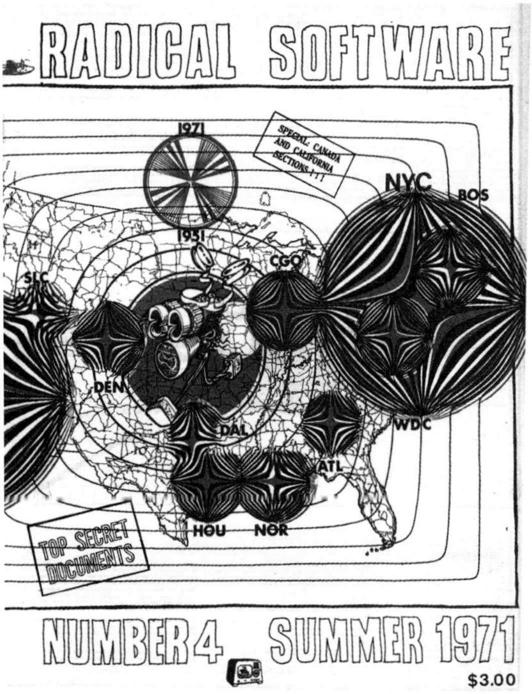

Covers from *Radical Software*, nos. 1, 3, & 4, 1970–71

While a videotaped encounter group is far from a work of art, Ryan's notion of infolding is useful as an alternative model of the relation between video and narcissism. Here the videotape releases a subject from the closed-circuit of herself rather than causing her to collapse into it. Ryan's notion of infolding helps to explain Vassi's analogy between video and LSD: like Ryan's therapeutic videotape, an acid trip both dissolves the boundaries of the self and offers it back as an object. Many of the writers who published in *Radical Software* saw video's capacity to mirror and therefore objectify experience as a prelude to political action. Community video was praised as an organising tool in Dorothy Hénaut and Bonnie Kline's 'In the Hands of Citizens: A Video Report', in the first issue. Recounting the collaboration between the video group Challenge for Change and the Comité des Citoyens de Saint-Jacques in downtown Montreal, the authors declared: 'Having seen people like themselves on the familiar TV screen, discussing their problems with utter frankness, removed much of the reticence and timidity people have in a group of strangers. They simply said, "I guess this is the place where I can talk freely," and talked at length of problems shared and possible collective solutions.'[13]

Radical Software's utopian placement of video may seem quaint today, but there are good reasons for revisiting it. First, the journal's embrace of art and activism under a single umbrella offers a refreshing corrective to the repressive disciplinary boundaries that structure current discussions of visuality in both the academy and the art world. Art historians and critics have sorted those Raindance affiliates who were identified as artists into one category and put activists into another. The freewheeling potential of video is thereby neutralised by confining it within a medium. This process of codification suggests the second rationale for looking again at *Radical Software*: it affords a cautionary tale regarding the Internet's claims as a site for radical democracy. Just as cable TV was once hailed as a new democratic forum, so the Internet is praised for its networked communities. The commercialisation of this space, like cable before it, is already abundantly apparent, but an acknowledgement of the history of various mediums' assimilation into commerce will help to ground and direct strategies for maintaining spaces for open interchange. Finally, *Radical Software* is worth reading because the fundamental tactic it elaborates — feedback — still works. Think of the grass-roots groups that came together to disrupt the meetings of the World Trade Organization in Seattle in 1999 by creatively and exuberantly seizing public space. They constituted a visually savvy, direct-action rebellion conceived and coordinated largely through the Internet, and they put into practice the dual dimensions of feedback — as interference or 'noise' and as communication. True to the tradition of *Radical Software*, these activists jammed the mutually imbricated systems of city streets and global capital. In short, they talked back.

13 Dorothy Hénaut and Bonnie Kline, 'In the Hands of Citizens: A Video Report', *Radical Software*, vol.1 no.1, Spring 1970, p.11.

DEPENDENT PARTICIPATION: BRUCE NAUMAN'S ENVIRONMENTS

Janet Kraynak

> I don't like the idea of free manipulation ... A lot of people had taken a lot of trouble educating the public to participate — If I put this stuff out here you were supposed to participate.[1]
> Bruce Nauman

> A lot of the work is about that, frustration and anger in the, with the social situation, not so much out of specific personal incidents but out of the world or mores or any cultural dissatisfaction, or disjointedness or something, and it doesn't always appear that way in the work, I think. Somehow it generates work. It generates energy from the work.[2]
> Bruce Nauman

Between 1969 and 1974 Bruce Nauman produced a series of hybrid sculptural installations that assertively engage and operate upon the beholder's body, senses and mind. Erected from temporary walls or permanent rooms, some of the sculptures direct the beholder's passage through space while video monitors play prerecorded imagery and/or channel live-feed images of the viewer as she circulates the sculptural arena. In others, video is replaced by swaths of intense coloured lights that illuminate the interiors, performing optical tricks or inducing woozy feelings of nausea. In some, empty space is rendered acoustical through recorded sounds of the artist yelling, laughing, exhaling; or through walls lined with thick acoustical materials that invite the viewer to touch and produce sound. In other installations textual 'instructions', in the form of prose writings, are mounted on the walls, serving as directives for the beholder's feelings and actions.

In Nauman's installations the sculptural meets the architectural, the former realised as an environmental arena in which the beholder's role is no longer one of passive witness. Instead, the viewer is directly, physically engaged — 'performing' rather than 'viewing' the object — and indeed the completion of the object is contingent upon such interactions. As such, they have a long precedent in the pre- and post-war avant-garde, in which methods of artistic production were investigated and transformed as a means of reconsidering the traditional relations between art objects and their audience, and as a means of envisioning a different type of subject than the modernist contemplative one. Examples cross the boundaries of time and meaning: from the Russian Constructivist doctrine of productivism and Brecht's concept

1 Bruce Nauman, interview by Lorraine Sciarra, 1972, published in Janet Kraynak (ed.) *Please Pay Attention Please: Bruce Nauman's Words: Writing and Interviews*, Cambridge, Mass.: MIT Press, 2003, p.167.

2 Bruce Nauman, interview by Michele de Angelus, 1980, *ibid.*, p.269.

of estrangement to John Cage's incorporation of the audience into the musical composition, Minimalism's phenomenological experiments and Conceptual art's rethinking of the networks of artistic distribution, among others.

While the shift toward audience participation historically has been motivated by diverse concerns, frameworks that emphasise its positive attributes as well as its potential for critical transformation dominate the art-historical interpretation. Whether the Marxian model of de-alienation (in which the redefinition of object relations leads to a politically emancipated subject); or post-Structuralist critiques of authorship (where the activation of the reader dismantles the aura of the individual work and authorial intention); or the ideological model of collectivism (as an antidote to the passive lull of bourgeois leisure and media), participation is seen as an interventionist gesture that furthers the ambitions of a progressive avant-garde.[3]

But here I want to consider the question of the participatory artwork in terms of a more limited art-historical framework of the late 1960s, as well as its specific expression in Nauman's early installations. Despite individual differences of materials or design, Nauman's environments consistently figure spectatorial participation as a strange, even alienating, encounter. The viewer is assaulted with sound, frightened with foreboding narrow spaces and cornered by video cameras recording her every move. Recorded images, moreover, are instantly played back to the viewer, whose body is often reduced to a partial fragment or fleeting shadow, resulting in a sense of corporeal dispossession. Physically and psychologically, the viewer continually confronts a collapse of identification between her experience as a body/subject and her image or representation. Technical devices, in conjunction with carefully conceived architectural structures, interrupt passage through space, yielding highly charged environments. In the process the viewer becomes almost an object — a sculptural element — while external space itself seems to assume agency: overwhelming the spectator not necessarily in terms of scale but as a controlling or disciplining factor.

In short, participation in Nauman's environments emerges as an oppressive concept that is at the *expense* of the viewer: or, at least, while his installations depend upon the viewer's interaction, they are nonetheless ambivalent about the possibilities such involvement affords and, as such, create uncomfortable experiences. Such wariness is echoed in the artist's frequent comments over the years regarding his 'mistrust' of audience participation. In the following exchange with Willoughby Sharp, for example, Nauman speaks of his work, *Corridor Installation (Nick Wilder Installation)*, from 1970:

3 Beyond the European/American context, in the South American post-War avant-garde the participant assumed an equal — if not more crucial — role in an explicitly political project: for example, Lygia Clark's interactive 'relational objects' and 'propositions' produced during the 60s; or Hélio Oiticica's 'quasi-cinemas' (a series of interactive, multimedia installations made in the early 70s) and *Parangolé*, which Oiticica describes as follows: '*Parangolé* is anti-art *par excellence*; and I intend to extend the practice of appropriation to things of the world which I come across in the streets, vacant lots, fields, the ambient world, things which would not be transportable, but which I would invite the public to participate in. This would be a fatal blow to the concept of the museum, art gallery, etc., and to the very concept of "exhibition".' Hélio Oiticica, 'Position and Program', *Conceptual Art: A Critical Anthology*, (eds. Alexander Alberro and Blake Stimson), Cambridge, Mass.: The MIT Press, 1999, p.9.

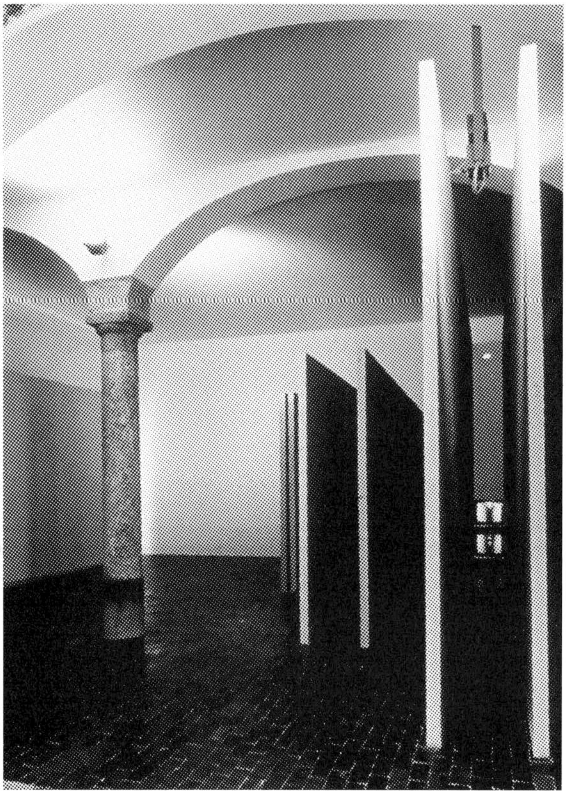

NAUMAN: The cameras will be set upside down or at some distance from the monitor so that you will only be able to see your back. I have tried to make the situation sufficiently limiting, so that spectators can't display themselves very easily.

SHARP: Isn't that rather perverse?

NAUMAN: Well, it has more to do with my not allowing people to make their own performance out of my art. Another problem that I worked out was using a single wall, say 20 feet long, that you can walk around. If you put a television camera at one end and the monitor around the corner, when you walk down the wall you can see yourself just as you turn the corner, but only then. You can make a square with the same function — as you turn each corner, you can just see your back going around the corner. It's another way of limiting the situation so that someone else can be a performer, but he can do only what I want him to do. I mistrust audience participation. That's why I try to make these works as limiting as possible.[4]

Bruce Nauman, *Live Taped Video Corridor*, 1970 © 2008 ARS, New York & DACS, London

Similarly, in another interview, Nauman disdains the creation of open-ended situations, which, he complains, reduce art to a form of 'game playing': 'I don't like to leave things open so that people feel they are in a situation they can play games with ... I think I am not really interested in game playing. Partly it has to do with control, I guess.'[5]

What to make of this apparent tension between the need (or desire) for reciprocal involvement on the part of the viewer and concomitantly a reluctance to allow for it or, at least, to preclude unfettered access? Because of the ways with which the spectator is compelled to perform certain tasks and is physically manipulated within the spaces, as well as the artist's comments (such as those cited above), there has been much speculation regarding not just the nature of Nauman's sculptures but also the artist's perceived relationship with, or even personal feelings toward, his audience — often with uneasy transpositions being made between Nauman's art and persona.[6] But I want to forgo this tendency to personalise — not the least because

4 Willoughby Sharp, 'Nauman Interview', *Arts Magazine* 44, no.5, March 1970, p.23. Reprinted in J. Kraynak, *Please Pay Attention Please*, *op. cit.*, pp.112–13.

5 Jan Butterfield, 'Bruce Nauman: The Center of Yourself', *Arts Magazine* 49, no.46, February 1975, p.55. Reprinted in J. Kraynak *Please Pay Attention Please*, *op. cit.*, p.182

6 For example, Paul Schimmel writes: 'Throughout Nauman's career he has baited, controlled, bored, infuriated, scared, insulted, angered, imperiled, experimented with and manipulated us — his viewers — into experiencing his work within his parameters.' Paul Schimmel, 'Pay Attention', in Neal Benezra, Kathy Halbreich and Joan Simon (eds.), *Bruce Nauman* (exh. cat. and catalogue raisonné), Minneapolis: Walker Art Center, 1994, p.69. A more extreme biographical leap is evidenced in the following observation by Andrew Solomon, from an article that profiles the artist on the occasion of the opening of his 1995 retrospective at the Museum of Modern Art in New York: 'Looking

the evidence of Nauman's artwork does not support such an approach, but also because I am interested in more consequential considerations of historical exigency: specifically, how Nauman's environments raise the very question of participation and how this involvement is interpreted.

Participation, this essay suggests, is a historical rather than a static concept, one that bears particular resonance with the emergence of technocratic society in the late 1960s. Characterised not simply by the pace and stuff of technological change (including computers, television and the familiar trappings of media culture), technocracy also specifically refers to the increasingly administrative order that accompanies these developments. Nauman's environments negotiate this new technocratic space, giving form to the acute anxieties with which it was greeted. The discussion will be guided by a number of contemporary sociological and philosophical writings that attempt to analyse the nature of these changes as well as the conflicts and fears engendered by a social system still in the making. In these writings, what emerges is that participation functions simultaneously as a source of seduction and controversy, touching upon a series of arising social tensions that are part of the larger history of the 60s and its lasting influence on contemporary culture.

Nauman's Environments

Typical of Nauman's production, the 1970 *Live Taped Video Corridor* is an elaboration an earlier work, in this case the artist's first environmental sculpture *Performance Corridor*. Employing the same simple structure of a plywood corridor with an entryway open at one end, in the later work, two video monitors are placed atop each other on the floor at the closed end of the corridor: a dead-end passage that leads to nowhere. As in *Performance Corridor*, the beholder performs the simple task of walking in and out of the corridor's interior, enveloped by its narrowly set walls. Here, however, visual and bodily experience is mediated by video: a pre-recorded image of the empty corridor as well as a continuous live feed from a recording camera that is mounted high on the wall near the structure's opening and tracks the viewer's movement through space. As the viewer works her way toward the corridor's mouth, walking closer to the picture, her body continually recedes, appearing ever smaller. This disconcerting effect is the result of a simple technical detail: because the monitor is placed at the far end of the corridor and the camera at its entry point, as the viewer moves forward, desiring to see and 'touch'

at Nauman's retrospective is like walking through someone else's psychoanalysis: it's full of patterns and recurring wishes, anxieties and obsessions; it's sometimes rather comical and often hostile; it keeps turning out to be about something other than what's apparently being said. Like someone else's psychoanalysis, Nauman's work is often boring and repetitive ... I had seen Nauman's work for years and had never wanted to meet him. I had thought he was probably sadistic and controlling and brilliant and unforgiving and cold.' Andrew Solomon, 'Bruce Nauman: Complex Cowboy', *The New York Times Magazine*, 5 March 1995, pp.29–30.

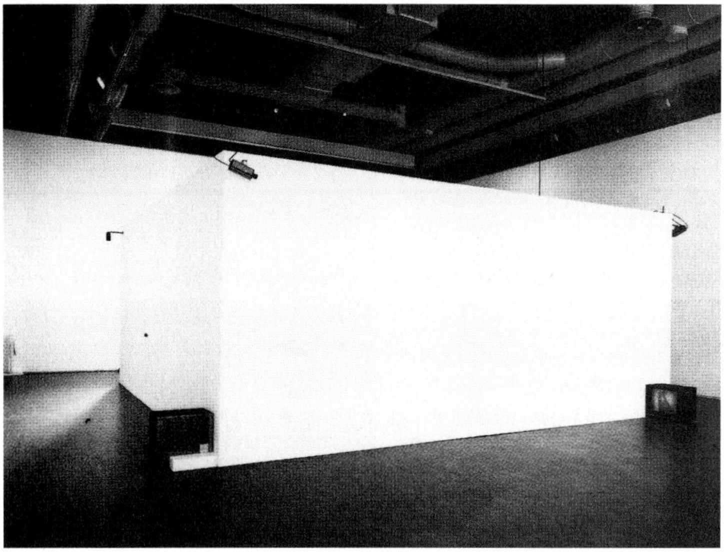

Bruce Nauman, *Going Around the Corner Piece*, 1970 © 2008 ARS, New York & DACS, London

her image, she is actually travelling further away from the recording device. Due to the orientation of the camera, moreover, the viewer can only see herself from behind: a perspective of one's body to which one is not normally privy.

In *Live Taped Video Corridor* a disturbing disjuncture results between vision and experience: I *feel* myself getting closer, yet I *see* myself receding further away. The two forms of sensorial information do not coordinate but rather contradict each other. Such strangeness is not only unfamiliar but unsettling: an uncomfortable space that welcomes me into its depths yet seems to mock me, subjecting me to its parameters. Concomitantly it depends upon me, however, and I am, technically, a desiring participant.

In subsequent pieces such perceptual effects continue with increasingly elaborate spatial configurations that generate new avenues of audience engagement. In *Corridor Installation (Nick Wilder Installation)*, 1970, the simplicity of the single corridor is multiplied into a sprawling construction consisting of six individual corridors of differing widths, only some of which the beholder can enter, as well as an enclosed, inaccessible room. The corridors are variously lit and unlit; some contain cameras and video monitors showing combinations of pre-recorded and real-time imagery, while others are empty, extremely narrow and unpassable. Shifting between access and prevention, each individual configuration explores different perceptual and phenomenal conditions. In the fourth corridor, for instance, a monitor sits at the far end of the passage, feeding a live picture of the floor and ceiling of the enclosed, empty room taken by a camera placed in its interior on an oscillating mount. As the beholder exits this corridor, turning a corner into the fifth passage, she encounters a television monitor that captures, for a brief instant, a fleeting, fragmentary image of the viewer's back. As if to heighten its destabilising effect, the image appears sideways, upsetting one's sense of bodily orientation.[7]

If *Corridor Installation* is descriptively confusing, it is experientially unwieldy. The beholder negotiates a maze of intricately designed spaces, arriving at physical impasses, but, even when entry is permitted, finds herself unable to move about freely and subjected to so many weird perceptual tricks. Reinforcing this sense of being 'cornered', Nauman shortly afterward created two related installations, *Four Corner Piece* and *Going Around the Corner Piece*, in which the beholder's passage from one place to another — as seen in the fourth and fifth corridors described above — becomes the basis of the sculptural installation. In the latter piece a full-scale square room is constructed and placed in the centre of a gallery, like an enlarged Minimalist cube. With no entry point the viewer instead circumnavigates its exterior, at each turn encountering a partial, momentary image of her back going around the corner that plays on a video monitor set upon the floor. Desperate to 'capture' the image — to *see* oneself properly — the beholder finds herself caught up in an endless cycle of replay, turning around and around and around the corners to no avail. As a result, the viewer is in the awkward — and ultimately frustrating — position of seeming to chase herself from behind, not unlike the proverbial dog hopelessly chasing its tail. (Perhaps, in light of an installation Nauman produced almost two decades later, a more apt analogy is a hapless rat.[8])

The subject's spatial discomfort, of being ill at ease in the external world, is a recurring theme in the literature on modernity: the notion of not belonging tied to both the physical and figurative displacements wrought by industrialisation, the architecture of urban life, and the sublime effects of overwhelming space.[9] Yet here I am less interested in the effects of estrangement than in those of solicitation; that is, the simultaneous beseeching and thwarting of the beholder that lies at the centre of Nauman's environments.

While, collectively, Nauman's sculptures might be the most systematic in this regard, numerous participatory artworks from the 60s and 70s are similarly characterised by a decidedly confrontational nature, in which the audience is subjected to various forms of manipulation or assault, yielding often unsettling, ambiguous experiences in which the goal of participation is not entirely clear. For example, in Allan Kaprow's *A Spring Happening* (1961) the audience was confined to the darkened interior of a small crate, while various — sometimes frightening — events took place outside, ones that were audible, but barely visible to the participants, who, as Judith Rodenbeck maintains, are figured as 'objects, collage elements, exchangeable tokens'.[10] In Vito Acconci's *Seedbed* (1972), the unsuspecting beholder, walking up a room-size ramp installed in a gallery, is caught off guard by the potentially embarrassing sounds of a private, sexual act. In Yoko Ono's *Cut Piece* (1964)

7 For further description of the piece, see entry no.172 in N. Benezra et. al., *Bruce Nauman*, *op. cit.*, p.241.

8 Referenced here are Nauman's two related 1988 pieces, *Learned Helplessness in Rats (Rock and Roll Drummer)* and *Rats and Bats (Learned Helplessness in Rats II)*. In both, a rat navigates the interior space of a Plexiglas maze, placed on the floor of a darkened gallery, while a combination of closed-circuit and pre-recorded imagery is projected onto the walls of the gallery. The rat essentially performs the same role as the beholder in the earlier corridor installations described above.

9 For example, architectural historian Anthony Vidler theorises modern space through the Freudian notion of the *Unheimlich* (uncanny). He writes: '[T]he labyrinthine spaces of the modern city have been constructed as the sources of modern anxiety, from revolution and epidemic to phobia and alienation ... ' See Anthony Vidler, *The Architectural Uncanny: Essays in the Modern Unhomely*, Cambridge, Mass.: The MIT Press, 1992, p.IX.

10 Rodenbeck further observes: 'This piece is often discussed in relation to the notion of "rebirth" — a mythic, even epiphanic reading ... [But] attendees recall the smell of fear — Kaprow himself admits he was interested in this as an element. The imagery — no, the actuality — of confinement as well as the assaultive violence of the audience's "liberation" by a roaring lawnmower has as much to do with the historically specific imagery of the Holocaust or of behaviorist experiments as it does with any mythical notion of "rebirth".' Judith Rodenbeck, *Crash: Happenings (as) the Black Box of Experience, 1958–1966* (PhD dissertation), New York: Columbia University, 2002, pp.105–06.

and Marina Abramovic's *Rhythm 0* (1974), on the other hand, the gesture to engage takes the form of a dare, in which the audience is confronted with the burden of *how* to act, with potentially serious — and violent — consequences for the artist.[11]

While such provocative relationships *vis-à-vis* the viewer constitute a significant tendency in the history of participatory artworks, in current practices the move toward audience involvement frequently manifests itself as a benignly *inclusive* aesthetic. For museums and other institutions, moreover, participation is promoted as a resolutely democratic enterprise, capable of rendering often inaccessible contemporary art less mysterious and more pleasurable for a general audience. The viewer engages in various light-hearted activities: relaxing on a lovely dock installed above a lake, eating food served by the artist or playing with an inviting mass of sculptural putty while listening to the music of the indie band Stereolab on a Walkman.[12] In these (and other) examples the once radical premises and potentially destabilising effects of participation are transmogrified into a user-friendly doctrine of artistic viewing. The artist is no longer producer but caretaker and nurturer who provides sustenance, entertainment and other pleasures for an audience that can enjoy such spoils without having to purchase anything.[13]

Because these artworks putatively circumvent the commodity system, providing an experiential encounter for the spectator, they are frequently positioned within a genealogy of 60s practices (such as decommodification, dematerialsation and institutional critique), invoking the language, if not the substance, of radical politics and progressive aesthetics. However, as I have argued elsewhere, such acts of social engagement and benevolence often mask what is in fact an *economic* relationship (i.e. one based upon return) that is identifiable if the model of economy is shifted: from the commodity to gift exchange.[14]

While the subject of my earlier discussion focuses on recent artistic practices and develops an alternative theoretical model, it shares with

11 Frazer Ward has written compellingly about the issue of performance and audience involvement through a theory of ethics exploring the nature of 'acts' rather than simply the entreaty 'to act'. Frazer Ward, 'Marina Abramovic's *Rhythm 0*: Performance, Audience, Ethics', paper presented at the College Art Association Annual Conference, Philadelphia, Pennsylvania, February 2002.

12 The works referred to here include Jorge Pardo's *Pier* (1997), installed in situ for the 'Sculpture Projects' exhibition, Münster, Germany, 1997; Rirkrit Tiravanija's *Untitled (Free)* (1992), as well as the artist's many other performances/installations in which he prepares and serves food; and Charles Long's *Bubble Gum Station* (1995), an installation (which is part of a series of sculptures collectively titled *The Amorphous Body Study Center*) consisting of a central pedestal holding a large blob of bright pink clay, which viewers are encouraged to manipulate while listening to music through headphones attached to the sculptural mass. Of course, not all contemporary works interpret audience participation in such terms: for example, Andrea Zittel's *A–Z Carpet Furniture* (1993; part of her *A–Z Designs for Living* series), among other works, touches upon the more oppressive or sinister aspects of design, controlling the viewer/inhabitant through domestic objects and spaces. Other pieces by the artist, however, such as *Escape Vehicles*, more readily approach the 'user-friendly' doctrine of participation. In *Escape Vehicles* the collector customises the interior of a small unit (the shell of which is designed by Zittel), creating a private space of personal taste and objects. Even this work, however, tarries between pleasure and oppression: as Stefano Basilico mentioned to me, in the *Escape Vehicle* one basically designs one's own coffin, a decidedly morbid task.

13 Miwon Kwon, in an important study of the historical and theoretical transformations of 'site-specific' practices, discusses this relatively recent phenomenon of the 'artist as service-provider'. Drawing upon — and inverting — Benjamin Buchloh's construct of the 'aesthetics of administration', which he developed in relationship to conceptual art, Kwon theorises the 'administration of aesthetics' in the art of the 1980s and 90s. Miwon Kwon, *One Place after Another: Site-Specific Art and Locational Identity*, Cambridge, Mass.: The MIT Press, 2002, p.51.

the current essay several key points: first, far from operating *outside* the dominant system, this 'gift economy' (as, it will be argued, 'participation') is structurally immanent to that system.[15] Second, they both propose a reading of *participation as obligation*: a tacit form of control in which reciprocity is all but guaranteed and desires and will are exploited, becoming, in effect, forms of submission — or dependency. Technocratic society, we shall see, is precisely built upon this dynamic: a dialectic of participation and control.

The Programmed Society

The notion of technocracy first widely arose in public discourse in the United States during the 1920s and 30s when a group of scientists and social engineers proposed a rationalistic, technological order as a means of curing the social and economic crises brought on by the Great Depression. For these self-described technocrats, however, faith rested not in technology as an isolated instrument but in its principles of efficiency, which, they believed, could be adapted to the social sphere. As historian William Akin notes: 'In the technocrats' minds the ills of the economy were traceable not to the machine *per se*, but to an *inefficient adjustment of the social order* to modern high-energy technology.'[16] For the technocrats, governmental and business institutions — the traditional corner stones of the capitalist system — were inadequate and inefficient systems that had led the nation to the edge of economic disaster. In their place the technocrats promoted the value of the 'technician' (or engineer) and enlisted the scientific management theories of Thorstein Veblen and Frederick W. Taylor, both of whom argued for a broad social application of the principle of technical rationality.[17]

While the technocratic period represents a relatively minor episode in social and political history, debates regarding the emergence of technocracy reached a fever pitch during the 60s.[18] In attempting to grasp the implications of the transformation from an industrial, production-based economy to

14 The argument was developed in relation to the work of Rirkrit Tiravanija, whose various projects entail serving food and drink, performing live music and re-creating a full-scale model of the interior of his apartment in a gallery, and so on — all of which generate spaces for social exchange. The 'generosity' often attributed to these works, is, however, misleading, in that, according to the structural logic of the gift, it demands reciprocity and fosters social contracts of obligation. See Janet Kraynak, 'Rirkrit Tiravanija's Liability', *Documents* 13, Fall 1998, pp.26–40.

15 In the essay on Rirkrit Tiravanija's work cited above, I draw upon Pierre Bourdieu's concept of symbolic 'capital', which represents an intangible, yet powerful, source of economic and political wealth, and contend that 'the gift' in fact constitutes a central economic force in late capitalist society.

16 William Akin, *Technocracy and the American Dream: The Technocratic Movement 1900–41*, Berkeley: University of California Press, 1977, p.x (emphasis added).

17 In *The Theory of Business Enterprise* (1904), Thorstein Veblen maintains that the rationality and objectivity of the scientist (or the engineer) was an antidote to the uncontainable self-centredness of the capitalist business-man, who, rather than aiding the economy, was detrimental to its smooth functioning. Frederick Taylor, whose theory of scientific management has been widely discussed, was similarly committed to scientific principles of rationality, which, he argued, could be applied to generate increasingly efficient models of work, the factory and, by extension, social life. Frederick Taylor, *The Principles of Scientific Management*, New York; W.W. Norton, 1911.

18 Referring to the 1960s as an important turning point, Andrew Feenberg, in his study on the philosophy of technology, writes: 'It is not easy to explain the dramatic shift in attitudes towards technology that occurred in the 1960s. By the end of the decade early enthusiasm for nuclear energy and the space program gave way to technophobic reaction. But it was not so much technology itself as the rising technocracy that provoked public hostility.' Andrew Feenberg, *Questioning Technology*, New York: Routledge, 1999, p.4.

an informational, service-oriented one, writers such as Daniel Bell speculated that a wholesale reconfiguration of the social structure was underway.[19] While Bell's tome (whose title, *The Coming of Post-Industrial Society: A Venture in Social Forecasting*, reveals the extent to which the future was perceived to be in the present) is one of the most influential on the subject, it ultimately amounts to an apologia for the new system. For Bell, technocracy represents merely one stage in the 'progress' of modern society, with the potential to realise the unfettered dreams of capitalism. For others, however, the advent of technocratic society ushers in a moment of profound social crisis. In the sociological writings of Jean Meynaud, Jacques Ellul and Alain Touraine, among others, techno-optimism is replaced by skepticism and even anxiety—a dystopic view of technology that recalls the philosophical writings of Heidegger, Adorno, Horkheimer and the contemporary work of Herbert Marcuse, in which technoscientific progress is viewed as inextricably bound to new forms of social domination and oppression.[20]

Technocracy's sceptics draw attention to the increasing value placed upon technical 'expertise' and the rise of ever more specialised forms of knowledge. As such, they maintain, traditional ideals give way to a relentless (and somewhat blind) pursuit of innovation and technical progress. Despite his otherwise rosy perspective, Bell himself identifies the emergence of technocracy as a historical crux, in which modernism's two models of social change—toward 'equality' (advocated in the writings of Alexis de Tocqueville) and toward 'bureaucracy' (anxiously elaborated by Max Weber)—meet and clash:

> In the last hundred and fifty years, the social tensions of Western society have been framed by these contradictory impulses towards equality and bureaucracy, as these have worked themselves out in the politics and social structure of industrial society. Looking ahead to the next decades, one sees that the desire for greater participation in the decision-making of organisations that control individual lives (schools, hospitals, business firms) and the increasing technical requirements of knowledge (professionalisation, meritocracy) form the axes of social conflict in the future.[21]

While Bell does not develop this reading beyond initial speculation, for Alain Touraine the interdependence of equality (i.e. the desire for a more inclusive society) and bureaucracy (i.e. technical, social and administrative hierarchisation) is the central principle of technocratic society and the main

19 Daniel Bell, *The Coming of Post-Industrial Society: A Venture in Social Forecasting*, New York: Basic Books, 1973.

20 Jean Meynaud, *Technocracy* (trans. Paul Barnes), New York: Free Press, 1968; Jacques Ellul, *The Technological Society* (trans. John Wilkinson), New York: Knopf, 1967; Alain Touraine, *The Post-Industrial Society: Tomorrow's Social History: Classes, Conflicts, and Culture in the Programmed Society* (trans. Leonard F.X. Mayhew), New York: Random House, 1971; and Herbert Marcuse, *One-Dimensional Man: Studies in the Ideology of Advanced Industrial Society*, Boston: Beacon Press, 1964. Martin Heidegger, *The Question Concerning Technology* (trans. W. Lovitt), New York: Harper and Row, 1977; Max Horkheimer and Theodor W. Adorno, *The Dialectic of Enlightenment* (trans. John Cumming), New York: Herder & Herder, 1972.

21 D. Bell, *The Coming of Post-Industrial Society*, *op. cit.*, p.8.

source of its disaccord. Both the tenor and content of Touraine's analysis is more typical of the literature, where the sense of urgency regarding the emergence of technocratic society is seen both in the passionate (and often paranoid) nature of the rhetoric and the extent of its reach.[22] Revealing his dim view, Touraine's study replaces the relatively neutral descriptives 'technocratic' or 'post-industrial' with the loaded term '*programmed*': 'the programmed society', he explains, more accurately captures 'the nature of production methods and economic organisation' of post-industrial culture. For our purposes here, however, it functions as a useful rhetorical shorthand, one that underscores the dual meaning of 'programmed': the technical sense (i.e. computer language or programming, systems logic, game theory) associated with a knowledge-based economy; and the social condition of being controlled or managed.

Touraine's book explores the three principle forms of domination, which, he argues, are characteristic of the programmed society: 'social integration', 'cultural manipulation' and 'political aggressiveness'. The latter speaks to the development of the techno-bureaucracy, while the two former relay the push-pull, so to speak, of the new system. Touraine writes: '[T]he individual is pressured into participating — not only in terms of his work but equally in terms of consumption and education — in the systems of social organisations and power which further the aims of production.'[23]

In short, Touraine argues that technocratic society, unlike earlier eras of industrialism, is contingent not upon *exclusion* but upon widespread *inclusion*. Participation is axiomatic to this system, but it is coerced. Moreover, its manipulative power rests upon the relative 'success' of the system, as well as its deviousness: the benefits and pleasures it affords and, as such, the needs it seemingly fulfils, all the while eschewing overt oppression. Whereas in Marxian theory economic exploitation of the workers or working classes results in their social alienation, in the programmed society, Touraine maintains, those of relative affluence — and, as such, with greater 'participation' in social, political and economic life — are nevertheless subject to the lure of propaganda, advertising and consumption. In short, in addition to the traditional oppressed classes, new ones are formed that cross a broad social strata, all becoming passive participants in their own domination.

Technocratic society, therefore, sees a dramatic shift, in which participation leads not to self-determination but, paradoxically, to *alienation*. 'Ours is a society of alienation,' Touraine writes, 'not because it reduces people to misery or because it imposes police restriction, but because it seduces,

22 For example, Theodore Roszak, in *The Making of a Counter Culture: Reflections on the Technocratic Society and Its Youthful Opposition* (New York: Anchor Books, 1969), argues that 'counter-culture' in the United States arose as a specific reaction to technocratic society. Similarly, Feenberg explores the relationship between the student revolts of May 1968 in France and technocracy, including their protest against the transformation of the university into a 'knowledge factory'. See, A. Feenberg, *Questioning Technology*, *op. cit.*, pp.21–43.

23 A. Touraine, *The Post-Industrial Society*, *op. cit.*, p.7.

manipulates and enforces conformism.'[24] In other words, alienation is wrought by complicity and conformity, which ultimately serve to nullify or 'manage' dissent. The programmed society, Touraine argues, amounts to an insidious yet potent system of '*dependent participation*'.[25]

Weak Participants

To be clear: I am not advocating a deterministic view; that is, that Nauman's controlling environments are a consequence of technocracy or can be 'framed' by its context. Rather, I want to suggest that Nauman's environmental sculptures share or are energised from one of the central principles of technocratic society — that of 'dependent participation'. Art historically this approach allows for an alternative model of explanation, destabilising the oppositional logic of the contemplative versus participatory artwork and their relative roles within the history of modernism. In contrast, through the model of dependent participation, participation itself represents a form of submission — one not so dissimilar to the slavishness of the seduced viewer that Brechtian distanciation seeks to counter, or the benumbed consumer of mass media that postmodern critiques, embracing semiotic theory, challenge. With this theoretical approach Nauman's environmental sculptures can be seen to question one of the stakes upon which much progressive sculptural work of the 1960s turned: namely the possibility (and benefits) of direct experience.

Central to the notion of 'presence' and the phenomenological aspirations of Minimalist sculpture (and famously derided by Michael Fried as its problematic 'theatricality'), the idea of direct experience was embraced as an antidote to modernism's transcendentalism.[26] Instead, meaning is grounded in the here and now of the temporal, material world, contingent upon the transient situations of encounter. Such forms of lived experience, in the critical thinking of the late 60s, undermined art's rarified (and artificial) aesthetic boundaries and, moreover, questioned the logic of medium specificity that preserved or accommodated this separation. The doctrine of presence reaches its apex in writings on performance, which is not simply

24 *Ibid.*, p.9.

25 *Ibid.*, p.9. The complete quote is: 'Alienation means cancelling out social conflict by creating dependent participation.'

26 In his essay (now equally as famous for the accuracy of its reading of Minimalist sculpture as for its decidedly negative assessment), Michael Fried posits an opposition between Minimalist 'presence' (defined as material and temporal) and modernist 'presentness', the latter an essentially atemporal construct in which time exists in an ideal, arrested state. Fried, 'Art and Objecthood', *Artforum* 5, no.10, June 1967, pp.12–23.

27 Guy Debord, *The Society of the Spectacle* (first English translation), Detroit: Black and Red, 1970. Debord writes: 'The spectacle is not a collection of images, but a social relation among people mediated by images.' Later on, Jean Baudrillard radicalised Debord's notion of spectacle, claiming that the 'real' itself no longer exists, rather it is atomised into an endlessly self-referential chain of signifiers. Jean Baudrillard, 'Simulacra and Simulations', *Selected Writings* (ed. Mark Poster), Stanford: Stanford University Press, 1988, pp.166–84.

28 See Jonathan Crary, *Suspensions of Perception: Attention, Spectacle, and Modern Culture*, Cambridge, Mass.: The MIT Press, 1999. For some recent studies that develop such themes in relation to television, technology and post-War media culture more specifically, see Anna McCarthy, 'From Screen to Site: Television's Material Culture, and Its Place', *October* 98, Fall 2001, pp.93–111; Pamela M. Lee, 'Bridget Riley's Eye/Body Problem', *October* 98, Fall 2001, pp.27–46; David Joselit, 'The Video Public Sphere', *Art Journal* 59, no.2, Summer 2000, pp.46–53; and Branden W. Joseph, '"My Mind Split Open": Andy Warhol's

insistently temporal but is heralded as the most immediate and 'present' of all forms—given the assumed structure of the copresence of artist and viewer, or, in case of interactive installations, the necessity of the viewer's immediate engagement in order to 'see' and ultimately create the work.

But if we consider Nauman's installations, direct experience is insistently, even aggressively, precluded. To recall one of the examples described above, *Live Taped Video Corridor* does not simply disturb phenomenal and perceptual states but seems to insist that experience can *only* be generated through representation and reproduction: a point reinforced in the semantic tethering of 'live' (presence) and 'taped' (reproduction) in its title.

The effects of media on perception, subjectivity and reality, of course, have been extensively addressed in critical literature, particularly in relation to the notion of spectacle culture.[27] In media society, to sum up these arguments, subjective experience and reality are not simply received but constructed through forms of mediation—such as television, advertising and other media. In the most extreme readings this leads to the derealisation of the real, its displacement by so much simulacra, as well as the dissolution or 'splitting' of the subject herself, who is caught within a mire of imagery and perceptual stimuli. Here, however, I want to leave aside this framework, which has been productively argued in other contexts,[28] as well as its potential focus on the literal presence of technology in Nauman's environmental installations, which is not my concern.[29] Rather, I am interested in a more circumscribed issue: how such mechanisms do not simply filter experience but render it largely *unmanageable*. In other words, the beholding subject, at the whim of forces that surpass desire or agency, becomes, to borrow Touraine's descriptive, a '*weak participant*'.[30]

Nauman's *Double Steel Cage Piece* (1974) operates on the edge of this premise, in which the possibility of 'willing'—but not necessarily free—participation is negotiated. The aspects of authority and control latent in the earlier, abstracted spaces are here thematised into a literal prison. Incarcerating the viewer between two parallel screens of thick wire, the work seems to give concrete form to the Foucauldian nightmare of disciplinary society, in which technology is not simply viewed as a dehumanising force

Exploding Plastic Inevitable', *Grey Room* 08, Summer 2002, pp.80–107 (in the same issue, see also David Joselit, 'Yippie Pop: Abbie Hoffman, Andy Warhol, and Sixties Media Politics', pp.62–79). Please note that Branden W. Joseph's essay is reproduced in the current volume.

29 One danger this approach poses is of lapsing into technofetishism, which, given Nauman's complicated relationship to new technologies, is highly suspect. Despite continually experimenting with different techniques and media, the artist often utilises outdated or outmoded techniques—such as neon, which in the 1960s, as Brenda Richardson notes, was already tainted by obsolescence. See Brenda Richardson, 'Bruce Nauman: Neons', *Bruce Nauman: Neons* (exh. cat.), Baltimore: Baltimore Museum of Art, 1982, pp.13–39. Furthermore, when Nauman employs newer technologies—such as the Sony Portapak video camera in the late 1960s and, most recently, infrared digital photography—he often subjects the medium to extreme forms of manipulation, harnessing it for decidedly dated visual effects such as filmic graininess. The futuristic and the retro are thus continuously inverted.

30 Furthermore, Touraine writes: 'A choice between returning to traditional cultural themes and memberships or the passive consumption of the mass media does not exist. These are two closely connected manifestations of cultural underdevelopment, which is itself *bound to the weak participation of the masses* in the values and products of technical civilisation and social democracy.' A. Touraine, *The Post-Industrial Society*, *op. cit.*, p.203 (emphasis added).

but gives rise to potent physical and institutional agents of control.[31] In *Double Steel Cage Piece* the viewing subject similarly emerges as a disciplined one, who acts — or, rather, behaves — accordingly.

Experience, in short, is not simply mediated and controlled, but it is *predetermined*. This structure, while characteristic of most all of Nauman's installations, is first, and most economically, realised in the 1969 *Performance Corridor*. Without the aid of technical devices, but simply due to the physical constraints of its narrow walls (built, moreover, to the measure of the artist's sweeping hips), a succession of like performances results: the 'original' one being a video of the artist's performance, which is subsequently re-enacted by the audience, whose autonomy is severely compromised by the nature of the physical structure. What results is a series of *programmed* iterations of the simple act of walking in and out of a corridor.

Heuristically speaking, the curtailing of direct experience — or its management — in Nauman's environments guarantees *repetition*: the outcome is largely determined in advance, and the most effective means of circumscribing the beholder's experience is put into place. All potential variations are carefully considered and reduced through a combination of architectural elements and technical devices so that — in *Going Around the Corner*, for example — the monitors are neatly positioned to face one direction, which, in turn, leads to the audience moving in lock-step, circulating the perimeter in an orderly line, without much interpretive modification. *Floating Room: Lit from Inside* (1972), to give another example, offers an equally guided experience. A square room, elevated several inches off the floor, is illuminated on the inside by glaring lights. Despite the disorienting nature of its interior space — in which walls fail to reach the floor and the intensity of the lighting induces nothing less than a pulsing headache — the viewer is nonetheless compelled to enter: because the only alternative is to remain within the physical unknown of a completely darkened gallery. As critic Jan Butterfield, referring to *Green Light Corridor* (1970), once remarked to the artist: 'I think it is a very frightening piece. The manner in which it was structured made it necessary to participate in it your way — and that is frightening.'[32]

Through highly prescribed details, Nauman's environments are structured by repetitious interactions. Repetition, however, is central to the principle of *efficiency*, the *sine qua non* of technological progress. In the 60s a widespread application of the technical notion of efficiency led to the formation or expansion of fields of knowledge, including game or decision theory, in which the ultimate aim (not unlike Nauman's environments) was to anticipate human responses — and, in so doing, to *manage* them.[33] Through an adaptation of scientific principles of rationality and theories of logic,

31 Michel Foucault, *Discipline and Punish: The Birth of the Prison* (trans. Alan Sheridan), New York: Vintage Books, 1979.

32 J. Butterfield, in J. Kraynak *Please Pay Attention Please*, *op. cit.*, p.179.

33 Game theory has a long history, but two key post-War texts are H.W. Kuhn and A.W. Tucker (eds.), *Contributions to the Theory of Games, Annals of Mathematics Studies* 24, vol.I, Princeton: Princeton University Press, 1950; and John Charles Mckinsey, *Introduction to the Theory of Games*, New York: McGraw Hill, 1952.

a means of envisioning and then limiting the range of possible behaviours was found, thereby ensuring a particular outcome.

While their pragmatic uses were numerous (military, scientific, economic, etc.), game or decision theory also demonstrates a more generalised characteristic of technocratic culture: its realisation of an information- or knowledge-based society, in which 'technical' expertise enters into areas hitherto largely immune to it. Information theory, cybernetics and decision theory (what Daniel Bell aptly terms 'intellectual technologies'), for example, operate according to a similar logic in which means and outcome — or input and output, to use the computer terminology — are calculated. Through computation, seemingly unquantifiable variables are parsed into discrete units of analysis, yielding a manageable order. 'The goal of the new intellectual technologies is, neither more nor less,' Bell exclaims, 'to realize the social alchemist's dream: the dream of "ordering" the mass society ... If the computer is the tool, then *decision theory* is the master.'[34]

In short, such knowledge systems, which are central to 1960s' technocratic society, are resolutely goal-oriented, working both prescriptively and predictively to ensure the most efficacious and expedient result. As such, they function as an analogue for technocratic culture as a whole — which may be described as a *society of performance*. Whether referring to economic activity, educational institutions or machines such as the computer, the goal of the given system or institution is one and the same: efficiency, or a graduated process of improving 'performance'.

If in his public comments Nauman disdains 'games' in the vernacular sense as non-serious 'play', his sculptural environments nonetheless incorporate the logic of game theory. Various restraints, both physical and mental, simultaneously anticipate and then circumscribe human response. In the process uncertainty and interpretive deviation are minimised as much as possible, a dynamic that economists, in an application of game theory, have described as 'minimax' — or the minimisation of maximum loss.[35] Nauman's installations constitute spaces of 'performance' — defined, that is, as *efficient interaction*. To emphasise *performance* here does not simply refer to the viewer creating *a* performance as a *participant*; rather, through the social theory of technology, *performance* acquires a very different meaning, one that concerns the formation of a rationalistic social order.

Whereas the Minimalist exploration of phenomenological conditions of perception banked on the ability to assert and engage the direct experience of the beholder, Nauman's installations aim to calculate and determine that experience through laws of probability. This perhaps explains why the artist often describes all aspects of his sculptural work (whether visual, conceptual

34 D. Bell, *The Coming of Post-Industrial Society*, *op. cit.*, p.33.

35 As cited in D. Bell, *The Coming of Post-Industrial Society*, *op. cit.*, p.31, the economic application of the principle of 'minimax' appears in John van Neumann and Oskar Morgenstern, *Theory of Games and Economic Behaviour*, Princeton: Princeton University Press, 1944.

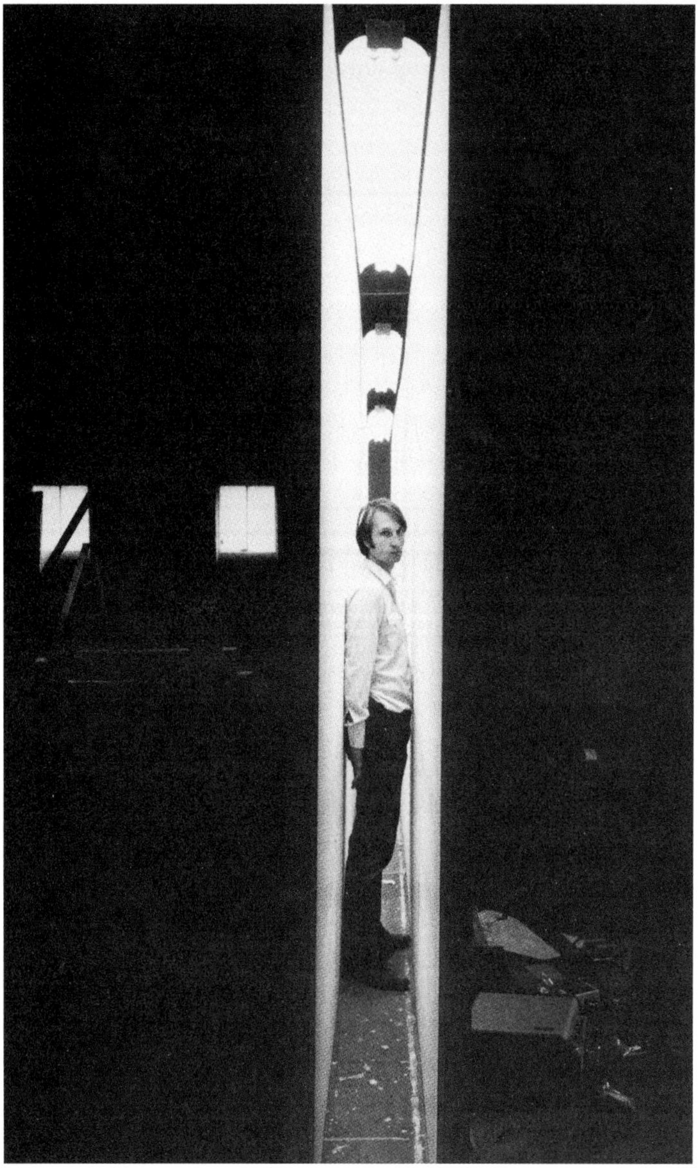

or perceptual) as 'modes of information': dry language that seems directly at odds with the highly experiential or material qualities of the works themselves.[36] But with this claim and the use of game theory — with its quasi-scientific mapping of responses and the mitigation of choice and conflict — as a theoretical model for performance (defined now as 'efficiency'), it may appear that this essay is proposing that Nauman's installations constitute embodiments of techno-rationality. Quite to the contrary, however, I am interested in the point at which the rationalisation of society comes under pressure. Rather than the realisation of reason, in other words, Nauman's 'performance' environments speak to the moment of reason's collapse, when technological change ushers in an acute crisis of legitimation — a topic of a philosophical debate that arises and is played out against the backdrop of technocratic society.

The Fate of an Idea: Technocracy and Reason

In the late 1960s, sociologist Jean Meynaud voiced his fear that 'politics' would be displaced by technocracy.[37] What Meynaud means by this is that the pursuit of traditional 'political' ideals, including those at the foundation of bourgeois society (i.e. freedom, self-determination, justice), will gradually dwindle away in favour of the singular mission to increase 'productivity'. Writing a decade later, with the benefit of hindsight and the present realisation of developments upon which earlier thinkers could only speculate, Jean-François Lyotard takes this sociological observation one step further, developing a philosophical account of the shifting nature of knowledge and society.[38]

Bruce Nauman, *Green Light Corridor*, 1970 © 2008 ARS, New York & DACS, London

In a not-so-subtle challenge to Jürgen Habermas's theory of communicative reason, Lyotard reflects upon what Andrew Feenberg describes as the 'technical turn' of contemporary knowledge.[39] Deftly marrying contemporary theory and the social discourse of technology, Lyotard specifically engages with the problematic of 'performance'. His subject is not simply computer and information technologies, however, but the reorientation of knowledge itself under the forces of technical change. He writes: 'Technology is a game pertaining not to the true, the just, or the beautiful, etc., but to efficiency: a technical "move" is "good" when it does better and/or expends less energy than another.'[40] Lyotard emphasises that the 'goal' of knowledge has ceased to be the revelation of truth or the realisation of human possibility and instead has become the optimising of 'performance'. Accordingly, he adapts the linguistic concept of *performativity* (i.e. the performative utterance or language game) as both a methodological model and the fundamental principle of contemporary, technocratic society—which being knowledge- or information-based is 'linguistically' oriented. According to the logic of the language game, ever-shifting rules produce a different outcome: hence Lyotard's now well-known notion of the local or 'little' narrative that displaces master or 'grand' narratives. But Lyotard not only argues that knowledge is subject to change and competing ideals; rather, with the advent of 'language' technologies (problems of communication, cybernetics, computer languages, information storage, to name a few of his examples), it is no longer even a product of individual 'knowing'. It is, in his words, 'exteriorized':

> We must thus expect a thorough exteriorization of knowledge with respect to the 'knower', at whatever point he or she may occupy in the knowledge process. The old principle that the acquisition of knowledge is indissociable from the training (*Bildung*) of minds, or even of individuals, is becoming obsolete and will become ever more so. The relationship of the suppliers and users of knowledge to the knowledge they supply and use is now tending, and will increasingly tend, to assume the form already taken by the relationship of commodity producers and consumers to the commodities they produce — that is, the form of value. Knowledge

36 For example, in the following, Nauman refers to two early sculptures: *A Cast of the Space under My Chair* (1965–68), a somewhat battered cubic form, and *Shelf Sinking into the Wall with Copper-Painted Plaster Casts of the Spaces Underneath* (1966), both of which are largely unreadable in the absence of their titles: 'I think, in a sense, a lot of the titles ... where there were titles like *Shelves Sinking into the Wall*, and all that, were sort of trying to give two pieces of information [...] And probably what I found out from that is that you can give two pieces of information and the piece is finally about that. It's about the tension of not being able to put them together.' interview by de Angelus, in J.Kraynak *Please Pay Attention Please*, *op. cit.*, p.265.

37 'Let us suppose that in a world in which the profit motive becomes more and more paramount,' Meynaud writes, 'the political authorities (as is already partly true) failed to keep a close watch on the activities of technologists, who do not all have the public interest at heart; in the end, the effect would be a barely perceptible evolution towards a regime which would be democratic only on the surface. The elected representatives would be deprived of the substance of their power [...] The democratic principle would then be nothing more than the "front" ... behind which the true leaders of the country would justify or disguise their domination.' J. Meynaud, *Technocracy*, *op. cit.*, pp.15–16.

38 Jean François Lyotard, *The Postmodern Condition: A Report on Knowledge* (trans. Geoff Bennington and Brian Massumi), Minneapolis: University of Minnesota Press, 1984.

39 Andrew Feenberg, *Alternative Modernity: The Technical Turn in Philosophy and Social Theory*, Berkeley: University of California Press, 1995.

40 J.F. Lyotard, *The Postmodern Condition*, *op. cit.*, p.44.

is and will be produced in order to be sold, it is and will be consumed in order to be valorized in a new production; in both cases, the goal is exchange. Knowledge ceases to be an end in itself, it loses its 'use-value'.[41]

In this passage not only does Lyotard renounce both subject-centred Hegelianism and the wilful humanism of Habermas, but he emphasises the commodification of knowledge itself—a subject of earlier speculation, which, he can now assert with some certainty, has come to pass.[42] With the removal of knowledge from the subject's control and the emphasis on 'performance' over 'truth', however, society loses its bases of legitimation. To recall Lyotard's statement cited previously, what is 'good' is no longer necessarily what is 'true'. Rather 'goodness' is gauged by productivity, while expending the least possible effort—an acutely passive condition. Due to this reorientation, Lyotard argues, society abdicates any claim to rationality. 'The games of scientific language become the games of the rich,' Lyotard inveighs, 'in which whoever is wealthiest has the best chance of being right. An equation between wealth, efficiency, and truth is thus established.'[43]

In this 'game'—one of struggle and conflict, and precisely *not* the Habermasian dream of trouble-free consensus—Lyotard finds a series of losses: of the possibility of resistance, of the actual fulfilment of human need and of political idealism. Lyotard's position, however, resists nostalgia, containing no dream of returning to a pretechnical past. Within this system, he counters, the source of domination and resistance are one and the same: the only path for the subject is opened up by an increased access to knowledge that technology affords; while at the same time technology (or rather, technical society) instills conformity. Hence the ambivalence of Lyotard's treatise, stuck in the dialectic of participation and control.

The Dream of Interactivity

The equivocality of Lyotard's argument, which distinguishes it from the wholesale technophobia of earlier philosophical accounts, is useful in understanding why we are not simply oppressed but are also seduced by Nauman's environments. What can be irritating lighting, as in the glaring yellow of the *Left or Standing, Standing or Left Standing*, is also the source of wondrous optical tricks: the simple juxtaposition of different lighting technologies (fluorescent and incandescent) produces painterly illusions in three-dimensional space.[44] What can be a terrifyingly narrow space in

41 *Ibid.*, pp.4–5.

42 And perhaps even more so in contemporary culture, where, for example, in educational institutions, the drive for 'efficiency' is equated with tangible evidence such as test scores rather than the acquisition of knowledge, and where the reward is not the creation of an educated or enlightened population, but money—in the form of additional school funding or salary incentives. Such outcomes of technocracy, only feared by earlier writers, are increasingly the rule of contemporary society.

43 J.F. Lyotard, *The Postmodern Condition*, *op. cit.*, p.45.

44 Formerly called *Installation with Yellow Lights, Left or Standing, Standing or Left Standing* (1971/99)—so named for the accompanying text written by the artist—it consists of a trapezoidal room whose walls do not extend to the ceiling and which is illuminated with bright, yellow fluorescent lights. Two corridors on either side of the central room are lit with incandescent lights; as a result, when the viewer looks up to the gap between the wall and ceiling, the two forms of light blend, yielding a purple afterimage.

Live Taped Video Corridor also induces a profound pleasure in the game it creates: no matter how much the beholder realises the futility of the task, she will repeatedly try to 'beat the machine' and somehow line up her image to match bodily experience. What can seem to be impossibly manipulative, as the illuminated cleave of space in *Green Light Corridor*, also reveals 'chinks' in the system — or the point where intervention is unable to completely dictate the outcome, as Nauman readily acknowledges.[45]

In Nauman's manipulative yet pleasurable spaces there is also a cautionary tale, one regarding participation as a panacea, a message that resonates perhaps even more intensely in contemporary culture where *dependent participation* is increasingly the reality — and even the operative principle — of a global information society. Advanced information technologies, such as the Internet, afford endless opportunity for interactivity; but hidden — and not so hidden — within them, are ever more insidious mechanisms of manipulation (browser tracking, personally targeted marketing, 'cookies', etc.). In this system choice is illusory and participation obligatory: after all, if we don't accept the mechanisms, we cannot purchase a book, a ticket or even view our own private records online. As Alain Touraine observed forty years ago, to refuse to participate is not a possibility. To be a subject in contemporary culture, one cannot simply reject the cards that historical possibility has dealt. There is little or no choice, which is why perhaps 'choice' — and its cousin 'customisation' — are now such ubiquitous buzzwords: forms of coercive management sporting a benign guise.

That the body of the spectator in Nauman's environments is the actor through which these dramas and conflicts are played out is not surprising. As a historical agent the individual is still the cornerstone, the pawn of a technocratic system that increasingly markets 'individual' desire and which, despite providing less autonomy and choice, proffers a fantasy of more and more. Likewise, in Nauman's installations the subject ultimately is the one who must navigate a minefield of participation and control, discovering those small opportunities where conformity breaks down and possibility, even if fleeting and limited, accrues.

45 In response to an inquiry by Jan Butterfield regarding whether or not he 'queries people afterwards' to check if the participant's reaction to any given installation is similar to his own, Nauman comments: 'People will tell me that they tried it and it didn't do what I said it would for them; or that they read a great deal about a given piece, but didn't have the response they were "supposed to"; or, conversely that they did not seem to relate at all to what I had written in the instructions. For example, I will say at some point that the exercise will become very sensual, or very sexual, and people will tell me that it didn't for them.' J. Butterfield, in J. Kraynak *Please Pay Attention Please*, *op. cit.*, p.181.

AFTER THE CULL
Elizabeth Bennett Hupp

World War II left North American and European artists in a new relational space, one in which artists — displaced and dislocated from former concepts of nationalism — faced a thorough re-investigation of established ideology. Until that point, the historical avant-garde had worked within the frames of an established narrative of art history as it had existed in the Western world. For the most part, artistic agendas were concerned with creating points of contact within this history, its artists, critics, art and institutions. For many citizens, the War represented a catastrophic failure on the part of the bourgeois nation-state and apathy within ideological institutions. As a result, many artists, intellectuals and theorists chose to align themselves with a brand of internationalist utopianism that criticised the continued dependency of national identity on a pre-War nationalism and aesthetic.[1] If Peter Bürger was correct to assert that an autonomous art existed in order for the historical avant-garde to abolish it, then the artists' shifted position after World War II would have been of relatively minor significance to society. Furthermore, if the neo-avant-garde's only success, as Bürger claimed, was to institutionalise the avant-garde as art, then both Minimalism and British sculpture of the early 1960s would have demonstrated the false autonomy of art and life praxes.[2] Bürger's assumption regarding an autonomous art has always been false; however, the neo-avant-garde's performance of this falsity will engage us for a moment and lead to the principle question.

It is impossible to think about mass-communication media without reflecting on velocity. In the early 1960s, television spread through Western Europe and the Americas at a rate comparable to the speed of modern information dissemination. This short period in the twentieth century that art historians deem high modernism may in part be characterised by the sudden rise of mass media, and, as Charles Baudrilliard suggests, also by the shift from societies of objects to societies of signs and simulacra. In both Minimalism and early British sculpture, one sees the pervasiveness of the shift materialise as an indignation on the part of these artists whose work resisted the increasingly mediated experience. These categorically high modern manifestations maintained the object; the avant-garde aesthetic; and thus an immediate, unmediated and tangible condition of communication. Artists'

1 Benjamin H.D. Buchloh, *Neo-Avantgarde and Culture Industry: Essays on European and American Art from 1955 to 1975*, Cambridge, Mass. and London: The MIT Press, 2000, p.307.

2 Peter Bürger, *Theory of the Avant-Garde* (trans. Michael Shaw), Minneapolis: University of Minnesota Press, 2004.

3 J. Martín-Barbero, *Communication, Culture and Hegemony: From the Media to Mediations* (trans. Elizabeth Fox and Robert A. White), London: Sage Publications Ltd, 1993, p.181.

4 Maria Carmen Ramírez, 'Tactics for Thriving on Adversity: Conceptualism

resistance to information's new principality in society led to a neo-avant-gardism that momentarily performed an autonomous art, separate (albeit desperately) from the real praxis of life.

Conceptualism, and specifically the genre of institutional critique, signaled the end of this temporary autonomy. To critique the institution of art was to fully absorb traditional conditions of art-making in order to re-emit them into society as questions formed outside the consensus. Allan Kaprow, Hans Haacke, Marcel Broodthaers and others produced art that privileged rhetorical association (an association of signs) over aesthetic relationships, in order to reveal the process by which art historically deferred to its own social potential for the sake of an illusory hegemony. Artists' critique of the institution was concurrent with larger critiques of other ideological state apparatuses. Thanks in large part to television, citizens of the United States actively protested against the political institution — and, more specifically, their federal government — during the Vietnam War. In this context, programmes of institutional critique were seemingly domestic affairs. For both artists and citizens, the institution and the adjacent strategies of critique were well within historically familiar territory. That is to say, the institutions of art, art-making, war and television were not foreign entities to those involved but highly established cultural ideals. In North America and Europe, institutional critique was a form of self-reflection.

The Cull

Between 1960 and 1976, six Latin American countries, including Argentina, Brazil and Chile, gave rise to military dictatorships. In 1960, three recently privatised Argentine television stations aired to the Argentine public syndicated television shows from the three most popular networks in the United States (NBC, CBS and ABC).[3] This act, orchestrated by the newly installed Argentine government, was part of a much larger Latin American project between 1950 and 1970 that sought to modernise the continent into an economic and cultural First World. During this period known as post-War *desarrollismo* (developmentalism or industrialisation), nearly every sector of society exemplified its commitment to the national ideology. Latin American artists actively participated in dialogues within an international avant-garde via cultural centres established in the 1950s, such as the Torcuato di Tella Institute in Buenos Aires and the first São Paulo Biennial.[4] The di Tella Institute harboured a group of young artists whose ideas attracted well-known critics, artists and theorists from the metropolitan centres of the United States and Europe.[5] In the 1960s, much of this attention was given to those artists working in the mediums of mass communication.

in Latin America, 1960–1980', in Sabine Breitweiser (ed.), *Vivências/Lebenserfahrung/Life Experience* (exh. cat.), Vienna: Generali Foundation, 2000, p.63.

5 I am thinking here of Lucy Lippard's interest in the work of the Mass Communications Media Group in the mid-1960s, Clement Greenberg's participation at the Torcuato di Tella Institute and Allan Kaprow and Wolf Vostell's collaboration with Marta Minujín in *Simultaneidad en Simultaneidad.*

Lea Lublin, Marta Minujín and David Lamelas are Argentine artists whose methods have been largely theorised as counter-media strategies. Undoubtedly, this is to some extent true. However, it would be too great a generalisation to envisage their work only in opposition to the commercial conditions of communication. Unlike in the United States and Europe, the shift from object to sign in Argentine society did not begin as a domestic process; rather, mass-communication media arrived as an imported novelty. In the context of *desarrollismo*, artists could, with proper vigilance, embrace and then exploit the strategies of mass media without compromising the national agenda. In this quickly changing political landscape, how are we to explain these artists' counter-institutional struggles against a non-indigenous institution? My rhetorical use of 'exploit' here does not refer only to the integration of mass-communication mediums into an artist's work. Instead, it must also suggest a unique process of selection, most acutely described as culling. Culling involves the deliberate removal of certain individuals from a group based on predetermined criteria, in order to achieve a desired final effect. The mediation of information through mass-communication technologies is a literal process of culling; observed world events compose the group from which undesirable individuals (blocks of information or 'stories') are deliberately removed by the media institution. While culling could be used to achieve an infinite number of final results, the media expressly culls for efficiency. Efficiency, of course, is the sole variable that allows for the practical dissemination of information on a colossal scale.

Culling for efficiency involves selecting information that conforms to the commercial and practical restrictions of time, space and format, as well as viewers' expectations. So, to say that Lea Lublin, Marta Minujín and David Lamelas all exploited mass-communication media is to suggest that their work inverted the media's culling process of time, space, format and consumer presence, in order to demystify or critique a foreign consumerism and establish a new Latin American aesthetic. Ultimately, it could be said that they employed a process of culling for latency in their work — deliberately selecting inactive information — which necessitated the viewer's interactive ontological presence. Instead of passively consuming mass-mediated information, in these works the individual viewer must actively pursue his or her own experience.

Fluvio Subtunal

In 1969, Lea Lublin constructed a 900-square-metre environment titled *Fluvio Subtunal.*[6] Participants were invited to navigate through the work, comprised of nine different spaces, and they came upon several conceptual snags along

6 There is no literal translation for the title of Lublin's work. *Fluvio Subtunal* is a play on words from the Spanish *Túnel Subfluvial*, meaning subterranean current.

7 The Hernandarias Subfluvial Tunnel was named after Hernando Arias de Saavedra (commonly known as Hernandarias), the first governor in Latin America to have descended from Europeans and been born in the Americas. Paraná is near his burial place in the city of Cayastá.

8 See https://home.no.net/lotsberg/data/subsea.html

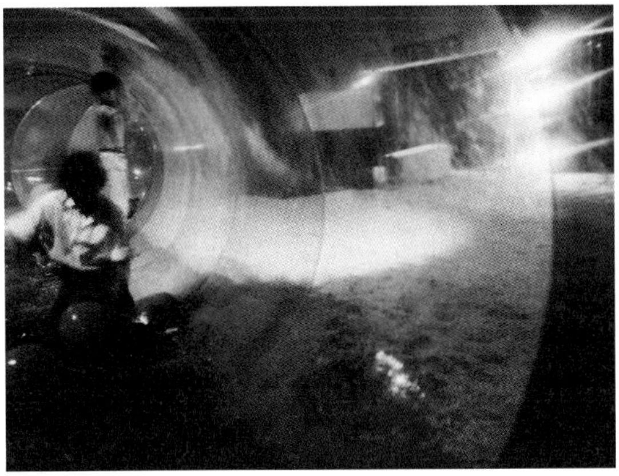

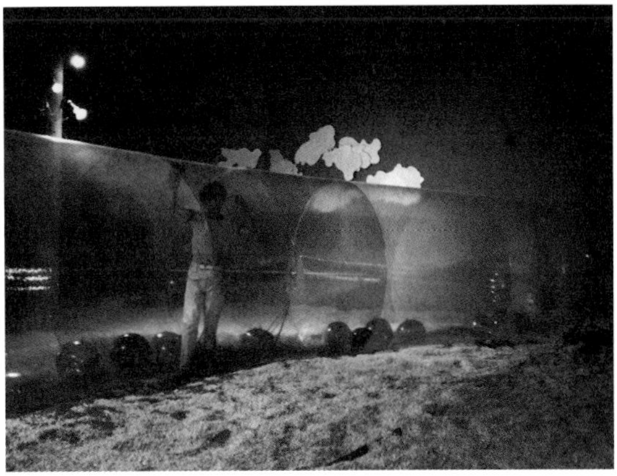

Lea Lublin, *Fluvio Subtunal*, 1969

the way. At these junctions, activities became tangible disruptions, suspending the viewer's physical movement and allowing for exaggerated empirical (re)discoveries of corporeality. Each temporary inhabitant experienced a heightened bombardment of the senses in order to awaken essential tensions between nature and human technology.

The title of Lublin's work rhetorically echoed the Túnel Subfluvial Hernandarias.[7] Completed only a few months before Lublin's exhibition, this 'ground tunnel' stretched 2,937 metres (1.8 miles) under the Paraná River between the Argentine provinces of Entré Rios and Santa Fé.[8] For the first time in Argentine history, commercial goods were transported between these discontinuous lands. Until the construction of the Rosario-Victoria Bridge in 1998, the tunnel remained the only connection between these densely-populated commercial areas. Not only did the tunnel modify the country's northeastern landscape ecologically, its existence posed significant possibilities for a growing national and increasingly-independent Argentine economy. It further enabled intra-national commerce and communication between Paraná (the capital city of Entré Rios), Santa Fé and the surrounding area.

In *Fluvio Subtunal,* the first meta-environment the viewer encountered was the 'Fountain Area'. Upon entering, he or she could only traverse the space atop up-turned buckets, which acted as stepping-stones across a floor inundated with water and covered with aluminium cans. In the second room, 'Wind' surrounded the viewer in the form of one hundred inflatable tubes hanging from the ceiling and moved by giant fans. At the end of this area was a translucent curtain. Once crossed, the participant stood in a space surrounded by photographs projected from slide projectors suspended from each wall. The walls, ceiling and floor of the 'Technological Area' were covered with photographs of the workers involved in the Hernandarias Tunnel project. Next was the 'Production Area', where visitors could construct their own objects from supplied natural and artificial materials. From here, one entered the only completely enclosed room, the 'Sensorial Area'. In this room, only black lights illuminated the space and various organic smells filled the visual void. In the 'Discharge Area', visitors could play with inflated toys in the shapes of animals before they made their way to the 'Nature Area'. A steady stream of water in a large, transparent tunnel bisected this room, which was otherwise filled with live animals and plants. The viewer's meticulous journey concluded in a fairground environment where games, such as 'Shoot the Picture', were set up for the participant's enjoyment.[9]

Lublin's work was directly indicative of a unique provision of space. This condition both explicitly manifests in the viewer's movement through a hyper-differentiated environment and more peculiarly resurrects a spatial latency within mass-communication media. Through the Hernandarias Tunnel's physical and conceptual position in the work, *Fluvio Subtunal* proposes a fundamental spatial and ideological dichotomy between the places of technology and nature in society. Moreover, a poignant discussion concerning the media's deliberate neutralisation of space remains endemic to Lublin's creation.

Mass media, specifically television, collapses spatial awareness for the consumer. Through mechanisms of proximity and familiarisation enacted through immediate similarities, television denies any real spatial difference between viewers and presented information. This is not to say that television is capable of emptying difference from information, but rather that it presents difference as a structuring frame, void of any implicit conflict. Communication theorist Jesús Martín Barbero states: 'As the spectacle of daily life is channeled into television, the hegemonic model of television reconstructs reality with a paradoxical control of differences.'[10] Thus, real differences between environs are easily absorbed in the production of television, fostering one of two likely effects on the waiting consumer.

First, absorption bridges physical and ideological difference (distance) between viewer and event, which in turn suggests the ready accessibility of what is actually far away. A single technology is able to make the world seem, if not homogenous and small, at the very least manageable by the individual. In Argentina, television programmes imported from the United States allowed the Argentine public direct access to North American popular culture as well as to coverage of events happening in their own country.[11] Second, the cumulative effects of television's projected proximity result in an apathetic immunity to mediation. The consumer displays apathy as indifference, a thoughtless condition that can lead to the further distancing of events from the viewer. Mass-mediated information, therefore, has both divisive repercussions for differing communities and unifying tendencies within a group composed of individuals with similar backgrounds. It is this latter effect that *Fluvio Subtunal* crystallised.

In one small sense, the Hernandarias Tunnel lessened the immediate differences between the provinces. Lublin's environment made this small

9 Jorge Glusberg, *Art in Argentina*, Milan: Giancarlo Politi Editore, 1986, p.76.

10 J. Martín-Barbero, *Communication, Culture and Hegemony*, *op. cit.*, p.181.

11 Consider, for instance, the exhibition 'Tucumán Arde', which was a collaborative effort by artists, sociologists and other activists who were outraged by the Argentine media's skewed perspective on the economically impoverished city of Tucumán. For a

step significant outside the more abstract aims of *desarrollismo*. In the 'Technological Area', the viewer shared the space with fellow visitors and other Argentines who actually made the idea of the tunnel a national reality. Mass media's empty differentiation was suppressed in this space and replaced with an immediate example of technology's role in nation building. Both environments, *Fluvio Subtunal* and its surrogate object, found solidity in difference, connecting seemingly disparate spaces with universal conditions of communication, the sensory and the physical.

Simultaneidad en Simultaneidad

Simultaneidad en Simultaneidad (*Simultaneity in Simultaneity*, 1966) was one of the first performance works in history to coordinate several mediums of mass media (simultaneously, of course). The work was originally conceived as an international collaboration between Marta Minujín in Buenos Aires, Allan Kaprow in New York and Wolf Vostell in Berlin. Nearly forty-years later, however, the artists' original intention is less significant than the work's completed form. Incidental modifications — and what can only be described as compassionate improvisations — rendered Minujín's performance an investigation into the informational latencies of mass media.

More than 750 people in Argentina alone participated in the work. It possessed two distinct yet highly interdependent parts and spanned ten days in October 1966. The earlier component, 'Enveloping Simultaneity', was prepared and performed in a theatre at the di Tella Institute. 'Instantaneous Invasion', in contrast, existed only later as mass-mediated information consumed at the theatre and, via television sets, within the homes of Argentine participants. On 13 October, sixty well-known Argentine media figures arrived at the di Tella Institute's theatre. Each individual was photographed and filmed entering and walking through the room to a designated space. Unfortunately, the taping process was fraught with technical problems and participants were forced to wait hours for their turn. As a result, only about 35 of them returned for the final performance ten days later, wearing the same attire as before.[12] Each individual entered the room as his name was called, was handed a radio and slowly moved to his assigned seat. As they walked, the previously prepared images 'followed' them. Pictures of the participant in profile visually accompanied his movement through the theatre as nine slide projectors turned on and off in sequence along adjacent walls. In the end, the movement of the images undermined the individual's actual progress. As the last participant took his seat in front of a personal television set, the first part of the performance ended.

full discussion of the work, see Maria Carmen Ramírez, *Del Di Tella a "Tucumán Arde": vanguardia artistica y politica en el '68 argentino*, Buenos Aires: El Cielo por Asalto, 2000.

12 See Inés Katzenstein (ed.), *Listen Here Now!*, New York: The Museum of Modern Art, 2004, p.237.

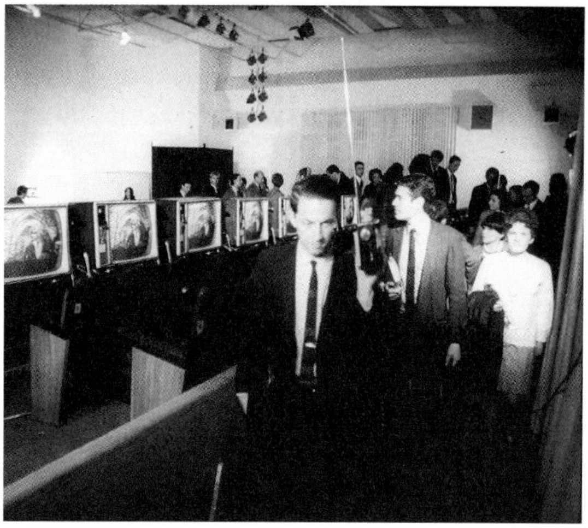
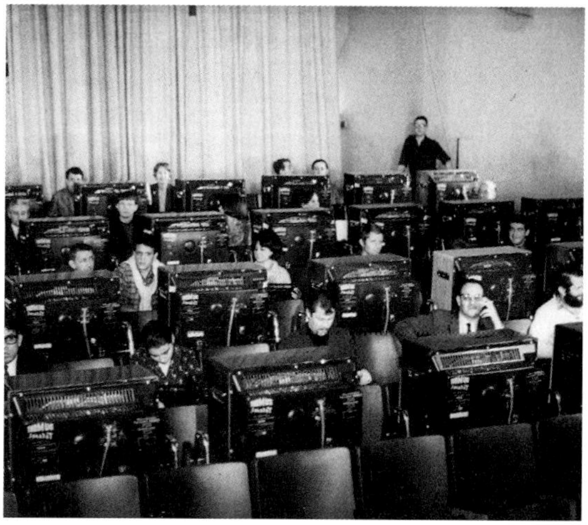

At four minutes past midnight on 24 October, Channel 13 aired a pre-recorded video to the theatre audience and the Argentine public. Minujín herself materialised on the screen, appearing to communicate with Kaprow and Vostell via radio and telex. As the artist disappeared, the audience heard a man (Vostell) describing a happening taking place 'live' in Berlin; a few moments later, the happening appeared on the television. Minujín was then heard reading a telegram from Kaprow describing another happening in New York, which subsequently surfaced on the screen.[13] During these events, the audiences in the theatre and at home were directed several times to switch between multiple events on different radio stations — once they were even told to read a newspaper for the television's missing audio. The final portion of the television recording showed three popular figures in Argentine society at home watching the performance. Minujín's voiceover called these individuals the 'invaded'. Additionally, five hundred people who owned a television and lived alone received what Minujín called the 'full invasion'.[14] During the work's 10 minutes of air time, each received a telephone call and some also received telegrams.[15]

Even in a textual description of Minujín's work it is difficult to comprehend the conceptual, technical and logistical complexities of *Simultaneidad en Simultaneidad*. Equally apparent is the lack of description regarding the significance of the individual viewer in experiencing this work. In 1968, performance theorist Michael Kirby noted that in the work 'each spectator [was] himself the subject matter of much of the presentation and therefore a "performer" without contributing anything more than his presence'.[16] This statement becomes even more illuminating when one considers the work's numerous 'inaccuracies'. At one point during the event, Kaprow could not get a phone call through to the theatre, though a dedicated line had apparently been set up. A little later than expected, Minujín talked to a man on the phone, whom she assumed to be Kaprow. A week later she discovered that she had actually spoken with a friend who had called to 'help out' after hearing that Kaprow was unsuccessful in reaching her.[17]

Marta Minujín with Allan Kaprow and Wolf Vostell, *Simultaneidad en Simultaneidad* (*Simultaneity in Simultaneity*), 1966

The happenings that the audience witnessed on their television sets, supposedly transmitted from New York and Berlin, were also somewhat falsely contrived. Unbeknownst to the audience at the time, these had been performed locally in Buenos Aires following descriptions of the actual events given by Kaprow and Vostell, and recorded prior to the performance. When Minujín was asked why this was necessary, she remarked that since the performance had been advertised as an international event, she felt she needed to fill in the missing elements herself.[18]

It is clear then that this work existed not only at the thresholds of mass mediums and unmediated experience, but also between truth and falsity. What began as an experiment in mass-communicated information in hindsight ended up being something more closely resembling a ruse. Ironically, this polemic tension is only validated in the physical realm of the beholder. In a conventionally 'objective' sense, truth and falsity are not applicable in any art-making process. So it is in the position of evaluating what is true and what is false that one finds the ontological presence of a viewer so immediately essential. On the one hand, it seems ridiculous to imply that mass-communication media does not take the viewer into account. But 'mass' in this context is an abstraction — a marketing aim or loosely targeted audience. The individual viewer is, for the most part, regarded only as a customer. This is an uncompromising condition of mass communication and may be understood as our 'sacrifice' for efficiency. Minujín's work refuses this sacrifice without entirely condemning the pragmatic value of this technology. It negotiates these positions by asking more from the individual. The messages received by the 'invaded' said: 'You are a creator. Look at your environment.' Yet Minujín's entire work directed the viewer to action, even through temporary passivity.[19] *Simultaneidad en Simultaneidad* demonstrated mass media's compromised efficiency and rejoiced in the individual when his or her latent presence was withdrawn from the mass.

Situación de tiempo

In order to fully appreciate David Lamelas's sense of perception, it is useful to think of his oeuvre as one long, unfinished thought. Nowhere is this analogy more palpable than in the relationship between his later sculpture and his earlier film. In *Situación de tiempo* (*Situation of Time*, 1967), he introduced a dialectic between public space and media technology and, more specifically, 'the conditions of communication governing social spaces'.[20] The di Tella Institute first exhibited Lamelas's installation in 1967 and the Witte de With

13 In Berlin, one-hundred milk bottles were placed around the city. In New York, the Argentine audience saw people licking whipped cream off a car while two participants wrapped in aluminum foil rolled out onto the street.

14 Michael Kirby, 'Marta Minujín's *Simultaneity in Simultaneity*', *The Drama Review*, vol.12 no.3, Spring 1968, pp.148–52.

15 Two-hundred people were hired to make phone calls and deliver telegrams to participants.

16 M. Kirby, 'Marta Minujín's *Simultaneity in Simultaneity*', *op. cit.*, p.150.

17 *Ibid.*, p.152.

18 *Ibid.*

19 *Ibid.*

20 B.H.D. Buchloh, *Neo-Avantgarde and Culture Industry*, *op. cit.*, p.317.

Center for Contemporary Art in Rotterdam recreated it thirty-years later. In a dark gallery, visitors viewed seventeen television sets displayed around its perimeter. Lit only by blank and glowing screens, the room became a jewel-like space starkly void of information.

Benjamin Buchloh often speaks of Lamelas's early mass-media installations as remnants of the artist's interest in Minimalist problems. In *Situación de tiempo,* however, Buchloh believes Lamelas transcended Minimalism's traditional questions regarding sculpture and architectural space in favour of forms of 'publicity'.[21] By this Buchloh means to suggest Lamelas's aesthetic 'branding' of the gallery's public space into a corporate environment. The most obvious evidence of this activity is the origin of the work's materials. State-of-the-art televisions were donated by di Tella Industries, the Institute's main sponsor and a major Argentine manufacturer of electronics.[22] Beyond this commercial consideration, one also finds the transformation of a formally social space into a uni-task environment, exclusively designed for the reception of mass-communicated information. However, the installation's profound lack of such information left only the work's indexical presence. It seemed that the artistic absorption of mass media technology required a larger shift in the social economy of communication. The object's relationship with and influence upon its environment—its publicity—advertised this changing condition.

For our purposes, Buchloh's concept of publicity exists within the format of culling for latency. This latent variable may be theorised as the formation of consensus. Cultural theorist Stuart Hall most thoroughly analysed this idea in his discussions of mass-communication research after Louis Althusser and Valentin Voloshnov. In order to reach a consensus in society, the interests of the masses must be, as Hall articulates it, appropriately 'squared' with the hegemonic policies of those theoretically outside and above.[23] Althusser suggested that a consensual ideology is achieved through the bureaucracy of ideological state apparatuses—methods by which institutions propagate ideology through willing compliance.[24] Although it seems practically impossible to genuinely align such disparate interests, all that is necessary is the repetition of format, which eventually becomes familiar. Mass-communication media is the most literal example of this phenomenon due in large part to its culling processes. To cull for efficiency is to select for the information most easily inserted into a predetermined and tested format. On the scale of mass communication, restrictions of time and space not only dictate the length and amount of information allowed, but also the rhetoric used for conveying it. In order for information to be understood,

21 *Ibid.*, p.319.
22 *Ibid.*
23 Stuart Hall, 'The Rediscovery of "Ideology": Return of the Repressed in Media Studies', (ed. Michael Gurevitch, Tony Bennett, James Curran and Janet Woollacott), *Culture, Society, and the Media*, London and New York: Methuen, 1982, p.85.
24 Louis Althusser, *Lenin and Philosophy and Other Essays*, London: New Left Books, 1989, pp.170–86.
25 S. Hall, 'The Rediscovery of "Ideology": Return of the Repressed in Media Studies', *op. cit.*, p.83.
26 *Ibid.*
27 *Ibid.*

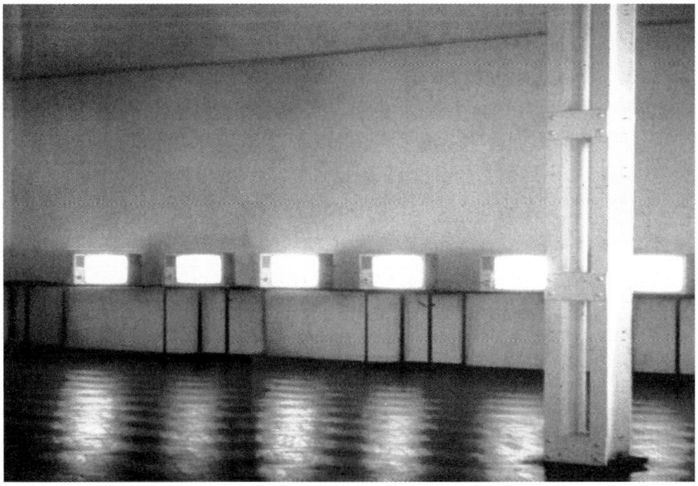

David Lamelas, *Situación de tiempo* (*Situation of Time*), 1967

mass media may only present information clearly and within a consensual format. Format takes precedence over content, and difference is presented void of implicit conflict.

In *Situación de tiempo,* Lamelas's method was one of reduction and the effect materialised as pure indexical process — a transformation of format into content. Two important achievements in the evolution of media studies clarify the significance of format attained through consensus formation. In 1973, Voloshinov noted that a sign, something that stands for something else, is an arena for struggle. At this site of struggle, the construction of meaning takes place, opening the door for consensus formation to potentially occur.[25] Hall noted that society ideologically contrives class and consensus formation, and should be 'understood as the complex result of the successful prosecution of different forms of social struggle at all levels of social practice, including the ideological'.[26]

Furthermore, a largely unexplored extension of Voloshinov's argument suggests that if social struggle could be conducted over the same sign, then neither side of the struggle could lay exclusive claim to any single sign.[27] The source of a sign's conflict, then, is its inflection or format as opposed to its whole being. It does not matter what the sign is, as long as we agree to its nature as a collectively compromised 'all'. This is how consensus is reached: the masses are ideologically formed, and format becomes the intentional act. The media's consensus is not gained through real emission, but rather through visual and discursive repetition. As an 'all', we only consider media's technologies as novelty, we mistake culled information for fact and we fail to recognise a sign's inflection. It is in this manner that television permeated Argentine society, and it was for this reason that *Situación de tiempo* easily reduced a potentially receptive environment into a container for blank repetition.

After the Cull

Let us conclude our discussion with a later work by David Lamelas that extends his earlier methods to a process of culling for universal latencies. Lamelas's first professionally produced film in the United States, *The Desert People* (1974), demonstrates the artist's furthering of 'format as content' to the utter validation of format as the only genuine aesthetic. Through the reintroduction of narrative as an anti-didactic variable, Lamelas departed entirely from any formal or linguistic conventions of representation. Instead of using the method of narrative to explicate visual information, the artist used it here as a format, simply a device that makes the information visual.

The Desert People presents the experiences of five people who visit a Native American reservation in the western United States. Each one is a professional actor who plays a character of an archetypal absolute (i.e. hippie, New York journalist, West Coast liberal, 'authentic' Native American and intellectual anthropologist). On the aesthetic surface, the film mimics the documentary genre. As each individual of the group speaks independently, the camera does not deviate from a single angle and there is little variation in the shots' setting and tone. In addition to these technical similarities, the only other elements that link the five characters are the car in which they travel together and a loosely gathered assumption that they have all shared the same experience. By the end of the film, however, even these last two elements vanish.

For the viewer, details of the actual visit to the reservation are fugitive and scarce. Each character speaks about the event but their inquiries yield nothing substantial beyond personal feelings. As these interviews progress, the film's chronology becomes increasingly muddled until the viewer loses his own place in the temporal framework. It is impossible to tell whether the characters are driving to or from the reservation, and the viewer is never able to confirm the actual existence of their destination. The film's spatial setting inversely compensates for these ambiguities, as the car flies through a desert that is a flat, monochromatic, 'anywhere' type of landscape. At the end of the film, the car drives off a cliff. In this single moment, the viewer's only spatial anchor is destroyed and finally the characters are joined by life's most inevitable and uncompromising event.

It is important to remember that unlike Lamelas's earlier films, *The Desert People* was a professional endeavour.[28] In commercially produced films, narrative is the primary tool by which indexical practice becomes intelligible to a mass audience. Narrative is the standard for which the producers of industry films cull information, and it's the organising tool by which they transform disjunctive scenes into a comprehensive story. Undoubtedly, some type of narrative exists in Lamelas's early sculpture, by way of its peripheral dialogue with Minimalism.[29] In *Situación de tiempo,* one begins to see the artist's first omission of narrative.[30] Despite his shameless

28 Interestingly, after the film's completion Lamelas moved to Hollywood. See B.H.D. Buchloh, *Neo-Avantgarde and Culture Industry, op. cit.*, p.330.

29 I am specifically thinking about *28 Placas Ubicadas en dos Formas no Convencionales* (*28 Plaques Placed In Two Unconventional Forms*, 1966–67), exhibited at the Museo Nacional de Bellas Artes in Buenos Aires in 1968, which consisted of 28 square, metal plates covering the floor of one gallery and a connecting intermediary walkway. The work tied one part of the museum to another and offered the viewer a logical procession of movement through the space — a narrative of movement, space and time.

30 Although it could be argued that an intransigent place is reserved for it by its very nature as an installation. Objects within architecture require spatial planning, which unconditionally leaves the viewer to experience the work as a spatial composition within a larger context of relative inside-ness and outside-ness. This dichotomy inherently possesses a beginning and an end.

31 This is where I see Lamelas's most significant break with conventional ideas of Conceptualism. The linguistic, like the narrative, in *The Desert People* is not used as a method for representation. In stark contrast, it is used as a non-representation or as something that interrupts a deceptive pretence towards representation.

reintroduction of narrative into *The Desert People,* its apotheosis promises nothing of traditional value to the viewer. In the film, he uses narrative to deliberately divide the work's material—its spatial, temporal and linguistic elements—into randomly constructed quotations.[31] This draws exclusive attention to the work's singular absolute: simply its existential presence.

As in North America and Europe, the end of World War II induced new spatial relationships for Argentine artists. *Desarrollismo* altered the citizen's place within society and heightened his or her role as a participant in a national project. Artists were called upon as cultural practitioners but chiefly as Argentine citizens, and this role presented them with a unique challenge. How could one reconcile mass media's practical usefulness as a national implement with its fundamental disavowal of what were believed to be art's primary conditions, singularity and uniqueness? By mimicking an institutionalised process, artists revealed mass media's essential lack while also validating its method. They affirmed the imported technology only through its own critique. However, unlike in the United States and Europe, this critique was not a self-reflection, but instead a critical deflection towards the influx of mass media and a larger foreign presence.

Culling for latency allowed Argentine artists to manipulate the malleable textures of perception, making entirely accessible what was not immediately perceivable. With this in mind, the new Argentine aesthetic substantiated format itself as a mode of visual inquiry. The discovered pliability of time, space and the presence of the individual in mass media further validated this philosophy. The result was a genuine Argentine artistic paradigm that existed at the very threshold of a burgeoning Argentine nationalism. In the 1960s, to invest in an autonomous art, as Bürger conceived of it, was an unproductive task, suited neither to the national project of modernisation nor to the more individualised resistance to North American culture that defined the post-*desarrollismo* period in Argentina. The work of Latin American artists in the high modern and postmodern period illuminates a larger, more complicated (but not at all unrelated) international strain of what has been too often narrowly defined as an insular and domestic practice of institutional critique in the United States and Europe.

LIVE ON TAPE: VIDEO, LIVENESS AND THE IMMEDIATE

William Kaizen

The Immediacy of the Medium

Friday, 30 July 1965: Andy Warhol was an hour into audio taping his superstar Ondine when a large package arrived at the Factory. Warhol was attempting to capture Ondine non-stop for 24 hours so he could transcribe the tapes into a book that would record a day in the life of the Factory's most flamboyant star.[1] The box held a videotape recording system, one of the earliest designed for use outside of a television studio. Warhol's audio tapes contain one of the first responses to video, one made long before the use of video by artists would be codified as 'video art', and even before Nam June Paik bought his first Sony video recorder later that year.[2] As such, these tapes record a point of emergence of one medium from another as video began to coalesce from audio, film and television. These portable video systems would soon open up the field of television production to amateur and artist alike.

Paul Morrissey arrived at the Factory and gave Warhol the low-down on his new machine:

> Morrissey: Are you excited about the new video camera?
> Warhol: ... Sit down here on the couch and tell me about it please ...
> Morrissey: [This is] the tape recorder, right? You ... aim ... this microphone at people. You aim the ... lens at the people.
> Warhol: Oh.
> Morrissey: And the picture goes onto the tape and then you [play] the tape ... just like you play back your tape recorder and the tape plays back through a television set.
> Warhol: Oh, man, and you get a picture too?
> Morrissey: Yes, immediately.
> Warhol: Oh, wow.
> Morrissey: So the sound ... [if it's not] adequate or the lighting is not good ...
> Warhol: You could fix it immediately.[3]

1 Eventually published as Andy Warhol, *A: A Novel*, New York: Grove Press, 1998.

2 While Paik was long given as the origin point for video art in America, recent accounts have begun to acknowledge Warhol's important early contribution, and that it precedes Paik's. See: John Allan Farmer, *The New Frontier: Art and Television, 1960–65*, Austin: Austin Museum of Art, 2000; Branden W. Joseph, 'Nothing Special: Andy Warhol and the Rise of Surveillance', *Ctrl Space: Rhetorics of Surveillance from Bentham to Big Brother* (eds. Thomas Y. Levin, Ursula Frohne and Peter Weibel), Cambridge, Mass.: ZKM/The MIT Press, 2002, pp.236–51; Michael Rush, *Video Art*, New York: Thames and Hudson, 2003; Steven Watson, *Factory Made: Warhol and the Sixties*, New York: Pantheon Books, 2003.

3 A. Warhol, *A: A Novel*, *op. cit.*, p.56.

In his typically deadpan way, Warhol hit the nail on the head: 'Oh, wow'. For Warhol the 'Oh, wow' of video was the fact that you got a picture immediately, that the moving image was represented in real time and instant replay. That little shock, of seeing what was being recorded at the very same instant that it was taking place, and then being able to change the picture afterwards, was an utterly new experience in 1965. Warhol was asked in an interview in *Tape Recording*, the magazine that sponsored his acquisition of the video equipment: 'What do you see as the essential difference between film and videotape?' He replied: 'Immediate playback. When you make movies you have to wait and wait and wait.'[4] To immediately see a moving picture with sync sound, to be able to monitor, record and replay one's self and the world right away—this was video's 'Oh, wow' when it was first introduced.

Throughout the history of early video art in America, artists repeatedly acknowledged the speed of video's immediacy.[5] Paik, who bought his equipment on 4 October 1965, also commented on this, writing: 'In my video-taped electrovision ... you see your picture instantaneously.'[6] With remarkable frequency the 'instantaneity' in Paik's account crops up as 'immediacy' in further descriptions of video. Bruce Nauman, when asked what interested him about video, responded: 'Well, initially, it was the immediacy of the medium.'[7] Jud Yalkut, in an interview with Raindance Foundation members Ira Schneider and Frank Gillette, described the difference between television and film as 'the immediacy of the television medium'.[8] Gillette said in the same interview: 'People see videotape and what they read in their skulls is "real"—it seems live, and has an unstored quality like the live immediacy of [...] the 7 o'clock news.'[9] Lynda Benglis wrote: 'Video was for me a way of presenting certain ideas that had occurred in film, but presenting these ideas in a more immediate, self-revealing way.'[10] Dan Graham wrote: 'Video is a present-time medium ... [It] feeds back indigenous data in the immediate, present-time environment.'[11] And recently Vito Acconci said: 'The immediacy of video was the most startling thing. The first video I made tried to make use of that ... I could use video as a mirror.'[12]

This sentiment was also echoed in the mainstream press as portable video was making its debut for a broader public. Various home video systems had been in the works throughout the early 1960s. On 8 June 1965, the first portable system for public consumption reached the United States from Sony in Japan.[13] A demonstration of the equipment by Akio Morita, Executive Vice

4 'Pop Goes the Videotape', *Tape Recording*, September/October 1965, p.16.
5 The issue of whether this was true in contexts outside of America remains to be explored.
6 Nam June Paik, *Videa 'n' Videology 1959–1973*, Syracuse: Everson Museum of Art, 1997, n.p.
7 Robert C. Morgan (ed.), *Bruce Nauman*, Baltimore: Johns Hopkins University Press, 2002, p.268.
8 Jud Yalkut, 'Frank Gillette and Ira Schneider, Parts I & II of an Interview', *Radical Software*, vol.1 no.1, Spring 1970, p.9.
9 Frank Gillette, *ibid.*, p.10.
10 'Video', *Art Rite*, no.7, 1974, p.12.
11 Dan Graham, *Video-Architecture-Television*, Nova Scotia: The Press of the Nova Scotia College of Art and Design, 1979, p.62.
12 Conversation with the artist, 20 June 2002. Acconci was describing his first video work, *Corrections* (1970), in which he burned hairs off the back of his neck using the monitor as mirror to access a spot that he could not otherwise see.
13 The Norelco unit used by Warhol was extremely heavy and never intended for widespread public use. Gene Smith, '$995 Home TV Tape Recorder to Be Introduced Here by Sony', *The New York Times*, 9 June 1965, p.64.

President of Sony and Chairman of the Sony Corporation of America, shows how indelibly the immediate was inscribed on portable video from the start. A newspaper reporter was sent to cover the story of Sony's latest gadget. As the reporter arrived and was introduced to Morita, an assistant videotaped their interaction. Just as the tape was about to be played back, they could hear sirens and smoke was visible outside the office window. The Sony showroom across the street was on fire! Morita and his assistant grabbed the video equipment and ran downstairs, taping the entire scene — fire, fire-fighters, crowd and all. Returning upstairs, they continued the interview with the startled reporter who had watched all this unfold from the window above. Morita played back the just-captured footage of the fire, saying: 'Now I'm going to show you how to have instant replay.'[14] The fire was still being extinguished while Morita replayed it for the reporter.

Another early public presentation of video also reiterated its immediacy, this time in a domestic setting. *Life* magazine ran a feature article on the new Sony equipment, accompanied by a large photograph of a prototypical suburban backyard with children playing in a swimming pool.[15] Dad looks on from the sidelines while Mum operates the camera, the rather heavy-handed implication being that since it's so easy to use even Mum can do it. The video-recording deck sits on the bottom edge of the picture, looming large in the foreground, with the image of the children that Mum shoots visible on the monitor above it. While the image's message is perfectly clear, it is reinforced by the accompanying caption which reads: 'New home video recorder, made by Sony Corp., makes a movie at a swimming pool and instantly shows it on a TV screen.' Further down, the article recapitulates this. Underneath a title that reads 'Betting on Instant Playback', the author writes that with video 'the home moviemaker can see the results immediately, erasing and reshooting scenes on the spot'. Video could immediately playback sounds and images, creating an instant, moving memorial even while it lingered on in the present.

Immediacy also surfaced in art criticism. John S. Margolies's 'TV — The Next Medium' discusses video's 'participation, simultaneity [and] spontaneity'.[16] While none of these qualities are particular to television or video, he also mentions, more specifically, how on video the image and sound can be 'changed immediately'.[17] Video artist and art critic Douglas Davis, in his

14 Nick Lyons, *The Sony Vision*, New York: Crown Publishers 1976, pp.186–88; Gene Smith, 'Trial by Fire Tests New Sony TV Unit', *The New York Times*, 14 July 1966, p.49.

15 'A New Pastime with a Big Future: Tape-It-Yourself-TV', *Life*, 17 September 1965, pp.57–60.

16 John S. Margolies, 'TV – the Next Medium', *Art in America*, September–October 1969, p.50.

17 *Ibid.*

18 Douglas Davis, 'Video Obscura', *Artforum*, vol.10 no.8, April 1972, p.62.

19 Gregory Battcock, 'Explorations in Video', *Art and Artists*, vol.7 no.11, February 1973, p.22. One of the best known formulations of the medium of video — although it came at the end of the history of early video — is Rosalind Krauss's claim: 'The medium of video is narcissism.' See Rosalind Krauss, 'Video: The Aesthetics of Narcissism', as reproduced in the current volume.

20 Donald Judd, 'Specific Objects', *Complete Writings: 1959–1975*, Halifax: The Press of the Nova Scotia College of Art and Design, 1975, pp.181 and 187.

21 I follow Jonathan Crary in taking technologies as assemblages of both material and discourse. He suggests that material does not drive discourse, but is coterminous with whatever possibilities emerge from particular material configurations. His work on the camera obscura is equally applicable to video when he writes that a given medium is discursive as much as material. A medium is as much 'an object about which something is said and at the same time an object that is used. It is a site at which a discursive formation intersects with material practices. [It] cannot be reduced either to a technological or a

essay 'Video Obscura', proposes that one of the most important distinguishing features of video is its 'immediacy' since 'no other medium allows [immediacy] to such an extent', but that it is this quality that is 'the most difficult to define'.[18]

Despite the difficulty that Davis proclaims, given the frequency of immediacy's occurrence in early descriptions of video, the term itself provides an answer to the problem of video as a medium. It says: 'Immediacy is the medium of video.' The question of the medium of video was raised repeatedly in the history of early video art. Gregory Battcock summed this up best when he wrote: 'Most of the activity in video, and the critical attention it attracts, has one principle goal: the very definition of video as a communicative (i.e. artistic) medium.'[19] The drive toward medium specificity in the history of early video art was the flip side of the endless possibilities that had entered the art world on the heels of Minimalism and the readymade-redux strategies of the 1950s and early 60s. As Donald Judd wrote in his essay 'Specific Objects', art circa 1965 'opens to anything' and any 'new materials' can be used.[20] In light of the seemingly endless parade of things that were finding a home in art galleries, it was as if, by defining video, critical discourse could grasp at least one point of purchase in a seemingly unlimited artistic milieu. While not necessarily apparent in the midst of video's emergence, given an examination of the historical record it becomes clear that immediacy was the one distinguishing characteristic claimed more frequently for video than any other. It emerges as a discursive clue bubbling to the top of what was said about how video was used.[21]

There is a paradox in the references to video as immediate: why would a system for recording be described as if it were unmediated? This is explained by the way in which video became its own format, distinct from live television and related to film. Stanley Cavell describes the immediate not as the medium of video but as that of television in his essay 'The Fact of Television'.[22] He understands medium as the definition given to a material support through continued social uses that produce particular types of affect.[23] While he follows Clement Greenberg, he is not caught up in the problems of taste that cause Greenberg to privilege high forms of art over low, or good works over bad. He is also not a technological determinist seeking essences that forever define

discursive object: it [i]s a complex social amalgam in which its existence as textual figure [i]s never separable from its machinic uses.' This implies that a thing is defined not by any inherent material qualities but by what is said about it or done with it, and that one can only confirm the nature of a given format in the persistence of both material and discourse. A format does not have an essence but rather a consensus over how it is used and understood, with consensus implying a kind of general, if contested, field rather than a single, monolithic, even if temporary, fundamental nature. This is in agreement with Stanley Cavell's take on the medium; see notes 22 and 23. Jonathan Crary, *Techniques of the Observer: On Vision and Modernity in the Nineteenth Century*, Cambridge, Mass.: The MIT Press, 1990, pp.30–31.

22 Stanley Cavell, 'The Fact of Television', *Themes Out of School: Effects and Causes*, Chicago: University of Chicago Press, 1984. He had first distinguished between television and film in his *The World Viewed*, Cambridge, Mass.: Harvard University Press, 1979, p.26.

23 S. Cavell, 'The Fact of Television', *op. cit.*, pp.31–32.

how a given technology works.[24] Rather, he is interested in whether new works either continue given conventions or push toward new norms, producing new media and so new conditions of possibility. He takes the medium of television, like all media, as a temporary stabilisation of materials, techniques and selves. Cavell writes of television that it has concretised around particular ontological possibilities as 'a current of simultaneous event reception'.[25] By this he means an immediate way of monitoring events at the same time as they take place. Television is a tele-technology. Like the telegraph, telephone or radio, it is a machine used for the real-time representation of an event with an unlimited distance between the event and its reception. With the addition of images, television made real-time representation at a distance seem closer to hand than ever before.[26] The response to video as immediate was conditioned by the immediacy of live television. Whereas film may also make distant events seem present, the events it depicts are understood as past. Filmic images are caught up in what Roland Barthes called photography's 'that-has-been' effect.[27] Photography and film generate their affect by returning the dead to life. Live television, on the other hand, operates in the present tense. It says about what it shows: 'this-is-going-on'. Compared to film, it seems even more alive.[28]

In the literature on video as a medium that preceded Cavell and Barthes, Davis and David Antin also make the distinction between live television's immediacy versus that of film. In the essay 'Time! Time! Time! The Context of Immediacy', Davis follows his earlier claim that immediacy in video is based on live television's 'sense of authentic presence'.[29] He further develops this in 'Filmgoing/Videogoing: Making Distinctions', writing that in film each diegetic step has been predetermined.[30] In live television, no matter how carefully scripted or composed the presentation, the threat of disaster lurks, waiting in the wings. Part of what captivates the audience is this possibility of failure, as they watch knowing that success depends on avoiding perceptible breakdown. Davis recalls the moon landing, shown live on television, and how the virtual event unfolded in the same time as the actual event, with no edited compression of time. It seemed as if 'anything could happen next' because on live television exactly how things would progress was unknown, both to the viewers and to the producers.[31] Antin, in his essay 'Video: The Distinctive

24 It is debatable whether or not Greenberg was a technological determinist in his proscription of flatness as the historical outcome of modernist painting. See Thierry de Duve, *Clement Greenberg between the Lines*, Paris: Edition Dis Voir, 1996.

25 S. Cavell, 'The Fact of Television', *op. cit.*, p.252.

26 This is an important distinction because film can also operate in real time, meaning that the time of representation is identical to the time of the original event, even though cinematic representation takes place after the fact. With television both sound and image could take place in real time at the same time as the event. Radar is the closest precedent and the context in which the term 'real time' was developed. See Paul N. Edwards, *The Closed World: Computers and the Politics of Discourse in Cold War America*, Cambridge, Mass.: The MIT Press, 1996, ch.3.

27 Roland Barthes, *Camera Lucida: Reflections on Photography* (trans. Richard Howard), New York: Hill and Wang, 1981, p.77.

28 Barthes's comments came at a time in the 1970s when they can be said to have been in reaction to television as much as to photography or film. They can be read as a response to the new mode of televisuality that had supplemented the photographic with an insistent present tense.

29 Douglas Davis, 'Time! Time! Time! The Context of Immediacy', *The New Television: A Public/Private Art*, Cambridge, Mass.: The MIT Press, 1977, p.79.

30 Douglas Davis, 'Filmgoing/Videogoing: Making Distinctions', *Video Culture: A Critical Investigation* (ed. John G. Hanhardt), Rochester: Visual Studies Workshop Press, 1986. Originally published in 1973 in the *American Film Institute Report*.

Features of the Medium', writes that in film, truth is always predicated on the past tense while on television truth seems more immediate because it seems to take place in the present.[32] This is despite the fact that by the early 1960s live broadcasting was the exception rather than the rule of television — reserved for news, sports and the president. Yet by then the 'live' had been indelibly stamped on television-image production, continuing, as Antin writes, the 'illusion of immediacy' even when on tape.[33] He quotes a handbook on television production that says that by 1961: 'The live production on videotape, though delayed in reaching the home by a few hours or days, was generally accepted as actual live television by the average viewer.'[34] This illusion of immediacy, he goes on, further quoting the handbook, is defined by 'the feeling that what one sees on the TV screen is living and actual reality, at that very moment taking place'.[35]

The confusion between real time and recorded time is borne out in the history of video's emergence as a medium distinct from television. This confusion had already been exploited in broadcast television with the introduction of magnetic-tape recording techniques in the 1940s. Before then all broadcasts had been live and had to be repeated across different time zones. Kinescopes, which were films made of live programmes, could be printed and distributed within hours of the original but they were neither instantaneous nor of good quality. By the early 1950s audio tape was adapted into videotape. 'Live' programming could be seen on the West Coast of America even when the event had taken place hours before on the East Coast, with no observable difference in quality between the two; thus the oxymoronic expression 'live on tape'.[36] Once videotape recording was introduced, it was used not only to delay broadcasts across time zones but throughout the broadcast day.[37] With 'video' (the shortened, colloquial version of the term for videotape-recording systems), television could move seamlessly between programmes that required live, local responses, such as the news, and those that had no need to be live. Television, as a format designed for live, real-time transmission, is saturated with the live presence of the things it puts on display. It is as if it were a window that tunnelled through to another place, opening directly onto the event shown. In this it is closer, both rhetorically and technically, to the present tense

31 *Ibid.*, p.273. This theme was further developed in Mary Anne Doane's 'Information, Crisis, Catastrophe' and Patricia Mellencamp's 'TV Time and Catastrophe, or Beyond the Pleasure Principle of Television', both in *Logics of Television: Essays in Cultural Criticism* (ed. Patricia Mellencamp), Bloomington: Indiana University Press, 1990.

32 David Antin, 'Video: The Distinctive Feature of the Medium', *Video Art*, Philadelphia: Falcon Press, 1975, pp.174–83; also published as 'Television: Video's Frightful Parent, Part I', *Artforum*, vol.14 no.4, December 1975, pp.36–45.

33 D. Antin, 'Video: The Distinctive Feature of the Medium', *op. cit.*, p.62.

34 *Ibid.*

35 *Ibid.*

36 This expression is also network shorthand for 'taped before a live studio audience'. Philip Auslander explores the ramifications of the relationship between live events and recorded events, noting that 'the live is actually an effect of mediatisation', and that the first use of the word live to refer to a performance only occurred after and in relation to the advent of tape recording. See Philip Auslander, *Liveness: Performance in a Mediatized Culture*, New York: Routledge, 1999, pp.50–54.

37 For more on the history of videotape recording, see Roy Armes, *On Video*, New York: Routledge, 1988; Brian Winston, *Media, Technology and Society, a History: From the Telegraph to the Internet*, New York: Routledge, 1998; and Siegfried Zielinski, *Zur Geschichte Des Videorecorders*, Berlin: Wissenschaftsverlag, 1986.

of theatre than to film. With magnetic-tape recording, television could move easily between the live and the not-live. As Cavell aptly notes, on television 'there is no sensuous distinction between the live and the repeat or the replay'.[38] Additionally, even when on tape (and even when edited after the fact or originally shot on film), there is always somebody in the broadcast-television studio standing by, prepared to 'go live' if necessary.

Television generates its reality effect from always seeming to be live because it always opens onto the possibility of continuous live transmission.[39] Media historian Jane Feuer uses the term 'liveness' to describe this effect and it perfectly suits the 'Oh, wow' of televisual immediacy: how it is that, even when not live, television seems live-like. Paradoxically, it was the intervention of video as a means of recording that produced 'the live' in live television, as liveness became an ideological as much as a technological limit condition. Video is indeed a record but, unlike film, it was seen as an instant record, and one that was, when it was introduced to artists, always already coded as live because of its use in broadcast television.[40] Rather than use video as a record, videotape had already been used to uphold the illusion of immediacy by closing the gap between live and recorded events.[41] Moreover, unlike film, videotape requires no processing. And video gains a further dimension of liveness because, with a monitor, what is being taped can be seen at the very same moment that the taping is taking place, appearing as it will in replay. With video there does not need to be any difference between the time of the event and its reproduction. The time of the event, its recording and its replay are collapsed. Video's immediacy, as it was repeatedly announced, came from this confusion between the live and the on-tape.

In their essay 'Television, A World in Action', Stephen Heath and Gillian Skirrow identify one of the major effects that televisual liveness produces for viewers. They write that the 'immediacy' of television (and they put 'immediacy' in quotation marks to acknowledge the distance it includes) functions to create an entirely different psychological connection to its viewers from other media; because of its liveness it is even more interpellative than film.[42] They write: 'The generalised fantasy of the television institution of the image is exactly that

38 S. Cavell, 'The Fact of Television', *op. cit.*, p.253. This overlooks the aging of recorded images, where dress and other markers give away the date of a particular image, but these types of distinction can be said to be meta- or supra-sensuous, and so beyond the scope of Cavell's claim.

39 Raymond Williams calls the continuous transmission of broadcasting 'flow' and its development in commercial broadcasting 'programmed flow'. As Williams acknowledges, this is not particular to television because it is also applicable to radio. See Raymond Williams, *Television: Technology and Cultural Form*, New York: Schocken Books, 1974, pp.86–96.

40 This would change to some extent with the introduction of video cassettes and their widespread usage by the mid-1980s.

41 'Reality TV' is only the latest symptom of this effect, and its origins go back to 1973 with the broadcast of *An American Family*. See Jeffery Ruoff, *An American Family: A Televised Life*, Minneapolis: University of Minnesota Press, 2001.

42 Stephen Heath and Gillian Skirrow, 'Television, a World in Action', *Screen*, vol.18 no.2, 1977, p.54. The authors follow Louis Althusser's exposition of interpellation in his 'Ideology and State Apparatus (Notes Towards an Investigation)', in *Lenin and Philosophy and Other Essays*, *op. cit.*, pp.85–126.

43 S. Heath and G. Skirrow, 'Television, a World in Action', *op. cit.*, p.54.

44 This had been noted before by Davis and Battcock, among others.

45 S. Heath and G. Skirrow, 'Television, a World in Action', *op. cit.*, p.56.

46 A larger history of the tension between immediacy and mediation in various technologies and especially in new media is tracked in Jay David Bolter and Richard Grusin, *Remediation: Understanding New Media*, Cambridge, Mass.: The MIT Press, 1999.

it is direct, and direct for me.'[43] Television hails its subject through a seemingly personal, one-to-one connection established between the viewer and what is on view.[44] They continue: 'Direct and for me. Television is the institution of an occupation: it occupies the viewer as the subject in a permanent arena of "communicationality" ... Little matter in this respect what is communicated, the crux is the creation and maintenance of the communicating situation. The subject of television is a citizen in a world of communication.'[45] Televisual immediacy, despite its mediation, seems to include viewers more than other media. It locks them in place as if they were called out to directly there and then, even when the event or person shown is miles away and days — or even years — in the past.

One of the primary concerns of early video art was to pry open video's immediacy, to make the viewer feel its mediation.[46] In many early video works — of which I will discuss two key examples below — video's immediacy is thickened until its intercession between selves as a means of communication becomes painfully apparent. Rather than act as a transparent mirror, in these works the video mirror screens the ways televisual immediacy mediates between the senders and receivers of information. By breaking immediacy down into im-mediacy, these works began to recognise how the conventions of televisual liveness produced a new set of limit conditions for the use of tele-technologies and the production of networked selves. They present a self that is live-like even as it is live on tape, re-presenting the self as a citizen in what was then still a strange new world of endlessly immediate information flow.

Outer and Inner Space

Warhol worked at the cusp of immediacy. His movie *Outer and Inner Space* made a first pass through the fields of liveness, moving from film to television and videotape recording. Made in the summer of 1965, it is a 16mm black-and-white film incorporating the video equipment that Warhol had received from Norelco. It shows Edie Sedgwick for half-an-hour as she becomes acclimatised — sort of — to the immediacy of video. She sits in front of a television set that replays her own image behind her. Warhol had just videotaped her and himself talking, shooting her close-up, in profile, looking to her left, her head entirely filling the screen. He then filmed her while the video played back as they continued their conversation, turning her in the other direction. Her videotaped image appears to be slightly larger than her actual head. It looks out across her filmed image, as though her televisual superego (or perhaps her id?) is speaking into and admonishing (or encouraging?) her filmed image's ear. Her past self interpellates her present self. Because of the different speeds of the television scan and the film shutter, her television image is evanescently flickering, the scanning fingers of the cathode-ray gun are revealed as they draw and redraw her image thirty times as opposed to 24 frames per second. The difference between video and film is made visibly present by the technical differences in the two formats. Warhol

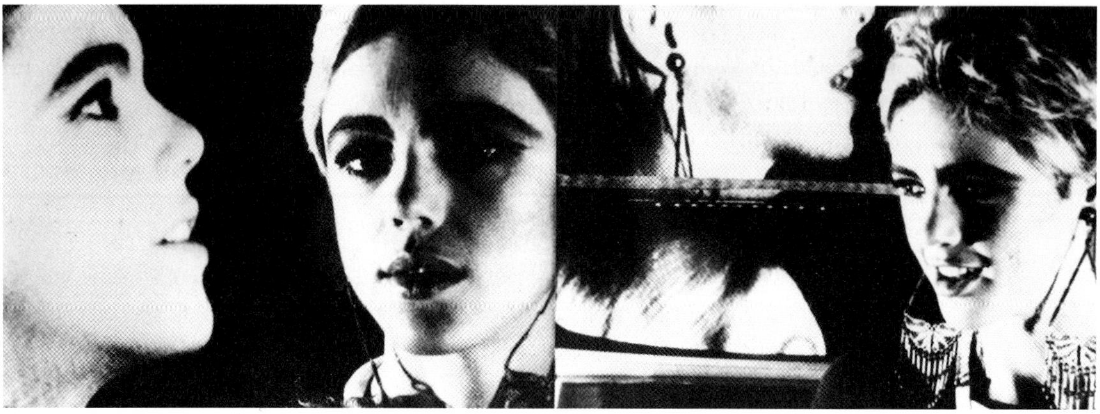

Andy Warhol, *Outer and Inner Space*, 1965. 16mm black-and-white film, sound, 33mins in double screen Courtesy The Andy Warhol Museum

shot two reels of film and the final version is shown with both reels projected simultaneously, side-by-side, optimally with the first reel on the left and the second on the right. The final film is a quadruple portrait of Sedgwick told in alternating video/film/video/film.[47] As much as Warhol gives us a portrait of Sedgwick, he has produced a portrait of the emergence of video caught on film, reflecting the new mode of televisual liveness erupting into and rupturing the filmic. By filming Sedgwick's interaction with her video image, Warhol captures video's 'this-is-going-on' in film's 'that-has-been'. He shows the viewer Sedgwick's psychological adaptation to video's liveness through the secondary mediation of film at just the moment when the latter was being eclipsed by the former.

While the soundtrack is often inaudible due to both the quality of Warhol's equipment and the babble that frequently occurs when multiple voices are speaking at once, much of their conversation can still be understood. Sedgwick spends most of the first reel upset about having to sit in front of her technologically mediated self as it speaks from behind her. She never turns around to look at her video self, despite her discomfort. She is uncomfortable with her video self because its voice demands a response as it calls out from behind her. Instead, she can only respond to Warhol. Pinned between them, she is the object of the look (really the voice) of both her past self and Warhol as the off-screen stand-in for the viewer.[48] She is the heroine who braves the treacherous waters of liveness, not only of these looks but also of her past made strangely present. Describing her video self early on, she says: 'It sounds like a lot of bullshit—it does ... I'm going to wait and see how bored everyone else will get ... Isn't that sad. I'm so fragile ... it makes me so nervous to have to listen to it. It really is rotten ... it's so pathetic. I never dreamed I was so pathetic.'[49] Her video head is an uncanny reflection. The monitor has become a mirror gone wild. The sound of her voice, whispering in her ear from the just-past, profoundly disturbs her.

47 As in some of Warhol's other 1964 films, such as *Henry Geldzahler* and *Empire*, *Outer and Inner Space* is an extension of his *Screen Tests* (1963–66) into longer form.

48 Here and throughout, I follow Kaja Silverman's distinction between the look and the gaze in cinema and camera-based works: the look is constituted by a specific, embodied point-of-view; and the gaze by the general conditions of visibility. Kaja Silverman, *Male*

In the second reel she is still uncomfortable about hearing her just-past voice. 'I find the voice very disturbing!' she exclaims.[50] She reacts as though her video self has its eye (and voice) on her immediately, in the present, as she sits there, forced to listen to it carry on. Midway through the second reel she has an epiphany and realises why she's been so bothered. She says, referring to her video self: 'It's so funny listening to this rather than remembering ... and it's so real. I could just think it all over again and be right.'[51] Her past self is immediately there, collapsed onto her present. The cinematic 'that-has-been', with its vestigial connection to history and memory, had been replaced by the televisual 'this-is-going-on', with its incessant presencing. After her epiphany she becomes more comfortable and is able to play with the new possibilities inherent to this condition. Her video image fakes a sneeze and she jumps in response, startled because she has forgotten that she had done this. She asks Warhol if he could tell if it was real or not, and then, remembering what comes next, she responds with another fake sneeze. And then her video image sneezes again and her film image responds and so on, in a chain of fake sneezes, concluding when she responds to her video image's final sneeze with a ridiculous cough. Throughout this interaction, Sedgwick turns an involuntary bodily response into a game, her sneeze-chain turning an allergic response to her video self into a state of acclimatisation. Video has given her the ability to interact with herself in a way that was overwhelming at first, triggering a mnemonic game where she could eventually accept the past as immediately present, sneezing with herself as if she were making faces in an actual mirror. Sedgwick is only able to come to terms with her video image when she accepts its liveness, as if, unlike film, it were a mirror or a present event. She becomes acclimatised when she can play with her video self as if it were actually present.

While Sedgwick may become used to video's immediacy, in projecting both reels at the same time Warhol further collapses the time of the event so that her accommodation to televisual liveness takes place alongside the confusion this liveness engenders. The double-screen projection mitigates her acclimatisation to televisual liveness because the audience sees her simultaneously lost in its immediacy even as she comes to terms with it. Warhol helps the audience negotiate this confusion through the use of two zooms made while filming, one moving towards her, the other away from her. Stills from the film generally show her only in close-up, but for most of the film one of the two reels is zoomed out and held in a medium shot. The effect is like that of a magic trick simultaneously shown and revealed. While filming, Warhol zoomed out about halfway through the first reel, revealing the set-up of the shot so that Sedgwick can be seen from the waist up with the entire television set visible behind her in the middle of the frame. The second reel begins from the same zoomed-out, medium-shot position but zooms back in

Subjectivity at the Margins, New York: Routledge, 1992, ch.3.

49 Bill Jeffries (ed.), *From Stills to Motion and Back Again: Texts on Andy Warhol's Screen Tests and Outer and Inner Space*, North Vancouver, British Columbia: Presentation House Gallery, 2003, p.28.

50 *Ibid.*, p.31.

51 *Ibid.*, p.34.

to the original position approximately five minutes later. When double projected, the left side begins in close-up and the right side begins in the medium shot. After five minutes the right zooms in to close-up and holds there for about ten minutes, and then the left zooms out to the medium shot. It is only for those ten minutes that the audience is plunged into the disorienting scene of Sedgwick in alternating video and film, with no exterior spatial context beyond the boundaries of her multiplied head. The zoom generates a structural narrative for the audience, first giving them the set-up of the trick, then plunging them into the strange new world of video presence, then releasing them from it by returning to the set-up. Through the zoom the audience shares Sedgwick's confusion but is able to overcome the temporal collapse that keeps her trapped. They are brought into and out of the new inner space where the self confronts itself through televisual liveness. They are then able to sit back and watch with a deeper understanding of Sedgwick's experience of being confronted with video liveness and the confusion of being forced to face one's immediately displaced self.

Warhol further reinforces the liveness of video through the manipulation of both the image and audio during their replay. Throughout the filming, Gerard Malanga moved around in the background (not really visible on camera, except here and there) manipulating both video player and television set. Since Sedgwick never turns around and cannot see these manipulations, they are only there for the benefit of the audience.[52] Malanga turns the vertical hold so that her image goes skipping up and down across the screen, rolling first slower and then faster, from top to bottom. He desaturates the image, freezing it by stopping the tape so that briefly only the faintest ghost of her television image is left. He stops and starts the tape so that the image becomes riddled with noise. With video, Warhol said in his *Tape Recording* interview, 'We like to take advantage of static', as in his silk screens, in which misalignment and maladjustments were a key part of his process.[53] Like Sedgwick's sneeze-chain, Warhol plays with video's liveness effect through Malanga, demonstrating for the audience the plasticity of the television image in a real-time manipulation that further reinforces the differences between television and film.

Throughout *Outer and Inner Space*, both Sedgwick and the audience know her taped image is not contemporaneous with her filmed image, and yet, despite her video image's being on tape, the film shows how the past is overcome by the present through video's liveness effect. At the very end of reel two, the videotape is turned off behind her and a static laced image of a cowboy film comes through from a television broadcast. The broadcast image erupts as a conclusion, as if to say the liveness of broadcast television is the cause of all this. Despite Sedgwick's seeming acclimatisation to all this liveness, her last words in the film stand as her final response to video: 'It's like being struck in the back of the head.' She then lies down and plays dead as the film ends.[54]

Centers

There was an interregnum between Warhol's and Paik's video work in 1965 and the more widespread uptake of video by artists. This was because the portable video systems advertised in 1965 were not widely available until the end of the decade. At this time, many artists who had been working in film, inspired by Warhol and underground cinema, switched to video. Liveness flourished in the work of artists who can be loosely grouped under the heading of post-Minimalism. Post-Minimalism undertook a critique of the metaphysics of presence that still clung vestigially to Minimalism as a hold-over from modernist notions of the autonomy of art. Minimalism had made the presence of the viewer's body part of the work of art itself, but only in a generic way. Both the gestalt and phenomenological readings of Minimalism assumed a kind of ideal viewer and neutral viewing situation, whereby all viewers would supposedly have the same experience of the work. In post-Minimalism, the system of artist, object, viewer and viewing context was no longer taken for granted but was itself opened up and put on display. Process took over from presence; the work of art emerged at the intersection of art institutions and the body as an epistemological site. The liveness of video post-Minimalism became another means by which to critique the kind of modernist presence espoused by Greenberg and Michael Fried. The post-Minimalists used video against the autonomy of art and the viewing subject. They made works that opened onto both television and art as institutions, moving into the spaces between live and recorded time.[55]

Of the many post-Minimalist videos to explore these issues, Vito Acconci's *Centers* points toward one way in which these issues were extended. Made in 1971, while Acconci was doing a residency at the Nova Scotia College of Art and Design, *Centers* is a single-channel, black-and-white videotape with no edits, which focuses on Acconci's head and shoulders. The artist faces the viewer, half visible and half hidden behind an extended arm whose finger points directly to the centre of the monitor and so out toward the viewer. Acconci has said of his first use of video, a year or so before: 'Video as a determinant of value: I need an action that can coincide with the feedback capacity ... I can sit in front of the monitor, stay concentrated on myself, have eyes in the back of my head, dwell on myself, see myself in the round.'[56] He could get at the monkey on his back — the closed-circuit video loop made parts of his body instantly accessible that were otherwise off limits. Video became an improved mirror — a hyper-mirror — that allowed the self to be examined from all angles and from every side. In *Centers*, the audience rather than the artist is reflected in the video monitor. Acconci has written of *Centers*: 'My attempt is

52 In one instance, Malanga turns up the volume, making Sedgwick cringe. This is the only time she is affected by his manipulations.

53 'Pop Goes the Videotape', *op. cit.*, p.18.

54 See B. Jeffries, *From Stills to Motion and Back Again: Texts on Andy Warhol's Screen Tests and Outer and Inner Space*, *op. cit.*, p.39, in which the transcription records this line as 'struck in the back of the neck'.

55 For more on Greenberg, Fried and post-Minimalism's critique of presence, see Pamela M. Lee, *Chronophobia: On Time in the Art of the 1960s*, Cambridge, Mass.: The MIT Press, 2004, ch.1.

56 *Avalanche* ('Special Issue on Vito Acconci'), Fall 1972, p.24. Acconci is referring to his piece *Corrections*. See also note 12.

to keep my finger constantly in the centre of the screen. I keep narrowing my focus into my finger. The result[ing] TV image turns the activity around: a pointing away from myself, at an outside viewer ... I'm looking straight out by looking straight in.'[57] For 20 minutes Acconci keeps his hand aloft. It covers most of his face, quivering as he tries to keep it raised. As the tape begins, it covers his face up to and including his eyes, becoming a second face that takes the place of his look. He is not the object of the look, as was Sedgwick, but the hyper-masculine subject, the father whose point commands obedience. In pointing through the television set he attempts to become pure look, his finger materialising the view from the monitor back out at the observer. This is a position uncommon for film, but quite common in live television, especially in the news and on talk shows, where talking heads speak to an observer who is absent or anonymous for them. Acconci sutures the observer into the image not through look, spoken word or cut but through body language. His emphatic gesture points like the person anchoring the news looks, fixing on the absent viewer who is addressed but who is neither there spatially nor temporally. This touch (hand substituting for eyes, eyes becoming hand) only reaches the observer at a distance. In pointing at the apparatus, he points out at the audience, his finger gesturing toward the centre of the camera eye, targeting — to use a word Acconci uses often — both machine and viewer.[58]

Despite the fact that this observer is absent for Acconci, both in the moment of the event and forever after as it has been recorded, *Centers* connects to his viewers in the present tense, as Warhol connected Sedgwick with her recorded self in *Outer and Inner Space*. Acconci's gesture says, inescapably, 'this-is-going-on' — 'I am pointing at you, now.' This is due in part to the fact that the viewer is conditioned by the direct look of the headshot in television as a condition of live news. In replicating the look of the direct address in television, *Centers* opens onto the ways in which 'phatic' communication works in television. Anthropologist Bronislaw Malinowski developed the notion of phatic communication in everyday speech.[59] He writes that phatic communication consists of speech 'used in free, aimless social intercourse ... in which ties of union are created by a mere exchange of words'.[60] He describes the kind of interactions used to open conversation (such as 'hello', 'how are you', 'nice day today') as statements designed not to communicate meaning *per se* but to simply confirm that the possibility

57 *Castelli-Sonnabend Videotapes and Films*, vol.1, New York, 1974, n.p.

58 He was not, as Rosalind Krauss would have it, looking at himself, but rather at the centre of the camera lens. Krauss, writing in 1976, at the tail end of the quest for the medium of video, writes that narcissism was the medium of video. She extrapolates this from a reading of *Centers* whereby she takes Acconci's point as directed at himself in the video monitor as mirror and not out at the viewer. As Anne Wagner has recently written in response to Krauss, Acconci's point is a rhetorical apostrophe, summoning both the absent viewer for Acconci and the absent artist for the viewer. He points not at himself, but at the viewer and so at televisual liveness. See R. Krauss, 'Video: The Aesthetics of Narcissism', *op. cit.*, and Anne M. Wagner, 'Performance, Video and the Rhetoric of Presence', *October*, no.91, Winter 2000, pp.59–80.

59 Bronislaw Malinowski, 'The Problem of Meaning in Primitive Languages', *The Meaning of Meaning* (ed. C.K. Ogden and I.A. Richards), New York: Harcourt, Brace and Company, 1923, p.315.

60 *Ibid.*, pp.313 and 315.

61 *Ibid.*, p.313.

62 Wagner notes that this can also be taken as a reference to Uncle Sam, and I would add that it is in response to the Vietnam War as it was brought live and direct to people's homes via television. See A. Wagner, 'Performance, Video and the Rhetoric of Presence', *op. cit.*, p.69.

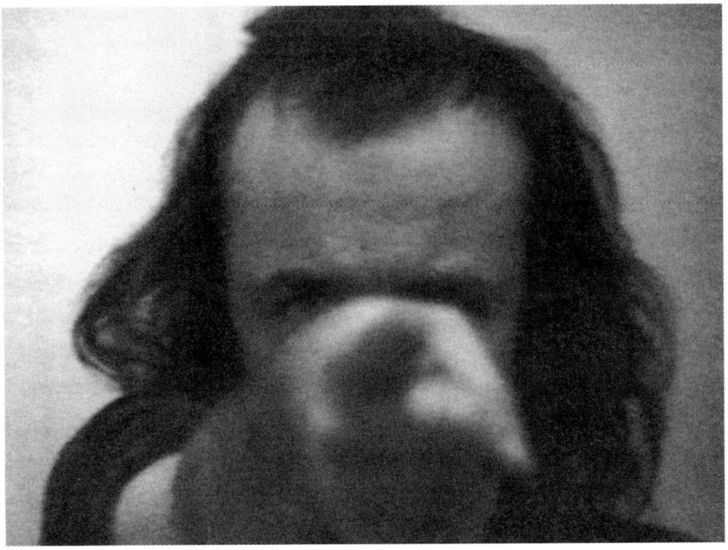

of communication exists. This extends to conversation in general, as it moves from topics of import back to gossip and to mutual 'affirmations of some supremely obvious state of things'.[61] The purpose of phatic communication is to open and keep open a social context for interaction. It is both a means of connection and a way to fill the silence as the connection is maintained. Phatic communication exists in broadcast television despite the fact that its connection only occurs in one direction. Live broadcast television has a variety of ways to cover over its uni-directionality and to keep the conversation going. News and talk shows have co-presenters and guests who chitchat amongst themselves, including viewers as if they were sitting with them and silently participating in their conversation. Live audiences are also used to heighten this effect—their murmurs and applause used so that viewers feel included, as if they were actually sitting in front of the event instead of a piece of furniture. Phatic communication allows television to provide company and comfort because the talking heads it presents seem to be there live, in viewers' living rooms despite their distance. Because of televisual liveness, this carries over into not-live programming as well.

Pointing is the most interpellative of gesticulations. It is the primary phatic gesture, an aggressive imperative opening onto the now-ness of communication. Pointing says: 'You! Pay attention to this thing! Here! Now!'[62] Acconci's gesture points toward the way in which the phatic is both opened and foreclosed in television. It heightens the non-reciprocity of the phatic contact that takes place between subjects on either side of the monitor's reflection, calling attention to how he can touch the viewer but cannot be touched in return. Over the course of the video, his finger increasingly wavers as his arm becomes exhausted. His hand slips downward and his eyes become visible—his look makes contact with the viewer only through his body's increasing exhaustion. The viewer cannot help but respond to these exertions as if they were taking place right there and then, watching as Acconci's embodiment of the male look strains and breaks down. Toward the end of the video, he struggles visibly to keep his finger aloft, making little snorts and grunts of exertion as the tip of his finger increasingly shakes. Watching, the viewer is sympathetically exhausted from this exertion. The tape ends before his arm gives out; there is no catharsis or conclusion, implying that this point is still going on, even after the screen goes black.

Vito Acconci, *Centers*, 1971. Black-and-white video, sound, 22mins 43secs. Courtesy Video Data Bank

At the centre of *Centers* is the blindness of the televisual eye, which prohibits any dialogical connection between sender and receiver. In film the direct address of the face into the eye of the camera is assiduously avoided because it only calls attention to the absence of the audience for the person on-screen. Because television is potentially live, however, this face-out becomes a significant formal strategy. As Acconci points at his viewers, in a virtual now, he accuses them, exhorting them to look at themselves and their own reflection in the video monitor, to think about the contradiction of responding to a past event as if it were present, and so to consider the kind of presence televisual immediacy produces. The work asks them to think about what it means to be confronted by an image's 'direct and for me' that is neither direct nor only for me. At the same time, it asks them to consider his position as the bearer of a pathetic televisual gesture, one whose phatic opening is both empathetic and full of pathos as he reaches out to touch someone whom he can feel and who feels him only in absentia.

THE ART OF THE POSSIBLE: NOTES ABOUT SOME INSTALLATIONS BY HARUN FAROCKI

Christa Blümlinger

A spectre is haunting Europe — the spectre of cinema. Cinema has invaded the realm of the museum; films are 'exhibited', as Dominque Païni has written, with increasing frequency; and a genuine 'cinema as exhibition', in the words of Jean-Christophe Royoux, has taken shape through the medium of the installation.[1] This leads us to wonder why films are 'exhibited' in one way or another. And we wonder all the more when the works in question are not the creations of media artists but installations realised by film-makers.

This shift of spatial context generates a number of effects which can, of course, be described as a kind of break in the thread of cinematic art, but which represent continuity as well. The apparent break is that the transposition of a film into a video installation not only takes possession of a new exhibition space — shifting an art form into a new context — but also and above all opens up new possibilities for the spatial and temporal transformation of visual images. In Harun Farocki's art, this change includes an approach in which a film is not projected at specified times on a movie screen or shown on a monitor or a television screen. Instead, two videotapes are run as endless loops in dual projection. This enables the viewer to confront both the parallel worlds of the assembled images and his own viewing position at the same time. Seen as a sequel in a progression of essayistic films, the medium of video assumes the function of an 'art of the possible' in Farocki's work — in the sense expressed by Francesc Torres, who emphasises the formal flexibility of the multimedia installation and the possibility of establishing links with other disciplines.[2]

When a film-maker reproduces moving images in installations, shifting them from the dark theatre space — where attentive viewers sit — to a more or less well-lighted exhibition room in which viewers walk around freely, there must be a reason for doing so. The motivation lies, perhaps, in the operation of the essayistic form as an ongoing, enquiring search, which can be pursued further in the museum 'using other means'. The motivation behind the work

1 Dominique Païni, *Le temps exposé: Le cinéma de la salle au musée*, Paris: Cahiers du cinéma, 2002. See also Jean-Christophe Royoux, 'Cinéma d'exposition: l'espacement de la durée/Cinema as Exhibition, Duration as Space', *Art Press*, no.262, November 2000, pp.36–41.

2 Francesc Torres, 'The Art of the Possible', *Illuminating Video: An Essential Guide to Video Art* (ed. Doug Hall and Sally Jo Fifer), New York: Aperture, 1990, pp.205–09; quotation from p.207.

of Atom Egoyan, for example, appears to come from this direction, as he has suggested in saying that he has 'always been attracted by films that relate to time and in which viewers are well aware that the passage of time generates a level of introspection and self-enquiry in response to their desire to know why and how the image is captured at a given moment'.[3] Yet the physical shift from the cinema to the installation can, as in the case of Harun Farocki, have a radicalising effect on the essayistic form at a different level, by no means a purely temporal one. If the ongoing, enquiring search is diverted to the montage, it can be articulated in specific ways at the point at which the linearity of image progression is suspended or at least subjected to relative interpretation, and at which the spatial arrangement of images challenges the viewer to discover new ways of seeing.

The shift from film cutting to video editing is of essential importance in this context. This is evident in *Schnittstelle* (*Section*), Farocki's very first installation and a kind of artist's self-portrait, which was realised for the Musée d'Art Moderne in Villeneuve d'Ascq in 1995.[4] In this retrospective look at his own works, Farocki exhibits the electronic editing panel as a laboratory in which the aesthetic difference between film 'editing' and electronic or digital 'compositing' (to quote Lev Manovich), or between film 'montage' and electronic 'mixage' (to use a distinction expressed by Philippe Dubois), becomes visible.[5] The visual and verbal insistence on abstract mathematical models makes it particularly clear in this context that digitised or electronic editing can be understood in the sense articulated by Gene Youngblood.[6] The Turing machine in *Schnittstelle* stands for new approaches to what were originally cinematographic image sequences, as the computer-addressable time code that turns the organisation of the cinematographic space into an abstract structure is derived from mathematics.

In one of his more recent installations, titled *Auge/Maschine* (*Eye/Machine*, 2001),[7] Farocki emphasised the calculable nature of digital images again in a spatial configuration installed as a dual projection. Here one experiences the comparison between analogue images created through the effects of light and recorded or altered by human hands and digitally recorded or processed images registered by machines and altered by computers. Based upon images transmitted by unmanned American surveillance aircraft during the Gulf War, Farocki unfolds a panorama

3 'Relocating the Viewer: An Interview with Atom Egoyan', *Parachute* 103, July/August/September 2001, p.53; quoted in Dominique Païni, *Le temps exposé*, *op. cit.*, pp.74–75.

4 See Christa Blümlinger, 'Harun Farocki, circuit d'images', *Trafic* 21, Spring 1997, pp.44–49.

5 Lev Manovich, *The Language of New Media*, Cambridge, Mass.: The MIT Press, 2001, p.293; Philippe Dubois, 'La question vidéo face au cinéma: Délacements esthétiques', *Cinéma et dernières technologies* (ed. Frank Beau, Philippe Dubois and Gerard Leblanc), Paris and Brussels: De Boeck, 1998, pp.189–205.

6 See Gene Youngblood, 'A Medium Matures: Video and the Cinematic Enterprise' (1984), *Ars Electronica: Facing the Future* (ed. Timothy Druckrey), Cambridge, Mass.: The MIT Press, 1999, pp.43–50; quotation from p.46.

7 *Eye/Machine* (2001) was first shown at the Carnegie Museum of Art in Pittsburgh and then at the ZKM, Karlsruhe, within the exhibition *Ctrl_space* (2001/02), curated by Thomas Y. Levin, Ursula Frohne and Peter Weibel. Farocki then made sequels of this installation, called *Eye/Machine II* (2002), shown in Brügge 2002 (Cultural Capital of Europe), and *Eye/Machine III* (world premiere at the ICA London). The three installations have also been shown together, as at the ZKM, Karlsruhe in 2004.

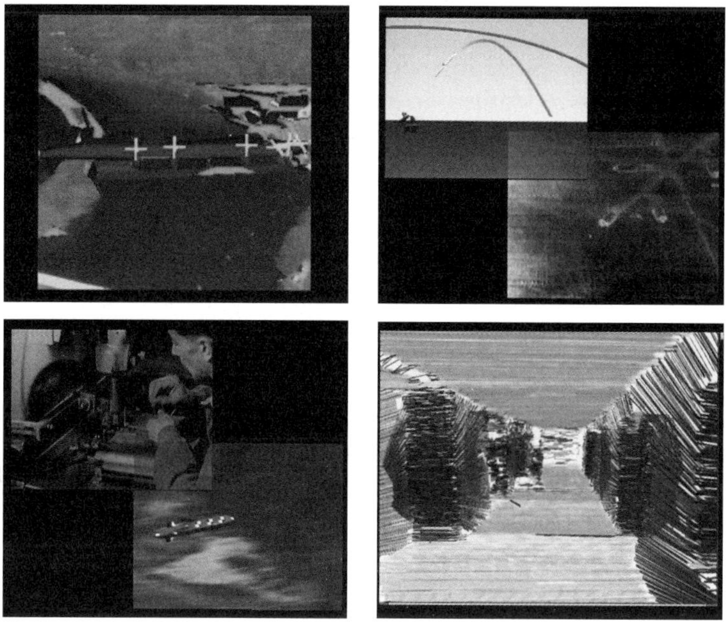

combining civilian and military surveillance technology in which the development of new machines of vision is sketched out as the autonomisation of the look. The artist's arguments are expressed in a montage between imagery and concept — that is between, on the one hand, the digital images and random-sound and, on the other, the intertitles and voices-off that give us a reading of the visual material. In this way, art forges a link to the discipline of technological historiography. This interdisciplinary conceptual approach and the subject of the calculated gaze are already characteristic of Farocki's earlier films *Bilder der Welt und Inschrift des Krieges* (*Images of the World and the Inscription of War*, 1988) and *Wie man sieht* (*As You See*, 1986). The difference between film and installation lies, in Farocki's case, in the mode of representation defined by the spatial setting.

Thus the iterative structure of the film montage becomes immediately obvious in the *Eye/Machine* installation by virtue of the possible coexistence of images. At the beginning of the roughly 20-minute loop, we see two identical images at the same time — military surveillance images of targets from the Gulf War. These recorded images, which Farocki refers to as 'operative', appear a total of four times during each run of the loop, always doubled at first, but then split into image and text and combined with different images each time. The first time they appear their lack of visual clarity is underscored. The emphasis shifts in the second appearance to their predetermined character and the process of deciphering them. In the third appearance, the political dimension of the remote-controlled invasion is associated with civilian simulation techniques used in architecture. The fourth and last time they appear, Farocki refers back to their publication in media coverage of the much-discussed Gulf War — an event some prophets of the Apocalypse say didn't happen, citing the lack of comprehensible visual images. 'Not propaganda, rather advertising for intelligent machines' is the message at the conclusion of Farocki's installation *Eye/Machine*. This summary is expressed in a condensed review of the accelerated progress of surveillance technology during the past ten years. Simulation, recording and presentation techniques that do not involve the human eye have long since found their place in the civilian world, where patients are monitored,

Harun Farocki, stills from *Eye/Machine*, 2000. Colour video, 23mins. Courtesy Harun Farocki Filmproduktion, Berlin

bridges simulated, spaces and objects identified by mobile, 'seeing' robots. Farocki arranges these new images — their visual comprehensibility being progressively perfected by technicians — in a game of repetition and difference that initially confronts the viewer as a puzzle.

If the industrial age replaced manual labour with machine labour, Farocki shows that this substitution is still oriented toward the product of manual labour. He sees machine vision in precisely the same way: the human eye still serves as the standard for certain algorithmically optimised forms of presentation. In the installation *Eye/Machine,* the viewer is offered the comparison between man-made images and technical simulation simultaneously. We see a model bridge rotating in virtual space and, next to it on the right, the film image of the real construction. The graphic structure is the same; only the movement in the picture is different. The bridge no longer moves, but traffic moves on the bridge instead. Here it becomes evident that the differences between the analogue and the digital image are differences of degree. The organisation of images appears much more important than the method used to record or generate them. In Farocki's works, the digital image is shown to be something that works like an information panel. It no longer refers, like the cinematographic screen mask (the famous 'cache' described by André Bazin), to something external, beyond the screen. Farocki aims at a difference between the qualities of being analogue and being digital, which is closely related to Gilles Deleuze's definition of the numeric image, in which 'the position is less similar to that of an eye than to that of an over-stimulated brain that is constantly taking in information: the brain/information pairing replaces the eye/nature pairing'.[8]

Through the doubling of centrally formatted image fields, Farocki pursued expanded cinema further through videographic means. The difference between showing the two tapes next to one another, as was done in the New York gallery Greene Naftali, or at right angles to each other, as was the case at the ZKM, Center for Art and Media in Karlsruhe and at the Le Plateau exhibition hall in Paris, is not merely one of degree for the viewer, who, to keep an eye on both sequences, must move his or her head more in one case and less in the other. The disposition of the images localises the viewer in relation to the exhibition space as well, pulling him or her into a corner (in the case of the right-angle projection) or holding him or her in place in front of a wall (in the side-by-side presentation). The double images may fix the viewer in position perhaps even more than the single-screen projections, due less to an idea of stereoscopic depth, which may emerge in the brief moment

8 Gilles Deleuze, *Cinéma 2: L'image-temps*, Paris: Minuit, 1985, p.349.

9 The work was also presented as an installation at multiple venues in 2001: in the exhibition 'Der Stand der Dinge' at the Kunst-Werke Institute for Contemporary Art, Berlin; in the retrospective 'Harun Farocki: Filme, Videos, Installationen, 1969–2001' at the Westfälischer Kunstverein, Münster; at the Frankfurter Kunstverein and other venues.

10 Farocki's montage system is essayistic, not only because of the complex image-sound relationship he develops, but also because it opposes the convention of linear narration in forming a coherent whole from a system of allusions, repetitions, oppositions and correspondences. I take the liberty of referring to a text of my own in this context: 'Zwischen den Bildern/Lesen', *Schreiben Bilder Sprechen: Texte zum essayistsichen Film* (ed. Christa Blümlinger and Constantin Wulff), Vienna: Sonderzahl, 1992, pp.11–32; quotation from p.18.

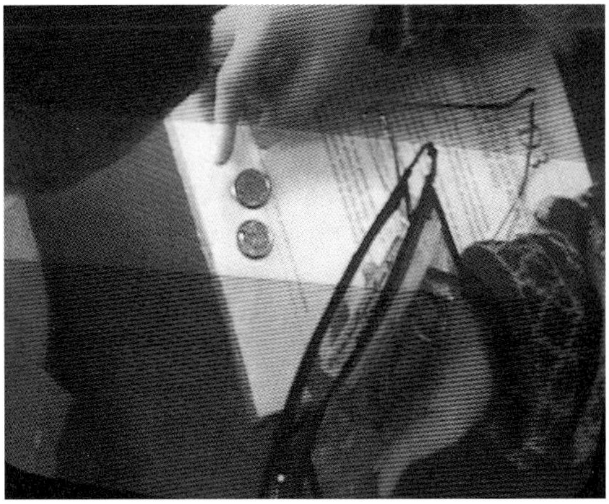
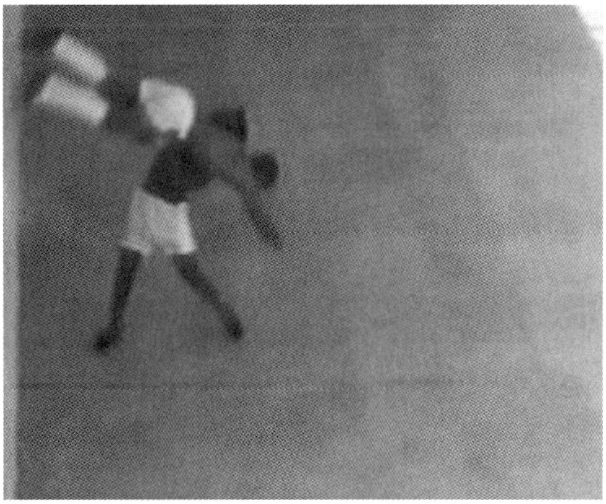

of figurative duplication, than to the direct appeal for heightened attention that is inherent in the exhibition setting.

The viewer of *Eye/Machine* is involved in reflection on the technical images not only by virtue of the written commentary or the specific sequence of images on the individual channels, but above all by the particular arrangement of the two image sequences running in parallel, which he or she is tempted to try to relate to one another. When Farocki feeds into these channels the 'found' machine images he calls 'operative' and at the same time displays their technical production within the context of experiments with robots, he is concerned less with the fascinating performance of new image machines than with the question of the cultural relationship between the human eye and the machines of vision.

In an earlier video installation titled *I Thought I Was Seeing Convicts*, which was realised on commission from the Generali Foundation in Vienna in 2000, Farocki turned his attention to a subject that allowed him to link the question of visual representation with the matter of the viewer's vantage point without losing sight of the political dimension of the represented subject itself.[9] In this installation, the spatial context of surveillance is also exposed to scrutiny as an architectural form of the kind Michel Foucault transposed from Samuel Bentham's Panopticon to other closed institutions for the purpose of analysing the microscopic workings of power in disciplinary societies.

'Found' images are removed from their original instrumental arrangement and used here as material for essayistic figuration.[10] However, the original spatial context remains present as a trace in the inserted intertitles; the printed words; and the part-narrative, part-descriptive and analytical commentaries or original sounds off-camera. In this way, one visual constellation is transported into another in order to be reinterpreted and viewed by the second one. Thus multiple images and visual contexts created independently of one another collide here. Interspersed with intertitles, the recorded images intersect and reflect one another. In complex sequences alternating between two parallel images, they generate a game of repetition

Harun Farocki, stills from *I Thought I Was Seeing Convicts*, 2000. Colour video, sound, 23mins. Courtesy Harun Farocki Filmproduktion, Berlin

and difference. As moments of crystallisation in the installation, such concepts as 'identity', 'surveillance' and 'searching' emerge and expose themselves clearly to view in the field of tension between body and machine, between manual and technical processing. We see not only videographed convicts but also their graphic equivalents in images registered and transmitted by electronic motion sensors. Between surveillance videos from a California high-security prison and computer simulations of movements performed by shoppers in supermarkets, a complex structure of the digital and the analogue, of simultaneity and succession, of the verbal and the visible emerges in Farocki's visual architecture. One could describe these paired arrangements in loops and rotating movements with reference to the structure of the double helix, in keeping with the use of this image in a visual montage-metaphor in Jean-Luc Godard's *Ici et ailleurs* (1974) as well as conceptually by Raymond Bellour.[11]

The basic material for *I Thought I Was Seeing Convicts* originated in various different surveillance contexts. Foucault defined this type of context in *Surveiller et punir* (*Surveillance and Punishment*, 1975) as a configuration of a certain relationship between seeing and visibility. Applied to the waning twentieth century, this surveillance situation can be understood as a model for the central context of the medium of video. In this sense, Anne-Marie Duguet sees the video context as the articulation of specific viewing orientations or modes of involvement on the part of the viewer, but also in a more general way in the sense of the Greek meaning of the word *mèchané*—as the technical configuration of a mechanical system that sets different instances of speech or visual representation in motion.[12] Whereas media artists such as Bruce Nauman, Bill Viola and Dan Graham place the viewer in alternating positions as the subject and object of seeing in their video feedback installations, Farocki, in accordance with his cinematographic principle, does not work in his installation with the loop of live transmission or the dissociation of seeing and being seen, but instead with 'found' surveillance material—that is, with images which were once actually transmitted live in prisons but have now become 'ready-mades' in the artist's archives.

Only at first glance does the gesture involved in working with found footage from surveillance cameras appear to resemble that of Michael Klier

11 See Raymond Bellour, 'La double hélice', *L'entre-images 2: Mots, Images*, Paris: P.O.L., 1999, p.24; first published in Christine van Assche, Catherine David and Raymond Bellour (eds.), *Passages de l'image* (exh. cat.), Paris: Centre Georges Pompidou, 1990. An English translation, 'The Double Helix', can be found in Timothy Druckrey (ed.), *Electronic Culture: Technology and Visual Representation*, New York: Aperture, 1996, pp.173–99.

12 Anne-Marie Duguet, 'Dispositifs', *Communications* 48, 1988, pp.221–42.

13 *Ibid.*, pp.226–27.

14 Marcel Duchamp, *Duchamp du Signe: Ecrits*, Paris: Flammarion, 1976, p.247; quoted in A. Duguet, 'Dispositifs', *op. cit.*

15 Farocki selected this configuration for the installation at the Kunst-Werke but not at the Generali Foundation, where the installation was presented previously as a dual, side-by-side projection of images onto suspended screens in space.

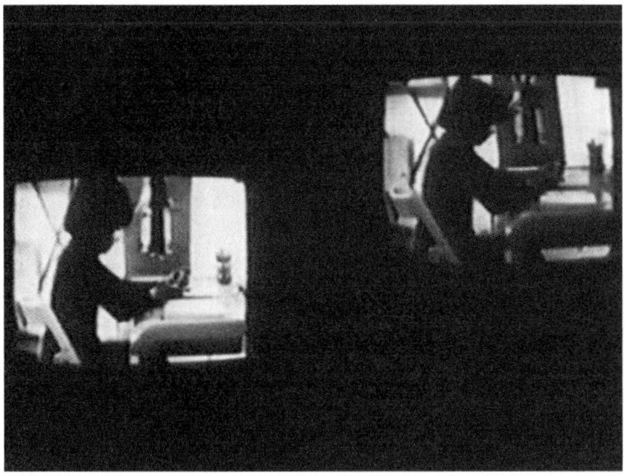

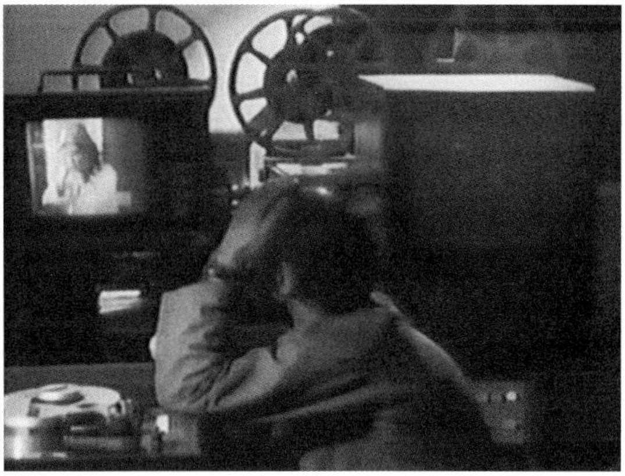

in his film *Der Riese* (*The Giant,* 1983), in which video material recorded automatically in hotels, public facilities and private homes is transformed into a kind of gigantic, fictionalising hyper-installation. A closer look reveals—apart from the difference in the original material itself—another essential distinction between Farocki's work and Klier's. Farocki does not use the cinema context but rather that of a videographic theatre as a medium. By changing spatial contexts, he creates a new visual structure in order to employ the medium of video in the inherent potentiality described by Duguet: as process and as pure visual virtuality, as well as in its metacritical function.[13] Duguet notes that in the context of a theatre of seeing and perceiving, it is, as Marcel Duchamp says, 'the viewers who make pictures'.[14]

The original cinematic principle of montage is both displayed and exposed to critical scrutiny in the installation by virtue of the simultaneous presence of two equivalent images which viewers cannot distinguish from one another. In this theatre of seeing and perceiving, the viewer is challenged to choose between two viewing positions or to shift back and forth between them. Thus, there is an essential aesthetic difference between two forms of presentation in these video works. In addition to the video installation, which exhibits two video screens or enlarges the presentation to a double projection so that the image itself is theatrically staged, in each case Farocki presents a single-channel version, which is shown on television. In this single-channel version, attention is distracted from the spatial constellation of the montage by means of image mixing, the encrustation of one image within the other, in contrast to the installation, which makes a kind of performance out of the montage.

By confronting the viewer with two parallel video images projected at right angles to one another, Farocki places himself virtually where the images *intersect*—at the point, that is, where a syntagmatic or paradigmatic choice must be made between two alternatives.[15] It is a situation which Godard staged symbolically as a question of the medium in his film *Numéro deux* (*Number Two*, 1975), in which two monitors appear again and again as coexisting images. In Godard's film, black frames appear from time to time, in which

Jean-Luc Godard, stills from *Numéro deux* (*Number Two*), 1975. Colour video, sound, 88mins

the position of the author as well as voyeur can be inscribed.[16] In Farocki's work, the intertitles assume this authorial function.

In contrast to Godard's film, the viewer of Farocki's installation finds himself in a theatrical situation by virtue of the spatialised presentation of the images 'facing' each other at right angles. The first task is to find a point of view. The shift of focus takes place in the viewer's gaze. In this way, the installation sets message and utterance in constant motion. A kind of dialogue between the moving-image sequences constantly emphasises the presence of that which is not visible at a given moment. This question clearly leads to the moment Pascal Bonitzer has referred to as the 'blind field'.[17] There is no counter shot of the convicts and consumers who are exposed to the gaze of the surveillance camera, for the viewers that see through the eyes of the camera remain invisible on-screen, like Fritz Lang's *Die Tausend Augen des Dr Mabuse* (*The Thousand Eyes of Dr Mabuse*, 1960). This is also evident in Farocki's prison material. A convict surprised during an attempt to make erotic physical contact leaves the visitors' room without turning his head. The watching eye is not worth a glance, as it cannot be located, even though the convict had previously attempted to build a screen against probing eyes out of chairs, as if there were only one identifiable other.

In contrast to the cinematographic image, the quality of the analogue in the video-surveillance image shifts from a spatial to a temporal level — namely one governed by the principle of real time. The long, static shot calls for action in the image or, as Farocki's commentary points out with respect to the presentation of several literally 'spectacular' scenes, the surveillance image tends, while showing the norm, to the deviation. Farocki derives a cinematic quality from the scenes of deviation by repeating, enlarging and commenting upon them at certain times. He does not claim to neutralise the context of power that is inscribed in the images, but instead seeks to analyse, entirely in keeping with the sense of a moral concept of a (cinematographic) scene. At this point, to which Bazin's equally famous and misunderstood formula 'montage forbidden' could well apply,[18] Farocki adds the external commentary of those who published the material for political purposes. He has an American civil rights activist describe the case of a convict who was shot to death by guards, a prisoner who was fired upon with excessive haste and then left lying unaided for much too long. Because the shooters are positioned like the video cameras and remain out of sight, Farocki provides no substitute for them, no counter-image. He remains in visual terms with the surveillance material in which the traces of violence and power are almost invisibly inscribed, and adds expert

16 See Serge Daney on Jean Luc Godard, 'Der Ton (Sie), das Bild (Er), die Stimme (Sie), das Auge (Er)', in Serge Daney, *Von der Welt ins Bild: Augenzeugenberichte eines Cinephilen* (ed. Christa Blümlinger, trans. Christa Blümlinger, Dieter Hornig and Silvia Ronelt), Berlin: Vorwerk 8, 2000, p.94; originally published in French as 'Le son (Elle), l'image (Lui), la voix (Elle), l'œil (Lui)', *Cahiers du cinéma* 262/263, 1976, p.40.

17 See Pascal Bonitzer, *Le champ aveugle. Essais sur le cinema*, Paris, Cahiers du Cinéma/Gallimard, 1982, especially pp.81–113.

18 André Bazin, 'Montage interdit' (1953–57), in *Qu'est-ce que le cinéma*, Paris: Cerf, 1990, pp.49–61. An English translation can be found in André Bazin, 'The Virtues and Limitations of Montage', *What is Cinema?*, vol.1 (trans. Hugh Gray), Berkeley and Los Angeles: University of California Press, 1967, pp.41–52.

voices-off and intertitles of his own to it. The verbal level opens a new angle of interpretation of the image and the possibility of incorporating an imaginary *off-screen space*. Thus the viewer learns, for example, that white plumes of smoke in the grey image of a California prison yard indicate that a shot has been fired. The unusual intertitles in *I Thought I Was Seeing Convicts* — and also in *Eye/Machine* — could more aptly be called 'lateral titles'; they function within a given image sequence as such, because they present an image that is always readable in co-presence with another image. In interaction with the repetition, this addition generates a deferred-action effect. Something becomes visible and recognisable after the fact. In this sense, the viewer experiences thought in an in-between space, in a disjunction of vision and speech.

'I thought I was seeing convicts' says a horrified Ingrid Bergman in Roberto Rossellini's *Europa 51* (1952), as she describes the frightening sight of factory workers.[19] Gilles Deleuze cites this scene from the film in a short essay on controlled societies, one of his many commentaries on Foucault.[20] His reference to the scene makes clear that the prison serves as a model for analogue systems in closed institutions, in which people are concentrated, distributed in space and regimented in time, and in which a productive power develops within a certain period of time, creating an effect which must be greater than the sum of its elementary powers. Farocki's film is Foucaultian in the sense that its lessons do not relate, as some critical reviews and catalogue texts summarily contend, only to the prison but also extend to an analysis of the disciplinary functions of other public spaces in order to derive an arrangement of power from the structuring of visibility in supermarkets, for example. Foucault describes the function of the Panopticon, which 'must be separated from every specific use' and which can also relate to other institutions, such as schools, military installations or hospitals, as a '*diagram*'.[21]

Characteristically, a series of comparable images appears at the beginning of *I Thought I Was Seeing Convicts* that emphasises the diagrammatic common ground shared by prisons and supermarkets: computer-generated ground plans of a penitentiary resemble the view of a self-service market seen from above; digital images that simulate movements in the shopping area look like digitised representations of convicts under electronic surveillance. 'Identity', as Farocki shows, is defined by a shopping list, by a number, by the location of a cell or the assignment to a tract. The diagrammatic image thus appears initially as a mental projection here, in contrast to the analogue image in the tradition of photography, which is based on the recording of light and time.

19 Rosselini's figures are not called 'convicts' but 'prisoners'. Deleuze refers to them in the original as '*condamnés*', or 'condemned'.

20 Gilles Deleuze, 'Post-scriptum sur les sociétés de contrôle', *Pourparlers: 1972–1990*, Paris: Minuit, 1990, pp.240–45.

21 Michel Foucault, *Surveiller et punir*, Paris: Gallimard, 1975; quoted in Gilles Deleuze, *Foucault*, Paris: Minuit, 1986, p.79.

The surveillance image is a real-time image that, if multiple cameras are involved, produces coexisting images on the editing panel. This montage technique of simultaneous selection, which is familiar to the viewer from various types of live television broadcasting as well as from the electronic culture of public space, is represented in Farocki's installation by the coexistence of two video images. They are opposed by the digital image, which is closely related to the logic of computer games and which, as a composed image, is not based on the Lumière's camera shot as a discrete unit. An early film in Farocki's collage tells the story of a prison visit in a scene filmed from a frontal perspective. This quotation is not merely a nostalgic allusion to a medium or a purely iconographic reference, but points instead to the precarious aesthetic status of the cinematographic image in the early years of the twentieth century, a status that also clings to the present 'post-photographic' images in the grey area between the digital and analogue worlds.

The conceptual opposition of analogue or videographic media and digital or post-photographic images, which is taken for granted as a postulate by media theorists arguing from a purely technical standpoint, is revealed as overly short-sighted in Farocki's figurative demonstration. For the graphically represented and numerically generated positions of figures come astonishingly close to the aesthetics of video-surveillance images, in which out-of-date or cheap optics, material deterioration, poor resolution and the effect of copying interact in a way that approaches the boundaries of figurative representation. The material quality of the use-worn video film thus leads to an almost graphic abstraction, whereas the computer simulation of people's movements strives toward a quality that is characteristic of what Bellour calls the '*virtual analogy*' of scientific model images from meteorology or biology.[22]

This paradoxical relationship between figuration and abstraction is revealed through the mental space that is created by the installation; for by imbuing projected images with spatial character, a view of an in-between space which corresponds to the invisible interval between two successive scenes in the cinema is opened. The highly symptomatic circulation of images between different media—which are transformed, distanciated and reflected according to specifications—is not only reiterated in Farocki's work by means of a cultural technique but also presented as an object of reflection and as a mode of thinking in terms of technological difference.

Translated by John Southard.

22 See R. Bellour, 'La double hélice', *op. cit.*, p.24; or R. Bellour, 'The Double Helix', *op. cit.*, p.185.

VIDEO, FLOWS AND REAL TIME
Maurizio Lazzarato

The book from which the following was excerpted is the product of my encounter with Angela Melitopoulos's work. Her method of filming, editing and contemplating the relationship between the image and the world inspired me to write an 'ontology' of video. Particularly in the following chapter, I limited myself to sketching out the views of various video artists on the nature of the video image and video technology. In Angela Melitopoulos's videotape *Passing Drama* (1999) you can 'see' this ontology instead of laboriously reading about it here.

The Recording (Or: 'Habit')

– I –

If cinema has already revealed that the world is a flow of images and this world of images is in a state of constant transformation, then video technology causes a further deterritorialisation of these flows. Video technology not only shows us the movement, the never-ending variation of images, but also the 'time-matter' from which the images are made (the electromagnetic waves). Video technology is a mechanical arrangement that establishes a relationship between a-significant flows (waves) and significant flows (the images). It is the first technical means of producing images that reflects the 'general decoding of the flows'.[1]

1 The electric flow, which can be considered the realisation of a random flow as such, can serve as an example of a technical means of expression that corresponds to the general deterritorialisation of the flows in capitalism. Marshall McLuhan puts it another way: 'Electric light is pure information, a medium without a message.' As a consequence, all images produced by electronic and digital technologies are transformations and combinations (composites) of intensities, forces, fields, taking place in the flow — the electromagnetic flow in the case of video, the optical flow in the case of the telematic, the algorhythmic flow in the case of the computer. The transition from the first to the last can be defined as an increasingly forced deterritorialisation. Fibre-optic cables replace copper. Lasers and silicon cables make the control and canalisation of light possible and now replace the electric shock as the vector of information bound to the net. The flow of information overcomes, again, matter, and light is just a mathematic (non-discursive) language. But in all cases, the relationship between a-significant and significant flows is the most interesting as a newly introduced paradigm — the images and sounds are produced by machines with matter consisting of new materials that are being endlessly and variably modulated, and from which the flows are made. Actually, 'these figures do not derive from a signifier nor are they even signs as minimal elements of the signifier; they are non-signs, or rather non-signifying signs, point-signs having several dimensions, flows-breaks or schizzes that form images through their coming together in a whole, but that do not maintain any identity when they pass from one whole to another. Hence the figures, that is, the schizzes or breaks-flows are in no way "figurative"; they become figurative only in a particular constellation that dissolves in order to be replaced by another one.' Gilles Deleuze and Félix Guattari, *Anti-Oedipus*, Paris: Les Éditions de Minuit, 1972 (here, mpls. 1977), p.241. 'Semiotics, languages, codifications that no longer pass through human subjectivity but open themselves to other processes of subjectification and other developments.' *Ibid.*, p.242.

Photography is already a technology that crystallises time because the image is bound to the shutter speed and, therefore, to the ability to capture time. It registers a development by fixating it. Film makes the still image run, thus causing the 'illusion' of movement (according to Henri Bergson's definition).[2] Yet video technology captures movement itself: not something moving in space, but the 'pure oscillations' of light.

Angela Melitopoulos summarises the specificity of this movement:

> For video, light is movement. The movement lies, above all, in the structure of the video image. It is often stronger in the structure of the image than in the object that is depicted and moving through the space. Video is directly bound to light because video transforms and codes light through a technology. Movement is produced with the electronic structure of the image, its lines, grid, its granulation. Movement, frequencies, atoms and energy exist in the objects. Video technology makes these energetic objects and thereby also another reality, visible.[3]

In terms of the technical creation of images, the genetic element of cinema is still the photogram. With montage, a further genetic element is introduced: a temporal element. Video, as stated by Nam June Paik, 'is time'.

From this point of view, cinematic technology still lies in the transition period before the epoch of the general deterritorialisation of flows. Cinematic technology couples the photographic image (the chemical impression of light on a carrier) to a process (the succession of images). The production of images by the machine is also not the result of an arbitrary (electronic) flow. It does not yet employ the endless variety of a-significant figures. It does not yet submerge itself in the matter of the images.

The video image is not an immovable still set in motion by a mechanical arrangement. Instead, it is a constantly reshaping profile painted by an electronic paintbrush. It takes its movement from the oscillations of matter; it is this oscillation itself. Video technology is a modulation of the flows — their image is nothing more than a relationship between flows. The video image is a result of contraction or dilation of the time-matter.[4]

> In the video, the arrangement of the shots is not what creates movement, but the movement of the light ... I not only work on the arrangement of the shots, but also on the movement of light and the molecular granulation of the video image. If the cinemagraphic patterns are too dominant it does not work. When I began working with video, I noticed that the movement of the images is not bound to the displacement of something in space ... that first became clear to me while I was working with video ... by slowing the video image down (dilating time) the movement did not lessen. Instead, it sped up through the movement of the granulation. In film, deceleration is due to a slower succession of shots — that has nothing to do with video.[5]

For the viewer, new speeds, which reflect just as many vectors of non-human subjectivisation, are made visible through the contraction or dilation of movement. The molecular 'becoming', the molecular alignments in Melitopoulos's video '*Passing Drama*' refer to minorities (migrants) and are the main origin of the hate Western societies hold for them. The video image becomes the echo of the movement of the great deterritorialised, of the migrant proletariat here.

The image presents itself to memory (the montage) not as an icon but as a chain of points and lines. The video image is a result of lines and intertwining. Different from a piece of woven material, the video image unceasingly weaves and intertwines with constantly new motifs. In *Passing Drama*, the images of looms not only serve as sociological descriptions but also simultaneously create a paradigm for the construction of images. Should one think of Plato here and his use of weaving as a metaphor for politics? Flows cannot be represented. They can only be compiled or arranged. One can dissolve flows in order to make others from them (hybridisation).

The difficulty of 'politically' representing minorities and the difficulty of using video as a means of 'aesthetic' representation have the same origin: the deterritorialisation of flows.

If real politics are to be searched for in ontology, as the classical period teaches us, then the politics of the video are also to be looked for in ontology. Weaving, dissolving and re-weaving flows — instead of representing them as the migrants as in *Passing Drama* — is radical constructivism in politics as well as in the video image.

– II –

Video artists already claimed the 'Bergsonic' characteristics of video technology and its specific difference to cinema in the 1960s. The film camera is too close to the illusion of perception as the impression of images on the medium, while the video camera must only be hooked up to see that there are images.

'One must not have a video recorder in order to make a video. One operates the video camera and the circuits are immediately put into action, something hums, something functions [...] everything is connected, a dynamic, living system, a field of energy.'[6] We find ourselves in the dimension of pure oscillations, the flowing of time-matter. The decision to record something means turning on the video recorder and not the camera. 'The camera always

2 It must be emphasised that Bergson, who limited himself to the critique of the illusion of movement, was not able to comprehend the crystallisation of time as an activity of cinema. As Andrei Tarkovski noted, 'for the first time in the history of the arts and culture, man has found the means to fix time and simultaneously reproduce it, to repeat it and return to it as often as possible. Man has a matrix of real time. Once it was seen and fixed, time could be conserved from now on in metal boxes, theoretically, forever.' Andrei Tarkovski, *Le temps scellé*, Paris: Cahiers du Cinéma, 1989, p.59. But the 'matrix of real time' first found its appropriate technological order in video.

3 Interview with Angela Melitopoulos by Maurizio Lazzarato, 'Vidéo, temps et mémoire', *Chimères*, no.27, Winter 1996.

4 In the film cut, the movement of the images is not determined by the projector as Bergson assumed when he compared human perception to the 'illusion of movement' created by cinematography. According to Bergson, the cinematographer records momentary poses (the photograms) and reconstructs the movement by adding mechanical movement to the images. Bergson neglected to see that the film cut distributes a past and a future, the actual appearance of time.

5 'Vidéo, temps et mémoire', *op. cit.*, p.96.

6 Bill Viola, 'L'espace à pleine dent', *Cahiers du Cinéma* (special issue 'Où va la Vidéo'), no.14, 1986, p.65.

works: there is always an image. There is always something that already works before it starts — like in the universe.'[7] When making a video production, one intervenes, connects to the continual process of universal change that already existed before one ever intended to use it. One ensconces oneself in the flow. This duration could be called 'real time', a duration that is unknown to film. Television made this feature of video technology, of the endless proliferation of images, 'visible'. With television, the world is always already an image. One must no longer represent, no longer create an image. 'We do not create images, we process them', say video artists.

– III –

In order to summarise the specific difference between the technical dispositives of film and video, we need analytical support.

Gilles Deleuze made a brilliant connection between the film image and Bergson's philosophy (I am indebted to his work for the consistence of my thoughts). Deleuze makes a very exact and original comparison between the term 'pure perception' and the fact that film depicts the world as a world of images for us.

With Bergson, we have defined pure perception as image-matter, but one must remember that this is about the image in principle, unseen by the human eye. It would be more exact to speak of flows of light or even of unlimited oscillations, pure stimulants, in order to make this term perceptible for our conscience (with an image). The image as we normally understand it is already a construction, the fixing of pure perception. The image is already a selection and contraction of pure oscillations that follows the need for action. 'But in truth this independent image is an artificial and belated product of our mind.'[8]

To use one of Bergson's lovely expressions, the image of our perception — like the video image — is created from 'visual dust'. Video technology allows us 'access' to something that belongs to the dimension of pure perception beyond the image, to the flows of light, to the flows of the flux-matter. Video assails and processes something of pure perception, which Bergson writes about. Pure perception exists only as abstraction for us because a filter that makes something visible is necessary for it to appear.

> A large sieve must intervene here like an elastic and shapeless membrane, like an electromagnetic field in order to have something emerge from this chaos ... from the physical point of view, chaos would be a universal attack of dizziness, the entirety of all possible perceptions as infinitesimal or endlessly small as they may be; the sieve extracts the differences that integrate themselves into regulated perception.[9]

7 *Ibid.*
8 Henri Bergson, *Oeuvres*, Paris: PUF, 1991, p.304.
9 G. Deleuze, *Le Pli*, Paris: Les Éditions de Minuit, 1988, p.104.
10 *Ibid.*, p.73.
11 *Ibid.*, pp.227–28.

According to Deleuze, there are countless filters or sieves placed on top of each other, with our senses as the top-most layer and leading down to the 'last filters beyond which would be pure perception (chaos)'. The electromagnetic sieve working in video is much closer to pure perception as the filter which is our senses.

According to Bergson, memory functions like Nam June Paik's synthesiser — namely as a capacity to reconstruct a continuity between what is dilated and what is not, quality and quantity. A new matter is thereby constituted, a new force of metamorphosis and creation.

– IV –

For Bergson, our concrete perception is the contraction of endless oscillations into an element of time, a synthesis of the flows of pure 'matter-perception' ... What is an image? It is the process in which millions of oscillations or pure vibrations are condensed or synthesised onto a receptive surface. The image is therefore a contraction of flows.

> The qualitative heterogeneity of our subsequent perceptions of the universe comes from each of these perceptions dilating itself to a specific density of duration. In this process, memory condenses an enormous variety of oscillations that all appear at the same time although they actually follow each other.[10]

In one moment we condense an extremely long 'history' that takes place in the outside world. If we take the example of 'red light', which has the longest wavelength and its oscillations therefore have the lowest frequency, we find that in a single moment 400 million oscillations follow each other. What we perceive as red light is a distribution, a contraction of this duration according to the contraction-dilation ability of our own duration; these abilities are not physiologically defined, but defined through the force of action.

> If we could dilate this duration, experience it in a slower rhythm, would we not then perhaps see — while this rhythm is gradually slowing down — how the colors become thinner and thinner, lengthening into subsequent impressions, each of which is doubtlessly still colored, yet increasingly tends to mingle with the pure oscillations?[11]

Bergson calculates that one would need 250 centuries in order to see the principal duration of a moment of the colour red. Memory then causes a contraction of 'pure duration' (which can save an endless number of phenomena) in a human duration which is solidified and distributed by it. This distribution takes place through space. Actually, Bergson claims that we cannot comprehend our perception as a relationship of temporalities because we habitually relate all of our movements to space. Our perception always covers a homogenous space via the uncertain variety (the infinite duration) of matter. Instead, one must observe movements in time. That is exactly what video does. From this point of view, video is closer to reality than natural perception — the disappearance of which is often lamented.

– V –

This explains Paik's assertion that 'video is time'. The dispositive of video technology 'imitates' the relationship between different temporalities that Bergson writes about. How does video produce colour? By modulating the flow of the flux-matter through technology in a specific way that influences the flow coming into being.

The video machine acts like the brain by translating movements, which are not perceivable in our categories of space and time, into movements that can be perceived. The pure perception of video technology, its energy-matter, exists in the electromagnetic waves, the pure oscillations from which images are 'produced'. The colour is an electromagnetic wave with specific 'oscillations' that are contracted by the video machine in a duration we can perceive. But, here, it is technology that operates like the mind (subjectivity) because it is the machine which translates the duration of pure perception into a human duration.

Let us listen to Paik:

> Since televisual space does not exist, all spatial information must be translated into undilated lines and points; then the signal can be wirelessly transferred to only one channel. All colors must be set to the same line. For this purpose, a kind of social contract has been created. A wave, called the 'color carrier wave', is equal to a second divided by 3.5 million. These very short waves are again subdivided into numerous phases: 7 colors represent, for instance, the colors of the rainbow. The first seventh of this wave is called 'blue', the next seventh 'yellow', the next 'orange' etc. A circuit opens and closes very fast (21 million times a second), whereby it lets the colors through according to their sequential order. In television, like in nature, color is created through a very fast temporal sequence. Making a film means letting nature be colored by chemical substances through the lens. But in television, there is no direct relationship between reality and images. Only code systems exist. Therefore, we enter the temporal dimension.[12]

The video image is a modulation-contraction in the flow of the flow of light. Memory does not determine this relationship in the machine, but rather the technological dispositive. Video perception is closer to the dispositive Bergson described than to the physiology of the eye. It is a technology that 'contracts' movement-matter and wave-matter into a human duration. By technologically processing duration and time, colour is returned to our perception. Natural perception exists in a transformation of the a-significant flows, which are made perceptible by the intervention of the brain and the memory. Video technology 'imitates' this relationship between flows and conscience.

In the relationship Bill Viola erects between our perception and the video camera, we also find remnants of Bergson's ontology.

The television image is a constant transit of waves of electric energy, a system of oscillation. Of specific frequencies as they are pictured in an object that oscillates. The image we see on the surface of the cathode tube is the trace of a point of light in movement, which is part of a flow of electrons that hit the back of the screen and light up the phosphorous on the surface in video technology, there is no constant (still) image. The weave of all television images, whether still or moving, is the radioactive bundle of electrons that are continually thrown out, an incessant flow of electric impulses arriving from the camera or the video recorder. The separation into lines or frames is only a division in time: the opening or closing of windows in time that demarcates the periods of activity on the inside of the progressing flow of electrons. This way, the image is a living and dynamic field of energy, an oscillation that only appears stable insofar as it goes beyond our ability to perceive such small units of time.[13]

Montage — 'Processing' (or Memory)

A video recording can be compared to the sensory-motor function of the body described by Bergson. The technical dispositive of a video recording actually transforms only one movement into another, even if the possibilities of the contraction-dilation are much more numerous than those of our body. The video camera only works within the realm of the present. The techniques of processing images (montage) allow us, however, to imitate the 'free' work of memory.[14] Similar to how the ('raw') perception of 'synthesising' activity of 'intellectual work' is processed, processing the 'recording' makes an 'endless' production of images possible through electronic image processing.

Technology then multiplies only the ability of intellectual work, although video is only the first step in endowing the machine with a memory that begins to resonate with the 'actual' object and can then reproduce the circuit between the 'actual' image and its memory. The technologies for processing images are technologies for the synthesisation of flows. The length of time determined by the video camera can be processed and therefore installs a degree of 'freedom'.

For Paik, only image processing can instil 'true memory' in video technology. He believed that the video camera is nothing more than a dispositive of input and output time that is tuned in to the flow (waves) of light, meaning a dispositive with absolutely no degree of freedom: it reproduced contractions and dilations as a matter of habit. If one limits oneself to letting the dispositive of the video camera function, then one finds

12 Nam June Paik, *Du Cheval à Christo et autres Écrits*, Paris: Lebeer Hossman, 1993, p.110.

13 Bill Viola, Valentina Valentini (ed.), *Vedere con la Mente et con il Cuore*, Rome: Gangemi Editore, 1993, p.73.

14 The work of the body and the brain is an automatic work, in which memory has no freedom. It is completely absorbed in the fulfilment of the goal-oriented action, the memory contracts and dilates time, but it is a repetitive 'habit'. Memory cannot 'freely' produce images, and it is only 'intellectual work' from the moment it is separated from the necessity of goal-oriented action. It can then introduce uncertainty, the unforeseen in the process of perception. The magnetoscope and the perfected techniques of image processing create a greater freedom in the contraction-dilation of the flows in the same manner.

oneself in the 'present' — namely, in the simple contraction-dilation and the perception-matter. But in order to contract or dilate the time of memory, one must employ the techniques of image processing.

> [Y]et it is real life (life 'live', so to speak) that makes the relationship of input and output time much more complicated. This is how, for instance, one's whole life can be relived in the fragment of a second in the form of flashbacks during extreme moments or in our dreams [...] or — like Proust — we can repeat a short period of our childhood over the course of our entire life practically in the isolation of a room with a cork wallpaper. That means certain fragments of the input time can be purposely dilated or contracted in the output time [...] exactly this quantitative and also qualitative metamorphosis is the function of our brain. The process of editing is nothing more than the simulation of this function of the brain.[15]

With Bergson, one could say that electronic image processing simulates memory and intellectual work more than 'the material syntheses'. The compression and dilatation Paik speaks of work with the duration crystallised by the video camera. Once again, the difference between this process and the film cut is remarkable.[16]

Based on the hypothesis that the video recorder already provides a — perhaps 'coarsening' — simulation of intellectual work, Viola defines the transition from video technology to digital technology as a further development of the relationship between perception and memory. 'After the first video camera (together with its recorder) gave us an eye combined with a primitive form of non-selective memory, we have now entered the next stage of development: the age of perception and the intelligent — though artificial — structures of thought.'[17]

Angela Melitopoulos experiments with the subjective bifurcations made possible through the work of placing images in a new order (montage): an ecology of the mind, an opportunity for resistance that resists the media's takeover of attention and memory:

> In the course of my work with video I have constructed something that could possibly be called a second niveau of memory that is bound to the machine. Aside from that, I also better understand my own memory through the work with video. I can reconstruct a chain of memory around an event that had been experienced but forgotten. I start to film and establish a relation to my experience then I scan the chains of images forwards or backwards at various speeds; simultaneously, various genres of images develop within the process. At the same time, other associations

15 N. J. Paik, *Du Cheval à Christo et autres Écrits*, *op. cit.*, pp.124–25.

16 'One should not say cut, but process, video processing (as said in English) in order to define the work of the electronic structure and images. Montage/cut are part of the cinematic language. It means bringing the shot and the sound together. Processing, on the other hand, means putting the image together. The image therefore begins to change somewhere, to become something else and something else again. You don't even have to see the image at the beginning, it is not predefined.' 'Vidéo, temps et mémoire', *op. cit.*

17 Bill Viola, *La Vidéo*, Paris: Communications, p.72.

18 'Vidéo, temps et mémoire', *op. cit.*

are called up and I can use them to construct a parallel path. Possible memories are sometimes more exact than 'real' memories. Through its vision, my memory is taken care of differently, by recoding the work referred to, I can create my own memory or at least something lying in my memory.[18]

The object of contemporary economy is linked to the question of how memory can be constructed; how one's attention can be steered towards the ability to be able to characterise one's wishes, beliefs and sensations, or to perceive their effects by dissolving flows and reassembling new ones. The public is the true customer of this economy. How to resist and create new worlds with a camera that is integrated in the flows (of cyberspace)?

Translated by Stephan Gregory, Angela Melitopoulos, Erik Stein, Stephan Geene and Rosanne Altstatt.

FIVE YEARS LATER
Bill Horrigan

Around the beginning of Lent in 2006, I was researching the film-maker Patrick Keiller when I came upon a back issue of the British journal *Vertigo*. It contained an article Keiller had contributed to a section on Jean-Luc Godard, in advance of the then-forthcoming Godard season at the National Film Theatre and a related conference at Tate Modern. (The text recounts how *Deux ou trois choses que je sais d'elle* (*Two or Three Things I Know About Her*, 1967) played a catalytic role in his own practice.) As I was about to close the journal, I glanced at the page directly following Keiller's piece and was struck to see it held a full-page advertisement for Tate Modern's next conference, in June 2001, titled 'Moving Image as Art: Time-Based Media in the Art Gallery'. More startling was seeing my name listed among the participating speakers.[1]

It's not that I'd forgotten the event or my attendance at it. It's just that the brief for the conference — the issues that justified, for those of us tending then as now to dwell on such things, this 'international conference [that] brings together artists, critics, historians and curators ... ' — seems today to belong to a different moment entirely. That's partly because the artistic practices of the five years since this conference, and the commentary greeting (or not greeting) them, have clarified the conference's issues as a last gasp made in the face of the inevitable, embodied in the occupation of the gallery by moving-image media.

To be clearer, here's what the conference set out to interrogate: ' ... the issues raised by moving images in art galleries, such as: What do galleries do to the moving image? In what context should history locate the moving image in art? What is the status of cinema in the light of gallery film/video?' Further instruction to the speakers elaborated: 'It can be argued that the now familiar use of film and video in the gallery is talked about as if they are a new art media. Are any connections with the past use of these media in fact trivial and epiphenomenal? I would ask you to take a view of within what histories, if any, film and video in the gallery could be seen.'

Embedded within those questions, and in the tones of voice in which they were posed, was the institutional admission (a 'conservative' one, coming as it did from a museum, although one in its behaviour actively accommodating a fuller range of opinion and action) that, like it or not, 'film and video in the gallery' was not a migration likely to be stemmed any time

1 *Vertigo*, vol.2 no.1, Spring 2001, pp.32–33.

soon; hence its history ought to be commissioned and its furtherance might be managed in an informed relation to that.

What follows here is an excerpt, more or less verbatim, of what I said at the Tate gathering in 2001, part of a longer address interspersed with a number of diversionary video clips.

—

In thinking about this occasion, I kept returning to wonder why, in fact, these questions were now felt to have a specific urgency. That is, why does the fact of moving images in the gallery now require interrogation as a phenomenal occurrence? And so to begin I thought it might be useful to speak in some fashion about that question, and in particular to wonder what exactly is 'new' about any of this such as to make the question itself 'new'.

The term 'film and video in the gallery' is an inelegant formulation, but at what point did we cease referring to this simply as video or as video art, which up until the early to middle 1990s still had widespread usefulness as a descriptive generic term? Hence this question: whither video? Last year, in the spirit of the millennial passage, both the Art Institute of Chicago and the Museum of Modern Art in New York announced symposia on 'The History of Video Art', each taking a multi-week format that would chart the form's emergence and development, from the 1960s to the present. (The MoMA event didn't take place due to a strike, but the symposium's structures and themes had nevertheless been clearly set out in its promotional material.)

What was striking in both instances was that each identified a golden age of video ending around 1990, with developments since then cast as a fallen state relative to its bygone glories. Each of these gatherings rested on the assumption that the practice of video art had a history able to be narrated with coherence and discretion — video certainly not unformed by its affinities with other postmodern tendencies but video enjoying a strong, unique identity as a tape-based medium for electro-mechanically producing moving images.

That's not to say that even to its practitioners had video ever fitted easily into a narrow niche; even within the limited and irreducible conditions of what technically qualified as video there have been during video's lifespan at least two great traditions: video deployed as an element within a gallery-based installation, or video as a single-channel programme — in other words, video as a museum practice involving objects and spectacle and implying a certain kind of contract with a presumed viewer, or video, more or less, as a television programme with viewing conditions more or less incidental.

This is, of course, already a simplification of the pre-1990 video landscape; all the same, video (meaning, video's producers) did gravitate to these fundamentally different usages, yet they were not felt to be in conflict with one another — simply two indications of video's adaptability and usefulness for artistically or didactically expressive purposes. Looking back on this period, the installation artist Rita Myers made this observation:

> That video emerged during the final stages of the modernist enterprise is crucial. While it did attempt to locate its 'inherent properties' like a good modernist medium, these properties were inextricably linked to subject matter, a natural consequence of the camera; but also a radical shift away from the other modernist media, painting, sculpture, etc. You can't really reduce a medium to its constituent elements when one of those elements virtually gives you back the world. Video challenged the modernist creed with content, and it continues to challenge the traditional museum/gallery world with moving parts and time, among other things.[2]

Myers's analysis dates from the 1980s, when video installation did represent a meaningful advanced practice within contemporary art, as artists incorporated video-based images into increasingly theatrical and sculptural demonstrations of *mise-en-scène*. One way of appreciating this ascent is by seeing it as the removal of video from the monitor—one obstacle to video's full integration into the art world having been its problematic reliance on viewing technologies essentially identical to those of television. For video to have entered the gallery system in the first place, it had to establish its specificity, and one way it did that was to differentiate itself from its apparent close relation, its first cousin, which was film. But video was different from film in two major ways: on the level of production, it had an immediacy and a different kind of malleability and reproducibility; and instead of being projected large, as cinematic spectacle, it was viewed small, contained in a box (hence, again, its kinship with television). These two material conditions were fed back into early formulations of the presumed aesthetics of video into video theory—video as individual experience versus cinema's narcotic mass spectacle.

But unlike film, video had a history of almost constant technological change, quite different from the relatively static or stable system of film technology. Incrementally in the late 1980s but then massively by the mid-90s, the technological means for aesthetically acceptable video projection became commonplace. Initially thought of as a mere technical development, the reality of video projection encouraged artists to realise the experiential differences between producing work meant to be viewed individually on a small TV monitor, and producing work that brought viewers face to face with wall-sized moving imagery. The video literature of the late 80s is rife with commentary and speculation on the theoretical ramifications of projection versus monitor, and it was not uncommon then for artists to refuse having their work seen via projection, an aesthetic principle maintained by artists whose use of video was allied precisely with the conviction that video was not cinema, i.e. not projected, not spectacle.

In my view, the increasing dormancy of what had been generally understood as 'video art' is tied closely to the triumph of projection over monitor-based presentation, which had been the guarantee of video's

2 Rita Myers, quoted in Marita Sturken, 'Paradox in the Evolution of an Art Form: Great Expectations and the Making of a History', *Illuminating Video: An Essential Guide to Video Art* (ed. Doug Hall and Sally Jo Fifer), San Francisco: Aperture and Bay Area Video Coalition 1990, p.19.

specificity within the gallery-based system. In turn, it is that dominance of projection that haunts this present discussion, to the extent that 'film and video in the gallery' — what used to be called video art — is now being brought back into the fold of one of its presiding aesthetic progenitors, which is that of cinema. By this I mean nothing other than the public consumption of projected, mechanically-produced moving images and video's incorporation as a historically specific dialect within that language, that history — cinema itself perhaps as post-photograph, but video certainly as post-cinema. The concluding mild irony here is that the triumph of video projection such as to welcome video back into the family of cinema is occurring at a moment when both those practices are being further transformed by the onslaught of digitality, an incomparably more revolutionary shift in terms of production and delivery than video represented *vis-à-vis* film.

—

So much for how it looked to me in June 2001. To circle a bit further around the 'mild irony' noted above, the concluding years of the last century also witnessed puzzled commentary within the culture and entertainment sectors on the death of cinema itself, an assertion made most public by Susan Sontag's serenely assured essay 'The Decay of Cinema' (1996).[3] Sontag spawned much response and counter-response, including, indirectly, a symposium at New York's Museum of Modern Art in 2000, at which it was more or less concluded that digital projection systems would, easily within a generation, become standard at commercial cinema venues. That prediction was far safer than the related ones having to do with home delivery eliminating the practice of movie-going altogether.

Still, it wasn't cinema's death that convened the panel at Tate a year later, but the migration of some of cinema's practices, affects and effects across the border into the gallery. As part of my talk, I chose a number of clips, gathered largely due to their assumed unfamiliarity to much of the audience (Warhol's double-screen film projection *Paul Swan*, 1965, and Todd Haynes and Christine Vachon's video loop *Domestic Violence*, 1996), but also grounded within my own curatorial practice of the past decade, much of which had been spent abetting the presence of moving images in the gallery (with the rest of my time spent putting moving images where they'd always been, on the cinema screen). In reflecting five years later on the Tate event and its wish to comprehend the new postures being assumed by video when institutionally framed, and on my own view of that in relation to cinema's establishing the gallery as a colony for itself, I was struck by how the succession of moving image-based projects I myself had been involved in presenting enacted unwittingly the transformational passage of video that my talk had, in part, been addressing.

3 Susan Sontag, 'The Decay of Cinema', *The New York Times Magazine*, 25 Febuary, pp.6–10.

I've worked at the Wexner Center for the Arts in Columbus, Ohio since it opened in 1989, and its first video installation, one of a series of events marking its inaugural exhibition, was the debut of Julia Scher's *Occupational Placement*, a building-wide, multi-monitor piece continuing the artist's explorations of surveillance technology. The installation offered viewers the sight of themselves live, intercut with pre-recorded textual overlays; the monitors also switched randomly to other live and pre-recorded views throughout the building. To that extent, Scher's piece (which also availed itself of fairly primitive computer technology to generate the random sequencing) fell squarely within the interactive sculptural installations of its time; but, having been given the entire building as her canvas, Scher also occupied its film theatre, training surveillance cameras on the seated theatre audience and then projecting the results on the theatre's screen so that viewers could gaze upon themselves via Scher's camera in scenes intercut once more with views of other parts of the building. Despite being state-of-the-art circa 1989, the video projection left much to be desired, providing an image with none of the clarity of film and much less sharpness than the same images had when viewed on video monitors elsewhere in the building. Yet one of the defining elements of Scher's piece was its embrace of a specifically cinematic *dispositif*.[4]

If Scher's piece prefigured her work of the 1990s, which became alternately more web-based and more theatrical and performative in its installation forms, Paper Tiger Television's project *Dream House* (1991) represented a translation into gallery form of their trademark television programmes. Designed to celebrate the New York City-based, progressive media collective's tenth anniversary, *Dream House* consisted of a cut-away construction of a 'typical' American house embedded within a single gallery, into each room of which were placed television sets (not the neutral monitors common to most museum presentational protocols) with Paper Tiger programmes constantly playing (their titles viewable upon request). As an environment it was entirely interactive, to the extent of encouraging visitors to take naps in the bedroom or living room, have coffee in the kitchen and hang out anywhere else. But Paper Tiger Television as a collective artistic entity had fundamentally never been about anything other than producing innovative, issue-based political programming. Hence an invitation to the collective to occupy a space at the Wexner was accepted and played out with inviting decorative gambits, but with an insistence finally on video as medium allied (ironically or adversely) to television. Indeed, in the history of American video, Paper Tiger Television has persisted as the most successful and influential champion of the medium as a politically allied agent for information and change. (Its subsequent spin-off Deep Dish Television provides satellite

4 Bill Horrigan, 'Absorption Complete', *Julia Scher: Always There* (ed. Caroline Schneider and Brian Wallis), New York: Lukas & Sternberg 2002, pp.3–27.

5 Daniel Marcus (ed.), *Roar! The Paper Tiger Guide to Media Activism*, New York and Columbus: Paper Tiger Television and Wexner Center for the Arts, 1991.

6 Chris Marker, quoted in Bill Horrigan, 'Another Likeness', *Chris Marker: Silent Movie*, Columbus: Wexner Center for the Arts, 1995, p.2.

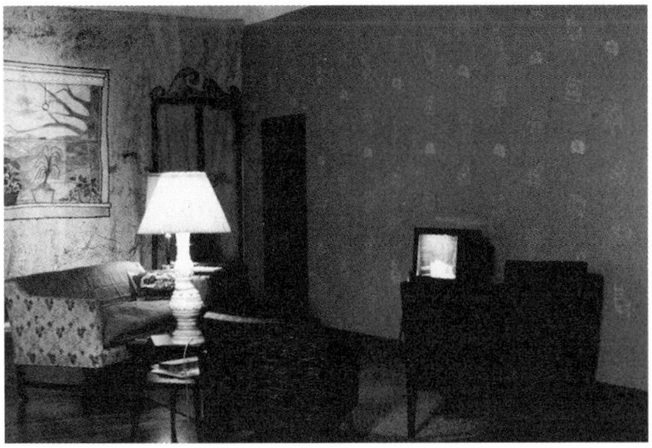 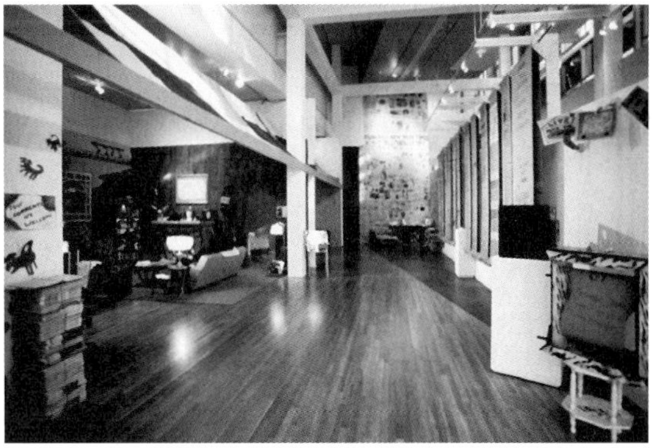

television and online platforms for the activist agenda originally executed simply through its video projects.)[5]

Scher and Paper Tiger Television, the first two large installations I worked on at the Wexner, now seem to me to have embodied the two dominant tendencies by which video had come to be defined during its relatively short life: video as one element in a sculptural elaboration and video as a television programme manoeuvring outside the system of dominant broadcasting.

After that, I was less often involved in presenting work by 'video artists' than by producers of moving images. From then on, those projects carried on a conversation with traditions of cinema, either through outward presentational apparatus or in forms of inner speech, and only secondarily to the accumulated legacy of video art. The film-makers whose work I helped place in the gallery, never abandoning traditional cinema forms entirely for the sake of the museum, all availed themselves of moving-image technology—the possibilities of its presentational apparatuses—to develop projects freeing spectators of cinema's fixed viewpoint dependency and defying cinema's conventions of duration.

Chris Marker's installation *Silent Movie* (1995), produced to mark the cinema's centenary, consisted of a Constructivist-like metal tower containing five stacked monitors, each of which played about 20 minutes of monochromatic imagery gathered around the separate themes of the journey, the gesture, the face and the waltz, with the middle monitor running textual fragments recalling the intertitles of silent cinema. On the walls surrounding the installation were hung a series of black-and-white frame captures of the actress Catherine Belkhodja as she figured, muse-like, within the video channels, as well as a dozen digitally-produced posters for imaginary silent films (e.g. *Hiroshima, Mon Amour*, starring Gloria Swanson and Sessue Hayakawa; a Lubitsch *Remembrance of Things Past*, with John Barrymore as Swann and Ramon Novarro as Morel; etc.) Because the computer interface piloting the installation generated perpetually different sequences and visual relationships across the five monitors, Marker's lyrical meditation was constantly self-altering, and he himself assessed the effect as 'the Kulechov experiment extended to writing'—here in tones variously whimsical, elegiac, awe-struck and bemused.[6]

Paper Tiger Television, *Dream House*, Wexner Center for the Arts, 1991. Photo © 2008 Richard K. Loesch

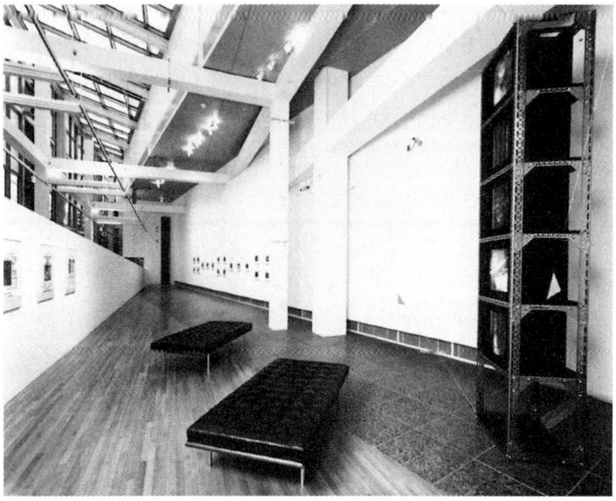

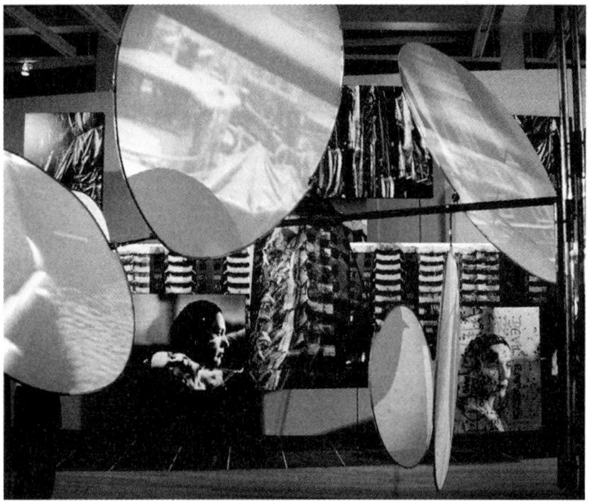

A photographer and film essayist drawn to open inquiry, Johan van der Keuken embarked on multimedia installations in the late 1990s — theatrical attractions combining large-scale photographs related to his films, which were then re-presented as a whole or in fragments on monitors and screens. In planning the show at the Wexner, he'd not let on that the cancer he thought he'd beaten (a battle he documented in *The Long Holiday*, 2000) had in fact returned. After his untimely death in January 2001, we worked with his collaborator, the designer Jeroen de Vries, on a reduced version of *The Body and the City* (1997–2000), intended to be an ambitious gathering of six separate installations shown in proximity to one another. Extracted and reconfigured principally from his film projects, *The Body and the City* argued strongly on behalf of the ultimate coherence of van der Keuken's lifelong project as an artist and world-citizen. It was an address aimed at an imagined museum-goer rather than at those aware of him primarily as a film-maker conversant with the non-Western world no less than with his native Holland. Our own space constraints allowed only three of the installations to be included, which were those focusing on Amsterdam, New York and Sarajevo. The first and third of these related respectively to *Amsterdam Global Village* (1996) and *Sarajevo Film Festival Film* (1993), augmented by a screening series aimed at conveying the scale of van der Keuken's artistic aspirations evident in the original version of *The Body and the City* . Van der Keuken's goal, as he saw it, stemmed from 'my pondering the intersection between photography and film and where the two can visibly coincide [...] The idea is to use image, projection, sound, and visual instruments to create individual and distinct worlds and atmospheres.'[7]

Likewise coming from a photography background, the Iranian-born Shiran Neshat found a wider audience in the late 90s when she began producing films for a gallery context — elegantly oblique, postmodern narratives joining the visual sparsity of her compatriot Abbas Kiarostami with a dramatic urgency relating specifically to women living in Islamic societies. Neshat's first two film installations, *Turbulent* (1998) and *Rapture* (1999), were both two-channel double-projections, with the images on one wall synched to the images on a facing wall, thereby situating viewers in the middle, looking back and forth as one set of images would be responding to, or elaborating upon, its opposite. For our commission of *Fervor* in 2000,

Chris Marker, *Silent Movie*, Wexner Center for the Arts, 1994–95. Photo © 2008 Richard K. Loesch

Below: Johan van der Keuken in collaboration with Jeroen de Vries, *The Body and the City* (Sarajevo), Wexner Center for the Arts, 2001. Photo © 2008 Richard K. Loesch

Neshat for the first time situated the double-projections not face to face but directly alongside each other, thereby not only moving closer to the viewing situation of conventional cinema (i.e. the spectator could enjoy an immobile viewing position for the piece's full duration), but also enacting a kind of visible montage between the 'woman's screen', on the one hand, and the 'man's screen', on the other. The literal walls holding women apart from men in traditional Islamic societies is given figurative form by Neshat in the thin blank space between the two projected images, a line further drawn within each of the projected narratives as both the woman and the man proceed to enter a religious gathering segregated by sex and with segregation imposed by a curtain wall. If Neshat's facing projections imposed, from the viewer's point of view, an either/or posture, the adjacent screens of *Fervor* advance a montage effect supporting represented events taking place at the exact same time.[8]

Cinema's traditional single-screen perspective, even if it is sometimes internally split into two or more separate quadrants (as in Mike Figgis's admirable, real-time *Timecode*, 2000), is at odds with a film-maker's wish to evoke not just simultaneity but also multiplicity and accumulation of a subject captured over time. Although he began and continues to work as an independent feature film-maker, Kutluğ Ataman captures documentary subjects in ways that are more easily presented within the terms available to the gallery than the cinema. This is not simply due to the often epic length of his portraits, but also to his understanding of human speech (and the construction of the self that each person illustrates by speaking directly) as an activity more faithfully represented as an ongoing stream rather than as a performance with beginning, middle and end, with truth values progressively emerging. In *The Four Seasons of Veronica Read* (2002), footage he shot during the course of a year is split among four projections arranged on double-sided hanging screens, with viewers then moving among them in an effort to construct the eponymous subject's story via her commentary to the off-screen Ataman. Although the running time of each of the four channels is modest by Ataman's standards, having them on view simultaneously abets — as a conventional film portrait of Veronica Read surely would not — the artist's view of identity as being perpetually in progress.[9]

Similarly, but less focused on individual subjectivity than on people set within social situations, Phil Collins's epic *they shoot horses* (2004) — a two-channel, seven-hour projection — sets up two perpendicular screens. One screen depicts five young Palestinians at life-size and the other screen four different kids at slightly smaller than life-size. All nine dance to the same music track in marathon dance sessions Collins produced over two days in Ramallah. The two screens are viewable from a single position, but one

7 Johan van der Keuken, quoted by Bill Horrigan in 'The Body and the City' exhibition gallery guide, Columbus: Wexner Center for the Arts, 2001.

8 Bill Horrigan, 'A Double Tour', *Shiran Neshat: Two Installations*, Columbus: Wexner Center for the Arts, 2000, pp.8–15.

9 Bill Horrigan, 'All Talk', *Image Stream* (ed. Helen Molesworth), Columbus Wexner Center for the Arts 2002, pp.2–29.

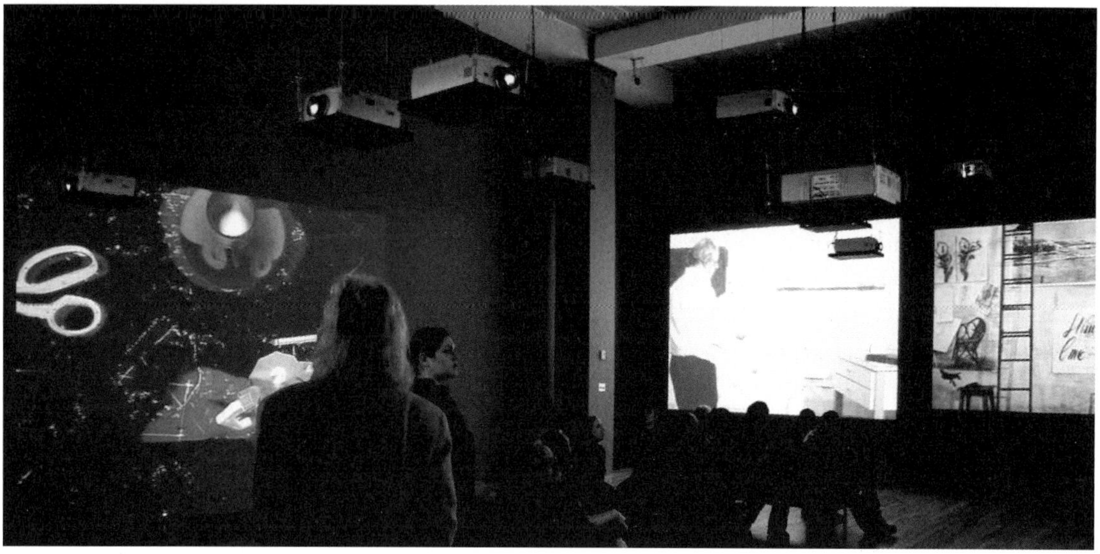

William Kentridge, *7 Fragments for Georges Méliès*, Wexner Center for the Arts, 2006. Photo © 2008 Sven Kahns

or the other draws the spectator's focus at any given moment. Over time and as individual 'characters' become discernible via their dance moves and from their wholly imagined, on the viewer's part, personal relationships (their voices are not heard at all until the final minute of the last hour), the work provides a theatrical scale and duration to the spectacle Collins engineered, first as a live gathering for the young participants, and then as an 'entertainment' documenting their play of energy and exhaustion on behalf of viewers elsewhere. As a rule-bound, task-based undertaking, and a counter-intuitive one at that (Collins: 'When we think about Palestine, it never seems to be in reference to modernity, or culture; in fact, it's relentlessly positioned as uncivilized'),[10] *they shoot horses* evokes Andy Warhol no less than the Judson Church Dance Theatre. As a 14-hour-long experience deeply opposed in essence to the form of gallery-based projection work into which one can idly wander and intuit no urgency or direction, its expressive effects can only be deeply earned by the time put into experiencing them.[11]

For *Domestic Violence* (1996), their first moving-image installation, the film-makers Todd Haynes and Christine Vachon (who usually function as writer-director and producer respectively) embarked on a remake, selecting ultra-violent and luridly verbal scenes from such films as *Clockwork Orange* (1971), *Natural Born Killers* (1994), *Dirty Harry* (1971) and the like. Haynes and Vachon spliced the actual audio tracks from the scenes onto shot-by-shot restagings, substituting babies, kittens and puppies in place of the original actors. With scenes separated from one another by the simulated buzz of a channel being changed, the film-makers conceived it as a loop intended to be watched on the television console that forms the centrepiece of a middle-class American living room they recreated in the gallery, complete with overstuffed furniture, filled candy dishes and an array of pet and parenting magazines — a welcoming environment accompanied by the psychopathic scream of Hollywood mayhem amplified to ear-splitting volume.[12]

Speaking back to cinema in a more conversational, comradely tone, William Kentridge's *7 Fragments for Georges Méliès* (2003) arrayed nine separate looped projections, from about 1-minute to 7-minutes long a piece, around the gallery's four walls, and set them to a single soundtrack—a solo piano piece evoking a silent film screening's musical accompaniment. Combining Kentridge's signature monochromatic animation with live sequences featuring himself enacting the role of the artist experimenting within his studio, the fragments illustrate the tricks of primitive cinema (magical transformations via stop-motion animation, gravity-defying feats via reverse-projection, etc.) The optical conceits each displays are then fed into the installation's longest individual projection, *Journey to the Moon* (2003), Kentridge's homage to the begetter of cinema's vocation to surpass or undermine the visible realm.

If an art can be said to 'advance', then the film-makers mentioned here use the genre of 'moving images in the gallery' to stage a progress on cinema's behalf, the gallery having become a far more receptive theatre for the unconventional than the viewpoint-dependent apparatus of traditional film-going. This would be a progress fuelled by cinema's own restless, supportable impatience, and that of its producers.

10 Phil Collins, 'The Loveliness of the Long-Distance Dancer', *The Independent on Sunday*, 6 June 2004.

11 Phil Collins, quoted by Bill Horrigan in 'Phil Collins: *they shoot horses*' exhibition gallery guide, Columbus: Wexner Center for the Arts, 2005.

12 B. Ruby Rich wrote about *Domestic Violence* in 'Violence to Glam Rock', *Sight and Sound*, December 1996, p.5.

-III- From Cinema to Post-Cinema

This final section examines the attraction that the moving image holds for contemporary artists. It explores what happens to the projected image when it is transposed from the black box to the white cube, and when cinema is 'exhibited' or re-contextualised within the museum. It analyses the relationship of film and video installation to classical cinema – to issues of image, narrative, reality, time and movement, for example – as it seeks to reconcile cinema's traditional concerns – i.e. with perspective and monocular narrative vision – with the more haptic, embodied or sculptural qualities of film and video installation art. A broad range of aesthetic, political, philosophical and ethical issues are raised by artists' engagement with and revitalisation of experimental documentary modes such as: What is the nature of the constitution of subjectivity under the conditions of our current media-historical landscape? What kind of subjects or sociality do different moving-image apparatuses address? What effects have new digital (computer-assisted-imaging) technologies had on artists since the 1990s, and how is this different from the rise of new electronic media such as television and video in the 60s and 70s? How is our role as a viewer altered; how does our experience change? What happens to the aesthetic field when film and video installation predominates? What are the challenges faced by this genre today? What is the future of film and video in the digital age?

Art and film debates have long hinged on competing views about how the cinematic has affected our idea of art and its relation to thought – this in fact was the question at the core of Walter Benjamin's famous essay from the 1930s on art and mechanical reproduction. John Rajchman takes on this complex problem in 'Deleuze's Time, or How the Cinematic Changes Our Idea of Art', an essay that develops from proceedings of a session on film and Gilles Deleuze from the 2005 Harvard University symposium titled 'Deleuze@20'. Referring to the basic philosophical notions of time and perception (in the philosophies of Kant and Deleuze), Rajchman situates the cinematic effect on contemporary art practice in the way that it participates in an 'aesthetics of movement and time' – how cinematic techniques or *dispositifs* forcibly introduce time into thought, where the past exceeds the present of a conscious self or collective.[1] What does it mean, he asks, to consider how the cinematic is part of a larger 'interference' among many arts and disciplines not based in 'medium' or 'modernism', or within 'post-cinematic', 'post-theoretical' time and societies of 'information'? His paper finds in Deleuze's conception of the cinematic – and in particular Deleuze's 'image of thought' – a valuable resource for thinking about the current potential of the cinematic in its ability to depart from cliché and informational control, tied up with the larger question of the role of perception in what it means to 'think and to think together'. Rajchman asks how this notion of the cinematic could lead to new thinking about figure and narration, violence and memory, image and reality, fiction and documentary, movement and time.

Italian philosopher Giorgio Agamben discusses the cinema of Guy Debord, considered by many to be an important touchstone for the idea of the cinematisation of society, and a key figure who marks the beginning of an iconoclastic movement against film's passive mode of spectatorship. In 'Difference and Repetition: On Guy Debord's Films', Agamben examines Debord's films in view of the proximity between cinema and

1 As T. J. Demos points out in 'The Art of Darkness: On Steve McQueen', *October*, no.114, Fall 2005, p.73, there has recently been a surge of Deleuzian readings of contemporary film and moving images. See George Baker, 'Reanimations', *October*, no.104, Spring 2003, pp.27–70; Jean Fisher, 'Intimations of the Real: On *Western Deep and Caribs' Leap*', *Steve McQueen: Caribs Leap/ Western Deep*, London: Artangel, 2002; Laura Marks, 'Deterritorialized Filmmaking: A Deleuzian Politics of Hybrid Cinema', *Screen*, vol.35 no.3, Autumn 1994; Rosalind Krauss, '"... And Then Turn Away?" An Essay on James Coleman', *October*, no.81, Summer 1997; pp.5–33.

history. Where does this closeness, this link, come from, Agamben asks, and what kind of history is involved? He begins by explaining that the difference between man and animal is that man is the only animal interested in images when he has recognised them as such. The image Agamben refers to is the image of cinema – a mobile image. Every image, he claims, can be seen in the light of cinema. The dimension of 'history' that has a tie with cinema, he suggests, is not chronological but messianic: each moment in time is charged with history, each image is a door through which the Messiah enters. Agamben discovers in Debord (and later in Godard) the power of repetition and montage. Within Debord's practice, montage is shown as such in itself. Repetition restores the possibility of what was; it makes, according to Agamben's reading of Benjamin, 'the unfulfilled into the fulfilled, and the fulfilled into the unfulfilled'. Herein lies the messianic dimension of cinema: to project power and possibility to what is impossible by definition towards the past. By placing repetition at the centre of his compositional techniques, on the one hand, Debord opens a zone of undecidability between the real and the possible. Stoppage, on the other hand, is related to Paul Valéry's sentence on poetry – 'a prolonged hesitation between sound and meaning' – which Agamben transforms into the realm of cinema as the 'hesitation between image and meaning', the being image of the image.

In 'Du Défilement au Defile' (republished in English in this book as 'From Movies to Moving'), Serge Daney analyses the relationships between mobility and immobility in the filmstrip (*défilement*) and the filming of figures passing by in the film itself (*défile*), and between the spectator and the image. He argues that there has been a reversal of mobility into immobility, meaning that film objects are no longer 'moved' by a force within themselves, for they stay fixed in place even if they are in fact moving. Daney transposes Pascal Bonitzer's notion of 'blocked vision' in the cinema – the process of pacification between the film and the audience ('the seat arrest') – to the contemporary situation of television and multimedia art. Daney's central point is that the possibility of the reversal itself and the existence of new cinematic objects are bound up with that reversal rather than with cinema itself. He rejects the notion of a possibility of cinema beyond cinema, beyond the history of cinema as such. Instead 'From Movies to Moving' describes something else: the question 'where are we going (where is the movement?)', Daney suggests, has been replaced by the question 'where have we come from (where does the movement come from)?' He writes of the triumph of programming over production: 'The movement is no longer in the images, in their metaphorical force or in our capacity to edit them together, it's in the enigma of the force that has *programmed* them ...'.

Jean-Christophe Royoux takes up this reversal from the mobile to the immobile image in 'The Time of Re-Departure: After Cinema, The Cinema of The Subject', against the force of narrative and beyond the *dispositif* of classical cinema, while underscoring the importance of Daney's historical argument. Such a transformation of cinema, Royoux says, has marked a generation of visual artists from Douglas Gordon, Pierre Huyghe and Philippe Parreno to Pierre Bismuth and Beat Streuli. What we have to understand, he argues, is how a new beginning can emerge from the *stopping* of cinema, to explore the other cinema (which is also and first of all the 'other' of cinema itself) whose roots can be discovered inside of cinema itself and far beyond. In short, the crisis of cinema – its confrontation with the point of no return (described as 'the unrepresentable that is the Shoah, "a moral point of no return"') – is also an opportunity to speak about representation itself. Cinema does not *go* somewhere; it stays within the responsibility of the viewer. 'Exhibition Cinema' – the term Royoux has given to this recent phenomenon – allows for a reconsideration of the end of cinema, its limitations and boundarles, as he articulates the potential of disassociated images, immobile images and the spatialisation of the cinematographic experience. His essay highlights the value of contemporary artworks that create a cinema for individual spectators, with the construction of sets that circumscribe the individual, the figure 'I'.

Ursula Frohne also considers the effects of contemporary video installation, such as changes in viewer perception, in 'Dissolution of the Frame: Immersion and Participation in Video Installations'. Taking up notions of the theatrical, performance, the *mise-en-scène,* the ruptured screen, temporality and repetition, Frohne argues that an essential lack of visibility in projection spaces poses challenges for spectators and transforms perception into participation. Tracing the history of immersive practices to eighteenth-century English gardens and the gothic novel and discussing various tropes – for example, the 'remake' – Frohne outlines two general tendencies: one that seeks to immerse and captivate viewers in 'a kind of hypnotising reality camouflage', the other that draws attention to the conditions of the medium and seeks to expose cinema and media culture as constructed spectacles. Arguing that the latter destabilises the viewer through new temporal conditions of visual awareness, Frohne identifies this fundamental dismantling of the medium and the destabilisation and mobilisation of the spectator as central characteristics of projected-image installations; she writes that 'the end of the illusion begins with the participation of the spectator'.

How, at this moment of technological transformation, can we attempt to theorise the medium of video, Liz Kotz asks in 'Video Projection: The Space Between Screens'. Commenting on how video has become dislodged from its technological support and historical confinement to the television monitor, and how all manner of electronically-produced moving images are now loosely referred to as 'video', Kotz offers a critical assessment of video projection. In particular, she focuses on Stan Douglas's *Hors-Champ*, Diana Thater's *Late and Soon, Occident Trotting* and Douglas Gordon's *24-Hour Psycho*, all from between 1992 and 1993, when video re-emerged into the gallery-museum context. Against a pervasive critical discourse that tends to situate such works as these in relation to the phenomenological, interactive and process-based concerns of early video, Kotz argues that these artists' pictorial and narrative concerns and the increasingly monumentalised installational format tend to align video more closely with large-scale, spectacularised photographic work – representing a certain convergence of painterly and cinematic practices. In response to such discourse, Kotz outlines a provisional theorisation of the phenomenon of 'projection', situating it in relation to the availability of new consumer technologies. With the current predominance of black-box viewing formats, Kotz argues, video is largely being assimilated back into older filmic conventions. Drawing on texts by David James, Jonas Mekas and Gene Youngblood, she makes the case that the recent move towards immersive and participatory environments represents an extension of an earlier project of 'expanded cinema', with its utopian desire to depart from constraints of the filmic apparatus. Kotz points to works by Lutz Bacher, Steve McQueen and Gillian Wearing as counter examples of more difficult and productive engagements with the durational and process-based structures of earlier video.

Concerned with the 'widespread rhetoric of anti-illusionism in the conceptualisation of artist's film and video since the 1960s [that] has caused critics to champion the rigorously self-reflexive practices of "Structural-Materialism" as an antidote to the regressive opiate of industrial narrative cinema', Andrew V. Uroskie notes, however, that 'a neglected alternative tradition has concerned itself with precisely those qualities of affective engagement and phantasmatic identification these critics have sought to dismiss'.[2] Far from demanding the defeat of illusionism, Uroskie's essay 'Siting Cinema' examines the work of artists who have 'employed film as a modality of transport away from the confines of a local material environment, even as they maintain a critical interest with the sedimented cultural and institutional histories of their chosen theatrical site. As in psychoanalytic philosophy, these works imply that a naive aversion to "illusionism" fails to advance either a sophisticated understanding of spectatorship or a pragmatic basis for political intervention.'[3] Through an analysis of *The Paradise Institute* (2001) by Janet Cardiff and George Bures Miller and *The Third Memory* (1999) by Pierre Huyghe, Uroskie's essay argues for the aesthetic and conceptual vitality of those contemporary art practices occurring within the hybrid institutional space between the white cube of the art gallery and the black box of the cinematic theatre. It concludes that a similarly hybrid approach bridging the disciplinary rhetorics of art history and film studies is now needed to address the sophistication of these works.

Acknowledging the prominent role of fractured and disjointed cinemas in contemporary art, and extending their dysfunctional, anti-illusory qualities, John Kelsey – one of three members of the artists' group Bernadette Corporation – proposes a cinematic aesthetics that broaches and complicates the multiple conditions, limits and possibilities of cinema: 'Cinema as a means without end.' In 'Moving Images Moving Images' (a new commission for this volume) Kelsey explores Bernadette Corporation's recent film and video work – *Get Rid of Yourself* (2001–03) and *Pedestrian Cinema* (2006–07) – within a broader discussion of the history of 'dismantled and vandalised cinemas'.

2 Email correspondence with the author, 8 July 2007.

3 *Ibid.*

As Raymond Bellour has sought to make clear, part of the present difficulty in experiencing visual art and cinema has to do with the increasing interconnection between art and cinema and the displaced capacity for specificity in the arts. Discussing the 'battle of ways and means' of such transformed, reinstalled and dismantled cinemas, he seeks to understand this 'impure art' and the 'aesthetics of confusion' it borders upon in his essay 'Of An Other Cinema'. Bellour has described the duelling that occurs amongst the diverse orders of images, structures and organisations as prerequisite for providing new resources for the imagination, as well as for a new ideology and politics of the image. In his text he examines the interplay of the cinematic with traditional and contemporary art practices to expose the tensions, differences and similarities of cinematic devices. Bellour provides an inventory of moving-image installations for this new theoretical film space: from, for example, the gestures of Pipilotti Rist to the photographic panoramas of Sam Taylor-Wood; from the subtle displacements and malleability of formats in Eija-Liisa Ahtila's films and videos to the successive screens of Gary Hill and the mutated projections of Douglas Gordon and Stan Douglas. Citing the 'so-called "crisis" within cinema' as one of 'the forces that animate[s]' projected art installations, Bellour examines their traditionally unassimilable qualities within the field of visual art, and in relation to changing experiences of the spectator.

The imprecise zone occupied by artists across disciplines is also the subject of Alexander Alberro's essay 'The Gap Between Film and Installation Art'. Here he argues that the emergence of the new type of audio-visual artist – whose mode of exhibition shifts effortlessly from single-channel to multiple-channel, from large screen to television monitor, from film to video to digital production – 'directly parallels the development of interdisciplinary visual studies programmes in the academy'. Like Bellour, he also expresses concern for how the historical specificity of this 'media crossing', the potential as well as the limitations of particular mediums at precise moments in their history, is often ignored. Alberro claims: 'Indeed, audio-visual production that is rigorously attentive to the inherent characteristics and histories of the medium in which it works is becoming a rarity.' The pressures of over-production and the metamorphosing of works into various versions for different exhibition contexts are some of the reasons Alberro gives for this lack of awareness. In his case study on Finnish artist Eija-Liisa Ahtila, he analyses the specific structural operations at play within audio-visual artworks, 'how the production of meaning is not only the result of a work's thematic content but also intricately dependent' on its formal elements and the way it 'dialogically negotiates the site of its display'. Alberro theorises on various aspects of montage: a horizontal montage of spoken sound and subtitled text as well as a mobile montage of the viewer now directing the order of cuts as he or she walks through the gallery.

Bound up with questions of what movement and time are themselves, both Gregor Stemmrich and Mark Nash continue an examination of the problems of exhibiting time in art spaces from the perspectives of their personal experiences programming and exhibiting films and videos within the art world context. Stemmrich's essay 'White Cube, Black Box and Grey Areas: Venues and Values' focuses on the changing relations between different contexts of art and cinema. He begins by building a historical perspective that confronts two concepts of how films have been integrated into the context of the international art exhibition, namely 'documenta 5' in 1972 and 'Documenta11' thirty years later. Stemmrich addresses the opposition between cinema and counter-cinema in the 1960s with its deconstruction in film and video works by contemporary artists, pointing out that artists today tend to reflect upon moments of film history. In the final section, Stemmrich elucidates the meanings that the concept of site-specificity had and still holds in relation to film.

Mark Nash, a member of the curatorial team of 'Documenta11' (a show critics proclaimed as the most 'cinematic' documenta ever), has republished his essay from the 'Documenta11' catalogue along with several new reflections on the production and reception of that exhibition and more recent projects, such as 'Experiments with Truth' (2004–05), his intervention at The Fabric Workshop and Museum in Philadelphia. Against a concern with formal aspects of contemporary art (the projected image included) and in contrast to what is seen to be a predominant draining away of social and political connotations in contemporary artistic practice, 'Documenta11' – and Nash's curatorial extensions of this work – set out to privilege a politics of the signified. Citing a range of politically and aesthetically oppositional film practices – with particular focus on issues of Third Cinema and collective practices – Nash aims to explicate reasons for the break in the indexical bond between image and referent, and the massive 'documentary turn' in the art world and the challenges viewers face when experiencing such works within the exhibition context.

The question we need to be considering now, Thomas Y. Levin argues, is less about the indexicality of the image or about whether digitisation has severed the link between the photograph and its referent, and more instead about how the digitised image might shape temporal-spatial relations for the viewer, in what he calls the '*tense* of the cinematic image'. In '*You Never Know the Whole Story*: Ute Friederike Jürss and the Aesthetics of the Heterochronic Image', Levin explores the dynamics of a post-photo-chemical image, specifically the temporal rupturing of the homogeneity of the image field into what he calls the 'heterochronic' (multiple-time) representation. It is precisely through such a shift in the '*tense*' of the projected image that one can map 'the rhetorical consequences of the proliferation of digital imaging'. He writes that '*the locus of its* [cinema's] *indexical foundation has changed*', noting how in the current context of so-called 'live' television and new media – such as webcams and CCTV – the rhetorics of cinematic verisimilitude have moved 'away from the now increasingly unreliable referentiality of the *image* to the increasingly indexically invested domain of an ostensibly un-edited, "instantaneous" or "real" *time*'. Through his close readings of a number of, in his words, 'semiotically heterodox' media works – such as Ute Friederike Jürss's three-screen installation *You Never Know the Whole Story* (2000) and David Claerbout's video installation *Ruurlo, Bocurloscheweg, 1910* (1997) – Levin demonstrates how their intermedial character raises the question of their status as images, and in so doing demands of the contemporary viewer – as do other works that invoke the rhetoric of 'real time' – an urgent new kind of media literacy.

DELEUZE'S TIME, OR HOW THE CINEMATIC CHANGES OUR IDEA OF ART

John Rajchman

After the War

How does the cinematic change our idea of art? Citing Paul Valéry, Walter Benjamin begins his great 1934 essay on mechanical reproduction with this question.[1] The problem was not so much whether cinema is an art, the so-called seventh one, but how, starting in the nineteenth century, it helped transform what we think art is, and in particular how one thinks in the arts or with the arts. For Benjamin, the problem of the cinematic was already inseparable from the whole question, at once aesthetic and political, of how one thinks with the new mass industrial audio-visual means of film and projection.

We might think of Gilles Deleuze as taking up this question again after World War II, when there arose not simply a new cinema in France but also new styles of thinking—a new 'image of thought'. The 'upheaval in general sensibility' that followed the War would lead 'to new dispositions of thought'.[2] Film-makers invented new ways of thinking with film and projection, at the same time as those in other domains started to invent related ideas, creating a whole new zone of interference and exchange. Deleuze's two volumes on cinema are a monumental attempt to see the new European cinema in terms of this constellation, to isolate the notions of image, space and time they involved and so show the distinctive ways film-makers took part in this larger mutation in thought.

Even though Deleuze wrote his study of cinema in the 1980s, the basic philosophical notions he uses go back to his 1956 essay on the problem of difference in Henri Bergson, written at a time when Alain Resnais was making documentaries like *Van Gogh* (1948), his great study of the artist's suicide, as well as, of course, *Night and Fog* (1955). These films would play a key role in Deleuze's analysis of cinema, in particular by demonstrating the principle that 'the cinematographic image is never in the present'.[3] Deleuze thought Resnais

1 Walter Benjamin, 'The Work of Art in the Age of Mechanical Reproduction', *Illuminations* (trans. Harry Zohn), New York: Schocken Books, 1969.

2 Such are the words that struck Deleuze in 'Correspondence with Dionys Mascolo', in Gilles Deleuze, *Two Regimes of Madness: Texts and Interviews 1975–1995* (ed. David Lapoujade, trans. Ames Hodges and Mike Taormina), New York: Semiotext(e), 2006, p.327. They are also suggestive for his larger encounter with Maurice Blanchot and Marguerite Duras.

3 Deleuze explicates this principle of the cinematographic image introduced in *Cinema 2*, ch.5 sec.2, in G. Deleuze, *Two Regimes of Madness*, *op. cit.* pp.290–91. See Gilles Deleuze, *Cinéma 2: L'image-temps*, Paris: Éditions de Minuit, 1985; or *Cinema 2: The Time-Image* (trans. Hugh Tomlinson), Minneapolis: University of Minnesota Press, 1989.

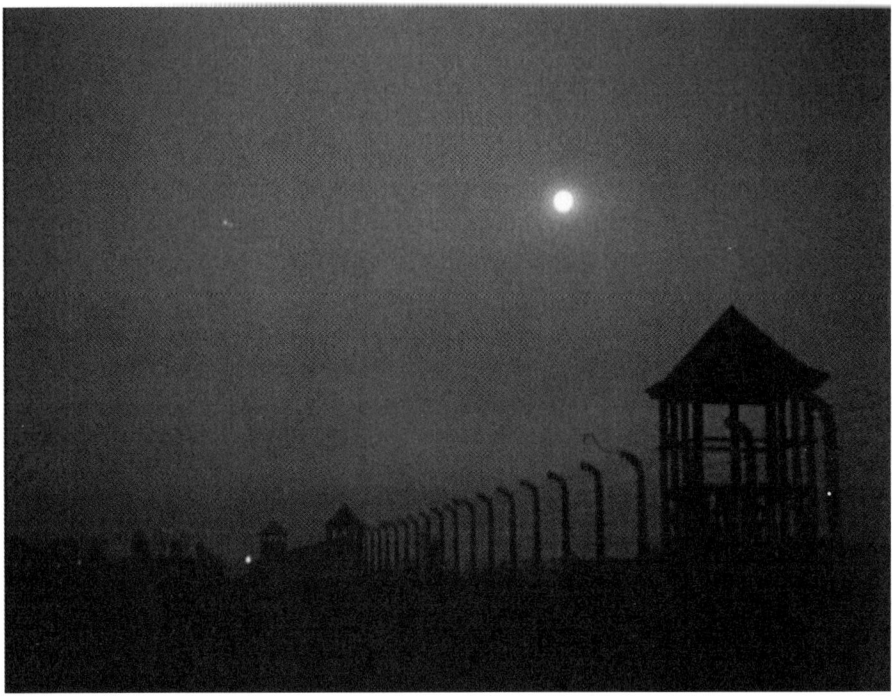

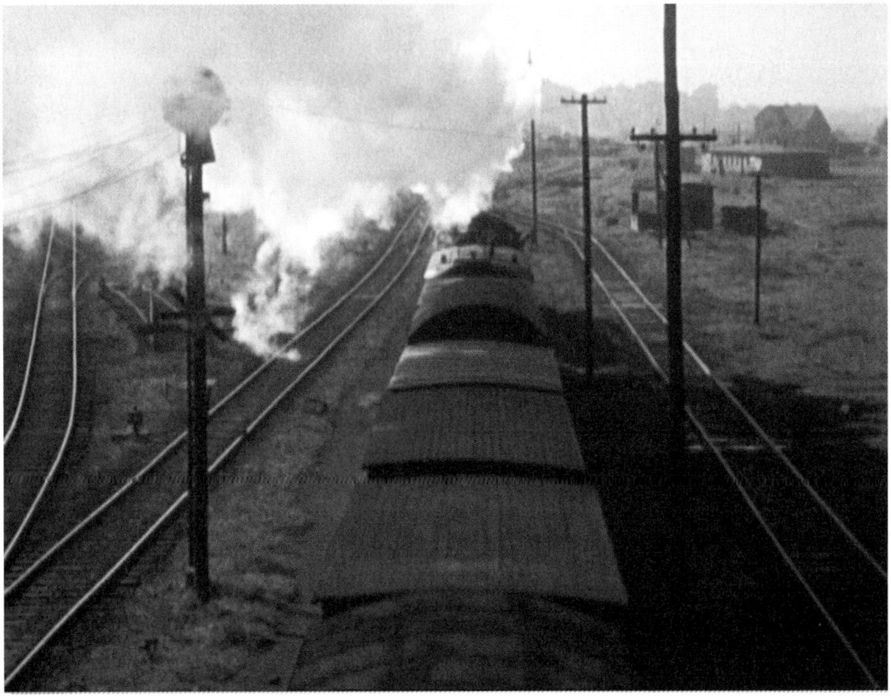

Alain Resnais, stills from *Nuit et Brouillard* (*Night and Fog*), 1955. 35mm black-and-white and colour film, 32mins

had perhaps gone the furthest with this principle for, in his documentaries as well as in the fiction films he would go on to make, we find not only new kinds of images but also a new function for them: that of rendering a past, at once indeterminate and violent, irreducible to anyone's memory, any *prise de conscience*.

The War is thus a dividing point not only for Deleuze's inventory of new signs and images in cinematic thinking, but also for his sense of a particular problem in post-War philosophy and in his philosophy: the problem of the peculiar 'time that takes thought'.[4] In effect, cinema makes visible the problem philosophy developed at the same time, for which Deleuze himself would try to work out a new logic of 'events' and their sense. If, especially in France, post-War cinema developed in tandem with post-War philosophy, following its peculiar twists and turns through psychoanalysis and Structuralism, it was because, Deleuze suggests, post-War cinema was itself an original audio-visual way of thinking — a peculiar relation of thought to *aisthesis*, a whole aesthetics. That is why the great film-makers needed to be confronted not simply with writers or painters but also with thinkers and questions of thought. The signs and images they invented involved a new sense of what a creative image is and what it means to think. Even the crisis in cinema brought on by television, and later by digital images, had to be posed on this aesthetic level — as a problem of images that don't force us to think or which keep us from thinking, as with the 'presentifying' tendencies Deleuze saw in most television.[5] He declared at the start of his study: 'What I call Ideas are images that make one think.'[6] To write about cinema was to identify these images and to examine the larger 'apparatuses', or *dispositifs*, through which cinema manages to pose them.[7] The problem of the new televisual-digital regime must be analysed in this way and

4 Gilles Deleuze, *Différence et répétition*, Paris: Presses Universitaires de France, 1968, p.216; my translation. For a full English translation of the text, see *Difference and Repetition* (trans. Paul Patton), New York: Columbia University Press, 1994; this note applies to p.166. At the end of his discussion of 'the image of thought', Deleuze captures with the words 'time into thought' the argument he elaborates throughout his study of cinema and the larger idea of 'aesthetics' it involves. Kant plays a key role in this turn; see note 8.

5 G. Deleuze, *Two Regimes of Madness*, *op. cit.*, p.291. Deleuze's view of the way television tends to 'presentify' everything is not simply a question of its broadcast medium. One of Deleuze's first writings on cinema is his discussion of Godard's television work. The link between 'present' and 'live' is nevertheless important, as found today in 'reality TV', for example.

6 *Ibid.*

7 In this essay I retain the French term *dispositif* for the manner in which cinematic space is put together. This sense of the term is part of the larger question of the 'regimes' of speaking and seeing that Deleuze extracts from Foucault in 'What is a dispositif?', in G. Deleuze, *Two Regimes of Madness*, *op. cit.*, p.338. In cinema theory, it might be said to belong to a series of notions of the 'cinematic apparatus' which descend from Marx, who stressed the ways in which automated production involves not simply forces but also relations of production (or what Deleuze would call a 'technical-social machine'). One variant is to be found in the Brechtian idea of '*Umfunktionierung*' that Benjamin developed, through which an author, more than a genius-fabricator of useless or autonomous works, becomes a 'producer' whose work alters the larger 'apparatus' of production and distribution in which it finds itself, posing the problem of the link between the 'collectivisation' of the means of production and the control of the Party; see note 13. Another is the notion of 'apparatus' that Baudry took over from Althusser's analysis of ideologies, where it is connected to an organisation of 'gazes' in the reproduction of social roles. Deleuze starts instead from a notion of 'machine' in which 'desire' functions not as prosthesis or projection of an inner state, but as itself a kind of 'programme' at work in larger socio-technical arrangements, the function of which is to undo the usual 'controllable' connections, for which he cites many artistic examples, notably Kurt Schwitter's *Merzbau*. See Gilles Deleuze and Félix Guattari, 'Balance Sheet-Program for Desiring Machines', *Semiotext(e)*, vol.2 no.3, 1977. With this example, one is close to the problem of cinema as a kind of 'installation', as in the debates about how cinema went 'into the light' of the gallery out of its darkened room *dispositif*. In this case, the cinema hall or gallery is 'architecture', just when architecture itself is seen in terms of a given *dispositif* — the darkened room itself deriving from a theatrical *dispositif* transformed by opera, the first modern mass form. Thus, for example, when

not simply 'media-logically', as more generally, in Deleuze's approach to the question of technology, and in particular, to the problems of information and control to which his study of cinema led him. For machines, unlike simple mechanisms, always have an indeterminate sensory or aesthetic component, through which they participate in larger fields, larger sorts of arrangements — our senses, our bodies, our brains. Cinema is a way of having ideas with images that introduces a new 'psycho-mechanics', a new way of affecting our nervous systems. Central to this arrangement was the invention of new determinations of space and time as forms of sensibility in relation to thinking. At the heart of Deleuze's analysis of cinematic images and their *dispositifs*, we find the problem of a determination of a time no longer defined by succession (past, present, future); of a space no longer defined by simultaneity (distinct elements in closed or framed space); and of a permanence no longer based in eternity (instead given as form of a complex variation).[8] Such were the new sorts of images that post-War film-makers gave us to think with and with which they started to work themselves.

Deleuze, then, might have responded to Valéry's question in the following way. Cinema changed the idea of art through the new ways it invented to show or render movement and time, participating in a distinctive manner in a larger aesthetics of duration, connected not simply with new technologies or new forces, but also with new ways of thinking, new questions and paradoxes, new political uses. Across all the arts, whether 'expanded' or not, we see these changes, these new sorts of determinations of space and time, this larger aesthetics, in which film-making, starting in its early spaces and with its early means, has played a key role.[9] As with Benjamin, there was an element of the philosophy of Immanuel Kant in this aesthetic field, but one that comes from Deleuze's new reading of Kant, or his new idea of the sense in which we are still Kantian. Indeed the crucial distinction between time and

Barthes stresses that 'cinema' refers to a place as well as what is shown in it, he opposes the 'eroticism' of that place to the awful familial setting of the television set. See Roland Barthes, 'On Leaving the Cinema'. Sartre stresses the 'democratic' appeal of the cinema hall to the hierarchical organisation of the bourgeois theatre in order to explain the source of his enthusiasm for it. See Jean-Paul Satre, *Les Mots*. To see such spaces as *dispositifs* is to see them as arrangements of sensibilia, which in turn can be analysed in terms of their relation to what 'forces us to think'. By that criterion, many 'darkened room' experiences are more intense than their equivalents in galleries.

8 See Gilles Deleuze, 'On Four Poetic Formulas', *Essays Critical and Clinical* (trans. Daniel W. Smith and Michael A. Greco), Minneapolis: University of Minnesota Press, 1997, pp.28–29. For Deleuze, Kant introduces the distinction between time and movement, as developed in and through the cinema volumes. The distinction is first introduced in G. Deleuze, *Différence and répétition*, *op. cit.*, pp.118 and 186, in passages devoted to the problem of introducing 'time into thought'; later, on pp.130 and 198, Deleuze already develops the consequences for the notion of 'aesthetics' that he puts into practice in his analysis of cinema. Prior to Bergson, Kant was the central philosophical figure for Deleuze's film aesthetic, to the point where he declares Bergson much closer to Kant than he allowed. 'On Four Poetic Formulas' resumes the lecture course Deleuze gave on Kant in 1978, which runs through his larger aesthetic enterprise in the 1980s, and directly concerns the 'paradox of inner sense' Kant elaborates on in *Opus Posthumum*.

9 In the essay 'La chambre' (1994), which takes off from Deleuze's analysis of the room in Samuel Beckett's *Film*, Raymond Bellour suggests one way of linking the problem of the 'room' in cinema to the room in which it is shown in 'the other cinema' of film and video installation. See Raymond Bellour, *L'Entre-images 2: Mots, images*, Paris: P.O.L., 1999, pp.281–316.

10 G. Deleuze, *Two Regimes of Madness*, *op. cit.*, p.252.

11 *Ibid.*, p.292.

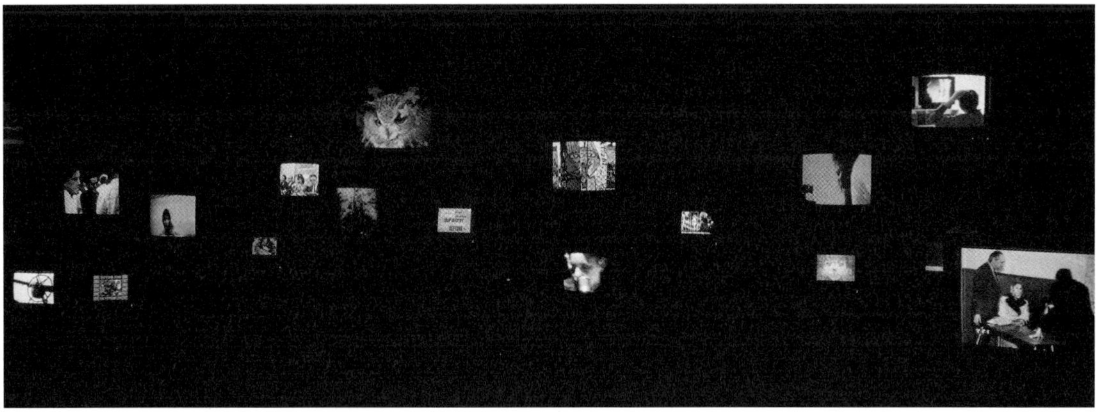

Chris Marker, *Zapping Zone – Proposals for an Imaginary Television*, Musée National d'Art Moderne, Centre Georges Pompidou, Paris, 1990–97. Photo © 2008 Philippe Migeat, CNAC/MNAM, Dist. RMN

movement elaborated in the books on cinema is first introduced in *Difference and Repetition* (1968), where he proposes to see as central to Kant's revolution the problem of a 'time out of joint'. Later, Deleuze would declare that the War offered cinema the condition to effectuate in a much shorter interval its own Kantian revolution, its own audio-visual way of freeing the idea of time from subordination to any prior movement, any extensive space.[10]

Kant had already taken space and time as forms of intuition, or as a priori conditions of an *aesthesis*, or of what he already called 'sensibilia'. The forms of sensation are thus distinct from the categories of the understanding, and can only be linked to them through the workings of a mysterious 'schematism' or through the 'productive imagination'. What matters for Deleuze is the independence of these forms from the understanding, not the way they figure in a unified consciousness. In freeing time from its subordination to the identities of movement in a closed world, and in associating it with forces or virtualities of another sort, the great post-War film-makers would thus free the forms of sensibilia themselves from any such schematic link with understanding, making them instead a matter of artistic experimentation or invention in relation to another kind of thinking — precisely that of 'ideas'. The 'time that takes thought' would be freed from categories of causality or even teleology; the post-War film-makers would link it instead to a whole new relation to character, milieu, space and action. What is new in Kant for Deleuze, then, is how, with the disjunction between our sensibilia and our categories for understanding substance or causality, there arises a new experimental zone where other sorts of determinations of space and time (such as when, in music or literature, one 'occupies without measuring' a sensory milieu) are linked to ideas.[11] Fyodor Dostoevsky's title character in *The Idiot* (1869), for example, not only moves in a much altered novelistic space and time, but in the process is also obliged to think, simply because there are no schemata to govern his actions — a situation Deleuze sees Akira Kurosawa later exploring in cinema. The cinematic lies in the distinctive ways film-makers invented to disjoin the forms of sensation from the understanding, using them instead to give us 'ideas' and so new 'personae' in thinking, like *The Idiot*.

We see this, for example, in Deleuze's demonstration of how Marguerite Duras or Jean-Marie Straub and Daniele Huillet turned the disjunction between sound and visual images into a veritable 'idea in cinema', a whole new exploration of the peculiar post-War intersection of 'stories without places' and 'places without stories'.[12] Indeed, it is precisely this sort of 'non-relation' between what we see and what we say that shows why it so misleading to think of cinema as language rather than as a 'signaletic material'. Deleuze was no textualist or narratologist; the signs and images he finds in cinema are given by no theory of language or code. Rather, in each case they are the result of a singular invention. He thought that even in literature we should look not to linguistics or narratology, but rather to the ways great writers invent a 'foreign language' in our language, tied up with the invention of new percepts and affects. His examples include the 'complicated time' in Marcel Proust; the 'crack-up' of the characters in F. Scott Fitzgerald; and the peculiar relation of the characters to a 'secret past' in Henry James's short stories, later exploited in film by Joseph Mankiewicz. The cinematic, in short, is this strange great complex of signs and images that film-makers invented to explore the problem that arises when space and time, regarded as forms of our sensibilia, are disjoined from the schemata that tie them to our understanding and are linked instead to another kind of thinking, governed by logic not of propositions and truths but of the sense (and non-sense) of what is happening to us.

Deleuze's study of cinema was his attempt to elaborate this problem, at once philosophical and aesthetic. He saw film-makers as developing an original way of exploring what Kant called the 'paradox of inner sense', or of the peculiar way we can be said to be 'in time'. This is a problem that Deleuze thought Resnais had explored further than Proust or Bergson. The question of the sense in which we are 'in time' was, of course, also a central one in modern philosophy; and, in his books on film, Deleuze takes up this issue by contrasting the ways Edmund Husserl and Bergson each formulated it in relation to science and mathematics. Husserl still imagined the forms of space and time to be centred in a consciousness, whereas Bergson offered a new idea of image freed from this assumption — closer to the way film-makers explore a-centred spaces prior to anyone's point of view. The cinematic is found in images that make visible or palpable this a-centred condition, or that 'sensibilise' us to it. The images in cinema are thus forms that explore a strange sort of movement in our lives that is irreducible to translation in extended space, the lines of which are freed from starting and ending points, instead tracing trajectories, at once fictive and real, in indeterminate milieus; they thus call for a time or a duration based not in chronology and succession, but rather in an interlocking topology or overlapping seriality. That is how cinema posed the question of how we actually think, how we are oriented and

12 G. Deleuze, *Cinema 2*, *op. cit.*, p.257; translation modified. Deleuze draws on the detailed analysis of Duras in Youssef Ishaghpour, *D'une image a l'autre*, Paris: Biblioteque Médiations, 1982.

disoriented in our thinking, our lives, our relations with ourselves and to one another. In *Cinema 1* and *Cinema 2*, Deleuze tried to analyse how, through the possibilities of camera-movement, framing, editing and projecting, cinema would invent a whole new 'psycho-mechanical' way to make visible such times and spaces in our worlds, situations or milieus, prior to (and immanent in) our conscious selves, as individuals or groups.

The principle that 'the cinematographic image is never in the present', for which Deleuze would find such a striking application in the troubling 'sheets of time' in *Night and Fog*, was thus part of a larger transformation in the very idea of the image itself in all the arts — in painting, photography or literature, as well as in new practices that would break away from such traditional mediums. We know, for example, that Soviet cinema would be seen to play a key role in the process in the 1920s and 30s that Walter Benjamin analysed in the avant-garde when he spoke of the new function of author as producer.[13] At the same time, the principle of 'not being in the present' was a philosophical matter that concerned the very concept of image and the way it presents things before they are represented for a unified subject or consciousness. Deleuze's conception of 'images' in cinema breaks from the idea that they are inner representations in our minds or brains, linking them instead with new questions explored in neurology and psychology — fields of knowledge, including especially psychoanalysis, with which cinema would have so many relations throughout the nineteenth and twentieth centuries.[14] To introduce movement and time into the very idea of the image was inseparable from the extensive neuroscientific literature on how images figure in our bodies or brains, or in the ideas of consciousness and of unconsciousness, in which the new memory sciences play a key role; one example of this is Deleuze's discussion of the dissociation theories of Pierre Janet. Indeed, that is how the 'cinematic' — regarded as a way of thinking with the forms of sensibilia — could be seen to extract itself from the great stupefying explosion of images in our lives that mechanical reproduction facilitated (before the 'control' of the post-War information-type machines) with its clichéd pictures, ordered words and relations with propaganda and advertising. If, as Deleuze proposes, the invention of a cinematic sensibilia arises from the crisis in psychology concerning the status of images, it is developed through and within the new industrial mass means, which we see at the same time in the psychological or social sciences.

13 Walter Benjamin, 'The Author as Producer', *Reflections: Essays, Aphorisms, Autobiographical Writing* (ed. Peter Demetz, trans. Edmund Jephcott), New York: Harcourt Brace Jovanovich, 1978, pp.220–38. See also Sergei Tret'iakov, 'Our Cinema' (1928), *October*, no.118, Fall 2006, p.27. There is something in the '*Umfunktionierung*' characteristic of author as producer that is akin to Foucault's analysis of the individualising 'function' of authorship, and his own attempts to get out of it; an important difference, however, concerns the way that the problem of 'power' in Foucault is purposefully posed in a way irreducible to any Party control. Deleuze relates the problem in Vertov to a new 'materialism of the eye'. See François Zourabichvili, 'The Eye of Montage: Dziga Vertov and Bergsonian Materialism', *The Brain is the Screen* (ed. Gregory Flaxman), Minneapolis: University of Minnesota Press, 2000, pp.141–49.

14 Jonathan Crary, in an analysis influenced by Deleuze, discusses Vertov and Cézanne in relation to the neuroscientific question of 'attention' in his *Suspensions of Perception: Attention, Spectacle and Modern Culture*, Cambridge, Mass.: The MIT Press, 1999.

In philosophy, Martin Heidegger had already shown in the 1920s how time and the problem of 'inner sense' was central to the Kantian enterprise and to his own attempt to move beyond its still metaphysical enclosure. But Deleuze's writings on difference in Bergson suggested a fresh way of taking up the question of time, which moves away from Heidegger's idea of a constitutive finitude or the *Dasein* of a *Volk* disclosed in and through the work of art. Deleuze tried to develop an ungrounded element in the kind of time and movement the cinematic image makes visible. In cinema, as in philosophy, he discovers something at once inhuman and vital. It is already to be seen in the kind of movement Dziga Vertov explored through the intervals in his editing or 'montage', or with the ability of the camera to capture a-centered worlds with 'indeterminate' zones in Orson Welles. He tried to work out an original notion of a world, closer to the perspectivism of Gottfried Liebniz than to Husserl's grounding in a life-world. Cinema not only invents images; it surrounds them with a world — a world that for Deleuze has become light or deterritorialised, irreducible to our 'being-there'.

We are thus 'in time' in a peculiar way, irreducible to the familiar division between subjective (or lived) and objective (or clocked) time. The problem is rather how we are affected by time and 'affect ourselves through it', at once objectively and subjectively; it is the problem of time itself as this uncontrollable potential in who we are or may become. The function of cinematic images is to show the workings of this time in our lives and our worlds. That is why the time-images in cinema are ones that defeat the presumed coincidence of subjective and objective images on which a whole tradition of story or narrative has rested. Such relations between space and viewing are undone as description of space frees itself from the presumption of a single objective viewpoint, and the form of narration frees itself from domination of a single narrative voice, as if in a free and indirect style. The forms of description and narration, in other words, depend on the role of mobility and indetermination in the images, and so with the sense and non-sense of what is happening. In Bergson (as well as in the Russian city of Vertov's *Man with a Movie Camera*), Deleuze finds a multiple, moving universe in which things appear without appearing as such *to* anyone, or to any one point of view. He finds images that make visible a world that can't be united or made fully present to our conscious selves, the sense of which nevertheless unfolds in time, through movement and the forms of sensibilia that are images. It is such a world of illumination without revelation that would later be taken up in time-image cinema. The topological superposition of 'sheets of time' in Resnais shows in particular, in a vivid way, the sense in which a terrible past coexists with the present, in a manner irreducible to flashbacks or conscious recollection, rendering the present uncertain and forcing us to think while dispossessing us of our ability to say 'I' or 'We'. Time is no longer a matter of either Man's finitude or God's infinite understanding — neither humanist nor salvationist, it is directly linked to questions of life and death themselves.[15]

In exploring how, through the means available to it, cinema makes sensible this kind of time in worlds, Deleuze thus develops an original view of space and time as forms of sensibilia that cause us to think. He frees those forms from their Kantian subordination to what he saw as the two great functions played by the philosophical idea of the subject: 'consciousness' and 'individualisation'.[16] The world that cinema shows us is an impersonal (or 'pre-personal') world prior to consciousness and to individualisation. In this way, cinema takes part in Deleuze's larger attempt to put the question of 'a life' in the place of the classical notion of the subject or of the self—a life that contrasts precisely with '*the* life of the corresponding individual' as with the conscious self, yet remains as a concrete question and possibility for our bodies as for our brains.[17] Thus the '*espaces quelconques*', or 'any-spaces-whatever', that Deleuze isolates, especially in post-War cinema (as well as in Structural film), involve spatial and temporal distributions which are indeterminate or '*quelconque*' just in the sense that they precede the supposed unities of conscious selfhood, or of static, grouped, definite or definable individuality, exposing worlds, situations or milieus prior to them. Indeed, that is why any-spaces-whatever are populated with a new, less definite kind of character and action that requires a new art of indefinite description that is realistic without being naturalistic. Cinema thus maps the workings of a time once pre-individual and un-conscious. Deleuze offers an inventory of images that show this time, irreducible to destiny, providence, causality or predictability, even statistical or probabilistic, which nevertheless affects us in ways we don't normally perceive. Such is the sort of time given by series and juxtapositions (rather than succession) and by indeterminate spaces of displacements and departures (rather than a 'situated' intersubjectivity or world). It is the kind of temporality that requires a change in the nature of belief—a turn to a more pragmatist belief-in-the-world, without need for salvation or historical destiny.

We see this time already in *Night and Fog*. Resnais's juxtapositions—of a past, shown through black-and-white archival materials, with a present given by cinematic mapping of mental spaces (in colour and with his famous tracking shots of the peculiar mental spaces of the concentration camps) and with the uncertain future given through Jean Cayrol's famous voice-over—form part of a larger constitution of cinema as a post-War kind of audio-visual thinking. If, as Deleuze argues, in this great documentary we can see the sum of the different ways of avoiding 'the piety of the recollection image', it is because of the way image and thinking discover in the film a new relation to the past and the way it figures in the present. The aim is no longer to re-capture or re-collect the past in a consciousness—individual

15 Deleuze develops this view as an original approach to questions of biology and technology in the appendix to Gilles Deleuze, *Foucault* (trans. Séan Hand), Minneapolis: University of Minnesota Press, 1988, pp.124–32. Daniel Birnbaum returns to this idea in his attempt to see Doug Aitken as part of an unwritten 'Cinema 3' in contemporary art. See Daniel Birnbaum, *Chronology*, New York: Lucas & Sternberg, 2005, pp.49–55.

16 G. Deleuze, *Two Regimes of Madness*, *op. cit.*, p.253.

17 *Ibid.*, p.386. The notion of an 'impersonal yet singular life' figures in Bellour's conception of 'the room'; see note 8.

or collective—which would have succeeded it but, on the contrary, to prevent any such closure within private memory or public commemoration, showing, rather, the sense in which it is still at work in the present. This function affects fiction as well as documentary film, undoing the usual distinctions between the two, and forming part of the new 'realism' in post-War cinema that Deleuze contrasts with an earlier naturalism. Indeed, Resnais would go on to explore in his great fiction films this past-coiled-with-the-present that seems to haunt our banal lives like a terrible secret; he would explore how it forces his characters to think, as if they had come back from the dead, moving about in a world without salvation or redemption, providence or phenomenological grounding. He would thus pose a new question, at once philosophical and cinematic, which, across a whole range of arts and practices, Deleuze sought to introduce into the very idea of what an image is, and of what it means to think in and with images in mass industrial society.

Cinema Today

Today it would seem that the situation of cinema is no longer quite what it was for Deleuze in 1984 any more than for Benjamin in 1934. Cinema is no longer alone; it no longer has the key role that fell to it between silent film and television. It forms part of a larger complex of images and spaces, where it discovers new roles to play, geared to altered geographies and responding to new forces on a global scale. Deleuze now belongs to world cinema rather than simply to European. As with anything new, there is nostalgic talk of a 'post-cinematic' condition. The history of film has itself become a matter not simply of preservation and distribution, but also of an art of obsolescence that looks back to what it has been, as if illustrating Marshall McLuhan's old dictum that when a technological medium is over it is turned into an art. Deleuze himself tried to resist such nostalgia back in 1984 when there was already much talk of a crisis of cinema. His quarrel with Jean-Luc Godard on the last pages of *Cinema 2* is one indication. The crisis meant not the death of cinema (with its corpse to be put into edited histories in melancholic anticipation of a more hopeful time), but, rather, the emergence of new possibilities inseparable from the larger fate of the kind of aesthetic thinking Deleuze had tried precisely to work out in cinema. The time had come to ask not simply 'what is cinema?' but also, and more importantly, 'what is philosophy?' The great film-makers had used new technical means to invent a mode of audio-visual thinking, which formed part of a larger aesthetic to which it then seemed important for Deleuze to turn. What, in fact, does it mean to 'have an idea' in and with the arts, in relation to other arts and other practices? This is the larger problem that Deleuze would go on to explore together with Félix Guattari in their 1991 volume *What is Philosophy?*

This problem of thinking in and with the arts is already to be found in Deleuze's treatment of the abstract, experimental or expanded cinema traditions that tried to use filmic techniques in ways closer to the practices of the visual arts. While Deleuze doesn't focus on these traditions, what he does say is suggestive. He was drawn to Antonin Artaud's enthusiasm for silent film (as seen in Artaud's role in Carl Theodor Dreyer's great *Joan of Arc*, 1928) when he argued for the superiority of such works with respect to an abstract cinema still content to ape developments in painting, still too 'cerebral'. Artaud thought that the peculiar 'witchcraft' of silent film was much closer to the 'cruelty' in gesture and word that he was seeking in the theatre; and Deleuze sees this idea as part of a larger invention of 'theatricality' peculiar to cinema, as seen in 'bodily attitudes' and their relation to time, explored in different ways in many arts. Abstract and experimental film figures in Deleuze's study when, not content to imitate what other arts are doing, it takes part in the ways the cinematic changes our ideas of theatre or of art, as Deleuze thought was the case for Structural film in its relations with the 'perception-image'.[18] In other words, abstract film is not abstract in a simple modernist or self-referential sense, but rather in the ways it experiments with the very spatio-temporal conditions of sensibilia and thought, which the great post-War film-makers exploited for their own purposes; in that sense, it is quite concrete. Indeed the very term '*espaces quelconques*', which Deleuze develops in a striking way, for example, in his discussion of Michelangelo Antonioni's work, derives from experimental film; and it is not hard to imagine extending the problem of empty, disconnected spaces that Deleuze already sees in another way in the films of Robert Bresson to a range of other arts and art practices occurring around the same time as Structural film. Rather than a stark opposition between narrative and abstract work, Deleuze identifies an exchange or connection made on the basis of a common exploration of forms of sensibility — an exploration taking place concurrently in different ways in many arts. It is perhaps something like this larger exchange that we see today in a situation where cinema no longer dominates or stands apart. What, then, would it mean to take up Deleuze's idea of the cinematic in today's altered circumstances, in relation to current or contemporary questions and to new wars and kinds of war? What role might cinema and philosophy yet play in a situation that some have perhaps been too quick to characterise as 'post-cinematic' and 'post-theoretical'?

I'd like to look at how this question might be formulated in relation to the visual arts. How did the cinematic — regarded as a post-War *dispositif* to render the workings of time — help transform the very idea of the 'visual' in the visual arts? And in what ways does it continue to be involved in the new 'conditions of visibility' today? No doubt this is a complex question with several parts that go off in a number of directions. First, there is the whole question of how to think with movement- and time-images? In what ways have they

18 Gilles Deleuze, *Cinéma 1: L'image-mouvement*, Paris: Éditions de Minuit, 1983, p.122; or *Cinema 1: The Movement-Image* (trans. Hugh Tomlinson and Barbara Habberjam), Minneapolis: University of Minnesota Press, 1989, pp.84–85. Deleuze amusingly suggests one sense in which the 'expansion' in Structural as well as expanded cinema was related to the 'expansion of consciousness' in taking drugs, as part of the larger 'community', rather unlike the Soviet case, with which these North American experiments were linked.

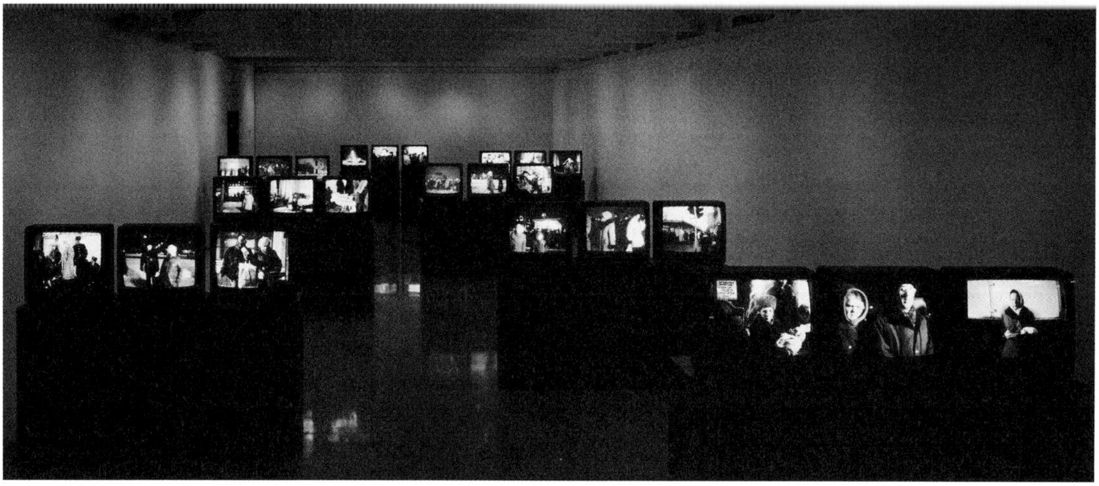

changed our understanding of what might be called 'un-moving pictures'? How do questions of time and movement change the very idea or sense of images in painting, photography or drawing, as well as our ways of seeing and talking about such things? Such questions have been explored in a variety of domains: in Sergei Eisenstein's discussion of Asian scroll-paintings as well as the Corbusian 'architectural promenade'; with the study of movement in Paul Klee's *Pedagogical Sketchbooks* (1923) or in Marcel Duchamp's *Gestalt*-defeating *Rotoreliefs* (1935) and *Nude Descending a Staircase* (1912); and, in another way, in certain practices of Kinetic art or in Futurism. More recently they have been taken up by Philippe-Alain Michaud in his analysis of Aby Warburg's *Mnemosyne Atlas* and his related Beaubourg theme show about the 'Movement of Images'.[19] Deleuze himself develops this question, of course, through his account of how Francis Bacon renders the forces of time in relation to figures through the a-signifying zones of possibility in the 'pictorial facts'.

Even Deleuze's treatment of the 'expanded' sensibilities in Structural film in terms of 'molecular perception' and the role of drugs can itself be read along these lines. This is also true of his account of the peculiar bodily, sexed or gendered theatricality of duration explored not only in the films of Andy Warhol but also those of Chantal Akerman, whose encounter with art and film experimentation in New York in the 1960s helped determine her own approach to questions of time in her cinema and later in her installations. At the same time, there is perhaps something peculiarly 'Asian' in the fixed frame and long duration, which Deleuze works out in Yasujirō Ozu's films, to be found in the early cinema techniques to which Warhol returned, and more generally in the priority Deleuze accords time with respect to narration; indeed Wu Hung has recently argued for a kind of proto-cinematic sense in Asian hand-scroll paintings.[20] We find a related strategy in Deleuze's treatment of the encounters of cinema with old-masters' paintings; take, for example, the striking pages in *Cinema 2* in which Deleuze connects the problem of depth of field in Orson Welles's invention of time-images to the decentrings of space in the Baroque

Chantal Akerman, *Bordering on Fiction: Chantal Akerman's 'D'Est'*, 1993/95. Collection Walker Art Center, Minneapolis, Justin Smith Purchase Fund

as read by Heinrich Wölfflin. Deleuze's many references to modernist painting include: the way the problem of the 'inhuman' in Paul Cézanne's sensations is taken up in turn by Vertov and the Kinoks; and the way that close-ups and affection-images in Eisenstein's film may be analysed in terms of the questions of pathos or of faciality — a key point in Deleuze's book on Francis Bacon, who himself was struck by images from *Battleship Potemkin* (1925) in his effort to paint the scream and not the horror.[21]

A context and impetus today for going back to look at such encounters of cinema with the visual arts is the wave of interest in moving pictures in art spaces today. Assisted by technical and distribution possibilities that appeared only after Deleuze wrote his cinema books, film-makers and artists now have a new exhibition arena outside the traditional darkened room of the movie theatre or familial televisual viewing spaces. Raymond Bellour and Giuliana Bruno have each analysed the role of the actual room and its architecture in such practices, and in their relation to earlier forms or *dispositifs* of image-installation.[22] Let me add to their analyses two brief remarks about how Deleuze's general picture of having ideas in cinema might be used in these circumstances. First there is the issue of how the new uses of art spaces to exhibit time intersects with larger questions that Deleuze develops in relation to post-War cinema of what movement and time are themselves; and it is perhaps significant that while Deleuze wrote nothing about such practices, his work remains popular among certain artists working with them — Pierre Huyghe, for example. In addition, these practices are tied up with the larger process through which 'contemporary' came to be distinguished from 'modern' art or art practices. Visual art and art spaces played a key role in the 1960s in their attempt to free the very idea of art from a series of distinctions and related practices in which it had been traditionally enclosed (traditional mediums and skills, studio production and exhibition in 'white cube' spaces) and, at the same time, from critical distinctions between art and mass or popular culture, critical discourse, information, or everyday life. Cinema participated in these attempts — in Robert Smithson's questions of site and non-site, in the violence of Gordon Matta Clark's 'anarchitecture', or, in another way, in Hélio Oiticica's interventions. Current work must also be understood in relation to such changes. In contrast to, say, Godard (who is still making great films), Huyghe uses film as part of a range of practices, similar to the way he uses Japanese Manga images — introducing advertising signs in urban spaces or orchestrating participation in parades.

19 Philippe-Alain Michaud, *Aby Warburg and the Image in Motion* (trans. Sophie Hawkes), Cambridge, Mass.: The MIT Press, 2004, pp.278–91; Philippe-Alain Michaud, *The Movement of Images* (exh. cat.), Paris: Centre Pompidou, 2006.

20 Wu Hung, 'The Painter Screen', *Critical Inquiry*, vol.23 no.1, Autumn 1996. The idea is developed further in Wu Hung, *The Double Screen: Medium and Representation in Chinese Painting*, Chicago: University of Chicago Press, 1997.

21 See Gilles Deleuze, *Francis Bacon: The Logic of Sensation* (trans. Daniel W. Smith), Minneapolis: University of Minnesota Press, 2003.

22 Raymond Bellour, 'An Other Cinema', *Black Box Illuminated* (ed. Sara Arrhenius, Magdalena Malm and Cristina Ricupero), Helsinki: NIFCA, 2003 — and reproduced in the current volume; Giuliana Bruno extends the analysis begun in her *Atlas of Emotion*, New York: Verso, 2002 in her *Public Intimacy: Architecture and the Visual Arts*, Cambridge, Mass.: The MIT Press, 2007.

Deleuze had posed the question of projection in terms of the larger *dispositifs* of camera movement, framing and editing as they appear in the early history of film and are later transformed. He was interested in how projection practices, along with editing and framing, freed themselves from the conventions of 'natural perception' (and from the mimetic conception of projection itself) to invent new sorts of images affecting our nervous systems. We see that from the start there is a sense in which the screen was less an illusionist window or *ersatz* classical stage than a moving frame with an 'out-of-frame' that allows movement and time to be rendered in new ways that would move beyond the conceptions of space in classical painting or theatre, suggesting alternatives to them. Thus Deleuze argues that the relation of cinema to a classical theatre space (and 'theatricality') is poorly posed as matter of a loss of or substitution for live presence. Rather, we find a new *dispositif* for creating images and spaces (and so of 'having ideas') with links or interferences with one another, which is connected to the two great efforts in theatre to create new kinds of image and space — Artaud's theatre of cruelty and Brecht's epic theatre, each of which is related to the cinematic exploration of time in 'bodily attitudes'.[23] Using the techniques of shooting, editing and projecting, cinema found a peculiar way to undercut the divisions between objective and subjective viewpoints or between the sound and image space in order to explore other spaces and times, which, even in darkened rooms, can strike our nervous systems in ways that are just as intense or cruel as live performances (which can often seem rather more predictable). If we try to then set current practices in a larger history of 'theatrical uses' of exhibition spaces, we need to include the whole problem in terms of the kinds of questions of 'images that force us to think' that Deleuze identified in post-War cinema.

The darkened room of theatrical cinema might then be seen as one highly successful *dispositif* in a larger history of image installation, itself conceived in terms of different ways of thinking in the arts. In this role, it became a laboratory to fabricate creative images — images to free our brains both to the patterns of clichés or *mots d'ordre,* which in turn serve to control our perceptions and affects, reducing them to easily identifiable opinions. Just as the filmic image is not, for Deleuze, a code or a language but rather an original way of expressing times and spaces that can't be contained in natural perception or affection, so filmic space, even in the darkened room, is more than a simple story-and-illusion apparatus. It is rather a *dispositif* that

23 Deleuze draws on Barthes's analysis of Eisenstein and the Brechtian 'gest' in developing his analysis of 'bodily attitudes' in cinema as seen, for example, in John Cassavetes's *Faces*, while he sees Carmelo Bene as close to Artaud. Ceremonial or everyday 'bodily attitudes' are time-images since the body shows them through the workings of time irreducible to plot or 'subject matter'. See G. Deleuze, *Cinema 2*, *op. cit.*, p.189; and Roland Barthes, *Music, Image, Text* (trans. Stephen Heath), New York: Hill and Wang, 1978.

24 Gilles Deleuze, *Proust and Signs* (trans. Richard Howard), New York: George Braziller, 1972, pp.5–7. Deleuze introduces in this study the question of the implications of 'showing time' for what he calls, for the first time, 'the image of thought'.

25 Deleuze discusses the problem of information in relation to Syberberg in 'What is a Creative Act?', in G. Deleuze, *Two Regimes of Madness*, *op. cit.*, p.322. He presents in terms of cinema the question of 'control' that he would later set-out more generally in his essay 'Postscript on Control Societies', in Gilles Deleuze, *Negotiations* (trans. Martin Joughin), New York: Columbia University Press, 1995, pp.177–82.

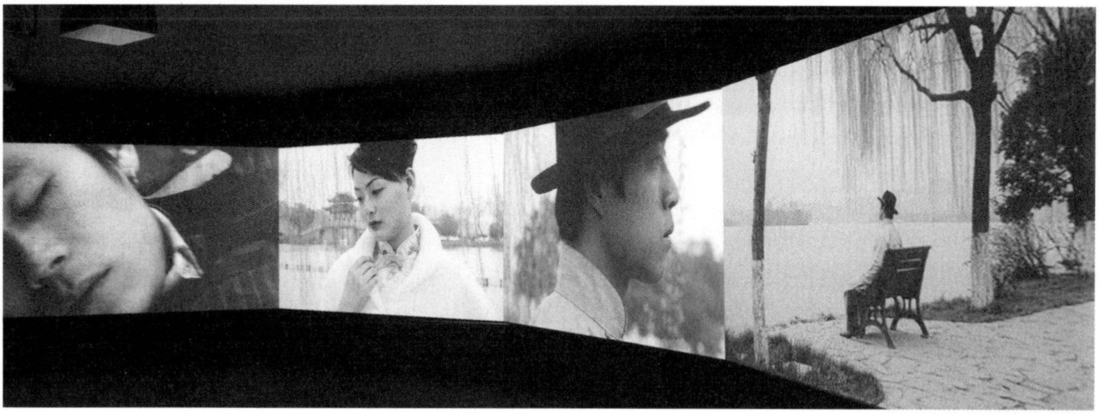

Yang Fudong, *No Snow on the Broken Bridge*, 2006. Courtesy Parasol unit, London

introduces a new 'psychomechanics' that directly affects the brain, as Eisenstein and then Artaud imagined, and to which Jean-Louis Scheffer would later attest in his picture of the post-War film-goer. The cinematic 'autonomisation' of images offered new ways to think and to make visible the role of time and space in thinking, and, indeed, it is just from this angle that Deleuze takes up the question of cinema as a mass, industrial art. He had already analysed the whole question of rendering a 'complicated time' in signs and images in relation to a new kind of 'intelligence' learned without prior method — an intelligence which always 'comes after', through encounters that force us think — in his study of 'signs' in the Proustian novel.[24] But when the same sort of problem (and notion of sign) is transferred, via the cinematic, to mass society, this kind of artistic intelligence encounters new enemies and rivals, and must be inserted into new circuits. It must also contend with a new conception of the public (typified in television ratings) — a 'statistical public' characterised by a whole new professionalisation of vision and a new massive machine of control over what we can see and say, think and do. In this way, Deleuze argues that, after the War, Hans-Jürgen Syberberg goes beyond Benjamin's preoccupations with mechanical reproduction and aura to ask more generally how cinema can create relations or arrangements of seeing, saying and acting irreducible to larger arrangements of information, communication and the public.[25] He thinks it is also why the history of cinema is a long 'martyrology' in the struggle to create new images, and why there is so often in cinema the dramatisation of a conspiracy against this attempt — an ongoing battle with the institutional forces of mediocrity from which an encounter with the visual arts or visual art spaces can offer one avenue of escape. The problem of cinema as mass art — 'post-industrial' as well as 'industrial' — is not simply a matter of the role that the cinematic *dispositif* plays in changing technical machines of production and reception; it has also to do with changing relations between having ideas and 'collective arrangements of enunciation' — hence, between intellectuals and the masses.

What is distinctive for post-War time-image cinema for Deleuze, in this regard, is a new political principle seen in altered relations between film-makers and their actors and publics. Unlike the 'mass-subject' of an Eisensteinian epic, the 'subjected masses' of a Leni Riefenstal rally or the much-calculated numbers of a Hollywood blockbuster, the problem Deleuze associates with 'thinking with cinema'—and, in a singular way, thinking with time-image cinema—is that the 'the people are missing'; they must yet be invented along with making the film itself. In his analysis of the new relations of directors to actors as well as to their publics in 'minority' and 'third-world' cinema, Deleuze tries to work out these changes, at once aesthetic and political. His sense of Straub-Huillet as great 'political' film-makers is a striking case of this view, but he elaborates it as well in his account of how the very idea of 'minority' breaks open the whole genre of ethnographic and documentary films toward a new aesthetic form beyond the fiction-document division. 'Mass' becomes indeterminate and irreducible to 'class' at the same time as there arise new ways of making it visible. We could imagine extending this idea to the global situation of the cinematic today; for example, beyond the division of fiction and documentary, contemporary artists and film-makers will invent images to get at 'events' in which an often violent, indeterminate past is tied up with the 'fabulation' of peoples moving in and across borders, irreducible to fixed classes or groups, related religious divisions or 'clashes of civilization'. Deleuze's study of post-War cinema may be read as a kind of aesthetic workbook for the questions of the multiplication of such situations in cinema and of their relation with the visual arts and visual art spaces.

New Analyses

How, then, does the cinematic change our idea of art? What would it mean to take up this question again today in new situations—for example, in relation to transformations in the visual arts? What role might theory or philosophy yet play with respect to notions of art to which the cinematic might be linked? To what kinds of new uses might we put this larger problem of 'showing time' through images that 'cause us to think'? In what ways, in the process, might we refashion the larger post-War image of thought that underlies Deleuze's analysis? One side of such questions concerns the style of analysis Deleuze forges in his cinema works. In the first place, there is a question of method. While Deleuze's books range over the entire history of cinema since the late-nineteenth century and are shot through with many historical, technical, social and political arguments, they are not history books or the books of a historian. They have another selective aim: to extract from the generality of films those singular non-linguistic signs and images invented by great film-makers to express time or movement in our own situations, milieus or worlds. They are thus not a-historical. Rather, they are abstract in another way, tied not to eternity but to the present and new problems, at once artistic and philosophical. It seems important to preserve this experimental aesthetic zone of questioning with which history is linked but to which it is not reduced.

In Deleuze's case, the new problems intersect in an increasingly complex spiral around the questions of time and thinking through which post-War cinema would be linked to post-War philosophy (and the 'theory' to which it gave rise). In this way, the War itself becomes more than an event in historical, legal or religious discourses. It becomes, at the same time, an 'aesthetic' matter — a turning point in the very nature of the images and having ideas, in which the cinematic would play a key role, especially, but not exclusively, in France. Thus the War — *this* War (with its mass destruction, its shame, the terrible secrets it left within and with respect to official histories) — figured in the cinema that came after it not simply in the manner Paul Virilio analyses — as a 'field of vision' or as a technological and propaganda machine anticipating the real-time wars of today — but precisely as the kind of upheaval in sensibility that called for the invention of new 'dispositions of thought'. Cinema would play a key role in the invention of a post-War aesthetic, exploring the ways a violent and indeterminate past figures in our very psyches, as in the early films of Resnais — for example, *Muriel* (1963), with its Boulogne-Algeria relations, and, of course, *Hiroshima Mon Amour* (1959).[26] For, along with camps, the questions of de-colonisation the War brought with it belonged to that aspect of the past with which cinema was concerned. Beyond his work with Duras, this is what links Resnais, in documentary and fiction, to the larger question developed in literature by Maurice Blanchot, who had his own sense of 'not-being-in-the-present', tied up with the disaster that would befall the very possibility of friendship in thought or of the 'philia' in philosophy. The philosophical concepts Deleuze forges in cinema — the idea of the image itself in its relations with fact, truth, 'realism', the space-time these images make visible, the peculiar role of body and brain in the way characters move about in them — no doubt derive from this larger context, even if they go off in other directions. Indeed, that is one reason why Deleuze insisted that the overlapping inventions and problems that he was trying to get at 'in cinema' nevertheless had to be fabricated independently of it and its history, in relation to other practices and inventions yet to come. To extract the peculiar kinds of philosophical creations which Deleuze called 'concepts' is to give them a life of their own, as indeed is the case for many of the conceptual inventions he works out in the course of his study. Theory departs from history in this way just when it ceases to be a reflective meta-discipline (as it still is with Kant), and instead becomes a source of new questions, encounters, interferences and exchanges, which cast older problems in a new light. That is what Deleuze seems to have had in mind when he declared that 'the life and survival' of cinema lies in its struggles with the informational regime of control, which he feared constituted a new rival to the very activity of thinking.

Deleuze's film books are thus not narratives, and to take up the problems or concepts that they work out in cinema doesn't require that one

26 Paul Virilio, *War and Cinema: The Logistics of Perception* (trans. P. Camiler), New York: Verso, 1989. In a larger discussion of these same themes, Virilio says that the paradox of the documentary treatment of war starting with Rossellini's *Rome, Open City* is one that has 'haunted me since I was born ... In 1959, *Hiroshima Mon Amour* provoked an upheaval comparable to the one caused by Seurat or Cezanne in the Impressionist period'. See Paul Virilio, *Politics of the Very Worst*, New York: Semiotext(e), 1999, p.29. The film is exemplary of the way artists use technologies to 'diverge' from the larger functions of propaganda or advertising.

insert oneself in any one story or history. They can be (and indeed have already been) used in many different ones. Deleuze's film books are rather 'montage books' of a roving philosophical spirit that try to introduce into the criticism (or reading) of film something of the collage approach and the 'stratigraphic time' that Deleuze had worked out for the history of philosophies, as in his famous image of a 'nomad' style of thinking. He thought there no more exists an intrinsic narrative in the history of the arts than in the history of philosophy, whose melancholy themes have long tended to overdetermine what Deleuze took to be the false problem of the 'end of art' (or 'the end of philosophy'). Part of the force of fabricating concepts 'in cinema' for uses outside of it was precisely to free them from a sort of intrinsic or internalising history, or a sense that cinema is a fixed language or medium whose only critical gesture would be to examine itself. The critical relation of the fabrication of concepts to the present is of a different sort. It is more a matter of introducing new histories into given ones. It supposes that there exist situations in which the usual stories no longer suffice once monolithic histories start to break off into many complicated paths. In this respect, the cinema books continue the strategy of many overlapping 'rubrics', which Deleuze adopted in his study of Francis Bacon, each going off in different directions, with sometimes unrecognised precursors and unforeseen applications, such that, in one such rubric, Deleuze can declare that each new painter recapitulates the history of painting in his or her own way. Against the search for a single great story or history in art or philosophy — reflected in the great nineteenth-century European dream of a great encyclopedic Library or Museum containing all words and images in ordered sequence — Deleuze proposed a new sort of pedagogy of images and concepts to complicate the present, disrupting its classificatory presuppositions in a process from which the invention of new kinds of images and thoughts is always emerging.

Deleuze adopts two interrelated principles in his cinema books to exemplify this approach. The first says that 'all criticism is comparative' and one must thus examine the cinematic in its larger overlaps with other arts and practices, since there is 'no work that doesn't have its continuation or its beginning in others'.[27] The second, found in the last sentences of his study, asserts that 'it is on the level of interferences with many practices that things happen, beings, images, concepts, all kinds of events'.[28] Together these principles encapsulate a preoccupation in Deleuze's writings in the 1980s with a reactive moment associated with the idea of 'postmodernism', in which, as if unable to create any further movement, thinking would retreat back into meta-reflection or meta-art, or else ironic re-appropriations of past inventions. The notion of 'interferences and resonances' worked out in Deleuze's analysis of the signs and images of cinema, then developed in *What is Philosophy?*,

27 G. Deleuze, *Two Regimes of Madness*, *op. cit.*, p.285; translation modified.

28 G. Deleuze, *Cinema 2*, *op. cit.*, p.280.

29 *'Intercesseurs'* is translated as 'mediators' in the essay by that title in G. Deleuze, *Negotiations*, *op. cit.*, p.121.

30 Deleuze writes: 'The limit common to all of these series of interventions ... is space-time. All of these disciplines communicate at the level of something that never emerges for its own sake, but

may even be regarded as a kind of antidote to this tendency, an attempt to get things moving again, to suggest sequences in which the cinematic might yet be inserted — 'we all need our interceders' he declared.[29]

Deleuze's study of cinema is itself filled with such interferences, and overlaps with many disciplines and practices, such that the cinematic lies precisely in the peculiarities of the way film figures in larger complexes, at once aesthetic, social, technical or political. When Deleuze calls post-War cinema 'modern', he doesn't mean 'modernist' in the sense of that word associated with medium self-reference, an idea he rejects or displaces in all of his studies of the arts. He doesn't at all see modern cinema as a melancholy retreat, turning in on itself in the face of kitsch. Its relation to 'clichés', its forms of abstraction, are of a different kind, linked rather to making visible new zones of space and time, and the new kinds of characters who inhabit them, using the *dispositifs* of mass industrial society. That is why the problem of 'meta-cinema' doesn't mean much to him, and why he is at such pains to distinguish the problem of the time-image from a simple opposition between narrative and non-narrative film. He insists that cinema's signs and images don't form a code or language that can be distinguished from others in some epic effort at differentiation and purification. André Bazin had spoken of an 'impurity' peculiar to cinema or the ways it turns to literature, or the visual arts, architecture or popular culture, for ideas to create its images. Deleuze extends this idea to include relations with philosophy or theory, as well as with sciences or techniques, as part of a larger image of thought. In the place of Kant's 'reflexive' idea of critique, Deleuze wanted to substitute a 'creative' one, in which the forms of sensibility that are space and time are themselves thrown open to experimentation across many different disciplines at once.[30] Deleuze adopted Klee's Bauhaus principle 'to make visible' as a watch-word for this process, and he associated it with a question in painting that Robert Delaunay formulated when he declared: 'Cezanne broke the fruit-dish; too bad the Cubists [stuck it together] again.'[31] It is in this sense that for the signs and images of cinema — for its logic, its peculiar manner of thinking with images — there pre-exists 'no determination technical or applied', not even a cultural or media-logical one; the signs and images must be precisely invented in a long and often difficult process.[32] For having an idea in cinema, there pre-exists no fixed sphere of competence, only available means and an inchoate necessity. As in any domain, an idea in cinema is something rare, given through many trials, moving back and forth, with many dead-ends, where one sometimes looks to other arts or disciplines for inspiration. Encounters across the arts, or through ideas in the arts, are not governed by fixed models, analogies or morphologies, but rather through the peculiar ways one invents to develop ideas, often through sensory means or in sensory spaces and time.

is engaged in every creative discipline: the formation of space-times.' See G. Deleuze, *Two Regimes of Madness*, *op. cit.*, p.315.

31 G. Deleuze, *Foucault*, *op. cit.*, pp.52–53.

32 G. Deleuze, *Cinema 2*, *op. cit.*, p.280.

It is not as if the 'contents' in each art could just be shuttled around from one 'form' or medium to the next. However, in making such invention possible, *dispositifs* like the cinematic are distinguished as something more than 'media' or technical supports, more than means of transmitting and receiving information; they are, rather, ways of disposing of our senses in such a way as to enable thinking, to make ideas possible.

The cinematic *dispositif* Deleuze isolates in the post-War period made possible the invention of new ways, beyond informing (through documentation) or narrating (through traditional characters and stories), to get at those events we can't make present through merely informing or narrating, or which require the invention of new kinds of 'image' that undo the classical division between the two. That is why it is so misleading to imagine that new kinds of *dispositif* simply take over or replace older ones. While it used new audio-visual technical means, the new cinema was not an attempt to supplant the book or the Guttenberg galaxy, as a hasty reading of Marshall McLuhan might suggest. It was a way of taking up the problems in the 'new novel' to create a 'new cinema', a way of linking creative ideas in books with those in darkened rooms. It was a way of breaking through the *sensus communis* supposed by our cliché-governed habits of thought, not only for the characters, but also for film-makers and spectators. For there is something 'dissensual' in the ideas that force us to think. That is why the new cinema led to the emergence of a new public, the sort of virtual audience that Serge Daney thought involved a critical 'supplement' of a sort. Deleuze thought critical thought should continue in relation to new conditions of informational control.[33] One is thus at some distance from the kind of communicational model of the public and public space, about which Alexander Kluge and Oskar Negt would challenge Jürgen Habermas in their search for another kind of 'public sphere'. In the place of a communicational sociability, Deleuze was interested in the way film-makers exploited the disjunctions of sound and image to expose another idea, developed philosophically by both Georg Simmel and Mikhail Bakhtin. Indeed, we find this notion already in Deleuze's analysis of 'wordly signs' in Proust, to which he returns in the passages in *What is Philosophy?*, where he is concerned more generally to contrast thinking and communication.[34] The problem of sociability in cinema might thus be linked to what might be called the sociability of cinema, or the way it creates new ways of thinking and thinking together. We thus find a larger principle that Deleuze developed in perhaps its most elaborate form in his study of cinema: the idea of a 'people to come' as a basic presupposition of philosophy, art, their relations with one another and their critical or political function.

33 See 'Letter to Serge Daney: Optimism, Pessimism, and Voyage', in G. Deleuze, *Negotiations*, *op. cit.*, p.72. Here the function of 'a little bit of art and thinking' is contrasted with the public as social consensus and the way it figures in the larger issue of information and control.

34 See Gilles Deleuze and Félix Guattari, *What is Philosophy?* (trans. Hugh Tomlinson and Graham Burchell), New York: Columbia University Press, 1994, pp.87–88. Here the problem of a 'sociability' in thought in opposition to imperial power is seen as the start of a problem of 'philia' in philosophy, taken up later through notions of 'fraternity' or 'solidarity' in relation to capitalism, and hence to Blanchot's attempt to rethink notions of 'community' and 'communism' after the disaster of the War.

How then does the cinematic change our idea of art? In looking at Deleuze's answer to this question from a number of different angles, we may start to better see the ways his conception of the cinematic fits with a larger series of transformations in the arts, and of the idea of art. These transformations suggest new zones for pursuing cinema's possibilities and, perhaps, new ways to play the singular game of art and thinking, for which Deleuze, in pursing his investigations and developing his ideas twenty years ago, offered a larger aesthetic frame.

DIFFERENCE AND REPETITION: ON GUY DEBORD'S FILMS
Giorgio Agamben

My aim here is to define certain aspects of Guy Debord's poetics, or rather of his compositional technique, in the area of cinema. I will purposefully avoid the notion of 'cinematographic work' with respect to Debord, because he himself declared it inapplicable. 'Considering the history of my life,' he wrote, 'I see clearly that I could not make what is called a cinematographic work' (*In girum imus nocte et consumimur igni*). Indeed, not only do I find the concept of work to be useless in Debord's case, but more importantly I wonder if it isn't necessary today, whenever one seeks to analyse what is called a work—literary, cinematographic or otherwise—to call into question its very status as a work. Rather than enquiring into the work as such, I think we should ask about the relation between what could be done and what actually was done. Once, when I was tempted (as I still am) to consider Guy Debord a philosopher, he told me: 'I'm not a philosopher, I'm a strategist.' Debord saw his time as an incessant war that engaged his entire life in a strategy. That's why I think that where Debord is concerned, we should ask about the meaning that cinema could have in this strategy. Why cinema, for example, and not poetry, as was the case for Isou, who was very important for the Situationists, or why not painting, as for another of Debord's friends, Asger Jorn?

What is at stake here, I believe, is the close tie between cinema and history. Where does the tie come from and what is the history involved? What is at stake is the specific function of the image and its eminently historical character. There are a couple of important details here. First, man is the only being who is interested in images as such. Animals are very interested in images, but only to the extent that they are fooled. You can show a male fish the image of a female fish and the male will eject his sperm; you can fool a bird with the image of another bird, in order to trap it. But when the animal realises it's dealing with an image, it loses interest completely. Now, man is an animal who is interested in images when he has recognised them as such. That's why he is interested in painting and why he goes to the cinema. A definition of man from our specific point of view could be that man is a movie-going animal. He is interested in images after he has recognised that they are not real beings. The other point is that, as Gilles Deleuze has shown, the image in cinema—and not only in cinema, but in modern times generally—is no longer something immobile. It is not an archetype, but nor is it something outside history: rather, it is a cut which itself is mobile, an image-movement, charged as such with a dynamic tension. This dynamic charge can be clearly seen in the photos of Etienne-Jules Marey and Eadweard Muybridge which are at the origins of cinema, images charged with movement. It was a force of this kind that Benjamin saw in what he called the 'dialectical image', which he conceived as the very element of historical experience. Historical experience is obtained by the image, and the images themselves are charged with history. One could consider our relation to painting in a similar way: paintings are not immobile images, but stills charged with movement, stills from a film that is missing. They would have to be restored to this film. (You will have recognised the project of Aby Warburg.)

But what is the history involved? Here it must be stressed that it is not a matter of a chronological history in the strict sense, but of a messianic history. Messianic history is defined by two major characteristics. First, it is a history of salvation: something must be saved. But it is also a final history, an eschatological history, in which something must be completed, judged. It must happen here, but in another time; it must leave chronology behind, but without entering some other world. This is the reason why messianic history is incalculable. In the Jewish tradition, there is a tremendous irony surrounding calculations to predict the day of the Messiah's arrival, but without ceasing to repeat that these were forbidden calculations, because the Messiah's arrival is incalculable. Yet at the same time, each historical moment is the time of His arrival. The Messiah has always already arrived, he is always already there. Each moment, each image is charged with history because it is the door through which the Messiah enters. This messianic situation of cinema is what Debord shares with the Godard of *Histoire(s) du cinéma* (1997). Despite their old rivalry—you may recall that in 1968 Debord said Godard was the stupidest of the pro-Chinese Swiss—Godard finally adopted the same paradigm that Debord had been the first to sketch. What is this paradigm, what is this

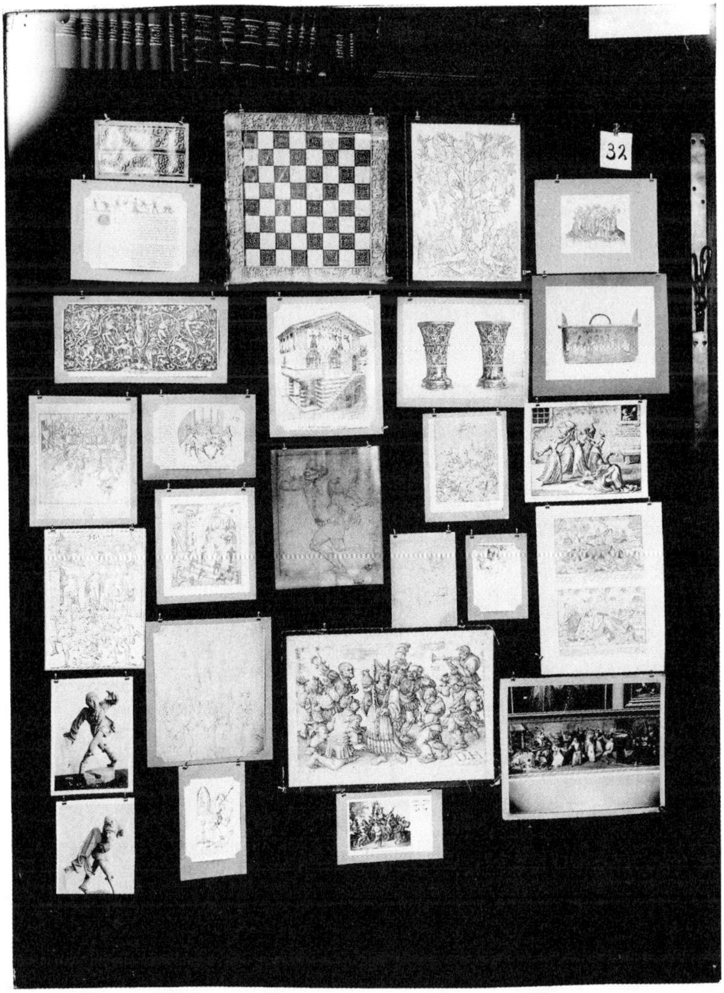

Aby Warburg, *Mnemosyne Atlas*, plate 32, 1929. Courtesy The Warburg Institute, London

compositional technique? Serge Daney, writing about Godard's *Histoire(s)*, explained that it is montage: 'Cinema was looking for one thing, montage, and this was the thing twentieth-century man so terribly needed.' This is what Godard shows in *Histoire(s) du cinéma*.

The specific character of cinema stems from montage, but what is montage, or rather, what are the conditions of possibility for montage? In philosophy since Kant, the conditions of possibility for something are called transcendentals. What are the transcendentals of montage?

There are two transcendental conditions of montage: *repetition* and *stoppage*. Debord did not invent them, but he brought them to light; he exhibited the transcendentals as such. And Godard went on to do the same in his *Histoire(s)*. There's no need to shoot film anymore, just to repeat and stop. That's an epoch-making innovation in cinema. I was very much struck by this phenomenon in Locarno. The compositional technique has not changed, it is still montage, but now montage comes to the forefront and is shown as such. That's why one can consider that cinema enters a zone of indifference where all genres tend to coincide, documentary and narrative, reality and fiction. Cinema will now be made on the basis of images from cinema.

But let's return to cinema's conditions of possibility, *repetition* and *stoppage*. What is repetition? There are four great thinkers of repetition in modernity: Kierkegaard, Nietzsche, Heidegger and Gilles Deleuze. All four have shown us that repetition is not the return of the identical; it is not the same as such that returns. The force and the grace of repetition, the novelty it brings us, is the return as the possibility of what was. Repetition restores the possibility of what was, renders it possible anew; it's almost a paradox. To repeat something is to make it possible anew. Here lies the proximity of repetition and memory. Memory cannot give us back what was, as such: that would be hell. Instead, memory restores possibility to the past. This is the meaning of the theological experience that Benjamin saw in memory, when he said that memory makes the unfulfilled into the fulfilled, and the fulfilled into the unfulfilled. Memory is, so to speak, the organ of reality's modalisation; it is that which can transform the real into the possible and the possible into the real. If you think about it, that's also the definition of cinema. Doesn't cinema always do just that, transform the real into the possible and the possible into the real? One can define the already-seen as the fact of perceiving something present as though it had already been, and its converse as the fact of perceiving something that has already been as present. Cinema takes place in this zone of indifference. We then understand why work with images can have such a historical and messianic importance, because they are a way of projecting power and possibility toward that which is impossible by definition, toward the past. Thus cinema does the opposite of the media. What is always given in the media is the fact, what was, without its possibility, its power: we are given a fact before which we are powerless. The media prefer a citizen who is indignant, but powerless. That's exactly the goal of the TV news. It's the bad form of memory, the kind of memory that produces the man of *ressentiment*.

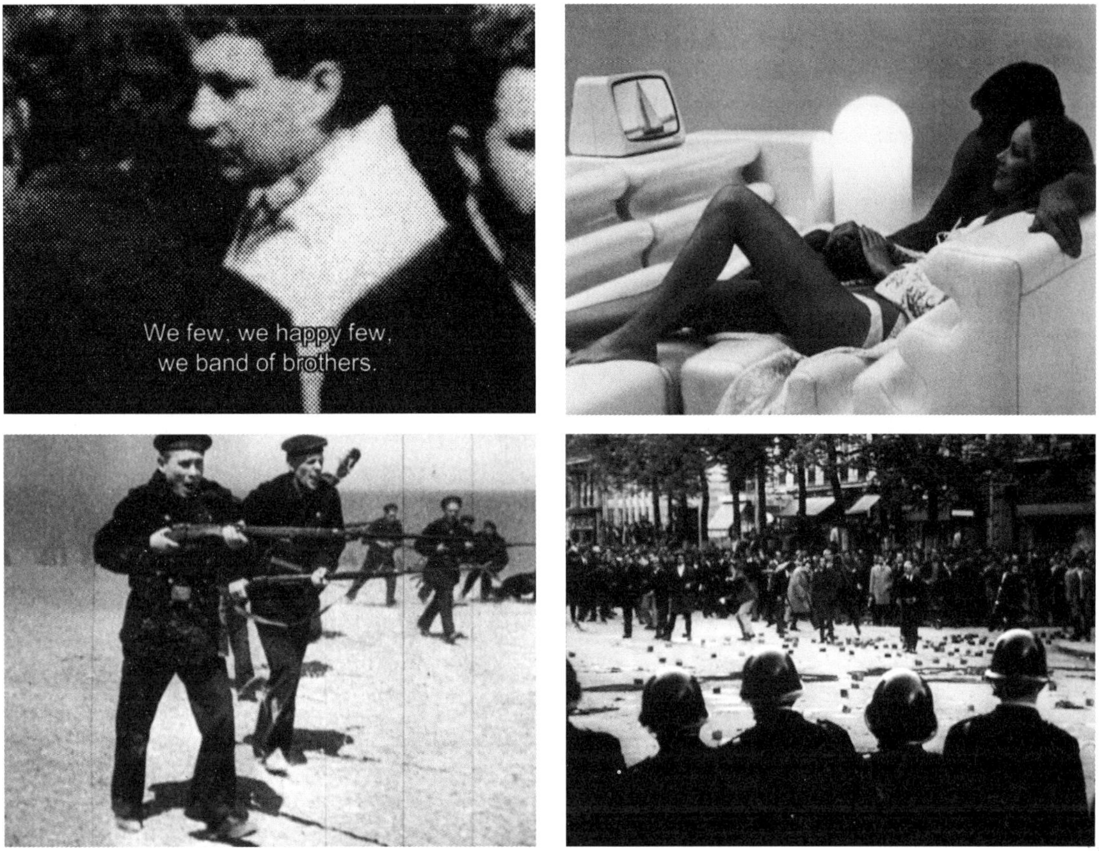

Guy Debord, stills from *La Société du Spectacle* (*The Society of the Spectacle*), 1973. 35mm black-and-white film, sound, 90mins

By placing repetition at the centre of his compositional technique, Debord makes what he shows us possible again, or rather he opens up a zone of undecidability between the real and the possible. When he shows an excerpt of a TV news broadcast, the force of the repetition is to cease being an accomplished fact and to become possible again, so to speak. You ask, 'How was that possible?' — first reaction — but at the same time you understand that yes, everything is possible. Hannah Arendt once defined the ultimate experience of the camps as the principle of 'everything is possible', even the horror we are now being shown. It is in this extreme sense that repetition restores possibility.

The second element, the second transcendental, is stoppage. It is the power to interrupt, the 'revolutionary interruption' of which Benjamin spoke. It is very important in cinema, but once again, not only in cinema. This is where the difference lies between cinema and narrative, the prose narrative with which cinema tends to be compared. On the contrary, stoppage shows us that cinema is closer to poetry than to prose. The theorists of literature have always had a great deal of trouble defining the difference between poetry and prose. Many elements that characterise poetry can also pass over into prose (from the viewpoint of the number of syllables, for example, prose can contain verse). The only things that can be done in poetry and not in prose are the caesura and the enjambment (that is, the carryover to a following line). The poet can counter a syntactic limit with an acoustic and metrical limit. The limit is not only a pause; it is a noncoincidence, a disjunction between sound and meaning. This is what Paul Valéry meant in his very beautiful definition of the poem: 'the poem, a prolonged hesitation between sound and meaning'. This is also why Hölderlin could say that by stopping the rhythmic unfolding of words and representations, the caesura causes the word and the representation to appear as such. To bring the word to a stop is to pull it out of the flux of meaning, to exhibit it as such. The same could be said of the stoppage practiced by Debord, stoppage as constitutive of a transcendental condition of montage. One could return to Valéry's definition of poetry and say that cinema, or at least a certain kind of cinema, is a prolonged hesitation between image and meaning. It is not merely a matter of a chronological pause, but rather a power of stoppage that works on the image itself, that pulls it away from the narrative power to exhibit it as such. It is in this sense that Debord in his films and Godard in his *Histoire(s)* both work with the power of stoppage.

These two transcendental conditions can never be separated, they form a single system. In Debord's last film there is a very important sentence right at the beginning: 'I have shown that the cinema can be reduced to this white screen, then this black screen.' What Debord refers to is precisely repetition and stoppage, which are indissoluble as transcendental conditions of montage. Black and white, the ground where the images are so present that they can no longer be seen, and the void where there is no image. There are analogies here with Debord's theoretical work. Take, for example, the concept of 'constructed situation', which gave its name to Situationism. A situation is a zone of undecidability, of indifference between a uniqueness and a repetition. When Debord says we should construct situations, he is always referring to something that can be repeated and yet is also unique.

Debord says the same thing at the close of *In girum imus nocte et consumimur igni*, where instead of the traditional word 'End' there appears the sentence: 'To be taken up again from the beginning.' The same principle is at work in the very title of the film, which is a palindrome that can be read both ways. A sentence that curls back into itself. In this sense, there is a kind of essential palindromy in Debord's cinema.

Together, repetition and stoppage carry out the messianic task of cinema I have described. This task essentially involves creation. But it is not a new creation after the first. One cannot consider the artist's work uniquely in terms of creation; on the contrary, at the heart of every creative act there is an act of de-creation. Deleuze once said of cinema that every act of creation is also an act of resistance. What does it mean to resist? Above all it means de-creating what exists, de-creating the real, being stronger than the fact in front of you. Every act of creation is also an act of thought, and an act of thought is a creative act, because it is defined above all by its capacity to de-create the real.

If such is the task of cinema, what is an image that has been worked on in this way, by repetition and stoppage? What is it that changes in the status of the image? We will have to rethink entirely our traditional conception of expression. The current concept of expression is dominated by the Hegelian model, in which all expression is realised by a *medium*—an image, a word or a colour – which in the end must disappear in the fully realised expression. The expressive act is fulfilled when the means, the medium, is no longer perceived as such. The medium must disappear in that which it gives us to see, in the absolute that shows itself, that shines forth in the medium. On the contrary, the image worked by repetition and stoppage is a means, a medium, that does not disappear in what it makes visible. It is what I would call a 'pure means', one that shows itself as such. The image gives itself to be seen instead of disappearing in what it makes visible. Historians of the cinema have noted, as a disconcerting novelty, the moment when the main character of Bergman's film *Monika,* Harriet Andersson, suddenly stares directly into the lens of the camera. Bergman himself has written of this sequence: 'Here, and for the first time in the history of cinema, a direct, shameless contact is established with the viewer.' Since then, pornography and advertising have made this procedure banal. We are accustomed to the gaze of the porno star who stares fixedly into the camera while doing what she has to do, as a way of showing that she is more interested in the viewer than in her partner.

Since his early films and ever more clearly as he went along, Debord has shown us the image as such, that is to say, according to one of his principles from *The Society of the Spectacle,* the image as a zone of undecidability between the true and the false. But there are two ways of showing an image. The image exhibited as such is no longer an image of anything; it is itself imageless. The only thing of which one cannot make an image is, if you will, the being-image of the image. The sign can signify anything, *except the fact that it is in the process of signifying.* What cannot be signified or said in a discourse, what is in a certain way unutterable, can nonetheless be shown in the discourse. There are two ways of showing this 'imagelessness', two ways of making visible the fact that there is nothing more to be seen. One is pornography and advertising, which act as though there were always something more to be seen, always more images behind the images; while the other way is to exhibit the image as image and thus to allow the appearance of 'imagelessness', which, as Benjamin said, is the refuge of all images. It is here, in this difference, that the ethics and the politics of cinema come into play.

Translated by Brian Holmes.

FROM MOVIES TO MOVING
Serge Daney

Photography is an immobile image, whereas the cinematic image has movement, different kinds of movements. In general, photography is contrasted to cinema as immobility to movement. True enough. But what's forgotten is that the movement of images in cinema could only be perceived because the people — the public — were immobile before those images. It's because people were put into theatres, locked into place before the screen and held in a situation of 'blocked vision' (as Pascal Bonitzer once put it) that they were able to *see* all kinds of movement: the (technologically fabricated) illusion of movement and a still more complicated movement, which, if you insist, can be called the 'language' of cinema, though it is much more a grammar: the movement consisting of everything that film-makers from Lumière to our day have proposed in order to make the jump from one element to the next. Cinema would never have been an art had there not been many different possibilities of *montage,* many different ways of forbidding oneself to pass from element A to element B without some underlying theory of editing that 'ensured' the transition.

But whatever the result (from Eisenstein's or Godard's ultra-sophisticated theories of montage to the practice of the linear narrative that seems to 'smooth over' all discontinuity), nothing of montage would have been perceived had there not been a movie theatre with immobile viewers, who furthermore did *not have the right to speak.* An audience that had been slowly trained to give up its 'bad' habits, to quit talking or interrupting the projection with its cries. This course of history, which must have taken considerable time, has left some traces, to judge by what still remains — here in France — of a truly popular cinema. It's enough to watch a kung fu film at Le Trianon cinema, near Barbès in Paris, to guess how the movie-goers must have played an interactive role with the film — taking advantage of the 'intermediary' scenes to go huff down a cigarette in the smoking room, making it back into the theatre just when the fight starts again. It's a highly archaic (and quite salutary) relation to the spectacle, one which television, in a sense, prolongs.

That said, what we call 'the history of cinema' is the history of the public's domestication, its 'immobilisation'. Broadly speaking: immobile people who became sensitive to the mobility of the world, to all types of mobility, the mobility of fictions (ahead to happier tomorrows and various other dreams), bodily mobility (dance, action), material and mental movements (dialectical and logical games).

My hypothesis (and as I state it, I'm trying to see if it 'holds up') is that a reversal has occurred. At the risk of reducing things to caricature, I'd tend to say that we've become very mobile in relation to images, which have become more and more immobile. Here's where we get back to the question of the relations between cinema and photography. The decline in the number of movie-goers results from the fact that more and more people are refusing 'blocked vision' — the seat arrest that sentences them to mutism and immobility, before an image which, in a sense, 'moves for two'. Audio-visual consumption (television, of course, but also video installations and things of the sort) tends to prove that we have learned how to pass by images the way people must have learned to pass by lighted window displays in the nineteenth century. The function of cinema as 'lighting', the implicit sale of desirable objects, the illumination of commodities for a bypassing public, this is what re-emerges. In a sense television shopping loops one of the loops that could be called 'cinema'. And one could even say that cinema has reconciled itself to one of its initial vocations, the *presentation* of things (which is perhaps a more primordial vocation than *representation*).

So we were immobile before moving images, and today we tend to move before increasingly immobile images. But what is an 'immobile' image? It should not only be understood as a 'freeze-frame', which a few years ago began to appear as a kind of death-drive instilled in film, which pushes the film-maker to reconcile himself with one of those 24 images per second, the ones Godard called 'the truth'. The freeze-frame marked a particular moment of cinephilic sensibility, but it was still a case of interruption, and of interruption as an action. Today it seems to me that we are in the presence of a new type of immobile image, a more 'serious' one, in a way.

Let's take Godard, a film-maker literally *transfixed* by the passion of the freeze-frame. Sequences of images, assembly lines, lines of jammed-up cars in a beautiful and premonitory film: *Weekend* (1967). But he also made another film, *Ici et ailleurs* (*Here and Elsewhere*), which slipped by more or less unseen in 1976, one of the most beautiful films ever made on the idea of *engagement,* of political commitment and intervention, or, more simply, of 'activism'. The film includes a quite long and excruciating scene whose 'meaning' has finally come to me today. You see people, people off the street, anonymous and average, managers, cleaning women, poorly dressed, fat, crushed, unhappy people ... all moving past a video camera which films each alone, one after the other. But each of them carries an image, a still photograph, and this is the image they come to have filmed, one behind the other, tapping each other on the shoulder and taking their turn. As if, in this scene, Godard were tempted to replace the '24 images per second' by '24 people carrying 24 images per second'; a veritable *mise en abîme*, infinite mirroring. No longer does the camera record things, but people come bearing their image like a cross before an indifferent video camera, set up there on a tripod, and it brings them into line, links one to the next. This idea of 'standing in line' with one's image so that it can be recorded (as if we were in the East and the image were

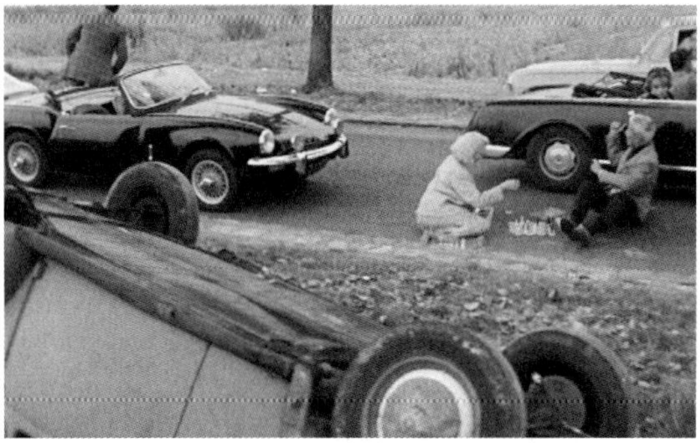

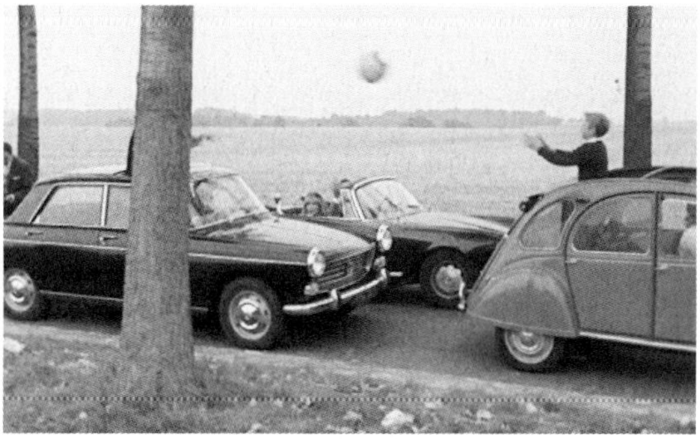

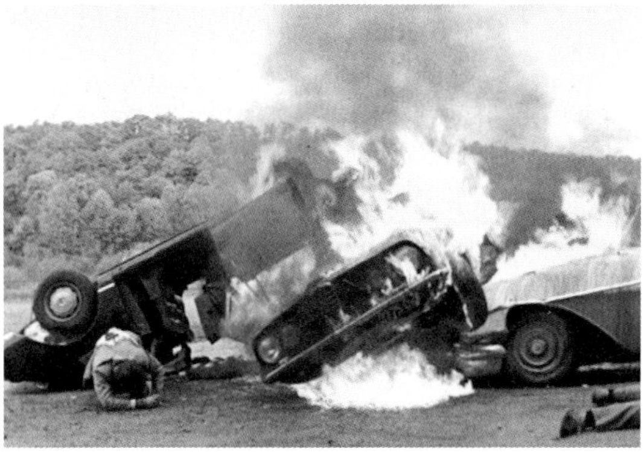

counted — Godard's dream — among the basic necessities) comes back in *Grandeur et décadence d'un petit commerce de cinema* (1986), made for television, where people move in line as well, but this time to intone, one by one, a long sentence by Faulkner.

In 1976, *Here and Elsewhere* came off as either a caprice or a gag. Yet the film spoke of how difficult it had become to intervene — from an activist's view point — with images. Though sympathetic to the Palestinian cause, having filmed in the camps, Godard could not find an organising principle for the images he brought back. He lacked a movement to organise the images. So, as always in such cases, he traded the question for the same question squared: 'Why can't I find the right montage for these images?' I think this was the last time a great film-maker joined forces with a political cause (and an organisation). A long period of film history came to a close.

In Godard's work the return to the inanimate (the freeze-frame) is clearly both a catastrophe and a pleasure (sadomasochistic, in a word). In his *Histoire(s) du cinéma (et de la télévision)* (1988–98), he takes the problem to the extreme. The idea is to salvage bits of cinema, sometimes in stills, sometimes reframed, at normal speed or in slow motion, to edit them together with words, music and texts, and then proceed to do an improvisation whose aim is no longer to relay the movement of the world but to recreate it from the tag ends (shavings, crumbs) that have filtered down from the filmed world: images already recorded, saturated with meaning and emotion. But it's true that Godard's ultimate question is 'How does cinema make us historians?'

Movement, the marching public, immobile images: another great example of premonition was given by a film-maker who is at first sight Godard's opposite, Fellini. We laugh uproariously at the parading people in Fellini's *Roma* (1972), especially the Vatican nuns on roller skates. But from *La Dolce Vita* (1960) onwards Fellini makes his actors not much more than bit players, only there to spend a brief moment before a supplementary character: the camera. There are no beginnings and ends in a Fellini film, those are questions he resolved once and for all, after *La Dolce Vita*. All the way until

Jean-Luc Godard, stills from *Weekend*, 1967. 35mm colour film, sound, 105mins

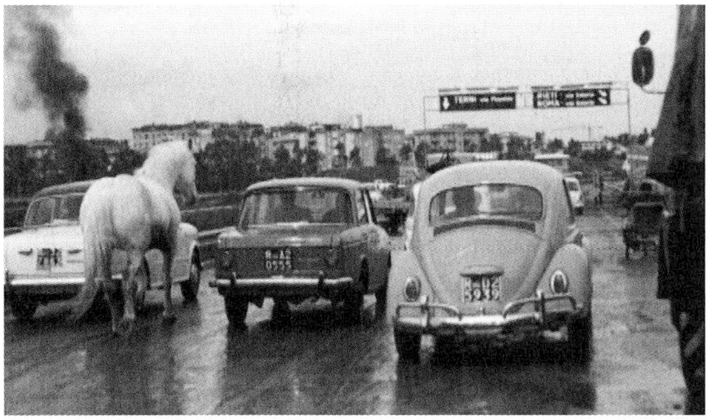

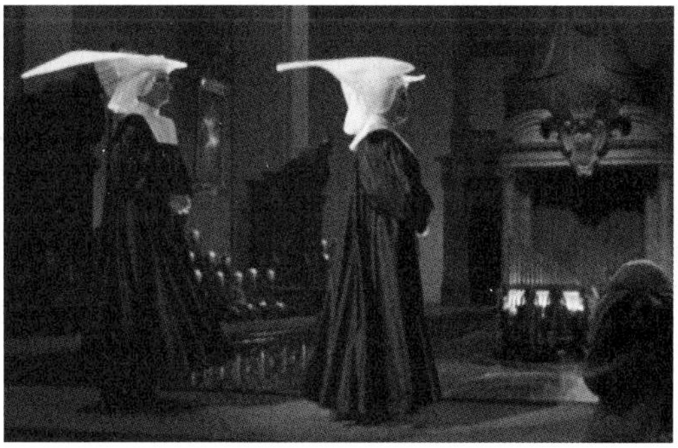

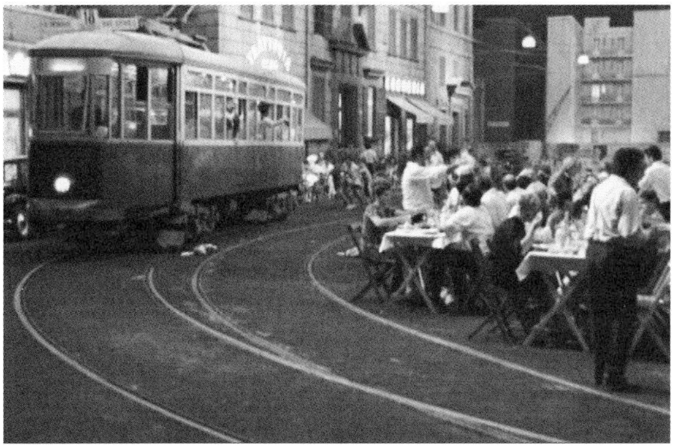

Ginger and Fred (1986), his films abound in parade scenes which are increasingly less affectionate parodies of what television does — in any case. *Ginger and Fred* is a major documentary on human stockpiling by television. And finally, with a bit of distance, two film-makers as different as Fellini and Godard seem much closer, like two journalists both saying the same thing: look, you can no longer film anything but parades!

Perhaps they say it at a time, from 1970 to 1975, which is a turning point in the history of cinema. And perhaps they are the last to possess such a cultural, craftsmanly memory of their instrument, the last before the amnesia. Each in his way, Godard and Fellini 'flirt' with advertising. The former sees it as obscenity, the second more like pornography — but both find it stimulating. Today, the advertising aesthetic seems to have triumphed in utter seriousness. Ten years ago it would have been a paradox to say that *Le Grand Bleu* (*The Big Blue*, 1988) and *L'Ours* (*The Bear*, 1988) were finally nothing more than advertising (I remember having said that about the first Lelouch films). Now the order of the day is no longer the 'contamination' of cinema by advertising (the question was resolved by *Diva*, 1981). Instead, the dominant form of cinema (the kind that 'works') has reached a *post-advertising* stage. Cinema now inherits prefabricated shots, ready-to-use 'clichés', in short — immobile images.

It's as though cinema had to *retrace* the path it has come by. This path was paved by the question: where are we going (where is the movement)? It now becomes: where have we come from (where does the movement come from)? The movement is no longer in the images, in their metaphorical force or in our capacity to edit them together, it's in the enigma of the force that has *programmed* them (and here the reference to television — the triumph of programming over production — is unavoidable). *The Big Blue* is far from being an innocuous film: it tells of the programming of the little ones ('*le petit d'homme*', as Lacan would say), of the new forms of totemism and the immobile unfolding of images which are already 'cliché'. If there is

Federico Fellini, stills from *Roma*, 1972. 35mm colour film, sound, 128mins a history of audio-visual communication — which will be increasingly harder to confuse with the more singular history of cinema — then *The Big Blue* is part of it.

It just so happens that in order to exist, such a 'product' necessarily inherits the movie theatre without inheriting the formal memory of cinema. The *fact* that such a film — or *The Bear*, which is even harder to stomach — can score such a tidal-wave success allows us to distinctly register the public's demand for cinema (something hardly possible before). It's no longer mysterious and I would say it consists in expecting cinema — and its rituals: dark room, big screen, group audience — to help establish the genealogy of the advertising image, in so far as advertising is now bound to the adventure of modern individualism. That the path should lead through mythology seems inevitable; that it should be a mythology of the *individual*, and no longer of *man*, must also be thought through. That on such a quest one should cross those who, for a century, have been its specialists, the Americans, seems equally destined. And that modern European (Franco-Italian) cinema — Godard, Fellini — whose greatness was to remain caught between 'myth and history', should meet with the respectful indifference of the public is, alas, just part of the picture.

And yet — that said — one needn't be Manichean. From 1945 to 1975, while 'modern cinema' (cinema coming out of the War, starting over from zero, from the ruins, in Japan as well as Europe, much more so than in the US) tried to save an ideal of man, and while television tried clumsily to save an ideal of the collectivity, the village and society, a third force — long unnoticed — was working toward the figurative safeguarding of the individual. This third force was advertising. When it became clear (only very recently in France, long ago elsewhere) that cinema depends economically on television and that the latter depends on advertising, then the loop was looped. Meaning that advertising could begin the 'adaptation' (that's what 'creatives' do) of a part — a small part — of the bodies and components inherited from cinema.

At the price of gradually losing its public (from which it asked too much maturity), modern cinema had nonetheless 'tamed' some rather tough realities, stretching the very limits of the spectacle: death, suffering, ugliness, everyday anonymity, dirtiness, dead time and so on. Once the public had been pretty much lost, advertising counter-attacked and set about fabricating a positive world, an always-better world, which, like the unconscious, would be unvisited by negation. The diver of *The Big Blue* is not a repeat of the diver in the advertising spot, the one who came up with a rose between teeth brushed in Ultra-Brite. No, he's the Ultra-Brite diver who had never before been taken seriously — figuratively and mythologically speaking. And what is serious, in the reign of immobile images, is the fabrication of a figure whose very principle is immobility, the immobility of he who knows only one movement, who cannot evolve, cannot be changed (by love or competition), who can do no more than disappear (it's actually quite touching) in the enigma of his own programming, in a mythical parity with the dolphins. Rather than speaking of immobile bodies (and images), we should speak of images and bodies as automatons, as does Philippe Quéau, whose latest book, *Metaxa*, joyously celebrates their arrival in our world.

The recomposition or 'reconfiguration' of the world is, as one might well suspect, the order of the day. Film-makers — the real ones — have been working at it relentlessly, and that's how one should analyse the *mannerist* wave that has washed over the best of cinema in the last ten years. Mannerism kept up a hysterical-affective relation with advertising (Wenders, Jarmusch, etc.). I get the impression this relation is running out of steam. The bodies of advertising are to cinema what those of religious trinketry were to sacred art: a terminal stage before the renunciation of the image (or its effective replacement by automatons). In other words: one can't tell much of a story through them, almost nothing is known of their innermost movements, nor anything of how they get along with others (even sexually). The ads, let's not forget, are not only 'little films', but they unfold in a deserted world, where at most two bodies fit on the screen, where the singularity of the bodies echoes no off-screen regularity (to the point where those abominable ads for Hollywood chewing-gum with their tonnes of joyous adolescents begin to seem like something out of Cecil B. De Mille). There is — to conclude — another, crassly sociological way of telling this story of mobility and immobility. It's that we're in a period of triumphant tourism, where everyone travels much more than in the past. It's no longer a question of 'discovering the world', its exotic and dangerous lands, through the window of 'documentary'. Or rather: the bar of exoticism has been lifted much higher. Here again, *The Big Blue* is contemporary with a moment when it's possible to go trekking in Bhutan with selected sherpas, yak-milk tea and personalised mystical experience. But precisely because this experience is no longer something special (just a product of the tourist industry), it may be unnecessary to ask cinema to give a desirable or convincing image for those who've stayed home. The proof? What do the kids say when they want to indicate that they've lived through things as complex as they are 'impossible'? They say: 'Man, I'm not even gonna tell ya!' And people complain about a crisis of fiction!

Translated by Brian Holmes.

THE TIME OF RE-DEPARTURE: AFTER CINEMA, THE CINEMA OF THE SUBJECT

Jean-Christophe Royoux

Early on, Serge Daney asked himself questions about the ends of cinema. That is why, working in the domain of contemporary art, on that thin line where sometimes it seems some of its practices have something to do with cinema, Daney's reflections interest me. Daney didn't flinch at inventing a few expressions meant to embrace cinema in its entirety based on the definition of what, for him, had been its characteristics, its historical sense. Still, as he was conscious of the dwindling of this destiny, he was always sensitive to what seemed to be, at the heart of cinema, the warning signs of its possible demise. He thus started by heeding Rossellini's words on the need for film-makers to take over the world of television, only to end up losing almost all of his illusions right away, like his film-making elders, while still holding onto a few powerful ideas on the relationship between cinema and information. He returns to this subject ten years later, with a new excuse, television having become in the meantime, for better or for worse, the repository of films intended for a large audience. But he also had concerns about what, for him, seemed to be a matter of putting the cinematographic apparatus into question. He wondered what could force cinema to go to its limits, and it seems to me that he took the chance — even if it was probably a difficult thing for him to commit himself to completely without offering a systematic exposé of it — to give a name to the primordial question of this cinema that was searching beyond itself. What I would like to try here is to reconstruct the main lines of this hypothesis instigated from inside the history of cinema itself, but the full testing of which probably requires the invention of another space of representation and therefore the connection to a different history: to be precise, the one seen on display in contemporary art for the last thirty years.

In this sense, Daney was right to say: 'Culture is a successful misunderstanding.'[1] It is in the very nature of photography, 'between the fine arts and the media', as Jean-François Chevrier puts it, to have made the status of images much more permeable. In this sense, it is completely justifiable to speak — as an exhibition had tried to, more than ten years ago — of 'passages of the image'. But unlike one of the more prevalent themes of this last decade,

1 Serge Daney, *Devant la recrudescence des vols de sacs à main*, Lyon: Aléas, 1991, p.112.

2 Here homage must be paid to the analyses of Raymond Bellour, collected in particular in the first volume of *L'Entre-Images*, Paris: La Différence, 1990, who made what he calls 'the photographic' one of the central subjects of his reflections on the transformations of the cinema-object.

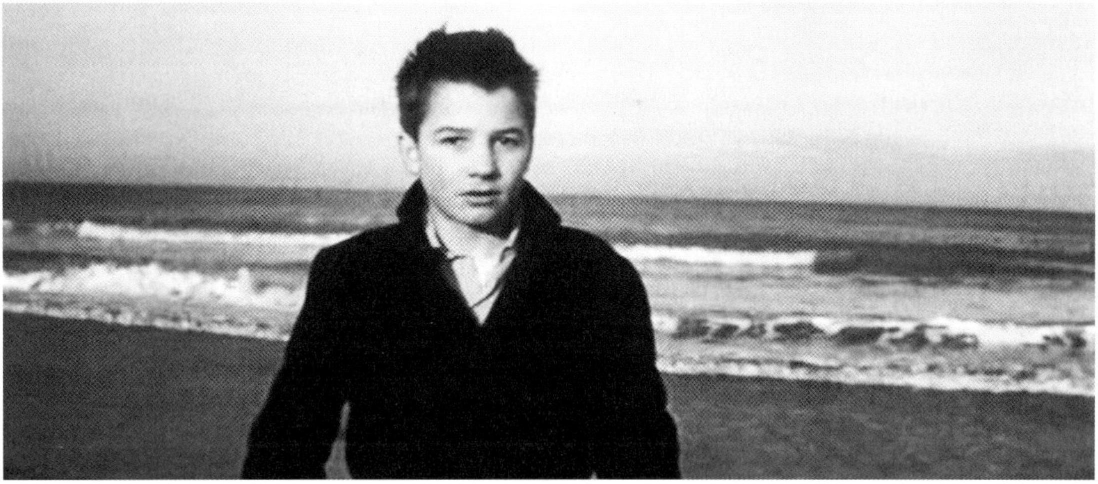

François Truffaut, still from *Les 400 coups* (*The 400 Blows*), 1959. 35mm black-and-white film, sound, 99mins

I don't think that there has been, or had been, real dialogues between cinema and the plastic arts, just as twenty or thirty years ago there was never a real line of communication between cinema and literature. We know that if cinema had been at first, for some writers, a source of inspiration for them, a way of extending the possibilities of literature, it had especially been, as Marguerite Duras put it, a way to be done with literature, to 'destroy' writing. It's not a matter of wanting to 'destroy' cinema, but to identify a reversal of perspective, the site of a conversion. All things considered, it is a fairly familiar phenomenon of the art history of this second post-War period that the most perspicacious critics have been those capable of identifying with the greatest assurance, in their particular privileged area of investigation, the fragile points, the points of tension where the endorsed model risked at any moment to shift over to its opposite. The most emblematic example is without a doubt Michael Fried's text on the emergence of Minimalist sculpture as a moment where the contradictions inherent in modernist theory are exacerbated. Why then, for 'we' who come from the so-called 'plastic' arts, should Serge Daney's commitment to a particular conception of cinema interest us today? To put it simply, we could sum up his intuition in the following way. At the beginning of the 1990s, Daney knew how to enunciate not the movement that comes to the image, as those interested in cinema do all the time, but the growing role played in these last few decades by the freeze-frame. After this stopping point, whose first appearance Daney observed in François Truffaut's *Les 400 coups* (*The 400 Blows*, 1959), precisely a half-second before the words 'the end' appear in the film, a passage is created that can no longer be described as an internal transformation to cinema, allowing for a new extension of it. This passage appears much more like an inversion, a return, for which Daney, not believing in 'an after-cinema from within cinema', is one of the few, with Jean-Luc Godard, to have perceived its ineluctable character.[2]

One could say that this is only another example in a history of critical writing constantly haunted by the work of death in cinema, as if death were cinema's privileged narrative substance. But Daney's knack, to a great extent, was to draw conclusions on the level of cinema as a whole on this permanent, almost insistent, presence of death in a multitude of exceptional films. He never stopped working at finding *the law* regulating the passage from the multitude of dead in cinema to the generality of the relationship between death and cinema, as if, just as he himself clearly put it, the cinema was born to maintain a 'kind of euphoria of mourning'.[3] So it seems to me that the tremendous love-hate complex that takes shape around the freeze-frame in Daney's writings goes well beyond the specific case of one of the expressions of death in cinema, and gets to the ontological heart of its essence and its ruin. In other words, the encounter between film and death, with the end of 'cinematism', in the freeze-frame, has functioned, in Daney's experience of cinema, as a decisive, founding experience, phobic *par excellence*. In Daney's world, a whole dialectic bases itself on the still image, one between two ideas, two genealogies, two conceptions of cinema that sum up the struggle around which his 'allegiance' to cinema and his 'belief' in it are structured. Far from some kind of melancholy toward a history of cinema that never seems to stop coming to an end, but also just as far from some kind of impatience to put a premature end to that very history, disentangling the misunderstanding that I have alluded to between art and cinema means exploring this hypothesis of a completely different kind of cinema where the freeze-frame, within the history of cinema itself, would have been one of the starting points identified by Daney. As a result, if the purpose of cinema is no longer to tell stories, if something is hindering the relationship, once obvious, between cinema, history and story, what we must understand is how it is possible to start again from that stopping point. In other words, by returning periodically to the question of the freeze-frame (since at least the first time he was asked to write about the relationship between 'photography and cinema' in 1984, by Raymond Bellour), Daney seemed to be preoccupied with the search for 'another time' whose culmination would simply be the inversion of the relationship between mobility and immobility inherent in cinema itself: immobility of the images (that, even when they move, constantly loop back to themselves, to ultimately go nowhere in point of fact, thus expanding the instant inordinately); and the intellectual, mental and/or physical and literal mobility of the spectator, who is asked to do a certain amount of work that is not at all incompatible with distraction.

Unfortunately, Daney's hostility towards 'experimenters'[4] kept him from noticing two borderline examples of films where the still image plays a crucial

3 Along these same lines, see Serge Daney, 'Le cinéma: ce qui ne retient qu'un moment (la mort au travail)', *La Rampe. Cahier critique 1970–1982*, Paris: Cahiers du cinéma/Gallimard, 1983, p.83. While discussing Vertov in *L'Entre-Images*, *op. cit.*, note 3, p.112, Bellour also stresses the idea of the freeze-frame as a first 'death' of cinema.

4 'In the area of cinema, undoubtedly under [Jean] Douchet's influence, we only liked the classics [...] I was never really interested by the avant-garde in cinema.' The cinema is the only art that never swung 'toward a dissenting relationship with large audiences'. See S. Daney, *Devant la recrudescence des vols de sacs à main*, *op. cit.*, p.118–19. Or again: 'The American underground, which is a sector with no connection to Hollywood, has never really existed for me, and that's not something I'm proud of. But, for me, cinema wasn't about finding itself in arrogant isolation, cut off from everything ... ' See Serge Daney, *Postcards from the Cinema* (trans. Paul Grant), Oxford: Berg, 2007, p.113.

5 Annette Michelson, 'Toward Snow: Part 1', *Artforum*, vol.9, June 1971.

6 Translators note: in English in the original text.

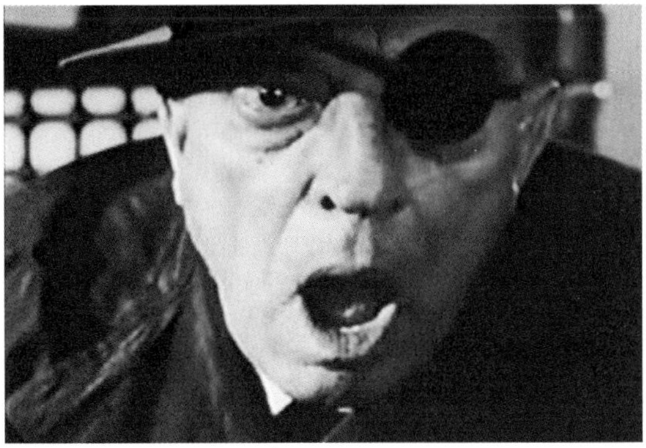

Samuel Beckett, still from *Film*, 1965, directed by Alan Schneider. 16mm black-and-white film, sound, 24mins

role in the success of the filmic project; bringing them to mind will allow me, from the outset, to formulate my hypothesis. First of all, Michael Snow's *Wavelength* (1967). Annette Michelson[5] describes this film as 'an inexorable advancing movement that seems to constitute the abstract spatial metaphor of the relationship between cinema and time, here reduced to its essence as a dramatic form of suspension'. The final fixed image, a black-and-white photograph of foaming sea waves, is the indispensable element to the film's self-referential closure. Through it, or thanks to it, the film loops back on itself in a metaphor of the process by which it was itself made. A parallelism develops between the film's self-referentiality and that of the spectator; one, sutured into the still image, is the condition of the other: the spectator's pure immobile presence, bound through his or her eyes to the slow, regular movement of the forward zoom. A perfect equivalence is established between the subject/spectator that the filmic situation's 'apparatus' takes hold of, and this very 'take', which manifests itself as the condition of filming this situation, as what is really at stake in it; as if the film were, to reuse one of Samuel Beckett's expressions, an attempt to capture that 'unnamable last person I'.[6] Stripped of the trappings of fiction, emptied of all other content except the dramatic tension through which the spectator, waiting for resolution, eternally suspended, becomes absorbed into the film, the image-duration becomes frozen, condenses itself into a block — the photographic image of the waves — about which one could say that it itself functions, metaphorically speaking, as the stand-in for the subject who was implicitly present throughout the 45 minutes of the film. The film coincides perfectly with this effect of pure spectatorial presence that the last image — the rippling of waves on the sea — prolongs *ad infinitum* on a metaphorical level. It is the inscription, in a metaphorical form, of the subject into the film. It is its *trace*. As if the 'gaze' of the camera, the active gaze of the spectator and the effect of co-presence that was their end result had finally been inscribed into the film itself. We find a similar construct in *Film* (1965), Samuel Beckett's first cinematographic experiment. Here again, even more explicitly, the camera's 'gaze' and that of the play's sole character coincide, in the form of a fixed image of his own face seen at the last minute in a reverse shot, after the character has struggled until the end to protect himself from seeing it. Here, literally, what makes the image stop, and the film along with it, is the subject's visual recognition of himself in the encounter. A mesmerising effect. The film, the unreeling of the images, stops when what constitutes its subject is the subject him or herself; in other words, when the construction of the person who perceives becomes more important that the construction of the presentation of the perceived subject. Today, among a whole generation of artists, we find a kind of development of the first formulations of this reversal of interest. Pierre Huyghe, for example, had the idea to make a film about the reception of a film (to remake an existing film on the basis of the collection of memories that it induced in its spectators). Philippe Parreno, as part of the 'Let's Entertain' exhibition at the Walker Art Center in Minneapolis (2000), tried to make a subjective, purely mental image materialise itself (the image of a state, of a moment), through the contribution of subjective images from a large number of associates. Pierre Bismuth in *From some folded shirts to ... (1,000 images)* (1997–98) presents the filmic unfolding of the succession, which was not predetermined, of photographic recordings from a strip of film as a sequence of 'slips of the film' liable to reveal the subjectivity of the person who, on the face of it, just put the shirts on without a preconceived programme or project (the opposite of cinema). We have here a principle of equivalence between all images — images of images, of films, of friends, of landscapes, of details — a quantitative principle of accumulation in place of montage.

1. The Founding Experience

As he made sure to let us know in his last interview, the screening of *Night and Fog* (Alain Resnais, 1955) in 1959 was a veritable revelation for Serge Daney. Cinema's confrontation with the unrepresentable that is the Shoah, 'a moral point of no return', was a first, radical experience of stopping before an image that, because one can barely stand to look at it, summed up all the others, while the film, partly comprised of still black-and-white images from archives — in sharp contrast to the shots of the camps, filmed more than ten years after the fact — kept spooling past, as one unwinds a ball of thread or wool. 'I saw, and in a sense, I've never recovered from that vision.' 'It is thus,' writes Daney, 'having chosen the cinema — supposedly "the art of moving images" — that I began my cinephagic life under the paradoxical aegis of a first *image-stilled*.'[7] Whatever the monstrosity of the facts recounted may be, the implacable visit of the camp goes on, without ever culminating in a dramatic interruption of the movement, which would be a truly unbearable sort of climax to the horrific story. It is precisely because things are this way, and that the film does not decide on its own to stop the image, that the moral responsibility of the spectator's memory is put into question. What is to be remembered, and how? But it is this very same paradoxical movement by which the film seems to be condensed into a single image that proves the irreplaceable justness of cinematographic experience. In the case of Alain Resnais's film, this movement is also expressed through a fragmentary writing style, disassociated from the film itself. For if all the elements work together to bring about the final success of the work — Jean Cayrol's text, Hanns Eisler's music — nonetheless, everything happens as if each of them followed its own logic. The film is torn between the information recounted by the matter-of-fact, detailed description of the tragedy and the monotonous, neutral tone of the voice-over presenting them; between the dissonance and harmony of the soundtrack, between the misleading image of a pacified present—the camp having become, ten years later, clean and silent, in the springtime sun—and the archival images in black-and-white, each one more unbearable than the next; between what little visibility there is of the material traces left by infamy today and the detailed recounting of the facts. Resnais's film is thus one of the first examples of a cinema that is not reconciled—a dissociated, divided, dismembered cinema, standard-bearer of 'the modern imperative' of an *other* cinema capable of not '[giving] the event back to fiction too early'.[8] One consequence of this sensitivity was a constantly sustained attention to the materials of film in all their uniqueness: on the one hand, insistence on the image as such; on the other, insistence on the lone voice, on a certain framing effect or on the skilfulness of the direction, perceived as so many detachable fragments of a totality in movement and whose characteristics permit any film to be redeemed, or on the contrary, affix a judgment to it definitively. So on the one hand, in opposition to the championing of American cinema by the cinephiles of *Cahiers du Cinéma*—in particular *film noir*, the championing of a special *tempo* of the action against 'le cinéma de qualité'[9]—and, on the other hand, in opposition to what will later appear to be, for Daney and for others, the very essence of television, one could say that the experience of cinema is first of all, for Daney, that of an image: not a 'beautiful image'—he stresses in his last interview that this is something foreign to him—but of a constructed image that one can feel, sense, one that condenses and stops the movement, opposing itself to any constant flow of visual information. *Night and Fog* is the paradigm of the realist art of cinema, which records and bears witness. In his last interview, with Serge Toubiana, one may assess the intimate and formative depth of this reference in Daney's critical development. One knew that the critic was hostile toward the increasing presence of signifiers characteristic of postmodern cinema, that he defended the recording, the 'block of image-sound'[10] that delivers 'some information about the world', the well-known message without code, the stubborn and literal presence of reality.[11] One now discovers that what founds film's subjective effectiveness for him involves an element that seems to be extracted

7 S. Daney, *Postcards from the Cinema*, *op. cit.*, p.25. Later, Godard/Gorin's famous quote, 'It's not a just image, it's just an image' (1969), participates in this same paradox where the multiplicity of images of which every film consists seems to reveal its end, its moral, its truth, through the exemplarity of a *single* image. As if, beyond the interest of the story, the creation of a continuous narrative line, the measure of every exceptional film, could be evaluated on the basis of any one example of its justness or its fatal mistake.

8 S. Daney, *Postcards from the Cinema*, *op. cit.*, p.30.

9 Translator's note: 'Le cinéma de qualité' was the term, considered as pejorative, that the writers of *Cahiers du Cinéma* gave in the 1950s to the French commercial cinema of the time, seen as excessively dominated by screenwriters and characterised by a 'psychological realism' that was 'neither real nor psychological'. François Truffaut's article 'Une certaine tendance du cinéma français', in *Cahiers du Cinéma* 31, January 1954, is typically considered the canonical text on the subject.

10 'Football with the sound of the ball and the players' conversations ... '

11 Incidentally, one may wonder if this is not the real cliché of a certain artistic modernity, encompassing the *Nouveau Roman*, Minimalism and, therefore, a certain cinema. On this point, a remark from Daney: 'A great film is, at best, a few years "ahead" of society. It can only record what begins to exist, it can only invent what is.' See S. Daney, *Devant la recrudescence des vols de sacs à main*, *op. cit.*, p.126.

from itself, as if the memory of a film let itself be entirely summarised in one shot, one image, one character, one line.[12] The concept of image would thus need to be enlarged, going beyond the strict domain of the visible. That would be one of cinema's real innovations, a redefinition of what an image is, that the concept of *trace* is perhaps the best at capturing. The image is what remains of the film once it is viewed. This is what the real dividing line would be today between this concept and the visual. If the visual for its part leaves few traces, Godard, for example, shows in his *Histoire(s) du cinéma* that, on the contrary, cinema is only an immense archive composed of the debris left behind by the subjective memory of films. In short, the opposition between still image and moving image is a bit contrived, somewhat rhetorical. After all, as Hollis Frampton pointed out, the celluloid strip of film is made up of nothing but a succession of fixed images. It is the apparently paradoxical connection between these two modes of the image that needs to be addressed today. As if the becoming of film was, inevitably, a becoming-freeze-frame. The distinction would be temporal rather than ontological: the still image would be either before — as its point of emergence — or after the film — what remains of it in the mind of the spectator.[13] The movement-image, conversely, designates the present experience of the confrontation with the film.

One may wonder if perhaps a recollection of the Rossellinian idea is at the heart of this conception of cinema. Daney's point of view on cinema, as a place for a practical experience of 'vision', is not very far at all from the Italian director's rehabilitation in the 1960s of the project of reinforcing the impression of the reality of cinema through 'direct vision', intended to remove the opposition between referent and signified. The basis of Rossellini's educational approach, at the point where he decided to abandon cinema for what he believed to be television's mission as a source of learning, boiled down to the idea of the 'essential image' for which the painting — a still image made of paint — would be the model. This only reinforces the proximity of Daney's position to that of Rossellini.[14] Clearly, the quote from Godard/Gorin in *Wind from the East* (1969), 'It's not a just image, it's just an image', strips the Rossellinian point of view of its essentialist and humanist pathos. Far from believing in a possible truth accessible through the image, it is the image itself that stands in for reality to the same degree as any one of its constituents. However, the idea (an ambivalent one, as always with Godard) of a justness of the image is not completely eliminated. Simply — as Godard sees it —

12 During a recent debate at the Femis [the French national film school] on the relationship between contemporary art and cinema, Chantal Akerman, commenting on a proposition by Douglas Gordon based on one of the most famous scenes from *Taxi Driver*, observed to what degree the artist's intervention had, in her eyes, the effect of condensing the film down to Robert De Niro's well-known line: 'Are you talking to me?' This is not the place to comment on the function of this line in the context of Gordon's work, but let us nevertheless observe, with regard to the logic that I employ in this text, to what extent the effect of reversal that I am attempting to highlight is comp-letely at work here, due to the structuring role of this ambiguous injunction. In the context of the film, this does indeed func-tion both as something addressed to the spectator and as something like the spec-tator's own interior monologue, exter-nalised. It is this confrontation that becomes the essential subject of the whole undertaking.

13 'The image is on the side of beginning.' See S. Daney, *Devant la recrudescence des vols de sacs à main*, *op. cit.*, p.134. In *La Rampe*, *op. cit.*, p.83, Daney defines the 'still photo' as follows: 'That which defies the intellect and never exhausts it, that which captures the gaze and the sense and focuses the scopic impulse: restraint in action.'

a just image can no longer be considered a transparent image, one that erases itself before the referent it exposes. It is as an image, no more no less, that an image can be called just. And this is precisely what distinguishes it from all the ideological undertakings that aim *past* the image and attempt to make it say something beyond itself. The 'good' image is a sample that has been taken without a preconceived intention to signify. It is an image that detaches itself from the continuum it comes from, 'imprints itself' into the consciousness and awakens it, allowing it to carry out a certain 'task'. If the intent of an immediately expressive image is greatly depreciated as a result, it is because, in the interim, the image-as-spectacle has taken its toll.

2. Cinema, Archive of the Present Day

And so, under the sign of the still image, a whole conception of the relationship to cinema becomes apparent. The 'regular deposit of mnesic traces' of which it consists is, as Godard says, not just the only way to become conscious of an unbroken history of the twentieth century, but it is also, from this very fact, the only way, for each of us taken one by one, to recognise that he or she has a history.[15] The psychic mechanism of the freeze-frame is merely an attempt to describe the relationship between cinema and memory, in other words the cinematographic articulation of the link between individual and collective memory, underlying all culture. It designates in cinematographic experience what Roberto Rossellini called 'the permanent education of the spectator'.

What is interesting about cinema, as many have insisted, is that it is an art that, more than any other, is firmly established in the social and cultural substance of an era. It is (it was?), it has been said, the whole of a society's imagination, the only real mass psychoanalysis of the twentieth century.[16] But Daney was no longer quite sure that cinema still had the means of carrying out this permanent task of X-raying society. This is why he said he got 'more pleasure out of writing about an old film, even a dreadful one, that was on TV and seen by many people, than about some deserving new release that premiered in an empty theatre'.[17]

It is with this somewhat retrospective look toward cinema that Daney appears in accord with a whole generation of artists for whom cinema is first and foremost an archive of information and sensations, of ways of seeing

14 I refer the reader to the text by Angel Quintana, *Mediación y transparencia. Un método didáctico para la utopia televisiva de Roberto Rossellini*, vol.134, Valencia: Ediciones Episteme, 1996, which gives a very general view of the topic. On the connections between the freeze-frame and the painting, see also R. Bellour, *L'Entre-Images*, *op. cit.*, p.120.

15 S. Daney, *Devant la recrudescence des vols de sacs à main*, *op. cit.*, p.107.

16 Félix Guattari, 'Le divan du pauvre', *Communication*, 'Psychanalyse et cinéma', no.23, 1975 (quoted by S. Daney in *Devant la recrudescence des vols de sacs à main*, *op. cit.*, p.112). But this is a widely shared idea, in particular by Roland Barthes in 'Upon Leaving the Movie Theater', *Apparatus* (ed. Theresa Hak Kyung Cha), New York: Tanam, 1980.

17 S. Daney, *Devant la recrudescence des vols de sacs à main*, *op. cit.*, p.107.

and showing that shows us not so much where we are going but where we are coming from.[18] As the widespread use by artists of *found footage*[19] — Douglas Gordon in particular — demonstrates as well, the intersection of the freeze-frame — as condensed experience of the world, lived through cinema — and the *archive* would thus be the true contemporary meeting place between art and cinema. The memory of cinema may actually be defined as *archive* of that which is shared by all. Cinema is the world's recorded double, a continent to inhabit. It is a way of informing us about what we are collectively, by reminding us about where we come from. It is the modern form through which a tangible conception of public space may be defined, the historical and imaginary space that is shared by all, which the salons and literary cafés of the eighteenth century brought into the world. Cinema is thus, by itself, the emblem of cultural identities. But in an era where various consumer products and collective imagery privatise public space, what one calls culture or collective memory is largely a matter of a culture of merchandise. Cinema marked the birth of this redefinition of culture, whose merchandise was the condition of its emergence. From the beginning, cinema has been connected in particular with the construction of basic figures, duly codified standards and narrative genres through which these figures evolve. As Erwin Panofsky has noted[20] — well in advance of a tendency that was, via Cindy Sherman's *Film Stills* in particular, one of the more characteristic forms of the renewed relationship between artists and cinema at the end of the 1970s — what is interesting about cinema is not the movement, the fiction, the story that is told. It is the accumulative dimension, the collection of archetypes, the typology of stereotypes and thus the 'figurative level of the filmic image'.[21] As with the style of criticism developed in the early years of *Cahiers du cinéma*, but in opposition to the importance of *auteurs* in that criticism, this is where he gets his particular interest — a somewhat paradoxical one for an art historian — in films produced by the big studios. His interest in cinema implies an increased receptivity toward representations, a sociological outlook that goes beyond taking the mastery of exceptional *auteurs* into account. It looks more toward the construction of a cultural history that requires an attentiveness to reality framed by standardised ideal figures. This is where the limit case of a cinema without film becomes possible, like the immense nomenclature of characters compiled in pre-War Germany by August Sander, who are so many incarnations of the synthesis that can exist between the uniqueness of individuals and the function or social status they occupy. Cindy Sherman — and the feminists — will take up this hypothesis and develop it fifty

18 This is notably the meaning of Douglas Gordon's cinémathèque project, collecting together the films that were screened in his hometown in the year of his birth, which he presented in particular during the exhibition dedicated to him at the Modern Art Museum in Paris.

19 Translator's note: in English in the original text.

20 Erwin Panofsky, 'Style and meaning in the motion pictures' (1937), *Three Essays on Style*, Cambridge, Mass.: The MIT Press, 1997

21 This fragmentation of the story in order to extract the constituent types is not unrelated to a certain perception of acting in cinema, from Rudolf Arnheim to Walter Benjamin, as 'broken down into a series of rearrangeable creations'; see my 'Expanded Spectatorship: Narrative Strategies in the Work of James Coleman', in *James Coleman*, Barcelona: Fondation Tapies, 2000, note 14.

years later. Incidentally, throughout the various versions of his essay, Panofsky emphasises the photographic rather than the cinematic dimension of films.[22] Didn't Daney himself have an amusing premonition in this direction, via the very strong personal attachment he had to postcards? Here again, through these 'imaginary extractions from a bit of landscape', it is a question of perceiving archetypes. 'The most beautiful postcards are obviously those in which the beauty seems neither planned nor willed by someone. I say "seems" because I could almost, and it's truly a perverse idea, reconstruct a *politique des auteurs* starting with the different types of shots and styles of framing [of] the main postcard producers.'[23] But, as if by chance and as he himself acknowledges, this 'film' woven from the succession of 1500 copies of freeze-frames sent to his mother, 'the collection of snapshots that is the proof of my existence', forms the 'only line' possible for establishing 'the chronological unfolding of my life'.[24] In other words, here again, as for the two examples cited at the beginning, the freeze-frame, as element of an archive that builds a bridge between collective representations and individual history, appears as one of the possible pivot points for a cinema that has become a means to tell one's own story rather than to hear and re-see-ve[25] the history of another.

3. From the Bad Image to the Cinema-Essay

As is generally known, in 1961, right about the same time as his fundamental encounter with Resnais's film, Daney discovered another point of view on the still image, which had become the 'bad object' *par excellence,* through a text by Jacques Rivette who excoriated a tracking shot in a film called *Kapo* that reframed the corpse of a victim of the camps (decidedly a 'test subject' for cinema) in a low-angle shot.[26] This spectacularisation of horror through the singularisation of a taken, stolen, extorted[27] image that is then exhibited as a 'powerful' moment of a dramatic plotline, was the early warning sign of the generalisation within cinema 'of pre-planned images, ready-made shots, in short immobile images'[28]—a process which incidentally led to the invention in contemporary art of one of the more convincing forms of cinema as seen in exhibitions. This form is exemplified by the work of Beat Streuli whose installations involving slide projections are comprised exclusively of snapshots of urban teenagers, often 'taken' without their knowledge using a zoom lens, whose aesthetic is not that far removed from that of a particular ad campaign for whom they are the target audience. However, unlike cinema, which functions unknowingly like advertising, this recycling on the part of the

22 Thomas Y. Levin, 'Un iconologue au cinéma, la théorie cinématographique de Panofsky', *Les Cahiers du Musée national d'Art moderne*, no.59, Spring 1997, p.44.
23 S. Daney, *Postcards from the Cinema*, *op. cit.*, p.63.
24 *Ibid*, p.61.
25 Translator's note: I stole this translation of 'rece-voir' (where it is clear the 'voir' is meant to stand out) from Channel 4's subtitles for Godard's *Scénario du film Passion*, where he says 'je veux voir, je veux rece-voir'.
26 S. Daney, *Postcards from the Cinema*, *op. cit.*, p.62.
27 *Ibid.*, p.62 and S. Daney, *La Rampe*, *op. cit.*, p.83.
28 Serge Daney, 'Du défilement au défilé', *La Recherche photographique*, special issue 'Le monde des images', 1989, p.50.

artist is not accidental. Rather, the assertion that advertising is the model for all of contemporary image production is a deliberate, and probably risky, act of re-appropriation that allows for the testing, more than the questioning, of how the inscription of each person into that very reality can take place.

As noted first by Daney, then by Pascal Bonitzer, the spectacular image is indistinguishable from 'the image as merchandise',[29] from 'the exhibition of merchandise for the public passing by',[30] which is actually a perfect definition of advertising. In other words, this advertising 'language' of the image attempts to momentarily interrupt the uniform monotony of the flow of juxtaposed heterogeneous fragments, cut off from any idea of connection and association, in which the image now finds itself trapped. This language, parenthetically, is an essential ingredient of that flow. As Fredric Jameson has suggested, the image is, as a result, reduced to a sort of logo that is a special kind of synthesis of image and word which refers to nothing but itself. Therefore, these logo-images represent the exact opposite of the image-as-recording, of that well-known ontology of the image — a proof that 'this has been'. The generalisation of the merchandise-form of the image and the transition to digital imagery — the coding of information — puts the image-as-recording into the minority even more than it already was. In a sense these new generations of images are synonymous with a liquid, regressive (immersion into sensations, privilege given to the ambiance, to the environmental aspects), dematerialised (they record the end to the specificity of media, a *post-medium age*)[31] and a-discursive state of the image (no longer any need to project oneself into a fictional world; now the goal is to produce an effect on the spectator directly). But when the images stop, it is always with the intention of taking the spectator hostage to 'sell' something to him or her, even if it is only the signs of his or her own (in)existence: 'I am melodramatic: cry! I am a lovely object to be enjoyed: buy!'

As a result, when the image has been absorbed into the visual, how can cinema remain the world's essential vector of presentation, how can one reconstitute the idea of cinema as the site for training the intellect and the senses?

Godard was right: the cinema can no longer do without reflecting on the image, on the way in which an image represents, through its exhibition value, 'the very act of "here is"' by which it presents itself.[32] This reversal of perspective thus implies the invention of a second cinematographic paradigm, complementing the first: it involves moving from the cinema of traces and of recording to the cinema-essay. It will now become necessary to apply oneself in all possible ways to removing every relationship of immediacy with the image's referent, every aim that is unable to question itself on the way in which it aims

29 As Pascal Bonitzer suggests, '*the image* [is the] *merchandise-form of the twentieth century*', in 'The Invisible Image', *Passages de l'image*, Paris: Editions du Centre Pompidou, 1991, p.18.

30 S. Daney, 'Du défilement au défilé', *op. cit.*

31 Translator's note: in English in the original text.

32 S. Daney, *La Rampe*, *op. cit.*, p.82.

33 Kaja Silverman and Harun Farocki, 'In Her Place, Number Two/Numéro deux (1975)', in *Speaking About Godard*, New York and London: New York University Press, 1998, p.159.

34 S. Daney, 'Du défilement au défilé', *op. cit.*

and to emphasise the rights of the metaphor, the natural medium of artistic thought. From now on cinema will have no other solutions than to 'speak in tongues', to show '[as] Freud tells us, and Godard repeatedly shows us, [that] the psyche can attach multiple and even contradictory signifieds to the same signifier'.[33] In a 1989 article, Daney presents Godard and Miéville's *Ici et ailleurs* (*Here and Elsewhere*, 1974), a film whose first half was filmed in Palestine at the invitation of the PLO, as one of the first examples (along with *Numéro deux*) of this reversal.[34] The film, which was intended to inform us about something — and what a 'thing'! one of the main political 'causes' of the second half of the century, thus one of the main objects of engagement that can be filmed — becomes a film on the film, questioning the reasons behind the impossibility of 'keeping' to the initial agreement. But *Here and Elsewhere* materialises this inversion of the aim by seeming to refuse the flow of the cinematographic image (the movement-image), replacing it with a procession of still images (held up by the characters in the film in front of a camera which is itself immobile), as if the cinema had to traverse the route it has taken backwards; as if, unlike what it usually does, it could no longer ask the question 'Where are we going (where is the movement going)?' and was condemned from now on to wonder 'Where are we coming from (where is it coming from)?', inviting us to go from the mobility of the image as necessary prerequisite for cinematographic experience to the immobility of the still image to try to 'recreate, from the bits and pieces that have already fallen from the filmed world, the world's movement'.[35]

This form of self-reflection is fatal to narrative coherence in film and, by extension, to cinema itself. It is no longer a matter of leading the spectator somewhere. The fact that the identification of a story with its end is *withheld* indefinitely amounts to an extension of duration. Doesn't the film, doomed to perpetual self-analysis, then lose its capacity to represent the real? As I have said, for a long time there was a large consensus on the fact that one of the fundamental interests of cinema was in giving an account of collective becomings, symbolising them, accompanying them, even clarifying them. This is probably why Daney, following Godard, was right to insist upon the intrinsic relationship between cinema and the act of *projection*. Today, conversely, as one recent exhibition in Paris (at the Grand Palais) has shown, the 'Visions of the Future' are displayed as a series of unordered parallel objects. What could be 'a next step after cinema' requires shedding new light on the articulation, the space between images — between the types or the constitutive levels of the image. This movement was mostly instigated by cinema itself, from Godard to Marguerite Duras.[36] But perhaps one should no longer expect it from *within* cinema before anywhere else. This dismemberment of the constitutive

35 As Thomas Y. Levin has noted, Panofsky suggested that there is a direct relationship between the cinema as mode of '*construction of space by or in time*' and the *perspectiva artificialis*, without however developing the analysis of the symbolic issues of such an association (E. Panofsky, 'Style and meaning in the motion pictures', *op. cit.*).

36 On Duras, Youssef Ishaghpour speaks of the work as 'exhibition space': 'Every level can detach itself, free itself from arbitrary unity, and develop itself within an autonomous sphere.' (*D'une image à l'autre, la nouvelle modernité du cinéma*, Paris: Denoël/Gonthier, 1982, p.285.)

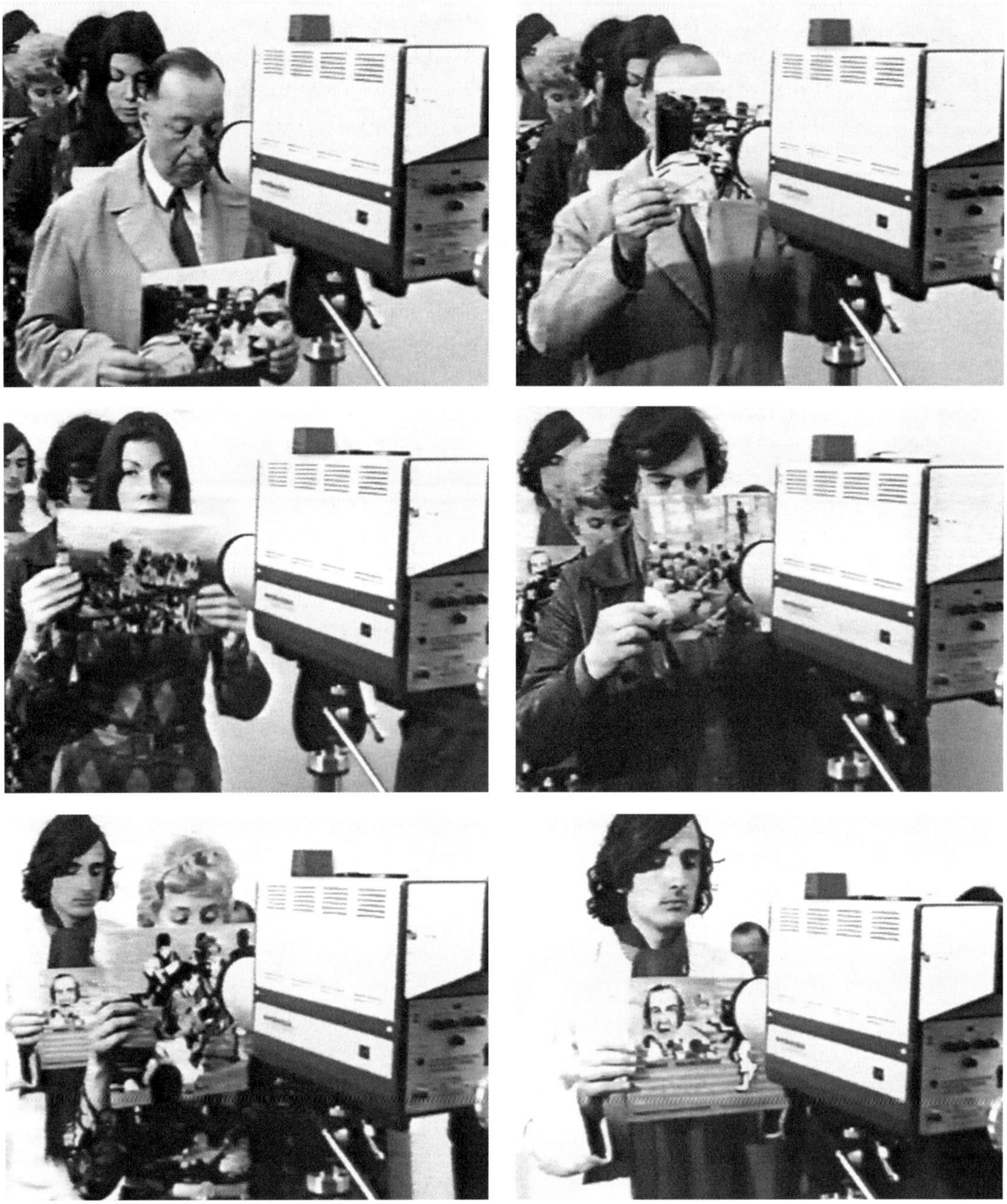

Jean-Luc Godard and Jean-Pierre Gorin, stills from *Ici et Ailleurs* (*Here and Elsewhere*), 1976. 35mm colour film, sound, 53mins

elements of film is one of the distinctive signs — alongside the form of the archive — of the interest artists have in cinema.[37] It means, for example, that attention is paid to the role played by sound effects or music in dramatic structure, independent of any fiction, or that the distance separating aspects of the film is brought to the fore: between the screenplay and its various interpretations, between the film's original and dubbed versions, or again, between a fictional, 'shortened' journey, filmed more than twenty years ago, and this same journey filmed today in its actual duration and inserted into the original footage to complete it. Opposing a homogeneous synthesis of the elements of film, the contemporary artists seen as having the closest relationship to cinema play with all the possibilities of disassociating these elements. The 'plot' no longer says anything on its own. Or rather, what it says can no longer be separated from the presence of the spectator in the space it also occupies. There is a movement of 'ingestion', of introversion or introspection that is no longer turned outside but inside, toward the viewing subject. What is left of the plot is nothing more than the support, the means, the medium of this constantly renewed attempt to turn the space already occupied by the plot into living space for the spectator as well. Cinema exposes itself:[38] a form (can it still be called narrative?) is established — that at this point can only be called 'story' for convenience's sake — for which horizontality, that is to say immobility and relativity, is the *sine qua non*.

Daney observed a certain tendency toward individualisation in post-War French cinema, and it irritated him. '[This] is precisely why we both love and hate it; it introduces us to a world-to-come which might no longer need the cinema; [it is a cinema] of individuals.'[39] Postmodern cinema, as Daney pointed out regarding the films of Luc Besson — although his films are of a different genre entirely — no longer presents anything but the impossibility for its autistic and narcissistic characters (Daney refers to them as *automatons*) to associate with others, and thus to tell stories.

In Besson's *Le Grande Bleu* (*The Big Blue*, 1988) Daney noticed one of the more characteristic symptoms, among others, of a profound paradigm shift in cinema's role in society: the actors'propensity toward being incapable of having a social life, or any sort of relationship to others. This is one of the reasons why, in Daney's view, the future of cinema within cinema was becoming increasingly uncertain. In a different way, work such as that of Beat Streuli, for example — typical, in my opinion, of one of the more obvious forms of cinema after cinema — shows how urgent it is to completely rethink our understanding of the experience of community; how detachment, and the withdrawal into narcissism it implies, is the prerequisite for a more just conception and representation of our relationship to others. In order to

37 I think in particular of propositions like Tacita Dean's *Volley Artist* (Tate Gallery, 1996) or *Feature Film* (Centre Georges-Pompidou, 1998) by Douglas Gordon, and of many of Pierre Huyghe's projects. One could also mention the specific details of the relationships established between the voices and the images in James Coleman's slide projections.

38 As is shown, for example, not only by the two screens within the screen but the equipment of the film and its director in *Numéro deux*.

39 S. Daney, *Postcards from the Cinema*, *op. cit.*, p.90.

continue thinking about 'what could follow cinema', it will now be necessary to change the question, to lose sight of what may have been cinema's destiny and leave oneself open to the possibilities of all other objects that allow for the subject's radical questioning of him or herself. Rather than wondering what kind of future film offers us, the issue now is wondering what the conditions are for 'the film to tell my story'. Still, this must be accomplished in a way that has nothing to do with either the projection of new role-models with which to identify, or with filmed autobiography, of course. With this new question, as set out by Daney, a new basis for fruitful dialogue between art and cinema may be established.

Translated by Allyn Hardyck.

DISSOLUTION OF THE FRAME: IMMERSION AND PARTICIPATION IN VIDEO INSTALLATIONS

Ursula Frohne

Vast as the dark of night and as the light of day
Charles Baudelaire

But inside, no more limits!
Jean Tardieu

In an early Sam Taylor-Wood photograph, the British artist appears in the role of Jackson Pollock, imitating the legendary pose of her historic colleague painting in his studio on Long Island. Barely recognisable as a female, Taylor-Wood restages Pollock's dance-like rhetoric, familiar from the Hans Namuth photographs that have become world-famous icons of the modern artist-subject. In *A Gesture Towards Action Painting* (1992), Taylor-Wood directs attention to this key moment in art and media history — the moment in which the artist-subject enters the picture via the physical act of painting ('action painting'), and thus bursts through the boundary separating self and representation, art and life. All this is indexed and inscribed on the canvas as moving traces of colour.[1] Taylor-Wood's appropriation of an artistic gesture that has crystallised into a myth can be taken as the starting point for a reflection upon the effects of contemporary video installation. In Pollock's gesture and its replication, a number of categories circulate, such as those of the theatrical, the notion of performance, *mise-en-scène*, repetition and the transformation of 'the image' (the screen) into a theatrical space or *mise-en-abyme*, as well as the transformation of the observer's perspective to a range of experiences made up of differing (art) historical perspectives.

Pollock's working method marked a turning point in the development of art, dissolving the traditional notion of the artwork into structures of action and performance. Film, photography and video — the 'new' media whose history is inseparable from that of the dark room, the technical and metaphorical transparency of the black box — made the concepts of such work accessible to a wider public. Pollock's drip technique — an act of painting liberated from the control of reason — eliminated the boundaries of the picture's surface,

1 On the relationship between work and artistic action, Harold Rosenberg wrote: 'On the screen, a picture should not be manufactured, but an event should occur.' See Harold Rosenberg, 'The American Action Painters', *Art News*, December 1952, p.76; and Regine Prange, 'Die mythische Geste', *Jackson Pollock. Number 32, 1950*, Frankfurt am Main: Fischer Verlag, 1996, pp.29–36.

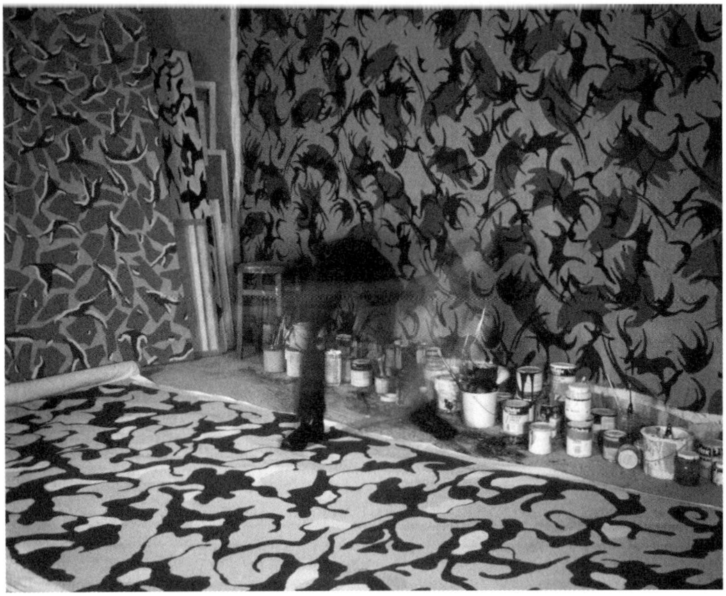

Sam Taylor-Wood, *A Gesture Towards Action Painting*, C-Print, 1992. Courtesy Jay Jopling/White Cube, London

and smoothed the path for a multiplicity of concepts of experience-oriented artistic pursuit, which steadily withdrew into dark environments as successive generations of artists increasingly improved their aptitude in the realm of new media. Taking the form of theatrical scenes and kaleidoscopic, large-format projections, these projects added the parameter of time to the space-defined visual parameter of the classical museum; indeed, the mechanical means of representation increasingly shifted the focus of visual perception from the experience of space to the experience of time. Pollock's colour diffusion — a seismograph for the artist's ecstatic osmosis (practising a kind of auto-immersion), which also visually dissolved the material basis of the painting — was a harbinger of this transformation of artistic practice. During the decades that were to follow, and aided by new technologies, artists perfected ways to stimulate the observer by creating spatial settings that engrossed him or her entirely. If the all-over effect of action painting triggered the potential dematerialisation of the support and included the physical presence of the body in the process of representation to the point at which, according to Pollock himself, the artist literally stepped 'into' the picture, then so, too, does the viewer today experience the reality-altering maelstrom of projected images in spaces of cinematic illusion.[2] Such images inscribe themselves in the viewer's mind either as emotional overkill or as detached moments of reflection, triggered not only by the inclusion of time as a point of reference in its own right, but also by the atmosphere generated by sequences of images lighting up in the dark, often with acoustic accompaniment.

From the White Cube to the Black Box

Sam Taylor-Wood belongs to the generation of artists whose working methods have absorbed the cinematic experience. Their installations transform the static, presentational space of the museum into a space for projection and illusion. Relating the all-encompassing effect of Pollock's paintings to the present, we can now say that the artistic practice of the past two decades has turned the black box into the new arena for the dissimulation of the frame. The black box has become a sphere for virtual events, where the public experiences moving pictures as engrossing images that stimulate the senses, while the boundary between the self and visual representation blurs. The museum itself is undergoing a metamorphosis, and is becoming a cinema in-process, in which, as Boris Groys has noted, the necessity for darkness creates a state of invisibility that often fuses with the structural impossibility of viewing a video work in its entirety.[3] This fundamental lack of visibility becomes a challenge for the observer as perception turns into participation.

Paradoxically, however, the power that unfolds in Pollock's action paintings connects the affective history of the white cube closely with that of its paradigmatic opposite, the black box. Since 1945, the reception of modern art has been inseparably united with the representative function of the white cube as a framing device. In a white cube, an object is dissociated from its real surroundings, and this de-contextualisation elevates the object to the status of an artwork. For Pollock's painting, the 'intensified presence' of the evenly lit, 'white, ideal space' became the setting for the performance of an existential aspect of expression — the embodiment of the artist-subject in the image — revealing a practically archetypical aesthetic effect.[4] Hans Namuth's visual characterisation of the screen as a 'stage' for the artist-actor has evolved in the contemporary context into the black box, the new field of action for the public. The black box reacts to the experience of projected images and sound dramaturgies, and, through the intensity of stimulated emotions, it ultimately interacts with narrative structures and numinous scenes. Brian O'Doherty, a leading analyst of the white-cube ideology, states that the white cube connects 'some of the sanctity of the church, the formality of the courtroom, the mystique of the experimental laboratory' with 'chic design to produce a unique cult space of aesthetics'.[5] If this is so, then the black box is the aesthetic that corresponds to the space of modernity, one that demands distance and embodies unity. The black box fascinates because its magic is of an entirely different order. It draws its power from the revitalisation of a stimulating aesthetic rooted in the immersive effect of the spectacle, which beckons with the theatrical allure of the unknown. Immersed in the illusory worlds of video spaces, viewers can cross the threshold of the immeasurable without jeopardising their own physical safety.

2 On the spatial relations between cinema and museum see Giuliana Bruno, 'Collection and Recollection: On Film Itineraries and Museum Walks', *Public Intimacy: Architecture and The Visual Arts*, Cambridge, Mass.: The MIT Press, 2007, p.41.

3 Boris Groys addressed the question of why contemporary artistic production follows a line of development toward the articulation of 'invisibility' by means of mechanical film-production methods, in so far as it traces the spatial parameters common to film reception by over-determining its temporal parameters and making it virtually impossible to see the whole work under the conditions of a museum display. See 'Immaterial Communication' (a conversation between Ursula Frohne, Boris Groys and Peter Weibel), in Annette W. Balkema and Henk Slager (eds.), *Concepts on the Move*, Amsterdam and New York: Lier en Boog, 2002. For more on 'Darkening Exhibition Spaces', see Boris Groys, *Die Logik der Sammlung*, Munich: Carl Hanser Verlag, 1997, p.22. For a reflection on video installations in the 1990s, see also Ursula Frohne (ed.), *video cult/ures*, Cologne: DuMont, 1999.

4 Brian O'Doherty, *Inside the White Cube: The Ideology of the Gallery Space*, Berkeley: University of California Press, 1986, p.14.

5 *Ibid.*

The Art of the Spectacle

Cinema itself is inextricably linked with modernism in our culture's metamorphosis into a cinephilic one through mass media. Regardless of whether its forerunners were the panorama, the wax museum, the amusement park or the architecture of nineteenth-century metropolises that brought about the *flâneur*, cinema evolved into the pinnacle medium of the twentieth-century entertainment industry, doing so despite (or perhaps because of) its popularisation through television. Cinema has decisively shaped the artistic developments of the past decades with an aesthetic that even Erwin Panofsky recognised as a 'necessity' of modern life rather than as an 'adornment'.[6] In spite of its technological sophistication, something survived in cinema that was uncanny to modernism: the popular rhetoric of nineteenth-century simulation embodied in the narrative style known as melodrama. To this day the core of the entertainment culture is based on this development — on people yearning to be in other places, taking on other identities. Viewers achieve such transitions and transformations by means of emotional affect and the perfect illusion — an illusion that uses optical effects and new visual technologies that make the frame of reference, by which the image is conventionally characterised, disappear. Blurring the boundary between spectator and spectacle allows viewers to imagine themselves as being part of what affects their perception.[7]

This sort of stimulating aesthetic first began to be investigated as early as the eighteenth century. For example, English gardens, imaginatively landscaped as living paintings through which one could stroll, can be regarded as immersion practices that foreshadowed the cinematic effects of Hollywood in their attempts to transport the visitor to different realities. Alexander Pope describes the artful concealment of fences in such gardens; the alternation of landscape accents; and creatively staged surprise-effects in the form of follies built to look like classical temples and monuments, ruins, illuminated fountains and bizarre grottos. His commentary documents a basic need for illusory effects that both imitate and exaggerate real life.[8] The emergence of the Gothic novel in this period heralds the theme of overwhelming attraction

6 See Erwin Panofsky, 'Style and Medium in the Motion Pictures', *Three Essays on Style* (ed. Irving Lavin), Cambridge, Mass.: The MIT Press, 1995, p.122. For a critical exegesis of Panofsky's essay, characterising his approach to the aesthetic experience of film as an attempt to safeguard a concept of reality, which had been lost in the destruction of the illusionary space in abstract art, see Regine Prange, 'Stil und Medium. Panofsky "On Movies"' (ed. Bruno Reudenbach), *Erwin Panofsky. Beiträge des Symposiums, Hamburg 1992*, Berlin: Akademie Verlag 1994, pp.171–90. For the relation between art and cinema, see also Thomas Hensel, Klaus Krüger and Tanja Michalsky (eds.), *Das bewegte Bild. Film und Kunst*, Munich: Wilhelm Fink Verlag, 2006.

7 Early film spectacles such as those by Anthony Griffiths, on the other hand, imitated the panoramas of English landscape paintings or Francesco Piransi's spatial caprices. They seem to quote the visual practices of the panorama, the forerunner of Cinemascope, which also attempted to convey a total illusion — suggesting to the viewer that he or she had reached another place simply by looking at something, and without having had to physically move location. See Kerry Brougher, 'Hitch-Hiking in Dreamscapes', *Notorious: Alfred Hitchcock and Contemporary Art* (ed. Kerry Brougher and Michael Tarantino), Oxford: Museum of Modern Art, 1999. Today's theme parks and hotels in Las Vegas and Japan are another variation on this particular pleasure: fairy-tale settings that provide a dream world for visitors, where the eternal boredom of ordinary life is temporarily set aglow by means of the absolute immediacy of the experience, in comparable fashion to a scene from a film.

and emotional stimulation as a medium of entertainment, a development that was to go far beyond Friedrich Schlegel's articulated prophecy of an 'escalation of the aesthetic of the interesting'.[9]

The Aesthetic of the Remake

Degraded to a mass medium by Hollywood, film has experienced its artistic elevation through the medium of video. Contemporary video installations do not simply employ the effects of audience identification that make commercial entertainment films successful; they also employ distancing approaches that consciously instil disillusionment within the observer, at the same time as creating a palpable detachment from the visual effects of cinematographic fictions, as has been shown by Juliane Rebentisch's illuminating analysis concerning the aesthetic phenomena of cinematographic installations.[10] Roughly one hundred years since the birth of film, the artistic 'remake' uses various methods and degrees of alienation to bring film classics back to their elementary structures, critically illuminating the history of the medium's effects through analytical procedures. Such strategies that alienate 'original' films are employed by contemporary artists as a means of exploring the reception of cinema, the technical aspects of which have become cultural constants for spectators (i.e. the 'cinematic character' of the black space, the conventional narrative that presents the flow of the plot in sequences of images, the montage techniques that create the illusion of 'real life').

Accordingly, for artists of the post-cinematic era, cinema and film are not interesting primarily as examples of particular genres, but as repositories of the raw visual materials that flood the pictorial worlds of ordinary culture.[11] Two general tendencies can be discerned in their working methods.[12] First, video installations by artists such as Pipilotti Rist and Doug Aitken respond affirmatively to the illusionary, affective principles of the cinematic parameters by creating spatial all-over effects through perfectly matched images and sounds that captivate the viewer in a kind of hypnotising reality camouflage. In order to attain such effects, they consciously draw on professional editing

8 See *The Works of Alexander Pope, esq.*, vol.IX, London 1757, Letter XL, 'A confutation about defining a garden, various opinions and some general reflections'. Also: http://books.google.de/books?id=lQcfAAAAMAAJ&printsec=frontcover&dq=inauthor:Alexander+inauthor:Pope&lr=#PPP1,M1

9 Friedrich Schlegel, *Über das Studium der griechischen Poesie. Kritische Friedrich-Schlegel-Ausgabe* (ed. Ernst Behler) Bd.1., Munich, Paderborn and Vienna: Schöningh, 1979, pp.217–367.

10 See Juliane Rebentisch, 'c) Die kinematographische Installation (Boris Groys, Walter Benjamin)', *Ästhetik der Installation*, Frankfurt/M: Suhrkamp, 2003, pp.179–207.

11 The emergence of non-linear structures and the possibility for interactive audience participation from expanded cinema through television, video and electronic media has been prompted by a desire to investigate communication structures and the relevant electronic possibilities. The disruption of the holistic cinematic experience is generally referred to by the term post-cinematic. See Peter Greenaway, 'Toward a re-invention of cinema', *Variety Cinema Militans Lecture*, The Netherlands, 2003; also cited by Matthew Clayfield, 'A Cinema Exploded: Notes on the Development of Some Post-Cinematic Forms', www.braintrustdv.com/essays/cinema-exploded.html

12 For the remake based on found-footage compilation or manipulation in contemporary art, see Stefano Basilico (ed.), *Cut: Film as Found Object in Contemporary Video* (exh. cat.), Milwaukee: Milwaukee Art Museum, 2005; and *Remakes* (exh. cat.), Bordeaux: CAPC, Musée d'art contemporain de Bordeaux, 2004.

techniques and the entire technological repertoire from MTV to Hollywood production, endeavouring to overwhelm the viewer, visually and acoustically. In such immersive installations, the exploration of mainstream themes are the focus of interest: the need for transcendence; the desire for extraordinary sensations, such as those experienced at a rave or a dance club; the permeation of technology; the magnetism of the information flood; mass media's influence on every area of contemporary culture; the attraction of velocity; and the fascination of potential omnipresence, which is the futuristic promise of the media.

Second, the other, more conceptually defined direction in video installation exposes cinema and media culture as constructed spectacles. Working with found footage and icons of film and television history, artists such as Douglas Gordon and Steve McQueen open up reflective approaches to the nature of cinematic images and their relevance for the patterns to be found within the viewer's inclination towards identification. These impulses, both iconophilic as well as iconoclastic, are inherent in the concept of the remake. They indicate an interest in transforming the usual models of representation in the cinema, a theme that is the focus of each formal reframing of found materials. Rather than pandering to the public's need for filmic spectacle in the manner of such famous cinematic hits as Alfred Hitchcock's *Rear Window* (1954), *Vertigo* (1958) and *Psycho* (1960), or David Lynch's *Blue Velvet* (1985), these approaches draw attention to the conditions of the medium itself, and by shifting the focus of the remake to the cinematic *dispositif*, the position of the observer becomes the actual subject of the work. Splintering the viewer's perspective (through multiple-viewers, double vision, split-screens, time-delay, etc.) invalidates Christian Metz's principle of identification with the camera (or actors).[13] The observer's position, which up until this point had experienced a defined frame of reference within the space of a museum or a cinema, loses its certainty regarding the object of reception because his or her ability to synthesise information when viewing images is challenged by the temporal conditions of visual awareness. The fundamental destabilisation of the spectator that this involves — further heightened by the spectator's freedom of movement in front of individual installations — is a prime characteristic of the paradigmatic transformation of the museum setting from a situation that focused on the viewer's optical reception of the work to one that focuses on the viewer's responsibility.[14]

13 See Christian Metz, *The Imaginary Signifier: Psychoanalysis and the Cinema*, Bloomington: Indiana University Press, 1982.

14 For more on this, see Groys's comments in 'Immaterial Communication', *op. cit.* For an anthology on current video-, film- and computer-based artworks, see Jeffrey Shaw and Peter Weibel (eds.), *Future Cinema: The Cinematic Imaginary after Film*, Cambridge, Mass.: The MIT Press, 2003. For collections of video art, see Ingvild Goetz and Stephan Urbaschek (eds.), *Fast Forward: Media Art Sammlung Goetz*, Munich: Kunstverlag Ingvild Goetz, 2003; and Joachim Jäger, Gabriele Knapstein and Anette Hüsch (eds.), *Jenseits des Kinos. Die Kunst der Projektion. Filme, Videos und Installationen von 1963 bis 2005, Werke aus der Friedrich Christian Flick Collection im Hamburger Bahnhof, der Kramlich Collection und aderen Sammlungen*, Ostfildern: Hatje Cantz Verlag, 2006.

15 Michael Fried, 'Art and Objecthood', *Artforum*, vol.5 no.10, Summer 1967, pp.12–23, reprint in Gregory Battcock (ed.), *Minimal Art: A Critical Anthology*, New York: Dutton, 1968, pp.116–47.

Representation as Visceral Experience

The experimental character of many video installations by younger generations of artists brings them close to the realms of performance art. The sense of immediacy achieved by the correlation between stage directions and space recalls the performative practices of the late 1960s and early 70s, which focused mainly on the body and the mind, while social and media conditions were explored through film and video. In this respect, the works of the 1990s differ fundamentally from early video works and the approach that shaped the artistic usage of the medium until well into the late 80s. On the one hand, the framework coordinates—which still remained more or less intact in the monitor sculptures of, say, Nam June Paik, Marie-Jo Lafontaine, Bruce Nauman and Bill Viola—increasingly dissolve into variable image fields. Multiple projections onto walls, ceilings, floors and free-standing screens transform the static framework of the black box into an experience of spatial infinity. Cinematographic formats allow for kaleidoscopic panoramas of moving images, in which the larger-than-life protagonists occupy the space with an almost tangible corporeality, like actors on a stage. On the other hand, the once minimal actions of early video works make a transition from a 'documenting aesthetic' almost entirely devoid of stage directions, towards theatrical micro-dramas that involve the audience in psychologically charged narrative structures and fictional sequences of dialogue. The role of the spectator thus oscillates between that of eyewitness and potential actor—as in the works of Tony Oursler, Monika Oechsler and Eija-Liisa Ahtila.

This form of 'reception aesthetic', which Michael Fried has criticised as being a 'fictitious viewing position' right from the start, is based on a distinctive psychology of reception with a performative disposition that recalls early documentary videos by Nauman, Vito Acconci, Chris Burden and Joan Jonas.[15] The recent works are comparable to the earlier ones in the sense that they use the medially heightened physical presence of the (virtual) protagonist to transpose a gripping sense of action to the (real) spectator, and also use physical, psychological and institutional framework conditions to imply a real-life situation. In the early 70s, by occupying the void between artist and audience, film and video broadened the visual spectrum of an art world dominated by performances and happenings. With an emphasis on 'presence and place', the immediate presence of both performers and spectators was originally the prime characteristic of these 60s art forms. The 'video performance' has taken these situationally-based artistic forms of expression a step further, creating complex compositions that interweave action and recording media without actually abandoning the 'aura' of the live act as the point of orientation for the audience. Fried criticised many works of Minimalist art for their 'theatricality'—for the importance that they placed on the viewer, how they depended on the presence of the spectator to experience a certain 'sense of duration', echo or 'endlessness'. However, his criticism was magisterially undermined by the deliberately theatrical approach of work in the 90s, which not only points out the significance of the time factor

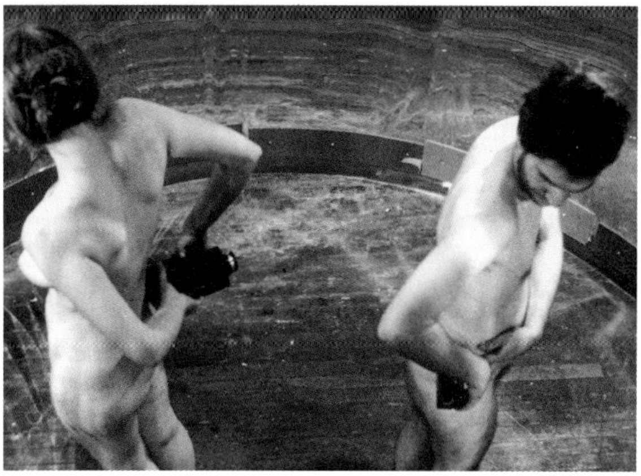

Dan Graham, *Body Press*, 1970–72. Black-and-white production still, 16mm colour film, 20mins. Courtesy Marian Goodman Gallery, New York & Paris

in video as a medium in itself, but actually accentuates the performative nature of the relationship between the spectator and the artistic formulation.[16]

An early attempt to experimentally investigate this transition or breach between representation and physical experience is Dan Graham's film installation *Body Press* (1970–72). In it, a man and a woman are standing back-to-back in a cylindrical room of mirrors, and each is guiding a camera around their naked body. After the actors exchange cameras at a certain point, they continue the performance, while the pictures are projected on the opposite walls of the room. The viewer is thus confronted with an almost life-size documentation of their bodies, in a treble mirroring that represents the three-fold viewpoint of actor, camera and spectator. The cubist fragmentation of perspectives helps to restore the physically tactile aspect of the performance to the filmic images, while intensifying the portrayal of the bodies — both in their relationship to real space and to the space of projection — in an 'image bursting' dynamic that shifts the filmic representation closer to that of sculptural presence.[17] In addressing the human body and its relation to architecture and to the medium as the virtual extension of the (public) space, *Body Press* foreshadows the time-delay video installations and mirrored, semi-transparent spatial constructions Graham later made, in which the viewer and the object viewed are brought together by multiple mirroring devices. The key no longer lies in the apotheosis of visual action, but, rather, in the transfiguration of the moving, active body and its reflected images. As in Graham's later mirrored environments, the spectators in the installations no longer see themselves in terms of the gaze alone, but actually perceive their own physical involvement. This dynamic transformation of space leads, in fact, to a spatialisation of the temporal, with significant repercussions for the projected image.

In his installation *Deadpan* (1997), Steve McQueen works with similar ways of affecting the viewer. As is the case with many works from the 1990s, McQueen's film image is shown in a closed, dark space, and it covers an entire wall from ceiling to floor. The black-and-white film shows a scene in which McQueen re-enacts a sketch from a popular American silent movie, taking on the role of Buster Keaton in the comedy *Steamboat Bill, Jr.* (1928). He stands

16 Whereas Fried stigmatised all art that included the beholder, many artists have been working since the 1960s on a systematic deconstruction of the myth of the disinterested viewer.

17 See 'Dan Graham, Body Press (1970–72)', in David A. Ross (ed.), *Seeing Time: Selections from the Pamela and Richard Kramlich Collection of Media Art* (exh. cat.), San Francisco: San Francisco Museum of Modern Art, 1999, pp.70–71.

18 See Chrissie Iles, 'Steve McQueen. Deadpan (1997)', in *ibid.*, pp.134–35, here p.135.

19 Rosalind Krauss on James Coleman's *Box (ahhareturnabout)* (1977), in Yve-Alain Bois and Rosalind Krauss, *Formless: A User's Guide*, New York: Zone Books, 1997, pp.161–65.

20 Michael Newman, 'McQueen's Materialism', *Steve McQueen* (exh. cat.), London and Zürich: ICA and Kunsthalle Zürich, 1999, p.60.

immobile with his back to the facade of a house that slowly falls towards him, only to leave him unhurt, to the viewer's surprise, due to a window aperture in the wall that falls precisely over the place where he stands. The lower edge of the projection is flush with the floor of the installation space, so that it looks as though the wall of the house were actually falling into the room where the viewer stands — which is to say, falling *out* of the projected space. The scene, which is silent and lasts 4 minutes, repeats itself as the film plays on in an uninterrupted loop. The splitting of the point of view represented in the image into a variety of camera angles, combined with the dramaturgy of the depiction — and intensified by means of the ever-increasing speed of the falling facade towards the end of the loop — causes the viewer to become increasingly physically aware of the repeated event. McQueen thus insists upon the physical tactility of the cinematic experience, by confronting the viewers with the time and space of their 'own physical reality'.[18] Viewers are pulled into the event, becoming aware of themselves while watching the scene — an effect that is emphasised by the reflection of the image on the floor of the black box. The black box can be freely entered by visitors, who are then allowed to experience the space-filling resonance of the projected light as a physical reality the closer they get to the image and, hence, to the event. Referring to James Coleman's installations, Rosalind Krauss once stated that the physical distance between the observer and the image is lost, as if in a 'lightning storm'.[19] Krauss's statement can be generalised as a commonplace phenomenon in any art involving projections of light, because of the fact that video images themselves create light in space. This explains their power to attract viewers into darkness.

The slapstick-like, yet claustrophobic repetition of the scene in McQueen's *Deadpan* functions as a quotation of the monotonous repertoire of performance of the 1970s, which aimed to 'hit the viewer in the centre of his physical presence'.[20] The moment of anxiety sensed by the viewer when the facade of the house drops dangerously towards the actor bears comparison with that felt in considering Chris Burden's spectacular performance *Shoot* (1971), the documentation of which shows him standing in anticipation of being shot in the arm — just one of many examples of performative approaches from the 70s that aimed at provoking physical and psychological reactions from audiences. Moreover, McQueen's work displays the characteristic suspense motive, to the extent that the facade's fall is a fear-inducing rather than humourous event. Differing from the logic of the 'original' — wherein Buster Keaton poses as the clueless hero notoriously privileged by his good luck — the 'replica' brings to light the construction of the typical rhetoric of naivety in this popular genre. This shift of meaning is revealed in the minimal signs of anticipation that precede

Steve McQueen, *Deadpan*, 1997. 16mm black-and-white film, video transfer, silent, 4mins 30secs. Courtesy Thomas Dane Gallery, London

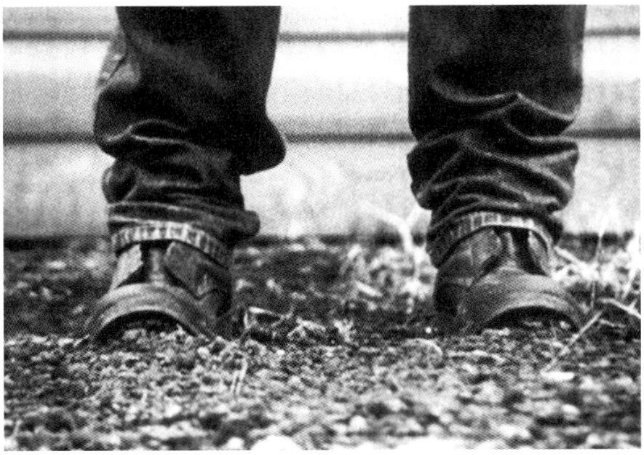

the threatening series of falls: McQueen's tense pose and perspiration marks can be read as traces of suppressed fear. By emphasising the physical threat and suggesting a psychological state of anxiety, McQueen revises the episode's feigned harmlessness, as it is achieved by the editing of the earlier film. The excluded human affects, which have been banned from the comical nature of the historical version, return in its remake as the off-screen spectres of filmic de-realisation techniques. Chrissie Iles has commented: 'The viewer is caught somewhere between the past memory of the original silent film, the phenomenological time of the sequence's reconstruction, and the time and space of the viewer's own physical reality.'[21] It is the remake that allows for what Hal Foster calls 'the return of the real' by demonstrating that one can only speak of a real when the effect of reality's representation collapses — as in abjective practices of shock, trauma and horror.[22]

The motive of the fear-inducing collapse (not to be confused with the calculated suspense of the Keaton film) turns McQueen's restaging into a symptom of suppression concerning a threatening reality by the illusionary character of filmic representation. The artistic imitation marks the boundary between filmic reality and life, between the artificiality of cinematic illusion and anticipated 'life-like' reality. Nevertheless, McQueen's scene is also based on the pretence of a performance solely staged for the camera; its relation to reality remains as much a construction as Keaton's performance because it also mediates its subversive message by emphasising the danger of the moment through its own repertoire of theatricality. As Erika Fischer-Lichte has pointed out, not even the 'performative aesthetic' that emerged during the 1960s by means of 're-defining the relation between the actor and spectators' was able to 'transgress the boundaries between art and life, between the aesthetic and the social, political and ethical'.[23] Nevertheless, McQueen's performative repetition, in subverting the controlled and directed logic of the narrative, brings the suppressed uncanniness and uncertainty of an amusement-geared destructive aesthetic into being. His physical appropriation of Keaton's scene — in practice a kind of meta-iconoclasm — robs the original of its fake harmlessness as created by its illusionary filmic features. Without

21 C. Iles, 'Steve McQueen', *op. cit.*, p.135

22 See Hal Foster, The Return of the Real', *The Return of the Real*, Cambridge, Mass.: The MIT Press, 1996, pp.126–168; also, Hal Foster, 'Obscene, Abject, Trauma', in *October* 78, Fall 1996,pp.106–124. On the relation between representation and reality in images, see also Michael Wetzel, *Die Wahrheit nach der Malerei*, Munich: Wilhelm Fink Verlag, 1997. Concerning the strategies of generating reality effects in visual media and contemporary art, see Ursula Frohne, 'Berührung mit der Wirklichkeit: Körper und Kontingenz als Signaturen des Realen in der Photographie der Gegenwart', in Hans Belting, Dietmar Kamper and Martin Schulz (eds.), *Quel Corps?: Eine Frage der Repräsentation*, Munich: Wilhelm Fink Verlag, 2002, pp.401–26.

23 Erika Fischer-Lichte, *Ästhetik des Performativen*, Frankfurt am Main: Suhrkamp, 2004, p.352.

24 See B. O'Doherty, *Inside the White Cube*, *op. cit.*, p.15.

25 For more information on Gordon's film adaptations, see Russell Ferguson, *Douglas Gordon*, Cambridge, Mass.: The MIT Press, 2001; Katrina M. Brown, *Tate Modern Artists: Douglas Gordon*, London: Tate Publishing, 2004; Philip Monk, *Double-Cross: The Hollywood Films of Douglas Gordon*, Toronto: Art Gallery of York University, 2003; Russell Ferguson (ed.), *Douglas Gordon* (exh. cat.), Los Angeles and Cambridge, Mass.: Museum of Contemporary Art and The MIT Press, 2002; and *Douglas Gordon: Kidnapping*, Eindhoven: Stedelijk Van Abbemuseum, 1998. Specifically on Gordon's *24 Hour Psycho*, see Ursula Frohne, 'Douglas Gordon, *24 Hour Psycho*, Anamorphosen des Kinos', *Kunsthistorische Arbeitsblätter*, vol.11 no.4, pp.15–24; and Ursula Frohne, 'Double Feature: Filmadaptation in Contemporary Art', *Fälschungen. Zu Autorschaft und Beweis in Wissenschaften und Künsten* (ed. Anne-Kathrin Reulecke), Frankfurt am Main: Suhrkamp Verlag, 2006, pp.364–89.

embezzling the fake character of his own restaging of the scene, McQueen preys on spectators' disillusionment, simply by re-inserting the unconscious and suppressed psychological dimensions of the filmic logic. With this slight but effective shift of focus, McQueen's seemingly banal adaptation of an iconic sequence from the filmic narrative breaks with the naturalisation strategies of a cinematic reality that has acquired the status of a second-order reality.

Spaces for Projection and Suggestion

The connections between repetition, drama and effect—so clearly highlighted by McQueen—distinguish the black box not only as a projection room, but also as space in which the psychological and the affective are evoked, in contrast to the contemplative cliché of the white cube. While recalling the affective characteristics of the white cube as 'shadowless, white, clean, artificial—the space is devoted to the technology of aesthetics', the metaphor of the black box consists of the return of the repressed.[24] Enabled by means of the aesthetics of new technologies, this return is not only the product of an affirmation of the flood of images common to popular culture, but also compensates for the deconstruction of areas that are otherwise excluded and suppressed in commercial media aesthetics. The museum thus becomes a new venue for cinematic experiments of a kind that have fewer and fewer possibilities of presentation in established film institutions. The film and video sequences of artistic installations develop their own visual dynamics by perpetuating themselves like traumatic events to the point of obsession. In the repetition of individual sequences as generated by the rejection of narration, the motif of time comes to the fore as an aesthetic experience somewhere between excess and reduction.

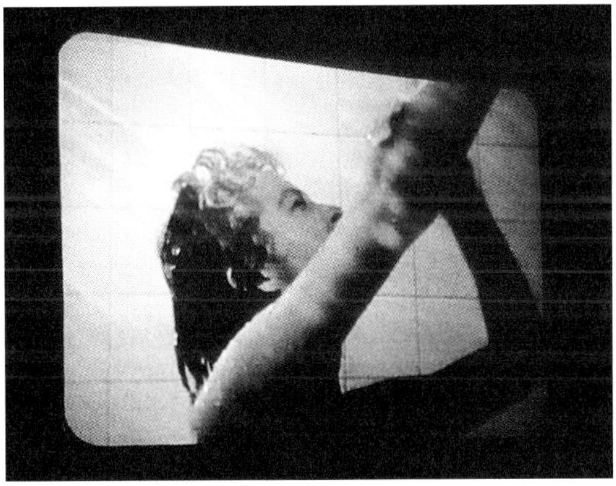

Douglas Gordon, *24 Hour Psycho*, 1993. Courtesy Gagosian Gallery

Douglas Gordon has emphasised this in his remakes of such films as Hitchcock's *Psycho* (1960), which he slowed down so that it takes 24 hours to play, thereby disturbing the continuum of the film. The almost static images in *24 Hour Psycho* (1993) return the medium to the state of a raw material whereby the narrative flow breaks down.[25] The double meaning of the word suspense corresponds to the dialectic of meaning that is an indicator of Gordon's process: by stretching the film and removing its sound, he de-activates the linear narrative that is of central importance to the build-up of tension, in Hitchcock's films in particular. In doing so, he shifts the emphasis to the absolute presence of the moment and the drama of details, gestures and poses, the isolation of which, in frozen schemes of expression, restructures the relationship between actor and viewer. The technical potential for this kind of structural dissection of film and its use as a ready-made was not available before the advent of video, which conceals the frame-by-frame structure that would normally appear in a slow playback. Gordon has taken advantage of this process of 'video analysis' in order to examine the 'symptoms' of the film scientifically as a touchstone of our cultural self-awareness. The fact that the aesthetic of some of his other works, specifically those using compiled archival film material, is dominated by extreme states of mind—psychoses, ecstasy, madness and euphoria—serves to intensify the space of projection and hence the viewer's experience. This is especially so when the projection screens are free-standing and the images are projected onto each side of a screen, prompting viewers to move around the space in order to view the work in its entirety. In these installations, the projector's rays inevitably hit the viewer at certain points, and the viewer's shadow falls on the projected image 'like a negative intrusion in the scene'.[26] Gordon holds up a mirror to the viewer's hidden fantasies in these deconstructive reframings of old footage.[27] Since Gordon's works are wrenched from their context and stripped of their scientific and educational function, the sensation of abnormality is experienced as a confrontation with the repressed areas of one's subconscious, or regarded with a detached and disinterested attitude towards the tormented character of the pictorial sequences. The deconstructive reframing of found film not only openly reveals the relationships connecting the director, artist and viewer and their exploitative desires, but also confuses the way that the viewers see themselves watching the (altered) film material, as they develop an awareness of their own synthesising function in the reconstruction of film history.

Beyond Illusion

Drawing the viewer into the work is, in many ways, typical of the way artists address the conventions of cinematic media. Rather than encouraging a critical distance from the Hollywood aesthetic—so familiar that it has been completely internalised by viewers—Doug Aitken speculates on the audience's total sensual absorption by appropriating and intensifying the industry's techniques. By sending the viewers of his installations on fictional journeys through passage-like visual scenarios, he turns an illusory effect into the vanishing point of scopophilic desire.[28] Generating overwhelming panoramas in a delirium of visual and spatial experience, Aitkin creates cinematic landscape views that emerge like *fata morganas*, and can best be described as vast. In his poem 'Correspondances' from *Fleurs du mal*, Baudelaire describes this vastness in terms of the sense of boundlessness and fascination he felt at entering into an 'other reality' without fundamentally

26 See Lynn Cooke, 'Douglas Gordon: Ein visueller Mensch, einer der sehen kann', *Douglas Gordon* (exh. cat.), Hannover: Kunstverein Hannover, 1998, n.p.

27 The voyeuristic relationship to the image is the focus of many works by artists whose media are photography, video and film. Victor Burgin, Stan Douglas, Pierre Huyghe, Cindy Sherman and Jeff Wall explore issues surrounding cinematic identity, which is connected with the public's expectations and the autocratic control of the director at the helm of the cinematic apparatus. For more on this, see Kerry Brougher, 'Hitch-Hiking in Dreamscapes', *op. cit.*

28 For more information on Doug Aitken's works, see Daniel Birnbaum, *Doug Aitken*, London: Phaidon, 2001.

29 From the monologue spoken by the protagonist in Doug Aitken's video installation *Electric Earth* (1996).

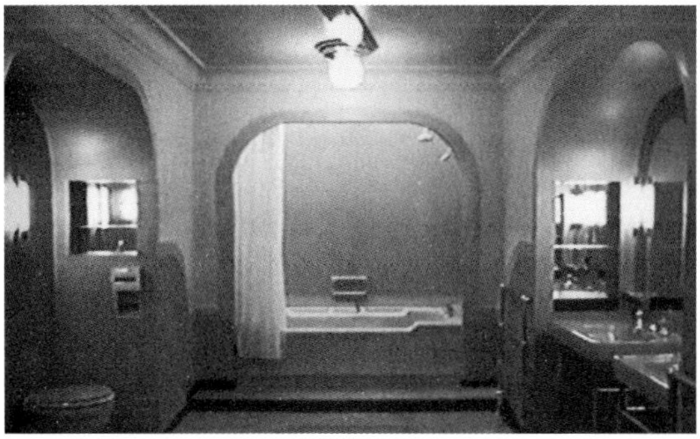

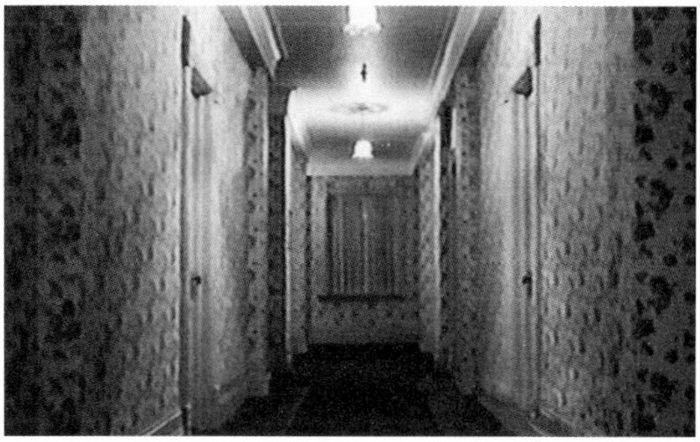

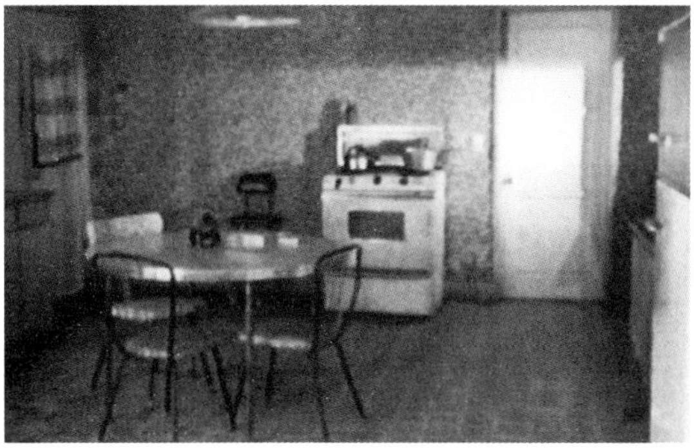

Isabell Heimerdinger, *Interior*, 1997–2000. C-Prints, 122×162.5cm each. Courtesy Meyer Riegger Galerie, Karlsruhe

departing from the coordinates of the 'real world'. This immersive attribute, which is vital to the experience of many an Internet user navigating through artificially generated spatial systems in the guise of a substitute persona, has converged with the frame-bursting, space-bursting visual rhetoric of Aitken's video installations as a horizon of cultural experience. Surrounded by visual backdrops made up of cinephilic projections of exotic and mysterious locations and cityscapes, the audience is enthralled by the immersive charm of the images, which are aimed less at revealing the machinations of filmic illusion than at conjuring up the experience of absolute presence within the projected scene. The visitors can bask in the glory of a film scene and sense the same electrifying effect described by the protagonist in Aitken's *Electric Earth* (1999) when he speaks about achieving ultimate oneness with his surroundings through dancing: 'A lot of times I dance so fast that I become what surrounds me, that's like food, like I absorb the images, absorb the information, that's like I eat it. That's the only now I get.'[29]

Isabell Heimerdinger's pictures of 'abandoned' film sets with the figures airbrushed out of them visualise the loss of reality in another way, linking it with the digital technique of special effects. Her film stills might be regarded as scenes in which the viewers imagine themselves as actors, and can also be read as images of the consciousness of the absent characters. Our cultural memory automatically occupies these empty spaces in her manipulated film stills, which can be visually decoded immediately as cinematic ambience, for they suggest to us that we know these places without ever having actually been there. Heimerdinger's images refer to that which is absent in much the same way as cinema itself invariably refers to an image originally recorded, whose transience is said to have prompted Cocteau to remark that film watches death at work.

This archetypal force by which film moulds the construction of reality also prompted Louise Lawler to create a cinema installation that takes to the extreme the theme of the black box as a culturally defined illusory space. In *A Movie Without the Picture* (1979), she showed Hollywood film classics,

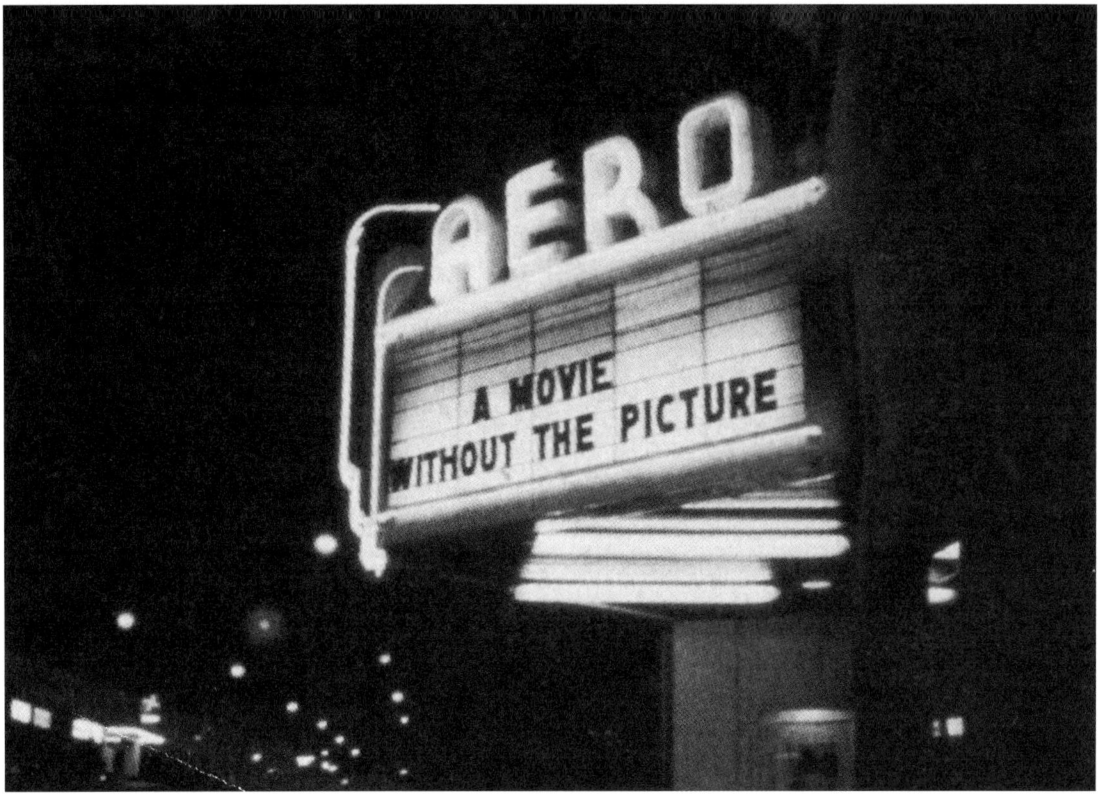

Louise Lawler, *A Movie Without the Picture*, 1979. Courtesy Monika Sprüth and Philomene Magers, Cologne, Munich & London

but removed the light bulb from the projector so that the film had neither light nor image and the audience had only the sound track as a point of reference for the plot. In the intimate atmosphere of Lawler's darkened room a new sense of cinema occurred that abstracted from the image-related dramaturgy of film and stimulated the associative capacity of the public acoustically. Whereas losing the picture would normally be regarded as a 'fault', in the context of this artistic presentation it actually heightened perception by mobilising inner processes of illusion that are never entirely uninvolved in our affective appropriation of our media culture's 'pre-produced dreams' — as already noted by Siegfried Kracauer in his description of film fantasies as 'the *daydreams of society*'.[30]

Framing the Viewer

Recent developments in the field of electronic images have provided new techniques of immersion and participation, opening up wide potential for artistic application. Multiple parallel projections and narrative strands in current works by Sam Taylor-Wood, Stan Douglas and Janet Cardiff explode space and time structures. Moreover, by overlapping various camera angles, image segments and audio impulses scenographically, they also achieve 'multiple sight and sound aesthetics', which require active interplay between the viewer, the video recording and the audio recording. According to the principle of multiplying viewpoints by using different cameras, all of which respond to one another as articulating apparatus, various perspectives of a scene are projected in parallel, thereby fragmenting not only the spatial continuity that exists in live television productions (which also use several cameras but broadcast only one angle at a time), but also the axial vision reproduced in television and cinema. This challenge to the normative syntax of the filmic medium also underlines the spatial presence of the plot, which increasingly appeals to the synthesising involvement of the audience. By dismantling the conditions of the medium in this way, the compositional involvement of the viewer is called upon to such a degree that the psychological and physical functions of the protagonist are completed only in the participatory reception of the spectator. Just as the viewer has become a participant in the scene, the parameters of the aesthetic of reception criticised by Michael Fried have become the actual principle of impact.

In the work of Taylor-Wood, the combinatory aspect of viewer involvement is the key motif. Although her life-size video projections are often distributed over all four walls of the room, they form a single story that becomes legible in the simultaneous juxtaposition of the individual picture segments, none of which are cut or montaged. This principle culminates in her work *Third Party* (1999), in which the viewer is surrounded by seven parallel scenes at a party. The individual images combine to create a spatial continuum in which people occasionally move through the fictional space and fluctuate between projections, as when the arm of one actress appears in the neighbouring screen to get a light from a man previously shown in isolation on an adjacent screen. This compositional technique of multiple projection screens whose spatial alignment replaces the diegetic frame actually crosses the 'aesthetic boundary between stage and auditorium'.[31] Such complex directing ultimately dissolves the classical order of the auditorium in which viewers sit still, watching what is happening on the screen, and replaces it with an all-embracing, almost tactile scenario in which the performative involvement of the viewer is a given from the moment he or she enters the room. By staggering the documentary segments in this way, the artist succeeds in almost literally transforming the black box into a party room. Physically encountering the life-size protagonists in the video sequences — as well as other spectators in the room — makes viewers aware of their own role as artists within the arena-like, all-round projection. Thus, the architectural ensemble, linked to the diegesis of the video projections, literally 'frames' the mobile spectator within the emotive space of moving images that Giuliana Bruno explores in her brilliant study of the relation between art installation, architecture and film.[32]

30 See Doris Mampe, 'A Movie Will be Shown without the Picture', *Moving Images, Film Reflexion in der Kunst* (exh. cat.), Leipzig: Galerie für zeitgenössische Kunst, 1999, pp.132–33; and Siegfried Kracauer, 'The Little Shopgirls Go to the Movies', *The Mass Ornament: Weimar Essays* (ed. Thomas Y. Levin), Cambridge, Mass.: Harvard University Press, p.292 (emphasis by Kracauer).

31 Martin Hentschel, 'Fotografie, Malerei, Film: Sam Taylor-Wood's Deklination der Gattungen', *Sam Taylor-Wood: Third Party*, Ostfildern-Ruit: Cantz Verlag, 2000, p.21.

32 See Giuliana Bruno, *Atlas of Emotion: Journeys in Art, Architecture and Film*, London: Verso, 2002.

Whereas Taylor-Wood achieves spectator involvement primarily by visual stimulation of the physical and spatial points of reference, Cardiff shifts the aspect of spectator involvement to the level of acoustic perception, as impressively demonstrated in *The Muriel Lake Incident* (1999) or *The Paradise Institute* (2001). Cardiff's work is also a return to the cinema space as a place of virtual travel — a kind of 'proto-spaceship', as Anne Friedberg once described the function of early cinema because of its capacity to allow viewers to forget their real environment and, seated on comfortable upholstery, even their own bodies for a while.[33] Dolby surround-sound systems transport the on-screen events into the cinema auditorium with such acoustic perfection that the spectators feel as though they are in the midst of what is happening, dissolving the membrane between the fiction of the screen and the reality of the auditorium to such a degree that the auditorium in the cinema functions as an extension of the projection screen. Cardiff has further emphasised this aspect of absorption by exaggerating the acoustic perception in her installations: visitors are provided with headphones so that the words they are hearing seem to be addressed to them personally, with the result that they tend to look around in surprise and astonishment at other members of the audience. In this way, the audience's visual and acoustic perceptions cross and shift in relation to one another, provoking constant parallel attention to the video image and to the other spectators. This touches on the theme of the spectacle that uses the fascination of the images to grasp the body and senses of the audience. At the same time, however, this deconstructive approach to the visual and auditory synchronicity of cinema creates feelings of (self-)alienation, which achieve a more complex way of visualising the increasing spectacularisation and homogenisation of cultural praxis in commercial media emissions. Hence, the end of the illusion begins with the participation of the spectator.

Translated by Ishbel Flett.

33 Anne Friedberg, *Window Shopping: Cinema and the Postmodern*, Berkeley: University of California Press, 1993.

VIDEO PROJECTION: THE SPACE BETWEEN SCREENS

Liz Kotz

How can we theorise the medium of video now, in the moment of its technological transformation — perhaps even its technical evanescence?

Some years ago, I recall overhearing a prominent curator acclaim the work of Tony Oursler, which used then newly available data-projectors to cast footage of obsessively talking heads onto small, puppet-like props, making the animated figures eerily appear to chant and rant. In effect, Oursler's flickering sculptures took the small puppet-show dramas of his earlier videotapes and moved them out into the gallery, where viewers could walk among the figures and encounter them in three-dimensional space and nearly life-like scale. For art-world viewers, Oursler's new projections succeeded in freeing video from its historical containment in the monitor or TV set. This long-standing desire of video art is not hard to understand: monitors are awkward, badly designed and a constant reminder of the medium's links to broadcast television, domestic furniture and all the degraded industrial uses of video technology. Mounted on the ubiquitous grey utility cart in institutional settings, monitors tend to disrupt the gallery or museum space. Is it no wonder video has so been often confined to the basement or the stairwell? Who among us would not prefer the luminous image freed from its ungainly technical support?

Largely invisible in gallery-based art of the 1980s, by the mid-90s video suddenly appeared everywhere, as increasingly monumental installations supplanted older, more modest forms like single-channel videotapes. In museum exhibitions, the divide was clear: while conventional tapes remained marginalised in physically segregated 'screenings', installational and sculptural projects could claim space on the main floor. Strolling through galleries, museum exhibitions and the ubiquitous international art fairs and festivals, viewers now encounter all manner of electronically-produced moving images that we still refer to or recognise as 'video'. In physical presentation, these range from miniaturised handheld gadgets and computer displays to closed-circuit systems, plasma screens and multi-image projections that immerse viewers in room-sized audio-visual environments.

Projection — from the Latin *projectionem* (from *pro* + *jacere*), meaning 'throwing forward, extension, projection' — indicates displacement, dislocation, transfer.[1] At its core, projection is a form of geometry modelled

1 *Oxford English Dictionary* (second edition), Oxford and New York: Oxford University Press, 1989; from *proicere*, *projicere* to throw forth, stretch out, expel, reject, give up, etc., from *pro* + *jacere* to throw.

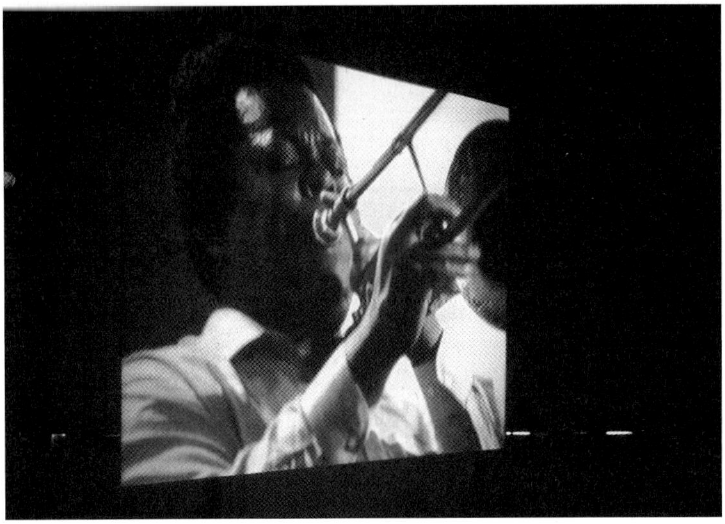

Stan Douglas, *Hors-champs*, 1992. Courtesy David Zwirner, New York

on the properties of light rays: it allows us to plot, from a fixed point, any number of regulated correspondences between two planes or between a two-dimensional picture plane and three-dimensional space. As such, projective geometry is a means of rationalising vision and space, under-pinning perspectival rendering, cartography and architecture. Yet the concept of projection can imply relations in both space and time, and the term carries old figural resonances of changing and transmutation as well as scheming and planning. For by its nature, projection carries inherent capacities for distortion and illusion as well as rational correspondence — by extension, the psychoanalytic concept implies a confusion between inside and outside, between interior psychic life and external reality. With roots going back to seventeenth-century magic lantern shows, modern forms of 'screen entertainment' rest on these very ambivalences. As we all know, projected images elicit fantasy: they invite us to see things that are not there. And they elicit specific forms of spectatorship, engendering a psychic mobility paradoxically dependent on physical immobility.

Drawing on decades of film theory, we can map how techniques of projection offer ways of joining a space, an image and a subject. These relationships are curiously intertwined: not only does the fixed position of the viewer seem to stabilise a system of visual relations, but theorists have been at pains to argue that the apparent unity and stability of this subject is itself a property of the optical system. Cinema, of course, most visibly demonstrates the power of this orchestration, but its effects are everywhere in our culture. In our present, while film exhibition remains confined to theatrical formats, severing the space of the image from other lived spaces, video potentially permits moving images to enter and interpenetrate all manner of architectural and urban spaces. With its greater mobility and technical flexibility, video would seem to offer all kinds of rich possibilities for rethinking and restructuring these core relationships — between viewing subject, moving or still image, architectural space and time — that are so fundamental to modern visual culture.

In New York, the re-emergence of video projection reached a threshold around 1993, with two exhibitions at David Zwirner Gallery that announced the spatial and sculptural ambitions of new work in video. In May, the Vancouver-based artist Stan Douglas presented *Hors-champs* (1992), an installation presenting two separate recordings of a free-jazz session onto opposite sides of a thin screen hanging diagonally across the middle of a room, which was empty except for two three-beam projectors mounted near the ceiling in opposite corners. It took viewers several minutes of circling around the work to register the differences between the two projections, which were loosely modelled on French *verité*-style television documentaries. As Scott Watson glosses the piece: 'On one side is Douglas's film of a session shot in 1960s style. The camera tracks each musician as the individual players take up the themes of the music and play. For the other side of the screen Douglas made a tape of what look like out-takes, the camera dwelling on players at rest.'[2] The work's title translates as 'out of field' or 'out of range', and, as Douglas notes, the bifurcated screening 'presents the spatialisation of montage'.[3]

In *Evening* (1994), Douglas continued the spatial juxtaposition of simultaneous tracks, projecting three fictional late-1960s newscasts side-by-side, causing their soundtracks to bleed and partly drown out one another. Using multiple screens to demarcate irreconcilable cultural spaces, both *Hors-champs* and *Evening* activate site and viewing position as spatial analogues of larger social topographies. Yet as subsequent projects attest, Douglas's deeper interest lay in recreating the codes and conventions of dominant media. Like photographer Jeff Wall, Douglas carefully restages and films scenes crafted to resemble historical artifacts, rather than using found footage. Over time, the technical virtuosity of these recreations has propelled Douglas toward film-making proper. In a 1997 interview, he described *Hors-champs* and *Evening* as his 'most sculptural [works] ... in as much as everything is in the room, like the three zones of sound in *Evening*, and the screen that you walk around in *Hors-champs*', acknowledging that his subsequent video projections had become 'more like pictures, like old-time screen practice'.[4] Indeed, Douglas's more conventionally cinematic projects, from *Subject to Film: Marnie* (1989) to *Win, Place or Show* (1998), reveal his investments in the narrative and formal preoccupations of Hollywood; and stagier works, like *Der Sandmann* (1995), show pictorial preoccupations that lie closer to the staged photographic tableaux of Wall or Gregory Crewdson than to the spatial or conceptual concerns of post-Minimalist visual art. For those old enough to recall the turn from the perceptual investigations of post-Minimalism to the 'new narrative' work of the late 1970s and 80s, the pervasive art-world embrace of narrative was not necessarily encouraging. Would video art yet again become just a way of making bad films?

Later that same year, the Los Angles-based artist Diana Thater presented *Late and Soon, Occident Trotting* (1993), a two-part projection that replicated the structure of her installation *Oo Fifi: Five Days in Claude Monet's Garden*

2 Scott Watson, 'Against the Habitual', *Stan Douglas*, London and New York: Phaidon, 1998, p.59.

3 Stan Douglas in 'Interview: Diana Thater in Conversation with Stan Douglas', *Stan Douglas*, *ibid.*, p.12. Such spatialisation of montage would soon become ubiquitous, in the far more conventionally narrative video installations of, for instance, Eija-Liisa Ahtila and Sam Taylor-Wood.

4 *Ibid.*, p.15.

(1992), which had been shown in Santa Monica the previous fall. In Zwirner's front room, psychedelically tinged landscape footage projected onto the gallery walls and out the front windows toward the street. Covered in semi-transparent neutral-density gels, the windows allowed ambient light in during the daytime — sometimes nearly washing out the projected footage — and permitted the projections to be glimpsed from outside. After nightfall, the silent pulsing patterns almost seemed to emanate from an empty club or dance space. As has become her custom, Thater threw the red, green and blue beams of the projector out of calibration, distorting the colours and abstracting the image into overlapping series of monochrome fragments. In the back room, the second part of the installation inverted this schema, as three, single-colour projections converged to produce an off-kilter composite image.

In texts and interviews, Thater has repeatedly related her work to the formal reduction and experimentation of Structural film. Yet, despite this rhetoric, her underlying formal and historical referents arguably lie closer to panoramic landscape painting. Using off-registration projection to render a sort of day-glow impressionism, Thater plays with the formal possibilities of ambient light and existing architecture. In contrast to, for instance, the outdoor works of Krzysztof Wodiczko, who in the 1980s was known for projecting politically-charged transparencies onto buildings and monuments, Thater's 'natural' landscape and quasi-pastoral motifs exclude public urban space and overt historical referents. While her projections explore the interpenetration of interior and exterior spaces, they employ these as scenic backdrops rather than as historical sites or structural parameters. Thus the displaced bourgeois interior of Monet's garden is emblematic of Thater's installations, which orchestrate casually dispersed interactions with those who move through the space. While writers have been at pains to celebrate the 'built-in instabilities' that disrupt Thater's system — cataloguing the 'skewed projector lenses', 'strobing color separations', '"defective" optical apparatus' and 'distorted image' that inhabit her work — such accounts overlook how these very instabilities are programmed, controlled and designed to generate pictorial effects.[5] Like Oursler, Thater insistently foregrounds her technical apparatus — strewing monitors, projectors, cables and equipment throughout the space — precisely because these materials function as props. Viewers' bodies may temporarily block the projected images, throwing shadows onto the wall, but such interruptions do not alter or generate the work in any significant way. Despite a Minimalist-derived rhetoric, these 'interactive' elements have little in common with, for instance, early video sculptures like Bruce Nauman's corridors, which required viewers to enter a pared-down architectural structure in order to activate the work.

5 See, for instance, Colin Gardner's 'No Guarantees, They're Wolves: Structure, Movement and the Dystopic in Diana Thater's *China*' and Timothy Martin's 'What Cyan said to Magenta about Yellow', both in *Diana Thater: China*, Chicago: Renaissance Society, 1996.

As has become a kind of *doxa* in the field, sympathetic critics and curators have aggressively sought to position new work in video projection as re-investigations of the phenomenological models articulated by artists of the late 1960s and early 70s like Nauman, Vito Acconci, Peter Campus and Dan Graham. Yet while Douglas and Thater incorporate three-dimensional space and mobile spectators into their installations, their underlying structures arguably derive from two-dimensional pictorial media (photography and painting, respectively) and not the procedural or durational structures that animated early video. Indeed, despite certain momentary resemblances to this earlier historical project, the pictorial and narrative orientations of artists like Douglas, Thater, Doug Aitken and Douglas Gordon align them more with the monumentally-scaled colour photographs of Jeff Wall, Cindy Sherman or even Andreas Gursky. It is no coincidence that Wall's work with enormous light boxes — staging a return to older pictorial functions with all the means of the contemporary mass media — is a touchstone for so many younger artists. With their carefully staged and mawkish 'cinematic' tableaux, both large-scale photography and video projection are strategically suspended between the high-culture aspirations of painting and the pop-culture appeal of Hollywood; and both trajectories vector toward the large, flat-panel monitor or plasma screen — technical means of presenting luminescent fields of colour that are, ultimately, high-tech paintings.

This proximity to painting and cinema is a big part of what has made video projection so appealing to contemporary artists. Technically, this shift was facilitated by the availability of smaller, cheaper portable data-projectors in the early 1990s. Designed for sales and display uses, these devices no longer required the darkened rooms and quasi-theatrical exhibition spaces associated with older three-beam systems. In effect, the new projectors freed the video image from its historical container — the box-like television monitor — and from its secondary siting, in box-like viewing rooms modelled on cinemas. Unhinged from these sites and the spectatorial conventions they inscribe, video footage proliferated in all manner of new configurations. For artists like Oursler, the new devices were a crucial enabling condition, allowing projected images to go beyond the box that had so long contained them. And although both Douglas and Thater used older, three-beam systems, their installations dislodged projection from conventional 'theatrical' settings and viewing conventions.[6]

Thater herself has called for work that would 'allow video to speak about itself — in a language endemic to it. Just as the Structuralist film-makers

6 The availability of consumer equipment allowed video to become 'a tool like any other', no longer requiring specialised technical training or expertise. Just as the post-War profusion of cheap 16mm-film equipment and educational devices like analytic projectors opened a space for amateur and experimental film-making in the 1950s and 60s, and as the late 70s availability of consumer-grade cameras and photo-processing helped liberate 'artists using photography' from the codified domains of fine art photography, the new array of camcorders, VCRs and desktop editing systems helped propel video outside the ghettoised domains of 'video art' that had consolidated by the 80s in isolation from wider visual art practice.

used "film" in such a way as to reveal a materiality, a shape and a form that characterise it, so we must be able to make the material "video" speak of a signal, tape, camcorders, monitors and projectors.'[7] Resorting to older, modernist discourses of medium-specificity, Thater protests that video 'played on a monitor like television ... subordinates itself to the codes of another medium'.[8] She strangely ignores that TV founded video's 'history and its language', even as video's forms and uses now extend far beyond the televisual.

This pervasive repression of the TV monitor and the medium's rather long entanglement with mass communication haunts work in video projection. Broadcast television derived from radio, not film, yet speech is curiously absent from what has become an emphatically pictorial practice. By configuring exhibition architecture to the size of the projection, artists effectively de-emphasise the rectangular structure of the image, sidestepping their use of video as a surrogate 'painting'. The shift to the wall as a pre-existing frame not only naturalises the rectangle via architecture, but also effaces the extent to which the structure of the tableau remains embedded in the very technology of video. Replacing a small box — the monitor — with a larger one — the room — hardly allows one to escape from the logic of the apparatus. By moving the mechanical device out of sight, newer types of projection routinely efface the technology manifested in the monitor. Yet it is clear that we can no longer convincingly turn to an older, modernist strategy of 'laying bare the device' as an antidote, since such displays have long since become mannerist gestures. As video technology moves toward incorporation into the wall and architectural container, artistic investigation of the medium must take this on.

Despite this wider set of possibilities, by the late 1990s the majority of work in video projection emphatically moved toward cinema as content and form. For so many artists, the actual technology of video is incidental, an efficient tool for delivering images, but not a medium *per se*. The narrative works of Eija-Liisa Ahtila, Shirin Neshat, Sam Taylor-Wood and Jane and Louise Wilson, for instance, harness video to generate new permutations of simultaneous, multi-screen cinema. Perhaps inevitably, critics bemoaned the confusing array of awkwardly partitioned and darkened rooms in which video was so often shown — most notably in the complaints about mazes of darkened cubicles with increasingly indistinguishable projection pieces at the 1999 Venice Biennale. The by-then ubiquitous 'black box' format of contemporary exhibitions suggested that video technology had been assimilated back into older filmic conventions, while simultaneously assimilating film into new mobile and ongoing — rather than stationary and event-based — forms of spectatorship.

The artistic relationship between video and cinema is not incidental. Equipped with slow-scan and single-frame pause, video viewing invites us to reread and reconstruct cinema — to break down the filmic flow, bring

7 Diana Thater, 'I wanna be your dog', in *Diana Thater: China*, *op. cit.*, p.12.
8 *Ibid.*, p.11.

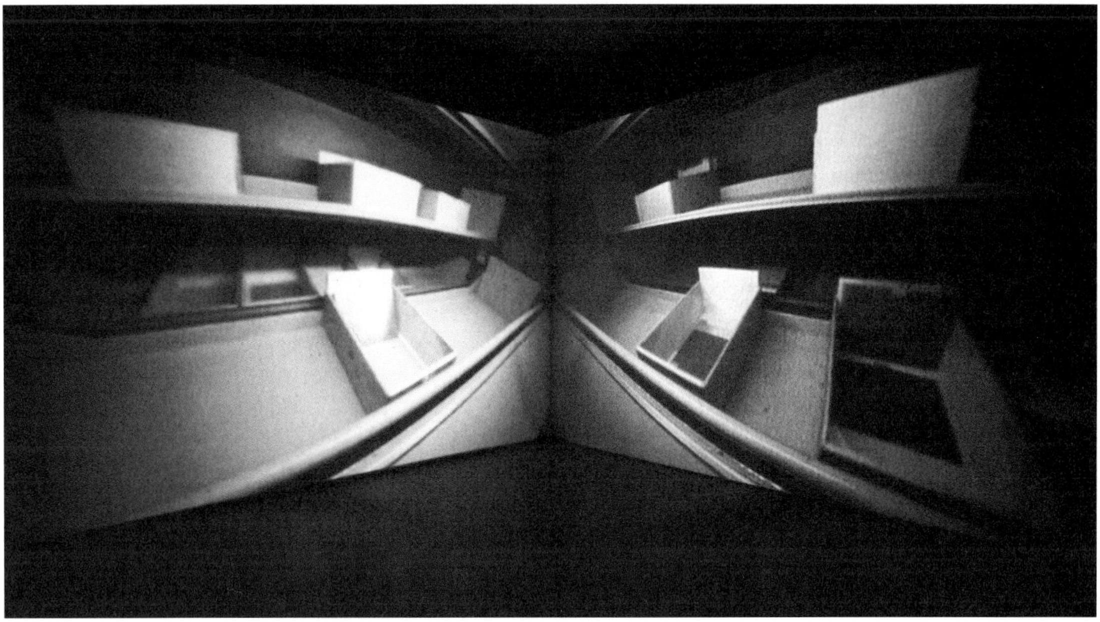

ephemeral passing frames to our attention and recompose its pieces into other forms. At one time, such opportunities to re-see and recreate cinema were rare, even precious. Ken Jacobs's legendary *Tom, Tom, the Piper's Son* (1969/71)—a projection performance later concretised as a rephotographed found-footage film—required years of painstaking labour with an analytic projector and optical printer. Now new consumer technologies perhaps make such procedures too easy, as so many recent projects of time-based 'rephotography' remain banal academic exercises, with countless younger artists re-shooting or restaging fetishised moments in classical cinema, or replaying the outdated codes of post-War documentary photography in newer electronic media.

Gordon's *24-Hour Psycho* (1993) is perhaps emblematic of artworks that employ video technology to dissect classic films—in effect, replaying the classic moves of early-1980s photo-appropriation in a time-based medium. Of course, part of the appeal of 'postmodern' photography lay in its canny spectacularisation of earlier conceptual practices. Using his low-tech 'eight track mix' (cropping, colour-shifting, shooting out-of-focus and so forth), Richard Prince framed and re-sequenced generic images from advertisements and amateur sources. But even when he worked with hyper-canonical materials like the celebrated Marlboro Man ads, Prince's peculiar copies found something new and even heartfelt in these clichés. In a somewhat analogous fashion, Gordon has used video to arrest narrative and render its flow as a series of graspable instants and sustained durations. His projects *Five Year Drive-By* (1995) and *through a looking glass* (1999) draw from John Ford's *The Searchers* (1956) and Martin Scorsese's *Taxi Driver* (1976), respectively. But Gordon's moves became formulaic, as he brought increasingly arbitrary procedures to already canonical films. In a marked departure from his peers' aversion to more difficult 'process' oriented operations, Steve McQueen's

Jane and Louise Wilson, *Stasi City*, 1997. Courtesy the artists and the Lisson Gallery, London

'Documenta11' installation *Western Deep* (2002) compellingly introduced present-day historical experience (a nearly 25-minute descent into a Southern African diamond mine) into durational models drawn from experimental film and early video. In comparison, *24 Hour Psycho* (1993) reads like the fortuitous discovery of a late-night VCR addict.[9]

In addition to providing a way to remake cinema, video has allowed artists to investigate projection itself as a kind of medium or material. As anyone who works with the format soon discovers, projection offers a tremendously seductive immateriality: the projected image both is and is not there. Recounting an early programme of expanded cinema at the Film-makers Cinematheque in 1965, Jonas Mekas noted the 'almost mythic drive toward pure motion, colour, light experience' that animated the work.[10] In video, too, glowing beams of light spray colour onto surfaces, yielding evanescent images seemingly freed from any technical support. While TV monitors and theatrical film projection tend to position viewers in a relatively-fixed, frontal relation to the image, environmentally-scaled projections envelop viewers, allowing them to enter image spaces not overtly mediated by the formality of frame or screen.

In so doing, the immersive environments produced by video projection and new imaging technologies inevitably extend and reconfigure 1960s projects of expanded cinema. Not unlike present-day video, that movement drew vastly conflicting aesthetic and social models into its practice. With roots in multimedia happenings and environments, dancers and artists affiliated with New York's Judson Church used films, slides and projections to accompany movement; their collage-based aesthetics tended to favour a profusion of images and overlays. At more or less the same time Structuralist film-makers like Tony Conrad, Paul Sharits and Michael Snow explored basic properties of the cinematographic apparatus, isolating every aspect — grain, filmstrip, frame, flicker, motion, screen, etc. — and subjecting them to sustained analysis and attention. In contrast to this medium-specific investigation of film, new multimedia artists like Stan VanDerBeek, Jordan Belson and Scott Bartlett aggressively used multiple means — film, slides, light, motion, sound — to produce maximum sensory impact. In an optimistic embrace of new perceptual capacities that merged McLuhan-esque techno-futurism with hippie drug culture, 1960s light shows and film performances harnessed projection to create audio-visual analogues of hallucinatory

9 While a degree of historical amnesia can free artists from blatant academicism, it also deprives them of the conceptual underpinnings of the strategies they use. For all the protests surrounding Martin Creed's 2001 Turner Prize for his installation *The Lights Going On and Off* (2000), no one in the art press even noted the work's resemblance to early-1960s projects by artists George Brecht or David Tudor — both close affiliates of John Cage, who of course cleared the ground for such durational acts of emptiness. Ommissions such as this are complicit with patterns of historical erasure. It would be hard to imagine Los Angeles's Museum of Contemporary Art, which granted a 'retrospective' to the then 34-year-old Douglas Gordon, mounting career retrospectives of generative artists like James Benning, Simone Forti or Yvonne Rainer. See Russell Ferguson, et. al., *Douglas Gordon*, Los Angeles and Cambridge, Mass.: The Museum of Contemporary Art and The MIT Press, 2001.

10 Jonas Mekas, *Movie Journal: The Rise of a New American Cinema 1959–1971*, New York: Collier Books, 1972, p.209.

11 Gene Youngblood, *Expanded Cinema*, New York: Dutton, 1970, p.41.

12 David James, *Allegories of Cinema: American Film in the Sixties*, Princeton: Princeton University Press, 1989, p.127. For James, the reconfigured exhibition formats and radically altered viewing experiences of the 1960s avant-garde represented a necessary extension of the New American Cinema's utopian project.

states, collapsing exterior and interior worlds. Championing 'the intermedia network of cinema and television, which now functions as nothing less than the nervous system of mankind', Gene Youngblood famously foresaw the perceptually-enhanced synaesthesia of new electronic technologies replacing older art forms like painting and facilitating new forms of subjectivity in their wake — 'when we say expanded cinema we actually mean expanded consciousness'.[11]

As film historian David James has argued, the expanded cinema movement was organised around two poles: more formally-oriented films providing 'meditational practice or visionary experience' and ritualistic works 'integrated into social situations more dynamic than those of the conventional theater'.[12] Both these 'visionary' and 'social situation' models resurface forcefully in the present—witness the integration of video into the kinds of recreated social spaces that periodically inhabit art fairs, museums and alternative spaces. Yet unlike their 1960s precursors, who sought technical means to generate new forms of collective life, current multimedia artists have largely appropriated pre-existing narrative models, commodity forms and gallery-based exhibition formats.

Although their tone may seem nostalgic, James's accounts of 1960s expanded cinema resonate uncannily with the claims made for present-day video and multimedia. 'Projection itself becomes the site of creativity,' he asserts, 'where the somatic passivity of theatrical consumption is replaced by ecstatic engagement.'[13] He continues: 'In place of the confining rectangle of the film frame and the closure of narrative ... light shows offered a three-dimensional visual field, matrixed neither spatially nor temporally, which dispersed rather than unified subjectivity.'[14] In this view, the new participatory spectacles held at countercultural venues and underground film spaces provided an atmosphere of collective improvisation and sensorial overload: 'all combined in a continuously transforming, enveloping, pan-sensual experience that could be entered and exited at will', indistinguishable from 'the interior projection of hallucination'.[15]

Nearly identical statements could be culled from the all-too-fawning literature on video installation, which unquestioningly affirms that newly immersive media spectacles provide genuine forms of desubliminatory, anti-disciplinary experience. Repressing the very psychoanalytic and theoretical

Yet James's tendency to equate physical arrangements with social and psychic relations leads him to overestimate the liberatory potential of these 'expanded' modes. Decrying the constrictive viewing booths that Austrian film-maker Peter Kubelka designed for Anthology Film Archives, which 'immobilized and imprisoned the spectator as a monadic visual consumer, repressing even the social interaction allowed in the commercial theater', James applauds the improvisatory, utopian dimensions of expanded cinema: 'Interrupting the history of cinema as authority and discipline, the multimedia light show discovered itself in a dance against somatic repression' (p.132).

13 *Ibid.*, p.132.

14 *Ibid.*, p.134. Despite his apparent embrace of such liberatory rhetoric, James is well aware of the complex techno-futurist entanglements of expanded cinema: 'The opening of the optical field, and the conceptual and kinetic liberation of the spectator within it, was often constructed as either analogous to or premonitory of' shifts in which 'the engineering of consciousness would parallel developments in the electronic communications industries' (p.134).

15 *Ibid.*, p.135.

models they cite, recent art-critical accounts employ emphatically reductive understandings of the filmic apparatus, equating the spectatorial position with a viewer's literal physical position — mobile, stationary, throwing a shadow on the image, etc. Daniel Birnbaum, for instance, suggests that Doug Aitken's mobile camerawork 'pushes the viewer's subjectivity to the point where the phenomenological model of experience breaks down', breathlessly proposing that in Aitken's multi-screen installations:

> This more complex space allows for the participation of the viewer but also brings the viewer's unity and stability into question. In works such as *electric earth* and *into the sun*, the complexity not only has to do with the multiple projections, but with the active involvement of viewers who decide their own pace when moving through the installations. Such kinesthetic and perceptual multiplicity can no longer be thought of in terms of a harmonious experiencing subject.[16]

That even the most normative products of classical Hollywood cinema can hardly be said to produce such a 'harmonious experiencing subject' seems to have escaped commentary.

By now we are all familiar with the contradictions Walter Benjamin diagnosed over seventy years ago between 'exhibition value' and the aura-producing attributes of the fine art object. Yet the situation of video *vis-à-vis* the museum manifests a new set of structural conflicts arising among different historical modes of 'exhibition'. As curator Chris Dercon suggests, part of the appeal that 'media-oriented displays' hold for museums is their capacity to attract different audiences addressed as spectators by using techniques drawn from popular entertainment, retail display and information delivery.[17] But as museums stretch to accommodate new media forms, transforming conventional white cubes into ubiquitous black boxes, high-tech formats of modern display culture merge awkwardly with older forms of connoisseurship associated with unique objects. Presented by growing museum education and publicity industries as technological supplements to conventional exhibitions, an ever-expanding apparatus of audio tours, exhibition websites, publications and guides gradually supplants the objects on view.[18]

16 Daniel Birnbaum, 'That's the Only Now I Get: Space and Experience in the Work of Doug Aitken', *Doug Aitken*, London: Phaidon, 2001, p.94.

17 See *Still/MOVING*, Rotterdam: Foto Instituut Netherlands, 2001, pp.28–31. As Dercon notes, many museums prefer to collect the secondary pictorial and photographic objects of media-based artists, rather than their more complicated (and more physically demanding) media installations; he mentions Douglas and Barney in this context, and one could add many others. Just as the current ascendance of photo-based art depended on escaping the narrow purviews (and limited budgets) of museum photography departments, a more central role for video, film, sound and other media arts would require institutional re-organisation as well as architectural reconfiguration.

18 With star-driven programming clumsily modelled on the blockbuster logic and entertainment values of Hollywood movies and big-ticket amusement parks, museum exhibitions must either fully differentiate themselves from the disposable novelty of the mass media or mimic their spectacular effects. Of course, the most reliable best-sellers — Van Gogh, Impressionist painters or the semi-annual David Hockney exhibitions that are a fixture in Los Angeles — always succeed in having it both ways at once. For video art, the viewer-friendly technological sublime of Bill Viola and Gary Hill has long filled a similar role, albeit to smaller audiences.

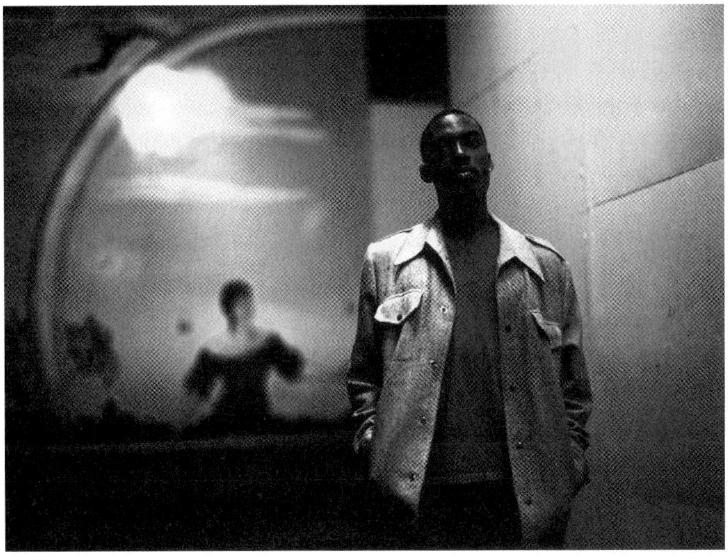

In what now seems like a distant past, earlier experimental film, video and performance practices sought to disturb the form and function of the gallery and museum, replacing collectible unique objects with a temporal experience that could be completely ephemeral or endlessly reproducible. Today's media-savvy art is designed for reproduction and display. Artists produce mural-sized video projections to fill the giant industrial spaces of contemporary museums, spaces themselves scaled to hold Minimalist and post-Minimalist sculpture. In a publicity-driven art world without any means of determining value except the market, a shrewd joining of technical skill, mannerist sensibility and photogenic appeal prevails. It is hardly a coincidence that media artists so often rely on 'secondary' products, particularly colour photographs, to subsidise their large-scale installations. Acutely stylised and designed for display, video projections often look staged to produce the striking colour photos that will appear in magazines, catalogues and gallery back rooms. Present-day ephemeral and site-specific forms have their bases covered: like all good tourist attractions, they offer a complete line of subsidiary products for collectors to take home.

With *Sleepwalkers* (2007) at the Museum of Modern Art in New York, which combined clichéd narrative content with flashy multi-screen technique, Aitken seems the avatar of video art as pricey, high-tech window dressing. Despite the enduring myth of the criticality or political-engagement of media-based art forms, today's commercially successful artists like Aitken gladly embrace the dictates of spectacle culture. If early projects by artists like Acconci and Nauman re-enacted the subjective experience of late capitalism as endurance, submission and disciplinary subjection, when recycled by contemporary artists like Matthew Barney, even these durational tropes can be cleaned-up, prettified and made entertaining. Yet this turn was far from self-evident — nor is it as exclusive as the all-too-visible success of certain types of work makes it seem. After all, the early, lower-tech projects of artists like Aitken, Barney and Thater were initially embraced as efforts to integrate procedural and pictorial dimensions. And despite the rapid turn to monumentality, the period of 1993 to 1994 also saw exhibitions of more demanding, durationally-based video projections by artists like Lutz Bacher, Steve McQueen and Gillian Wearing, whose work evidences deeper links with earlier Minimalist and Conceptual projects.

Doug Aitken, *Electric Earth*, 1999. Courtesy 303 Gallery and Victoria Miro Gallery

In an essay on video first published in the mid-1980s, the critic Fredric Jameson proposed that a 'medium' is defined by the conjunction of three distinct components: 'an artistic mode or specific form of aesthetic production'; 'a specific technology, generally organized around a central apparatus or machine'; and 'a social institution', including a set of vernacular forms, functions or uses.[19] Unlike older forms such as painting, whose historically entrenched role stabilises a relatively coherent field, for newer media these conditions perpetually go in and out of sync, producing different momentary formations of 'video' that soon dissolve into technical obsolescence. The incessant technical mutations of what we might call its 'material support' render efforts to define or theorise video particularly precarious — especially now, as videotape, monitor and cathode-ray tube give way to DVDs, digital storage devices and electronic screens. In digital cinema, the differential specificity of video *vis-à-vis* film (and vice versa) all but disappears, as the necessary relations between recording, storage, editing and release formats erode. How can video be a medium if it no longer has a central apparatus or machine, much less a specific form of aesthetic production or set of social or vernacular uses? We might follow Rosalind Krauss's early diagnosis and decide that video is not a medium at all, but merely a structure, the way that narcissism is a psychic structure.[20] Yet to do so seems to prematurely close down a still-emerging form.

For anyone who has studied early cinema and the larger history of screen practice, the present moment seems uncannily familiar. As film historian Charles Musser notes, moments of profound technological transformation tend to provoke trafficking with other media: 'when the screen enters a period of flux, it is particularly receptive to new influences from other cultural forms'.[21] Early in the twentieth century, the new motion picture adopted myriad exhibition formats, from panoramas and vaudeville shows to individualised, jukebox-like booths. Initially oscillating between peephole devices and projective formats, and between private viewing and collective spectatorship, cinema gradually achieved the codification of exhibition formats that grounds its current form. By its second decade, American narrative cinema had 'established a relation between producer, image and audience that has remained fundamentally unaltered ever since' — a relation whose structure and limits are now rendered more apparent though the incursions of 'interactive' and computer game models.[22]

As Krauss has proposed in recent texts on 'the post-medium condition' of contemporary art-making, cinema manifests a fundamentally 'aggregate' condition that cannot be reduced to its physical support:

19 Fredric Jameson, 'Reading without Interpretation: Postmodernism and the Video-text' (1986), *Postmodernism, or, The Cultural Logic of Late Capitalism*, Durham, North Carolina: Duke University Press, 1991.

20 Rosalind Krauss, 'Video: The Aesthetics of Narcissism', *October*, no.1, Spring 1976. Please note that this essay is reproduced in the current volume.

21 Charles Musser, *The Emergence of Cinema: the American Screen to 1907*, New York: Scribner, 1990, p.16.

22 *Ibid.*, p.19.

23 Rosalind Krauss, *'A Voyage on the North Sea': Art in the Age of the Post-Medium Condition*, London: Thames & Hudson, 1999, pp.24–25.

24 Richard Dienst, *Still Life in Real Time: Theory After Television*, Durham, North Carolina: Duke University Press, 1994, pp.4 and 5.

> the medium or support for film being neither the celluloid strip of the images, nor the camera that filmed them, nor the projector that brings them to life in one motion, nor the beam of light that relays them to the screen, nor that screen itself, but all of these taken together, including the audience's position caught between the source of the light behind it and the image projected before our eyes.[23]

Precisely because of its internal complexity and variability, the cinematic apparatus offers a non-reductive means of understanding a medium as a set of procedures, structures and operations — a kind of relation to the viewer — that allows artists to probe and articulate its structures in critical, compelling, yet self-referential ways. This may be precisely what contemporary video lacks, in its quest for maximum 'aesthetic impact' of a very different sort, one that harnesses the televisual capacity for the profuse diffusion of images — what Richard Dienst terms TV's 'all encompassing putting-into-view of the world', its production of 'a field of near total instantaneous visibility' — and that uses new digital and projective technologies to proliferate these throughout architectural space.[24]

Such images find their natural home in the emerging world of 'information architecture', in which every building functions as a kind of image and every built surface promises to contain some type of networked display. As flat-screen technologies allow the picture to return to the space of the wall from which it had long ago been detached, it does not reinsert this image into a wall whose architectonic solidity and immobility remain intact. Indeed, one of the key lessons of decades of 'experimental' architecture has been the historical interpenetration of the tectonic and the semiotic. A host of functions for the transmission of information (signage, windows, corporate logos, transparency) — once peripheral to the structural, load-bearing capacities of the wall — have now been integrated into the building's interior and exterior surfaces. The very emergence of public urban space as a computerised convergence of surveillance, communication and entertainment might propel critical projects in video, as artists attempt to address the electronic image and its mutating relation to new forms of architectural space and subjectivity.

New media theorist Lev Manovich has argued that transcoding — the technical possibility of transferring an image or composition or 'work' from one format to another — is 'the most substantial consequence of the computerization of media'.[25] Despite the lure of electronic transfer without loss, Manovich acknowledges the technical impossibility of absolute fidelity. What artists since John Cage have understood, however, is not merely that transfer and transcoding entail distortion, but that this breakdown, reprocessing and information loss (which occurs across digital and analogue modes) is remarkably generative and productive. In Lutz Bacher's *Olympiad* (1997), for instance, a modestly scaled projection of a 'corrupted' tape of a walk

25 Lev Manovich, *The Language of New Media*, Cambridge, Mass.: The MIT Press, 2001, p.45.

through the Olympic Stadium in Berlin displays myriad tracking problems and signal disruptions that erratically destabilise the video image. As the artist recounts, the resulting tape was 'resurrected' through reprocessing by a time-base corrector, leaving it playable only in black-and-white due to signal loss.[26] Drawing on the Cagean principle that 'once anything happens it authentically is', Bacher embraced the artwork as a structure that can incorporate accident, damage and decay. The difficulty of the work — its jarring perceptual disruption — results from the unanticipated investigation of the degraded video image and video signal and 'the ways in which these recurring technical breakdowns both enhance and disrupt the classical aspirations of the site'. Nothing could be further from the mannerism of Thater's increasingly contrived projection distortions, or Aitken's over-produced spectacles of post-apocalyptic collapse and decay, in which his own technology (after a crucial early piece) never fails or falters.[27]

In *Olympiad*, the breakdown of the video signal foregrounds the pixilated grid structure — the 'raster' — recalling visual art analogues like Sigmar Polke's 1960s *Rasterbilder* ('dot paintings') or Warhol's early silk screens, which systematically explore the poignancy produced by image degradation. No mere pictorial device, this pixilated grid is the very structure of the transmissible image. It is the matrix through which images must pass before they can inhabit the same surface as printed text; pixels also comprise the screen through which the two-dimensional image must pass before it can be transmitted electronically. As Dienst notes, the 'transmission of a moving picture' by broadcast, metal wire or laser technology entails the 'de-screening' and 're-screening' of light through a video signal:

> What is transmitted, at the simplest level, is simply a stream of pulses that scan a field at a certain speed: light entering the camera hits a plate where it can be registered line by line, translating a two-dimensional spatial arrangement of light into a sequential signal. When this signal reaches the other end, it is translated back into a field by projecting the electrical intensities line by line onto another screen.[28]

In video, scanning and projection are means of translating electronic signals into a two-dimensional picture: what was previously inside the monitor (phosphorescent pixels on an enclosed glass screen) is now transferred to the larger container of the room or screen. As Dienst notes, 'scanning mediates at

26 Unpublished notes of the artist, 1998.

27 In *inflection* (1992), Aitken launched a small rocket with a film camera attached; the footage, played back in slow-motion, records the blurry and enigmatic landscape viewed from the rocket's flight. As Daniel Birnbaum notes: 'Here, essential elements of Aitken's work are already present: a moving vehicle; speed made tangible; an abstract landscape unfolding through contemporary technologies of vision.' See D. Birnbaum, 'That's the Only Now I Get: Space and Experience in the Work of Doug Aitken', *op. cit.*, p.40. What he fails to note is that, after this piece, accidental and process elements drop out of Aitken's work, replaced by the aestheticisation of the ruin. And while Thater's early projects appear organised around unforeseen accidents introduced by process, technology and site, such disruptions seem to recede in her recent, more technically-polished works.

28 R. Dienst, *Still Life in Real Time: Theory After Television*, *op. cit.*, p.17.

29 *Ibid.*, p.21.

30 My thanks to Eric de Bruyn, Simon Leung and Federico Windhausen for discussing these materials with me.

both ends between visible screens and electrical currents; it is above all a way of translating and framing light as information'.[29] Thus the pixel and scan lines are the visible marks of the intervention of technology and its abstracting effects (hence the very goal of 'high definition' television is to repress this structure, to make video look more like film by reducing pixilation below the threshold of visibility). Video, as a temporally generated grid, produces a continual transformation of the image. Signal interference and disruption are integral to its workings, as are the decays and distortions introduced by recording and storage processes. It is in the interplay between this screen of scanning — that translates electrical signals into moving images — and the screen of projection — that transmits these optical images into architectural space — that video occurs. As we continue to wait for artists to explore the unpredictable things that happen there, perhaps we are beginning to see that the video-projection work that was so celebrated during the past decade was less of a disruption of mass-media signal than a sign of the times.[30]

SITING CINEMA
Andrew V. Uroskie

Getting Framed

Everything that's of any importance takes place outside the room.
But the room reminds us of the limitations of our condition.[1]
Robert Smithson

Upon approaching *The Paradise Institute*, a work first exhibited at the 2001 Venice Biennale by the Canadian artists Janet Cardiff and Georges Bures Miller, we find ourselves in a doubly framed space. Already within the white cube of the gallery, we encounter a large, two-level plywood box, complete with stairs and doorways leading in and out. Looking inside from a distance, we might be able to just make out the kind of stadium seating more commonly associated with the local multiplex. There is nothing slick or manufactured about the large, plywood construction — on the contrary, it seems to have been quickly thrown together. Yet the seating inside, with its plush red covering and — as we will soon discover — adjustable backs, is obviously not the most economical option. Both this box and its interior seem out of place in a gallery setting, albeit for different reasons. While the box is not without a certain Minimalist aesthetic, it fails to hold our attention as a form. Circumnavigation does not lead to a reflection on the structure *per se*, so much as heighten our anticipation of discovering what lies within. The kind of theatricality invoked is not in the phenomenological sense that Michael Fried famously designated as the pull of Minimalist sculpture; rather, it is in the more prosaic sense of suspense that we might experience in advance of seeing a fairground attraction or a theatre spectacle. As with such attractions, one may not simply enter, but must first obtain a ticket and wait for the performance to commence.

Climbing the steps, we find headphones on the seats awaiting us. Placing them over our ears, the exterior sounds of the gallery are quickly muffled, and our immediate aural environment is swallowed up in the projected static of white noise. The doors to the outside close, and darkness follows. Simultaneously relaxed by the seating and made anxious by the claustrophobic enclosure (how can we leave if we need to get out?), we wait for something to begin. But just as the noise of our fellow audience members falls away, sounds and conversation begin anew. Over to the left and just behind us on the right, people are talking again. Cardiff and Miller recorded the audio component of the piece using binaural technology, which gives

1 Liza Bear and Willoughby Sharp, 'Discussions with Michael Heizer, Dennis Oppenheim and Robert Smithson' (held December 1968–January 1969), *Avalanche*, 1, Fall 1970; reprinted in Jack Flam (ed.), *Robert Smithson: Collected Writings*, Berkeley: University of California Press, 1996, p.250.

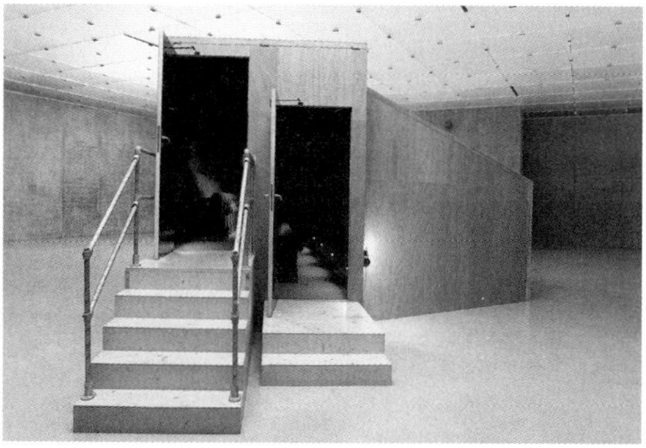

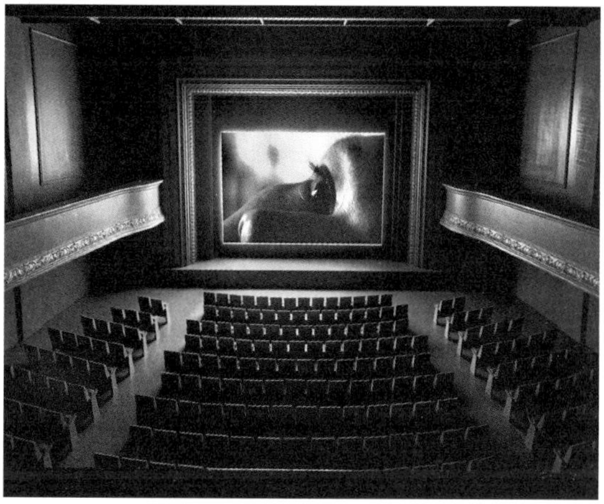

a powerful illusion of spatial presence to the sound we hear. Thus, while aurally isolated from the real people around us, we continue to overhear the conversations of people who seem to surround us. There is a sense of uncanny doubling as real and recorded sounds overlap and coalesce. We hear people rustling in their seats, taking off items of clothing and whispering to one another — all preparing for the main attraction. A mobile phone goes off and a woman quickly tells her caller that she has to go — 'she's in a movie'. Occurring in eerily precise stereo-sound and seemingly at discrete spatial locations, this all seems quite realistic. Yet this is not to say that it is taken for reality. Even the binaural recordings cannot perfectly evoke the manifold sensory experience of a real phenomenal environment, and spectators quickly recognise that they are listening to an illusion. Yet far from ruining the work, the spectator's double-consciousness — his or her simultaneous experience of real and recorded sounds and continued ability to distinguish between them — will prove fundamental to the experience the work seeks to generate. Within the *Paradise Institute*, reality will not be banished so much as redoubled, creating a spectatorial environment that is distinct yet coexistensive with the physical space of the theatre.

As the screen lights up in front of us, its glow illuminates a miniature diorama of seats, a proscenium and a balcony, at the far edge of which we might understand ourselves to be seated. Cardiff and Miller have here constructed an alternative universe, a heterotopia in miniature. Gazing upon the tiny diorama, seated on our full-sized chairs, we can comfortably give ourselves over to the spectacle, secure in the knowledge that it is merely spectacle, and that we remain outside of it looking in. The headphones we are given to wear — like the diorama before us and the makeshift theatre in which we sit — specifically draw attention to the staged character of the illusion. Yet this acknowledgement should not be understood as a way of simply 'foregrounding the apparatus'. This notion, originally stemming from Russian Formalist literary criticism and the dramatic theories of Bertolt Brecht, has operated from within a rhetorical economy invested in sharply distinguishing reality from illusion. *The Paradise Institute* does not allow such secure boundaries to be maintained. While the apparatus is explicitly foregrounded, this is not done simply to dismiss illusion in the name of a contravening reality, but rather to throw the certainty of this very demarcation into doubt.

Janet Cardiff and George Bures Miller, *The Paradise Institute*, 2001. Exterior photo © 2008 Markus Tretter. Interior photo © 2008 Jens Ziehe. Courtesy the artists and Luhring Augustine, New York

Suddenly we are addressed by a woman's voice just to our left: 'Here's your drink ... have some of my popcorn.' Eating noisily, she tells us that she has heard of this film, that it was based on a real story, that the experiments carried out in it were made by North Americans in World War II. But she may be mistaken — that may be another movie. On the screen, the film begins. But with this voice beside us, it is as if we have already been placed in the centre of the fiction, rather than simply before it. Dramatic elements are now erupting all around us, even though it is not clear they all belong to the same drama. On-screen a nurse approaches a bare-chested man strapped to a bed. While he begs her not to, she slowly bends down and presses her lips to his chest, kissing and then lightly biting his chest. The scene is emotionally charged, even arousing — but, like the voices, it merely solicits our attention without grounding it in a coherent, linear narrative.

A voice from the audience behind us crudely interjects: 'Now that's nursing!' Our attention is grabbed away from the characters on-screen, towards those 'seated' in the audience. The female voice beside us wonders aloud at several points whether you or she might have accidentally left the stove on at home; as she does so, we pull out from the disjointed, *noir* narrative to witness shots of a burning house — a scene which somehow feels completely extra-diegetic, even though the original diegesis is never fully established. The burning house comes to emerge as our own, even as we consciously disown it. It is, as Freud once described the subject of the unconscious, a house of which we are an uncertain or absent master. Likewise, when we are repeatedly asked 'do you want some more popcorn?', it begins to feel as if we are *choosing* to answer with our silence. Repetition performatively works to assign ownership and responsibility, and we find that we cannot help but be involved in this strange form of 'communication'. As the elements of the narrative become introjected one by one, we leave behind the safety and comfort of a distanced spectatorship and begin to occupy an awkward space inside the fiction.

As the film narrative evolves, the distinction between what is occurring on- and off-screen begins to break down completely. A diabolical man evoked in the story starts to become detached from it and crosses over into the audience. The patient in the film does not leave his bed — just as we, the spectators, do not leave our seats. A sense of vertigo overtakes us as we are constantly thrust into new and different locations. As the suspenseful music builds and the screen goes blank, we seem to have lost all ability to discern where this fiction starts and stops. The diabolical man, now beside us in the audience, laughingly describes our predicament: 'You thought you were pretty smart — playing both sides. How long did you think it could last?' We hear a crowd of people pounding on the plywood theatre within which we are seated, demanding that we get out. As the crowd begins shouting a countdown, a burning house appears on-screen and the film abruptly ends. The doors to the outside open up, and we file out of the black box into the freshly comforting white cube of the gallery.

Within *The Paradise Institute*, we struggle not to separate fact from fiction so much as to establish a firm locus for that fiction to *take place*. We never confuse fact and fiction, because we always understand that we are being presented with a fiction. But it is not a consistent fiction. It is fractured, multiple, existing in too many places at once. As we lose track of the boundary or frame where the diegetic world starts and stops, our phenomenological sense of wholeness and interiority gives way to a kind of paranoia. It seems no accident that the work begins with the admonition that spectators will not be able to leave the theatre once the performance has begun. Unlike traditional theatres, *The Paradise Institute* contains no brightly glowing exit sign reassuring us that (in a physical or psychological emergency) the space of the fiction can be quickly and definitively left behind. The word 'paradise' stems from the Ancient Persian for 'walled-off space', and *The Paradise Institute* stages what is ultimately a crisis of boundaries for its spectator. We are allowed to exist neither inside nor outside of the spectacle. This liminal staging of subjectivity is one that is familiar in psychoanalytic theory, wherein the inner space of the psyche and the outer space of the world can no longer be definitively separated as in classical philosophy, but come to form an overlapping or chiasmatic structure. *The Paradise Institute*—which in its very name conflates fantasy with containment, ancient myth with modern medicalisation—confronts the cultural locus of the spectacular with a markedly different economy of spectatorship. Haunted by levels of fiction without a clearly marked escape, the work presents this experience as ambivalently pleasurable and nightmarish at one and the same time.

Trapped within the Fiction

On a hot day in August 1972, 'Little John' Wojtowicz found out that his boyfriend, Aron, lacking the funds for a desperately wanted sex-change operation, had become suicidal and was interned at a mental hospital against his will. Believing that nothing but the operation could ultimately keep Aron alive, Wojtowicz and two friends staged a robbery at a Chase Manhattan Bank in Brooklyn. As a robbery, it was a spectacular failure. But, as a spectacle, it was a fantastic success. Trapped in a stand-off with the police after his escape was prevented, Wojtowicz became a cult hero amongst the crowds that gathered to watch. Newspaper and television reporters quickly arrived on the scene, and, as a result of its extended duration, the robbery became the first to be broadcast over network television as it occurred in real time. Following the ordeal, newspapers, magazines and a talk show told and retold this basic story in different ways; a screenplay was written and rewritten; and within a few short years, Warner Brothers brought the story to the big screen in Sidney Lumet's *Dog Day Afternoon* (1975). Winning both popular and critical acclaim, that film immortalised Al Pacino as John Wojtowicz, even as the real Wojtowicz languished unknown in jail.

In his video *The Third Memory* (1999), Pierre Huyghe seeks to trace the mediation of this event within both Wojtowicz's individual memory and the collective memory of history. In a split-screen film approximately 10-minutes long, Wojtowicz — having served a twenty-year jail sentence — is asked to re-enact the robbery on a stripped-down studio set. The set recreates the space of a bank, but, because of its minimal decoration, it is not clear whether it is meant to recreate the bank set of *Dog Day Afternoon* or the original Chase Manhattan Bank in Brooklyn where the robbery took place, or both. Within the installation, strategic juxtapositions draw attention to the ways in which subsequent news and Hollywood coverage have reshaped even the original participants' recollections of actual events. As Wojtowicz recounts a story that is no longer his alone, fiction and reality, the imagined and the documented, become inextricably intertwined.

From a first memory of the original crime to a second memory achieved through the media's interpretation of that crime through television, print and cinema, Huyghe presents Wojtowicz's recreation of the original event as a third memory — one in which the multiple layers of mediation emerge for both the actor and spectator. *The Third Memory* presents the past as a continuously shifting field within the present, an ongoing struggle to mine and decipher meaning from an increasingly opaque sedimentation of characters and actions. As we discover within Wojtowicz's narrative for *The Third Memory*, the foiled bank robbery was itself inspired by Martin Scorsese's *The Godfather* (1972); and, ironically, Wojtowicz's acting-out under the adrenaline surge provided by Marlon Brando and Pacino in that story inspired Sidney Lumet's award-winning *Dog Day Afternoon*, again starring Al Pacino. Cinematic drama gives birth to real life drama, which, in turn, replicates the cycle. For Wojtowicz, Pacino's cinematic success serves to bookend, and thus bracket out, his own dramatic failure — illustrating the porous boundary between self and other forged through affective identification.

Since *Dog Day Afternoon* was released, there has been a general confusion between Pacino's character Sonny Wortzik and the real-life John Wojtowicz. Lumet's film intentionally precipitated this confusion with its

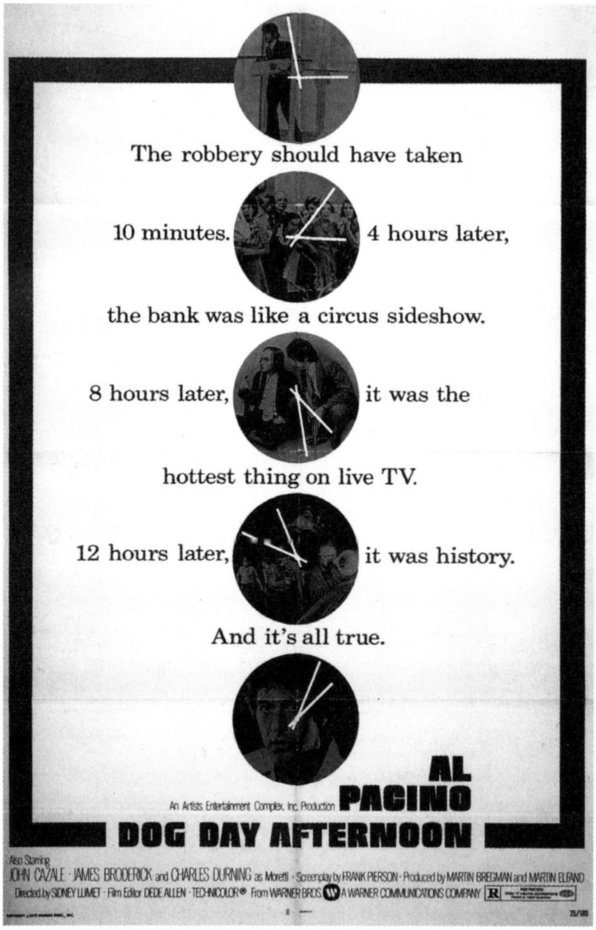

Film poster for *Dog Day Afternoon*, 1975

Facing page: Pierre Huyghe, *The Third Memory*, 1999. Courtesy the artist and Marian Goodman Gallery, New York & Paris

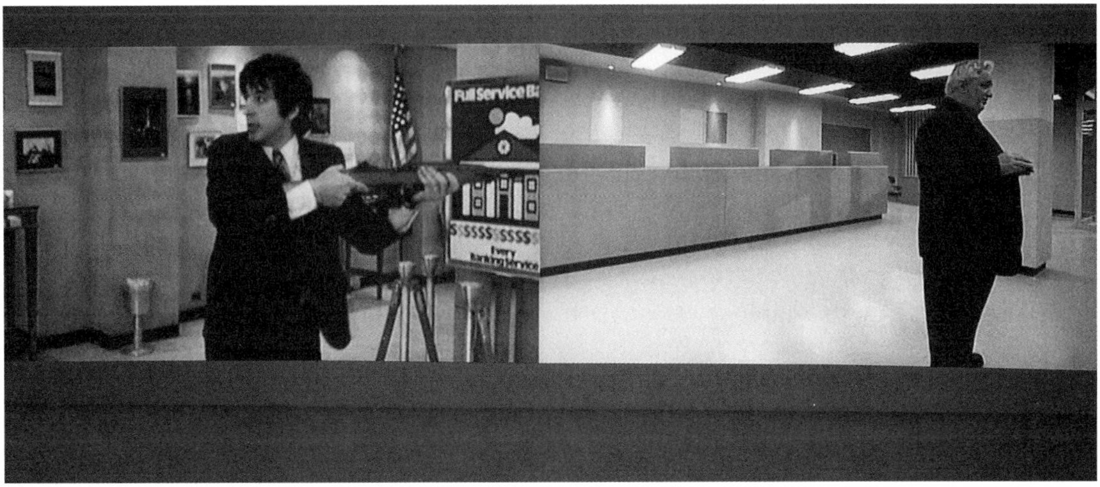

beginning title sequence: 'What you are about to see is true. It happened in Brooklyn, New York on August 22nd, 1972.' The film presents itself as it came to be understood — as a representation of history. But it is a representation that does not acknowledge its character as representation, which contains and delimits the real life event within its fictional frame. Thus no reference is made, even in the final credits, to John Wojtowicz. Within Huyghe's reconstitution, by contrast, Wojtowicz is placed at centre stage. Yet the stage he is given is only schematic, deliberately unfinished. In this, Huyghe presents his remake of the robbery in a resolutely de-spectacularised manner. As twin cameras track and pan across the unfolding action, the scene is depicted from two perspectives at once, depriving the viewer of a single locus of cinematic identification. Focusing our attention only upon Wojtowicz's character and his narrative, Huyghe's reconstitution provides its image of this history only through the subjective lens of Wojtowicz himself — through the visible scars these memories have etched upon him as he goes about re-enacting the primal scene. Rather than the 'high drama' through which this story has so often been told, what stand out in Huyghe's reconstruction are the human qualities of 'Little John' as a person — his humour, his compassion, his intelligence and the underlying simplicity of his love for another man.

But Huyghe is not content to simply let Wojtowicz 'tell his side of the story', as it were — he is not interested in recreating the debased spectacle of the talk-show format. Rather, he creates a quasi-fictional space within which Wojtowicz is allowed to 'replay' events: to play the role of the bank robber within what he himself refers to as 'the real movie' of his life. Wojtowicz re-enacts his bank robbery on a movie set, amongst sound and lighting technicians, with two cameras capturing his every move from different angles. Wojtowicz is given the injunction to set the record straight, but while doing so he cannot help but blend fact and fiction. His memory of that fateful day is overwhelmed by the hundreds of stories he has read, interviews he has given and the indelible performance of Pacino resonating within his head. Given the opportunity to re-enact his own bank robbery, it is as if the bank robbery is no longer his to re-enact. Thus we cannot simply say, as has been argued, that Wojtowicz is allowed to 'reclaim' his reality from the grip of its media (mis)representation.[2] Huyghe understands that any 'undoing' of this mediation — reconstituting Wojtowicz's story, as it were — cannot be simply *opposed* to the cinematic, for Wojtowicz's performance had been constituted through the language of the cinematic imaginary from the very beginning. In seeing the original release of *The Godfather* to 'inspire the troops', as Wojtowicz puts it in *The Third Memory*, he sought to emulate the same actor who was eventually cast to play his part. But even taking Pacino out of the picture, as it were, the whole *idea* of holding up a bank with a shotgun — like his phrase 'inspire the troops' — comes straight out of Wild West movies and *Hogan's Heroes*-style World War II films. Cinematic and extra-cinematic history would seem here to be hopelessly entangled.[3] It is not simply that fact and fiction become blurred, but that history itself becomes incomprehensible outside the phantasmatic worlds of cinematic narrative when there is no longer a meaningful distinction between news and entertainment.[4]

In coming to grips with Huyghe's practice, we can no longer rely on a reductive conception of cinematic 'deconstruction' through which the hidden ideological structures are revealed and contested. Yet neither can we rely upon the model of the visionary avant-garde film-maker expressing his particular creativity. Huyghe's *Third Memory* might be more productively considered as a complex form of performative documentation. It is concerned with industrial cinema insofar as this cinema provides a nodal point from which to engage a larger field of questions concerning the imbrication and codependence of subjectivity, media and representation within the modern era. While offering a critique of *Dog Day Afternoon* and other media narratives of the event, it does not pretend to offer a final, clear, authoritative view — even, ironically enough, when the subject of these narratives is finally allowed to

2 Jean-Charles Massera, author of the companion text to Huyghe's *The Third Memory*, contends that the work models and effects a form of Situationist 'reconstitution' of lived experience over and against the mediation of spectacle culture.

3 The political implications of this confusion have been traced extensively within contemporary film scholarship. An early and important reference point is Michael Rogin's *Ronald Reagan, The Movie: And Other Episodes in Political Demonology*, Berkeley: University of California Press, 1988. A more general argument is presented in Mark Crispin Miller's *The Bush Dyslexicon: Observations on a National Disorder*, New York: Norton, 2002.

4 A somewhat analogous story from this same period illustrates this point quite precisely. Nik Cohn, an early pioneer of rock journalism in the London Mod scene of the 1960s, came to America to reinvent himself as a hard-boiled journalist. He sold a story titled 'Tribal Rites of the New Saturday Night', about a suave dance-hall king from Brooklyn, to *New York Magazine* for their 7 July 1976 issue. The fantastic true-life story of this 'Italian Stallion' gave rise to the Hollywood film *Saturday Night Fever*, which itself went on to define the era within American popular consciousness, eventually becoming a Broadway hit musical. Cohn was widely praised for having his finger on the pulse of a generation. The only problem is that the 'Italian Stallion' never existed outside Cohn's imagination. Cohn had originally stated: 'everything described in this article is factual and was either witnessed by me or told to me directly by the people involved. Only the names of the main characters have been changed.' Yet in 1997, for a *New York Magazine* story on the film's twentieth anniversary, Cohn finally admitted that his story was a complete fabrication: 'I'd only recently arrived in New York. Far from being steeped in Brooklyn street life, I hardly knew the place. As for Vincent, my story's hero, he was largely inspired by a Shepherd's Bush mod whom I'd known in the Sixties.' The original article had, tellingly, used illustrations rather than photographs. By the time of the second article, of course, it hardly mattered, for *Saturday Night Fever* had already claimed iconic status as a historical document, fictional or not. Fascinatingly, Cohn seemed to undertake a similar dissassociation from reality as Wojtowitcz: 'Spurred in part by retroactive conscience, I began to put in hard time in Brooklyn, steeping myself in Bay Ridge lore. Gradually, my invention became real to me; my hero came to life. In my imagination, I kept a detailed log of his progress, tracking him as he changed jobs, moved away from home, grew out of disco, left the neighborhood and then

speak directly. In fact, *The Third Memory* seems to point to the relative naivety of this earlier aesthetico-political ideal, because Wojtowicz, despite having been cheated by Warner Brothers, continues to identify with Pacino. While languishing in jail, Wojtowicz wrote of the great pleasure he continued to take in the occasional private screenings granted to him of *Dog Day Afternoon*.

If this is a form of alienation, it is not something that can simply be opposed to the spectacular culture of the cinematic. As Huyghe put it in a recent interview:

> [S]pectacle has always been linked with illusion, with manipulation, with the culture industry ... simply rejecting the spectacle or entertainment as bad; this is a form of escapism. Nor is the point just to incorporate spectacle ... saying, 'I will also just be an entertainer'. The point is to take spectacle as a format, and to use it ... to 're-scenarize' the real.[5]

As Huyghe goes on to clarify, his work involves 'the reformulation of protocols of exhibition and representation' because these protocols have 'shifted the [very] notion of representation. Today, an event, its image and its commentary have become one object.' In so doing, Huyghe specifically rejects a longstanding paradigm within theories of film and visual culture by which the task of the critic is conceptualised as wholly anti-spectacular — locating and revealing media illusions so as to return us to an unmediated reality. Within Huyghe's work, suffused as it is by the complex affective identifications of cinematic culture, there is no clear and simple bedrock of 'reality' to which we can return. The work does locate, however, the changing protocols of exhibition and display through which media culture is born.

In attending to these protocols, *The Third Memory* ultimately directs our attention to the political control of information itself and the changing nature of news in the era of the ubiquitous broadcast stream. For Wojtowicz's bank robbery was not only the first ever to be captured live on national TV as it unfolded, it also took place on the very evening that then-President Richard Nixon was making a major political calculation. Rejecting both widespread expectations and the explicit advice of many within his party to balance the presidential ticket by nominating a moderate for his running mate, Nixon shocked the nation — and inaugurated a new Republican strategy — by nominating another hard-line conservative. Newspapers posted within *The Third Memory* show the two events competing for headlines. Though left out of the fictionalised account of *Dog Day Afternoon*, Wojtowicz alleges that the FBI was under direct orders from Nixon to keep the 'gay bank robber' from compromising the President's media attention. Later, he claims, the FBI shot his partner in cold blood, and his own life was saved only by the local New York Police's demand that the FBI surrender Wojtowicz into their custody. It's hard

returned. I noted his marriage, the birth of his two daughters; watched him pick up a gambling problem; saw him slither toward middle age.' Nik Cohn, 'Saturday Night's Big Bang', *New York Magazine*, 8 December 1997.

5 George Baker, 'An Interview with Pierre Huyghe', *October*, no.10, Cambridge, Mass.: The MIT Press, 2004, pp.80–106.

to know what to make of Wojtowicz's assertion, though given our subsequent knowledge of Nixon and Agnew's long list of criminal activities — Nixon was forced to resign during the shooting of *Dog Day Afternoon* — it is certainly not implausible. Whether or not we believe Wojtowicz's assertions, we will never know either way. And this access to information, or lack thereof, is precisely the point. With our access so explicitly mediated, we are uncomfortably positioned in the realm not of knowledge but of belief.

Yet Huyghe's subtle opening sequence again calls our attention to the importance of the protocols of exhibition that lie invisibly anterior to the image itself. *The Third Memory* begins with an image from *Dog Day Afternoon*, but not one from its theatrical release. Instead, we first see the familiar FBI copyright warning prohibiting the film's unauthorised remediation through home-viewing technology. Over the familiar image, we hear Wojtowicz's voice as he begins to recount his own troubled history with the FBI. Juxtaposed with the opening title of *Dog Day Afternoon*, we begin to sense the precarious status of our access to information: while *Dog Day Afternoon* presents itself as historical fact, even Huyghe's modest attempt to contest this history is prohibited by monopoly copyright. Just as *Time Magazine* was once on the verge of purchasing history itself by acquiring exclusive copyright to Abraham Zapruder's film of JFK's assassination, so Warner Brothers' control of Wojtowicz's true story is, ironically enough, enforced by the FBI. Whether actively enforced through copyright law or passively propagated through the consolidation of a privatised media industry, the increasingly pervasive corporate monopoly over information is depicted by Huyghe as a literal matter of life and death.

In the face of an increasingly constrained and intimidated news media, consider journalist Ron Suskind's description of his meetings with two senior advisors to President Bush at the inauguration of his 'war on terror':

> The aide said that guys like me were 'in what we call the reality-based community', which he defined as people who 'believe that solutions emerge from your judicious study of discernible reality'. I nodded and murmured something about enlightenment principles and empiricism. He cut me off. 'That's not the way the world really works anymore,' he continued 'We're an empire now, and when we act, we create our own reality. And while you're studying that reality — judiciously, as you will — we'll act again, creating other new realities, which you can study too ... We're history's actors ... and you, all of you, will be left to just study what we do.'[6]

6 Ron Suskind, 'Without a Doubt', *The New York Times Magazine*, 17 October 2004, sec.6 p.44. Suskind continues: 'Mark McKinnon, a longtime senior media adviser to Bush ... started by challenging me. "You think he's an idiot, don't you? ... all of you do, up and down the West Coast, the East Coast ... Let me clue you in. We don't care. You see, you're outnumbered 2 to 1 by folks in the big, wide middle of America, busy working people who don't read *The New York Times* or *Washington Post* or *The L.A. Times*. And you know what they like? They like the way he walks and the way he points, the way he exudes confidence. They have faith in him. And when you attack him for his malaprops, his jumbled syntax, it's good for us. Because you know what those folks don't like? They don't like you!" In this instance, the final "you", of course, meant the entire "reality-based community".'

7 In her analysis of the 'Pentagon Papers', Arendt writes of the architects of the Vietnam War: 'the ultimate aim was neither power nor profit. Nor was it

Suskind's interlocutor foregrounds the manner in which the production and circulation of images has emerged as the very goal of contemporary politics. It is a situation that political philosopher Hannah Arendt had presciently described in 1972, the year of Wojtowitz's televised bank robbery, with the phrase 'Image-making as global policy'.[7] But while I sympathise with Suskind's concern for something we might want to call 'reality-based' governance, I am wary of the way this kind of rhetoric inscribes a familiar trope of political modernism — from Marxist through post-Structuralist criticism — which is bound up with rigorously distinguishing 'reality' from 'illusion', whilst placing its collective energy in a naive aspiration to dispense with 'illusionism' once and for all. The resulting criticism has inhibited not only our knowledge of individual artists and works, but the possibility of a more sophisticated understanding of spectatorship itself — one which acknowledges, after a century of psychoanalytic philosophy, that a rational distinction between 'reality' and 'illusion' is often one of the *least* important considerations for a study of either aesthetics or politics. *The Third Memory* speaks to profound social and political questions within our time *from deep within* the phantasmatic worlds of the cinematic. Far from offering a simple deconstruction of the media spectacle, Huyghe illustrates just how dependent we have become — as individuals and as institutions — on the forms of exhibition and identification articulated within a century of moving-image culture.

Disciplinary Archaeologies: Beyond Film and Video, an Expanded Cinema

For artists of Warhol's generation, the cinema was the very site for the collapse of the modernist ontology of medium specificity. As a sickly child, Warhol experienced the glamour of the 'silver screen' not within the great picture palaces of yore, but isolated in his bed, through the interlaced lines of the cathode ray tube. In *The Philosophy of Andy Warhol*, he describes the most formative of his youthful activities — watching movies on television — as inherently paradoxical, because in appearing on television they seemed to be no longer movies, but television.[8] Warhol was here less interested in making the now-familiar critique of television's uniformity than he was in calling attention to the processes — both formal and historical — by which the golden age of cinema was being remediated within the post-War televisual society. Rather than going out to the social space of the cinema theatre,

even influence in the world in order to serve particular, tangible interest for the sake of which prestige, an image of the "greatest power in the world", was needed and purposefully used. The goal was now the image itself, as is manifest in the very language of the problem-solvers, with their "scenarios" and "audiences", borrowed from the theatre ... Image-making as global policy — not world conquest, but victory in the battle "to win the people's minds" — is indeed something new in the huge arsenal of human follies recorded in history.' Hannah Arendt, 'Lying in Politics: Reflections on the Pentagon Papers' in *The New York Review of Books*, vol.17 no.8, 18 November 1971.

8 Andy Warhol, *The Philosophy of Andy Warhol: (From A to B and Back Again)*, New York: Harvest Books, 1977.

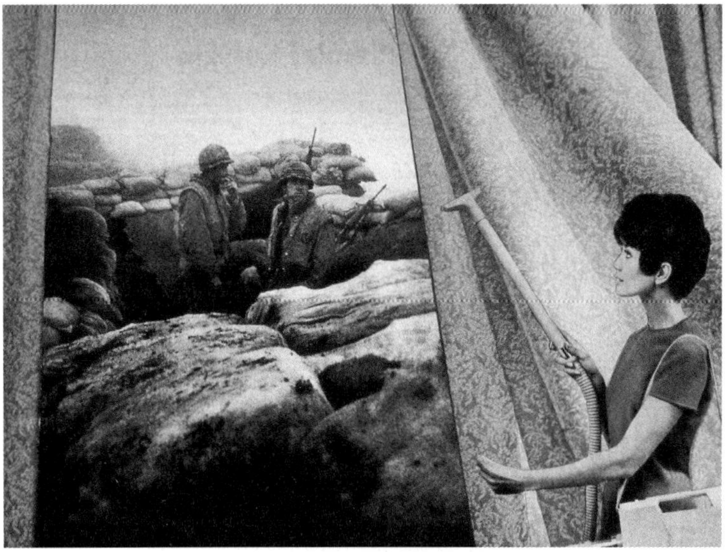

movies were originally a private experience that reached him in the most intimate of domestic spaces. For Warhol, the dislocation of the moving image was importantly bound up with a concomitant dislocation of subjective interiority within a post-War televisual society.

The generation of artists who began working in the early 1960s witnessed the incredible transformation of their newly televisual world when images of Kennedy's assassination met them at home or at their local bar. Walking along a city street, one might be suddenly and decisively transported by the television in a shop window to those horror-filled streets of Dallas, Texas. Soon it would be Birmingham, Alabama. Later it would be the jungles of Indochina. As the ubiquitous televisual image brought that which was spatially and psychologically distant into precarious proximity, traditional psychological borders became less distinct, more permeable. The inner space of the psyche and the outer space of the world seemed to become interwoven through the ever-present display of the moving-image screen.

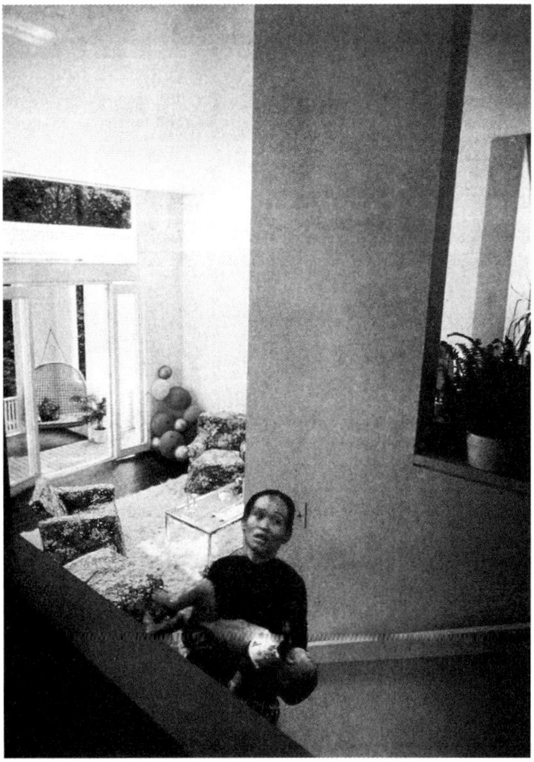

Bringing the War Home: House Beautiful, the photographic series that Martha Rosler began in 1967, succinctly illustrates the way in which the inner and outer spaces of both the post-War subject and the domestic space had become imaginatively shot-through with such affective televisual imagery. While the first image in the series shows the atrocities to be uncomfortably proximate, they still remain outside the picture window, with the possibility of closing the drapes and exiling them from the home. In the second image, the window has been broken and a pleading villager holds her wounded baby within this elegant, modernist space. Standing upon or perhaps ascending a staircase which we have been invited to think of as our own, she transforms an image of purity into a paranoiac vision of a haunting. That such an image would immediately provoke ideas of mental disturbance is at the heart of my argument, for what was at stake with the incorporation of television as both material and metaphor in the art of the 1960s was a psychodynamic reconceptualisation of the self-contained modernist subject, a reconceptualisation which found fertile ground in the post-War reappraisal of Freud's legacy in the seminars of Jacques Lacan.

Compelled to deal with this newly mediated reality in their artistic practices, artists of the 1960s went beyond the mere incorporation of media imagery into painting, taking up moving-image technology itself — its temporal rhythms and visual logic — as a medium for artistic practice. In so doing, they looked to the 'intrusive' quality of the moving image — its brazen link with the local and the distant — to reconceptualise the location, or 'sitedness', of aesthetic practice itself within a newly interconnected world. As images became unfixed as never before from the specificities of *physical* location, artists and critics were beginning to consider the institutional site within which images were encountered as perhaps the predominant frame through which those images would be experienced and understood.

When artists of the early 60s turned their attention to the technology of cinema, they discovered a pre-established cultural site that could never have the aesthetic or conceptual autonomy of painting or sculpture. Due to the economic importance of Hollywood's industrial practice, as well as the tradition of independent film-making that had already developed in opposition to this practice, the idea of film had already become a well defined domain of inquiry. Yet coextensive with the radical gestures of Pop and Minimalism, the artists who began to incorporate moving-image technologies into their practice in the 1960s were engaged primarily in an act of aesthetic and conceptual refusal. Refusing both the commercial cinema as well as its expressive, 'visionary' counterpart, they sought to reconsider both the institutional site and the affective economy of moving-image spectatorship as a novel and important domain of inquiry. This meant rethinking the embodied phenomenology of physical and perceptual transactions with the cinematic screen, as well as the social, cultural and political institutionalisation of cinema and what it had come to mean for the post-War audience. It meant considering the black box of the cinematic theatre together with the white cube of the gallery or museum space — attempting to discern in what ways they might be brought together, or how one might be approached from the perspective of the other.

Previous page: Martha Rosler, *Cleaning the Drapes*, 1967/72
Below: Martha Rosler, *Balloons*, 1967/72, both from *Bringing the War Home: House Beautiful*, 1967/72. 20 photomontages as C-Prints, 61×51cm each. Courtesy the artist and Galerie Christian Nagel, Cologne and Berlin

The interest and anxiety over the cultural location of the moving image — the sense that it was no longer confined to the theatrical site but had spilled out into everyday life and precipitated a more general cinematisation of society — constitutes a rich and fertile terrain within post-War artistic practice. Yet the discursive and institutional promiscuity of moving-image art — its failure to establish itself solely within the institutions of the theatre or the gallery, or within the discourses of either film studies or art history — has occasioned a critical blindness that cannot be remedied through the simple reintroduction of a few neglected artists or works. The peripheral location of these practices is no accidental sign of neglect, no mere historical oversight. Rather, the difficulty of locating artist film-making in the aesthetic discourse of the 1960s and in the later discourses of art and film criticism is inextricably bound up with the difficulty of locating these practices within the physical, institutional or discursive space of either the art gallery or the cinematic theatre. This interstitial location has frustrated attempts to understand artist film-making since the 60s, as well as relegating it to the disciplinary periphery of post-War art-history and film studies. Any critical recovery of this important body of work must first work to bridge the unproductive and unnecessary chasm that has been built up between the art- and film-historical accounts of this period.

For many years, Structural film was considered to be the epitome of artistic modernism in the cinema. Breaking with the traditions of narrativity and theatrical representation within industrial cinema, it attempted to constitute a self-referential practice of 'pure film'. This dream of aesthetic purity had its discursive corollary in an unfortunate tendency within film and media studies to downplay or simply bypass the art historical context in a quixotic attempt to manufacture an autonomous history of experimental film. Thus the films of Michael Snow and Paul Sharits are considered in terms of their basic continuity with Maya Deren's 'visionary' cinema of the 1940s — or even Germaine Dulac's work of the 20s — but not in terms of the theories and practices in Minimalism, Op art, Conceptualism or Fluxus that were contemporaneous with their production. Within this historiography, even the most radical filmic practices are folded into a basic continuity with older traditions of underground cinema, or viewed in terms of their opposition to mainstream industrial practices. Despite the fact that so-called Structural film-makers — Snow, Sharits, Warhol, George Landow and Hollis Frampton among them — were artists whose work was not exclusive to film, and despite their profound links to the aesthetic and conceptual transformations of art in the 1960s and early 70s, the critical investigation of these artists' films tended to situate them within an understanding of the medium as conceptually and historically autonomous.

Correlatively, contemporary art historians and theorists have tended to consider video and performance art as if these practices were aesthetically and conceptually autonomous and unrelated to developments in avant-garde film and intermedia art. This reductive conception of medium specificity has lead to serious historical omissions, when it has not lead to outright factual error. Thus, while Bruce Nauman, Richard Serra, Dan Graham and Vito Acconci are widely regarded as pioneering figures in the development of a domain called 'video art', it is seldom mentioned that much of this work was actually done on film rather than videotape, and that it was often in self-conscious dialogue with aesthetic and conceptual developments in avant-garde film. Neglect of the multiple contexts within which many of these artists worked has only increased the marginalisation of new media artistic practices, isolating them from the larger development of post-War art and film history, and ultimately hindering attempts to understand the historic and conceptual roots of artists' film and video in the present era. The pervasive rhetoric of medium specificity has too long acted as a barrier to understanding the aesthetic and conceptual sophistication of these early hybrid modes of practice. The rich aesthetic and conceptual field to which these works gave rise only becomes accessible once we are able to recover a sense of the difficulty that the incorporation of the time-based media technology of film caused for artistic practices from the early 1960s to the early 70s. The fundamental question with which we might begin is not 'how was film (or video) imagined as an artistic medium?' but rather 'how is the very *idea* of the artistic medium transformed through its encounter with moving-image technologies?'

While the Minimalist paradigm that has dominated art-historical discussion of these years was largely involved in reconceptualising the gallery as a phenomenological space of perceptual transactions, a neglected theory and practice of expanded cinema was involved in a much broader re-evaluation of aesthetic institutions in the televisual age. Within this alternative tradition, it was not simply the material of film but the whole institution of cinema that was taken as the site of conceptual and aesthetic interrogation. Like the white cube of the gallery space, the black box of the cinematic theatre was understood as a historically sedimented cultural space of perception, one with longstanding codes of representation dictating what could transpire on the screen, as well as codes of behavior dictating how the spectator must relate to the screen. In attempting to reconceptualise and rearticulate these codes, the artists and critics of this tradition were interested in taking not the celluloid strip but this entire spectatorial economy as its medium. In so doing, expanded cinema constituted a bold and prescient shift away from the autonomous, medium-specific practices we tend to associate with high modernism, towards the more environmental, mediated and site-specific conceptual practices that came to follow in its wake.

Early in this century, the German critic Walter Benjamin wrote about how technologies become uniquely visible in their birth and obsolescence. The 1960s were a seminal moment for the emergence of the moving image in North American art because of a dramatic conjunction of birth *and* obsolescence within the cultural life of moving-image technologies: as broadcast television surged forward, the film industry was in a precipitous decline. The old glamour of the 'silver screen' was being presented between commercials on TV. Cheap B-movies and theatrical gimmicks signalled ever more desperate attempts to lure back the theatrical audience. Yet the generation of artists who first experienced this decline in the theatrical cinema were the first to grasp the possibility for its radical reinvention. With inexpensive small-gauge film becoming widely available, and video technology just around the corner, many established artists took up moving-image technologies while possessing little or no previous experience in the medium. Because Hollywood had already colonised society's relation to the moving image, it became necessary for these film artists to deal with the cinematic *theatre* in contesting that naturalisation. Within their hybrid cultural and institutional location, these cinematic 'amateurs' gave birth to a conceptually rich and aesthetically compelling body of work that has, nevertheless, been forgotten in the history of post-War art and film. Yet the difficulty of definitively locating this work within traditions of art and film history is, in fact, a direct index of its contemporary relevance. For in their sustained effort to give birth to a radically new way of experiencing the moving image, these artists both necessitated and helped to create a novel institutional and discursive location between the white cube and the black box. Caught between these two sites, the dialectic of location and dislocation — both physical and psychological — was perhaps destined to become the dominant theme in the emergence of the moving image in contemporary artistic practice.

MOVING IMAGES
MOVING IMAGES

John Kelsey

It's not only rage that drives children to break their favourite toys. Sometimes it's the urge to release the productive potential trapped inside a product, sometimes it's simply the joy of wasting them. A history of dismantled and vandalised cinemas would include, among many others: Lettrist and Situationist attempts to liberate cinematic materials from their spectacular function by scratching the print, blacking the screen and disjoining sound from image; Warhol's non-stop screen tests and his multi-projector film happenings; Joan Jonas's opening up of cinematic time and space to live performance; Tony Conrad's preparation of cooked celluloid, meat and vegetables for 'projecting' onto — or hurling at — a blank movie screen; etc.

But cinema has always been broken and in pieces — it was even born that way. At the very first cinematic spectacles at the end of the nineteenth century, Parisian audiences encountered not only the screen and its magic, but also the noisy *bête lumineuse* — the projector — which was itself a spectacle to behold, and which for this reason was situated in the midst of the audience. This was before the fixed-viewing arrangement we know today, before the seats were lined up in rows and bolted down, before the projector was hidden away in its booth. In the beginning, the audience, the screen and the projector were mobile elements in an open arrangement. There was no rule dictating the number or sequence of reels that made up a film, and sometimes scenes from different pictures were shuffled and combined in one programme. So no two screenings of a film were ever the same. And the audience could move about, talk, fight and arrange the furniture according to their impulses. These events did not take place in proper cinemas, but in pubs, dance halls or whatever common dives could be made available for the night. There was no 'cinema', there was no finished version of any film, no distribution system and no official control over either the business or the presentation of film. There were simply the moving images, the machines that produced them and the festive, informal gatherings of the first movie-going public. And cinema continues in pieces. The difference today is that its fragmentation is rarely festive or epic. Dismantling cinema and using its materials to construct a contemporary art installation, for example, and then installing this new arrangement in a museum only liberates cinema in order to lose it once again. No matter how immersive and kaleidoscopic the image environment, no matter how cleverly appropriated the material or how brutally cinema has been fractured or derailed from itself, to encounter moving images in the form of a contemporary art installation is only to encounter their usual unavailability —another kind of window shopping. True, cinema has not been itself for some time now—since it went digital—and its recent mutations have been a sort of adventure. It's easier today than ever before for anybody at all to intervene in its processes, and everybody agrees that now is the time for piracy, hacking and the free use of cinematic information. But the question is *how* to use it once you get your hands on it, and what kinds of subjective worlds this free use can make available to us.

Bernadette Corporation's film *Get Rid of Yourself* (2001–03) elaborated a politics of subjectivity linked to the emergence of anonymous and antagonistic life-forms within the anti-globalisation movement. The film borrowed techniques from its subject—the so-called anarchist 'black bloc'—in order not to simply document the street violence, property damage and rioting that took place in Genoa, but precisely to make itself riot-like and to put its own processes in contact with the chaotic rhythms and de-subjectivising encounters of the event. In other words, not to present an image of resistance but to produce an image problem; to make moving images move away from themselves; and to arrive at the cinematic equivalent of a burning bank, a looted supermarket, a line of flight opening up a provisional free zone in the midst of an intensely controlled and programmed confrontation. *Get Rid of Yourself* became a fast favourite among curators of contemporary art, an example of the 'new politics of aesthetics', and has since found its place in the museum with all the others.

To create a cinema equal to our present desires would mean not only causing it to dysfunction, not simply interrupting its illusory continuity in order to expose the traumatic real it prefers to hide, but opening cinematic production (and reception) to other kinds of events—social, collective, intersubjective—and to the vertigo or joy of its own dispersal in lived time and space. For cinema is not only moving images, it is a system of productive relations and a chance to intervene in the specific rhythms and distances that determine these from without and within. Is this a 'relational' cinema? Only if the relationality it produces is not foremost and, finally, aesthetic. Between the street and the seat, the recording and the projection, the actor and the viewer, the soundtrack and the bedroom, the museum and the graveyard, play and rewind, original and copy, doing and not doing, countless potential sites of production and interruption remain to be discovered. To disperse cinema in this way is to create and multiply cinematic possibilities both on and off the screen where the finished product normally appears.

Pedestrian Cinema was conceived as a temporary underground film studio operated by Bernadette Corporation in Berlin. Since its inception in 2005, it has travelled to Mexico City, Paris and New York, and has been presented in exhibitions at the Witte de With in Rotterdam (*Bernadette Corporation*, 2005), the Hamburger Kunstverein (*King Kong*, 2006) and Kunstlerhaus Stuttgart (*Multiplyplex*, 2007). As part of this work-in-progress, Bernadette Corporation recently published a screenplay, *Eine Pinot Grigio,*

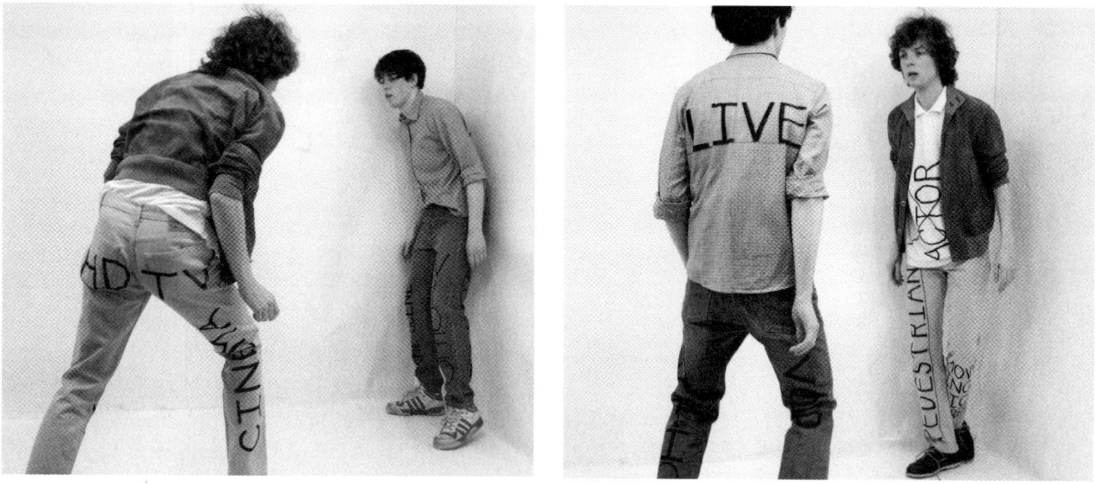

Bernadette Corporation, stills from *Out of Space*, 2006. Colour video, 30mins

Bitte (Sternberg Press, 2007), which the artist had no intention of ever producing as a film.

In Hollywood, the memorandum has always been a preferred means of informal, inter-office communication. Written during the early stages of *Pedestrian Cinema*, the following memos accompanied the partly fantastical work of elaborating an underground film studio of epic proportions, an invisible film factory to fill the wide-open void of Berlin.

—

Our first fiction is that we are doing cinema at all, and not just any cinema but a collective cinema dispersed across the time and space of a year in Berlin.

—

Each day, *Pedestrian Cinema* confronts the question of fabricating itself. It focuses its processes as a motor for thinking and working on a cinema happening 'here', among us, not falling from the stars.

—

The fact that *Pedestrian Cinema* is a non-stop, year-long activity does not mean that it cannot be at the same time a cinema on strike (strike here meaning not a work stoppage but a suspension of the relations that support what we normally think of as cinema). Suspending the relation that ensures our habitual distance from professional cinema draws cinema into a state of exile, in which going 'underground' is not a disappearing act but the discovery of an empty, wide-open cinema whose first thought is its own repopulation.

—

The casting call, for example, is an obvious first step towards peopling our fiction. Like Kafka's 'Nature Theater of Oklahoma', everybody is welcome. And Berlin is full of idle young bodies.

—

Berlin, a city of voids and deserts, is where *Pedestrian Cinema* will discover an underground film studio as immense as MGM or Universal.

—

To practice a kind of 'offensive retreat' (T.E. Lawrence) and at the same time to be right here in the city, conducting casting calls and auditions, location scouting, writing scenarios, shooting screen tests, screening dailies, producing our production, etc. Hollywood began this way too: a few streetwise, ambitious sons of immigrants arriving in the desert of California with an idea of setting up facilities for the production of an industrial-strength glamour that would be more contagious than anything.

—

Pedestrian Cinema is the desire to set up a place and activity that becomes a device for intersubjective experience. By looking at places, encountering people, making an appointment to film, keeping the borders of the film open, the idea of an outside is revived — this exterior that the film studio runs into in its work. It is a relationship of the local, in which the people who enter into the production process also elaborate it, sending it in different directions. Once the script is thrown away, what remains is the relations of the film studio trying to make a new cinema and the world it will be made from. These will not be films 'about' something, but films that 'run into' something.

—

Making cinema mobile to the point of instability. Where it can take off in the same second as any thought or whim. I is had gone. Discovering a half-cooked actor. An excuse for a scene.

—

If culture and the conditions we live and work in come at us as rhythm — not just discourse or signs but as rhythmic discourse and signs — our function is also to play these rhythms back at different speeds and tempos. The question of 'how to make something happen' is at once critical/interpretive and musical/poetic. *Pedestrian Cinema* responds in a musical and machine-like way to the deadening rhythms of commerce and urban life by excavating other rhythms within them, sometimes by slowing and interrupting them. So when we say 'cinema' we mean an attention to on- and off-screen rhythms (from the way an actor crosses a shot to the way global capital flows through a city) and a politics of rhythmic intervention. Cinema is a means of engaging both the system of movements — of bodies, of information, of capital, of thought — that our cinema is immersed in and of injecting new and mutant speeds back into the flow of the present.

—

There is the glamour of launching new stars. There is also the glamour of the death of the audience. Once the audience realises it is dead, *Pedestrian Cinema* will immediately begin (if you are there, you are making it too).

—

Distribution is the business of circulating cinematic products. Dispersion is something else. To disperse cinema across a collective activity and over the time of a year is to scrap the notion of a complete and finished product. *Pedestrian Cinema* is both a relational space and a process that continuously produces and modifies this space.

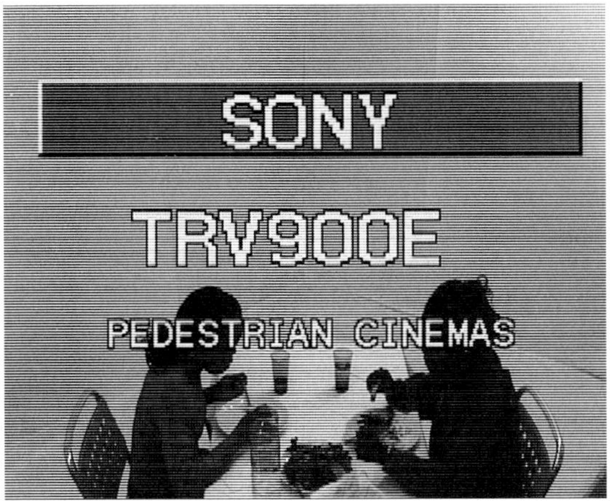

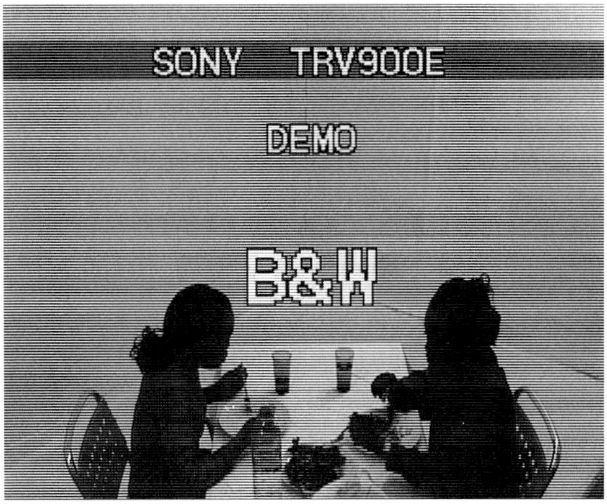

—

A visit to the studio by a group of potential buyers — a journalist, a curator, an agent, etc. — all the possible parties interested in the idea of 'new cinema'.

—

Pedestrian Cinema is an open door, a strange sign of production. Under the guise of cinema. Under the guise that is cinema.

—

Pedestrian Cinema undoes the efficient, linear logic of pre-production/production/post-production, elaborating instead a system whereby multiple films, activities and relationships can be improvised within its overall topology. One film-in-progress can be usurped by or added to another at any point. Material from any production can be recycled and put to new uses by any other. The making of one film can unmake the others.

—

How to keep the air circulating without the power of fans? *Pedestrian Cinema* is a 'production of production', continuously multiplying the very conditions and possibilities of cinema. Cinema as a means without end.

—

We are all moving images colliding with other moving images. *Pedestrian Cinema* sets itself up as a place where one image moves another, as a sort of 'backroom' where images can get together and move if they feel like it. Here we are all moving images moving images.

Bernadette Corporation, stills from *Out of Space*, 2006. Colour video, 30mins

OF AN OTHER CINEMA
Raymond Bellour

How can one make two incompatible scenes of fog merge into one another? How can one even imagine doing it? In Antonioni's *Identification of a Woman* (1982), two human beings, both victims of some vague, *fin-de-siècle* torment, drift through the fog on a road and become nearly invisible. The film's alternating shots, which—up to the point that they get out of their car—have brought them to confront themselves as much as the forces of nature, become more intangible and dangerous. For as their melancholic bodies seem increasingly close to disappearing into the fog, so too does the camera more often seem to enter alone (as is the intention of the cinematic reverse shot) into this white mass, which in turn alters the representation in a slyer, stealthier manner than any attempt ever made by painting to represent clouds. Affected, as if in itself, by the off-screen gazes of the man and the woman (whose gazes also become those of the spectators), or by enveloping the heroes of the formless drama, the blinding fog becomes (by fixing the image of its fluid substance) the kind of symbol of the abandonment of souls that fascinated Antonioni. In contrast, in Ann Veronica Janssens' untitled installation for the Belgian Pavilion at the 48th Venice Biennial in 1999, the visitor is led to wander errantly and endlessly in a real fog. This fog is not, however, any more real than that of the film, since it too becomes material for a work of art; but unlike the fog of the film, it permits no fiction other than the very event of its strange incarnation that every visitor experiences. There are indeed some images and photographs present on evanescent walls. But these images bear witness to the gaze as much as they differ from it. They belong to the regime of affective impression, which transforms the least significant elements of the rooms' setting (elements like the skirting boards and the doors) into spectacular and intimate material of which the visitor becomes a part, progressively displacing it through arbitrary and involuntary movements. So it is with every visitor to this opaque, transparent, milky space—acting on one's own, yet publicly and with respect to other visitors. From one fog to another, from one device to another, one obviously thus senses that a radical separation persists. But it is modulated according to its own motif by the insistence of a growing indecidability of human affect.

Let's look at things from another side. Why did Bill Viola choose to call one of his most powerful installations *Slowly Turning Narrative* (1992)? In it one sees a large, rotating screen, one side of which is a mirror; on the other side we see a close-up shot of a man looking straight ahead and a random series of images of the world behind him. As the screen turns, we hear several hundred verbal phrases. The virtual relations between the two sources of images are thus marked as eventful. The spectator is incorporated into the plan of action, is reflected in the mirror-screen and, due to the progressive movement of the mirror-screen, is vaguely projected onto the walls with fragments of images. Why this very strong term, *narrative*: narration, story, fable, tale? And why a revolving story? Why so slow? Is it in order to differentiate itself from cinema, or that, in its own way, this device shows that film is a narration in images that does not revolve like this?

It seems time for a new inventory (necessarily modest, random and subjective), the occasion for which has already been provided by the richness of installations of every kind at the 1999 Venice Biennial.[1] To fix the terms of it is a delicate task. In effect, one would have to describe the explosion and dispersal by which that which one thought to be or have been cinema (if one accepts to see things through its eyes) now finds itself redistributed, transformed, mimicked and reinstalled. These particular devices belong less to a typology that would permit a reassuring classifying of them; rather, they show the differences from and similarities to cinema's devices, which inspire them or which they approximate. One must therefore evaluate them as they present themselves, without discarding any grouping that appears justified, but also without imposing merely illusory identities on them. And two things at least are certain. While remaining conceptual in their own way, by means of the attention with which they multiply and vary their devices, these installations inherit from cinema its premiere double vocation of recounting and documenting, and of thus being linked to the so-called realities of the world. On the other hand, these installations more or less rework the figures from which films have drawn their forms of expression. By both duplicating cinema and differentiating itself from it, the installations thus also make cinema enter into a history that exceeds it. The history of installations begins with the invention of the camera obscura and projection, and unfolds through its many different devices (from phantasmagoria to the diorama) throughout the nineteenth century. Cinema can thus be viewed (retrospectively and probably too simply) as an installation that succeeded in capturing for itself alone the energy appropriate to the animated image, dominating it for half a century until the advent of the competition of what television has been for so long, namely, a 'projection-without-projection'.

1 Like the 'strolling-essay' by Vincent Dieutre, 'Gran Canale', in *La lettre du cinéma*, no.12, Winter 2000, and the perspective of Dominique Païni, 'Le retour du flâneur', in *artpress*, no.255, March 2000. We must at least add to this two related essays that have appeared over the last few years by Stéphanie Moisdon Trembley, 'L'image avec sa perte', in *Cinémathèque*, no.10, Autumn 1996, and 'La belle équipe', in *artpress*, no.227, September 1997; as well as two essays by Jean-Christophe Royoux, 'Narration et paysage: ce que devient le cinéma à l'heure de sa reproduction — Quelques remarques à partir du travail de six jeunes artistes britanniques', in *Perfect Speed* (exh. cat.), Ontario and Tampa: Macdonald Art Centre and University of South Florida Contemporary Art Museum, 1995–96; and 'D'une boucle à l'autre: activité artistique, post-cinéma et télévision', in *Journal de l'Institut Français de Bilbao*, no.8, April 1998. For a view of the whole, see Ursula Frohne (ed.), *Video cultures. Multimediale Installationen der 90er Jahre* (exh. cat.), Cologne: Museum der Neue Kunst/ZKM Karlsruhe and Dumont BuchVerlag, 1999.

The throng of installations today is defined mostly along the lines of video art or of the somewhat forgotten history of film-installations that are now beginning to reassert themselves.[2] These installations, and the forces that animate them, may seem to be the effect of the so-called 'crisis' within cinema and to the difficulties of contemporary art, of which installations are probably the most vivid manifestation. But if it is difficult to assimilate these works to the tradition of the plastic arts, the very framework of which they explode, it is no less difficult to take them as belonging to traditional cinema or as a supplement of cinema; it would rather be better to continue (to the extent that it will be possible) to recapture cinema in the historical and formal singularity of its own device. The strange force of these works is thus to open ever more clearly the indefinable expansion of an *other cinema*, according to which the conditions of an *aesthetics of confusion* are clarified and amplified. It is better to try to describe its nuances than to pretend to be able to escape them.

Subjected to an incessant transformation, the already ample work of Tony Oursler furnishes a model for an *other cinema*, crossing two principles with limitless forces. The first principle is a reinvention of projection, divided and multiplied. Oursler projects faces or scenes that he has filmed or borrowed (accompanied by monologues and dialogues) onto materials with an exaggerated polymorphism. Secondly, within these elaborated stagings, he assembles these beings, victims of their frantic destiny of images, mixing them into one or several rooms, taking advantage of the opportunities offered by the architecture of museums (doors, windows, beams, stairs...), arranging objects or minute decorative elements like a theatrical scene, in order to elaborate, by means of their variation, horribly inhabited worlds. He thus invents a kind of cinema, just as metaphysical and social as fragmented and permanent, between the elements around which one circulates, but in front of which one also pauses, subjected to the anguished throes of a generalised mini-projection. The being who sees all this is no longer a spectator of the sort fashioned by traditional theatre and cinema. But nor do I think that this being is truly the type of *flâneur* that Dominique Païni has reinvested with Baudelarian affects. There would need to be a real crowd for that, and the street is not the Salon. As random and often uncertain as it is, in the situation of a semi-spectacle inferred by the museum, the work fixates that which one could call its visitor — but there is no right word with which to grasp this dissolved, fragmented, shaken, intermittent spectator.

2 As the exhibition conceived by Dominique Païni titled 'Projections, les transports de l'image' testifies. The exhibition was installed from November 1997 to January 1998 at Le Fresnoy, Studio National des arts contemporains (catalogue by Hazan/Le Fresnoy/AFAA).

The Three Gestures of Pipilotti Rist

During the 1999 Venice Biennial, Pipilotti Rist chose to oppose two gestures. The first one, titled *Nothing*, gathered the curious visitors in front of an unusual machine, from which every three minutes comes some enormous soap bubbles, rolling towards the viewers, breaking at their feet. The vanity of art, of contemporary art. The second gesture is an installation delimited by a semicircular ramp in front of which a bench had been placed, welcoming some visitors. It is called *Vorstadthirn* (*Suburb Brain*), 'a miniature model of the periphery of Zürich'. There is loud, aggressive music. At the centre of the arrangement, the viewer can survey a very elaborate model of a suburban house, on the edge of a forest, with its garden and outhouses. Everything is there: street lamps along the alleys, a lawnmower, garden furniture, a plastic pool, the garden hose. In sum, the setting of a life. There are also three projections that partially illuminate the room. Beyond the house, on the large wall at the end, an interminable stream of landscapes flows to an abrupt and slowed rhythm. To the right is a small screen drawing from the lack of definition of the big screen: a very close-up shot of a mouth and of a face oscillate at the leftmost limit of the frame, against a landscape in movement. A young woman (played, as is almost always the case, by the artist) performs a monologue: her life within the house, brother and sister, her parents, her difficulty as a woman, her rebellion. The third projection takes place on a de-centred window of the house (one need only turn a bit to perceive red or white curtains on the side of the house, indicating two other windows that light up intermittently). The scene, in violent and overexposed colours, involves a festive meal with cake and candles; the scene is continuously filmed, like home movies, punctuated by passing close-ups of ecstatic or pained faces. The party is intercut with brutal sketches, streaming by in a manipulated, accelerated fashion, with little, destructive and jumpy characters or bodiless heads or decapitated bodies populating the same setting.

Who am I, before this nameless presentation, among the conglomerate of visitors, many of whom remain for several repetitions of the image loop? Of course I put the three screens into relation with one another: the large one, which seems composed of parts of the landscapes in the second one; the second one, which tells me of the third; the third one, where I seek the heroine in her domestic life. I then project this relation on the two mini window-screens of pure light. The whole house, the set, seems to explode from within, under the pressure of the mixing of images; each of the objects that surround it becomes a promise of a fictional

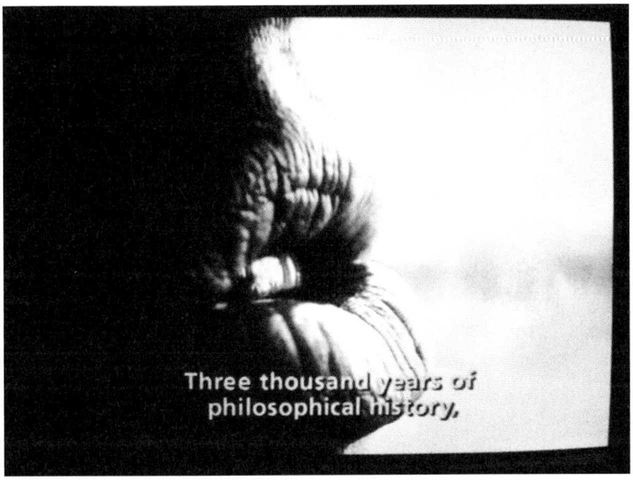

Pipilotti Rist, still from *Vorstadthirn* (*Suburb Brain*), 1999. Colour video installation. Courtesy Hauser & Wirth, Zürich and London

narrative. The device leads me to combine and recombine fragments of images and words that the spectacle aims at me, starting from the elements that it procures. Definite, limited interaction, but more forced and more lively than that which we experience at the cinema. We are indeed in *an other cinema*.

But Pipilotti Rist has also devised a third gesture (among many others) that she restructures with respect to each of the cities in which she installs her *Remake of the Week-End* (installed during the summer of 1999 at the Musée d'Art Moderne de la Ville de Paris). The description of the installation would be interminable. The mega-Durasian name — Himalaya Goldstein — of the fictional occupant of the place struck many visitors who viewed the work, as if everything in this composition consequently unfolds (over seven rooms or spaces haunted by projections) bearing the mark of the dispersed heroine: the garden, the kitchen, the bedroom, the living room. Four principles above all seem to be at work in order to seduce and overwhelm. The first is that everything is a possible motif for a projection: floors, ceilings, furniture, objects, even the bottles in the bar (there are thus thirteen different 'screens' in the room, in which we could pretend to follow a soccer match on the label of a bottle). The second principle is that the 'real' habitat rejoins cinema on an unexpected side: in the living room, the main space, lit like an antique shop, one can easily feel oneself to be in a studio or on a set, with its surfeit of available props, ready for a shoot. But this principle is made to be discarded for the third: in the empty room, at the end of the route, iron bare walls and, in semi-obscurity, images swallowed up by the very movement that gives rise to them are projected — volatile image-objects of fragments of bodies and sexual organs. Then we come to the last principle: if projection is extended onto everything, if everything becomes a screen, then the body is also a site for a frenetic expansion of projection. A wildly sexual, truncated and internal body, by which visitors (if they walk on the image projected on the floor) would be swallowed by the gaping mouth of the heroine (as always, Pipilotti), who seems to ascend towards them. A naked, automated body, panned by the camera, but also worked over by a contorted play with its setting, over the tiling and amenities of the kitchen, a body that is too white and benumbed like the Duchampian mannequin in his *Étant Donnés* (1946–66).

Sets Without Images

From these three gestures by Pipilotti Rist could flow two opposed problematics, which leisurely criss-cross in her work: first, pure sets without established images; and, second, several rooms with multiple images, or, if there is only one room, with two or several images.

One could have also seen Martine Aballéa's *Hôtel Passager*, just opposite the *Remake of the Week-End*, in the other wing of the Musée d'Art Moderne. A simulacrum of a hotel, in real or near-real space, like a film set ready to be used. One can write or receive messages at the reception desk, arrange meetings in the bar-restaurant, relax in the rooms, even if one can visit only five of the 99 rooms announced. There is a 'honeymoon suite', and in some rooms there are closets; but there is never any running water and nowhere can one turn off the lights: it is obviously impossible to spend the night there. The visitor becomes a singular sort of *flâneur*, ironically constrained to discount the divergences between the simulacrum and a supposed reality. Here again, as in all the installations that refer first to a contrived situation, the faded spectacle is rewoven through the eyes and the bodies of fellow visitors.

A more restrained, more precise work with a giddiness for nothingness is *El Living* by Argentinian Leandro Erlich (Kent Gallery, New York, autumn 1999). People enter and exit having seen nothing. Art degree zero. A small, simple, well-kept living room, identically reproducing itself on both sides of two horizontal windows, a room in which the left wall (as one enters) is simulated. The first window is a simple mirror, but the second is an exposure or opening (to verify this, one passes first one's hand, then one's head, through it), which suggests an absent and paradoxical mirror, since all the elements of the setting are also found there, inverted. The limited but suddenly endless shock comes from the evasion of a supposed reality.

Several Rooms

Doug Aitken's innovation in Venice in 1999 was to conceive several rooms no longer simply in order to arrange the phases of a series of installations as the many variables of a device (as did Bill Viola at the Biennale four years earlier with his *Buried Secrets*), but rather in order to simulate the recounting of a story. To achieve this effect, he conceived a huge corridor with an entry/exit at each end, and divided it into three or four rooms (depending on whether one takes the central space, which is divided by two transparent half-sized walls, as one or two rooms). There are thus eight image-screens arranged on the walls all along the four spaces, in such a way that one can always see at least two images at once, and sometimes one can catch sight of up to six, by turning oneself around at a few select points within the corridor. The interest of *Electric Earth* is furthered by the actor/hero, a black youth named Ali Johnson, about whom the film (Aitken usually shoots in film — carefully shot images that he then projects in video) recounts or exposes the physical and doubtlessly mental trajectories. A first screen shows him laying on his bed playing with the remote control, recalling the American thematic of video art obsessed with television; the question is no longer one of a critical relation, but rather of a pure expansion of information and flux. A last screen, at the other end of the corridor, suggests the end of something, via the closed image of a tunnel. In the temporal and spatial interval between these two screens, an imagery is narrated around his vibrant body: the city, drugs, machines, screens that go on and off, images are shown, events accumulate, so many flickerings all along this rhizome-work.

Doug Aitken, who was awarded the Biennial's Lion D'Or for *Electric Earth*, is a Californian American. He began his career in advertising and music videos. He recognises no ready-made definition of his art, and especially not the category of video artist, describing himself first and foremost as close to cinema. He has shown certain works successfully in the form of continuous projections, and more often as installations (he likes to mark the difference, on which he always works, between the voyeur and the active participant).[3] His 1998 installation, *Eraser*, shows clearly how he constructs a process that stages the fiction of the documentary gaze through the unfolding of space. Aitkin undertook and filmed a seven-mile trek on the Ile Montserrat in the Antilles, an area evacuated in 1995 after the devastating eruption of a volcano. He divided his progression along these seven miles into three segments, three rooms: two screens at right angles in the first two rooms, three screens in the third; and always a biased perspective in order to glimpse the route that links them.

Two or Several Images

Is it possible in a single room? This is the question, concerning the cinema of fiction, that the English artist Sam Taylor-Wood poses.

Already five years ago, in the work *Travesty of a Mockery*, two shots are brought together at the juncture of two walls, one shot on each wall, showing a man and a woman, in order to reinterpret one of the great scenes in the history of cinema, the domestic quarrel, to which both Rossellini and Godard have given a modern fullness. The force of the arrangement is that its symbolism is, in this case, too simple — the separation of the two screens suggesting the separation of two beings — and this simplicity clashes with the separation between two shots, which cinema takes as its law. The semblance of absurdity that most often encloses each of the characters in their own framework thus makes the temporal succession of shots, the connection of which becomes visible at the angle where the walls meet, surge forth between the shots in a virtual manner. The objects that move from one frame to the other — a glass of milk, a frying pan — or the rare, sudden and violent confrontations between two bodies in one frame are perceived as a transgression with respect to the split spaces that the gaze of the film spectator commonly conceives, both despite the segmentation and because of it, as participating in a principle in a homogenous space. (Significantly, during the presentation of *Travesty of a Mockery* at the White Cube Gallery in London, one sees in a second room two photographic 'panoramas', due to which the carefully arranged intervals between the actor-figures seem to echo those cuts that are absent from the installation.) Sam Taylor-Wood repeated and complicated the operation this

3 See in particular two interviews with Aitken, the first by Francesco Bonami, 'Doug Aitken: Making Work without Boundaries', in *Flash Art*, May–June, 1998; the second by Giovanna Adamasi, in *-cross*, no.2, 1999.

4 The two screens to the left and right can be reversed, as they were when moved from the 1997 Venice Biennial to the 1999 Karlsruhe Biennial (see *Video cultures*, *op. cit.*)

time by making use of three walls, one image per wall, reserving the fourth wall for the spectator (*Atlantic*, 1996). When spectators enter the room, to their left there is an extremely close-up image of woman addressing a man with a miserable vehemence; on their right, a wide-angle shot shows the hands of the man moving nervously (cigarette, bread crumbs); facing the spectator, in the general shot of a room in a restaurant, one more or less quickly recognises the couple seated at a table.[4] One understands fragments of their conversation through the background noise. Here again, the device is simple, almost too simple, yet severely contorted: one never stops imagining not only the possible combinations between these three symbol-shots of the cinematic editing, but also the intermediary choices that they call forth, and the possible variations of proportions and figures that they infer.

Shot/Reverse Shot

In both cases, it is the shot/reverse shot, which in cinema is the premiere trope of the rotating identification between the characters, that is redesigned in a void and thus disfigured—in a manner very different from the great modern cinematic stagings of it (Oliveira, Godard, the Straubs).

The installation tends to confront the relation of a mirrored separation between two shots (which cinema treats by succession or superimposition) in the unitary division of its spaces and the paradox of its arrangements. The shots are thus symptomatically back-to-back, but in such a way as to be attracted to one another by the swirling of the rotating double mirror-screen in *Slowly Turning Narrative*. Or even better, the effect created by *Interval*, in the second room of *Buried Secrets*. Two alternating shots or series of shots are projected on two opposite walls in the room, contrasting thematically (the calmness of a man in his bathroom/the brutality of intense and catastrophic images); a parallel and displaced composition is thus formed. But the time of projection on each screen, very slow at first, is progressively reduced to the point of reaching the threshold-limit of the photogram, and these opposing shots come to form a common block in the bedroom where the visitor is trapped—a mass in fusion that recalls the effect of Godardian flickering, maintained at a distance in the fictive and unitary light of the projection.

But this contracted equivalence of alternating or parallel composition of which cinema is fond can, on the contrary, be extended to and carried by another violence. This is the case in *Turbulent* (1998), by the Iranian artist Shirim Neshat, critically noticed in Venice by Vincent Dieutre, who exclaimed:

> Two gigantic screens face each other. One sings, the other does not. In black-and-white, the Iranian singer looks straight ahead, his singing fills up the space and seems to charm a group of men seated behind him ... connoisseurs, no doubt ... what he stares at is the other screen: the same room, a sort of old, trashed, but empty Olympia ... empty if it were not for the feminine silhouette that hides from the male gaze. Then the singer will

fall silent, his public will loudly applaud him, and the woman on the other screen will turn towards him and begin another song, even more ancient, more raucous, a song from before Islam and the mullahs, a song for the empty room and the other singer facing her, astounded and overwhelmed ... the camera turns to the aquiline face of the woman shrouded in darkness ... and then everything stops (credits) ... starts again ... and the heart-rending singer takes his turn again.

The power of the work, whose political effect is carried by this simple and hard form, is to take hold of the visitor, who has become nearly a spectator, both in succession as well as in simultaneity. One can imagine that the '*other cinema*' is in the midst of inventing an equivalent of what Griffith sought in his great parallelisms, the culmination of which is *Intolerance*. One eminent contemporary French critic, somewhat skeptical of these comings and goings between installations and cinema (a cinema that has once again become very inventive this last decade) pointed out to me that one would not find in the art collections of museums a work equivalent to that of Kiarostami. The comparison, or its impossibility, makes us speculate. Would one also say this about *La Dentellière* in relation to *The Princess of Cleves* or to *Bérénice*? Or in contrasting Vermeer with Racine? Obviously not. But today, the proximity of materials and the overlapping of devices requires making relations that slip away, pushing Dieutre to underline (and Iran obliges it) inversely that: '*Turbulent* approximates for the better the cinema of someone like Makhmalbaf. The "arty" arrangement, more in the style of New York than Iran, only reduces the physical impact by making the spectator into the centre of the experience, more so than does a traditional film.'

If, in the installations where it is reworked in many diverse ways, the shot/reverse shot technique engages in a fictionalisation that is rooted in the kind practiced by cinema, it is always its device that is targeted by those who displace and reinvent it. One of those artists who displace and reinvent cinema is Douglas Gordon, about whose mining (*mises en abime*) of cinema, itself also multiplied, I will briefly comment, as I have done elsewhere.[5] It is the power of the scanty but striking idea of his installation at Venice, *Through a Looking Glass*. He simply chose a moment from the famous shot in *Taxi Driver* (1976), where Robert De Niro pretends in the mirror to shoot himself with his Colt ('Are you talking to me?'), and projected two loops of it, facing one another but not synchronised, on the walls of a large, dark room in order to discover at what moment in cinema that any and every shot involving a mirror always refers to the spectator and to his dependence on the screen. It is this link that the installation undoes, in order to re-do it, more physically, as something new: the discordant accord between two images perceived as identical yet different, but that cannot be seen at once.

5 See 'L'instant de voir', in *L'Entre-Images 2*, P.O.L, 1999, and 'le corps de la fiction', in *Trafic*, no.30, Summer 1999, concerning his 'remake' of *Vertigo*.

The aim of the film-installation *To Derive an Approach* by Finnish-American Liisa Roberts (also in Venice, just a few yards from Gordon and Rist) is of another sort, without the mediation of third or fourth generation (i.e. post-TV) cineophilia. The mirror is once again the theme: two reverse shots are projected facing each other on two small suspended screens, made of translucent photographic paper joined by a glass partition that circumscribes the place of the projections letting everyone see everything in the room. The shots show a banal scene — two women seated one evening at a café table. But the scene is filmed once from within the café, and then again from the exterior, in such a way that the great glass facade of the café separating the two spaces is also the site of their convergence, due to the reflections through which the direct view of the street in one image is redoubled on the other image. Perfectly synchronous, the shots oppose and complete one another, according to a confusion that progressively increases and that one seeks to dissipate. And each visitor is supposed to produce this confusion (which worked poorly in Venice): the looped and silent projection is interrupted as soon as one enters the room; it starts again when, already closer to the two images between which one pauses, one cannot see them together, neither physically nor mentally.

Eija-Liisa Ahtila

What is particularly interesting in the work of this other Finnish artist is that it no longer takes as granted the hiatus between installation and film, museum or cinema. Thus, *Today* (1996–97) is 'a short film and a video-installation formed in three episodes. It is intended to be presented on television, at movie theatres and film festivals, as well as in art galleries and museums.' Even better, '*Me/We*; *Okay*; *Gray* (1993) are three short audiovisual stories/film productions. The films are shown both as independent works, and as a short at the movies and on different television stations, between commercials and TV shows.' Since 1995, Ahtila's catalogues also list in their references just as many selections in film or video festivals as in individual and collective exhibitions. Her work often includes real credits, identifying it as 'film/installation video', and mentioning the distributors and technicians and the formula 'written and directed by'. To visit one of Ahtila's exhibitions is to submit to a series of subtle displacements that make one doubt how to identify it. This is the degree to which the *other cinema* takes itself as real, but also detaches itself from it, as if by a principle of malleability, or by an endless porosity of the experience (as in her exhibition in 2000 at the sumptuous Neue Nationalgalerie designed by Mies van der Rohe in Berlin).

A series of photographs stands out from among five displayed works (recalling a previous exhibition at the Fridericianum in Kassel). Six well-lit series, each composed of three or four images, bring into play the divergences of time and action within a theme or a situation, as a way of once again recalling that one inevitably and always passes from photography to cinema. One also notices *Me/We*, *Okay* and *Gray* shown on three monitors in a fleeting space; one must make an effort to concentrate on the very structured and very dense ninety-second films that bring into play situations of familial, sexual and environmental alienation.

The three other works each occupy an independent room. Two of them are pure projection spaces, with two screens for *Consolation Service* (24mins, also shown at the 1999 Venice Biennial) and three for *If 6 was 9* (10mins, 1995). In one of the two rooms, a sofa has been placed in the middle to accommodate four privileged spectators, while the rest have to stand (as was also the case with *Suburb Brain*); in the other room, armchairs have been arranged in a discontinuous fashion against the back wall, as if to suggest the antechamber for the movie theatre. The 'show times' are announced for *Consolation Service*, and it is striking to notice the extent to which the quality of attention and thus also of the work itself changes depending on whether the black drapes at the two entries are fully closed. For *Consolation Service* is a film that recounts the difficult history of the separation of a couple with a child on two screens. The sound and the dialogues (and the subtitles) are identical on both screens; only the images continually change. All of the implications of the strange supplement that the double screen creates with respect to perception, identifications and emotion would have to be approached in detail, which entails much more difficulty than does a traditional analysis. Scenes at the social worker's or psychotherapist's office are striking because of the diversity of editing and staging solutions, in particular when threaded panoramic shots allow the woman to pass into the same frame as the man, and vice-versa, which most often a compositional cut between two screens guarantees. And of course, the care-giving character also enters each of the two screens as a possible common third party. Not to mention the variable proportion of the size of the shots, fixed just as much in an elliptical simultaneity and in their succession.

But the strongest effect depends on or results from memory. In Venice, strolling aimlessly (let's say I was stricken by the festival fever), I walked too quickly by this film-installation that demands a spectator, and had kept only a depressing blur of a memory of these bodies in conflict. Only after having watched *Consolation Service* a second time, more carefully, did I take into account that these filmic bodies now live on in me, like the lives of so many other bodies more or less, destined to remain depending on the form-giving or structuring power of the film, of which this anomalous device has become a fascinating example. There is something similar in *If 6 was 9*, which reveals, on three screens and in a serial fashion, the sexual discoveries of a group of adolescents. The play of the screens is more varied here; the story is more fluid, treated as a ballet of situations and impressions, with multiple voices. One of the screens serves to detail a fragment of the second (on the screen at the right, a close-up of a cake that one of the heroines is eating on the middle screen), while the third screen circles in on another motif (in this case, a second girl); the three screens can, by being added together, form a continuous landscape, the beginning of a panorama. So many combinations are possible, with a certain musical sense in which music itself participates, that the memory of images is made difficult. But one nevertheless recalls faces and landscapes having been included in the shots — real cuts, stable and reliable in their framing and relations.

I still think of *Today*, which I first saw in a video festival, a story shown on a monitor or a screen; I encountered it again later, along with two other videos, as an installation (at the Chicago Museum of Contemporary Art, autumn 1999). Once again, three screens, this time on three walls, as in Sam Taylor-Wood's installation. But here the three screens concern three different points of view on the same story or event: the death in an accident one summer night of the grandfather. Once again, one imagines the three versions of Mankiewicz's *A Letter to Three Wives* (1949) or André Michel's *Trois Femmes* (1952), unfolded over three screens. An obviously deceptive analogy: the story concerns assured memory and integrates its past times into one single time, as if there were the virtuality of the image-crystal (Mankiewicz is one of Deleuze's strongest examples). But Ahtila's three screens themselves suppose an exploded story, a random sense of configurations, gestures, identities and words that make and unmake them. Here, three chairs announced the challenge issued to the spectator: one in the middle, lost and alone; another upside down in the corner; the third turned against the wall.

The desire for installations thus makes use of the desire for film in order to explode it, when the device doesn't glide into the situation of cinema. In Berlin, *Anne, Aki, and God* (1998) occupied this place. A large room, lit by a multiplicity of projections. Two different screens, one set up near the entry facing an armchair (as if for one single spectator), the other above an analyst's couch (on which some visitors sit). And six monitors reducing all around, through the fiction-monologue of six different masculine characters, the faces of the case of Aki, the psychotic whose portrait the installation presents. On the wall, posters show the credits and develop the installation's 'scenario' in progress, the structure that Aki makes around the figure of Anne, the woman he has invented. One striking thing in this very architectural configuration: the most fictional scenario of this ensemble of works (although based on real facts) is that in the face of which the *other cinema* responds by means of the most honest dynamic of the installation, rather than by those of film, which doubles it.

One or Several Devices

Twice in his long career, Abel Gance wanted to address the monologic nature of the cinematic screen. The first time was in 1927, in *Napoléon vu par Abel Gance* (*Abel Gance's Napoléon*) the premiere of which was on the symbolic date of 7 April at the Opera. On that night and subsequently exclusively at the Cinéma Marivaux, amazed spectators were able to see two lateral screens suddenly emerge during the final sequence, when Bonaparte undertakes his Italian campaign. These two lateral screens project different shots or reduce the effect of one same shot into a panorama. The 'talkies' will be justified

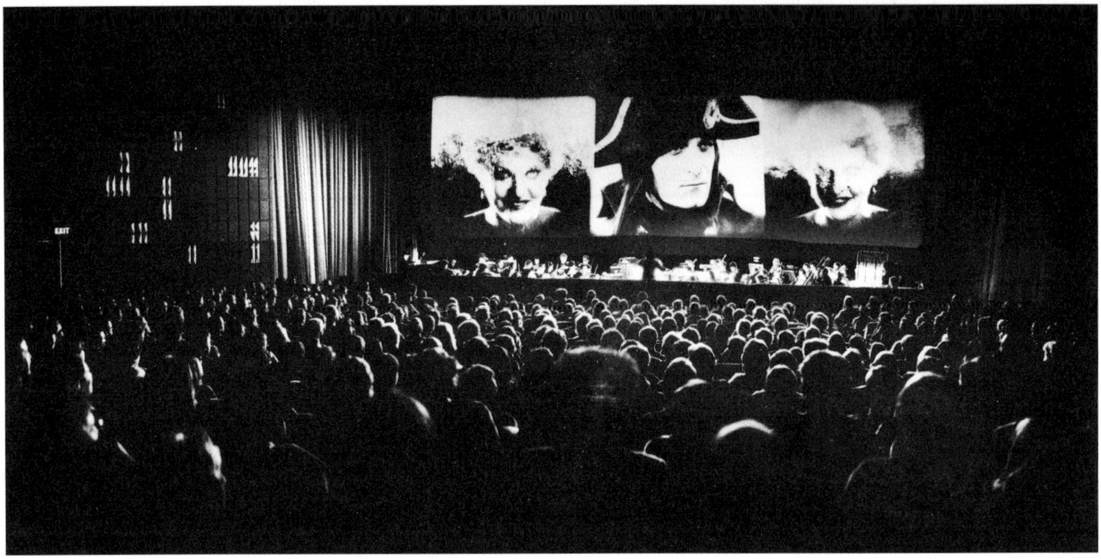

Performance of *Abel Gance's Napoléon,* (1927) at the Empire, Leicester Square, 1984. 35mm black-and-white film, silent, 235mins. Photo © 2008 Laurie Lewis. Courtesy British Film Institute

in the madness still attached to the unforeseeable spectacle linked for a long time to the early days of its history. Cinema consequently, and despite the thousands of variations associated with the architecture of theatres, will remain what it has been ever since Lumière's first showings, as if in spite of the multiple variations of its 'primitive' period: the projection of a unique image on one single screen. And logically, this will be the case until the small screen of television, in its perfidious manner, will have broken once and for all the monopoly attached to the production of the animated image, which will allow Gance to reformulate his dream in 1953 as 'polyvision'. Indeed, 'The Time of the Broken Image', as he predicted, by 'the spark that flies from the simultaneous shock of two or several images', is for him a hyper-hypnosis, intended to fix its spectator to the point of 'total identification'. What Gance conceives is a hyper-film-device. And yet, when he opposes 'images that are multiplied' to 'images that are added together', he enters, in his own way, into an expanding logic that will oppose the 'blocked vision'[6] of the cinema's spectator to the vision of *an other cinema*, an *expanded cinema*, lacking identifications and the identity of which is less simple to take hold, since its arrangement changes with every occurrence.[7] Because one cannot claim to be able to fix an identity whose variation defines its very meaning and value, one can at least try to distinguish some models of it, as a way of terminating an adventure by making other works enter into it, works that have in common with the first ones the opening of a limitless malleability of devices to the supplements of fiction and the documentary gaze.

6 This formulation is Pascal Bonitzer's, taken up again by Serge Daney in 'Du defilément au défilé', in *La Recherche photographique*, no.7, 1989, which tracks, under other names, what we could call a certain installation-effect in the true films of cinema.

7 With these words, Gene Youngblood predicted in his famous book *Expanded Cinema*, London: Studio Vista, 1970, a global mutation of human subjectivity in the 'paleocybernetic age'. We can more modestly take from it the idea of an endless variability of the modes of projection, of diffusion and of reception of images, around the idea/word of cinema.

THE WALL. It is one of the oldest figures of video art. It was useful to Paik's planetary simultaneism and to Chris Marker's historicism. It is moving to see that it was able to open itself to an auto-portrait of old age and contemplation. The *Solo Scenes* of the Swiss artist Dieter Roth, whose death marked the 1999 Venice Biennial, show this on dozens of monitors forming an immense and crazy rectangle, a super-screen of the details in which one finds God, as the empty and extraordinary equality of every instant.

THE ROOM. Though many other spaces lend themselves to installations, the closed, dark room seems to be the place where that experience is best played out, since it mimics more than others the new beginnings of cinema through the detours and the disguises that we have seen. Showing himself to be sensitive to this aspect, Dominique Païni suggested that such a varied and repeated device would relate less to cinema than to the romantic dream, splendidly formulated long ago by Caspar David Friedrich, exposing each of his works only in a black box with appropriate lighting, and even music.[8] The idea is seductive if we take sides with the fine arts and museums; and were there no more painting, one could imagine that a desire to eternalise it today takes this route through animated images. But things seem contrary with respect to *an other cinema*, a new cinema that owes to the old form so many of its obsessions and figures. The back wall where part of the projection probably takes place does not have the mystery of a true, forbidden projection booth with respect to the spectator. But the visitors who use this wall to lean on, seated or standing, and the seats that appear here and there, show that a mimetic of the spectator lives with an overly simple errancy, and often substitutes for it, in the same moment making so many new, paradoxical and quasi-Bazinian windows opened on the world out of the diverse projected images.

The room also shelters, as we have seen, some environmental projections according to which the images penetrate differently, by simultaneities of which 'polyvision' exceeds the frontality of one or several different screens, while continuing to bring dramas and scripted places into play, contrary to the speculative-thematic polyphonies of Viola's rooms. Let's think in this regard of the installations of the English twins Jane and Louise Wilson: *Stasi City* (1997) and *Gamma* (1999). Without mentioning the photographs and the sculptures that accompany it, the spaces, or the moving images, the singularity of these installations is to multiply uninterrupted movements and compositions of several shots assembled in both vertical and horizontal networks. A form-imposing and almost literal physicality of terrible places — headquarters of the political police or military bases — is thus transmitted within the room, and on two or three entirely covered walls

8 In the diverse examples given by Roland Recht and by which Païni is inspired, there are four transparent images on paper, lit like wagons, in which Recht sees the equivalent of a 'magic lantern' or the effect of a 'true diorama' (*La Lettre de Humboldt*, Paris: Christian Bourgeois, 1989, pp.109–11). This already puts the experience midway between painting and (pre-)cinema.

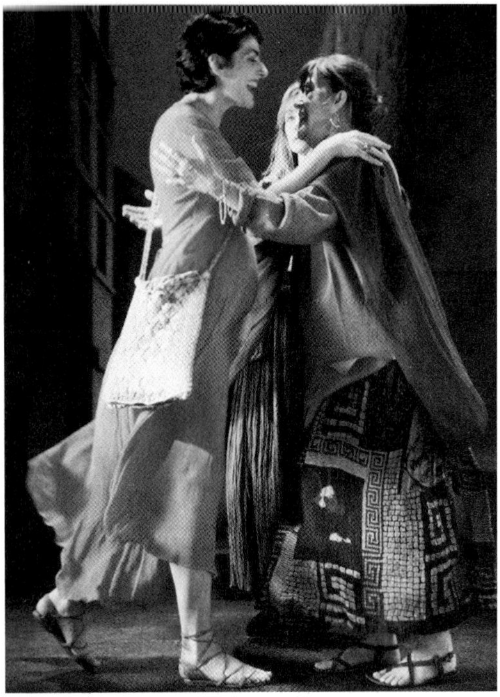

Bill Viola, still from *The Greeting*, 1995. Photo © 2008 Kira Perov

at the same time. The camera bears witness to these terrible places in order to create a spectacle in which one finds oneself both trapped and intensely aware.

As to video work that wants to be painting, in the overt competition that it has with the picture, it is revealing that it could finally penetrate the true space that haunts it. Thus, Viola's *The Greeting*, the fifth of the installations of *Buried Secrets* (1995), inspired by one of Pontormo's *Visitations* (c.1514–16), was shown last autumn, isolated from his large retrospective in a room at the Art Institute of Chicago, to the astonishment of many visitors: right in the middle of the Pontormos, the Titians and other assembled works, as tradition of the museum of painting wants.

THE SERIES. Wandering from room to room has become a programmatic act in an *other cinema*, according to which vision operates by jumps and fixations. It is striking that midway between *Buried Secrets* and *Electric Earth*, between a paradigm of devices and the fluctuations of a story, the possibilities of series has recently attracted Gary Hill for the first time, the title of whose work is a bit like a chest of drawers: *A name, a kind of chamber, two weapons and a still life* (Barbara Gladstone Gallery, New York, 1999). Without lingering here too long, let's say that the five devices brought into play participate in the genesis of a body— the auto-portrait of the artist as a great image-maker. On the one hand, a truly dark room criss-crossed with blinding flashes, where a stroboscopic projection hits a visible table (the eye is reduced to the state of an automatic and wild machine); on the other hand, four more or less well-lit rooms or spaces. Three of them shelter corporeal images to differing degrees and according to various strategies, on two or three screens (one notices on two mirrored screens a false shot/reverse shot, the same close-up shot of the artist from the front and from the back, with the voice that names himself: 'Gary, Gary ... '). The last room stands out for two extreme gestures, inducing an unmasterable tension. This time, the image is no longer analogical; it is rather an image of synthesis, coldly and endlessly assembling objects, due to an interminable movement. The interest of this inhuman image comes from the chosen device: the continuous shot passes successively across thirteen screens (eight monitors and five real screens) without its movement appearing to be interrupted. A hitherto unseen form of composition is thus put into place: no longer from shot to shot, but from screen to screen, jumps of the eye inscribed in space, gaping jointures exhibited by the machinery. One moves from the explosion of the body to the explosion of perception and its reference.

SCREENS EVERYWHERE. In the *other cinema*, everything becomes a screen, and the screen can appear everywhere. The most humorous and torturous epiphany is the miniature screen, sometimes only a few inches, installed by Pipilotti Rist in a floorboard at PS1 (the large museum in Queens, New York). As soon as one leans down, one sees the face-body coming up vertically, as if from the pit into which it falls again. One finally understands that a page has been turned and that humankind has grounds to worry: instead of walking in the image, as Augustine believed because he always took himself as standing before the image, humankind can now walk, often without even noticing, on the image.[9]

THE PROJECTION. But the image also resides in the indeterminate distance of its projection, the great frontal projection of a single image on a single screen. In the *other cinema* the image itself can either undertake its own transformation, its self-destruction, or metamorphose its power to fascinate.

The coupled installations of Stan Douglas and Douglas Gordon (Dia Art Center, New York, 1999) propose this work of mutation. *Double Vision* does it twice. Stan Douglas decided to use a pastiche style for a Canadian television show (two men confronting each other in a room), but in such a way that the image slides from its overly simple realist illusion to a continual and variable unfolding of its motifs, to the point of producing contradictory perceptions. These are extraordinary images, never before seen, of a savagely cruel degree with respect to the eye that perceives them. As to Douglas Gordon, faithful to his programme of revisiting American cinema, he takes over *Whirlpool*, a classic of *film noir* in which hypnosis is the central theme. The destruction/transformation supposes here projecting Preminger's entire film in order to produce a mechanical hyper-hypnosis by two means of two mixed techniques: a constant stroboscopic effect and, more importantly, the invention of enantiomorphic images that endlessly unfold in relation to their central axis. It is not certain that lovers of Gene Tierney will find that seeing her doubled is really tolerable, nor that the amateur of the falsely realistic density of such beautiful black-and-white will tolerate seeing it so Vasarelised. But so it is that art senses itself constrained to respond to a much-loved cinema, which itself is disliked by television.

Cinema can also be reinvented, an *other cinema*, by other means. I can think of nothing that does this better than *Photograph*, the installation by James Coleman (which arrived in Paris at the Marion Goodman Gallery in the spring of 2000, after New York and Barcelona). Imagine a deep and dark room into which visitors enter and become visitors pinned to the walls like butterflies. The screen is far away, the projection shows a difficult image with profound contrasts. The sound is also very beautiful, the voice of a very young girl reciting an enigmatic text to the rhythm of intercut breaths, an address in

9 Saint Augustine: 'Although man worries in vain, he does however walk in the image.'

classically arranged old English. As is often the case with Coleman, a projection of diapositives are chained together according to a wisely measured rhythm, according to the fiction that it inaugurates. This time its subject is a group of very young girls participating with some boys in rehearsals for a school play in a poor suburb. Rarely have still photographs appeared animated, each by their own internal quality as if due to the agency of their composition. Rarely have human beings been grasped with such intensity. Coleman underlined this tension with an inaugural moment, a prelude briefly reshown twice in order to stress its evocation and perpetuate its effect: quasi-insensible movements are produced by superimposition of several slides on a background that evoke certain bookbinder themes like clouds or fog. In order to not be so obsessed with it, I quickly thought of the faces of barely animated women at the end of the opening credits of Ingmar Bergman's *Persona* (1966). In a strangely proximate way, such imponderable movements affect both the mobile shots of Bergman's films and the immobile shots of Coleman's imagistic story. One wonders also what differentiates *Photograph* from *La Jetée* (1962). There is of course a story in Marker's film, the story of a man marked by his childhood image; the story is recounted in voice-over, and music works for dramatic effect. The text composed by Coleman is, in appearance, very far from its image, and refers to an art of the counterpoint. But he also works this image, contributes to carrying along its fiction. The suspended breaths and the gasping of the voice participate in suspensions of photography, its flow from affects to the illusions of the movement that it produces. Rather than inventing cinema, the distance manifested between text and image comes close to the cinema of Straub, in the first part of *Trop tôt, trop tard*, for example. The effects on the senses created by distance, the sensual intelligence of the expressive shots. One is thus led to think that the eminent contemporary critic mentioned earlier was not right, and that the art of installations, this *other cinema*, can just as easily approximate as be equal to the art of cinema.

One also dreams of this when looking at Thierry Kuntzel's *Venises*, shown in a haphazard fashion at the Venice Biennial of 1995, and reprojected today as it should be, in a narrow room facing a bench offered to spectators (this occasion was his exhibition *Si Lent* last spring at the Yvon Lambert Gallery). The image flows as in Promio's historic 'travelling' shot on the Grand Canal. But the movement comes above all from the objects — boats of all sizes — which pass intermittently back and forth within a fixed framework. It becomes the trembling of a life, trapped and transfigured. For due to the quasi-invisible links and its accelerated time, this view of the lagoon insensibly animates the endless but syncopated rhythm of all that is shown in the image, as in a vision of variable painting — Monet's cathedrals and deserts captured in a single block. It is the time that one red and foggy night falls in the flow of water and that the spectator no longer knows who he is.

Translated by Robert Vallier.

THE GAP BETWEEN FILM AND INSTALLATION ART

Alexander Alberro

There has been a virtual explosion of film and video projections in museums, galleries and other exhibition spaces since the early 1990s. These audio-visual artworks are in and of themselves difficult to classify, for in their expansion of traditional media such as painting, sculpture and photography they enter the nebulous zone of multimedia installation art. Some of these works are produced by film- and video-makers such as Chantal Akerman, Harun Farocki, Ulrika Ottinger and Chris Marker, whose works are usually screened in independent cinematheques, cineclubs and film forums, but who have recently taken to showing in museums and other gallery spaces. Then there is the phenomenon of artists who directly comment on and often incorporate cinematic history in their works, such as Pierre Huyghe, Rodney Graham and Steve McQueen. But in the past decade there has emerged a third group of relatively young artists who seem to shift gears effortlessly in their mode of exhibition: moving from single-channel to multiple-channel, from large screen to television monitor, from film to video to digital productions.

The emergence of this new type of audio-visual artist directly parallels the development of interdisciplinary visual studies programmes in the academy. The rubric of visual studies seems to provide scholars tired of the particular disciplines in which they were trained with the justification to work in an expanded field of scholarship. And while most would baulk, for instance, at the work of an expert on sculpture or painting who writes on Cervantes or Faulkner, the reverse isn't true — today there seems to be the assumption that anyone can speak with authority on a visual artefact regardless of one's training and expertise. Indeed, this general crossing into other disciplines is symptomatic of what Marjorie Garber refers to as 'discipline envy'.[1] Writing about visual art is sexy, trendy and reaches a broader and more diverse public than more traditional academic venues. These are, I might add, also some of the same reasons why many film-makers are turning to galleries and museums to show their work. Just as the young academic is expected to be prolific, so, too, the young artist's success is measured by the number of venues in which his or her work is shown. One of the immediate results of this phenomenon is overproduction, especially of works that can metamorphise into several different versions and employ different media depending on the viewing context. Unfortunately, this type of media crossing

1 Marjorie Garber, *Academic Instincts*, Princeton: Princeton University Press, 2001, pp.53–95.

often ignores the historical specificity — the possibilities and limits — of a particular medium at a given moment in its history. Indeed, audio-visual production that is rigorously attentive to the inherent characteristics and histories of the medium in which it works is becoming a rarity. This has recently led some to call for a diligent alertness to the specific structural operation of each medium employed, and for an increased awareness of how the production of meaning is not only the result of a work's thematic content but also intricately dependent on the way a particular work comes together in formal terms and dialogically negotiates the site of its display.

What does this mean practically? Well, let me examine this problem by focusing specifically on the work of a Finnish artist, Eija-Liisa Ahtila. Ahtila's oeuvre provides a particularly good example because she has produced work for television, videos, single- and multi-channel projections and 35-mm films. Her early work of the 1980s consisted primarily of text-based installations that foregrounded her interest in feminism and gender theory, and in the formation of identity by the mass media.[2] But following her studies in film at the University of California, Los Angeles, she began to make audio-visual productions. What's striking about Ahtila's work, and why I'm focusing on it, is that she often produces the same idea and footage in multiple formats, adjusting and changing the work according to each exhibition context. Thus, in 1993 Ahtila made three separate but interconnected 90-second, 35-mm, black-and-white films: *Me/We*, *Okay* and *Gray*.[3] All of the elements in this triptych exist in the formats of both film (intended for cinema projection or television transmission) and video (for gallery or museum installation).

As films, the three shorts are very fast, condensed narratives designed to be shown as trailers with feature films or as advertisements, either in succession or interspersed with other programming. Filmed at a pace resembling MTV, the shorts feature extremely concise if pithy narratives laden with audio-visual imagery, much like novellas, short stories, information bulletins or dreams. Each is tightly edited: every detail is an integral component of the narrative. *Me/We*, for example, resembles a television commercial — more specifically, a laundry detergent advert, with a close-up of a coffee cup spilling staining liquid onto a table cloth; a sequence of a family hanging linen to dry on a clothes line; and another sequence in which two

2 A collaboration with artist Maria Ruotsala, *In His Absolute Proximity* (1988), which consisted of an ensemble of large colour photographs and enlarged texts, drew heavily on the stereotypes and clichés located in both language and visual representation to examine how the female body is looked at and represented; and Ahtila's *Dog Bites* (1992) featured a series of photographs of a naked woman imitating the expressions and positions of a dog eager to please its master.

3 The division of work into three roughly equal parts characterises many of Ahtila's audio-visual dramas. The films *If 6 was 9* (1995) and *Today* (1996–97) both require three separate projections. In the former, Ahtila revisits her earlier investigations into gender and sexuality, now focusing on the erotic world of adolescent girls coming of age. The piece, consisting of a series of monologues, is projected in a loop, at once reinforcing the idea of a continuous narrative circle without build-up or development and obliterating conventions of beginning and end. Both the installation (a DVD projected on a single wall with a three-way split screen) and film version feature three separate moving pictures. But unlike the operation of *Me/We*, *Okay* and *Gray*, there is a clear thematic link between the sections of *If 6 was 9*, as the same characters, places, narratives and images respond and react to one another. Thus, for example, on one screen that is isolated from the rest the camera focuses on a self-confident and promiscuous girl who is fully aware of her body's allure. She expresses contempt for her self-righteous, 'bookwormish' peers, some of whom are shown on the other two screens. Their body positions, gestures and activities (e.g. reading, playing piano) all seem to indicate a different

women snap dry sheets in preparation for folding. But the voice-over narrative spoken by the father, which describes his psychological alienation from his family, is subverted through a deft slippage on Ahtila's part: when other family members address the camera, they actually ventriloquise the father's voice-over so that their voices become his projections.

Similarly, in *Okay*, which focuses on a couple's tempestuous relationship and estrangement, Ahtila manipulates the audio track by gradually transforming a woman's voice into a man's, thereby underscoring the complex psychological transference, projection and erasure of individual identity at play in any intimate relationship. The voices on the soundtrack of *Gray*, which features three suitably manic women caught in an industrial elevator during a nuclear disaster, overlap then separate as each responds to the fear of contamination. At one point, referring to the emergency broadcast announcing the disaster, one woman says: 'I do not understand the foreign language.' Nor do we, though certain words are recognisable, such as 'reactor', 'radium', 'boron' and 'gamma'. The implication is that although the terminology of nuclear science is universal — like panicked body expressions — words dealing with emotion are different in every language.[4] *Gray* also represents the felt sense of powerlessness during a catastrophe when the mass media is the only source of information.

As installations, the three videotapes play on separate monitors placed on simple wooden tables, chairs or on the floor with the cables of the apparatus clearly visible. The effect is thus of a makeshift viewing space, such as the kind customarily assembled for television viewing at home, and the information conveyed is mediated by the viewer's phenomenological relationship with the site in which the work is installed. Rather than heightening the cinematic illusion providing the viewer with a privileged position in relation to the filmic action and created reality — the installation makes no attempt to efface the physical context, neither by disguising the surroundings nor by employing illusory cinematic devices. Instead, the 90-second shorts create a disjointed, dizzying effect — much like channel-surfing or information overload — even though their repetition allows the viewer to process each narrative. The installation's environment is meant to evoke the everyday private sphere of the spectator's personal physical space.[5]

relationship to their as of yet unawakened sexuality. Structurally the effect of viewing the three projections on one screen is similar to flipping through the pages of a magazine, which in turn parallels the experience of several of the girls who leaf through glossy publications in search of clandestine information. As they learn about the mysteries of male anatomy and eroticism, we, too, come to know more about the secret desires and fantasies of female teenagers.

4 Yet it is not just the body language or verbal communication that conveys the pressing urgency, but also the subtle inclusion of details caught fleetingly by the camera, such as when we notice that one of the women is pregnant, which thereby adds a future dimension to the mini-narrative. The scene changes from the elevator to a poetic underwater drowning sequence as the carefully thought-out and lucid response to a scientific disaster shifts to a real terror which defies rational depiction, and, in its very unreality, better captures the truth of the moment.

5 As Timothy Corrigan has observed: 'When any movie is watched as a television show, that is, the domestic setting of the experience may create a kind of immediacy and complicity between the television image and the viewer, but that imagistic immediacy is very significantly redefined across the fragmentation that is either built into the television text (such as commercial interruptions and the cuttings or reductions of the image) or simply intrude upon and invade it as part of the distractions of a domestic environment (conversations or the ringing of a phone).' Timothy Corrigan, *A Cinema Without Walls: Movies and Culture After Vietnam*, New Brunswick, New Jersey: Rutgers

In contrast, the effect of seeing one of these shorts in a cinema before a feature presentation is very different. There the context of viewing is a formalised one: conventionally the spectator is rendered passive for the duration of the programmed screening. When projected on a large screen, the shorts take on an added dimension. The formal features are all exaggerated, and one is much more aware of the televisual style, such as the speed, technique of editing and framing of individual shots. What fits perfectly and seems absolutely appropriate within the context of a television monitor now appears slightly distorted. As cinematic projection, then, Ahtila's work reveals ways in which the characteristics of television drama, music videos and advertising have transformed not only the narrative structure of the moving image, but also the relationship between viewing practices and the construction of meaning.

Ahtila's *Today* (1997) provides another good example of this. The film is about an elderly man who is run-over by an automobile driven by his son. It is presented either as a single, one-channel film or as three narrative perspectives projected in large format on three different walls of the gallery. In the film version of this Oedipal drama the narratives follow one another. The first narrative is that of a granddaughter, the next of an older female neighbour and then, finally, that of the father. We soon discover that it's the latter who is responsible for the accidental death of the elderly man, his own father. The triad of the three generations depicted inevitably recalls the riddle of the sphinx initially posed to Oedipus, who then sets forth to unwittingly kill his father, marry his mother and produce children, the most celebrated of which is Antigone. Indeed, it's the Antigone-like character of the girl throwing her yellow rubber ball against a wall that's most intriguing in this short, for it's she who mediates between the three generations and inherits the family trauma; just as the father recollects his father's inability to express physical warmth, so, too, the daughter stands completely detached and unmoved by her father's tears.[6] The montage, or the cuts, are contained within the rectangle of the film itself.

However, the effect of the installation is very different. For instead of a strict ordering of sequences beyond the control of the seated spectator,

University Press, 1991, pp.27–28. The television spectator, according to John Ellis, 'glances rather than gazes at the screen; attention is sporadic rather than sustained', John Ellis, *Visible Fictions: Cinema: Television: Video*, London: Routledge, 1982, p.24.

6 Here Ahtila works with the Freudian concept of the 'uncanny', in which a former and often traumatic event resurfaces or re-emerges in an unconscious way in the present; see Sigmund Freud, 'The "Uncanny"' (1919), *The Standard Edition of the Complete Works of Sigmund Freud* (ed. and trans. James Strachey), vol.17, London: Hogarth Press, 1955, pp.219–52.

7 With this in mind, it is interesting to note that Ahtila's *Anne, Aki and God* (1998), which includes five 21-inch (53cm) television monitors, two large screens, a bed and an armchair, exists only in the form of an installation. The intricate narrative concerns Aki, a Nokia-computer technician, who becomes schizophrenic and obsessed with finding or creating a woman named Anne (the performances of several actors who audition for her role are projected on the smaller monitors). In addition, Aki receives guidance in his search for Anne from two gods with whom he is in continuous dialogue (these conversations are featured on the two large screens). In a manner that parallels the predicament of Flaubert's Emma Bovary, who could no longer distinguish her real emotions from those produced for her by pulp romances, Aki's psyche is entirely overdetermined by the mass media. In a particularly revealing sequence, Aki is told by one of the gods that he will be 'in charge of Hollywood because Hollywood controls all emotional fantasies of human beings'. This acknowledgement of the role of the mass media — and especially narrative cinema — in the creation and manipulation of the human

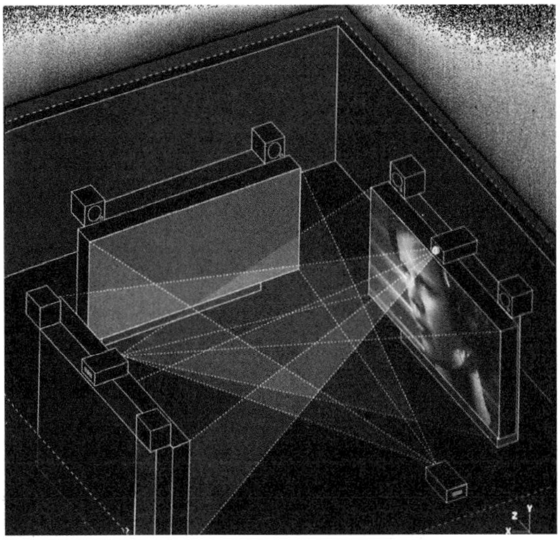

Eija-Liisa Ahtila, study for *Today*, 1996/97. Photo © 2008 Crystal Eye Ltd, Helsinki. Courtesy Marian Goodman Gallery, New York & Paris

now the latter is physically required to move through an architectural space, in which the three-channel work is projected, in order to understand the narrative. The piece thus operates as a kind of ambulatory arrangement of cuts with the spectator phenomenologically moving through the architectural space. But, in turn, the viewer is much more in control of this narrative, for now it is he or she who decides on the order of the cuts or montage. The spectator thus functions as the fourth wall, the final screen completing the narrative. Yet, just as the ordering of the information presented and the alignment of the spectator's body in relation to the work determine the meaning of the narrative, so, too, the medium through which the work is communicated — as installation, film or both — effects the story's interpretation.[7] This is stressed when, through a camera shift, the rubber ball bounces off the position occupied by the filmic apparatus. For, if in the one-channel version this act seems to constitute an aggressive confrontation with the gaze of the spectator, then in the three-channel version, by contrast, it serves to accentuate the viewer's notion of their own physical space in order to more fully draw the viewer into the drama as a participant onto whom meaning is transferred. Of course, as opposed to the cinema version, if the viewer feels at all confronted by the act of a ball thrown in the direction of his or her gaze in the installation version, they can turn away and look at another screen.

Let me turn to a more recent audio-visual work by Ahtila, her 20-minute *Consolation Service* (1999), in order to buttress these points. The installation of this piece features two interrelated though separate simultaneous projections. But in contrast to her earlier work, here the screens depict the same scene viewed from slightly different camera angles. The 'split' image thus relates directly to the topic of the narrative: the divorce of a young couple. However, the film rendition is composed of only one projection and a filmic text that

psyche begins to explain Ahtila's decision to not participate directly in the dream-machine by making a film version of *Anne, Aki and God*. The story of Aki, though based on a 'true' case, bears a strong resemblance to Freud's celebrated study of Daniel Paul Schreber, a judge on the Saxon Supreme Court who in 1893 suffered a psychotic break with delusions that included bedside visitations from God, confused sexual identity and general schizophrenia; see Sigmund Freud, 'Psychoanalytic Notes on an Autobiographical Account of a Case of Paranoia (Dementia Paranoides)' (1911), *The Standard Edition of the Complete Works of Sigmund Freud* (ed. and trans. James Strachey), vol.12, London: Hogarth Press, 1958, pp.9–82. The case has been interpreted as demonstrating how Schreber's blurring of fantasy and reality reflects the 'madness' of the society he inhabited; see Eric L. Santner, *My Own Private Germany: Daniel Paul Schreber's Secret History of Modernity*, Princeton: Princeton University Press, 1996. However, although the parallels between Aki and Schreber are striking, in *Anne, Aki and God* the psychosis of modernity has been replaced by the pathology of an utterly mediatised and technologised world.

presents a coherent narrative whole. The result is a short film that closely approximates conventional narrative cinema, as it multiplies the shots of Anni, the young woman, suturing us into her identity, while J.P., her soon-to-be-ex husband, operates as the antagonist. The difference in the rigidity of the ensuing stereotypes and clichés when seen through the mono-vision of the film version versus the double-vision of the installation reveals the way these social constructs are dependent on — and perpetuated by — single points of view. From this perspective, *Consolation Service* critiques the process by which a complicated, highly individual and specific problematic (the collapse of a marriage) loses its complexity when filtered through the genre of narrative cinema.

Consolation Service also includes the invisible yet audible presence of a female narrator who foregrounds the general difficulty of beginning a story about an ending. Redoubling the artist's own perspective, the narrator starts from a documentary fact — that in her apartment complex a young couple with a child are separating — and increasingly moves into the realm of fiction and over-the-top spectacle (such as when J.P. rematerialises in *Star Trek*-like fashion). This effortless, extravagant fusion of documentary and fiction evokes the staged conventions of television documentary, in which people ostensibly represent their own 'reality' when, in fact, the information is channeled through a technological medium and many long-established conventions. The slippage between fiction and documentary is doubled in this work by the confusion of television and everyday life. For instance, when an image of a desert landscape complete with parched horses suddenly appears during a surreal underwater drowning scene, the viewer is still in the realm of the drowning world. But just as quickly the transition to a third part of the narrative occurs, as the desert landscape scene radiates from a television screen in a living room. Yet Ahtila does not let the televisual elements eclipse the conventions of narrative cinema. As in the films of Ingmar Bergman, John Cassavetes or Rainer Werner Fassbinder, the emotions and psychological interplay between the characters of Ahtila's films are captured less through conversation than through silent gazes, muted expressions and banal, everyday objects.[8]

8 Thus the look on Anni's face when a lewd joke is told by an attractive blonde at J.P.'s birthday party reveals the true discomfort, pain and humiliation she is enduring in the present.

9 Just as Freud's theories have become clichéd and reified in a manner parallel to the relentless, nearly mechanical tendency of the dominant style of feature film-making to reduce complex historical events to love stories discussed by Raymond Bellour 'Psychosis, Neurosis, Perversion' (1986), *A Hitchcock Reader* (ed. Marshall Deutelbaum and Leland Poague), Ames, Iowa: Iowa State University Press, 1986, pp.311–31.

10 *Ibid.*

11 The character Vera cynically observes in *Today*: 'Exactly the ideas which start to clot are merchandise.' In other words, what sells is precisely that which inhibits the flow of thoughts and can be easily contained within the trope of cliché. One possible key to the formally labile nature of Ahtila's work is her return to what might be ur-narrative themes, all heavily inflected with contemporary theories of psychoanalysis. Ahtila's emotional landscapes are populated with generational struggles, miscommunication and alienation between the two genders, and coming-of-age anxieties. For Western audiences, these tropes are so familiar and compelling that their sheer force overshadows the medium in which they are conveyed. The slippage between media that Ahtila performs prompts us to reconsider the dialogical relationship between form and content. Of course, one might question whether Ahtila in her audio-visual practice is participating in or countering the contemporary trend to cross over indiscriminately between narrative film, MTV and video installations; or whether she is successful in producing work that can operate in multiple formats. These interesting questions will have to wait for another moment.

In addition to presenting formal features that bring to mind a contemporary televisual style, Ahtila's new work reveals not only ways in which the characteristics of television drama, music videos and advertising have transformed the narrative structure of the moving image, viewing practices and the construction of meaning, but also the role of television in the construction of identity. In this regard *Consolation Service* addresses the present impossibility of creating the type of realistic psychological dramas common on celluloid screens during the 1940s and 50s, before television permeated into all realms.[9] The medium of television, Ahtila's work seems to suggest, has completely trivialised all representations of everyday life, including cinematic ones.[10] It's in ways such as this — by, for instance, addressing the transformation of the possibilities of a particular medium due to the development of another — that Ahtila's films open up to interpretations and meanings that derive from the critical investigation of the intrinsic formal characteristics of distinct media.[11]

To sum up, then, the formal aspects of exhibition and transmission significantly affect and inform a work of art's meaning. More often than not, however, in discussions of audio-visual work these differences are overlooked in favour of content-based analyses. This focus on a more thematic methodology, while concomitantly overlooking the formal constituents of the work, is symptomatic of a more basic problematic that I find in the practice of visual studies generally. Because of an all-too-common lack of knowledge on the part of the writer of the specific histories and parameters of different media and genres, what is left is the narrative.

Now, it's not unusual for this type of problem to occur in translation. For, as any translator knows, even though broader audiences may be reached by translation, all acts of translation constitute a loss. We only need to think of the inherent difference of, for example, Shakespeare in different languages or in different media — for instance, as written text, live staged performance or on film — to be aware that although the core story may remain the same, significantly different texts are produced in each language and in each medium. And so it should be with the field of visual studies — just because a text exists as a film doesn't mean that it's the same as a video or CD-ROM or sculptural installation. Each particular display apparatus has its own history, its own parameters, its own limits and its own language and grammar. We need to be attentive to these particulars if we want to advance interpretations that grapple with the objects in their entire complexity and to treat the formal components as not just as equal to but, indeed, integral to the thematic dimension.

WHITE CUBE, BLACK BOX AND GREY AREAS: VENUES AND VALUES

Gregor Stemmrich

In his essayistic reflection 'The Semiotics of the Built World', the British artist Liam Gillick explains, or, better, complains:

> Cinema and art are one of those double acts, which provoke endless bad seminars, dull conferences and boring exhibitions based on art and something similar. The desire to enter the world of mainstream cinema is extremely attractive to artists who have flirted with the meanings generated by the medium.[1]

Gillick expresses a certain disappointment with the way many artists look for a cultural importance in cinema that art cannot offer in quite the same way, but he is also critical of the fact that curators, art critics and theorists take the fact that cinema is attractive to artists as a reason for relating art to 'something similar', while thinking exclusively in terms of art. Gillick also expresses disappointment with reference to cinema itself:

> In some ways cinema is one of the grave disappointments of the twentieth century in terms of the way it has become formalised. Yet the experience and potential of cinema is completely different.[2]

This last sentence does not quite cancel out the disappointment, but identifies a viewpoint from which it can be treated in a different way. The cinema has established various codes, some more obvious than others, but ultimately this does not impinge on our experience of cinema. This experience relates to a potential for cinema that is not captured or exhausted by any kind of formalism.

In the course of the twentieth century, both film-makers and visual artists have repeatedly tried to release this potential. They were well aware of the cinema's and art's heterogeneous cultural connections — a heterogeneous quality that cannot be denied by simply claiming cinema as another art. Both cinema and art open up exceptional perspectives, but there is little reason to separate the two contexts when the aim is to establish a historical perspective

1 Liam Gillick, 'The Semiotics of the Built World', *Liam Gillick — The Wood Way*, London: Whitechapel Art Gallery, 2002, p.87.
2 *Ibid.*, pp.86–87.

on the complex attempts that have been made to recognise such potential and to articulate it aesthetically.

It is impossible to address all the divergent ambitions to unleash the potential of cinema here. For an initial understanding of this history, however, it might be helpful to focus upon the venues and related ideas of value that have been set up within the art world in order to deal with cinema as an institution and film as a medium. This focus can be sharpened quite specifically if we compare — or rather confront — 'documenta 5' in 1972, curated by Harold Szeemann and the first documenta to include a film programme, with 'Documenta11', curated by Okwui Enwezor in 2002, which promoted an unprecedented amount of moving images. Seeing the differences between then and now will help to clarify the changes that took place. Farther into this essay I shall elucidate these differences with respect to various artistic approaches to cinematic experience.

Then and Now: the Film Sections in 'documenta 5' and 'Documenta11'

The integration of films into the exhibition concept of 'documenta 5' was based upon a sharp distinction between films made by artists and films made by film-makers. Those by artists were either made on or transferred to video and shown continuously within the context of the exhibition, while the other films were shown only once and screened in the Kino Royal in Kassel, outside the exhibition area.[3] The defining criterion that a film was made by an artist, however, didn't imply that the film itself was seen as a work of art in its own right; instead it was seen as a by-product. The term 'artist' meant that the person was best known for his or her works of art, and not for film-making. Films that were shown within the exhibition area were thus mostly documentaries — for instance, land art projects and performances, like Joseph Beuys's *Eurasienstab* (1968). Film was understood as a means of documentation and reproduction, not as artwork in its own right. It seemed to be the only possible way to present the documented works in the exhibition, and, as art critics pointed out,one shouldn't expect any elegance or fine art of editing from a film that was made by an artist.[4] Yet the definition used — that a film was made by an artist — could never constitute a genre in itself. Indeed, at that time there already existed many films by artists that were not only documentation of their works but were intended to be regarded as works of art in their own right. Artists such as Dan Graham, Richard Serra, Paul Sharits, Michael Snow and Andy Warhol, to name just a few, focused upon the medium of film and on its sculptural processes. These films were not shown in 'documenta 5'.

3 See Roland Nachtigäller, Friedhelm Scharf and Karin Stengel (eds.), *Wiedervorlage d5. Eine Befragung des Archivs zur documenta 1972*, Ostfildern-Ruit: Hatje Cantz Verlag, 2001.

4 In a symposium organised by the Documenta-Archiv Kassel (25 July 2002), Birgit Hein, curator of the film programme of 'documenta 5', explained that this was common opinion among critics around 1972.

The general motto of 'documenta 5' — '*Befragung der Realität — Bildwelten heute*' ('Questioning reality — pictured worlds/worlds of pictures today') — led to the integration of a film programme within the conceptual structure of the exhibition.[5] All kinds of films were shown in the Kino Royal: the pornographic films of Russ Meyer, political propaganda films, documentary films, socialist-realistic films, avant-garde and experimental films, private family films, newsreels, home movies, commercials and so on. It is difficult to understand today what exactly the programme looked like because none of these films were listed in the catalogue of 'documenta 5', and none of the director's names were included alongside the list of artists. The exhibition's motto about 'questioning reality' simply meant that all kinds of pictures had to be questioned in relation to reality, and what is taken as reality had to be questioned in relation to a large array of different pictures and products. Art was understood as something that can initiate such questioning, but film was not understood as art. Experimental and avant-garde films, which were shown in the film programme during 'documenta 5', were announced as 'art films' ('*Kunstfilme*'), not as art. Their status was different and their integration into 'documenta 5' was based on two contrasting ideas. On the one hand, art films as well as other films could 'question reality'. On the other hand, their status was based on the Greenbergian idea of formalistic purity and the self-definition of the medium. A film in which such self-definition appeared was an art film, but as art it was defined as distinct from the tradition of painting and sculpture and from things that were no longer painting and sculpture but were still derived from that tradition. So an art film was not catalogued as a work of art but presented as one more item in the questioning of reality. In the side-programme of films there was a split, or polarisation, between art films that followed the idea of the self-definition of a medium and more or less propagandistic films with a political message. Birgit Hein selected the art films and argued that the formalistic self-definition of film as an art had a political meaning, too; but in the context of a polarisation with more or less propagandistic political films this argument does not seem very convincing.

If we compare the documenta of 1972 with that of 2002, thirty years later, we can see that the distinctions that were operating in 1972 have collapsed. There was no polarisation between self-reflexive art films and films with a clear political intention. All the films were shown inside the exhibition and listed in the catalogue. There was also no official distinction between films by artists and films by film-makers. All the different categories seemed to have been merged or condensed into the same format. The concept of an integration of films in the documenta of 1972 was surely a restrictive one, but one should admit that it implied much respect for film-making as an art in its own right — as a unique practice and profession that could not simply be adopted by the art world. It was a great open gesture to show all these different

5 The German expression '*Bildwelten*' provokes both readings.

kinds of films within the context of documenta, and the public was invited to make up its own mind.

If the concept of art film at 'documenta 5' was problematic in some ways, it was just as problematic at 'Documenta11' for other reasons. In the 2002 exhibition, different modes of presentation for moving pictures existed side by side, and it was not always clear how these related to each other and to the content of the films presented; nor was it readily apparent what these different modes of presentation said about the traditional categories of art and cinema and how they had changed. Comparing a multi-screen installation in a gallery space — in terms of how it relates to the architecture of the white cube, or fits into an installation that includes sculptural objects — with a film projection in a cinema makes it clear that an art exhibition is the best possible venue for the presentation of such work. Many interesting questions arise as to how these installations relate to the experience of cinema, but there is still a clear distinction of venues, which is also a distinction between art and cinema. Other modes of film presentation at 'Documenta11', however, did not respect these distinctions. There were rooms where one could see documentary or essay films on television or projected on a white wall. In some cases movies (longer than an hour) were projected onto the wall of a white cube without seats or announcements of the beginning or end of the film. In other cases white cubes were redesigned as provisional cinemas. These cinemas, however, did not function as normal cinemas because they were conceived for the presentation of only one particular film. The format and function of the cinema was adapted to the format and function of the white cube, and vice versa.

Elsewhere — for example, in the presentation of a film by Ulrike Ottinger — a provisional cinema was built in order to show a film that was obviously made for presentation in a regular cinema. In the presentation of a film by Steve McQueen, however, a provisional cinema was built for a film that was made for an art context. Since the beginning of their careers both Ottinger and McQueen have regarded galleries and museums as the adequate venues to achieve cultural prominence for their films. Maybe the distinction is just a question of duration: Ottinger's film lasts several hours, McQueen's film about 20 minutes. Both films, however, are made to be seen from beginning to end; and in the case of McQueen's film, the public was even forced to wait for the beginning of the film in order to enter. So these films were shown in provisional cinemas despite being made in formal terms more closely associated with a regular cinema setting. However, the status of a provisional cinema raises the question of what an adequate situation for showing and viewing would be — a question that cannot be answered by the same provisional solution in all cases. For instance, a provisional cinema was arguably totally adequate for showing McQueen's film *Western Deep* (2002), because the completely dark room and wooden structure without comfortable seats created an almost claustrophobic sense of enclosure that corresponded perfectly to his film about miners, enhancing and supporting the immense, phantasmatic, bodily response that the film produced. Through the rest of the exhibition, however, all the other provisional cinemas confused this functional relationship.

Artists have been making films for a rather long time, but they do not typically express the idea that they regard provisional cinemas as an adequate venue for their presentations. The concept of the provisional cinema within an art exhibition suggests that you can have the cinema inside the context of art, as a Trojan Horse, which implies that the context of art may not be totally adequate for the presentation of these films. One should admit, however, that such provisional cinemas do offer an opportunity simply to see films that otherwise might not have been shown. An art exhibition is just a platform for the discussion of art and for the discussion of the platform as well. The point about provisional cinemas is a point in the discussion of the platform — so it is also necessary to approach issues that relate to the art itself.

The Artist as Film Director — Cinema and 'Counter-Cinema'

For some time a distinction has been made between films by artists and films by film-makers, yet strong competition has not existed between them because they have used the medium in completely different ways. However, these different roles and ways to use the medium now seem to have converged, or appear exchangeable. There are cases of artists and film-makers trying to work in both fields — that is, within the context of cinema and within the context of art. For example, the film-maker Chantal Akerman also presents work derived from her experience as a film director in the form of multi-screen video installations. She presents her films as art, and they look like art, but there is a contradiction in terms. The imagery suggests a desire for a kind of meaning, a kind of continuing narration, a deep psychological involvement, a poetical intimacy of experience that is related to the experience of cinema and its three-dimensional representation. This response is not enhanced or supported by a multiplication of filmic images on an array of video monitors that come into view as sculptural objects. The filmic image here looks rather flat, almost a cliché that is objectified in its distribution. In fact, Akerman's video installation *From the Other Side* (2002) looked more like an advertisement for her film of the same title than an independent work. One shouldn't mind an advertisement for a great film, but one might ask whether the art context is then just the lobby of a cinema. Furthermore, the fact that the video monitors function as obstacles for the visitor and that this could be related (rather intellectually) to the topic of the film — the borderline between Mexico and the US — seems to imply a false idea of 'real experience'.

This does not mean, however, that it should be regarded in principle as impossible for an artist or a film director to work on 'the other side', so to speak. Film as a medium has some rather 'sculptural' properties: as a light cone in its projection; as a field of vision that is related to depth and also can

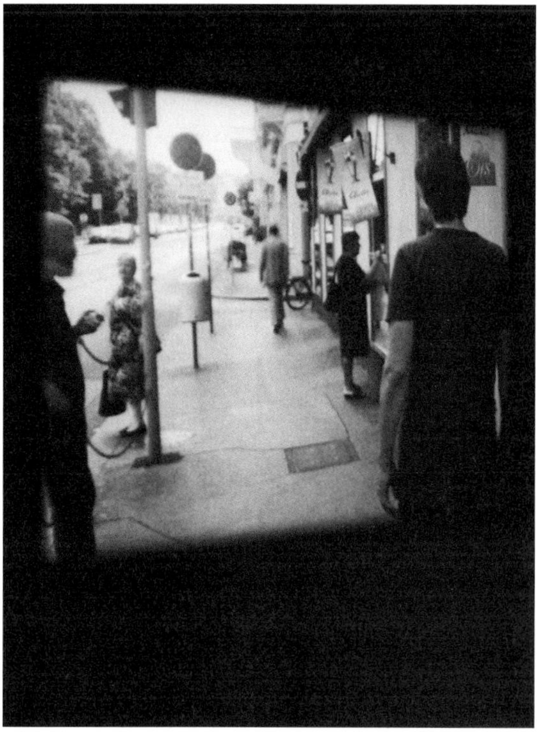

Matthew Buckingham, *A Man of the Crowd*, 2003. Installation view. Courtesy Murray Guy, New York

be flattened to a degree that relates to the sense of touch; as a filmstrip that is cut and quite plastically splices together various aspects of space; as something that is based on contrasts of light; and as something that relates to movement. There are very subtle ways to provide a sense of filmic narration and of the sculptural presence of the filmic, and at the same time provide the possibility to work with few adaptations in the context of both art and cinema. Matthew Buckingham, for instance, has often done so quite convincingly while refusing to show some films, such as *A Man of the Crowd* (2003), without the set-up of the installation. Another example would be Eija-Liisa Ahtila, who was trained as an artist using film and video; she often works in connection with sculptural installations, while also screening pieces in the cinema and on the film festival circuit. Sometimes, however, the relationship of her work to the different spaces is not clear. In *Consolation Service* (1999), she tells the story of a divorced couple with both partners traumatised by the experience in different ways. The DVD of the work offers a choice between two different modes of presentation: the viewer can either see the film as a normal movie or as a split screen with two different pictures side by side. The one-picture format seems to relate to the cinema and the two-picture format to installation art, even if double-screen projection is also possible in the cinema. There are a few moments of lucidity when the two pictures correspond and imply a sort of comment on each other, but for the most part their correlation seems totally banal and the two-picture format comes across just as an added gadget to a normal movie.

Of course, one may criticise this or that film that is presented as a work of art, and this or that work of art that uses film, but after seeing 'Documenta11' one may also ask whether or not the art context has become an expanded cinema — not in the psychedelic terms of the 1960s but on the level where any distinction between art and cinema is denied and art gets 'cinematised' while the cinema gets 'artified'. If the term 'expanded cinema' can be reused in this respect, one may also ask what happened to that other idea of the 60s — the idea of a 'counter-cinema'. Can the avant-garde films that were presented in 'Documenta11' in any sense be aligned with the notion of a counter-cinema?

In order to bring this question closer to an answer one may focus on a work by Lorna Simpson that was shown in the 2002 exhibition. Titled *31* (2002), it consists of 31 flat-screen monitors presented on a wall in a grid-like structure that is to be read as a calendar month. Each flat screen represents

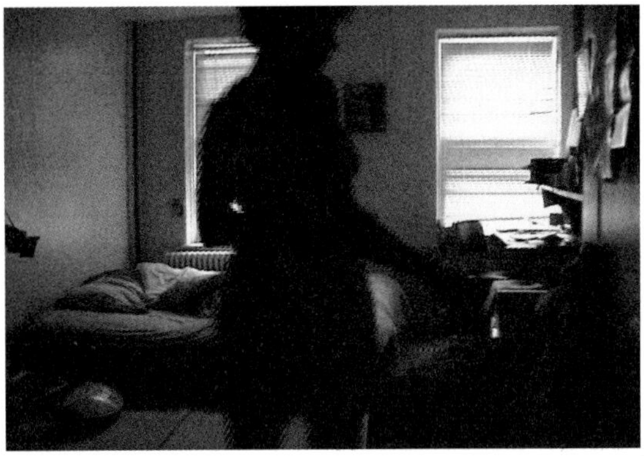

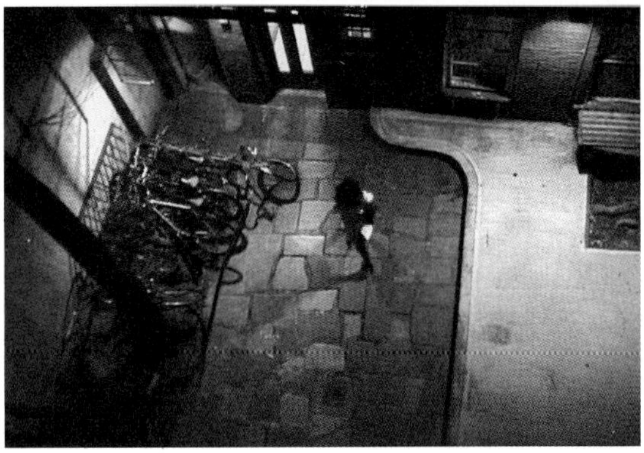

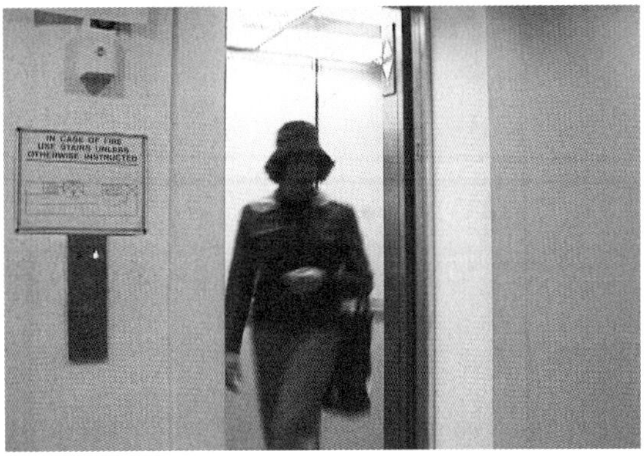

one day in the month of the professional and private life of a black woman. There are situations that appear and reappear nearly every day, and there are things occurring that are not just aspects of a daily routine. We can see, for instance, changes of atmosphere and can imagine details that may become emblematic for a situation. The film, if one may call it a film, was shot on video and transferred to DVD. One gets the impression that we see scenes of real life through the eyes of surveillance cameras. The camera angle and its movement in relation to the movement of the characters, however, are too filmic to support such a view for long. Everything seems to be based on a *mise-en-scène* that cannot be achieved with surveillance cameras. So another model comes to mind, that of a soap opera on TV. A soap opera is connected with the idea of the normal life of a person or family. It only functions as a soap opera if there is a continuing narrative with surprising turns and shifts of comical or dramatic interactions. Such turns and shifts are lacking in Simpson's work and there are many gaps in the narration. The whole thing looks very sterile in relation to the idea of a soap opera, and it looks very cinematic in relation to the view of a surveillance camera. The film lasts only 20 minutes, and uses a very subtle kind of editing through which viewers are invited not just to focus on one screen after another, but to let their eyes traverse several screens at once in order to work out possible correlations. The overall impression you receive is that 'you can never know the whole story', giving the film an enigmatic quality, an experience enhanced by the fact that it is impossible to watch all screens at the same time. The flat screens themselves, when seen from certain angles, change colour and become totally artificial, inverting light and dark or fading out completely. Every flicker of our eyes or turn of our heads brings a new aesthetic configuration. We cannot relate these pictures to our normal visual experience nor to our normal experience of cinema. We may relate them, however, to other moving pictures — to electronic billboards in urban surroundings, to screens that are connected to a computer or to surveillance cameras.

Lorna Simpson, stills from *31*, 2002

Simpson's film installation can be compared and confronted with Jean-Luc Godard's film *Deux ou trois choses que je sais d'elle* (*Two or Three Things I Know About Her*, 1966).[6] Both films are about the daily activities of a woman, but in quite distinct ways. Godard's film is a typical example of 'counter-cinema'. (Other examples that focus on the daily activities of women are films by Chantal Akerman, Laura Mulvey and Yvonne Rainer. But Godard's film seems to be one of the earliest examples and the most adequate choice for a comparison.) Godard's 'her' refers both to *la région parisienne* (the outskirts of the city) and to one woman that lives there. The film is an investigation about the general conditions of life as it focuses upon one particular individual who is exposed to those conditions, while not being completely determined by them. It is based on episodes that are combined with filmic documentation, essayistic reflections and commentary, with Godard always present — as the title makes clear. In an interview Godard gave in the mid-60s, he explained that it is impossible to live in Paris without prostituting oneself in one way or another. His film focuses upon a woman who, from time to time, works as a prostitute. Lorna Simpson's film focuses on a woman who does not get up every morning in the same bedroom, which of course does not mean that she works as a prostitute.

Peter Wollen has defined the principles of counter-cinema in terms of an antithetical construction. The seven vices of normal or classical cinema are contrasted with the seven virtues of counter-cinema. For the purpose of brevity this list can be repeated here:

1. Narrative Transitivity v. Narrative Intransitivity
2. Identification v. Estrangement
3. Transparency v. Foregrounding
4. Single Diegesis v. Multiple Diegesis
5. Closure v. Aperture
6. Pleasure v. Unpleasure
7. Fiction v. Reality[7]

The seven virtues of counter-cinema can be applied to Godard's film very easily. What is interesting, however, is that if one tries to determine Simpson's position in respect to this list it always seems to fall between Wollen's poles. For instance:

1. 'Narrative Transitivity versus Narrative Intransitivity.' The whole installation seems to be directed towards narrative transitivity: one thing follows another. That can be applied to the scenes on each screen and to the whole sequence of screens. But, at the same time, the installation seems to be directed towards narrative intransitivity: the construction

6 Alfred Guzzetti, *Two or Three Things I Know about Her: Analysis of a Film by Godard*, Cambridge, Mass. and London: Harvard University Press, 1981.

7 Peter Wollen, 'Godard and Counter-Cinema: Vent d'Est', *Afterimage*, no.4, 1972; reprinted in Philip Rosen (ed.), *Narrative, Apparatus, Ideology: A Film Theory Reader*, New York: Columbia University Press, 1986, pp.120–29.

of scenes and screens is a construction of gaps, digressions, interruptions and episodes.

2. 'Identification versus Estrangement.' It's a neither-nor situation. The fact that the presence of the same woman affects us in all scenes and on all screens comes close to provoking an emotional response that might result in empathy. But, because we can see this woman simultaneously in so many different situations, the impression of multiple or divided characters seems unavoidable.

3. 'Transparency versus Foregrounding.' The filmic language might be transparent on each screen and it might not at first sight be directed towards a foregrounding of its own mechanics, but the whole installation does exactly that. And this, of course, affects the perception of what can be seen on each screen.

The same is true with the other points—there is no difference here between single diegesis and multiple diegesis, or between closure and aperture. The installation is neither directed towards entertainment nor towards provocation, and it is neither about fiction as fiction nor about reality as reality. It would be more adequate to say it is about a *mise-en-scène* that connects the opposing sides of an antithetical construction without being either one. That is, it counters or deconstructs the opposition of cinema and 'counter-cinema' without losing touch with the tradition of the latter.

Towards the Notion of an 'Absolute' Reality – Moments of Film History

This field of discourse has long seemed to be based upon clear-cut categorical distinctions: between art and cinema; between cinema and 'counter-cinema'; and, as Peter Wollen pointed out in his essay 'The Two Avant-Gardes', between an avant-garde critically and creatively dealing with the established language of cinema and an avant-garde formalistically focused upon the self-reflexive use of the medium, or what has been termed Greenbergianism as applied to film.[8] A further distinction has lain between an avant-garde film-making that focused upon formal devices that could have political implications and a kind of predominantly essayistic and documentary type of film-making that tried to foreground a political message.

While one could very easily take a stance and argue in favour of only one category within this field, taken together the different categories have a tendency to hold each other in check. It is therefore rather significant that programmatic, political film-making as a movement broke down at roughly the same time as the formalistic film movement. These seemingly opposed categories actually required and mediated each other. In our present situation there is no longer a desire for clear-cut categories but for integration, diffraction, deconstruction or paradoxical adaptations of seemingly opposite intentions. As such, mediation is taken into consideration on more than one level. There is a kind of 'media literacy' and an awareness of media history that earlier avant-gardes could not deal with in the same way. In order to understand this, one has to focus not only upon the shifting relationship between art and cinema, but also on how technical media such as photography, film, video and computers are integrated into the general context of art, and how art relates to the predominant or institutionalised cultural use of such media.

The history of photography is very significant in this respect. As Jeff Wall pointed out in his lucid essay '"Marks of Indifference": Aspects of Photography in, or as, Conceptual Art', photographers such as Walker Evans worked as photojournalists in the 1930s while striving to achieve the status of a modern artist, while vanguard artists in the 60s — such as Dan Graham, Ed Ruscha or Robert Smithson — used the model of the photojournalist to reject the false heroism and formalism that was part of the image of the modern artist.[9] This reversal was mirrored to a large extent by the simultaneous integration and exclusion of film in 'documenta 5'. Here it was supposed that photographers and film-makers might strive to achieve the status of a vanguard artist, but 'real' vanguard artists use the media of film and photography without fine-art ambitions, simply to provide and contextualise visual information and, implicitly, to satirise fine-art ambitions. Towards the end of the 1970s, however, artists like James Coleman, Tracy Moffat, Cindy Sherman and Wall replaced the conceptual model of photojournalism with the model of the film production still — that is, a photograph where every single detail, every gesture and facial expression is part of a *mise-en-scène*.

Wall argued further that Conceptual art — as important as it was — had led to an impasse. Whereas he and others tried to get out of it through a new use of photography as a kind of filmic *mise-en-scène*, most artists in the late 70s sought to overcome this impasse in the outburst of Neo-Expressionist mythological painting. Even here, however, one can sense the growing impact of the experience of cinema. The painter Markus Lüpertz, for instance, explained that he got his ideas about using emblematic configurations in the centre of his paintings from the sequences that film corporations such as Twentieth Century Fox or Columbia Pictures used to announce themselves at the beginning of a movie. We can also think here of the pathetic historical fiction and panoramic illusion of depth in the paintings of Anselm Kiefer that reflect cinematic experiences, or of the New York painting star Julian Schnabel who went to Hollywood to make a movie about another star,

8 Peter Wollen, 'The Two Avant-Gardes', *Studio International*, vol.190 no.978, November/December 1975, pp.171–75. Please note that this essay is reproduced in the current volume.

9 Jeff Wall, '"Marks of Indifference": Aspects of Photography in, or as, Conceptual Art', in Ann Goldstein and Anne Rorimer (eds.), *Reconsidering the Object of Art: 1965–1975* (exh. cat.), Los Angeles, Cambridge, Mass. and London: The Museum of Contemporary Art and The MIT Press, 1995, pp.246–67.

Jean-Michel Basquiat. The 'new spirit in painting', as it was called, seemed to revive an expressionist gesture of authenticity, centred on the private feelings of the artist, but this authenticity had a source outside itself in the pervasive experience and role models of commercial cinema. The art world of the 1980s was largely centred on the commercialism and consumerism of the art market, using the glamour and gossip of the film industry as a model for its behaviour. Artists like Robert Longo, Sherman and Schnabel, among others, were welcomed by Hollywood and encouraged to make commercial films. This was in contrast to Warhol's experience in the 60s, when he combined underground, pop and queer culture into a kind of mimicry of Hollywood, but stayed outside its methods of circulation and economy. From the 80s onwards, it seems the art world has been driven towards the experience of cinema not only as subject but also as predominant model for its behaviour.

In video art we can observe a shift from a phenomenological use of the medium, refering to real-time bodily experience, towards a cinematic use, refering to phantasmatic modes of imagery provoking imaginary identifications in the viewer. Early video art was to a large extent about real time in terms of perception, representation, behaviour and duration. The apparatus as object was exposed as a part of performances and installations. When video technology was first available in the 60s it could easily be integrated into the art context because it seemed to have no history — at least no art history. Video was welcomed as a means to get rid of overburdened art-historical precedents for image-making. It could also be used to analyse and criticise television with its own technology, as in several works by Nam June Paik, Dan Graham and Dara Birnbaum. Video, like television, is about present time, not about history.

Things are much more complicated when artists try to relate the institution of art to the institution of cinema, however. Cinema as an institution has a rather complex history, and film as a medium establishes a contemplative mode of seeing — a mode that is about things that happened in the past. Over the last fifteen years we have seen numerous film and video installations that precisely use the mediums in order to contemplate the history of cinema — installations by Douglas Gordon, Stan Douglas and Pierre Huyghe for instance. They restage or utilise paradigmatic moments in the history of cinema, and initiate a kind of meta-discourse on that history that is centred on neither the institution of cinema nor the institution of art. Instead, there is an implicit assumption that collective historical experiences are foregrounded and condensed in the history of film. Looking back at certain moments in film history is always like looking back at history itself. That is not to say that films represent historical reality objectively, but by becoming cult objects they achieve an absolute reality because so many real fantasies come into play around their production and reception. Artists strive to develop methodologies in order to deal with and analyse this absolute reality, enabling them to deal with cinema as an institution and to relate its history to the context of art.

'Sight-Specific' Site-Specificity

What we see in cinemas and on TV or hear on the radio can, to a large extent, simply be read as the dominant cultural media. It seems to be totally formalised. This reading can be challenged, however, if we emphasise the idea that a film is made in order to build a socially desired configuration. In this way the true potential of cinema can be addressed, and because there exists no differentiation in film between fantasy and so-called reality, this foregrounding conveys a 'sight-specific' idea of total reality.[10]

This idea, however, might be related to the concept of site-specificity as it was first formulated in the 1960s. Site-specific art initiates a kind of 'reality-effect', and evokes an idea of totality in the sense that it uses a site in order to build a new configuration that intervenes in it as it specifies it, making the work an inseparable part of an existing but now transformed site. From the earliest days of site-specific art onwards, the basic idea was that a work of art should be an integrated part of a situation, a place, a location — not in order to harmonise the relationship between the artwork and its surroundings, but rather in order to give the artwork the capacity to disrupt its surroundings and evoke complex issues, possibly interconnecting various discourses related to it that would normally be barred from consciousness. Site-specific art has always had a complex relationship to the use of media. It often has two different venues: the site of the intervention in an urban or some other space — for instance, the museum or the landscape — and the representation of that intervention in film and photography that reflects its intent and enhances the scope of issues to which it can be related. Robert Smithson's film *Spiral Jetty* (1970), for instance, documents his sculpture as well as being documentation of the production of a film. It is also a hyperbolic chain of associations and essayistic reflections including allusions to Hollywood cinema. In this way it focuses upon a filmic idea of 'sight-specific' site-specificity.[11] Gordon Matta-Clark, who created sculptural cuts into the architecture of the urban and suburban landscape, similarly used film as a means of documenting his work, but also as a means to cut into space itself. In his film *City Slivers* (1976), he reflects aesthetically on the urban experience and projects re-filmed filmic cut-outs ('slivers') of various films on a screen or on the architectural wall of the gallery itself.[12]

The concept of site-specificity was first understood as an artwork's intervention into one specific site, but later 'site' was redefined as a venue or place that allows seemingly different discourses to cross and influence each other. Therefore, the use of media could become even more important than an artwork's integral relation to a spot on the geographic map. In this respect

10 'Lawrence Weiner — Show (&) Tell, Interview by Bartomeu Mari', *Having Been Said — Writings & Interviews of Lawrence Weiner 1968–2003* (ed. Gerti Fietzek and Gregor Stemmrich), Ostfildern-Ruit: Hatje Cantz Verlag, 2004, pp.262–70.

11 Tom Holert, 'Strudel und Wüsten des Politischen: *Zabriskie Point*, *Spiral Jetty* und die Grammatik der Entgrenzung', *Kunst/Kino* (ed. Gregor Stemmrich), Köln: Oktagon 2001, pp.94–119.

12 Marc Glöde, 'Den Raum zerschneiden — den Raum denken. Zu den Filmarbeiten von Gordon Matta-Clark', *Umwidmungen. Architektonische und kinematographische Räume*, (ed. Gertrud Koch), Berlin: Vorwerk 2005, pp.88–98.

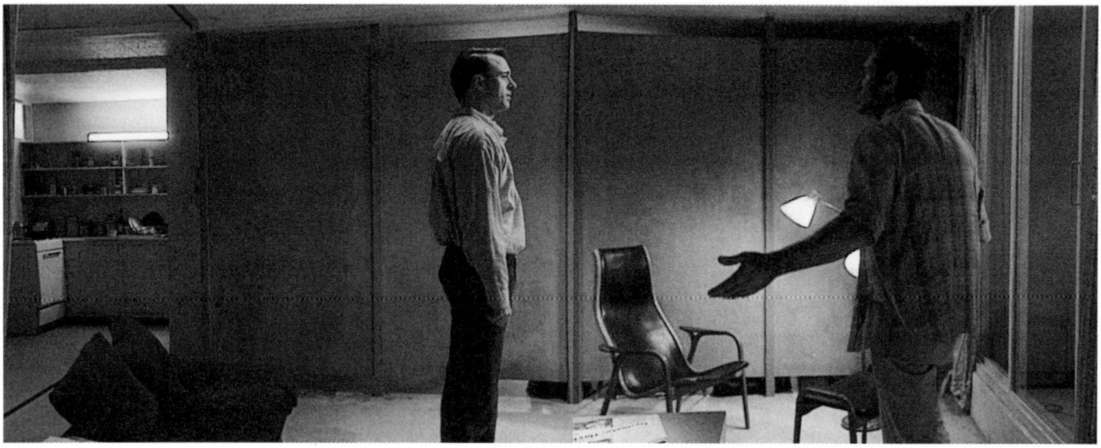

Stan Douglas, still from *Win, Place or Show*, 1998

the concept of site-specificity can be useful for understanding various artistic approaches to film and installation art involving film.

The work of Stan Douglas is a suitable example. He almost always makes reference to a specific location and to things that happened there in the past. Most of his film installations are focused upon settlements and on desires or utopian aspirations that are connected to a specific place on the earth, particularly ruined or discarded places. This reference is established in his use of film to reflect or restage moments of film history, often in direct relation to the history of the chosen location. The restaging or recreation of a cinematic space opens up the possibility of including further references to the history of music, literature, architecture and politics. Diverse issues, memories, experiences and discourses are allowed to overlap, becoming sampled and condensed. This cinematic space relates to both the white cube of the gallery and the black box of cinema, but its site cannot simply be equated with either one of these spaces. It is folded into itself at the same time as it unfolds itself—pictures and screens are transparent, doubled or divided, and constant alternation and repetition occurs. In this way, the screened filmic image becomes its own site and its own site-specific intervention simultaneously. There is always a kind of splitting and doubling and a reversal and deference that provoke an idea of a total reality that is not completely accessible. In *Win, Place or Show* (1998), for instance, Douglas makes reference to single-male workers' dormitories that were proposed for Vancouver's Strathcona district in the 1950s but never built. This reference is combined with a reconstruction of the style and atmosphere of a famous TV series, *The Clients*, shot in Vancouver and aired in 1968.[13] In contrast to the TV series, however, every scene is filmed from various camera angles whose views are projected randomly on a split screen that disrupts the continuity of filmic narration. Douglas possibly

13 For more specific information see: William Wood, 'Secret Work', *Stan Douglas* (exh. cat.), Vancouver: Vancouver Art Gallery, 1999, pp.107–22.

14 Lawrence Weiner, *ON THE ROCKS. Some questions + 5 answers relative to moved pictures*, Lund: Edition Sellem—Archive of Experimental and Marginal Art, 1976.

alludes, in this respect, to the infinite mirroring of Robert Smithson's *Enantiomorphic Chambers* (1965). Together these chambers bring about an idea of a view (a sight as well as site) that is totally self-reflexive — that is, the notion of a stage where total reality happens although it is not accessible to human eyes. Douglas's concept is less restrictive than traditional narrative moving image, breaking up the scenario by introducing different, random angles while still offering a space for narration.

Film builds and uses its own narrative framework, but the culture is a narrative framework, too. Culture exists because it supports, frames, determines and maintains its own narration. Art and cinema both participate in culture, but traditionally build different relations to it. Both, however, present aesthetic configurations that might change the culture and also, therefore, change their relationship to one another. Today there exists a kind of confusion about this relationship and how it has changed, or might change, and the question of what art and cinema's common configurations could be prevails. In 1976, Lawrence Weiner asked in one of his books: 'Is there a parallel between the synthetic (art) and the synthetic (cinema) when imposed upon a narrative framework (the culture in the case of art; the plot in the cinema)?'[14] If the question is still valid today, we might have to take not only the parallel into consideration, but also strange ellipsoids and hyperboles.

ART AND CINEMA: SOME CRITICAL REFLECTIONS

Mark Nash

Over the last thirty or so years, moving-image practices and the critical and theoretical debates surrounding them have transformed the space of contemporary art and curatorial practice. In this essay I want to examine some aspects of this contribution and revisit a key moment — that of the mid-1980s cultural theory in Britain — as a way of situating more clearly the work that has already been done in this area. The questions raised then, I argue, are still pertinent for discussions of contemporary visual-art practice and international exhibitions today.

'Two Sides to Every Story'[1]

Visitors to recent contemporary art exhibitions, notably the Venice Biennial 2001, cannot fail to have been struck by the series of 'dark rooms' provoking encounters with a wide range of video and film practices, albeit often murkily presented by DVD video projection.[2] I want to explore some of the paradoxes or contradictions engendered by the presence of artists' film and video in the gallery, which challenges both our relationship to the museum and our perception and interpretation of moving images. In particular, our relationship to the dominant moving-image regimes of film and television is brought into question.

At the same time I want to explore what I perceive as a tension between advocates of the single-channel cinema (or TV) experience and those of gallery installation work, which I think comes down to both a mistrust and a misunderstanding of cinema. Mistrust because cinema is often felt to embody the claims of the popular against the more elite pleasures of the traditional art gallery, although this distinction is becoming increasingly irrelevant; misunderstanding because the cinema is an integral if not generative part of twentieth-century art and the cinematic a key mode of twentieth-century subjectivity. We are always already in cinema, one way or another.

1 Also the title of a work by Michael Snow from 1974, included in Chrissie Iles, *Into the Light: The Projected Image in American Art, 1964–1977* (exh. cat.), New York: Whitney Museum of American Art, 2001.

2 Cinephile moving-image curators have argued persuasively that video and film have their own medium specificities, even though cash-strapped galleries currently prefer to move works over to DVD. Luckily there are certain artists such as Tacita Dean or Liisa Roberts who insist on continuing to use celluloid.

In discussing the role of the moving image in the art-gallery context it is necessary to ask which kind of cinema we are talking about. The history of cinema in the twentieth century is a history of a plurality of cinemas. Indeed, even the arrival of sound film was considered such an epistemological break that many critics (such as Erwin Panofsky) were inclined to define it as a distinct art form, sharing the same support medium as silent film. I am adopting a tripartite division of the field of cinema: narrative, avant-garde and documentary, derived from recent discussions of genre theory.[3] This has the effect of liberating the experimental and the avant-garde from the binary opposition to mainstream 'Hollywood narrative' posed both by theorists and practitioners[4] and enables us to think more rigorously about its role in the history of contemporary art. It also allows us to analyse documentary cinema's indexical relation to reality independently from the 'reality effect' of the classic realist narrative.

Artists' film and video has emerged as a major if not dominant moving-image discourse in the museum and gallery circuit: avant-garde and experimental moving-image practices are reconfigured and restaged; Hollywood narratives are reworked and represented (Pierre Huyghe, Douglas Gordon) in forms of critical or cynical pastiche. Documentary has also emerged as a major reference point. The twentieth-century archive of photographic and magnetic (film and video) images is preserved and reworked in a range of artists' work: e.g. in the work of Yervant Gianikian and Angela Ricci Lucci, Pere Portabella, Trinh T. Minh-ha or Fiona Tan — several of whom have developed a practice of deconstructing and reworking the colonial archive, insisting that the possibility of rereading and engaging with this 'past' is as important as creating a present or imagining a future. Film-makers Chris Marker and Jean-Luc Godard have eloquently and consistently developed a practice of preserving the history and memory of cinema through the intervention of new technologies.

Chris Dercon has described a developing gallery-based cinema as neither experimental nor classical, but a cinema of fragments:[5] 'Young artists ... from all over the world imitate a wide variety of Western visual expression, avant-garde techniques and, inevitably, the cinema ... Significantly many young artists are responding to existing forms of mimesis in cinema itself. So we can now speak of a secondary mimesis, which is becoming recognizable in films

3 See Alan Williams, 'Is a Radical Genre Criticism Possible?', *Quarterly Review of Film Studies*, vol.9 no.2, pp.121–25, quoted in Steve Neale, *Genre and Hollywood*, London and New York: Routledge, 2000, p.20. One can imagine these fields as an overlapping series of circles, and it is often at the overlapping points of the avant-garde with other kinds of cinema that significant work takes place (viz. avant-garde/documentary, e.g. Trinh T. Minh-ha; avant-garde/narrative, e.g. Chantal Akerman and Ulrike Ottinger; avant-garde/narrative/documentary, e.g. Jean-Luc Godard and Tomás Gutiérrez Alea).

4 See, for example, film-maker Peter Gidal's attempt to produce and theorise a non-representational image in experimental films and writings (see his *Materialist Film*, London and New York: Routledge, 1989).

5 It is worth remarking that this fragmentation of vision was already implicit in the Cubist and Duchampian project, and we may indeed now be seeing a 'modernisation' of moving-image practice delayed for so long by the domination of realist narrative. However, this new fragmentation is also bound up with a resistance to and redefinition of narrative temporality as duration (Andy Warhol, Michael Snow) in the development of what Gilles Deleuze in *Cinema 2: The Time-Image*, London: Athlone, 1989, has defined as the time-image — essentially a post-World War II phenomenon.

made by visual artists.'[6] New kinds of cinemas are being developed, entailing new visual and sonic conditions in the production of subjectivity.

In his essay 'The Machine in the Museum or the Seventh Art in Search of Authorization', Bruce Jenkins argues that cinema has redefined the way in which we understand contemporary art, which indeed is much more deeply indebted to cinema and the moving image than some critics and artists would like to admit.[7] Experimental cinema in particular, he argues, internalised key questions of modernism very early on (viz. Duchamp's founding critique of cinema's illusionism in *Anemic Cinema*, 1926, and Joseph Cornell's detemporalisation of the cinema in *Rose Hobart*, 1939). I would extend Jenkins's argument to include pre-World War II documentary (think of Dziga Vertov or Joris Ivens), which, I would argue, was equally adept at responding to the challenges of modernism in the 1920s and 30s, whereas narrative cinema, in the guise of art cinema, responded rather later. Antonioni's *L'Avventura* (1960) is a key instance in art cinema's incorporation of modernism.[8] Antonioni is important because of his rigorous separation of the look and the gaze. He breaks the relay between actor, character and audience, while at the same time elaborating a more fragmented regime of looking. Jenkins makes a further key point that the social organisation of film production itself also posed a challenge to artists: 'namely the "unusual and unnatural" situation of an artistic enterprise based on cooperation' — an issue I shall return to shortly.[9]

In a recent catalogue essay, 'On the aesthetics of video installations', Boris Groys focuses on two ways in which the moving image changes the gallery-going experience.[10] The first concerns illumination — the fact that moving-image exhibits are not illuminated by the museum's light but emit their own source of light or darkness: 'Video and film installations have now introduced deepest night or dusk into the museum.' The artist, as Groys points out, now controls the light by which we see their work. The second concerns a shift in the temporal conditions influencing our perception of art. Moving pictures have begun to suggest to the viewer how much time they should spend on contemplation. However, should we 'interrupt our contemplation of some video or film work in order to return to it at a later point, we will inevitably be filled with that very same feeling of having missed something crucial and will no longer be sure what is really happening in the installation'. Moving images, in other words, return us to the experience of real life, 'that familiar place ... where one is forever haunted by the feeling of being in the wrong place at the wrong time'. Moving-image installations create an anxiety in

6 Chris Dercon, 'Gleaning the Future from the Gallery Floor', *Vertigo*, vol.12 no.2, Spring 2002, p.3.

7 Bruce Jenkins, 'The Machine in the Museum or the Seventh Art in Search of Authorization', *Witte de With Cahiers*, no.3, Rotterdam and Düsseldorf: Witte de With Center for Contemporary Art and Richter Verlag, 1995.

8 The film, you will recall, is about the search for a missing person, Anna, but halfway through, the film loses interest in this narrative and abandons itself to an exploration of the spaces of southern Italy and the alienation of erstwhile comedienne Monica Vitti.

9 B. Jenkins, 'The Machine in the Museum or the Seventh Art in Search of Authorization', *op. cit.* — Jenkins is quoting from Arnold Hauser, *The Social History of Art* (trans. Stanley Godman), New York: Vintage Books, 1958, p.250.

10 Boris Groys, 'On the aesthetics of video installations', in Peter Pakesch (ed.), *Stan Douglas: Le Detroit* (exh. cat.), Basel: Kunsthalle Basel, 2001, n.p.

the viewer for which there is no adequate and satisfactory solution: 'Whatever the individual's decision, either to stay put or to keep moving, his choice will always amount to a "poor compromise".' In the cinema, on the other hand, the audience is traditionally immobile, secure in the knowledge that, provided they didn't miss the beginning of the film, they will have seen everything they need to see to understand the work.

Curators who work with moving images also insist on Groys's point that the installation of film and video in the gallery context represents a freeing up of the spectator from what they regard as the restrictions of traditional cinema. Lynne Cooke, writing on Marijke van Warmerdam, comments '... since there is no fixed seating, spectators must determine their own vantage points, a process in which they become conscious of their activity as viewers. In this her works are far removed from the classic, passive cinematic experience in which the audience, cocooned in a darkened chamber, traditionally forfeits all self-consciousness, becoming totally immersed, discarnate observers.'[11] Similarly Chrissie Iles, in a major moving-image exhibition catalogue, *Into the Light: The Projected Image in American Art, 1964–1977*, after pinpointing a range of aesthetic strategies (Cézanne, Cubism, Duchamp) which 'laid the ground-work for the postminimalist decentering of the viewing subject', continues: 'Cinema becomes a cocoon, inside which a crowd of relaxed idle bodies is fixed, hypnotized by simulations of reality projected onto a single screen. This model is broken apart by the folding of the dark space of cinema into the white cube of the gallery.'[12]

This metaphor of a darkness folded into or inserted into the white cube is a potent one. While for Groys it spells the end of the white cube, for Iles the white cube spells the end of a particular kind of cinema experience. Of course in the gallery context the moving image reads differently and the artists' and curators' insistence on refusing the viewer a safe, protected, old-fashioned cinema space should not be underestimated. However, my feeling is that much writing on film and video in the gallery can too easily gloss 'sitting in a cinema' with 'passivity', or 'mobility' with 'freedom', overlooking the often overtly political single-channel film work concerned with creating an active spectator in the traditional cinema setting.

Indeed, to watch a film in a cinema in Puerto Rico, Lagos or Bombay is to encounter a very different, active call-and-response approach to spectatorship not a million miles away from that which Third Cinema struggled to create in developing (in Bertolt Brecht's phrase) a cinema of 'pleasure and instruction'.

Psychoanalytic-based film theory was developed through an analysis of a spectatorial regime — classic Hollywood cinema focused on the role of the gaze sutured into the shot-reverse-shot figure — and a historically specific mode of spectatorship: the regular movie-goer, supported by a panoply of

11 Lynne Cooke, 'B(e)aring Meaning', in *Marijke van Warmerdam: Single, Double, Crosswise* (exh. cat.), Eindhoven: Van Abbemuseum, 1997, p.8.

12 C. Iles, *Into the Light*, *op. cit.*, p.34.

magazines as well as the architecture of the picture palace. However, its key concepts of the gaze and subjectivity as theorised through the experience of cinema were developed to explain the ideological hold of mass cinema: 'The goal of the theoretical project was to disengage the spectator from his/her habitual, pre-designated location in the dominant cinematic apparatus through a process of critical unravelling of the apparatus and thereby produce a politically conscious audience for another cinema.'[13]

One of the reasons for film theory's focus on Hollywood was to find — in Michael Hardt and Antonio Negri's phrase — 'alternatives to Empire'.[14] In its move from theorising sexual difference to issues of race, 1980s film theory began an ongoing theorisation of difference which extended into cultural and critical studies *tout court*.[15] Despite the importance of this move there is considerable unfinished business in the relative theoretical neglect of other regionally dominant cinemas — Iran, Nigeria and India, for example. It is no accident that this theoretical project continues today in the Indian subcontinent.

These cinemas propose a range of aesthetics and politics that differ from those of mainstream Hollywood or art cinema: a nostalgia for a rural, religious past in the video theatrics of Nigerian soap opera which emerged out of the Yoruba travelling theatre movement (Ola Balogun); continuing feudal relations of power and identity in Hindi narratives; an attempt to develop a theocratic modernism in Iranian art cinema (Mohsen Makhmalbef); and so on.

In Godard's account there is an acceptance of this major shift in the spectatorial regime of narrative cinema:

> Woman: When did the gaze collapse?
> Man: 10 years ago? 15 years? Maybe 50, before TV? Who knows?
> Woman: Be more precise.
> Man: Before TV took precedence.
> Woman: Over what? Over current events?
> Man: Over Life?
> Woman: Yes.[16]

For Godard the loss of cinephilia is compensated for by his investing video with many of the qualities of painting,[17] evidenced, for instance, in his framing of subjects against the light, a device familiar from German Romantic artists such as Caspar David Friedrich or Karl Friedrich Schinkel. Godard's critique refers to the end of the classic Hollywood system and the interlocking aesthetics of National European Cinemas (which he explored in his *Histoire du Cinema* shown in 'documenta X').

13 M. Madhava Prasad, *Ideology of the Hindi Film*, New Delhi and Oxford: Oxford University Press, 1998, p.2.

14 See Michael Hardt and Antonio Negri, *Empire*, Cambridge, Mass. and Oxford: Harvard University Press, 2000.

15 See, for example, these issues of *Screen*: 'Other Cinemas, Other Criticisms', vol.26 no.3–4, 1985; 'The Last Special Issue on Race?', vol.29 no.4, 1988.

16 Dialogue from Jean-Luc Godard's *Éloge d'Amour* (2000).

17 One should point out that this equation, not *camera-stylo* but *video-peinture*, has a longer history, viz. Michelangelo Antonioni's *The Oberwald Mystery* (1980).

18 Manthia Diawara, lecture, 4 October 1999, published in Gareth James, Annette Schindler and Florian Zeyfang (eds.), *I said I love. That is*

Godard's own practice involves the three modes of cinema (avant-garde, documentary and narrative, as already referred to), e.g. a modernist reworking of Hollywood narrative by the *Nouvelle Vague*, or an attempt to produce another way of seeing and thinking about the documentary image as in his and Anne-Marie Miéville's short-lived (and utopian) project to produce images to protect newly independent Mozambique from the international media by creating 'an autonomous image which of itself would be a challenge to any new image that they anticipated would soon arrive in Africa'.[18]

Spectatorial positioning is complex and relational. Ella Shohat and Robert Stam have coined the phrase 'transnational or cross-cultural spectatorship' to emphasise the fact that 'spectatorial identification is culturally, discursively, and politically discontinuous, that it is fissured, even schizophrenic, suggests a series of gaps; the same person might be crossed by contradictory discourses and codes'.[19]

The ideological functioning of cinematic spectatorship has, over the past fifty years, shifted to the wider, more fragmented and dispersed regime of the visual, encompassing advertising, television, mass circulation magazines and so on. Consequently, curatorial and artistic practices that are concerned with deconstructing and reconstructing spectatorship have had to find approaches that are not merely architectural. The construction and problematisation of the subject involves a series of discursive relays in which curatorial practice has played an essential role in opening up the signification of individual works into discursive frameworks that have inevitably moved beyond the gallery setting. But I would argue that there can be no necessary connection between a particular formal approach to the conditions in which a work is experienced (e.g. creating a mobile spectator) and a presumed radicality.

The key question is whether the new physical mobility that the spectator is offered in gallery and museum installations really involves a critique of dominant spectatorial regimes of cinema. Do gallery-based moving-image practices participate in the construction and problematisation of the subject in this way? Do they explore the discontinuities inherent in spectatorship, in the sense in which Homi K. Bhabha defines it, as an overcoming of binary oppositions and the opening up of a 'process of translation'?[20]

My argument here, though restricted to a particular issue concerned with the claims being made for film and video in the gallery space, is part of a wider argument about the terms and conditions for radical film and video work in the post-Cold War era, and the kinds of spectatorial engagements they propose. I would argue, for instance, that Stan Douglas's *Win, Place or Show* (1998) is precisely political in its hyperbolic engagement of the cinematic

the Promise. The tvideo politics of Jean-Luc Godard, Copenhagen: Ojeblikket, 2003. *Cinema Novo* film director Ruy Guerra had invited both Godard/Miéville's company Sonimage and Jean Rouch to work with him in accord with the newly independent Mozambique government's desire to establish a kind of television that would empower Mozambican viewers rather than recolonise them.

19 Robert Stam and Ella Habiba Shohat, 'Film Theory and Spectatorship in the Age of the "Posts"', *Reinventing Film Studies* (ed. Christine Gledhill and Linda Williams), London, Oxford and New York: Arnold, 2000, p.398.

20 Homi K. Bhabha, *The Location of Culture*, London and New York: Routledge, 1991, p.33.

machine with his construction of an endless series of shot variations within a televisual narrative format. Whereas Douglas Gordon's *left is right and right is wrong and left is wrong and right is right* (1999), a reworking of Otto Preminger's *Whirlpool* (1949) into a feature-length flicker film (à la Bruce Conner), is to my mind more formalist. Both works — presented together in New York's Dia Center for the Arts exhibition 'Double Vision' (February 1999–March 2000) — force the spectator into gallery-style mobility. However, one of them, I would argue, proposes the terms of a critique quite absent in the other.

It can be argued that Third Cinema has provided a discursive space for a range of different cinematic practices that contemporary art has not been able to emulate and that the processes of deconstruction and reconstruction of aesthetic discourse in the visual arts have taken a different course to those alternative, experimental and political cinemas included under the general rubric of Third Cinema. Indeed, one of the aims of this 'Documenta' is to draw our attention to this alternative tradition.

Hamid Naficy has developed the intriguing concept of an 'accented' cinema to describe and define a post-colonial cinema of exiled and diasporic subjects based on a 'double consciousness' — 'constituted both by the structure of feeling of the film-makers themselves as displaced subjects and by the traditions of exilic and diasporic cultural productions that preceded them'.[21] An offshoot of the Third Cinema movement, accented cinema is more situated, less polemical but nevertheless still political.

Let me give some other examples of such accented Third Cinema practices. Shirin Neshat's video and film narratives are engaged in a complex dialogue with the representational schemas of Iranian cinema. Her veiled women protagonists do not simply function as representatives of repression and inequality; her use of the veil acts as a spectatorial lure, drawing the audience's attention to the fact that a different regime of looking as well as power is being questioned in her work. These issues are explicit, too, in the work of Indian film-maker Amar Kanwar, whose *A Season Outside* (1997) uses the confrontational performance of national identities enacted on an India-Pakistan border crossing as a starting point for the investigation of the construction of an Indian masculinity divided between the demands of the nation state and the family and the very different tradition presented by Buddhism. Isaac Julien moves between the single-channel avant-garde and art-cinema format and the multi-channel installation with its attendant proposition of a mobile spectator. His work in both formats, I would argue, exposes, deflects and reconstructs the cinematic gaze (e.g. through the use of the sequence or *le travelling*) and, in so doing, opens the audience to other

21 Hamid Naficy, *An Accented Cinema: Exilic and Diasporic Filmmaking*, Princeton and Oxford: Princeton University Press, 2001, p.22.

22 R. Stam and E. Shohat, 'Film Theory and Spectatorship in the Age of the "Posts"', *op. cit.*, p.374.

23 Hal Foster, 'What's Neo about the Neo-Avant-Garde', *October*, no.70, Fall 1994; quoted in Geeta Kapur, *When Was Modernism: Essays on Contemporary Cultural Practice in India*, New Delhi: Tulika, 2000, pp.374–75.

24 *Ibid.*, p.374.

25 Vanguard film practices have continued to take place at the fault lines of the Soviet empire, for example: the 1960s Czech New Wave; or the films of Dusan Makavejev in Yugoslavia or Sergei Paradjanov in Georgia. Equally,on the Indian subcontinent,

concerns: to make questions of race or sexual difference a matter of indirect reference rather than embodiment.

Contemporary cinematic practices propose a series of scopic regimes, some voyeuristic, others exhibitionistic, with a concomitant range of aesthetics. This makes it imperative to re-examine the heritage of avant-garde and experimental film and video and in particular the contribution of, to adopt Naficy's term, 'accented' artists to these debates.

When Was the Avant-Garde?

> If the avant-garde is a historically conditioned phenomenon and emerges only in a moment of real political disjuncture, it will appear in various forms in different parts of the world in different times.[22]

While it is generally agreed that the collapse of the project of the 'historic avant-gardes' coincided with the changed political climate in post-World War II Europe and North America, critics and art historians are sharply divided on whether the notion of the avant-garde is appropriate for post-War art at all. Hans Magnus Enzensberger and Peter Bürger have argued that the avant-garde project is dedicated to the destruction of bourgeois art, and that the post-War avant-garde is, in the words of Hal Foster, 'merely neo ... so much repetition in bad faith that cancels the pre-War critique of the institution of art'.[23] Foster takes a position in favour of successive vanguards precisely to make contemporary artistic practice viable. Geeta Kapur extends or rather 'deflects' this argument in order to unpick its '(Euro)Americanist' bias:

> An African or Asian avant-garde will come into its own if at least two moves take place simultaneously. One, a move that dismantles the hegemonic and conservative features of the national culture itself. Two, a move that dismantles the burdensome aspect of Western art, including its endemic vanguardism. That is to say, such an avant-garde would have to treat the avant-garde principle itself as an institutionalized phenomenon, recognizing the assimilative capacity of the (Western) museums, galleries, critical apparatuses, curators and media.[24]

What is interesting and useful about Kapur's position is that it allows one to bracket off contemporary art practices which have abandoned any dialogue with issues of politics, the state or national culture and whose avant-gardism has become institutionalised, while simultaneously investigating other sites where it can be argued that avant-garde work is indeed going on today or was disregarded in the recent past.[25]

film-makers such as Mani Kaul or Kumar Shahani have questioned the political and aesthetic framing of the investigation of national identity begun by Satyajit Ray under the aegis of Jawaharlal Nehru.

In an influential paper, 'The Commitment to Theory',[26] Homi K. Bhabha proposed the concept of a 'third' space which he made the condition for the articulation of cultural difference: 'It is the "inter"—the cutting edge of translation and negotiation, the *in-between* space—that carries the burden of the meaning of culture.'[27] In seeking to overturn the dualism underlying much contemporary and theoretical practice, Bhabha further sets out the enunciative terms for a vanguard artistic practice, supplementing those of Kapur:

> The language of critique is effective not because it keeps forever separate the terms of the master and the slave, the mercantilist and the Marxist, but to the extent to which it overcomes the given grounds of opposition and opens up a space of translation ... In such a discursive temporality, the event of theory becomes the negotiation of contradictory and antagonistic instances that open up hybrid sites and objectives of struggle ... [28]

In the years that have passed since that initial formulation, this notion of a third space has become something of a mantra for artists committed to exploring social-political questions in their work while at the same time working to maintain the notion of autonomy in their artistic practice. What was important about Bhabha's formulation at that time was that it broke open a number of binary positions which were constantly being returned to in the cultural field and keeping it mired in its Zhdanovian heritage.[29]

In insisting on a semiotic interpretation of cultural production, Bhabha was building on a line of reflection from Soviet linguists such as Mikhail Bakhtin who asserted the importance of the social in their analyses while insisting on the autonomy of the linguistic or semiotic instance. By deploying Bakhtin, Bhabha was also building on the work of the British film journal *Screen,* which, in the 1970s, had initiated a major epistemological break in the ways we think about visual culture, but at the time had been unable to extend its thinking from psychoanalytically inflected discussions of sexual difference to broader questions of cultural difference.

Subsequent development of cultural theory has made notions of cultural difference and 'other'-ness almost commonplace—even the mainstream US media such as CNN after September 11 are beginning, albeit in a limited way, to acknowledge differences under the *pax* (or, as we should now rename it, *bellum*) *Americana*. Although, as Bhabha would undoubtedly point out, much of the burgeoning discourse concerning racism, migration, human rights violations, the 'war against terror' and so on is in fact an attempt to foreclose the enunciative spaces that are constantly opening up. Difference cannot be written out, but it can be managed.

26 Homi K. Bhabha, 'The Commitment to Theory', first delivered at the 1986 Third Cinema Conference held in Edinburgh and subsequently published in its proceedings *Questions of Third Cinema* (ed. Jim Pines and Paul Willemen), London: British Film Institute, 1989. 'The Commitment to Theory' is also published as the opening chapter in Bhabha's *The Location of Culture, op. cit.*

27 H. Bhabha, *The Location of Culture, op. cit.*, p.38.

28 *Ibid.*, p.25.

29 Andrei Alexandrovich Zhdanov's theses on Soviet Socialist Realism re-established the primacy of the social in cultural debates in the Soviet Union and of state control of artistic matters, putting an end to the experimentation of the historic Soviet avant-gardes.

The Edinburgh International Film Festival conferences from the 1970s until 1986 were probably the most important single location in the anglophone world for the development of theoretical debates on cultural production, with a specific focus on film. 'Documenta11' could be seen as also participating in the tradition of these combative, theoretically informed cultural events — 'Documenta11' is first and foremost a series of frameworks, platforms within which issues can be discussed. And we need to approach the exhibition in Kassel and the contributions of its artists in that light, and focus on the enunciative specificity of the works and projects presented.

Collective Practice

Walter Benjamin, Bertolt Brecht and Arnold Hauser have all pointed to the collaborative aspect of cinema and its potential for de-individualising art practice and dislocating regimes of authorship, ownership and control. In Britain, even as late as the 1980s, a film and video workshop movement enshrining notions of collective practice was established in an alliance between activist film-makers, the then fledgling Channel 4 Television and the film and television trade union ACTT.

This was a direct descendant of the Third Cinema debates in the New Latin American Cinema movement. In their manifesto 'Towards a Third Cinema', Fernando Solanas and Octavio Getino argue that the New Third Cinema 'of liberation' will not be that of Hollywood (first cinema), nor *cinema d'auteur* (second cinema), but a cinema which makes films '*that the System cannot assimilate and which are foreign to its needs or ... that are directly and explicitly set out to fight the System*' and in which films are produced as part of collaborative politico-cultural work.[30]

The aesthetic strategy of the New Latin American Cinema combined Italian Neo-Realism and *Nouvelle Vague verité* realism (e.g. Glauber Rocha's *Terre em Transe,* 1967) with anti-Realist montage drawing heavily on the avant-garde and militant documentary tradition (e.g. Solanas and Getino's *The Hour of the Furnaces*, 1968; or Tomàs Gutiérrez Alea's very different *Memories of Underdevelopment*, also 1968). The 1980s workshop movement in Britain was able to embark on an analytical, critical and theoretical debate with the Realist premises of the British documentary movement and art cinema, drawing on advanced work in film theory and cultural studies that had emerged in London and Birmingham in the 1970s.[31] See, for example, Black Audio Film Collective's *Expeditions: Signs of Empire/Images of Nationality* (1982–83), a semi-abstract tape-slide performance juxtaposing fragments of colonial discourse; or Isaac

30 Fernando Solanos and Octavio Getino, 'Towards a Third Cinema' (1969), *New Latin American Cinema, Volume 1: Theory, Practices and Transcontinental Articulations* (ed. Michael T. Martin), Detroit: Wayne State University Press, 1997, p.43. Emphasis in original.

31 My reference is to the Centre for Contemporary Cultural Studies in Birmingham, and the journals *Screen* and *Theoretical Practice* in London.

Julien and Sankofa Film and Video Workshop's *Looking for Langston* (1989), which synthesises several visual genres including documentary footage, fictional narrative and the *tableau vivant*. A number of workshops (Black Audio, Ceddo, Retake, Sankofa) were also concerned with fighting the exclusionary and often racist practices in the British media industry.

At that time I was part of a London-based group, the Society for Education in Film and Television, and the journal *Screen,* both of which were challenging the terms of the debates on the role of the mass media in contemporary society — through a massive importation of mainly French theoretical work from linguistics, semiotics and psychoanalysis. The possibility of political and social change through ideological struggle in culture was very much on the agenda in the early 1970s — whence we used to paraphrase Karl Marx, 'the point is to change things'. Louis Althusser's work, combined with both Soviet and Chinese writing about the social function of art, was very important for us then.

This was the time of 'documenta 5', which uniquely brought together avant-garde film and video practices with these elaborate politico-cultural schemas. In the UK, these discourses and their practitioners kept themselves very separate. There were in fact two avant-gardes: the film co-op movement, which was concerned with formal experimentation — Greenbergianism in the cinema, if you will — and a looser political cinema concerned with struggles in representation, as in the work of Godard or Danièle Huillet and Jean-Marie Straub. These were soon to be joined in the *Screen* avant-garde by an unlikely mix of a range of art cinema film-makers, such as Miklós Jancsó and Nagisa Oshima.

In the thirty years that have passed, one would agree with Godard that the project for a political avant-garde cinema appears to have collapsed. The end of the Cold War and the failure of 'actually existing socialism' were major factors. The aesthetico-political practices of film collectives — the films and videos produced internationally by the women's movement, *Cinema Novo* in Latin America or the wide range of film and video associated with working-class struggles such as the UK miners' strike or Cinétracts in France in 1968 — have disappeared from view. Most of the film co-ops and their supporting institutions closed down, due to both a lack of institutional support and a change in the audience as attention shifted to the major re-articulation of moving-image practices in the gallery context.

My argument, however, is that the project for a political avant-garde cinema continues to inform new work staged in the gallery context, and that its debates and issues are being re-articulated and restaged by artists and film-makers for our 'bad new times'. Much of the tension and hostility that the moving image engenders in the gallery can be attributed to anxiety about restarting a series of political and aesthetic encounters that were both bruising but ultimately productive in the 1970s and 80s.

In 'Documenta11', we want to refocus attention on a range of historical and contemporary collective or collaborative practices. However, it is also important to remember the important tradition of the political documentary, central to militant Latin American cinema: 'The cinema known as documentary with all the vastness that the concept has today, from educational films to the reconstruction of a fact or a historical event, is perhaps the main basis of revolutionary film-making. Every image that documents, bears witness to, refutes or deepens the truth of a situation is something more than a film image or purely artistic fact; it becomes something which the system finds indigestible.'[32] The Chilean *Colectivo Cine Ojo* based their name on that of the formative Cine Eye movement in Soviet Russia associated with Dziga Vertov. Its *Memoirs of an Everyday War* (1986) reworks 1980s Chilean media footage to provide an analysis of the bizarre language of the Pinochet dictatorship in which the terms of revolution and fascism were completely reversed (Pinochet was revolutionary; the opposition fascist).

The work of Igloolik Isuma Productions, an Inuit production company in Nunavut, Canada, is about renewing traditional oral narratives in new media, and in so doing provides a support for the cultural survival of a first nations people. Fareed Armaly's collaborative project *From/To* is exemplary in its attention to the wide range of oppositional media strategies in the Palestinian struggle for autonomy and independence. As well as the complex work of reading the traces of the struggle that *From/To* enacts, Armaly also provides a framework, a kind of virtual 'pavilion', for a range of other film-makers and activists. Where else can one find information on Palestinian film history or activist films?

These issues are not the province of groups and collectives alone. Film-maker Trinh T. Minh-ha, for example, has consistently engaged a feminist and anti-ethnocentric gaze in her single-screen projects, starting from her seminal *Reassemblage* (1982/83).

In his essay, 'The Black Box' [for the Documenta11 catalogue], Okwui Enwezor refers to the uneven way past 'Documentas' have engaged the issues that emerged globally in the second half of the twentieth century, the search for freedom propelled by independence and liberation struggles, the rethinking of the project of modernity among previously dominated and colonised societies, the reconceptualisation of the relationship between the West and the non-West. In attempting a diasporic understanding of modernity, 'Documenta11' is attentive to this issue of locality emblematically formulated by Hardt and Negri and which needs to be brought into play with Kapur and Bhabha's insistence on the importance of locality or location — location in the sense of Paul Gilroy's Black Atlantic,[33] or Enwezor's Trade Routes,[34] referring to the process of movement through which the contemporary diasporic subject is constituted.

32 F. Solanas and O. Getino, 'Towards a Third Cinema', *op. cit.*, p.69.

33 Paul Gilroy, *The Black Atlantic: Modernity and Double Consciousness*, Cambridge, Mass.: Harvard University Press, 1993; London and New York: Verso, 1993.

34 *Trade Routes: History and Geography* (exh. cat. for the 2nd Johannesburg Biennale), Johannesburg and The Hague: Greater Johannesburg Metropolitan Council and the Prince Claus Fund for Culture and Development, 1997. Okwui Enwezor was the exhibition's artistic director.

Examples of this diasporic consciousness raised in some of the film and video work in the exhibition are the border crossings of Mexican illegal immigrants in Chantal Akerman's *The Other Side*; the traces of the expulsion of Ugandan Asians in Zarina Bhimji's new work *Out of Blue;* Isaac Julien's exploration of the imaginary of the post-World War II Afro-Caribbean diaspora's 'circum-atlantic' peregrinations in *Paradise Omeros*; Ulrike Ottinger's journey to Odessa (*Südostpassage — Southeast Passage*) in a reversal of the routes of Eastern-European migration, and so on.

Jean-Marie Teno's film *Vacances au pays — A Trip to the Country* (2000) is emblematic here. Teno develops the term 'tropical modernity' to explore the effects of colonial and post-colonial modernisation on Cameroon society, a modernism that was at the same time imposed, longed for and never achieved. The two small skyscrapers of Yaoundé come to stand in for the longed-for modernism represented by the Manhattan skyline. However, this film, like so many others in Africa, can only be made from the position of the exile. As Edward Said has pointed out, 'Modern culture is in the large part the work of exiles, emigrés, refugees' since the cultural and political conditions for critical artistic production are not available in the artist's country of origin.[35]

In *Empire*, Hardt and Negri argue that 'Globalization, like localization, should be understood instead as a *regime* for the production of identity and difference, or really of homogenization and heterogenization'; and that what needs to be critically addressed today is 'the *production of locality*, that is, the social machines that create and recreate the identities and differences that are understood as the local'.[36] Art practice, in particular moving-image art practice, has a key role in this endeavour.

35 Edward W. Said, 'Reflections on Exile', *Reflections on Exile and Other Essays*, Cambridge, Mass.: Harvard University Press, 2000, p.173.

36 M. Hardt and A. Negri, *Empire*, *op. cit.*, p.45.

Postscript (2005)

This essay is in two parts: the first is concerned with the moving image in the gallery context — crudely summarised as how the black box relates to the white cube — and the second deals with issues of Third Cinema and collective practices. Both issues informed 'Documenta11' in Kassel in 2002. In the three years since I wrote the following essay for that exhibition's catalogue there has been a massive 'turn to documentary'. The range of artists, aesthetic practices, debates and issues 'Documenta11' introduced into the mainstream contemporary art world have been taken up in biennials and exhibitions all over the world. Our work as co-curators, and that of the many artists and critics we were in dialogue with, preceded the massive change to the world polity that the events of September 11 brought about; yet, perversely, 'Documenta11' and September 11 have both been credited with this renewed interest in documentary.

I subsequently continued to explore the issues raised in this essay in both my curatorial and critical projects. For instance, in the 'Other Cinemas' section of the Berlin Biennial in 2004, hosted by the Kino Arsenal at the Sony Center in Potsdamer Platz, I presented a range of politically and aesthetically oppositional film practices to provide a 'broadened understanding of the critical realism of East German cinema and art practice'.[37] As in Kassel, we took advantage of a purpose-built cinema.

In a more recent exhibition, 'Experiments with Truth', which took place during 2004 and 2005 at The Fabric Workshop and Museum in Philadelphia, I explored a range of approaches to notions of the 'documentary' and of the 'indexical' in the practice of contemporary moving-image artists, while contributing to debates on the presentation of moving-image work in a gallery setting. Sound penetration was a major issue in the installation of the exhibition spaces for 'Documenta11' and I learnt from this in designing the exhibition spaces for 'Experiments with Truth' with Lynn Rice of Open Office, where we were able to establish a similar axial corridor design. This time we lined the surfaces with acoustic foam and provided a light and sound lock for each entry, so that we did not need to use curtains to separate the individual spaces. Coincidentally, another moving-image show that was presented in London in 2004 — 'Time Zones' — provided something of a counterpoint to my show. All of its works were impressively installed in an open-plan fashion in the vast, loft-like spaces of the Tate Modern's temporary exhibition halls. Sound penetration was not an issue, in this instance, given the size of the gallery spaces. 'Experiments with Truth' focused on work that dealt with issues of documentary that, in my view, required dedicated viewing spaces so that the audience could engage with the work under the best conditions

37 Mark Nash, 'Hub Anderes Kino/Other Cinemas', *3rd berlin biennial for contemporary art* (ed. Ute Meta Bauer), Cologne: Verlag der Buchhandlung Walther König, 2004, p.37.

possible. The Tate exhibition was more concerned with formal aspects of recent moving-image work, which the open-plan presentation foregrounded.[38]

My catalogue essay for 'Experiments with Truth' continues the debate on the challenges spectators face when viewing documentary work, which I broached in the 'Documenta11' essay:

> If issues of time and duration constitute a formal challenge to the spectator's position, documentary cuts through this by combining duration with narration, thereby forcing the viewer to engage with a range of contents which appear to be located in the real world, rather than that of fiction or fantasy. I say 'appear' because in recent years I believe we have been witnessing a break in the indexical bond between image and referent.[39]

That essay goes on to explore what I perceive to be a tension between the work of those artists who are still interested in some kind of figuration of political and social reality and those artists where this link has been broken and artistic enunciation is foregrounded. Of course, this is a delicate balance, and one in which the stakes are important.

It seems to me now that the art world is more comfortable with documentary work that makes claims for formal experimentation than work that makes demands on its audience to understand the specificity of a conjuncture with which they may not be familiar. An example of the former could be Albanian artist Anri Sala's single-screen installation *Time after Time* (2003), in which an apparently dying horse struggles along the side of a road against the glare of oncoming headlights. As in Robert Bresson's film *Au Hasard Balthazar* (1966), Sala's installation makes allegorical reference to the Christian passion. There are no markers of place enabling one to identify the location with any precision, indeed no other information is required of the audience for an effective affective identification.

On the other hand, Sala's earlier video *Intervista* (1998), in which he confronts his mother with evidence of her involvement with the Albanian Communist Party, takes pleasure in its use of archival film to connect to the past of Albanian communism, and contrasts it with a contemporary interview with his mother. Sala thereby makes the points that communism was not a monolithic institution, and that the post-Cold War transition is being experienced differently in diverse locations.

This is not to value one piece over the other, but rather to simply point out that one offers an ease of address that the other does not. For the individual artist, especially one coming from Eastern Europe, this poses the dilemma of what Hal Foster has defined as 'critical distance'.[40] If one is too much the native informant, one is too close. If one is too much the ethnographer, one is too far. The struggle for the artist is to find the correct distance.

While 'Experiments with Truth' was concerned with showing the work of artists who were actively engaged in this dilemma, there are other approaches — for example the Exhibition 'Reprocessing Reality',[41] recently presented at the Chateau de Nyon near Geneva and curated by Claudio Spinelli in association with the Documentary Film Festival 'Visions du Réel'. In this collaboration, the film festival continued to explore film and video documentary while the exhibition explored what it means to be a spectator of documentary images through apt juxtaposition of moving-image work, photography and related documentation. Christoph Büchel's video *AC-130 Gunship Targeting Video (Afghanistan) 12/8/2002* is a record of an attack by an American bomber on a village in Afghanistan, downloaded from the Internet and presented unedited. It was juxtaposed with a series of photographs and a video of interviews by Taryn Simon, depicting people in the US wrongfully convicted and subsequently released as a result of DNA evidence, filmed in locations relating to the alleged crimes.

Whereas single-screen film and television documentaries tend to disengage critical distance simply by the weight of the conventions and expectations that the audience has of documentary narrative and cinema viewing situations, the exhibition context can create a dialogue between works and positions which has quite radical potential. In the examples above, the indifference in Büchel's video of US imperialism to human suffering (the 'too far' of aerial photography) complements Simon's critique of an overly subjective investment in memory and the photograph ('too close'), which produces convictions but not justice.

The range of aesthetic, political, philosophical and, indeed, ethical issues raised by this turn to documentary demands attention. How to reconcile cinema's historic concern with perspective and monocular narrative vision with one that is more haptic, embodied, sculptural? How do we think about sound and image in an age of digital reproduction when the indexical bond between image and referent is loosened?

Most importantly, perhaps, to what extent are we still involved in the paradox of what Walter Benjamin called the 'optical unconscious' — namely, the move to a subjective register which accompanies depiction once it is separated from a critical frame? Benjamin critiqued the *Neue Sachlichkeit* (New Objectivity) photography as saying 'the world is beautiful', in opposition to Bertolt Brecht's imperative that 'the point is to change it'. One might argue that much of the work involved in the contemporary 'documentary turn' is involved in an analogous but dystopian move. This time the affect produced is one of horror rather than wonder: the world is no longer beautiful, and we are in the process of witnessing the destruction of the world as we know it. Crucially then, where is the position for critical engagement in all this?

38 See Mark Nash, 'Questions of Practice', *What Makes A Great Exhibition?* (ed. Paula Marincola), Philadelphia: Philadelphia Exhibitions Initiative, 2007.

39 Mark Nash, 'Experiments with Truth — the Documentary Turn', *Experiments With Truth*, Philadelphia: The Fabric Workshop and Museum, 2005, p.16.

40 Hal Foster, 'Whatever happened to Postmodernism?', *The Return of the Real*, Cambridge, Mass.: The MIT press, 1996, p.225.

41 http://reprocessingreality.ch/

YOU NEVER KNOW THE WHOLE STORY: UTE FRIEDERIKE JÜRSS AND THE AESTHETICS OF THE HETEROCHRONIC IMAGE

Thomas Y. Levin

The trio of silent, large-screen video projections in the ZKM's Museum für Neue Kunst [*You Never Know the Whole Story* (2000) by Ute Friederike Jürss] catch one's attention right away. Not, however, because of any flashy movement but rather, just the opposite: in their odd, somehow dynamic stasis they are fascinatingly hard to read, difficult to identify generically. Formally the black-and-white projected images invoke the iconography of the news photograph in the chaotic intensity of the scenes that they capture seemingly *in medias res*. Although somehow inviting one to read them in a (photo- and cinematographically) narrative fashion as fragmentary evidence of some very agitated 'real-world' drama, these images not only withhold the elusive 'whole story' (whatever that might be) invoked in the installation's title, they don't even divulge *part* of the story or stories of which they are ostensibly a trace. Unless, of course, one is looking in the wrong place, i.e. unless the 'whole story', or rather, the story of the 'whole' is not one that necessarily can be discovered by readings that remain resolutely at the level of referential narrative. Indeed, in a dynamic of retrospective revision that will itself prove to be crucial to the understanding of this work, further inspection reveals that the initial intermedial impression of the installation (a video projection of a news snapshot) is somewhat more complicated than at first glance: for while the projected images do indeed recall highly charged photo-reportage stills, they do so by invoking the longstanding tradition of the *tableau vivant*. What we see on second glance, in other words, seems to be a projection of a video of a theatrical *staging* of a still news photograph.

1 Godard's is hardly the first cinematic restaging of the *Night Watch* (1642) as *tableau vivant*: besides Jos Stelling's 1976 *Rembrandt fecit 1669*, the topos is explored at length in the 1942 Nazi bio-pic *Ewiger Rembrandt* by Hans Steinhoff (of *Hitlerjunge Quex* fame). Interestingly, while Steinhoff's cinematic biography does give us a visual account of the moment when Rembrandt supposedly gets the inspiration for the painting (a chance night-time surveillant observation of the company of Lt Banning Coq leaving their regular drinking establishment), it also explicitly parodies the idea that the painting originated as an (effectively photographic) rendering of the group posing as a *tableau vivant*. Instead — and this is not uninteresting for the present context — we are shown Rembrandt painting each individual in costume and holding a pose, but entirely alone and one after another.

2 See Joachim Paech, 'Eine Szene machen: Zur räumlichen Konstruktion filmischen Erzählens', in Hans Beller, Martin Emele, Michael Schuster (eds.), *Onscreen/Offscreen: Grenzen, Übergänge und Wandel des filmischen Raumes*, Stuttgart: Hatje Cantz Verlag, 2000, pp.107–08; translation and emphasis by the author. Compare also Paech's more extended treatment of the *Nightwatch* scene in his *Passion oder die Einbildungen des Jean-Luc Godard*, Frankfurt am Main: Dt Filmmuseum, 1989, pp.11–14; and Alan Bergela's reading in 'The Other Side at the Bouquet', in Raymond Bellour and Mary Lea Bandy (eds.), *Jean-Luc Godard: Son+Image 1974–91*, New York: Museum of Modern Art, 1992, pp.60–65.

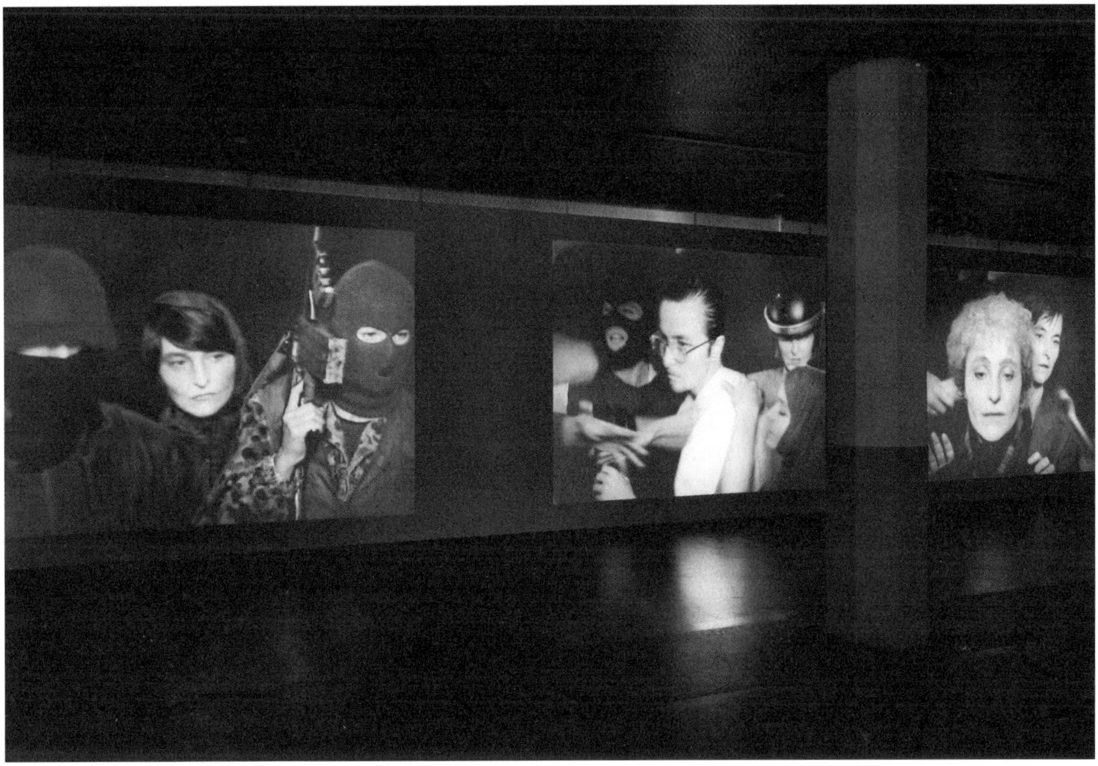

While such performance of frozen time is not entirely unfamiliar—one encounters it in major metropolitan centres, for example, in the form of mimes striking the motionless poses of classical statues in hopes of inspiring passer-by donations—the stasis invoked in such touristic theatricality is almost always specifically and unmistakably beaux arts in character. As such, it is at first glance quite similar in its art historical intertextuality to the staging of Rembrandt's *Night Watch* in Godard's 1982 film *Passion*—there a sculpture, here a historical painting.[1]

Godard's cinematic *tableau vivant* is further complicated, however, by the fact that its production is itself rendered diegetically as a media event, i.e. it is presented as a scene being shot in a movie studio as part of a film in the making. Leaving aside the amusing genre auto-referentiality of this 'art film'-within-an-'art film' structure, what is of interest in this context is the fact that the cinematic rendering of the painting—the mediatic *mis-en-scène* of a canvas—fundamentally *changes* its conditions. Exploiting the painting's theatrical configuration as a narrative space, Godard's photographic/cinematic recasting of the *tableau vivant* imposes on the familiar subject matter an *hors cadre* which the canvas never had, and offers the spectator, by means of camera movement, previously 'unavailable' points of view from within the assembled mass. As Joachim Paech has argued in his extensive work on this scene, 'the film's moving image dynamizes the represented space and *expands it*, in the manner of a theatrical stage, so that it also includes an invisible (back-stage) space [...]'[2] Read media-historically, this rendering of the *Nightwatch* as

Ute Friederike Jürss, *You Never Know the Whole Story*, ZKM, Karlsruhe, 2000. Installation view. Photo © 2008 Volker Naumann

a diegetic space which can be traversed both by the camera and by the tableau 'characters' themselves is, as such, a form of intermedial trumping, exploiting the dynamics of cinematic narrative to 'play out' the painting in a manner that both profits from the significant cultural cachet of the famous canvas while simultaneously retroactively recasting its stasis as profilmic (in the sense that the photographic is always capable of being subjected to post-factum 'extrapolation' or 'expansion').

This all-too familiar gesture seems strikingly absent in the Jürss projections which do not seem to exploit the temporal capacities of video to elaborate upon, or render narrationally dynamic, the stasis of the still journalistic images which they invoke (in the manner, to take a familiar example, of Oliver Stone's 1991 film *JFK*). This comparative *lack* of movement stems not least from the important difference in the respective media intertexts: because *pace Laocoön,* unlike both sculpture and painting, the news photograph is itself already *qua snapshot* an image of frozen time *by virtue of its very conditions of production*, its iconographic invocation by the *tableau vivant* is itself already a theatricalisation of an instant that was previously part of a temporal continuum which it always already implies *in and through its stasis.* At first glance — an initial take that by now we have learned (rightly) to distrust — this would seem to imply that the intermedial dynamic staged by the Jürss projections is both different from — and also similar to — the one staged in Godard's *Passion*: different, in the way that cinema recasting painting is different from video recasting photography; similar in that they seem to share both a temporal vector (newer media commenting on older ones) and the ultimately theatrical means employed. Unless of course the theatricality of the video re-staging of the photo-chemical images is not as simply thespian as it appears to be.

Indeed, given the questions of time raised by the specifically photographic media intertext in the Jürss projections (i.e. the iconographic invocation of the news photograph), they may well be better compared, both in terms of their formal constituents and their complex rhetorical strategies, with some of the concurrent work by the Belgian video artist David Claerbout. The affinity between the work of these two contemporaries is most evident in Claerbout's 1997 video installation *Ruurlo Bocurloscheweg, 1910*, whose title names the location and year of production of the 'vintage' photograph which serves at some level as the basis of this silent black-and-white big screen projection. Even simpler than the Jürss projections at first glance, this installation seems to be just a video of an auratic photographed landscape, an exploration of the comparative patinas of sepia-toned early photo-chemicality and contemporary digital video projection. As one studies the image and the tiny figures that populate its bucolic Dutch country scene complete with the *de rigeur* windmill, one is suddenly struck by the fact that the leaves of the large tree that dominates the composition are very subtly, but unmistakably, blowing in the wind. Cued by this unexpected dynamic feature to revise one's assumptions about the media genre of image — and recalling Claerbout's 1997

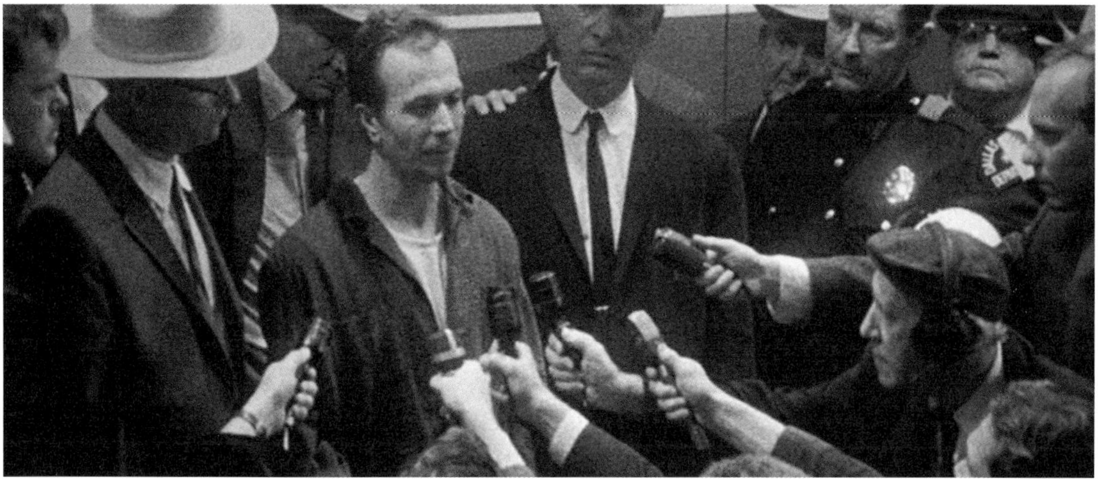

video projection *Tree* which is a 20-minute 'real time' silent Hi8 colour film of the aleatoric movements of a voluptuous tree's branches in the wind — one scans *Ruurlo Bocurloscheweg, 1910* for further evidence of its status as a film, rather than a photograph. But this micrological search for semiotic identity is in vain, since the only thing that moves in the otherwise decidedly still projection is the tree. This is disconcerting in that it violates what we now recognise is a key assumption about photo-chemically based media: *the semiotic homogeneity of their signifying surface.*

What we are seeing, it turns out, is an 'animated photograph', a video projection of a semiotic hybrid consisting of an old photo-chemical image in which one of the central elements has been subjected to the animatronic magic of digital post-production. This incursion into the field of the image, the introduction of movement into the otherwise uniformly static temporality of the photograph, complicates it enormously: the moving leaves, as a readable trace of a 'post-production' intervention, throw into question the ostensible 'reliability' of the photo-chemical indexicality of the photographic image as such. This in turn has a corrosive effect on our reading of the remainder of the image whose referential claims now seem curiously undermined. How do we know that other elements, while still, have not also been subjected to a similar — even if not animated — post-factum digital revision? But this doubt, while it has haunted photography in some form since its inception, is now more than ever *the* semiotic anxiety of the current transitional media-historical moment, marked as it is by the increasing affordability, sophistication and proliferation of digital imaging in the domains of both photography and cinema. Indeed Claerbout's installation points in a particularly efficient manner to what Lev Manovich has called the increasing 'modularity' of contemporary media practices, i.e. the construction of images out of discrete and potentially semiotically very different signifying parts or 'modules'. While hardly new as a technique — one need only recall Stellan Rye's 1913 *Der Student von Prag*, The ur-*Doppelgänger* film in which the hero Balduin constantly encounters his uncannily autonomous — optically composited — mirror

Oliver Stone, still from *JFK*, 1991. 35mm black-and-white and colour film, sound, 189mins

image, both of whom are played by Paul Wegener[3] — modular compositing has increasingly become *the* paradigmatic logic of early twenty-first century media.[4]

Attuned by Claerbout's *Ruurlo Bocurloscheweg, 1910* to the potential complexities involved in video recastings of photographs, one re-examines the theatricality of the mediatic *tableaux vivants* in the Jürss installations. Just as, in *Ruurlo Bocurloscheweg, 1910*, it was the barely visible, silent rustling of the leaves that alerted us to that installation's media hybridity, in Jürss's projections it is the rather odd, ever-so slight, silent bobbing of the limbs and poses as they are held over the course of a ten-minute loop that suddenly seems to call out for further interrogation. The most unambiguous, foregrounded and polysemic element of this economy of subtle movement — whose first effect is to undermine the assumption that we are watching a still image — is, of course, the blinking of the eyes. In each of the Jürss projections at least one of the central characters clearly blinks, albeit at irregular intervals that suggest a wilful resistance to the regularity of the normal somatic urge and, as such, deprive the viewer of what could have been a reliable bodily index of elapsed time. This ocular movement also simultaneously invokes a well-known media-historical intertext in which the same gesture plays a very similar and crucially media-disambiguating role: this scene is, needless to say, in Chris Marker's *La Jetée*, that seminal celluloid experiment of 1962 whose rigorous reduction to a series of black-and-white stills poses in a most efficient manner André Bazin's famous question: 'qu'est-ce que c'est le cinema?' The one and only point in the entire film where *La Jetée* violates its own static formal constraint is the magic moment when the (phantasmatic?) slumbering female object of mnemonic desire suddenly and oh-so subtly — indeed, one must make a point of attending to it or else one is unsure of whether it actually took place — seems to awaken and return the (viewer's?) gaze. To the extent that this barely visible transition from the 'still' to the 'full-motion' image — which is to say, from one logic of stills to another — is readable, it is so thanks to the fact that after opening her eyes,

3 See Helmut H. Diederichs, *Der Student von Prag: Einführung und Protokoll*, Stuttgart: Verlagsgemeinschaft Fischer, Kress, Wiedleroither, 1985. The important link between the narrative possibilities of compositing and both the legitimation and profitability of the new cinematic medium as an 'art' are best captured by the scriptwriter Hans Heinz Ewers who observed in 1925 that *Der Student von Prague* 'was a thoroughly extraordinary success not only for Germany but worldwide. It was the first artistic film ever. I had clearly proven to the critics, artists and the audience that one could make art out of film — and also provided the no less important proof to the film industry that one could make lots of money with art on film.' (Hans Heinz Ewers, 'Anfänge des Films', 1925), reprinted in *Hätte ich das Kino! Die Schriffsteller und der Stummfilm*, Marbach/N., 1976, p.106.) On the question of the double, see also Heide Schlüpmann, 'Je suis la solitude. Zum Doppelgängermotiv in Der Student von Prag', *Frauen und Film* 36, February 1984, pp.10–24.

4 See Lev Manovich, 'What is Digital Cinema?' in Peter Lunenfeld (ed.), *The Digital Dialectic: New Essays on New Media*, Cambridge, Mass.: The MIT Press, 1999, pp.173–92; this text is one of numerous excerpts from Manovich's book *The Language of New Media*, Cambridge, Mass.: The MIT Press, 2001.

5 Indeed, the blink is a rather remarkably polysemic gesture: a bodily gesture that recalls the condition of possibility of the cinema's illusionary production of an effect of motion (i.e. the hiatus between one image and another that requires a very brief closure of the projection apparatus such that the film can advance to the next image without the movement of the celluloid being seen as such), it is also the brief break between two instances of seeing, an automatic *techne* of topical moisture refreshment for the somatic visual apparatus, a moment of blindness — possibly phenomenologically different from a narcoleptic interlude only in degree, not kind — that effectively makes the continuum of so-called 'real time' into a series of discrete instants, punctuated by almost invisible but at some level constitutive interruptions.

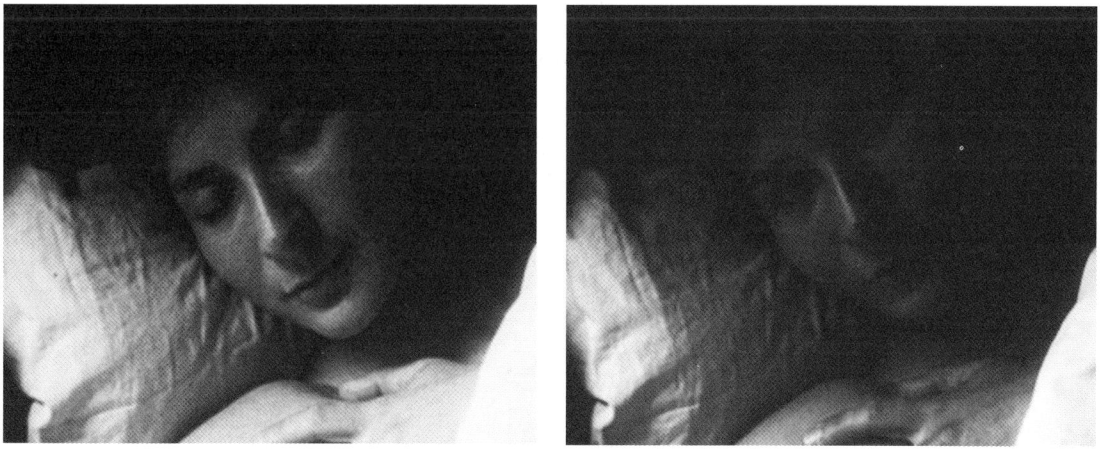

the woman clearly and repeatedly blinks. It is thus the very same gesture whose colloquial meaning is (understandably) akin to instantaneity ('in a blink') whose rapid repetition here functions as a very efficient signifier of extended or so-called 'real' cinematic time.[5] In the Jürss projections, the blinks seem to have a similar function, 'exposing' the temporal dimension of the theatrical *mise-en-scène*—unless of course a blink means something fundamentally different in cinema than in video. And it does.

Besides the important—indeed essential—automatic quotidian functioning of the blink in what one could call 'background mode', this ocular gesture can also serve various sorts of signifying functions when it is read as invested with a modicum of agency. This sort of signifying (because intentional) blinking could well be what we see in both Marker's film and Jürss's projections: in the former, the wakened sleeping beauty blinks with a 'fluttering' rapidity that one is tempted to read as a sort of flirtatious modesty, while the blinks in the Jürss projections, despite (or perhaps precisely because of) the clear effort to keep their number to an absolute minimum, are so clearly manifest when they do occur that they could be read as a double-eyed version of the ironic variant of the blink known as the wink. But if the wink signals that something 'is up', if it lets us in on the joke, or registers the fact that wherever it is invoked what is going on ought not be taken at face value—something of the order of 'get it?'—one wonders what exactly there is to 'get' in the Jürss projections? Cued by this question to re-examine the projection for what previously may have been taken at face value, one returns to what one had already registered as the strangeness of the projection's depth effect, recognising now why this oddly excessive and yet discontinuous recessionality seems somehow so familiar: it is the very same effect that characterises that hugely popular, late-nineteenth-century virtual reality technology—the stereoscopic image. Because such '3-D' photographs are only possible thanks to the difference 'between' their parallax-shifted twin images, and only actually arise in the act of their 'synthesis' by a viewer, the perceptual experience characteristic of the stereoscopic illusion is, as Jonathan Crary has so insightfully described it, 'essentially an apprehension

Chris Marker, stills from *La Jetée* (*The Pier*), 1962. 35mm black-and-white film, sound, 28mins

of differences; the relation of the observer to the object is not one of identity but an experience of disjunct or divergent images'.[6] While this synthetic perception produces a powerful illusion of depth, this virtual depth is further marked by a very characteristic uncanniness due to the fact that the space between the foreground, middle and background planes is essentially absent. Because the recession in the virtual space of stereoscopic illusion is effectively discontinuous, this simulated depth could be said to be haunted by a series of voids. Despite the powerful capacity of spectatorial disavowal to overlook such discrepancies, this quality was already registered in the late-nineteenth century and may well, so Crary speculates, have been responsible for the ultimate demise of the stereoscopic craze.

What is suggested by the formal similarity of the uncanniness of early stereoscopic virtuality and that of the Jürss projections is that, like the former, the latter are also the product of a synthetic depth-effect. Having been sensitised by the 'wink' to question what one had taken at face value — for example, the value of the faces on the screen — one takes a closer look at the figures comprising the *tableau vivant* only to discover that, despite the superficial differences in appearance and costume, the fundamental physiognomy of every one of the 'characters' is in fact the same. As it dawns on one that all the figures in the *tableau vivant* are in fact the same person, it becomes clear that what *appears* in the projection as visually simultaneous is in fact of necessity the product of a series of temporally *sequential* takes subsequently integrated into one image. Just as stereoscopic virtuality is generated by means of the spectatorial synthesis of the two *spatially* non-congruent (but temporally simultaneous) still images, the virtuality of Jürss's projections is produced by the post-production synthesis of a number of *temporally* distinct (but spatially integrated) barely moving-image fragments. Thus the fundamental assumption of the spatio-temporal homogeneity of the signifying field which was undermined by the Claerbout projections with regard to the photograph is here being thrown into doubt with regard to the recorded video image. Just as the assumed semiotic homogeneity of the photograph was a function of the mistaken presumption that the indexicality of its photo-chemical basis necessarily pertained across the entirety of the image's surface, so too the assumed semiotic homogeneity of the Jürss projections is a function of the mistaken presumption of the necessary spatial and temporal coherence of the moving video image. The Jürss projections are thus fundamentally marked by what one could call the condition of *semiotic hybridity*: Despite the seeming coherence of their visual fields, they are in fact thoroughly fractured both spatially (the constellation of figures that we see never occupied a shared space) and temporally (every one of the different figures was recorded at a different time). Since every figure in each of the Jürss

6 Jonathan Crary, *Techniques of the Observer: On Vision and Modernity in the Nineteenth Century*, Cambridge, Mass.: The MIT Press, 1990, p.120.

projections is also none other than the artist herself, the installation also could be said to recast Cindy Sherman's mobilisation of narcissistic masquerade as a means of restaging media genres. What Jürss has done is to displace the *physical* seriality of Sherman's film stills onto the *temporal* seriality of the production of the composite video *slices* that constitute the different component figures of each projection.

To get a sense of the specificity of what is at stake here, it may be useful to compare the projections to another (slightly older) set of examples from the iconographic tradition of the self-portrait-as-multiple. Consider first the 1917 photograph which Marcel Duchamp took of himself in front of a hinged mirror; here the prismatic multiplicity is still entirely pro-filmic in the sense that the image is a spatio-temporally coherent photograph of Duchamp and a series of his actual, optical reflections. Contrast this with the later press photograph of a superimposed series of time-lapse images of Duchamp descending a staircase: here the temporal hybridity is clearly readable as a visual condensation of the sequential Muybridgean/Mareyian technique which Duchamp openly credited as a key intertext for the well-known oil canvas which the photograph invokes. In both cases the threat posed by the image of the multiple self—which is emphasised by the fact that Duchamp is recognisably the same in each of his iterations—seems mitigated today (although it may not have been at the time) by a more-or-less readable production narrative (optical reflection of the mirror in the former; time-lapse photography in the latter). As a result, both images can be said to have a certain spatio-temporal homogeneity: Duchamp in front of a mirror = homogeneity of place and time; Duchamp descending the stairs = homogeneity of place (the visibly constant stairs) and an intelligible relationality of time (a temporal multiplicity that is comprehensible because both linear and uniformly sequential). The Jürss projections stand in stark contrast to both these images first and foremost because, unlike Duchamp, whose multiple appearances are readably identical, Jürss appears multiply but always *as an other*. As a result, unlike the 1917 Duchamp self-portrait which appears to be a composite montage but is not, the Jürss projections do not appear to be composite images but are; and if the composite nature of the later Duchamp image is readable in its linearity, the composite nature of the sequentiality as contiguity (*nacheinander nebeneinander*) logic of the Jürss projections, even when recognised as such, remains entirely inscrutable.

This dynamic of readable versus unreadable compositing is, of course, also the hallmark of the domain in which such techniques are most widely used today—big-budget commercial cinema. Given the large number of feature films that depend on both spectacular and very mundane 'special effects' to construct their narrative spaces, it is hardly surprising to learn that the technical means used to create the simulated recessional space in the Jürss projections (the *Inferno* programme) is in fact a staple of high-end Hollywood post-production studios. In general, this sort of programme operates 'invisibly', serving as a means of erasing the visible traces of the material conditions of possibility of spectacular cinematic feats such as — to take a well-known example — the guy-wires that supported the actors during their gravity-defying leaps in *The Matrix* (Andy and Larry Wachowski, 1999). Since the final cinematic product bears no traces of the post-production incursions — except, perhaps, the sheer spectacularity of the effects themselves — this would seem to have consequences for the referential status of the cinematic image, to the extent that its reality-effect is based on the presumed indexicality of its photographic basis. Indeed post-production interventions play a central role in fuelling Baudrillardian anxiety about the referentiality of images in the age of their digital simulatability — as is evident in everything from the resurgent pro-filmic piety of the Dogma 95 credo to the Joel Schumacher film *8mm* (1999) whose central narrative concern — to establish whether a reel of small-guage film is in fact 'really' the snuff film it purports to be — is nothing more and nothing less than the question of celluloid referentiality (which the film of course fully confirms). The referential drama of modular compositing is perhaps rendered most explicitly in the memorable scene from Barry Levinson's 1997 film *Wag the Dog* where we are shown the 'blue screen' mechanics of how to fabricate a pathos-invoking television 'news' image of an 'ongoing conflict' that never took place. This diegetic foregrounding of the simulational capacities of digital special effects is only possible, however, because the epistemic consequences are shifted away from cinema and onto television: in a classic instance of the dynamic of intermedial displacement, cinema here 'exposes' the truth about TV and thereby seems somehow free of such 'manipulation'. But of course, it isn't — a fact that, curiously enough, an increasing number of contemporary films have begun not only to admit, but to celebrate. Indeed, while post-production effects are usually rendered invisible in the final cut, in a striking development of great theoretical interest in this context, the semiotic hybridity of digital post-production effects has become a central, indeed a *foregrounded* feature in a number of films from *The Adventures of Rocky and Bullwinkle* (Des McAnuff, 2000) to *King Kong* (Peter Jackson, 2005) and *Speed Racer* (Andy and Larry Wachowski, 2008).

Of course the cinematic spectacle of *readable special effects* is neither new nor in any way exclusively a function of digital post-production; in fact, one can trace the principles of mechanical image compositing back at least to the proto-cinematic optical devices such as the Thaumatrope from the early-nineteenth century and the pioneering cinematic wizardry of Georges Méliès and Ferdinand Zecca from the late nineteenth/early-twentieth century.[7] Indeed, almost one-hundred-years later, the practice of foregrounded visual devices — as manifested so charmingly, for example, in *Who Framed Roger*

7 Invented by Dr. William Henry Fitton in 1826, the Thaumatrope consisted of a cardboard disc with two different images on each of its faces; when spun on the string attached to its two sides, the persistence of vision effect produced a momentary but compelling perceptual synthesis of the images (for example, a bird and a cage).

8 On the technical aspects of the post-production in *Who Framed Roger Rabbit?*, see Mark JP Wolf, 'In the Frame of Roger Rabbit: Visual Compositing in Film', *The Velvet Light Trap* 36, Fall 1995, pp.45–59.

9 See L. Manovich, 'What is Digital Cinema?', *op. cit.*, pp.175 and 180.

10 The media hybridity of the Disney film *Dinosaur* (Eric Leighton and Ralph Zondag, 2000), in which hyper-realist computer graphic renderings

Rabbit? (Robert Zemeckis, 1988) — still invokes this early cinema genealogy in its celebration of what one could call a cinema of composite attractions. Far from the use of technical devices to heighten some sort of 'reality-effect', here the animated central figure and his 'live-action' environment are clearly and rigorously distinguished as a condition of possibility of the film's key conceit — the seamless interaction of two media-epistemically distinct spaces. However, while the semiotic hybridity of *Roger Rabbit* — a film which was unprecedented at the time both in the sheer number of composites (1031) and its extremely complex use of camera movement[8] — depends on the readable distinction between the domains of animation and live-action cinema, any threat to the latter's status which this might pose is contained by the fact that these two semiotic economies are hardly weighted equally: with the exception of the opening, which begins in the animated 'world' and then pulls back to 'reveal' the 'real world' of live-action, at every point the optically composited animation *inhabits* the live-action space whose traditional status as narrative space, as the semiotic *frame* or ground, is thereby maintained entirely intact.

It is this longstanding subordination of animation to live-action which is irrevocably reversed with the advent of digital imaging: once all images — whether animated or live action — can be artisanally manipulated, then, as Manovich has put it, 'cinema can no longer be clearly distinguished from animation' and digital cinema becomes defined as 'a particular case of animation that uses live-action footage as one of its many elements'.[9] Cinema is born out of animation, disavows it and then finally, a century after its birth as a medium, becomes a subset of it. In this light it is tempting to read the continued proliferation of reassuringly readable media hybrids such as *Space Jam* (Joe Pytka, 1996) and *Rocky and Bullwinkle* in which a foregrounded — although now digitally instead of optically composited — semiotic hybridity clearly subordinates the — albeit now digitally produced — animation to the live-action, as a nostalgic yearning for a bygone cinematic episteme in which the photographic had not yet been relegated to the status of a subset of a more general *graphic* digital media condition.[10]

Equally foregrounded in its readable semiotic hybridity, yet different in the specificity of its means, is the *tour-de-force* of thespian genius and post-production effects in Eddie Murphy's 1996 and 2000 revisitings of the *Nutty Professor* topos. In both films, and in his more recent iteration of the same topos in *Norbit* (Brian Robbins, 2007), Murphy simultaneously plays a wide range of different characters (fat/thin, male/female, young/old, etc.) many of whom appear together in the same scene — another instance of the multiplicity of self as 'other' (and a powerful corporeal materialisation of

of ur-creatures are inserted more-or-less seamlessly into a vast range of photographed environments shot at exotic locations around the world, is importantly different yet still entirely readable. While not foregrounded as animations, the animatronic constructions are recognisable as the technical wonders that they are both through a simple plausibility inference (dinosaurs were not around to be photographed) and because of the cheesy anthropomorphisation. Nevertheless, the combination of the clearly digital fabrications and seemingly referential spaces (the length of the list of location sites almost seems like an overcompensation) makes it often hard to decide on the status of what one is seeing — the result being a media-historically new form of *Unheimlichkeit* [the uncanny].

W.E.B. DuBois's theorisation of the double consciousness of the black man).[11] Such on-screen doubling (which deserves more extensive treatment than is possible here) is of course a longstanding cinematic phenomenon that ranges across various genres and periods and includes — besides the German *Doppelgänger* movies of the teens and 20s mentioned above — films such as *Sherlock Jr.* (Buster Keaton, 1924), *Meshes of the Afternoon* (Maya Deren, 1943), *The Parent Trap* (David Swift, 1961), *Futureworld* (Richard T. Heffron, 1976), *Dead Ringers* (David Cronenberg, 1988), *Double Impact* (Sheldon Lettich 1991) and *Timecop* (Peter Hyams, 1994). The semiotic hybridity which is their shared hallmark, however, is no longer intermedial (as in the animation/live-action contrast of *Space Jam* and *Roger Rabbit*) but resides entirely *within the domain of the (post-)photographic itself* and is readable to the extent that the spectator can 'recognise' Eddie Murphy in all his various guises. What this means is that, much like the Jürss projections, the hybridity of the *Nutty Professor* films is a function of the *heterochronicity* — i.e. multiple temporalities — of its images: the media-savvy audience sees Murphy's various characters interacting 'with' each other even as it realises that the rendering of these various figures *must* have taken place in temporally sequential episodes, i.e. one 'after' another. Thus the fascination of such composite multiplicity at some level resides in its presentation of temporal sequentiality as visual simultaneity in a manner structurally analogous to the acoustic phenomenon of overdubbing, where one singer performs all instruments, or sings all the parts of a multi-part harmony: listening to the final product we hear as a phenomenal simultaneity a sound whose condition of production was entirely of the order of sequentiality. On the one hand, compared to *Roger Rabbit*, the *Nutty Professor* films appear thoroughly semiotically homogenous in their live-action even though, on the other hand, the apparent seamlessness of what one could call their heterodox polyindexicality is entirely a function of digital post-production effects.[12]

How then is one to read images assembled out of multiple and discontinuous photographic zones? Such poly-photographic constructs certainly no longer function simply like a photograph (not that a photograph ever functioned simply, which it surely didn't): the foregrounded artisanality of their production (i.e. the fact that the production and coordination of the various post-production elements requires a complex technical and thus also intentional intervention) replaces the ostensibly 'simply mechanical' conditions (which were never simply mechanical) governing the production of the 'traditional' photograph with a renewed emphasis on artistic agency (expression instead of simply reproduction). One can also point to another more reflexive quality of this readable photo-hybridity, an almost neo-Brechtian formalist foregrounding of their constructedness of the sort

11 See W.E.B. DuBois, *The Souls of Black Folk* (1903), New York: Dodd and Mead, 1979.

12 Of course, not all forms of heterochronicity are the product of post-production, as is evident, for example, in *The Kid* (Jon Turteltaub, 2000), a Disney film released at almost the same time as *Nutty Professor II*, in which a white man (who works as an 'image manager'), also confronts himself as 'other', but here it is himself as a child (i.e. a diegetic heterochronicity).

13 See David N. Rodowick, *The Crisis of Political Modernism: Criticism and Ideology in Contemporary Film Theory* (1988), reprinted by Berkeley: University of California Press, 1994.

celebrated in 1970s modernist political cinema and film theory.[13] Of course neither of these takes explain much about how the *Nutty Professor* films function in terms of their popular reception: in fact, thanks to the powerful effects of their very classically narrative flow (and the remarkable capacities of disavowal), both of these Hollywood cinematic spectacles operate much like they always have — and seemingly despite their clearly foregrounded heterochronic character. This is due, at some level, to the fact that the temporal structure of the photograph as such was, in a sense, always already heterochronic, simultaneously combining, as Roland Barthes once noted, a 'there-then' (the moment of the photograph's genesis) and a 'here-now' (the moment of its reception). The 'reality effect' of the moving cinematic image, in turn, is a function not only of the indexical and iconic character of its (heterochronic) photograms but also — indeed even more so — of the rhetorics of its temporality. This explains why the heterochronicity of an image containing Eddie Murphy as various characters does not in itself undermine the 'reality effect' of a masterfully edited Hollywood narrative production.

As Thomas Elsaesser has put it: 'vision is only part of what makes the moving image "real" to a viewer, so that the question one needs to ask is not so much whether the digitised image severs the link between the material trace of the real in the photograph and its power to resemble the real, but how digitisation might affect the time-space relations for the viewer, and thereby the "tense" of the image.'[14] And it is precisely through a decidedly noticeable shift in the *tense* of the cinematic image towards a temporality of so-called 'real time' that one can track the rhetorical consequences of the proliferation of digital imaging. What the general undermining of the status of photo-chemical indexicality means is thus not simply, as Manovich claims, that cinema is 'no longer an indexical media technology',[15] but rather that *the locus of its indexical foundation has changed*, shifting away from the now increasingly unreliable referentiality of the *image* to the increasingly indexically invested domain of ostensibly un-edited, 'instantaneous' or 'real' *time.* From the striking proliferation of films such as *The Truman Show* (Peter Weir, 1998), *Caché* (Michael Haneke, 2005) and *Deja Vu* (Tony Scott, 2006) in which surveillance is not only a thematic focus but also informs the narrative structure itself, to the explosion of so-called 'reality TV' shows such as *Real World* and *Big Brother*, there is increasing evidence of a new aesthetics of surveillant indexicality whose 'authenticity' is a function of the absence of any intervening agency supposedly guaranteed by the *instantaneity* of its technical conditions of production (the same quality previously attributed to the photo-chemical iconico-indexicality of the image). While I have examined some of the issues involved in this development at greater length elsewhere,[16] what is of particular

14 Thomas Elsaesser, 'Digital Cinema: Delivery, Event, Time', in Thomas Elsaesser and Kay Hoffmann (eds.), *Cinema Futures: Cain, Abel or Cable?*, Amsterdam: Amsterdam University Press, 1998, p.209.

15 See L. Manovich, 'What is Digital Cinema?', *op. cit.*, p.175.

16 See, for example, my essay 'Rhetoric of the Temporal Index: Surveillant Narration and the Cinema of "Real Time"' in Thomas Y. Levin et. al., *CTRL [Space]. Rhetorics of Surveillance from Bentham to Big Brother* (Cambridge, Mass.: The MIT Press, 2002): pp.578–593.

interest in this context is how this new temporal economy of the 'live' image also serves to contain and render palatable significant levels of semiotic hybridity. This is already evident, for example, at various points in Phillip Noyce's 1993 classic of panoptical cinema titled *Sliver* which takes place in a high-class Manhattan high-rise that, unbeknownst to the dwellers, has been completely wired for continuous, remote PTZ (pan-tilt and zoom) surveillance of their private domestic lives. At one point early on, the evil surveillant yuppie is walking down a street with the heroine when he comes across a store window with a closed-circuit video camera and monitor which he immediately employs (symptomatically) as a means to speak 'to' her. The image of him and his 'real-time' double is a diegetic surveillant recasting not only of the classic reverse-shot but also of the image of the multiple self which, emptied of its post-production heterochronicity, now reads like a technologically updated version of the photograph of Duchamp and his reflections in the hinged mirror — with 'live' video transmission replacing the mirrored reflections.[17]

Even more striking as a feature-length example of the shift from visual to temporal indexicality (and of the capacity of the latter to contain foregrounded semiotic hybridity) is Mike Figgis's remarkable film *Time Code* (2000). Dividing the screen permanently into four 'real time' quadrants each of which contains a more-or-less autonomous narrative — a formal invocation of the by-now familiar iconography of the classic surveillance set-up — the film was constructed using, as the publicity materials announce: '4 cameras. No edits. Real time.' At 3pm on 19 November 1999, so the final credits explain, four cameramen started their synchronised digital video cameras and each followed one of the four central characters (or character groups) who, over the course of the next uninterrupted 90 minutes, encounter each other both acoustically (cell-phone/audio surveillance) and visually in ways that often link — and sometimes briefly merge — some of their respective quadrants. The product of this remarkable choreography of real-time camerawork and semi-improvised acting — effectively a new (literal) take on the hackneyed 'docu-drama' genre — is a spectacular excess of visual information. While one's ocular attention is at some level guided by the soundtrack whose shifting volume levels across the quadrants cue the viewer as to which is narrationally salient at any given moment, the film as a whole nevertheless remains thoroughly and deliciously overwhelming. You never, as it were, know the whole story. In a curious recasting of Bazin's argument about the 'truth' of long take, however, *Time Code*'s unambiguous celebration of semiotic excess is explicitly justified as a new form of realism, in contrast to the 'fake reality' supposedly created by the 'distorting' selectivity of montage. Despite (or perhaps because of) the seemingly heterochronic character of its more-or-less independent digital-video quadrants — a visual challenge even for graduates of the spectatorial

17 The same diegeticisation of post-production by means of a pro-filmic monitor is also evident in the effect-intensive first *Nutty Professor* film where, for example, the rotund professor to his surprise encounters himself in his more slender gestalt via a video gone amok.

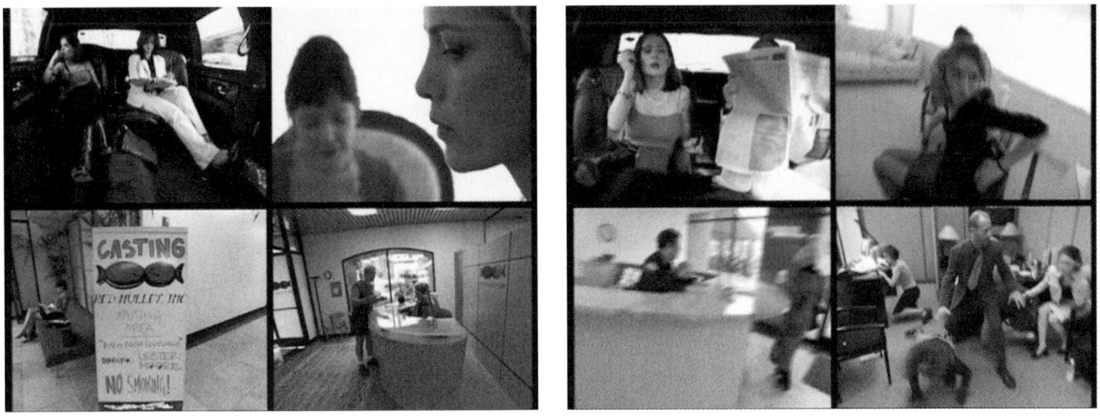

Mike Figgis, stills from *Time Code*, 2000. 35mm colour film, sound, 97mins

boot camp of MTV hyper-montage — *Time Code*'s realist claims are based, as the film's publicity materials never fail to remind us, on the unprecedented *temporal* coherence of its conditions of production: 'For the first time, a film shot in real time' boasts the slick website at www.sony.com/timecode. The film's very title not only invokes the technical means employed to achieve the 'sync' of sound and image (and, in this case, of image and image as well); it also points to the fact that here time is the key, or code, to both the multi-tasking challenge posed by the four images and their coherence as a quartet.

The challenge, of course, is how to make the conceit of a supposedly synchronous 'real time' *visible* within the film's own formal constraints, i.e. how to convey the ostensible *homo*chronicity of the four thoroughly independent images employed to relate the quotidian drama of Hollywood studio life which is the film's satirical reflexive narrative. Within each quadrant, *Time Code* takes up the signature jerky, hand-held camerawork of a visual rhetoric that one could call strategic dilettantism which had already been explored in earlier dramatic appropriations of the *cinema-vérité* idiom such as *David Holtzman's Diary* (Jim McBride, 1970) and, more recently, the *Blair Witch Project* (Daniel Myrick & Eduardo Sanchez, 1999). But in order to extend the 'authenticity of unprofessionalism' across the four quadrants in such a way that they are unequivocally foregrounded as being *in sync*, *Time Code* must push even further this willful appropriation of the shaky image that was for so long both the bane of Hollywood professionalism (witness the imperative of the Steadicam), and the hallmark of *cinema-vérité* anti-professionalist 'authenticity'. The result is a rather ingenious geographically motivated variant: given that *Time Code* is 'set' in Southern California, it is not entirely surprising when, at various random points during the multi-camera docu-diegesis, an earthquake 'occurs' and, consequently, *all four of its images shake.* It is this 'docu-diegetic' trembling, a sudden quivering that convulses the entire screen, freezing everyone in their tracks in response to the momentary recognition of the fragility of their (terrestrial) ground, that periodically re-establishes the temporal homogeneity of this quartered carnival of semiotic superabundance. 'Real-time' synchronicity is manifested, in other words, by literally shaking the very images themselves. That is, in order for *Time Code* to establish *visually* the *temporal* homogeneity that governs its otherwise visually disparate images, in order for it to stage something akin to temporal *stability,* the film must invoke fundamental *instability*—both the instability of the fundament (the quaking earth) and the instability of the signifier itself (the shaking image).

It is this very same gesture—which Werner Hamacher has called 'das Beben der Darstellung' (the quaking of presentation)[18]—that, in an admittedly more subtle manner than discussed above, also marks the Jürss projections. Unlike *Time Code,* however, where the hybridity of the constitutive quadrants is very readable and the equally foregrounded shaking across the disparate fields serves to emphasise their (temporal) *homogeneity,* in the Jürss projections the hybridity of the constitutive slices is largely *un*readable and the comparatively minimal yet still noticeable movement of the static figures serves, upon closer analysis, to signal their *heterogeneity.* But it does so precisely because it refuses the very economy of movement, of action, whose temporal character effectively serves to occlude the readability of post-production heterochronicity or other sorts of semiotic hybridity. This is why it is so crucial that we see the blinking in the Jürss projections, that we experience the quivering in their stillness: for it is through this rigorous staging of stasis *in time* that they expose the suturing rhetorics of 'real' time, of temporal indexicality, as the new regime of motivated signification. In the age of digital imaging—i.e. at the moment when Barthes's punctum has become a pixel—the insistence of the Jürss projections that one never knows the whole story may well be because there never was a whole about which a/the story could have been known. But if previously it was the rhetorics of photo-chemical indexicality that helped maintain the fiction of the possibility of both that story and that whole, then now, at a juncture when the rhetorics of indexicality have become more temporal than visual, it may well require a trio of quivering heterochronic projections to tell the 'you never know the whole' story.

18 Werner Hamacher, 'The Quaking of Presentation: Kleist's "Earthquake in Chile"', *Premises* (trans. Peter Fenves), Cambridge, Mass.: Harvard Univ. Press, 1996, pp.261–293. I am very grateful to Deborah Esch (Toronto) for kindly calling my attention to this text in this context.

About the Authors

Giorgio Agamben is Professor of Aesthetics at the University of Verona, Italy. He also teaches philosophy at the Collège International de Philosophie in Paris and at the University of Macerata in Italy. He has published a large number of books on philosophy, political theory and art, including *Homo Sacer: Sovereign Power and Bare Life* (Giulio Einuadi, 1995; Stanford University Press, 1998) and *Infancy and History: On the Destruction of Experience* (Verso, 2007).

Alexander Alberro is Associate Professor of Art History at the University of Florida, Gainesville. He is the author of *Conceptual Art and the Politics of Publicity* (The MIT Press, 2003). He is the editor of *Two-Way Mirror Power: Selected Writings by Dan Graham on His Art* (The MIT Press, 1999) and *Museum Highlights: Selected Writings on Andrea Fraser* (The MIT Press, 2005), and co-editor of *Art After Conceptual Art* (The MIT Press/Generali Foundation, 2006; with Sabeth Buchmann) and *Conceptual Art: A Critical Anthology* (The MIT Press, 2000; with Blake Stimson).

Raymond Bellour is Director of Research Emeritus at the Centre National de la Recherche Scientifique in Paris. He was one of the founders of the French film review *Trafic*. He is the author of many publications on film, video and new media, including *The Analysis of Film* (Albatros, 1979; Calmann-Lévy, 1996), *L'Entre-Images* (La Différence, 1990) and *L'Entre-images 2* (P.O.L., 1999). He is the editor of *Jean-Luc Godard: Son + Image, 1974–1991* (The Museum of Modern Art, 1992) and the complete works of Henri Michaux (La Pléiade/Gallimard, 1998–2004). He was co-curator, with Christine Van Assche and Catherine David, of the 'Passages de l'image' exhibition at the Centre Georges Pompidou in 1990.

Elizabeth Bennett Hupp is a PhD candidate in the History of Art department at the University of California, Berkeley.

Christa Blümlinger is Senior Lecturer in cinema studies at the Université de la Sorbonne Nouvelle, Paris. Her most recent books include *Von der Welt ins Bild. Augenzeugenberichte eines Cinephilen* (Vorwerk 8 Verlag, 2000 – an edition of writings by Serge Daney), *Das Gesicht im Zeitalter des bewegten Bildes* (Sonderzahl, 2002; with co-editor Karl Sierek) and *Reconnaître/Poursuivre* (Théâtre Typographique, 2002 – a selection of writings by Harun Farocki). She is currently completing *Kino aus zweiter Hand* (Vorwerk 8, 2008) – a book on archival film and media art.

Sabeth Buchmann is Professor of Art History in the field of modernism and post-modernism at the Academy of Fine Arts Vienna. She is a member of the editorial board of *Texte zur Kunst* and a co-founder of the magazine *ANYP*. Her writing has been published in various magazines, catalogues and books. Recent titles include *Denken gegen das Denken. Produktion – Technologie – Subjektivität bei Sol LeWitt, Yvonne Rainer und Hélio Oiticica* (b-books, 2006) and *Art After Conceptual Art* (The MIT Press/Generali Foundation, 2006; with co-editor Alexander Alberro).

Beatriz Colomina is Professor of Architecture and Founding Director of the Program in Media and Modernity at Princeton University. She is the author of *Domesticity at War* (ACTAR and The MIT Press, 2007), *Doble exposición: Arquitectura a través del arte* (Akal, 2006), *Privacy and Publicity: Modern Architecture as Mass Media* (The MIT Press, 1994) and *Sexuality and Space* (Princeton Architectural Press, 1992).

Serge Daney (1944–92) was a French film critic and co-founder, with Raymond Bellour, of *Trafic*. He began writing for *Cahiers du cinéma* in 1964 and later served as Editor-in-Chief from 1975 to 1981. Daney joined the French newspaper *Libération* in 1981. He published four collections of his articles during his lifetime: *La Rampe* (Gallimard/Cahiers du cinéma, 1983), *Ciné-journal* (Cahiers du cinéma, 1986), *Le Salaire du zappeur* (P.O.L., 1988) and *Devant la recrudescence des vols des sacs à main* (Aléas, 1991). Since his death, several other books have been released, including *L'Exercice a été profitable, Monsieur* (P.O.L éditeur, 1993), *L'Amateur de tennis* (P.O.L éditeur, 1994), *Persévérance* (P.O.L éditeur, 1994) and *L'Itinéraire d'un ciné-fils* (Éditions Jean-Michel Place, 1999).

Eric de Bruyn teaches contemporary art and media theory at the University of Groningen. He was co-curator, with Chrissie Iles, of the exhibition 'Flashing into the Shadows: The Artist's Film in America 1966–76' (2000–03). Recent writings include 'Topological Pathways of Post-Minimalism', in *Grey Room*, no.25 (Autumn 2006); 'A Film in Five Episodes', in *David Lamelas* (Secession, 2006); and 'The Expanded Field of Cinema, of Exercise on the Perimeter of the Square', in *X-Screen* (2004). He is currently completing a book titled *Film as Anomaly* on filmic practices in post-Minimalism.

Ursula Frohne is Professor for Art History at the University of Cologne. She edited *Video Cult/ures* (DuMont/ZKM, 1999), *CTRL [SPACE], Rhetorics of Surveillance from Bentham to Big Brother*, (The MIT Press, 2002; with co-editors Thomas Y. Levin and Peter Weibel) and *Present Continuous Past(s): Media Art: Strategies of Presentation, Mediation and Dissemination* (Springer, 2005; with co-editors Mona Schieren and Jean-Francois Guiton). Since 2007, she has been chair of the research project 'Reflective Spaces of Cinematographic Aesthetics'.

Bill Horrigan is Director of Media Arts at the Wexner Center for the Arts, The Ohio State University, Columbus. Previously, he worked at the American Film Institute in Los Angeles and at Walker Art Center in Minneapolis. He recently curated 'Chris Marker: Staring Back', the first museum presentation to be drawn from the French film-maker's photographic archive.

Bruce Jenkins is Professor of Film, Video and New Media at the School of the Art Institute of Chicago. He previously served as the curator of film and video at the Walker Art Center and as the Stanley Cavell Curator of the Harvard Film Archive. His recent writings include 'Bruce Conner's REPORT: Contesting Camelot', in *Masterpieces of Modernist Cinema* (Indiana University Press, 2006); and 'The Impossible Cinema of Marcel Broodthaers', in *The Unsilvered Screen: Surrealism on Film* (Wallflower Press, 2007). He is the editor of *On the Camera Arts and Consecutive Matters: The Writings of Hollis Frampton* (The MIT Press, 2008).

David Joselit is Professor in the Department of the History of Art at Yale University. He worked as Curator at the Institute of Contemporary Art, Boston in the 1980s, and has a longstanding practice as a critic for such publications as *Artforum* and *Art in America*. He is the author of *Infinite Regress: Marcel Duchamp 1910–1941* (The MIT Press, 1998), *American Art Since 1945* (Thames & Hudson, 2003) and *Feedback: Television against Democracy* (The MIT Press, 2007).

Branden W. Joseph is Associate Professor of Modern and Contemporary Art in the Department of Art History and Archaeology at Columbia University. He is the author of *Random Order: Robert Rauschenberg and the Neo-Avant-Garde* (The MIT Press, 2003) and *Beyond the Dream Syndicate: Tony Conrad and the Arts after Cage* (Zone Books, 2008). His writings have also appeared in *Artforum, Bookforum, Art Journal, October, Critical Inquiry, Texte zur Kunst* and *Les Cahiers du Musée national d'art moderne*.

William Kaizen is Assistant Professor of Aesthetics and Critical Theory at the University of Massachusetts, Lowell. He is currently writing *The Immediate* (Duke University Press), a book on early video art and telecommunication. His writing has appeared in *Bomb, October, Grey Room* and *Texte zur Kunst*. He has also written on the legacy of Gregory Bateson in post-War American art for *Art Journal* and on Nam June Paik's work in computing for a forthcoming book on early computer art to be published by the University of California Press.

John Kelsey is a writer and artist based in New York. He is a regular contributor to *Artforum* and a member of the artists' collectives Bernadette Corporation and Reena Spaulings. Recent projects include *Radio Danièle*, a radio programme organised in collaboration with the artist Christopher Williams, and 'How To Cook a Wolf', a year-long exhibition series at Kunsthalle Zürich Parallel. Versions of Bernadette Corporation's *Pedestrian Cinema* have been exhibited at the Witte de With (2005), Kunstverein in Hamburg (2006) and Kunstlerhaus Stuttgart (2007). Bernadette Corporation's screenplay *Be Corpse* was published by Lucas-Sternberg Press in 2007.

Liz Kotz teaches in the Department of Art History at University of California, Riverside. She is the author of *Words to Be Looked At: Language in 1960s Art* (The MIT Press, 2007). She writes on post-War and contemporary art and media, and has contributed articles to *Artforum, October, Texte zur Kunst* and other publications.

Rosalind Krauss is Meyer Schapiro Professor of Modern Art and Theory in the Department of Art History and Archaeology at Colombia University. She is one of the founding editors of *October* and the author of a number of books, including *The Originality of the Avant-Garde and Other Modernist Myths* (The MIT Press, 1985), *The Picasso Papers* (Farrar, Straus & Giroux, 1998), *Bachelors* (The MIT Press, 1999), *The Optical Unconscious* (The MIT Press, 1993) and *'A Voyage on the North Sea': Art in the Age of the Post-Medium Condition* (Thames & Hudson, 1999). Krauss co-organised 'Formless: A User's Guide' with Yve-Alain Bois at the Centre Georges Pompidou in Paris in 1996, and co-wrote the seminal volume that accompanied the exhibition (Zone Books, 2000).

Janet Kraynak is Assistant Professor of Contemporary Art at The New School University in New York, with a joint appointment in the Department of Art and Design Studies, Parsons the New School of Design and the Department of Arts in Context, Lang College. Kraynak has published widely on performance, alternative media and technology, feminism, participatory aesthetics and art in relation to globalization. She is the editor of *Please Pay Attention Please: Bruce Nauman's Words: Writings and Interviews* (The MIT Press, 2003), and is currently completing a critical study of Nauman's art of the 1960s and 70s.

Maurizio Lazzarato is a sociologist and philosopher. He is one of the founders of the *Multitudes* review and a member of its editorial board. His publications include *Videofilosofia. La percezione del tempo nel postfordismo* (Manifestolibri, 1997), *Immaterial Labour* (University of Minnesota Press, 1996), *Puissances de l'invention. La psychologie économique de Gabriel Tarde contre l'economie politique* (Les empêcheurs de penser en rond, 2002) and *Les Révolutions du Capitalisme* (Les empêcheurs de penser en rond/ Seuil, 2004).

Pamela M. Lee is Professor of Art and Art History at Stanford University. Her writing has been published in *Artforum, Grey Room, October, Res: Anthropology and Aesthetics, Les Cahiers du Musée national d'art moderne, Texte zur Kunst* and *Word and Image*. She is the author of *Object to Be Destroyed: The Work of Gordon Matta-Clark* (The MIT Press, 1999) and *Chronophobia: On Time in the Art of the 1960s* (The MIT Press, 2004).

Thomas Y. Levin is Professor in the German Department at Princeton University, where he teaches media theory, cultural theory, intellectual history and philosophy. His essays and translations have appeared in *October, Parkett, Grey Room, New German Critique, Screen, Critical Inquiry, Assemblage, From, Open, Insi(s)tu, The Yale Journal of Criticism, The Musical Quarterly, ARCH+, Les Cahiers du Musée national d'art moderne* and *Texte zur Kunst*. Levin has edited and translated books on the work of Siegfried Kracauer, including the critical edition of *The Mass Ornament: Weimar Essays* (Harvard University Press, 1995). As a curator Levin was part of the team that put together the first exhibition on the Situationist International, which began at the Centre Pompidou in 1989 and toured to the ICA, London and the ICA, Boston.

Mark Nash is a film-maker, theorist and curator. He is Professor and Head of Department, Curating Contemporary Art at the Royal College of Art, London. He was an editor of *Screen* from 1978–81; co-curator of 'Documenta11' in Kassel (2002); film curator for 'The Short Century: Independence and Liberation Movements in Africa 1945–1994' at Villa Stuck, Munich, Berlin, Chicago and New York (2001/02); and curator of the Other Cinemas 'hub' for the 3rd Berlin Biennale (2004). He also curated 'Experiments with Truth' at The Fabric Workshop and Museum, Philadelphia, (2004–05).

John Rajchman is Associate Professor and Director of MA Programmes in the Department of Art History and Archeology at Columbia University and Visiting Professor in the School of Architecture, Princeton University. He is author of *Truth and Eros: Foucault, Lacan and the Question of Ethics* (Routledge, 1991), *Constructions* (The MIT Press, 1998) and *The Deleuze Connections* (The MIT Press, 2001). He is editor of *The Identity in Question* (Routledge, 1995).

Jean-Christophe Royoux is a curator, art critic and an advisor on visual arts to the French Ministry of Culture. He is the author of many essays on post-cinematographic practices and co-editor of *Cosmograms* with Melik Ohanian (Lukas & Sternberg, 2005). He curated 'Multipistes' (Argos, Brussels, 2005) and is currently writing a book on 'exhibition cinema'.

Gregor Stemmrich is an art historian at the Free University of Berlin, where he specialises in modern and contemporary art. He is the editor of *Minimal Art. Eine kritische Retrospektive* (Verlag der Kunst, 1995), *Jeff Wall. Szenarien im Bildraum der Wirklichkeit* (Verlag der Kunst, 1997), *Kunst/Kino. Jahresring 48* (Oktagon, 2001) and *Having Been Said: Writings & Interviews of Lawrence Weiner 1968–2003*, (Hatje Cantz, 2004; co-edited with Gerti Fietzek).

Andrew V. Uroskie teaches Art History and Criticism at Stony Brook University, where he is Assistant Professor of Modern and Contemporary Art and affiliate faculty in Cinema and Cultural Studies. His writing on photography and the moving image has appeared in numerous anthologies as well as the journals *Cinema et Cie* and *Grey Room*. He is currently finishing a book on expanded cinema for the University of Chicago Press titled *Between the Black Box and the White Cube: The Emergence of the Moving Image in Contemporary Art*.

Stan VanDerBeek (1927–84) was a film and video artist. He began making independent art films in 1955 and was a pioneer in experimentation with the use of multiple screens, animated collages, drawn animation, live action, film loops, found footage and video and computer images.

Jonathan Walley is Assistant Professor in the Cinema department at Denison University. He has published essays on avant-garde film in *October*, *The Velvet Light Trap* and *Senses of Cinema*. He is currently working on a book about the history and theory of 'paracinema'.

Federico Windhausen is Assistant Professor at California College of the Arts, where he teaches the history of experimental film and video and Latin American cinema. He has published essays on the work of Hollis Frampton, Morgan Fisher, Matthias Müller and Christoph Girardet, and on the London Film-Maker's Cooperative. He is currently writing a book on the renewal of Argentinean cinema since the mid-1990s.

Peter Wollen is a film-maker and film theorist. His books include *Readings and Writings: Semiotic Counter-Strategies* (Verso, 1982), *Singin' in the Rain* (British Film Institute, 1992), *Raiding the Icebox: Reflections on Twentieth Century Culture* (Indiana University Press, 1993) and *Signs and Meaning in the Cinema* (British Film Institute, 1998). He wrote the screenplay, with Mark Peploe, for Michelangelo Antonioni's *The Passenger* (1975), co-directed *Riddles of the Sphinx* (1977; with Laura Mulvey) and directed *Friendship's Death* (1988).

Gene Youngblood is Professor of Moving Image Art at the College of Santa Fe. He is a theorist of electronic media arts and a scholar in the history and theory of experimental film and video art. He has published widely and is the author of *Expanded Cinema* (E.P. Dutton, 1970), the first book about video as an art medium. He is currently writing a book on the history of video, and is also completing two other books, titled *The Challenge to Create on the Same Scale As We Can Destroy*, about the career of Kit Galloway and Sherrie Rabinowitz, and *The Broadcast and Its Discontents*, about the critique of corporate media.

About the Editors

Tanya Leighton is an independent editor and curator. She recently curated the international travelling exhibition 'In The Poem About Love You Don't Write The Word Love' and edited an accompanying collection of essays (Sternberg Press, 2006). She also co-edited, with Pavel Büchler, *Saving the Image: Art After Film* (Manchester Metropolitan University, 2003).

Charles Esche is Director of the Van Abbemuseum, Eindhoven and Research Fellow at Central Saint Martins College of Art and Design, London. He is an editor of *Afterall* journal with Mark Lewis, Thomas Lawson and Dieter Roelstraete and Series Editor of Afterall Books with Mark Lewis. He co-curated Istanbul Biennale 2005 with Vasif Kortun and has published a collection of his essays, *Modest Proposals* (Baglam Press, 2005).

Editor's Acknowledgements

Art and the Moving Image was initiated by Charles Esche, Mark Lewis and Caroline Woodley at Afterall, London. I would like to express my gratitude to them for inviting me to realise this idea, and for their vision, guidance and support throughout the various stages of this project. Thanks are due to Mark Dunhill and Martin Woolley at Central Saint Martins College of Art and Design; Chris Wainwright at the University of the Arts London; and James Attlee, Judith Severne, Celeste Stroll and Roger Thorp at Tate Publishing. I would also like to thank the designer Kaisa Lassinaro.

I am indebted to the generosity of all the authors and artists who permitted the reproduction of their work in this book, so many of whom also contributed invaluable suggestions and recommendations for the contents of this book as a whole. I would especially like to thank our two key advisors, Eric de Bruyn and Liz Kotz, as well as William Kaizen and Andrew V. Uroskie – their insights, critiques and collaboration have made this book possible. Special thanks go to François Bucher, Charles Esche, Branden W. Joseph, William Kaizen and Keith Sanborn, whose comments greatly improved the organisation and substance of my introduction. I would also sincerely like to thank Emily Zimmerman for her initial work on this project, particularly on the bibliography and authors' biographies, and Fiona Bate for continuing this important work. Verena Kaminiarz also made an invaluable contribution to the project overall with her meticulous work in translating and summarising key texts and sourcing many articles and essays. I would like to acknowledge Gregory Williams for his help with translation and Gemma Sharpe for her hard work sourcing and securing the rights for reproducing the texts and illustrations contained in the book. Thanks, too, to Deirdre O'Dwyer for copy-editing the texts and Lucy Steeds for pulling the final copy together.

This book would not have been possible without the advice and recommendations of countless individuals; I am deeply grateful for their kindness and generosity. While this is undoubtedly an incomplete list, thank you to: Rodrigo Alfonso, Callie Angell, Saul Anton, Magali Arriola, Yann Beauvais, Karen Beckman, Joost Bolten, Nicolas Bourriaud, Matthew Buckingham, Cemeti Art House, Weng Choy, Shim Chung, Lynne Cooke, Alison Cornyn, Timothy Corrigan, Jonathan Crary, Melanie Crean, Douglas Crimp, Erika Dalya Muhammad, Stefaan Decostere, Timothy Druckrey, Thomas Elsaesser, Michael Eng, Ruth Ewan, Nuno Faria, Morgan Fisher, Zuzana Flaskova, Hal Foster, Catherine Fowler, Brian Frye, Rene Gabri, Gridthiya Gaweewong, Peter Gidal, Jennifer González, Rita González, Melissa Gronlund, Boris Groys, Alfred Guzzetti, Susanna Haddon, Hou Hanru, Mark Hansen, Nanna Heidenreich, Birgit Hein, Thomas Hensel, Sofía Hernández, Wulf Herzogenrath, Kathy High, Petra Hinck, Daniel Hoffman-Schwartz, Agung Hujatnika Jennong, Pierre Huyghe, Gloria Hwang Sutton, Kim Hyun Jin, Melle Jaarsma, Maryam Jafri, David James, Jesal Kapadia, Gülsün Karamustafa, Thomas Keenan, Ryszard Kluszczyński, Gertrud Koch, Vasif Kortun, Surasi Kusolwong, Pablo Lafuente, Kim Lamm, Barbara London, Geert Lovink, Anthony McCall, Scott McQuire, Arlindo Machado, Lev Manovich, Ivonne Margulies, Laura Marks, Adrian Martin, Saloni Mathur, Marina Grzinic, Mónica Mayer, Christine Mello, John Menick, Matthias Michalka, Philippe-Alain Michaud, Kate Mondloch, Vanessa Joan Müller, Krisna Murti, Irene Nierhaus, Olu Oguibe, Robin Oppenheimer, Peter Osborne, Pedro Paixão, Nikos Papastergiadis, Zhang Qing, Walid Raad, Ashish Rajadhyaksha, Raqs Media Collective, Juliane Rebentisch, Jose Alejandro Restrepo, Ruang Rupa Grupa, Catherine Russell, Domeniek Ruyters, Piotr Rypson, Jayce Salloum, Delfim Sardo, Stefanie Schulte Strathaus, Hannah Sharpe, Simon Sheikh, Shelly Silver, Jeffrey Skoller, Pooja Sood, Maria Rosa Sossai, Nancy Spector, Julian Stallabrass, Caspar Stracke, Chris Strayer, Xu Tan, Claire Tancons, Christine Tohme, Jalal Toufic, Ho Tzu Nyen, Jonathan Unglaub, Dimitri Vilensky, Rinaldo Walcott, Antek Walczak, Maria Walsh, Michael Walsh, Apichatpong Weerasethakul, Graham Weinbren, Paul Willemsen, Kaelen Wilson-Goldie, Hendro Wijanto, Benjamin Young, Akram Zaatari, Florian Zeyfang, Siegfried Zielinski, Maxa Zoller, Michael Zryd and Thomas Zummer.

For Richard J. Leighton.

Tanya Leighton
Editor

Text Sources

All texts are courtesy the author unless otherwise indicated. All rights are reserved. We are very grateful to all the authors, authors' estates, translators, publishers, galleries and museums for their assistance in reproducing these essays.

Alberro, Alexander, 'The Gap Between Film and Installation Art', first presented at the conference 'Beyond the Screen' organised by Nora Alter at the University of Florida, Gainesville, April 2003.

Agamben, Giorgio, 'Difference and Repetition: On Guy Debord's Films', first presented as a lecture at the 'Sixth International Video Week' at the Centre Saint-Gervais, Geneva, November 1995. First published in Tom McDonough (ed.), *Guy Debord and The Situationist International*, Cambridge, Mass.: The MIT Press, 2004.

Bellour, Raymond, 'Of An Other Cinema' (revision), *Trafic*, no.34, Summer 2000. This version: Sara Arrhenius, Magdalena Malm and Cristina Ricupero (eds.), *Black Box Illuminated*, NIFCA, IAPSIS and Propexus, 2003.

Bennett Hupp, Elizabeth, 'After the Cull', new commission.

Blümlinger, Christa, 'The Art of the Possible: Notes About Some Installations by Harun Farocki', first published in *Trafic*, no.43, Autumn 2002 (revised version of 'Dis positivwechsel', *Nach dem Film* 2: www.nachdemfilm.de, 2001). This version: Ursula Biemann (ed.), *Stuff It: The Video Essay in the Digital Age*, Zürich: Edition Voldemeer, Vienna/New York: Springer, 2003.

Bruyn, Eric de, 'The Museum of Attractions: Marcel Broodthaers and the *Section Cinéma*' (revision), Gregor Stemmrich (ed.), *Kunst/Kino* Jahresring 48, Cologne: Oktagon Verlag, 2001.

Buchmann, Sabeth, 'Leisure 73', written for the X-Screen panel organised by Matthias Michalka, Birgit Hein, Helmut Draxler and Ruth Noack, February 2004, Museum Moderner Kunst Wien (Mumok). First published as 'Da Antropofagia ao Conceitualismo' ('From *Antropofagia* to Conceptualism') in Paula Braga (ed.), *A arte de Hélio Oiticica*, São Paulo: Perspectiva, 2008.

Colomina, Beatriz, 'Enclosed by Images: The Eameses' Multimedia Architecture', *Grey Room*, no.2, Winter 2001 © *Grey Room*, Inc. and Massachusetts Institute of Technology.

Daney, Serge, 'From Movies to Moving', *La Recherche photographique*, no.7, 1989. This version: Catherine David (ed.), *documentadocuments* 2, Ostfildern-Ruit: Cantz Verlag, 1996.

Frohne, Ursula, 'Dissolution of the Frame: Immersion and Participation in Video Installations' (revision), *Black Box. Der Schwarzraum in der Kunst* (exh. cat.), Kunstmuseum Bern, 2001. This version: '"That's the Only Now I Get": Immersion and Partizipation in Video Installationen', Gregor Stemmrich (ed.), *Kunst/Kino* Jahresring 48, Cologne: Oktagon Verlag, 2001.

Horrigan, Bill, 'Five Years Later', new commission.

Jenkins, Bruce, 'Fluxfilms in Three False Starts', Janet Jenkins (ed.), *In the Spirit of Fluxus* (exh. cat.), Minneapolis: Walker Art Center © 1993 Walker Art Center, Minneapolis.

Joselit, David, 'Tale of the Tape: *Radical Software*', *Artforum*, May 2002.

Joseph, Branden W., '"My Mind Split Open": Andy Warhol's Exploding Plastic Inevitable', *Grey Room*, no.8, 2004 © *Grey Room*, Inc. and Massachusetts Institute of Technology.

Kaizen, William, 'Live on Tape: Video, Liveness and the Immediate', new commission.

Kelsey, John, 'Moving Images Moving Images', new commission.

Krauss, Rosalind, 'Video: The Aesthetics of Narcissism', *October*, no.1, Spring 1976. This version: Gregory Battcock (ed.), *New Artists Video*, New York: E.P. Dutton, 1978.

Kotz, Liz, 'Video Projection: The Space Between Screens' (revision), Zoya Kocur and Simon Leung (eds.), *Theory in Contemporary Art Since 1985*, London: Basil Blackwell, 2004.

Kraynak, Janet, 'Dependent Participation: Bruce Nauman's Environments', *Grey Room*, no.10, Winter 2003 © *Grey Room*, Inc. and Massachusetts Institute of Technology.

Lazzarato, Maurizio, 'Video, Flows and Real Time', *Videophilosophie*, Berlin: b_books. This version: Søren Grammel (ed.), *videonale9* (exh. cat.), Bonn: videonale9, 2001.

Lee, Pamela M., 'Bare Lives', *X-Screen: Film Installations and Actions in the 1960s and 1970s*, Cologne and Vienna: Verlag der Buchhandlung Walter König and Museum Moderner Kunst Stiftung Ludwig Vienna, 2004.

Levin, Thomas Y., '*You Never Know the Whole Story*: Ute Friederike Jürss and the Aesthetics of the Heterochronic Image' (revision), *Ute Friederike Jürss: 'You Never Know the Whole Story'* (exh. cat.), Ostfildern-Ruit and Karlsruhe: Hatje Canz and ZKM Center for Art and Media, 2000.

Nash, Mark, 'Art and Cinema: Some Critical Reflections', *Documenta11* (exh. cat.), Ostfildern-Ruit: Hatje Cantz, 2002.

Rajchman, John, 'Deleuze's Time, or How the Cinematic Changes Our Idea of Art', first presented at the symposium 'Deleuze @ 20' organised by David Rodowick at Harvard University, Cambridge, Mass., May 2005.

Royoux, Jean-Christophe, 'The Time of Re-departure: After Cinema, the Cinema of the Subject', *Trafic*, no.37, Spring 2001.

Stemmrich, Gregor, 'White Cube, Black Box and Grey Areas: Venues and Values', first presented at the conference 'Beyond the Screen' organised by Nora Alter at the University of Florida, Gainesville, April 2003.

Uroskie, Andrew V., 'Siting Cinema', previously unpublished.

VanDerBeek, Stan, '"Culture: Intercom" and Expanded Cinema: A Proposal and Manifesto', *The Tulane Drama Review*, vol.11 no.1, Autumn 1966.

Walley, Jonathan, 'Modes of Film Practice in the Avant-Garde', previously unpublished.

Windhausen, Federico, 'Paul Sharits and the Active Spectator', new commission.

Wollen, Peter, 'The Two Avant-Gardes', *Studio International*, vol.190 no.978, November/December 1975. This version: Peter Wollen, *Readings and Writings: Semiotic Counter-Strategies*, London: Verso, 1982.

Youngblood, Gene, 'Hardware: The Videosphere', *Radical Software*, vol.1 no.1, Spring 1970.

Illustration Notes

 We are very grateful to all the artists, artists' estates, artists' studios, galleries and museums for providing the images that illustrate this book.

Ahtila, Eija-Liisa, *The House*, 2002. DVD installation for 3 projections, colour, sound, 14mins

—— *Today*, 1996/67. 35mm film and DVD installation for 3 projections, colour, sound, 10mins

Aitken, Doug, *Electric Earth*, 1999. 8-laserdisc installation, 18mins

Akerman, Chantal, *Bordering on Fiction: Chantal Akerman's 'D'Est'*, 1993/95. 25-channel video installation, 16mm colour film, sound

Broodthaers, Marcel, detail from *Section Cinéma*, 1971. Photograph of Broodthaers holding Georges Sadoul's *L'Invention du Cinema*, 1971. One of 11 elements of *Section Cinéma* contained in a chest – itself one of 12 main elements (inner room)

—— *Ceci ne serait pas une pipe*, 1969–71. Frames from 35mm black-and-white film, silent, 2mins 20secs

—— detail from *Section Cinéma*, 1971. Photograph of a chest including 11 elements of *Section Cinéma*, itself one of 12 main elements (inner room)
All images © 2008 Maria Gilissen

Buckingham, Matthew, *A Man of the Crowd*, 2003. 16mm black-and-white film installation, sound, 20min-loop

Cardiff, Janet and George Bures Miller, *The Paradise Institute*, 2001. Wood, theatre seats, colour video projection, head-phones and mixed media, 299.72×1772.92×533.4cm

Coleman, James, *Box (ahhareturnabout)*. 16mm black-and-white film, continuous loop with synchronised voice-over

Douglas, Stan, *Hors-champs*, 1992. Two double-sided laser CAV laserdiscs, 13mins 20secs each rotation

—— *Win, Place or Show*, 1998. Four double-sided CAV laser discs with 8 back-ups, 2-channel colour video projection, 6mins each, soundtrack

Fudong, Yang, *No Snow on the Broken Bridge*, 2006. 35mm black-and-white film, 8-10 screens, 8-10 or 10-12mins

Gordon, Douglas, *24 Hour Psycho*, 1993. Video projection of *Psycho* directed by Alfred Hitchcock, Universal Studios © 2008 Universal

Graham, Rodney, *Vexation Island*, 1997. Laserdisc, laserdisc player, AC-3 amplifier, 5 speakers, 1 subwoofer, 156×366cm Pearlescent Da-Snap screen, Barco projector 701 S HQ, 400×1200×600cm

Guerrilla Television, cover courtesy Michael Shamberg and Raindance Corporation © 2008 Henry Holt & Company, Inc.

Huyghe, Pierre, *Streamside Day*, 2003. Digital video projection from film and video transfers, colour, sound, 26mins

—— *The Third Memory*, 1999. Double projection, beta digital, 9mins 46secs

Jürss, Ute Friederike, *You Never Know the Whole Story*, 2000. 3-channel video installation transferred to DVD loop, silent, 10mins

Marker, Chris, *Silent Movie*, 1994–95. Computer-controlled, 5-channel video/sound installation with five 25-inch monitors stacked on metal shelving and steadied with guy wires

Nauman, Bruce, *Going Around the Corner Piece*, 1970. Wall-board, 4 video cameras, 4 video monitors, walls 305×610cm each

—— *Green Light Corridor*, 1970. Wallboard, green fluorescent light fixtures, dimensions variable

—— *Live Taped Video Corridor*, 1970. Wallboard, video camera, 2 monitors, videotape player, videotape, dimensions variable

Nicolson, Annabel, *Reel Time*, 1973. 16mm black-and-white film documenting performance with sewing machine and projections, variable duration

Oiticica, Hélio and Neville D'Almeida, *01-CC1 (Trashiscapes/Cosmococa Programa in Progress)*, 1973/2003. C-print mounted on aluminum 75.6×113.7cm

—— *01-CC5 (Trashiscapes/Cosmococa Programa in Progress)*, 1973/2003. Installation view

—— *23-CC3 (Maileryn/Cosmococa Programa in Progress)*, 1973/2003. C-print mounted on aluminum 75.6×113.7cm

Radical Software, covers and inside spread courtesy Beryl Korot, Davidson Giglotti, Ira Schneider and the David Langlois Fondation

Rigby, Jane, *Ambient Vision*, 1979. 16mm film installation

Taylor-Wood, Sam, *Travesty of a Mockery*, 1995. Two-screen video installation, 10-min loop

Schneider, Ira and Frank Gillette, *Wipe Cycle*, 1969. Two 30min edited tapes, 2 video time delays, live camera, mixing the audience into the artwork as active participants

Simpson, Lorna *31*, 2002. 31 short films transferred to 31 DVDs played simultaneously on 31×38cm flat screen televisions

Videofreex, paperback book cover. Courtesy Black Dome Press

Viola, Bill, *The Greeting*, 1995. Colour video and sound installation

Wilson, Jane and Louise, *Stasi City*, 1997. 4-channel colour video installation, 4mins 59sec-loop

Bibliography – Publications

Selected Books, Exhibition Catalogues and Dedicated Magazine Issues

Agamben, Giorgio, *Means Without End: Notes on Politics* (trans. V. Binetti and C. Casarino), Minneapolis: University of Minnesota Press, 2000.

Alberro, Alexander (ed.), *Two-Way Mirror Power: Selected Writings by Dan Graham on His Art*, Cambridge, Mass. and London: The MIT Press, 1999.

Allen, Richard and Malcolm Turvey (eds.), *Camera Obscura, Camera Lucida: Essays in Honor of Annette Michelson*, Amsterdam: Amsterdam University Press, 2002.

Andrew, Dudley, *Concepts in Film Theory*, Oxford: Oxford University Press, 1984.

——, *Film in the Aura of Art*, Princeton: Princeton University Press, 1984.

——, *The Major Film Theories: An Introduction*, Oxford and New York: Oxford University Press, 1976.

Angell, Callie, Avis Berman, Arthur Danto et al., *The Andy Warhol Museum*, Pittsburgh: The Andy Warhol Museum; Carnegie Institute, 1994.

Armes, Roy, *On Video*, London and New York: Routledge, 1988.

Arnheim, Rudolf, *Film as Art*, Berkeley: University of California Press, 1957.

——, *Film Essays and Criticism*, Madison: University of Wisconsin Press, 1997.

Artforum. Special: 'Film' (ed. Annette Michelson), vol.10 no.1, Sept 1971.

Artpress, no.14, 1993.

Arts Magazine. Special: 'Video', vol.49 no.4, Dec 1974.

Baker, George (ed.), *James Coleman: October Files 5*, Cambridge, Mass. and London: The MIT Press, 2003.

Balázs, Béla, *Theory of the Film: Character and Growth of a New Art* (trans. E. Bone), New York: Roy Publishers, 1953.

Barthes, Roland, *Image-Music-Text* (trans. S. Heath), New York: Hill and Wang, 1977.

Battcock, Gregory (ed.), *The New American Cinema: A Critical Anthology*, New York: E.P. Dutton, 1967.

—— (ed.), *Idea Art: A Critical Anthology*, New York: E.P. Dutton, 1973.

—— (ed.), *New Artists Video: A Critical Anthology*, New York: E.P. Dutton, 1978.

Battcock, Gregory and Robert Nickas (eds.), *The Art of Performance: A Critical Anthology*, New York: E.P. Dutton, 1984.

Baudry, Jean-Louis, *L'Effet cinéma*, Paris: Éditions Albatros, 1978.

Bazin, André, *What Is Cinema?*, vol.1 (trans. H. Gray), Berkeley: University of California Press, 1967.

——, *What Is Cinema?*, vol.2 (trans. H. Gray), Berkeley: University of California Press, 1971.

Bellour, Raymond, *The Analysis of Film* (ed. Constance Penley), Bloomington: Indiana University Press, 2000.

——, *L'Entre-Image*, Paris: Éditions de la Différence, 1990.

——, *L'Entre-Images 2*, Paris: P.O.L. éditeur, 1999.

——, *L'Entre-Images: Photo, Cinéma, Vidéo*, Paris: Éditions de la Différence, 2002.

Bellour, Raymond and Mary Lea Bandy (eds.), *Jean-Luc Godard: Son + Image 1974–1991* (exh. cat.), New York: Museum of Modern Art, 1992.

Benjamin, Walter, *Illuminations* (ed. Hannah Arendt, trans. H. Zohn), New York: Schocken Books, 1968.

Berger, John, *About Looking*, New York: Pantheon Books, 1980.

——, *Ways of Seeing*, London: British Broadcasting Corporation; Penguin Books, 1972.

Bergson, Henri, *Matter and Memory* (trans. N. M. Paul and W. S. Palmer), New York: Zone Books, 1991.

Biemann, Ursula (ed.), *Stuff It: The Video Essay in the Digital Age*, Zürich: Edition Voldemeer; Vienna: Springer, 2003.

Bonitzer, Pascal, *Le Champ aveugle: Essais sur le cinéma*, Paris: Cahiers du cinema; Éditions Gallimard, 1982.

——, *Peinture et cinéma: Décadrages*, Paris: Cahiers du cinéma; Éditions de l'Etoile, 1987.

——, *Le Regard et la voix: Essais sur le cinéma*, Paris: Union Générale d'Éditions, 1976.

Bordwell, David, *Making Meaning: Inference and Rhetoric in the Interpretation of Cinema*, Cambridge, Mass. and London: Harvard University Press, 1989.

——, *Narration in the Fiction Film*, Madison: University of Wisconsin Press, 1985.

Bordwell, David and Noël Carroll (eds.), *Post-Theory: Reconstructing Film Studies*, Madison: University of Wisconsin Press, 1996.

Bordwell, David and Kristin Thompson, *Film Art: An Introduction*, New York: Alfred A. Knopf, 1986.

——, *Film History: An Introduction*, 2nd edition, Boston: McGraw Hill, 2003.

Braudy, Leo and Marshall Cohen (eds.), *Film Theory and Criticism: Introductory Readings*, Oxford and New York: Oxford University Press, 1979.

Breteau, Gisèle, *Abécédaire des films sur l'art moderne et contemporain, 1905–1984*, Paris: Centre Georges Pompidou, 1985.

Marcel Broodthaers: Cinéma (exh. cat.), Barcelona: Fundació Antoni Tàpies, 1997.

Browne, Nick, (ed.), *Cahiers du Cinéma, 1969–1972: The Politics of Representation*, Cambridge, Mass. and London: Harvard University Press, 1990.

Bruno, Giuliana, *Atlas of Emotion: Journeys in Art, Architecture, and Film*, New York: Verso, 2002.

Buchloh, Benjamin H.D. (ed.), *Dan Graham: Video-Architecture-Television: Writing on Video and Video Works*, Nova Scotia and New York: The Press of Nova Scotia College of Art and Design and NYU Press, 1979.

Burch, Noël, *Theory of Film Practice* (trans. H.R. Lane), New York: Praeger, 1973.

Bürger, Peter, *Theory of the Avant-Garde* (trans. M. Shaw), Minneapolis: University of Minnesota Press, 1984.

Burnham, Jack, *Beyond Modern Sculpture: The Effects of Science and Technology on the Sculpture of This Century*, New York: Praeger, 1972.

——, *The Structure of Art*, New York: Braziller, 1970.

Cahiers du cinema. Spécial: Godard, hors série, no.300, Paris: Les Éditions de l'Étoile, 1979.

——, *'Où va la video?'*, hors série, no.14, Paris: Les Éditions de l'Étoile, 1986.

——, *'Vidéo art exploration'*, hors série, no.10, Paris: Les Éditions de l'Étoile, 1981.

Canongia, Ligia, *Quase Cinema: Cinema de Artista no Brasil, 1970–80*, Rio de Janeiro: Fundação Nacional de Arte, 1981.
Carroll, Noël, *Interpreting the Moving Image*, Cambridge: Cambridge University Press, 1998.
——, *Theorizing the Moving Image*, Cambridge: Cambridge University Press, 1996.
Casebier, Allan, *Film and Phenomenology: Toward a Realist Theory of Cinematic Representation*, Cambridge: Cambridge University Press, 1991.
Cavell, Stanley, *The World Viewed: Reflections on the Ontology of Film*, New York: Viking Press, 1971.
Celant, Germano, *Offmedia, nuove techniche artistiche: video disco libro*, Bari: Dedalo libri, 1977.
A Century of Artists' Film in Britain (exh. cat.), London: Tate Publishing, 2003/04.
Cha, Theresa Hak Kyung (ed.), *Apparatus, Cinematographic Apparatus: Selected Writings*, New York: Tanam Press, 1980.
Chion, Michel, *The Voice in Cinema* (trans. C. Gorbman), New York: Columbia University Press, 1998, pp.17–29.
James Coleman: Projected Images: 1972–1994 (exh. cat.), New York: Dia Center for the Arts, 1995.
Communications. Special: 'Video', no.48, 1988. *2000 BC: The Bruce Conner Story* (exh. cat.), Minneapolis: Walker Art Center, 1999.
Crary, Jonathan, *Suspensions of Perception: Attention, Spectacle and Modern Culture*, Cambridge, Mass. and London: The MIT Press, 1999.
——, *Techniques of the Observer: On Vision and Modernity in the Nineteenth Century*, Cambridge, Mass. and London: The MIT Press, 1990.
Crimp, Douglas (ed.), *Joan Jonas: Scripts and Descriptions, 1968–1982*, Berkeley: University Art Museum, 1983.
——, (ed.), *Pictures* (exh. cat.), New York: Artists Space, 1977.
Cubitt, Sean, *The Cinema Effect*, Cambridge, Mass. and London: The MIT Press, 2004.
——, *Timeshift: On Video Culture*, London: Comedia; London and New York: Routledge, 1991.
——, *Videography: Video Media as Art and Culture*, London: MacMillan; New York: St Martin's Press, 1993.
Curtis, David, Philip Drummond and Richard Francis, *Film as Film: Formal Experiments in Film, 1910–1975* (exh. cat.), London: Arts Council of Great Britain, 1979.
Cut: Film as Found Object in Contemporary Video (exh. cat.), Milwaukee: Milwaukee Art Museum, 2004.
D'Agostino, Peter (ed.), *Transmission: Theory and Practice for a New Television Aesthetics*, New York: Tanam Press, 1985.
D'Agostino, Peter and Antonio Muntadas (eds.), *The Un/Necessary Image*, New York: Tanam Press, 1982.
Daney, Serge, *Ciné-journal*, Paris: Cahiers du cinéma, 1986.
——, *L'Exercice a été profitable, Monsieur*, Paris: P.O.L., 1993.
——, *L'Itinéraire d'un ciné-fils*, Paris: Éditions Jean-Michel Place, 1999.
——, *La Maison cinéma et le monde. 1. Le Temps des cahiers 1962–1981* (eds. Patrice Rollet, Jean-Claude Biette and Christophe Manon), Paris: P.O.L., 2001.
——, *La Rampe*, Paris: Gallimard and Cahiers du cinéma, 1983.
——, *Le Salaire du zappeur*, Paris: P.O.L. éditeur, 1988.
——, *Persévérance*, Paris: P.O.L. éditeur, 1994.
Daniels, Dieter and Rudolf Frieling (eds.), *Media Art Action: The 1960s and 1970s in Germany*, Karlsruhe: ZKM Center for Art and Media; Vienna: Springer, 1997.
——(eds.), *Media Art Interaction: The 1980s and 1990s in Germany*, Karlsruhe: ZKM Center for Art and Media; Vienna: Springer, 2000.
——(eds.), *Media Art Net/1 Survey of Media Art*, Karlsruhe: ZKM Center for Art and Media; Vienna: Springer, 2004.
——(eds.), *Media Art Net/2 Key Topics*, Karlsruhe: ZKM Center for Art and Media; Vienna: Springer, 2005.
Danino, Nina and Michael Mazière (eds.), *The Undercut Reader: Critical Writings on Artists' Film and Video*, London: Wallflower Press, 2003.
Davis, Douglas, *Art Culture: Essays on the Post-Modern*, New York: Harper and Row Publishers, Inc., 1977.
——, *Art and the Future: A History/Prophecy of the Collaboration Between Science, Technology and Art*, New York: Praeger, 1973.
Davis, Douglas and Allison Simmons (eds.), *The New Television: A Public/Private Art*, Cambridge, Mass. and London: The MIT Press, 1977.
Debord, Guy, *Complete Cinematic Works: Scripts, Stills, Documents* (ed. and trans. Ken Knabb), Edinburgh: AK Press, 2003.
——, *Comments on the Society of the Spectacle* (trans. M. Imrie), London: Verso, 1990.
——, *The Society of the Spectacle* (trans. D. Nicholson-Smith), New York: Zone Books, 1992.
Debray, Régis, *Transmitting Culture* (trans. E. Rauth), New York: Columbia University Press, 2000.
——, *Media Manifestos: On the Technological Transmission of Cultural Forms* (trans. E. Rauth), London: Verso, 1996.
Delehanty, Suzanne (ed.), *Video Art*, Philadelphia: Institute of Contemporary Art and University of Philadelphia, 1975.
Deleuze, Gilles, *Cinema 1: The Movement-Image* (trans. H. Tomlinson and B. Habberjam), London: The Athlone Press, 1986.
——, *Cinema 2: The Time-Image* (trans. H. Tomlinson and R. Galeta), London: The Athlone Press, 1989.
Derrida, Jacques and Bernard Stiegler, *Echographies of Television*, Cambridge: Polity Press, 2002.
Dixon, Wheeler Winston, *The Exploding Eye: A Re-Visionary History of 1960s American Experimental Cinema*, Albany: State University of New York Press, 1997.
Dixon, Wheeler Winston and Gwendolyn Audrey Foster (eds.), *Experimental Cinema: The Film Reader*, London and New York: Routledge, 2002.
Doane, Mary Ann, *The Emergence of Cinematic Time: Modernity, Contingency, the Archive*, Cambridge, Mass. and London: Harvard University Press, 2002.
——, *Femmes Fatales: Feminism, Film Theory, Psychoanalysis*, London and New York: Routledge, 1991.
Doane, Mary Ann, Patricia Mellencamp and Linda Williams (eds.), *Re-Vision: Essays in Feminist Film Criticism*, Frederick, Maryland: University Publications of America; Los Angeles: The American Film Institute, 1984.
Druckrey, Timothy (ed.), *Electronic Culture: Technology and Visual Representation*, New York: Aperture, 1997.
Duguet, Anne-Marie, *Vidéo, la mémoire au poing*, Paris: Hachette, 1981.
Eco, Umberto, *The Open Work* (trans. A. Cancogni), Cambridge, Mass. and London: Harvard University Press, 1989.
Ehmann, Antje and Harun Farocki (eds.), *Kino wie noch nie. Cinema like never before* (exh. cat.), Vienna: Generali Fondation; Cologne: Verlag der Buchhandlung Walther König, 2006.
Eisenstein, Sergei M., *Cinématisme: Peinture et cinéma* (trans. A. Zouboff), Brussels: Éditions Complexe, 1980.
——, *Film Form: Essays in Film Theory* (ed. and trans. J. Leyda), New York: Harcourt Brace, 1949.
——, *The Film Sense* (ed. and trans. J. Leyda), New York: Harcourt, Brace, Jovanovich, 1970.
Elsaesser, Thomas (ed.), *Early Cinema: Space, Frame, Narrative*, London: British Film Institute, 1990.
——, *Harun Farocki: Working on the Sight Lines*, Amsterdam: Amsterdam University Press, 2004.

Fell, John L. (ed.), *Film Before Griffith*, Berkeley: University of California Press, 1983.

Film Culture. Special: 'A Guide to Independent Film and Video', no.62, 1976.

—— *'Paul Sharits'*, nos.65/66, 1978.

Foster, Hal, *The Return of the Real: Art and Theory at the End of the Century*, Cambridge, Mass. and London: The MIT Press, 1996.

—— (ed.), *The Anti-Aesthetic: Essays on Postmodern Culture*, Seattle: Bay Press, 1983.

Frampton, Hollis, *Circles of Confusion: Film, Photography, Video: Texts, 1968–1980*, Rochester, NY: Visual Studies Workshop Press, 1983.

Fried, Michael, *Art and Objecthood*, Chicago: University of Chicago Press, 1998.

Friedberg, Anne, *Window Shopping: Cinema and the Postmodern*, Berkeley: University of California Press, 1993.

From Receiver to Remote Control: The TV Set (exh. cat.), New York: The New Museum of Contemporary Art, 1990.

Future Cinema: The Cinematic Imaginary After Film (exh. cat.), Karlsruhe: ZKM Center for Art and Media; Cambridge, Mass. and London: The MIT Press, 2003.

Gale, Peggy (ed.), *Video by Artists*, Toronto: Art Metropole, 1976.

Gidal, Peter, *Materialist Film*, London and New York: Routledge, 1989.

—— (ed.), *Structural Film Anthology*, London: British Film Institute, 1978.

Gillette, Frank, *Aransas: Axis of Observation*, Houston: Points of View, 1978.

——, *Between Paradigms: The Mood and Its Purpose*, New York: Gordon and Breach, 1973.

Godard, Jean-Luc, *Godard par Godard: Les années Cahiers*, Paris: Éditions de l'Étoile and Cahiers du cinéma, 1985.

——, *Godard par Godard: Les années Mao aux années 80*, Paris: Éditions de l'Étoile and Cahiers du cinéma, 1985.

——, *Jean-Luc Godard par Jean-Luc Godard: Tome 2, 1984–1988*, vol.2, Paris: Cahiers du cinéma, 1998.

——, *The Future(s) of Films: Three Interviews 2000/01* (trans. J. O'Toole), Bern: Gachnung and Springer AG, 2002.

Goldstein, Ann and Anne Rorimer (eds.), *Reconsidering the Object of Art: 1965–1975* (exh. cat.), Los Angeles: Museum of Contemporary Art; Cambridge, Mass. and London: The MIT Press, 1995.

Jack Goldstein (exh. cat.), Grenoble: Magasin – Centre national d'art contemporain de Grenoble, 2002.

Graham, Dan, *Rock My Religion: Writings and Art Projects, 1965–1990* (ed. B. Wallis), Cambridge, Mass. and London: The MIT Press, 1993.

——, *Two-Way Mirror Power: Selected Writings by Dan Graham on His Art* (ed. A. Alberro), Cambridge, Mass. and London: The MIT Press, 1999.

——, *Video-Architecture-Television: Writings on Video and Video Works, 1970–1978*, Halifax: The Press of the Nova Scotia College of Art and Design, 1979.

Greenberg, Clement, *Art and Culture: Critical Essays*, Boston: Beacon Press, 1961.

——, *The Collected Essays and Criticism: Perceptions and Judgments, 1939–1944*, vol.1 (ed. John O'Brian), Chicago: Chicago University Press, 1986.

——, *The Collected Essays and Criticism: Modernism with a Vengeance, 1957–1969*, vol.4 (ed. John O'Brian), Chicago: Chicago University Press, 1993.

Groos, Ulrike, Barbara Hess and Ursula Wevers (eds.), *Ready to Shoot. Fernsehgalerie Gerry Schum. Videogalerie Schum* (exh. cat.), Düsseldorf: Kunsthalle Düsseldorf; Cologne: Snoeck, 2003.

Guattari, Félix, *Chaosmosis: An Ethico Aesthetic Paradigm* (trans. J. Pefanis), Sydney: Power Publications, 1995.

Hall, Douglas and Sally Jo Fifer (eds.), *Illuminating Video: An Essential Guide to Video Art*, New York: Aperture, 1991.

Hamlyn, Nicky, *Film Art Phenomena*, London: British Film Institute, 2003.

Hanhardt, John G. (ed.), *Video Culture: A Critical Investigation*, Rochester, NY: Visual Studies Workshop Press and Peregrine Smith Books, 1986.

Hansen, Mark B. N., *New Philosophy for New Media*, Cambridge, Mass. and London: The MIT Press, 2004.

Heath, Stephen, *Questions on Cinema*, Bloomington: University of Indiana Press, 1981.

Heath, Stephen and Patricia Mellencamp (eds.), *Cinema and Language*, Frederick, Maryland: University Publications of America, 1983.

Hedges, Inez, *Breaking the Frame: Film Language and the Experience of Limits*, Bloomington: Indiana University Press, 1991.

Heidegger, Martin, *The Question Concerning Technology and Other Essays* (trans. W. Lovitt), New York: Harper Colophon Books, 1977.

——, *Being and Time* (trans. J. Stambaugh), Albany: State University of New York Press, 1953.

Hein, Birgit and Wulf Herzogenrath (eds.), *Film als Film. 1910 bis heute* (exh. cat.), Cologne: Kölnischer Kunstverein, 1977.

Henderson, Brian, *A Critique of Film Theory*, New York: E.P. Dutton, 1980.

Hendricks, Jon (ed.), *Fluxus Codex*, Detroit: The Gilbert and Lila Silverman Fluxus Collection, 1988.

—— (ed.), *Videokunst in Deutschland: 1963–1982*, Stuttgart: Verlag Gerd Hatje, 1982.

Herzogenrath, Wulf and Edith Decker (eds.), *Video Skulptur. Retrospektiv und aktuel 1963–1989*, Cologne: DuMont, 1989.

Herzogenrath, Wulf and Barbara Nierhoff (eds.), *Peter Campus: Analog + Digital Video + Foto 1970–2003* (exh. cat.), Bonn: VG Bild-Kunst; Bremen: Kunstverein Bremen, 2003.

Hillier, Jim (ed.), *Cahiers du cinéma: 1960–1968. New Wave, New Cinema, Reevaluating Hollywood*, Cambridge, Mass. and London: Harvard University Press, 1986.

——, *Cahiers du cinéma: The 1950s: Neo-Realism, Hollywood, New Wave*, Cambridge, Mass. and London: Harvard University Press, 1985.

A History of the American Avant-Garde Cinema (exh. cat.), New York: The American Federation of the Arts, 1976.

Notorious: Alfred Hitchcock and the Contemporary Art (exh. cat.), Oxford: Museum of Modern Art, 1999.

Hollander, Anne, *Moving Pictures*, New York: Alfred A. Knopf, 1989.

Horrigan, Bill (ed.), *The Media Arts in Transition*, Minneapolis: Walker Art Center, 1983.

Howard, Brice, *Videospace and Image Experience*, San Francisco: National Center for Experiments in Television, 1972.

Huffman, Kathy Rae (ed.), *Video: A Retrospective, 1974–1980* (exh. cat.), Long Beach: Long Beach Museum of Art, 1984.

Hulten, Pontus K.G. (ed.), *The Machine as Seen at the End of the Machine Age* (exh. cat.), New York: Museum of Modern Art, 1968.

Pierre Huyghe (exh. cat.), Rivoli-Torino: Castello di Rivoli Museo d'Arte Contemporanea; Milan: Skira, 2004.

Pierre Huyghe: The Third Memory (exh. cat.), Paris: Centre Georges Pompidou; Chicago: The Renaissance Society at the University of Chicago; Paris: Éditions du Centre Pompidou, 2000.

Iles, Chrissie (ed.), *Into the Light. The Projected Image in American Art 1964–1977* (exh. cat.), New York: Whitney

Museum of American Art, 2001.
James, David E., *Allegories of Cinema: American Film in the Sixties*, Princeton: Princeton University Press, 1989.
—— (ed.), *To Free the Cinema: Jonas Mekas and the New York Underground*, Princeton: Princeton University Press, 1992.
James, Gareth and Florian Zeyfang (eds.), *I Said I Love. That Is The Promise: The TVideo Politics of Jean-Luc Godard*, Berlin: b_books, 2003.
Jameson, Fredric, *Postmodernism, or, The Cultural Logic of Late Capitalism*, London: Verso, 1991.
——, *The Cultural Turn: Selected Writings on the Postmodern 1983–1998*, London: Verso, 1998.
Jay, Martin, *Downcast Eyes: The Denigration of Vision in 20th-Century French Thought*, Berkeley: University of California Press, 1993.
Jenkins, Bruce, *Film Reader 3*, Evanston: Northwestern University, 1978.
Jenkins, Bruce and Susan Krane (eds.), *Hollis Frampton: Recollections/Recreations*, Cambridge, Mass. and London: The MIT Press, 1984.
Jenkins, Bruce, and Melinda Ward (eds.), *The American New Wave, 1958–1967*, Minneapolis: Walker Art Center, 1982.
Jenkins, Janet (ed.), *In the Spirit of Fluxus* (exh. cat.), Minneapolis: Walker Art Center, 1993.
Joselit, David, *American Art Since 1945*, London: Thames & Hudson, 2003.
——, *Feedback: Television against Democracy*, Cambridge, Mass. and London: The MIT Press, 2007.
Joseph, Branden W., *Beyond the Dream Syndicate: Tony Conrad and the Arts after Cage*, New York: Zone Books, 2008.
Judson, William D. (ed.), *American Landscape Video: The Electronic Grove* (exh. cat.), Pittsburgh: The Carnegie Museum of Art, 1988.
Kaplan, E. Ann (ed.), *Psychoanalysis and Cinema*, London and New York: Routledge, 1990.
——, *Women and Film: Both Sides of the Camera*, London: Methuen, 1983.
Kaprow, Allan, *Assemblage, Environments and Happenings*, New York: Harry N. Abrams, 1966.
Kirk, Kara (ed.), *Seeing Time: Selections from the Pamela and Richard Kramlich Collection of Media Art* (exh. cat.), San Francisco: San Francisco Museum of Modern Art, 1999.
Kirshner, Judith Rossi (ed.), *Vito Acconci: A Retrospective, 1969–1980* (exh. cat.), Chicago: Museum of Contemporary Art, 1980.
Klüver, Billy, Julie Martin and Barbara Rose (eds.), *Pavilion by Experiments in Art and Technology*, New York: E.P. Dutton, 1972.
Knight, Julia (ed.), *Diverse Practices: A Critical Reader on British Video Art*, London: Arts Council of England and University of Luton Press, 1996.
Kostelanetz, Richard (ed.), *Moholy-Nagy: An Anthology*, New York: Praeger, 1970.
Kracauer, Siegfried, *Theory of Film: The Redemption of Physical Reality*, Oxford and New York: Oxford University Press, 1960.
Krauss, Rosalind, *'A Voyage on the North Sea': Art in the Age of the Post-Medium Condition*, London: Thames & Hudson, 1999.
——, *The Optical Unconscious*, Cambridge, Mass. and London: The MIT Press, 1993.
——, *The Originality of the Avant-Garde and Other Modernist Myths*, Cambridge, Mass. and London: The MIT Press, 1985.
Kraynak, Janet (ed.), *Please Pay Attention Please: Bruce Nauman's Words*, Cambridge, Mass. and London: The MIT Press, 2005.
Kriesche, Richard, *Art, Artist and the Media*, Graz: AVZ–Graz, 1978.
Kubelka, Peter, *Une Histoire du cinéma*, Paris: Centre Georges Pompidou, 1976.
Lamelas, David, *David Lamelas: A New Refutation of Time*, Düsseldorf: Richter Verlag, 1997
Lauretis, Teresa de, *Alice Doesn't: Feminism, Semiotics, Cinema*, Bloomington: Indiana University Press, 1984.
——, *Technologies of Gender: Essays on Theory*, Bloomington: Indiana University Press, 1987.
Lauretis, Teresa de and Stephen Heath (eds.), *The Cinematic Apparatus*, London: Macmillan, 1980.
Lauretis, Teresa de, Andreas Huyssen and Kathleen Woodward (eds.), *The Technological Imagination*, Madison, Wis.: Coda Press, 1980.
Lawder, Standish, *The Cubist Cinema*, New York: NYU Press, 1975.
Latour, Bruno and Peter Weibel (eds.), *Iconoclash: Beyond the Image Wars in Science, Religion, and Art* (exh. cat.), Karlsruhe: ZKM Center for Art and Media; Cambridge, Mass. and London: The MIT Press, 2002.
Lee, Pamela M., *Chronophobia: On Time in the Art of the 1960s*, Cambridge, Mass. and London: The MIT Press, 2004.
Le Grice, Malcolm, *Abstract Film and Beyond*, Cambridge, Mass. and London: The MIT Press, 1977.
——, *Experimental Cinema in the Digital Age*, London: British Film Institute, 2001.
Levin, Thomas Y., Ursula Frohne and Peter Weibel (eds.), *CTRL Space: Rhetorics of Surveillance from Bentham to Big Brother* (exh. cat.), Karlsruhe: ZKM Center for Art and Media; Cambridge, Mass. and London: The MIT Press, 2002.
Lippard, Lucy, *Six Years: The Dematerialisation of the Art Object from 1966–1972*, New York: Praeger, 1973.
—— (ed.), *Conceptual Art*, New York: Praeger, 1973.
London, Barbara (ed.), *New Video Japan* (exh. cat.), New York: The Museum of Modern Art, 1986.
Mignot, Dorine (ed.), *The Luminous Image* (exh. cat.), Amsterdam: Stedelijk Museum, 1984.
MacCabe, Colin, *Godard: A Portrait of the Artist at Seventy*, New York: Farrar, Straus & Giroux, 2003.
——, *Godard; Images, Sounds, Politics*, London: British Film Institute; Bloomington: Indiana University Press, 1980
——, *High Theory/Low Culture: Analyzing Popular Television and Film*, New York: St. Martin's Press, 1986.
MacDonald, Scott, *Avant-Garde Film: Motion Studies*, Cambridge: Cambridge University Press, 1993.
——, *A Critical Cinema: Interviews with Independent Filmmakers*, Berkeley: University of California Press, 1988.
——, *A Critical Cinema 2: Interviews with Independent Filmmakers*, Berkeley: University of California Press, 1992.
Mannoni, Laurent, *The Great Art of Light and Shadow: Archaeology of the Cinema* (ed. and trans. Richard Crangle), Exeter: University of Exeter Press, 2000.
Manovich, Lev, *The Language of New Media*, Cambridge, Mass. and London: The MIT Press, 2001.
Marcus, Daniel (ed.), *Roar! The Paper Tiger Guide to Media Activism*, Columbus: Paper Tiger Television; Wexner Center for the Arts, 1991.
Chris Marker: Silent Movie (exh. cat.), Columbus: Wexner Center for the Arts, The Ohio State University, 1995.
Marks, Laura U., *The Skin of the Film: Intercultural Cinema, Embodiment, and the Senses*, Durham and London: Duke University Press, 2000.
Masséra, Jean-Charles, *The Lesson of Stains (Towards An Aesthetics of Reconstitution)*, Paris: Centre Georges Pompidou; Chicago: The Renaissance Society, 2000.
McCarthy, Anna, *Ambient Television: Visual Culture and Public Space*, Durham and London: Duke University Press, 2001.
McDonough, Tom (ed.), *Guy Debord and the Situationist*

International. Texts and Documents, Cambridge, Mass. and London: The MIT Press, 2002.
McLuhan, Marshall, *Understanding Media: The Extensions of Man*, New York: McGraw-Hill, 1964.
——, *Verbi-Voco-Visual Explorations*, New York: Something Else Press, 1967.
McLuhan, Marshall and Quentin Fiore, *The Medium Is the Massage*, New York: Bantam, 1967.
——, *War and Peace in the Global Village*, New York: Bantam, 1968.
McShine, Kynaston (ed.), *Information* (exh. cat.), New York: The Museum of Modern Art, 1970.
Mekas, Jonas, *Movie Journal: The Rise of a New American Cinema, 1959–1971*, New York: Macmillan, 1972.
Mellencamp, Patricia, *Indiscretions: Avant-Garde Film, Video, and Feminism*, Bloomington: Indiana University Press, 1990.
—— (ed.), *Logics of Television: Essays in Cultural Criticism*, Bloomington: Indiana University Press, 1990.
Merleau-Ponty, Maurice, *Phenomenology of Perception* (trans. C. Smith), New York and London: Routledge and Kegan Paul, 1962.
Metz, Christian, *Film Language: A Semiotics of the Cinema* (trans. M. Taylor), Oxford and New York: Oxford University Press, 1974.
——, *The Imaginary Signifier: Psychoanalysis and the Cinema* (trans. C. Britton, A. Williams, B. Brewster and A. Guzzetti), Bloomington: Indiana University Press, 1982.
——, *Language and Cinema* (trans. D.J. Umiker-Sebeok), The Hague: Mouton, 1974.
Michelson, Annette (ed.), *New Forms in Film* (exh. cat.), Montreux: Corbax, 1974.
Millennium Film Journal. Special: 'A Montage of Voices: Twenty Years of Filmmakers' Statements. 20th Anniversary Edition' (ed. Tony Pipolo and Grahame Weinbren), no.16/17/18, Fall/Winter 1986/87.
Minh-ha, Trinh T., *Cinema Interval*, New York and London: Routledge, 1999.
Mitry, Jean, *Le Cinéma experimental: Histoire et perspectives*, Paris: Édition Seghers, 1974.
——, *Esthétique et psychologie du cinéma*, vol.1, *Les structures*, Paris: Éditions Universitaires, 1963.
——, *Esthétique et psychologie du cinéma*, vol.2, *Les formes*, Paris: Éditions Universitaires, 1965.
Morse, Margaret, *Virtualities: Television, Media Art, and CyberCulture*, Bloomington and Indianapolis: Indiana University Press, 1998.
Mulvey, Laura, *Death 24 x a Second: Stillness and the Moving Image*, London: Reaktion Books, 2006.
——, *Visual and Other Pleasures*, Bloomington: Indiana University Press, 1989.
Bruce Nauman: Exhibition Catalogue and Catalogue Raisonné (exh. cat.), Minneapolis: Walker Art Center, 1994.
Nichols, Bill (ed.), *Maya Deren and the American Avant Garde*, Berkeley: University of California Press, 2001.
Noguez, Dominique, *Le Cinéma, autrement*, Paris: Les Editions du Cerf, 1987.
——, *Cinéma: Théorie, lectures*, Paris: Editions Klincksieck, 1973.
——, *Trente Ans de cinéma expérimental en France (1950–1980)*, Paris: A.R.C.E.F., 1982.
Oetterman, Stephan, *The Panorama: History of a Mass Medium* (trans. D.L. Schneider), New York: Zone Books, 1997.
Hélio Oiticica (exh. cat.), Rotterdam: Witte de With; Paris: Galerie nationale du Jeu de Paume; Barcelona: Fundació Antoni Tàpies; Lisbon: Centro de Arte Moderna da Fundação Calouste Gulbenkian; Minneapolis: Walker Art Center, 1992.
Parfait, Françoise, *Vidéo: Un art contemporain*, Paris: Éditions du Regard, 2001.
Peltry, Robert H. and Mary Hall-Pelfry, *Art and Mass Media*, New York: Harper and Row Publishers, 1985.
Penley, Constance, *The Future of an Illusion: Film, Feminism, and Psychoanalysis*, Minneapolis: University of Minnesota Press, 1989.
—— (ed.), *Feminism and Film Theory*, London and New York: Routledge, 1988.
Pincus-Witten, Robert, *Postminimalism into Maximalism: American Art 1966–1989*, Ann Arbor and London: UMI Research Press, 1987.
Price, Jonathan, *Video Visions: A Medium Discovers Itself*, New York: New American Library, 1977.
Projected Allegories (exh. cat.), Houston: Contemporary Arts Museum, 1988.
Projected Art (exh. cat.), New York: Finch College Museum of Art, 1966.
Projected Images: Peter Campus, Rockne Krebs, Paul Sharits, Michael Snow, Ted Victoria, Robert Whitman (exh. cat.), Minneapolis: Walker Art Center, 1974.
Prospect '69 (exh. cat.), Düsseldorf: Städtische Kunsthalle, 1969.
Prospect '71: Projection (exh. cat.), Düsseldorf: Städtische Kunsthalle and Art-Press, 1971.
Rainer, Yvonne, *Work 1961–73* (ed. Kasper König), Halifax: The Press of the Nova Scotia College of Art and Design, 1974.
——, *The Films of Yvonne Rainer*, Bloomington: Indiana University Press, 1989.
Rancière, Jacques, *Film Fables* (trans. E. Battista), Oxford and New York: Berg Publishers, 2006.
Rebentisch, Juliane, *Ästhetik der Installation*, Frankfurt a.M.: Suhrkamp, 2003.
Reck, Hans Ulrich, *Mythos Medienkunst*, Cologne: Verlag der Buchhandlung Walther König, 2002.
Rees, A.L., *A History of Experimental Film and Video: From the Canonical Avant-Garde to Contemporary British Practice*, London: British Film Institute, 1999.
Renan, Sheldon, *An Introduction to the American Underground Film*, New York: E.P. Dutton, 1967.
Renov, Michael and Erika Suderburg (eds.), *Resolutions: Essays on Contemporary Video Practices*, Minneapolis: University of Minnesota Press, 1995.
A Report on the Art and Technology Program of the Los Angeles County Museum of Art, 1967–1971 (exh. cat.), Los Angeles: Los Angeles County Museum of Art, 1971.
Resolution: A Critique of Video Art/TV Generation (exh. cat.), Los Angeles: Los Angeles Contemporary Exhibitions, 1986.
Return of Guerrilla Television: A TVTV Retrospective (exh. cat.), New York: International Center of Photography, 1986.
Rieser, Martin and Andrea Zapp (eds.), *New Screen Media: Cinema/Art/Narrative*, London: British Film Institute, 2002.
Riviere, Daniele (ed.), *Paysages virtuels. Image video, image de synthese*, Paris: Dis Voir, 1988.
Rodowick, D.N., *The Crisis of Political Modernism*, Berkeley: University of California Press, 1994.
——, *Reading the Figural, or, Philosophy after the New Media*, Durham and London: Duke University Press, 2001.
Rosen, Philip (ed.), *Narrative, Apparatus, Ideology: A Film Theory Reader*, New York: Columbia University Press, 1986.
Ross, David, *Artists' Video*, New York: Art Information Distribution, 1975.
Ruiz, Raúl, *Poetics of Cinema* (trans. B. Holmes), Paris: Éditions Dis Voir, 1995.
Rush, Michael, *New Media in Late 20th-Century Art*, London: Thames & Hudson, 1999.

——, *Video Art*, London: Thames & Hudson, 2003.
Russell, Catherine, *Experimental Ethnography: The Work of Film in the Age of Video*, Durham and London: Duke University Press, 1999.
Schneider, Ira and Beryl Korot (eds.), *Video Art: An Anthology*, New York: Harcourt Brace Jovanovich; The Raindance Foundation, 1976.
Schwarz, Hans-Peter (ed.), *Medien Kunst Geschichte* (exh. cat.), Karlsruhe: ZKM Center for Art and Media; Munich: Prestel, 1997.
Screen Reader 2: Cinema and Semiotics, London: The Society for Education in Film and Television, 1981.
Shamberg, Michael and Raindance Corporation, *Guerrilla Television*, New York: Holt, Rhinehart and Winston, 1971.
The Filmic Art of Paul Sharits (exh. cat.), Buffalo: Burchfield-Penney Art Center, Buffalo State College, 2000.
Shohat, Ella and Robert Stam, *Unthinking Eurocentrism: Multiculturalism and the Media*, London and New York: Routledge, 1994.
Silverman, Kaja, *The Acoustic Mirror: The Female Voice in Psychoanalysis and Cinema*, Bloomington: Indiana University Press, 1988.
——, *World Spectators*, Stanford: Stanford University Press, 2000.
Sitney, P. Adams, *Visionary Film: The American Avant-Garde, 1943–2000*, Oxford and New York: Oxford University Press, 1979.
—— (ed.), *The Avant-Garde Film: A Reader of Theory and Criticism*, New York: NYU Press, 1978.
—— (ed.), *The Essential Cinema: Essays on Films in the Collection of the Anthology Film Archives*, New York: Anthology Film Archives and NYU Press, 1975.
—— (ed.), *Film Culture Reader*, New York: Praeger, 1970.
Situationist International Anthology (ed. and trans. K. Knabb), Berkeley: Bureau of Public Secrets, 1981.
Sklar, Robert, *Film: An International History of the Medium*, New York: Harry N. Abrams, 1993.
Skoller, Jeffrey, *Shadows, Specters, Shards: Making History in Avant-Garde Film*, Minneapolis: University of Minnesota Press, 2005.
Smith, John, *Film and Video Works 1972–2002* (exh. cat.), Bristol: Picture This Moving Image and Watershed Media, 2002.
Sobchack, Vivian, *The Address of the Eye: A Phenomenology of Film Experience*, Princeton: Princeton University Press, 1992.
Spielmann, Yvonne, *Video. Das reflexiv Medium*, Frankfurt a.M.: Suhrkamp, 2005.
Spellbound: Art and Film, London: Hayward Gallery; British Film Institute, 1996.
Stam, Robert, Robert Burgoyne and Sandy Flitterman-Lewis, *New Vocabularies in Film Semiotics: Structuralism, Post-structuralism, and Beyond*, London and New York: Routledge, 1992.
Stemmrich, Gregor (ed.), *Jahresring 48: Kunst/Kino*, Cologne: Oktagon Verlag, 2001.
Studio International. Special: 'Avant-Garde Film in England and Europe', vol.190 no.978, November–December 1975.
Suderburg, Erika (ed.), *Space, Site, Intervention: Situating Installation Art*, Minneapolis: University of Minnesota, 2000.
Top Value Television (TVTV), *The Prime Time Survey*, San Francisco: TVTV, 1974.
Town, Elke (ed.), *Video by Artists 2*, Toronto: Art Metropole, 1986.
TV as a Creative Medium (exh. cat.), New York: Howard Wise Gallery, 1969.
Tyler, Parker, *Underground Film: A Critical History*, New York: Grove Press, 1969.
Ulmer, Gregory L., *Applied Grammatology*, Baltimore: John Hopkins University Press, 1985.
——, *Teletheory: Grammatology in the Age of Video*, London and New York: Routledge, 1989.
Video Art: Expanded Forms (exh. cat.), New York: Whitney Museum of American Art, 1998.
Videofreex, *The Spaghetti City Video Manual: A Guide to Use, Repair, and Maintenance*, New York: Praeger, 1973.
Vogel, Amos, *Film as a Subversive Art*, New York: Random House, 1974.
Vostell, Wolf, *Happening und Leben*, Berlin: Hermann Luchterhand Verlag, 1970.
Wallis, Brian (ed.), *Art After Modernism: Rethinking Representation*, New York: The New Museum of Contemporary Art; Boston: David R. Godine, 1984.
Weber, Samuel, *Mass Mediauras: Forms, Technics, Media*, Stanford: Stanford University Press, 1996.
Wees, William C., *Light Moving in Time: Studies in the Visual Aesthetics of Avant-Garde Film*, Berkeley: University of California Press, 1992.
White Cube/Black Box (exh. cat.), Vienna: Generali Foundation, 1996.
Wild Walls (exh. cat.), Amsterdam: Stedelijk Museum, 1995.
Williams, Linda (ed.), *Viewing Positions: Ways of Seeing Film*, New Brunswick: Rutgers University Press, 1995.
Williams, Raymond, *Television: Technology and Cultural Form*, New York: Schocken Books, 1974.
Winston, Brian, *Media, Technology and Society. A History: From the Telegraph to the Internet*, New York: Routledge, 1998.
——, *Misunderstanding Media*, London: Routledge and Kegan Paul, 1986.
Wollen, Peter, *Paris Hollywood: Writings on Film*, London: Verso, 2002.
——, *Readings and Writings: Semiotic Counter-Strategies*, London: Verso; New Left Books, 1982.
——, *Signs and Meaning in the Cinema* (1972), London: British Film Institute, 1998.
Michalka, Matthias (ed.), *X-Screen: Film Installations and Actions in the 1960s and 1970s* (exh. cat.), Vienna: Museum Moderner Kunst Stiftung Ludwig; Cologne: Verlag der Buchhandlung Walther König, 2003.
Youngblood, Gene, *Expanded Cinema*, New York: E.P. Dutton, 1970.
Zielinski, Siegfried, *Audiovisions: Cinema and Television as Entr'actes in History*, Amsterdam: Amsterdam University Press, 1999.
——, *Video/Apparat, Medium, Kunst, Kultur. Ein internationaler Reader*, Frankfurt a.M.: Peter Lang, 1992.
——, *Zur Geschichte Des Videorecorders*, Berlin: Wissenschaftsverlag, 1986.

Bibliography – Articles

Selected Articles and Essays

Agamben, Giorgio, 'Face au cinema et à l'historie, à propos de Jean-Luc Godard', *Le Monde des livres*, 6 October 1995, p.11.

Albera, François, 'Anomique cinéma, le cinéma au delà de l'esthétique', *Artpress*, no.14, 1993, pp.10–17.

Allan, Michael, 'The Location of Lebanon: Portraits and Places in the Videography of Jayce Salloum', *Parachute*, no.108, October/November/December 2002, pp.165–76.

Antin, David, 'Television: Video's Frightful Parent', *Artforum*, vol.14 no.4, December 1975, pp.36–45.

Anton, Saul, 'One More Step', *Parkett*, no.69, 2003, pp.32–43.

Arthur, Paul S., 'Creating Spectacle from Dross: The Chimeric Cinema of Ken Jacobs', *Film Comment*, vol.33 no.2, March/April 1997, p.61.

——, 'Structural Film: Revisions, New Versions, and the Artifact', *Millennium Film Journal*, no.2, Spring/Summer 1978, pp.5–13.

——, 'Structural Film: Revisions, New Versions, and the Artifact. Part Two', *Millennium Film Journal*, nos.4/5, Summer/Fall 1979, pp.122–34.

Baker, George, 'An Interview with Pierre Huyghe', *October*, no.110, Fall 2004, pp.80–106.

——, 'Artist Questionnaires: 21 Responses', *October*, no.100, Spring 2002, pp.6–97.

——, 'At the Limits of Sculpture', *Art Journal*, vol.60 no.3, Fall 2001, pp.105–07.

——, 'Reanimations', *October*, no.104, Spring 2003, pp.28–70.

——, 'The Space of Stain', *Grey Room*, vol.1 no.5, Fall 2001, pp.5–37.

Battcock, Gregory, 'Celluloid Sculptors', *Art and Artists*, vol.6, October 1971, pp.24–27.

——, 'Explorations in Video', *Art and Artists*, vol.7, February 1973, pp.22–27.

——, 'Greening of Televideo and the Aesthetics of Boeing', *Domus*, no.509, April 1972, pp.50–53.

——, 'Informative Exhibition at the Museum of Modern Art', *Arts Magazine*, vol.44 no.8, Summer 1970, pp.24–27.

Baudry, Jean-Louis, 'Ideological Effects of the Basic Cinematographic Apparatus' (trans. A. Williams), *Film Quarterly*, vol.28 no.2, Winter 1974/75, pp.39–47.

——, 'Writing Fiction, Ideology', *Afterimage*, vol.5, Spring 1974, pp.22–39.

Beauvais, Yann, 'Deconstructing Cinema', *Artpress*, no.262, November 2000, pp.42–47.

——, 'Un cinéma mineur, de moeurs, d'humeur', *Artpress*, no.14, 1993, pp.148–52.

Bellour, Raymond, 'An Interview with Bill Viola', *October*, no.34, Fall 1985, pp.91–119.

——, 'Autoportraits', *Communications*, no.48, 1988, pp.327–87.

——, 'I Am an Image', *Camera Obscura*, nos.8/10,1982, pp.116–23.

——, 'The Film Stilled', *Camera Obscura*, vol.24, 1990, pp.98–123.

——, 'The Moving Image: A Battle of Ways and Means', *Modern Painters,* vol.14 no.1, Spring 2001, pp.66–69.

——, 'Thierry Kuntzel et le rétour de l'écriture', *Cahiers du cinéma*, no.321, March 1981, pp.40–50.

Bishop, Claire, 'Video Killed the Radio Star', *Flash Art*, vol.36, January/February 2003, pp.70–73.

Blümlinger, Christa, 'Harun Farocki: Strategies Critiques', *Parachute*, no.111, July/August/September 2003, pp.112–25.

——, 'Image(circum)volution: On the Installation *Schnittstelle (Interface)*' (trans. R. Hillman and T. Mathieson), *Senses of Cinema*, vol.2 no.21, 1998, www.sensesofcinema.com/contents/02/21/farocki_blumlinger.html

Bourdon, David, 'Warhol as a Filmmaker', *Art in America*, vol.59, May 1971, pp.48–53.

Boyle, Deirdre, 'Juan Downey's Recent Videotapes', *Afterimage*, vol.6 nos.1/2, 1978, pp.10–11.

——, 'Subject to Change: Guerrilla TV Revisited', *Art Journal*, vol.45 no.3, Fall 1985, pp.228–32.

Bruyn, Eric de, 'David Lamelas: Passing Time', *Texte zur Kunst*, vol.7 no.26, June 1997, pp.100–07.

——, 'On the Museum as Film Décor: Marcel Broodthaers and *La Bataille de Waterloo*', *Trans no.* 8, Fall 2000, pp.76–91.

Bucher, François, 'Television (an Address)', *Journal of Visual Culture*, vol.4 no.1, 2005, pp.5–15.

Buchloh, Benjamin H.D., 'Allegorical Procedures: Appropriation and Montage in Contemporary Art', *Artforum*, vol.21 no.1, September 1982, pp.43–56.

——, 'Critical Reflections', *Artforum*, vol.35 no.5, January 1997, pp.68–69, 102.

——, 'From Gadget Video to Agit Video: Some Notes on Four Recent Video Works', *Art Journal*, vol.45 no.3, Fall 1985, pp.217–27.

Buchsbaum, Jonathan, 'Peter Wollen: In Search of Political Film', *Millennium Film Journal*, nos.14/15, Fall/Winter 1984/85, pp.61–71.

Buergel, Roger M., 'Arbeiten an den Grenzen des Realen', *Texte zur Kunst*, no.43, September 2000, pp.66–75.

Burnham, Jack, 'Problems of Criticism: Art and Technology', *Artforum*, vol.9, January 1971, pp.40–45.

——, 'Systems Aesthetics', *Artforum*, vol.7, September 1968, pp.30–35.

Burris, Jon, 'Did the Portapak Cause Video Art? Notes on the Formation of a New Medium', *Millennium Film Journal*, no.29, Fall 1996, pp.3–28.

Camper, Fred, 'Film: The Front Line', *Millennium Film Journal*, nos.14/15, Fall/Winter 1984/85, pp.48–56.

——, 'The End of Avant-Garde Film', *Millennium Film Journal*, nos.16/17/18, Fall/Winter 1986/87, pp.99–124.

Carroll, Noël, 'Avant-Garde Film and Film Theory', *Millennium Film Journal*, nos.4/5, Summer/Fall 1979, pp.135–43.

——, 'Causation, the Ampliation of Movement and Avant-Garde Film', *Millennium Film Journal*, nos.10/11, Fall/Winter 1981/82, pp.61–82.

——, 'Medium Specificity Arguments and Self-Consciously Invented Arts: Film, Video and Photography', *Millennium Film Journal*, nos.14/15, Fall/Winter 1984/85, pp.127–53.

Cavell, Stanley, 'The Fact of Television', *Daedalus*, vol.111 no.4, Fall 1982, pp.75–96.

Chomont, Tom, 'Radical Form: Radical Content', *Millennium Film Journal*, no.22, Winter/Spring 1989/1990, pp.124–26.

Connolly, Maeve, 'The Doubled Space of Willie Doherty's *Re-Run*', *Filmwaves*, no.23, Winter 2004, pp.8–10.

Cooke, Lynne, 'Rodney Graham: A Tale of a Hat', *Parkett,* no.64, 2002, pp.96–105.

Copjec, Joan, 'India Song/Son nom de Venise dans Calcutta desert: The Compulsion to Repeat', *October*, no.17,

Summer 1981, pp.42–43.
——, 'The Orthopsychic Subject: Film Theory and the Reception of Lacan', *October*, no.49, Summer 1989, pp.53–71.
Cornwell, Regina, 'Art in the Agora: Dara Birnbaum', *Art in America*, vol.79 no.2, February 1991, pp.134–37, 169.
——, 'Interactive Storytelling: A Pioneering Work of High-tech Video Art', *Art in America*, vol.76 no.1, January 1988, pp.43–45.
——, 'Oppenheim's Delirious Operations', *Artforum*, vol.17, November 1978, pp.36–40.
——, 'Paul Sharits: Illusion and Object', *Artforum*, vol.10 no.1, September 1971, pp.56–62.
——, 'Some Formalist Tendencies in the Current American Avant-Garde Film', *Studio International*, vol.184 no.948, October 1972, pp.110–14.
——, 'Spectacle, Attention, Counter-Memory', *October*, no.50, Fall 1988, pp.97–107.
——, 'Techniques of the Observer', *October*, no.45, Summer 1988, pp.3–35.
Crimp, Douglas, 'About Pictures', *Flash Art*, nos.88/89, March/April 1979, pp.34–36.
——, 'Joan Jonas's Performance Works', *Studio International*, vol.192, July 1976, pp.10–12.
——, 'Pictures', *October*, no.8, Spring 1979, pp.75–88.
Cubitt, Sean, 'Cartographic Instruments, Narcissist Illusions, Regimes of Realism in CGI', *Millennium Film Journal*, no.34, Fall 1999, pp.44–64.
Curtis, David, 'English Avant-Garde Film: An Early Chronology', *Studio International*, vol.190 no.978, November/December 1975, pp.176–82.
Davis, Douglas, 'Art and Technology: The New Combine', *Art in America*, vol.56 no.1, January/February 1968, pp.28–47.
——, 'Art and Technology Conversations. Billy Klüver: The Engineer as a Work of Art', *Art in America*, vol.56 no.1, January/February 1968, pp.38–46.
——, 'Avant-Garde Is Dead! Long Live the Avant-Garde', *Art in America*, vol.70, April 1982, pp.11–19.
——, 'Conversations with Gyorgy Kepes, Billy Klüver and James Seawright', *Art in America*, vol.56 no.1, January/February, 1968, pp.38–45.
——, 'Media/Art/Media: Notes Toward a Definition of Form', *Arts Magazine*, vol.46, September/October 1971, pp.43–45.
——, 'Post-everything', *Art in America*, vol.68, February 1980, pp.11–14.
——, 'Post-performancism', *Artforum*, vol.20, October 1981, pp.31–39.
——, 'Provisional Overview of Artist's Television in the US', *Studio International*, vol.191, May 1976, pp.265–72.
——, 'Video Obscura', *Artforum*, vol.10, April 1972, pp.65–71.
——, 'What Is Content? Notes Toward an Answer', *Artforum*, vol.12, October 1973, pp.59–63.
Debevoise, Clay, 'Mirror Spaces: A Review of Video Spaces, Eight Installations', *Millennium Film Journal*, no.29, Fall 1996, pp.68–78.
DeJong, Constance, 'In Between the Dark and the Light (Television/Society/Art: A Symposium), *Artforum*, vol.19 no.5, January 1981, pp.25–29.
Deleuze, Gilles, 'Qu'est-ce que l'acte de création?', *Trafic*, vol.7, Autumn 1998, pp.133–42.
Demos, T.J., 'The Art of Darkness: On Steve McQueen', *October*, no.114, Fall 2005, pp.61–89.
Dercon, Chris, 'Gleaning the Future from the Gallery Floor', *Senses of Cinema*, vol.2 no.28, 2002, www.sensesofcinema.com/contents/03/28/gleaning_the_future.html
Dewey, Ken, Henry Geldzahler et al., 'Expanded Cinema: A Symposium. N.Y. Film Festival 1966', *Film Culture*, no.46, Winter 1966, pp.1–2.
Dietz, Steve, 'Public Sphere's', *Media Art Net*, 2004, www.medienkunstnetz.de/themes/public_sphere_s/public_sphere_s/
Duguet, Anne-Marie, 'The Luminous Image: Video Installation', *Camera Obscura*, nos.13/14, Spring/Summer 1985, pp.28–49.
Dusinberre, Deke, 'On Expanding Cinema', *Studio International*, vol.190 no.978, November/December 1975, pp.220–24.
Eleftheriotis, Dimitris, 'Video Poetics: Technology, Aesthetics and Politics', *Screen*, vol.36 no.2, 1995, pp.100–12.
Elwes, Catherine, 'Northern Exposure', *Art Monthly*, no.217, June 1998, pp.7–11.
——, 'Videoscan: Video Art, Who Needs It?', *Art Monthly*, no.196, May 1996, pp.8–11.
EXPORT, VALIE, 'Expanded Cinema as Expanded Reality', *Senses of Cinema*, vol.3 no.28, 2003, www.sensesofcinema.com/contents/03/28/expanded_cinema.html
Fargier, Jean-Paul, 'Nam June Paik et Shigeko Kubota', *Cahiers du cinéma*, no.341, 1982, pp.28–34.
——, 'Vidéo, vitesse, technologie. La troisième fenêtre. Entretien avec Paul Virilio', *Cahiers du cinéma*, no.322, 1981, pp.35–40.
Farocki, Harun, 'Influences Transversales', *Trafic*, no.43, September 2002, pp.19–25.
——, 'Reality Would Have to Begin', *Documents*, nos.1/2, Fall/Winter 1992, pp.136–46.
Field, Allyson, 'Hurlements en faveur de Sade: The Negation and Surpassing of "Discrepant Cinema"', *SubStance*, vol.28 no.3, 1999, pp.55–70.
Field, Simon, 'Film Is...?', *Art and Artists*, vol.6 no.9, December 1971, pp.24–29.
Fleischer, Alain, 'Du cinéma considéré comme moyen de transport', *Artpress*, no.14, 1993, pp.50–54.
Fowler, Catherine, 'Double Visions, Double Frames', *Filmwaves: Art in-sight*, vol.23, Winter 2004, pp.5–7.
——, 'Room for Experiment: Gallery Films and Vertical Time from Maya Deren to Eija-Liisa Ahtila', *Screen*, vol.45 no.4, Winter 2004, pp.324–43.
Frampton, Hollis, 'Eadweard Muybridge: Fragments of a Tesseract', *Artforum*, vol.11 no.7, March 1973, pp.43–52.
——, 'For a Metahistory of Film: Commonplace Notes and Hypotheses', *Artforum*, vol.10 no.1, September 1971, pp.32–35.
——, 'Letter From Hollis Frampton to Stan Brakhage', *Millennium Film Journal*, nos.16/17/18, Fall/Winter 1986/87, pp.212–13.
——, 'The Withering Away of the State of Art', *Artforum* vol.13 no.4, December 1974, pp.50–55.
Frampton, Hollis, Ken Jacobs and Michael Snow, 'Filmmakers versus the Museum of Modern Art', *Filmmakers' Newsletter*, vol.2 no.7, May 1969, pp.1–2.
Freed, Hermine, 'Video and Abstract Expressionism', *Arts Magazine*, vol.49 no.4, December 1974, p.67–69.
Fried, Michael, 'New York Letter', *Art International*, vol.8 nos.5/6, Summer 1964, p.82.
——, 'Shape as Form: Frank Stella's New Paintings', *Artforum*, vol.5 no.3, November 1966, pp.18–27.
Furlong, Lucinda, 'Notes Toward a History of Image-Processed Video: Steina and Woody Vasulka', *Afterimage*, vol.11 no.5, December 1983, pp.12–17.
——, 'Tracking Video Art: "Image Processing" as a Genre', *Art Journal*, vol.45 no.3, Fall 1985, pp.233–37.
Gever, Martha, 'An Interview with Martha Rosler', *Afterimage*, vol.9 no.3, October 1981, pp.10–17.
——, 'Pressure Points: Video in the Public Sphere', *Art Journal*, vol.45 no.3, Fall 1985, p.238–43.

——, 'Video Politics: Early Feminist Projects', *Afterimage*, vol.11 nos.1/2, Summer 1983, pp.25–27.
Gever, Martha and Marita Sturken, 'Mary Lucier's Elemental Investigations', *Afterimage*, vol.9 no.7, February 1982, p.8.
Gidal, Peter, 'Film as Film', *Art and Artists*, vol.7 no.9, December 1972, pp.12–43.
——, 'Interview with Hollis Frampton', *October*, no.32, Spring 1985, pp.93–117.
——, 'Samuel Beckett's "Ghost Trio"', *Artforum*, vol.17 no.9, May 1979, pp.53–57.
——, 'Theory and Definition of Structural/Materialist Film', *Studio International*, vol.190 no.978, November/December 1975, pp.189–96.
Gilbard, Florence, 'An Interview With Vito Acconci: Video Works 1970–1978', *Afterimage*, vol.12 no.4, November 1984, pp.9–15.
Godard, Jean-Luc and Anne-Marie Miéville, 'France/Tour/Detour/Two/Children', *Camera Obscura*, nos.8/9/10, Fall 1982, pp.61–73.
Godfrey, Mark, 'Light Years: Mark Godfrey talks to Anthony McCall', *frieze*, no. 99, May 2006, pp.124–29.
Goodeve, Thyrza Nichols, 'The Mobile Muse: Giuliana Bruno Walks with Her Tongue Through Her "Atlas of Emotion"', *Parkett*, no.66, 2002, pp.6–10.
Grace, Sharon, 'An Interview with Shigeko Kubota', *ArtCom*, vol.4 no.15, 1981, pp.22–26.
Graham, Dan, 'Artists Pages', *Interfunktionen*, no.8, 1972, pp.27–33.
——, 'Artists Pages', *Interfunktionen*, no.9, 1973, pp.57–64.
——, 'Eight Pieces by Dan Graham 1966–1972', *Studio International*, vol.183 no.944, May 1972, pp.210–13.
——, 'Performance as Perceptual Process', *Interfunktionen*, no.7, 1971, pp.84–85.
——, 'Theater, Cinema, Power', *Parachute*, no.31, Summer 1983, pp.11–19.
——, 'TV Camera/Monitor Performance', *Interfunktionen*, no.7, 1971, p.88.
Griffiths, Alison, '"Journeys for Those Who Can Not Travel": Promenade Cinema and the Museum Life Group', *Wideangle*, vol.18 no.3, 1996, pp.53–84.
——, '"Shivers Down Your Spine": Panoramas and the Origins of the Cinematic Reenactment', *Screen*, vol.44 no.1, Spring, 2003, pp.1–37.
Grundmann, Roy, 'Masters of Ceremony: Media Demonstration as Performance in Three Instances of Expanded Cinema', *Velvet Light Trap*, no. 54, Fall 2004, pp.48–64.
Gunning, Tom, 'The Cinema of Attractions: Early Film, Its Spectator and the Avant-Garde', *Wide Angle*, vol.8 nos.3/4, 1986, pp.63–70.
Hall, David, 'British Video Art: Towards an Autonomous Practice', *Studio International*, vol.191 no.981, May/June, 1976, pp.248–52.
——, 'Video', *Studio International*, vol.191 no.979, January/February 1976, pp.61–63.
Hall, Sue and John Hopkins, 'The Metasoftware of Video', *Studio International*, vol.191 no.981, May/June 1976, pp.260–64.
Hanhardt, John G., 'Film Image/Electronic Image: The Construction of Abstraction, 1960–1990', *Visible Language*, vol.29 no.2, 1995, pp.138–59.
——, 'The Passion for Perceiving: Expanding Forms of Film and Video Art', *Art Journal*, vol.45 no.3, Fall 1985, pp.213–16.
Hanhardt, John G. and Maria Christina Villaseñor, 'Video/Media Culture of the Late Twentieth Century', *Art Journal*, vol.54 no.5, Winter 1995, pp.20–25.
Hansen, Miriam, 'Benjamin, Cinema, and Experience. "The Blue Flower in the Land of Technology"', *New German Critique*, vol.40, Winter 1987, pp.179–224.
——, 'Reinventing the Nickelodeon: Notes on Kluge and Early Cinema', *October*, no.46, Fall 1988, pp.179–98.
Hein, Birgit, 'Film as Art: Part 1', *Heute Kunst*, no.13, February/April 1976, pp.5–6.
——, 'Return to Reason: On Experimental Film in West Germany and Austria', *Studio International*, vol.190 no.978, November/December 1975, pp.197–202.
——, 'The Avant-Garde and Politics', *Millennium Film Journal*, no.2, Spring/Summer 1978, pp.22–28.
Hermange, Emmanuel, 'Pour nous le cinéma est mort. Notes sur quelques stratégies cinéphiles de l'art', *Parachute*, no.103, July/August/September 2001, pp.13–24.
Herzogenrath, Wulf, 'Video Art in West Germany', *Studio International*, vol.191 no.981, May/June 1976, pp.217–22.
——, 'Video-Kunst [documenta 6, Kassel]', *Kunstwerk*, June 1977, pp.42–44.
Horn, Laurence, 'On Video and its Viewer', *Millennium Film Journal*, nos.14/15, Fall/Winter, 1984/85, pp.155–64.
Iles, Chrissie, 'Reflections: Video Sculpture Past and Present', *Performance Magazine*, no.58, Summer 1989, pp.45–53.
James, David E., 'Artists as Filmmakers in Los Angeles', *October*, no.112, Spring 2005, pp.111–27.
——, 'Hollywood Extras: One Tradition of "Avant-Garde" Film in Los Angeles', *October*, no.90, Fall 1999, pp.13–17.
——, 'Peregrinations of the Avant-Garde: The Chelsea Girls Go to Russia', *Millennium Film Journal*, no.38, Spring 2002, pp.9–18.
Jenkins, Bruce, 'A Case Against "Structural Film"', *Journal of the University of Film Association*, vol.33 no.2, Spring 1981, pp.9–14.
——, 'Hollis Frampton: The Red and the Green', *October*, no.32, Spring 1985, pp.77–92.
Joselit, David, 'An Allegory of Criticism', *October*, no.103, Winter 2003, pp.3–13.
——, 'Inside the Light Cube', *Artforum*, vol.42 no.7, March 2004, pp.154–59.
——, 'Into the Light: Image in American Art 1964–1977, Whitney Museum of American Art, New York', *Artforum*, vol.40 no.5, January 2002, pp.135–36.
——, 'No Exit: Video and The Readymade', *October*, no.119, pp.37–45.
——, 'Plastic Empathy: The Ghost of Robert Whitman', *Grey Room*, no.25, Fall 2006, pp.64–91.
——, 'The Play of Repetition: Andy Warhol's *Sleep*', *Grey Room*, no.19, Spring 2005, pp.22–53.
——, 'The Video Public Sphere', *Art Journal*, vol.59 no.2, Summer 2000, pp.46–53.
Kaplan, Ann E. and Jeff Halley, 'One Plus One: Ideology and Deconstruction in Godard's *Içi et ailleurs* and *Comment ça va*', *Millennium Film Journal*, no.6, Spring 1980, pp.98–102.
Kaprow, Allan, 'Video Art: Old Wine, New Bottle', *Artforum*, vol.12 no.10, June 1974, pp.46–49.
Keenan, Thomas, 'The Push and Pull of Rights and Responsibilities', *Interventions*, vol.4 no.2, 2002, pp.191–97.
Keller, Marjorie, 'Women and Film', *Millennium Film Journal*, nos.14/15, Fall/Winter 1984/85, pp.43–47.
Kirby, Michael, 'The Uses of Film in the New Theatre', *Tulane Drama Review*, vol.11 no.1, Fall 1966, pp.49–61.
Kittler, Friedrich, 'There Is No Software', *Stanford Literature Review*, vol.9 no.1, Spring 1992, pp.81–90.
Kluge, Alexander, 'Why Should Film and Television Co-operate?' (trans. S. Liebman), *October*, no.46, 1988, pp.96–102.
Korot, Beryl, 'Language as Still Life: From Video to Painting', *Leonardo*, vol.21 no.4, 1988, pp.367–70.
Kozloff, Max, 'Pygmalion Reversed', *Artforum*, vol.14 no.3, November 1975, pp.30–37.
Krauss, Rosalind '"...And Then Turn Away?" An Essay on James Coleman', *October*, no.81, Summer

1997, pp.5–33.
——, 'Impressionism: The Narcissism of Light', *Partisan Review*, vol.43 no.1, 1976, pp.102–12.
——, 'Paul Sharits', *Film Culture*, nos.65/66, 1978, pp.65–66, 89–102.
——, 'Paul Sharits: Stop Time', *Artforum*, vol.11 no.8, April 1973, pp.60–61.
——, 'Problems of Criticism X: Pictorial Space and the Question of Documentary', *Artforum*, vol.10 no.3, November 1971, pp.68–71.
Kurtz, Bruce, 'Artists' Video at the Crossroads', *Art in America*, vol.65 no.1, January, 1977, pp.36–40.
——, 'Fields: Peter Campus', *Arts Magazine*, vol.47 no.2, May 1973, pp.25–29.
——, 'Video Is Being Invented', *Arts Magazine*, vol.47 no.3, December/January, 1973, pp.37–44.
Langford, Michelle, 'Alexander Kluge', *Senses of Cinema*, 2003, www.sensesofcinema.com/contents/directors/03/kluge.html
Lebredt, Gordon, 'Stan Douglas: Living the Drive', *Parachute*, no.103, July/August/September 2001, pp.27–40.
Le Grice, Malcolm, 'Kurt Kren', *Studio International*, vol.190 no.978, November/ December 1975, pp.183–88.
——, 'The History We Need', *Experimental Cinema in the Digital Age*, London: British Film Institute, 2001, pp.29–37.
Lestocart, Louis José, 'Chris Marker: Truth, First Person Singular' (trans. C. Penwarden), *Artpress*, no.224, May 1997, pp.48–51.
——, 'Syberberg, le cinéma comme installation', *Artpress*, no.14, 1993, pp.86–89.
Levin, Thomas Y., 'Iconology at the Movies: Panofsky's Film Theory', *The Yale Journal of Criticism*, vol.9 no.1, Spring 1996, pp.27–55.
Levine, Les, 'Camera Art', *Studio International*, vol.190 no.976, July/August 1975, pp.52–54.
——, 'The Information Fallout', *Studio International*, vol.181 no.932, April 1971, pp.264–67.
Liebman, Stuart, 'Apparent Motion and Film Structure: Paul Sharits' *Shutter Interface*', *Millennium Film Journal*, no.2, Spring/Summer 1978, pp.101–09.
——, 'Paul Sharits' S:TREAM:S:ECTION:S:ECTION:S:S:ECTIONED: Paradigm Lost, or Adventures of the Dialect', *Millennium Film Journal*, nos.16/17/18, Fall/Winter 1986/87, pp.190–94.
——, 'Surrealism and Cinema: A Conversation with Annette Michelson', *Millennium Film Journal*, no.1, Winter 1977/78, pp.52–59.
——, 'Why Kluge?', *October*, no.46, Fall 1988, pp.5–22.
London, Barbara, 'Independent Video: The First Fifteen Years', *Artforum*, vol.9 no.19, September 1980, pp.38–41.
——, 'Time As Medium: Five Artists' Video Installations', *Leonardo*, vol.28 no.5, 1995, pp.423–26.
London, Barbara and Lorraine Zippay, 'A Chronology of Video Activity in the United States: 1965–1980', *Artforum*, vol.9 no.19, September, 1980, pp.42–45.
Lord, Chip, 'TVTV: Video Pioneers 10 Years Later', *SEND*, Summer 1983, pp.18–23.
Lupton, Catherine, 'Terminal replay: Resnais revisited in Chris Marker's Level Five', *Screen*, vol.44 no.1, Spring, 2003, pp.58–70.
MacDonald, Scott, 'Morgan Fisher: Film on Film', *Cinema Journal*, vol.28 no.2, Winter 1989, pp.13–27.
Manovich, Lev, 'Database as a Symbolic Form', *Millennium Film Journal*, no.34, Fall 1999, pp.24–43.
Margolies, John, 'TV – The Next Medium', *Art in America*, vol.57 no.5, September/October, 1969, pp.48–55.
Marks, Laura U., 'Giuliana Bruno, *Atlas of Emotion: Journeys in Art, Architecture and Film*', *Screen*, vol.44 no.3, Autumn 2003, pp.337–42.
——, 'How Electrons Remember', *Millennium Film Journal*, no.34, Fall 1999, pp.66–80.
——, 'Video's Body: Analog and Digital', *nach dem Film*, no.2, March 2002, www.nachdemfilm.de/no2/mar02eng.html
Marshall, Stuart, 'Television/Video: Technology/Forms', *Afterimage*, vols.8/9, Spring 1981, pp.70–85.
——, 'Video Art: The Imaginary and the Parole Vide', *Studio International*, vol.191 no.981, May/June 1976, pp.243–47.
——, 'Video-Technology and Practice', *Screen*, vol.20 no.1, Spring 1979, pp.109–19.
McCall, Anthony, 'Line Describing a Cone and Related Films', *October*, no.103, 2003, pp.42–62.
McCarthy, Anna, 'From Screen to Site: Television's Material Culture, and Its Place', *October*, no.98, Fall 2001, pp.93–111.
——, 'The Misuse Value of the TV Set: Reading Media Objects in Transnational Urban Spaces', *International Journal of Cultural Studies*, vol.3 no.3, 2000, pp.307–30.
McDonough, Tom, 'No Ghost', *October*, no.110, Fall 2004, pp.107–30.
Menick, John, 'Real-Time Futures: Five Notes on the Work of Wolfgang Staehle', *Parachute*, no.113, January/February/March 2004, pp.120–27.
Metz, Christian, 'The Fiction Film and Its Spectator: A Meta psychological Study', *New Literary History*, vol.8 no.1, Autumn 1976, pp.75–105.
Michaud, Philippe-Alain, 'La Technique du Chiffonnier ou le Cinéma Déplacé', *Artpress*, no.21, 2000, pp.92–95.
——, 'Line Light: Le cinéma géométrique de Anthony McCall', *Les Cahiers du Musée Nationale d'Art Moderne*, no.85, Fall 2003, pp.78–89.
Michelson, Annette, 'Bodies in Space: Film as Carnal Knowledge', *Artforum*, vol.7 no.6, February 1969, pp.54–63.
——, 'Camera Lucida/Camera Obscura', *Artforum*, vol.11 no.5, January 1973, pp.30–37.
——, 'Foreword in Three Letters', *Artforum*, vol.10 no.1, September 1971, pp.8–10.
——, 'Paul Sharits and the Critique of Illusionism: An Introduction', *Film Culture*, nos.65/66, 1978, pp.83–89.
——, 'Screen/Surface: The Politics of Illusionism', *Artforum*, vol.11 no.1, September 1972, pp.59–62.
——, '*The Man with the Movie Camera*: From Magician to Epistemologist', *Artforum*, vol.10 no.7, March 1972, pp.60–72.
——, 'Toward Snow', *Artforum*, vol.9 no.10, June 1971, pp.30–37.
——, 'What Is Cinema', *Artforum*, vol.6 no.10, Summer 1968, pp.67–71.
——, '"Where Is Your Rupture?": Mass Culture and the Gesamtkunstwerk', *October*, no.56, 1991, pp.42–63.
——, 'Yvonne Rainer, Part 1: The Dancer and the Dance', *Artforum*, vol.12 no.5, January 1974, pp.57–63.
——, 'Yvonne Rainer, Part 2: Lives of Performers', *Artforum*, vol.12 no.6, February 1974, pp.30–35.
Michelson, Annette, Richard Serra and Clara Weyergraf, 'The Films of Richard Serra: An Interview', *October*, no.10, 1979, pp.69–104.
Minh-ha, Trinh T., 'Mechanical Eye, Electronic Ear and the Lure of Authenticity', *Wide Angle*, vol.6 no.2, 1984, pp.58–63.
Morris, Robert, 'Notes on Sculpture, Part 1', *Artforum*, vol.4 no.6, February 1966, pp.42–44.
——, 'Notes on Sculpture, Part 2', *Artforum*, vol.5 no.2, October 1966, pp.20–23.
——, 'The Present Tense of Space', *Art in America*, vol.66 no.1, January/February 1978, pp.70–81.
Morrissey, Paul and Derek Hill, 'Andy Warhol as a Film-maker: Paul Morrissey Interviewed by Derek Hill', *Studio International*, vol.181 no.930, February 1971, pp.57–61.
'Movie Mutations: correspondance avec et entre quelques

enfants des années soixantes par Jonathan Rosenbaum, Adrian Martin, Kent Jones, Alexander Horwath, Nicole Brenez et Raymond Bellour', *Trafic*, no.24, 1997, pp.5–44.
Mulvey, Laura, 'Passing Time: Reflections on Cinema from a New Technological Age', *Screen*, vol.45 no.2, Summer, 2004, pp.142–55.
Murray, Timothy, 'Debased Projection and Cyberspatial Ping: Chris Marker's Digital Screen', *Parachute*, no.113, January/February/March 2004, pp.92–99.
Nash, Michael, 'AFI Video Festival', *Artscribe International*, no.76, Summer 1989, pp.86–87.
——, 'Bill Viola's Re-Visions of Mortality', *High Performance*, vol.10 no.1, 1987, pp.60–65.
Nauman, Bruce, 'Body Works', *Interfunktionen*, no.6, September 1971, pp.2–8.
——, 'Notes on Projects', *Artforum*, vol.9 no.4, December 1970, p.44.
Negt, Oskar and Alexander Kluge, 'The Public Sphere and Experience', *October*, no.46, 1988, pp.60–82.
Nesbit, Molly, 'Chris Marker', *Artforum*, vol.34 no.8, April 1996, pp.96–97.
Nicholson, Annabel, 'Artist as Filmmaker', *Art and Artists*, vol.7 no.9, December 1972, pp.20–28.
Orléan, Matthieu, 'L'art contemporain nous raconte des histoires', *Trafic*, no.34, 2000, pp.50–58.
Osthoff, Simone, 'Lygia Clark and Hélio Oiticica: A Legacy of Interactivity and Participation for a Telematic Future', *Leonardo*, vol.30 no.4, 1997, pp.279–89.
Paik, Nam June, 'Random Access Information', *Artforum*, vol.19 no.11, September 1980, pp.46–49.
Paik, Nam June and Paul Schimmel, 'Abstract Time', *Arts Magazine*, vol.49 no.4, December 1974, pp.52–53.
Païni, Dominique, 'À propos d'un coloque et d'un livre: Le cinéma est la peinture, le cinéma haï la peinture: Entretien avec Jacques Aumont', *Cahiers du cinéma*, no.421, June 1969, pp.60–62.
——, 'La trace et l'aura à propos Benny's video', *Artpress*, no.14, 1993, pp.18–23.
——, 'The Return of the Flaneur/le retour du flâneur', *Artpress*, no.255, March 2000, pp.33–41.
Pelzer, Birgit, 'Vision in Process', *October*, no.10, Fall 1979, pp.105–19.
Perreault, John, 'Bruce Nauman', *Art News*, vol.67 no.1, March 1968, p.22.
——, 'The Act of Seeing', *The Village Voice*, 8 February 1968, pp.19–21.
Perrone, Jeff, 'Ins and Outs of Video', *Artforum*, vol.14 no.10, Summer 1976, pp.53–57.
Pincus-Witten, Robert, 'Bruce Nauman: Another Kind of Reasoning', *Artforum*, vol.10 no.6, February 1972, pp.30–37.
——, 'Keith Sonnier: Video and Film as Color-Field', *Artforum*, vol.10 no.9, May 1972, pp.35–37.
——, 'Open Circuits: The Future of Television', *Artforum*, vol.12 no.8, April 1974, p.70.
——, 'Theatre of the Conceptual: Autobiography and Myth', *Artforum*, vol.12 no.2, October 1973, pp.40–46.
'Pop Goes the Videotape: An Interview with Andy Warhol', *Tape Recording*, vol.12 no.5, September/October 1965, pp.15–19.
Rajadhyaksha, Ashish, 'Spilling Out: Nalini's Recent Video's Installations', *Third Text*, vol.17 no.62, 2003, pp.53–61.
Rajchman, John, 'The Postmodern Museum', *Art in America*, vol.73 no.10, October 1985, pp.110–17, 171.
Rancière, Jacques, 'History of the Art System', *Artpress*, no.258, June 2000, pp.18–23.
——, 'Le cinéma, art contraire', *Cahiers du cinéma*, April 2002, pp.56–63.
——, 'Le cinéma dans la "fin" de l'art', *Cahiers du cinéma*, December 2000, pp.50–51.
Reeve, Charles, 'Time and the Image: A Conversation with Jonathan Crary', *Parachute*, no.103, July/August/September 2001, pp.42–50.
Roca, José Ignacio, 'TransHistories: Myth and History in the Work of José Alejandro Restrepo', *Cinémas d'Amérique Latine*, no.10, 2002, pp.101–16.
Rosler, Martha, 'Video: Shedding the Utopian Moment', *Block*, no.11, 1985, pp.27–33.
Ross, Christine, 'The Disappearing Screen: An Incomplete Matter', *Parachute*, no.113, January/February/March 2004, pp.15–29.
Ross, David A., 'A Provisional Overview of Artists' Television in the US', *Studio International*, vol.191 no.981, May/June 1976, pp.265–72.
——, 'Douglas Davis', *Flash Art*, May 1975, pp.24–26.
——, 'Paik, Gillette, Downey: Process and Ritual', *ArtsCanada*, vol.30 no.4, October 1973, pp.41–44.
'Roundtable: Obsolescence and American Avant-Garde Film', *October*, vol.100 no.1, Spring 2002, pp.115–32.
'Roundtable: The Projected Image in Contemporary Art', *October*, vol.104, Spring 2003, pp.71–96.
Royoux, Jean-Christophe, 'Cinema as Exhibition, Duration as Space', *Artpress*, no.262, November 2000, pp.36–41.
Sanborn, Keith, 'Modern all too modern', *Cinematograph*, vol.3, 1988, pp.107–16.
Schulte-Strathaus, Stefanie, '"Showing Different Films Differently": Cinema as a Result of Cinematic Thinking' (trans. N. Heidenreich and R. Rossi), *The Moving Image*, vol.4 no.1, Spring 2004, pp.1–16.
Serra, Richard, [Documents], *Avalanche*, no.2, Winter 1971, p.20.
——, 'Statements', *Artforum*, vol.10 no.1, September 1971, p.64.
Sharits, Paul, 'Hearing: Seeing', *Film Culture*, nos.69/75, 1978, pp.43–68.
——, 'Movie Cookbook', *Film Culture*, nos.109/112, 1978, pp.29–43.
Sharp, Willoughby, 'Body Works', *Avalanche*, no.1, Fall 1970, pp.14–17.
——, 'Bruce Nauman', *Avalanche*, no.2, Winter 1971, pp.23–31.
——, 'Jack Burnham Interview', *Arts Magazine*, vol.45 no.2, November 1970, pp.21–23.
Sicinski, Michael, 'Michael Snow's *Wavelength* and the Space of Dwelling', *Qui Parle*, vol.11 no.2, Fall/Winter 1999, pp.59–89.
Silverman, Kaja, 'The Author as Receiver', *October*, no.96, 2001, pp.17–34.
Simon, Joan, 'Breaking the Silence: An Interview with Bruce Nauman', *Art in America*, vol.76 no.9, September 1988, pp.140–49, 203.
Sitney, P. Adams, 'Structural Film', *Film Culture*, no.47, 1969, pp.1–10.
Sitney, Sky, 'The Search for the Invisible Cinema', *Grey Room*, vol.19, Spring 2005, pp.102–13.
Smithson, Robert, 'A Cinematic Atopia', *Artforum*, vol.10 no.1, September 1971, pp.53–55.
Snow, Michael, 'A Statement on *Wavelength* for the Experimental Film Festival of Knokke-le-Zoute', *Film Culture*, no.46, 1967, p.1.
——, 'Hollis Frampton Interviewed by Michael Snow', *Film Culture*, nos.48/49, 1970, pp.6–12.
Sontag, Susan, 'The Decay of Cinema', *The New York Times Magazine*, 25 February 1996, pp.6–10.
Spiegl, Andreas, 'Empire as Cinema', *Afterall*, no.8, 2004, pp.5–8.
Stam, Robert, 'Numero Deux: Politics, Pornography, and the Media', *Millennium Film Journal*, no.3, Winter/Spring 1979, pp.72–78.
Stemmrich, Gregor, 'Dan Graham's *Cinema* and Film Theory',

Media Art Net, 2004, www.medienkunstnetz.de/themes/art_and_cinematography/graham/1/
Sturken, Marita, 'An Interview With Barbara Buckner', *Afterimage*, vol.12 no.10, May 1985, pp.6–9.
——, 'Feminist Video: Reiterating the Difference', *Afterimage*, vol.12 no.9, April 1985, pp.9–11.
——, 'James Byrne's Video Projects: The Aesthetics of the Subject', *Afterimage*, vol.10 no.9, April 1982, pp.7–11.
——, 'Private Money and Personal Influence: Howard Klein and the Rockefeller Foundation's Funding of the Media Arts', *Afterimage*, vol.14 no.6, January 1987, pp.8–15.
——, 'TV as a Creative Medium: Howard Wise and Video Art," *Afterimage*, vol.11 no.10, May 1984, pp.5–9.
——, 'What Is Grace in All This Madness: The Videotapes of Dan Reeves', *Afterimage*, vol.13 nos.1/2, Summer 1985, pp.24–27.
Sutton, Gloria H., 'Tactical Media: Re-Interpreting VALIE EXPORT's Tapp und Tastkino (1968–1971) as a Model of Communication in Expanded Cinema', *New German Review*, vol.18, 2002/03, pp.76–90.
Tucker, Marcia, 'PheNAUMANology', *Artforum*, vol.9 no.4, December 1970, pp.38–44.
Uroskie, Andrew V., '"La Jetée en Spirale": Robert Smithson's Stratigraphic Cinema', *Grey Room*, vol.1 no.19, Spring 2005, pp.54–79.
VanDerBeek, Stan, 'Re:Vision' [1965], *Perspecta*, no.11, 1967, pp.113–19.
Vasulka, Woody, 'Syntax of Binary Images', *Afterimage*, vol.6 nos.1/2, Summer 1978, pp.20–24.
Wagner, Anne, 'Performance, Video and the Rhetoric of Presence', *October*, no.91, Winter 2000, pp.59–80.
Walley, Jonathan, 'An Interview with Anthony McCall', *The Velvet Light Trap*, no.54 (Fall 2004), pp.65–75.
——, 'The Material of Film and the Idea of Cinema: Contrasting Practices in Sixties and Seventies Avant-Garde Film', *October*, vol.103, Winter 2003, pp.15–30.
Weibel, Peter, 'Avant-Garde Film in Austria: Current Activities', *Studio International*, vol.190 no.978, November/December 1975, pp.214–18.
Whitney, John H., 'A Computer Art for the Video Picture Wall', *Art International*, vol.15, September 1971, pp.35–38.
Windhausen, Federico, 'Words into Film: Toward a Genealogical Understanding of Hollis Frampton's Theory and Practice', *October*, vol.109, 2004, pp.76–95.
Wollen, Peter, 'Landscape, Meteorology, and Chris Welby', *Millennium Film Journal*, nos.16/17/18, 1986/87, pp.208–11.
Wooster, Ann-Sargent, 'An Armory of Mirrors: Juan Downey's "Looking Glass"', *Afterimage*, vol.10 nos.1/2, Summer 1982, pp.24–27.
——, 'Video Art: Expanded Forms', *High Performance*, vol.11, Autumn 1988, pp.62–63.
——, 'Why Don't They Tell Stories Like They Used To?', *Art Journal*, vol.45 no.3, Fall 1985, pp.204–12.
Wyver, John, 'Video Art and Television', *Sight and Sound,* vol.57 no.2, Spring 1988, pp.166–72.

Index